BIG BAND JAZZ

BIG BAND JAZZ

Albert McCarthy

PEERAGE BOOKS

First published in Great Britain by Barrie & Jenkins

This edition published in 1983 by Peerage Books
59 Grosvenor Street
London W1

By arrangement with Cameron Books Ltd
2A Roman Way
London N7 8XG

ISBN 0 907408 70 2

Printed in Czechoslovakia

50511/1

ACKNOWLEDGEMENTS
The author is particularly indebted to Max Jones, Jazz
Journal and the Melody Maker for pictures used in this
book. He would also like to express his gratitude to the
following people who have made available pictures
included in this book:
Eddie Barefield, Edgar Battle, John Bartlett, John
Blowers, Jack Bladley, Milt Buckner, Charles Delaunay,
Bertrand Demeusy, Roger Prior-Dodge, Mike Doyle,
Franklin Driggs, Bjorn Englund, Don Gazzaway, Claude
Hopkins, Mack McCormick, Hughes Panassie, Charles
Payne Rogers, Sylvia Pitcher, Gene Ramey, David
Redfern, Brian Rust, Duncan Schiedt, Joyce Stone,
Edward S. Walker, Valerie Wilmer, and Tiny Winters.
Also, Jazz Hot, France; and Record Research, U.S.A.
and the author's collection.

Contents

Introduction

The bands covered in this book concentrated primarily on jazz in the broad sense of the term. I know that a hard and fast definition is difficult to come by. Inevitably there are inconsistencies here, such as the inclusion of Paul Whiteman on the strength of the recordings with Bix Beiderbecke and a few other jazz musicians. Some people, of course, would question whether swing bands are truly jazz groups, but I prefer to regard them as such. My own criteria put such bands as those of Will Hudson and Bob Zurke just within the limits of jazz, but place Glenn Miller's outside. Although the Miller band sometimes played a form of big band jazz, its musical policy generally lay in another area. The fact that a band did not pursue a concentrated jazz policy is certainly no cause for condemnation. The finest of the 'commercial' bands—Isham Jones's for example—was musically superior to the poorer jazz-orientated units. My concern here has been simply to work within some definable criteria for big band jazz.

One of my major objectives has been to make it clear that big band jazz was not a phenomenon of such major cities as New York, Chicago and Los Angeles, but a music that could be heard almost anywhere in the United States. I therefore wanted to draw attention to as many of the lesser known bands as possible, not only to the territory groups but to those that worked in the entertainment centres yet were overshadowed by the big name units. As I came to write the book, I realised that however hard I tried to include all the bands on my original list, space reasons would inevitably result in a fair number having to be omitted. Also, my suspicion was confirmed that at this very late date an enormous amount of research is still needed before the full story of the big band era can be documented. If there is ever to be anything like a definitive work on the subject, research must be carried out in the near future, preferably by a whole team of enthusiasts; their task will be of encyclopaedic proportions.

In dealing with bands other than the major ones, I have given, as far as is practical, personnel listings. To the not too deeply committed reader, this may appear finicky: lists of musicians' names hardly make for interesting reading. However, I feel that these listings are important in showing how musicians worked their way through numerous bands, the luckier and/or more talented finally making their reputations with the name groups.

Over the years, I have interviewed many dozens of musicians, in some instances taking down hours of their reminiscences on tape. For their patience and courtesy in answering what must have seemed a never-ending flow of questions, I am particularly indebted to the following: Henry Allen, Eddie Barefield, Edgar Battle, Emmett Berry, John Blowers, Russell Bowles, Milt Buckner, Jacques Butler, Don Byas, Happy Caldwell, Doc Cheatham, Buck Clayton, Bill Coleman, Jimmy Crawford, Harry Dial, Vic Dickenson, Eddie Durham, Roy Eldridge, Neal Hefti, Milt Hinton, Claude Hopkins, Budd Johnson, Harold 'Money' Johnson, Taft Jordan, John Letman, Al Lucas, Alton 'Slim' Moore, Snub Mosley, Gene Ramey, Ben Richardson, Eli Robinson, Hal Singer, Willie Smith, Buddy Tate, Clark Terry, Joe Thomas, Charles Turner, Earle Warren, Ben Webster, Paul Webster, Dicky Wells, Francis Williams and Teddy Wilson.

Many other musicians have contributed to this book through their reminiscences and clarification of personnels to such researchers as Bertrand Demeusy, Kurt Mohr and Johnny Simmen, whose published material has been of great value. Amongst such musicians are Cat Anderson, Curby Alexander, Bernard Archer, Billy Brooks, Gus Chapell, Leon Comegys, George Corley, Ray Culley, Eddie Davis, Bill Doggett, Joe Evans, Charlie Gains, Frank Galbreath, Lloyd Glenn, A. G. Godley, Earle Howard, Paul Howard, Quentin Jackson, George Johnson, Lem Johnson, Lenny Johnson, Porter Kilbert, Ed Lewis, Jack McVea, Freddy Mitchell, Phatz Morris, Red 'Mack' Morris, Glyn Paque, Jerome 'Don' Pasquall, Jay Peters, Ed Preston, Gene Prince, Caughey Roberts, Marshal Royal, Ben Smith,

Floyd Smith, Don Stovall, Buster Tolliver, Tommy Turrentine, Amos White, Joe Wilder, Walter Williams and Britt Woodman.

Unhappily, several of these musicians have died in the past few years; the toll amongst the big band era stalwarts has been unbearably heavy in recent times.

For help in listing little-known personnels and in generally setting out chronological sequences on many of the less publicised bands, I am greatly indebted to Bertrand Demeusy. Without his assistance, the coverage of some of the territory bands would be considerably briefer. To Walter C. Allen, I owe a debt of gratitude for his permission to reproduce information' in the form of press reports and news items that he has assiduously researched in newspapers produced for a black readership. Without the pioneering work of Frank Driggs, our knowledge of much that took place in the Midwest and Southwest would probably still be rudimentary. Mr Driggs has been working on a book on this area of jazz for several years; its appearance is eagerly awaited as the definitive study of the subject. I have made frequent reference to the standard discographical works—Brian Rust's 'Jazz Records 1897–1942' (Storyville Publications, London, 1970) and Jorgen Grunnet Jepsen's 'Jazz Records' (eleven volumes dated 1942 to various years in the 1960s, Karl Emil Knudsen, Copenhagen), and above all to John Chilton's 'Who's Who of Jazz' (Bloomsbury Book Shop, London, 1970). The latter remains one of the finest research volumes in the literature of jazz, and whenever I have wanted to check biographical material, I have unashamedly made use of it. In addition, I have read all the literature on the subject of big bands that I could find, both well known books and magazine articles, common and uncommon. Where they have been of use, they are listed as reference material in the bibliography for the relevant chapter. I have tried conscientiously to list source material whether it be in written or oral form, and to acknowledge its use. If I should inadvertently have omitted any credit I hope that the oversight will be forgiven.

Finally, records (12in. mono LPs unless otherwise indicated) are listed chapter by chapter at the end of the book. No attempt has been made to give all LPs by the artists mentioned, but rather to give brief details of those that are relevant to the text. I have attempted to discuss only recorded examples that are available in LP form, but in a very few cases have had to fall back on 78 rpm items; these are not included in the reference details. Many of the LPs listed are deleted, but the pattern of record issues is so swift changing that in the same or slightly different form, the contents might well reappear by the time this book is in print.

ALBERT McCARTHY

1 Early Syncopated Bands

Syncopation developed as the most outstanding characteristic of popular music between about 1890 and 1910. There was a logical progression from the early cake walks, through ragtime in both its classical and more commercialised forms, to early dance music and jazz. In due course, jazz was to benefit immensely by its additional incorporation of elements of the rural blues. Inevitably, though, before any degree of formalisation can make it easier to distinguish specific areas of popular music, an interim period occurs, in which a variety of approaches are evident. Past, present and future then co-exist simultaneously within the work of certain artists. In this situation, the pioneering syncopated orchestras appear to deserve a little more sympathetic consideration, musically as well as historically, than they have received in most of the standard jazz histories.

It is curious that research into the development of black American music has concentrated on the backgrounds of ragtime, jazz and blues pioneers, rather than that of the early syncopated orchestras. The information we have results almost solely from the efforts of Samuel B. Charters and Leonard Kunstadt, published in their book 'Jazz—A History of the New York Scene' and in their contributions to the magazine Record Research. Anyone who writes at all on the subject is indebted to these two researchers. The position is not helped by the extreme rarity of the records made by these early orchestras. Some were vertical-cut items, unplayable on conventional record players. However, there is a gathering interest in the music, and reissues of a few items are becoming available. Obviously, such performances cannot be judged in strict jazz terms, but the verdict, 'not jazz', often pronounced by less liberal jazz fans is no final condemnation, merely an irrelevance. The links between orchestras like those led by Jim Europe, Ford Dabney and Wilbur Sweatman, and the great jazz orchestras of a decade or more later, may be tenuous, but their existence can hardly be denied by any unbiased researcher.

It is rather ironical that the first microgroove release to contain material by Jim Europe should finally appear well over a half-century after his death, at a time when the companies are pouring out reissues of the most obscure blues and jazz artists of the past. Aside from his music, Europe is an important figure in the history of American entertainment, for he was without doubt the first black bandleader to achieve a nation wide reputation. I am indebted to Messrs Charters and Kunstadt for the following information on his regrettably short career.

Jim Europe was born in Mobile, Alabama, on 22nd February 1881. His family moved to Washington D.C., ten years later. There, he completed his education and musical training. In 1904, he went to New York, hoping to find a job as musical director in one of the Negro touring companies. It appears, though, that he was not successful until 1906 when he went out with a revue entitled 'Shoo Fly Regiment'. It is to be presumed that he

Jim Europe with the U.S. 369th Infantry Band outside the Tunis Hotel in Paris during 1918.

was not associated in any way with syncopated music at the time and, like the older coloured musicians, looked upon it with distaste. After returning to New York in 1909, he survived initially by accompanying singers, playing in small dance orchestras and teaching piano. He soon became aware of the conditions suffered by coloured musicians, most of whom were poorly paid for work in Harlem clubs and second class downtown hotels, in contrast with their white counterparts who played at the better restaurants and hotels. Europe came to the conclusion that part of the problem lay in the lack of a strong organisation to represent the coloured musicians, and in 1910, he became involved in the formation of the Clef Club.

The Clef Club was not the first attempt to organise coloured musicians and entertainers, for four years earlier the New Amsterdam Musical Association of New York had been founded. It met with limited success, apparently because its members were generally of an older school than the Clef Club group and wished to maintain musical standards that excluded ragtime and other forms of syncopated music. Europe made the vital decision that his future lay largely in popular music. To attract attention to the club, he formed an orchestra and gave a concert at the Manhattan Casino in May 1910. The group's repertoire consisted of light classics, popular songs of the day and a few ragtime pieces. Some of the ragtime numbers were written and conducted by Joe Jordan. The concert, followed by a variety programme and dancing, was a great success and received enthusiastic reports in the Harlem press. Others followed, each one more spectacular than the last. A concert in the spring of 1913 attracted an audience of close on four thousand. Encouraged by his success, Europe now set about achieving his greatest ambition, the organisation of a concert at the Carnegie Hall downtown. Various problems had to be faced, but Europe's determination resulted finally in a concert presented in March 1914. Fronting an extraordinary line-up that included forty-seven mandolins, twenty-seven harp-guitars, eleven banjos, thirteen cellos, eight violins, eight trombones, seven cornets and ten pianos, Europe offered a programme that ranged from religious songs (after initial misgivings, two church choirs agreed to take part in the concert) to popular music which was considerably influenced by ragtime. Needless to say, the concert attracted a great deal of attention and brought Europe's name before a much wider public. It probably also increased the jealousy displayed towards him by some Harlem musicians, however, for he suddenly announced that he was leaving the Clef Club to form a rival organisation called the Tempo Club.

Europe's greatest break had come in 1913 when the celebrated dancing team of Irene and Vernon Castle had appointed him as their musical director. The Castles changed the style of dancing in the United States to a remarkable extent during the period prior to America's involvement in World War I. The dances they introduced became fashionable in every American ballroom. At the height of their fame, they were reputed to earn $31,000 a week for a series of one-night appearances. In 1915, they featured in silent films and stage shows. Irene Castle, whose beauty and personality won over the whole of America, was important as a symbol of a more tolerant and enlightened social attitude that finally crystallised in the 'Jazz Age' of the 'twenties. After the death of her English husband in a flying accident early in 1918, Irene continued to be a popular figure in the entertainment world into the 'thirties. In the mid 'sixties, she made one of her rare public appearances when Dance Magazine threw a birthday party in her honour, and, still as slim as she had been in her heyday, she claimed that she 'could have danced all night'.

Europe regularly backed the Castles at their dance saloon, normally leading a six piece group instead of the somewhat larger line-up of his Society Orchestra. It has been claimed that Europe brought the fox-trot to the Castles' attention. If this was the case, they had reason to be grateful to him. Though they were not at first too impressed with the new dance, their performances made it the rage in America within a very short time. In 1913, Europe signed a contract with the Victor Record Company, thus becoming the first black American bandleader to record. With his Society Orchestra, he made ten titles, of which two were never issued. In 1915, the year in which Europe's association with the Castles was at its peak, his booking office was producing an extremely high revenue, and he must have felt that his future was

assured. His usual flair for self-advertisement had asserted itself at the second of his Tempo Club concerts, held in the autumn of 1914, when he persuaded the Castles to judge a dancing contest. Beforehand, they presented him with a bronze statuette of themselves in recognition of his services. At the close of this event, a picture of Europe was projected on a screen, whereupon the orchestra turned round their chairs and went into a version of *Castle Walk* under the direction of his screen image. Europe was generally described as a courteous but very reserved man, although there are indications that he did not feel modesty to be too relevant an asset in the advancement of his career.

Early in 1917, the United States entered World War I and Europe, in common with millions of his fellow citizens, had the pattern of his life entirely changed. He soon enlisted in a New York coloured regiment and received a commission. Within a short time, he was ordered by his commanding officer to organise the finest regimental brass band that he could muster. Europe assembled an outstanding group of some fifty musicians, including dancers, singers, and entertainers. He secured the services of the renowned Bill 'Bojangles' Robinson as drum major. The band personnel did not exist on ordinary army pay. Europe was able to use high salaries as a bait to attract the men he wanted, and in the autumn of 1917, the resulting 369th Infantry Band (taking the regimental nickname of The Hellfighters) set sail for Europe.

From the moment of its arrival, the band was a sensation; General Pershing, commander of the A.E.F., ordered it to be sent to his headquarters. During the next year, the band travelled widely to play for Allied personnel. In February and March 1918, it undertook an extensive tour of French cities to perform before wider audiences. Its greatest triumph was scored with its 'jazz' numbers, and these might be responsible in part for the French interest in jazz which was to be manifested in so many ways in the years ahead. After the armistice was signed, the band returned to a tremendous New York welcome. A million people watched it march down Fifth Avenue on a day that ended in a special Carnegie Hall reception in its honour.

It had always been Europe's intention that the band should continue as a civilian unit once the war was over, and after recording some thirty titles for the Pathe Record Company it set out on an immensely successful tour of many major American cities. There seemed little doubt that Europe was now in a unique position to capitalise on his fame. Not only did he enjoy a considerable reputation amongst white Americans, but he was also widely admired in his own community for his pioneering efforts in opening up a whole new field of employment opportunities for black musicians. It came, then, as a shock to the nation when the news was released that Europe had been murdered, on the night of 9th May 1919, by Private Herbert Wright, a drummer in his band. Wright had been showing signs of mental disturbance since the start of the tour and, on the night in question, had disobeyed earlier warnings not to walk across the stage while vocal groups were performing. Europe called the drummer to his dressing room in a Boston hall, were he lunged at his leader and stabbed him in the neck with a small penknife. At first, Europe was not thought to have been seriously injured. However, when he was taken to a local hospital, the doctors discovered that his jugular vein had been severed. He died within an hour or two and was buried with full military honours at Arlington Cemetery five days later.

It is impossible to know the direction Europe's musical involvements would have taken, had he lived, but it seems probable that in due course his sharp awareness of what was most in demand would have made him a part of the jazz scene. In many ways, this dignified, somewhat withdrawn man was as far removed from the stereotype of the black entertainer of his period as could be imagined. One of his greatest achievements to prove by example that there was no reason for well-schooled musicians to despise popular syncopated music.

The issued titles by Europe's Society Orchestra, recorded in December 1913 and February 1914, are a mixed bag. Best are *Too Much Mustard* and *Down Home Rag*. These performances are strongly syncopated, and the rhythm is set by banjo-mandolins; there is a degree of variation in the playing of the lead instruments. The vitality of the whole is impressive, despite the inadequate recording techniques of the period. *Too Much Mustard* evokes curious echoes of later Eastern European dance music. The fast tempos are surprising, calling one would think for more than the normal skill in dancing.

The recordings by the 369th Infantry Band are interesting in a number of ways. The material ranges from popular songs of the day, often indifferently sung by Noble Sissle, to novelty numbers such as *That Moaning Trombone*, and standards of the calibre of *Ja Da* or *Clarinet Marmalade*. Of particular note are versions of several W. C. Handy numbers, including *St Louis Blues* and *Memphis Blues*. The playing of syncopated music by brass or military type bands was quite well established by the time of the Europe recordings. Such famous bands as Sousa's and Arthur Pryor's extensively featured ragtime numbers. Blues, though, were certainly not attempted by these groups. In outline, the Europe recordings of *Memphis Blues* and *Hesitating Blues* employ a conventional brass band approach, but there are some notable differences. For example, on *Memphis Blues* there are a number of short breaks which suggest that Europe and his musicians may have listened to records by the Original Dixieland Jazz Band, while a clarinet featured on *Hesitating Blues* is not at all dissimilar in style to the playing of some of the early jazz musicians. It is not difficult to imagine the astonished reaction of European audiences when they first heard the band. For all the occasional ponderousness of its recorded performances, the links with jazz are clearly evident. Early jazz history is a great deal more complex than some writers would allow.

Though Europe dominated the scene up to the time of his death, his contemporaries were far from inactive. The most prominent were Will Marion Cook, Ford Dabney, Tim Brym, Eubie Blake, Noble Sissle and Wilbur Sweatman. After Europe left the Clef Club, it continued to function, organising a number of quite ambitious concerts. One of its best known members was the composer Will Marion Cook, born in Washington, D.C., on 27th January 1869. He studied at Oberlin College and later in Europe, then began his musical career by writing for stage shows that featured comedian Bert Williams. In 1898, he was responsible for the music of an all-coloured show 'Clorindy' which played both in New York and London.

By inclination, Cook was conservative and viewed the increasingly popular syncopated music with suspicion. However, its obvious popularity forced him to come to terms, and in 1919 he led his New York Syncopated Orchestra on a tour of major American cities. A handbill of the period stressed that the music of the orchestra was 'educational as well as artistic'. Apparently, it drew only limited audiences. In June of the same year, Cook brought his Southern Syncopated Orchestra to England at the start of a European tour which was to last until 1922. Details of this orchestra and events surrounding the tour will be discussed later, but it is worth noting that Cook's personnel included the late Sidney Bechet and one or two others who went on to make significant contributions to jazz. After his return to the United States, Cook's career was chiefly restricted to the straight musical field, and he died at the age of seventy-five in New York City on 19th July 1944.

Europe's immediate successor as musical director at the Clef Club was Tim Brym, a man of similar age and background who hailed from South Carolina. During the war years, he organised and led a seventy piece brass band for the 350th U.S. Field Artillery Regiment that won considerable acclaim when it performed for President Woodrow Wilson at the peace conference. It gave concerts during 1919 and its publicity referred to it as a 'jazz band'. The band was nicknamed the Black Devils, and when Brym recorded for the Okeh label with a more orthodox line-up of approximately ten pieces during March-May 1921, he retained the name. The titles were issued as by Tim Brym and his Black Devil Orchestra. Most of these records feature blues numbers. Those that I have heard are rhythmically stiff and somewhat unconvincing as jazz performances. Brym last recorded early in 1923, with a male vocal quartet called Tim Brym's Black Devil Four. His subsequent career is obscure.

Ford Dabney, Europe's assistant director at the Tempo Club, recorded fairly frequently between 1917 and 1922 and was certainly one of the pioneers of syncopated music. As early as 1914, he had made some piano rolls at the same time as Europe himself, but his first major break came at the beginning of 1917 when Florenz Ziegfeld engaged his band to appear in the 'Midnight Follies' at the Amsterdam Roof in New York City. This led to a recording contract with the Aeolian company, for whom he made over forty titles between about August 1917 and November 1919. At this time, the Aeolian company issued their output on vertical-cut recordings, with the result that performances by Dabney's band are little known. The few that I have heard are rhythmic, rather formally arranged, and contain elements of ragtime, marches and Tin Pan Alley blues. The most interesting musician in his band was trumpeter Crickett Smith, who worked in

Europe from 1919 until he settled in India late in 1936. He died in Bombay seven years later. Leonard Kunstadt has reported that Dabney's version of *Darktown Strutter's Ball* features some spirited playing by Smith. If a selection of Dabney's better titles were to be reissued, it is likely that he would be given more credit for his contributions during an important transitional period in the history of syncopated popular music.

Wilbur Sweatman is remembered as the man who played three clarinets at once. His most famous number for this presentation was apparently *The Rosary*. On a slightly less eccentric level, it is sometimes recalled that he wrote *Down Home Rag*, a theme still played regularly today. In fact, he is another important transitional figure who embraced both the ragtime and jazz eras. Though his recordings hardly suggest that he was an outstanding clarinettist—whether playing the instrument singly or in triplicate—Buster Bailey and Gene Sedric, among others, were far from scornful of his abilities.

Sweatman was born at Brunswick, Missouri, on 7th February 1882. He started out as a violinist. Towards the end of the nineteenth century, he toured with circus bands, then with Mahara's Minstrels at a time when one of his companions was the late W. C. Handy. He formed his first orchestra in Minneapolis during 1902. For the next ten years or so, he toured the vaudeville theatres extensively, and alternated this work with residencies in Chicago, where he was widely praised for his direction of the orchestra at the Pekin Theatre in 1911. Two years later, he opened for the first time in New York at Hammerstein's Victoria Theatre, billed as 'The Minstrel Marvel of the 20th Century'. From this time, he was a

Wilbur Sweatman in 1923 with Maceo Jefferson, Ralph Escudero, Duke Ellington, Flo Dade, Sonny Greer, Ian Anderson and Otto Hardwick.

Wilbur Sweatman's band in 1928. Cozy Cole is standing on the far right in the back row Right: *Eubie Blake and Noble Sissle, 'The Dixie Duo', in 1919.*

leading performer on one of the major vaudeville circuits, but spent a great deal of time appearing at theatres and dance halls in New York. He topped the bill in a show at the Lafayette Theatre in March 1923; the advertisement read 'Originator And His Most Imitated Rag Time And Jazz Band'. In his band at this time, were Duke Ellington, Otto Hardwick and Sonny Greer. Other personnels that he led included a number of famous jazz instrumentalists. With his Original Jazz Kings, he opened Connie's Inn in the summer of 1923, and was popular at such ballrooms as the Savoy for several years afterwards.

During the 'thirties, Sweatman concentrated on business interests. Among them were a music publishing firm and a booking office. He was the executor for Scott Joplin's estate. As late as the 'forties, however, he still continued to perform in public quite regularly. At some time during the following decade, he was involved in a severe car accident that left him unable to play for the rest of his life, and he returned to music publishing as his major activity. He died in New York City on 9th March 1961 at the age of seventy-nine. In view of his lengthy and extensive career,

the autobiography on which he was working at the time of his death should have been fascinating, particularly as he was noted for his good memory and concern with fact. Sweatman's records strongly feature him playing clarinet in a hokum style, even those such as *Battleship Kate* and *Florida Blues,* which stem from a comparatively late stage of his career. It is unfortunate that his records failed to capture the straightforward clarinet playing of which by all accounts, he was entirely capable.

The team of Eubie Blake and Noble Sissle must be one of the most venerable in the history of popular entertainment. Blake, who was born in Baltimore on 7th February 1883, is today a sprightly ninety-year-old, who still makes public appearances and records. His early jobs as a pianist included appearances in sporting houses and medicine shows, and his association with Noble Sissle began around 1917. They moved from Baltimore to New York together, for many years working as a vocal-piano duo, joint orchestra leaders and composers. They wrote and produced the famous show 'Shuffle Along' (1921), and contributed material to numerous revues during the next decade. Their paths diverged from 1928, when Sissle began to concentrate on bandleading, which he made his career for more than twenty years. They did come together again during the World War II, however, and appear as a duo in many U.S.O. shows. Sissle's career is given in more detail elsewhere in this book, and the length of his bandleading days can be gauged by the fact that his most famous sidemen were Sidney Bechet and Charlie Parker, though not of course at the same time.

Blake first recorded in 1917, as leader of both a trio and an orchestra. His early work is strongly in the ragtime tradition. *Sounds of Africa* is one of his most interesting compositions in this vein. He recorded with a band for Victor and Emerson in 1921 and 1922. The two Victor titles were *Baltimore Buzz* and *Bandana Days* from 'Shuffle Along'. The performances are rather straightforward, with slight jazz content, like most of the titles he made with a band for the Crown label in 1931.

Blake's real value lies in his composing and piano playing. He has written many songs that have become standards. Amongst the best known are *I'm Just Wild About Harry, Memories of You* and *You're Lucky to Me.* Equally important are his ragtime compositions such as *Chevy Chase, Fizz Water* and *Troublesome Ivories.* His piano style, particularly on more recent recordings, is ragtime based and closely linked to the Harlem stride school. Although the early years of Blake and his associate Noble Sissle were largely spent working in vaudeville, they are both artists whose long lives have spanned a considerable part of the history of popular syncopated music. Whatever the deficiences of their earliest band records, they were a part of that small group of pioneers whose music helped, by forming a link between ragtime and jazz, to create the musical climate in which big band jazz could take root and flourish in due course.

William Christopher Handy is best known as 'The Father of the Blues', a rather contentious title in the eyes of many blues authorities. That he was the first person to publish

W. C. Handy

a considerable body of blues material can hardly be disputed, though whether it was truly original or part of a common residue is debatable. I am less concerned here with Handy's song publishing that with his early years as a bandleader, for it is sometimes overlooked that he was one of the earliest coloured leaders to record.

Handy was born in Florence, Alabama on 16th November 1873. His initial musical career was spent as a solo cornetist with a brass band and as musical director for Mahara's Minstrels. From about the mid 1900s, Handy led his own orchestra throughout the South, bringing it to New York in 1917 to record for the Columbia Record Company. When he moved to New York a year later, he established a song publishing business in partnership with Harry H. Pace and became less active as a leader. After the onset of his blindness in the early 'twenties, he rarely fronted a band. Around 1926, he used Jelly Roll Morton's group for a short tour. In the following decade, he was with Clarence Davis's band, and a group of his own with violinist Billy Butler as its musical director. These occasions were for limited engagements and, for the rest of his life, Handy concentrated on his business interests, working until his death in New York on 28th March 1958 despite suffering, in addition to his blindness from severe disabilities that resulted from his falling on a New York subway track in 1943. His book 'Father of the Blues' contains some interesting material on his early days. After

his death, a statue of him was erected in Memphis and he was the subject of a commemorative postage stamp.

In the much publicised clash between Jelly Roll Morton and W. C. Handy over their conflicting claims to be the man most responsible for the early development of blues and jazz, Morton made great play on Handy's own limitations as a cornet player. Certainly, he was in no sense a jazz cornetist as his rather embarrassing contributions to a 1939 recording date make painfully obvious. However, his early bands did include jazz musicians such as Darnell Howard (then playing violin), saxist Nelson Kincaide and cornetist Johnny Dunn. Although such recordings as *Ole Miss Rag, Livery Stable Blues, Yellow Dog Blues, St Louis Blues* and *Panama* may be deficient in many, or indeed most, aspects of jazz, as early examples of orchestral syncopated music in a very transitional phase they are not without historical interest. Despite Morton's taunt that Handy could not even play jazz, he did contribute to it a large body of material that has become standard, and in his early bandleading days laid some of the groundwork for a later generation of musicians.

It might be objected that some of the bands mentioned here were too far removed from the mainstream of big band jazz, even given the benefit of historical lineages, really to merit the attention of contemporary listeners. In terms of straightforward jazz it is true that the bands dealt with here had little to offer. Of greater relevance is the fact that they helped to create a musical climate that made possible the subsequent developments of the big band as a norm of jazz. It is easy to be contemptuous of the recordings of the early bands, while in fact the best of Jim Europe's military band performances have a great deal more rhythmic drive than, say, the first records by Fletcher Henderson. It is all too simple to hear only the naïvety and imperfections of records from bands such as the one led by Europe and forget that they represent the burgeoning of a new popular music form that would already have produced its fair share of masterpieces in ten years' time. No doubt there were other unknown orchestras paving the way for the later public acceptance of big jazz bands, but at least when something is known of their activities it is only right that the pioneers should receive their due share of credit. Musically, what the Jim Europes and Wilbur Sweatmans had to offer might have severe limitations. Nevertheless, had they not primed the public to accept what was to follow, the subsequent history of big band jazz might have flourished a great deal less.

Left: *The caption to this advertisement reads: 'The costly dining-room in Miss Arlington's, 225 Basin Street. Panels in wall and wood (sic) carpet in at great expense'. Miss Arlington's was a New Orleans pleasure house where early syncopated music would certainly have been featured. Above: Louis Armstrong* (arrowed) *with the Colored Waif's Home Brass Band, 1911. Armstrong learnt to play the bugle at the home. Below: another Colored Waif's Home band in 1913 with Peter Davis, Henry Rene (probably 'Kid' Rena), Jeffrie Harris, Gus Vanzan, Isaac Smooth and James Brown.*

2 Chicago—Pioneers & Pre·Swing Era Bands

The coloured population of Chicago, approximately 40,000 in 1910, rose 150 per cent by 1920, when it exceeded 100,000. Since then it has, of course, continued to increase. Black entertainers arrived with each wave of migration from the South, and pianists such as Tony Jackson and Jelly Roll Morton were working in Chicago by 1910. In 1915, the white Tom Brown's Dixieland Band was attracting a great deal of attention and the next year the Original Dixieland Jazz Band arrived. It is from around this time that the influx of New Orleans jazzmen really got under way, and the pattern was sustained over the next decade. The greatest single event in Chicago's early jazz history was the arrival of King Oliver in 1918. Four years later it led to the opening of his Creole Jazz Band at the Lincoln Gardens on 17th June 1922. A year later Louis Armstrong joined the band there.

By the early 'twenties, the South Side, the black quarter of Chicago, was well provided with theatres, cabarets and clubs. State Street, alone, was the headquarters of the Pekin Theatre, the Dreamland Cafe (not to be confused with Paddy Harmon's Dreamland Ballroom), the two Elite Cafes, and innumerable bars that featured music.

Vaudevillians such as Wilbur Sweatman, established in Chicago in the first decade of the century, spread a taste for syncopated music that was to help the burgeoning big bands considerably in a few years' time. The pioneer leaders of big bands in Chicago were Charles Elgar, Clarence Jones, Charles 'Doc' Cooke, Carroll Dickerson and Erskine Tate. All but Cooke were leading orchestras by 1920. One aspect that differed somewhat from the big band scene in New York was the importance of the theatre bands, a field in which, for example, Clarence Jones, Sammy Stewart, and particularly Erskine Tate made their names. These bands featured an extensive repertoire that covered light classics, popular songs of the day, and jazz standards. However, the demand for 'hot' playing ensured that they employed a contingent of jazz musicians. From the musicians' viewpoint, such bands had the advantage of finishing comparatively early at night, enabling them to double at night clubs and other late hour spots. Before the depression, musicians could earn good salaries. Milt Hinton once mentioned that trumpeter Joe Suttler—not a major name by any means—earned seven hundred dollars a week in the late 'twenties, a vast salary at that time.

Chicago is a town with inevitable gangster associations, and most of the major clubs and theatres where the big jazz bands played were at one time gangster owned. The prohibition era in Chicago has been the subject of many books and films, but the domination of the drinking joints by gangsters did not hurt the musicians, who found employment opportunities plentiful.

The depression hampered the development of jazz, particularly among big bands. Even so, many continued to function, though some newcomers rapidly found survival beyond their capacity. Chicago appears to have suffered the same lack of progress in jazz as the rest of the United States during the depression. However, the World Fair of 1933-34 provided welcome relief for Chicago musicians who found employment available again. By the time that this was over, the swing era was not far distant, and big band jazz was really to come into its own.

Few of the Chicago-based bands, even among those working from time to time in New York or on extensive tours, achieved a national reputation. In the jazz field, the one big exception was the Earl Hines band which opened at the Grand Terrace late in December 1928 and played long residencies there throughout the 'thirties. From the outset, it was modern in its musical outlook, clearly pointing the way to the swing era, a few years later. Most Chicago jazz musicians, except the few whose careers were spent almost exclusively in small groups, considered the Hines band to be superior to all other local units. By the early 'thirties, when it had really become established, it must have made such theatre orchestras as Tate's begin to sound dated. This fact, combined with the depression, certainly helped to make life difficult for many of the pioneer big band organisers.

Regrettably, very few of the early Chicago big bands recorded with any frequency; indeed some of them never recorded. For this reason, hardly any evaluation of their music is possible. We have to rely on the opinions of musicians who heard them. However, whether they were outstanding, average or mediocre, all played their part in making the big band era an exciting one in the history of popular music. In spite of the lack of adequate documentation of the bands' histories and personnels, it is better to report the little that is known about them than to overlook them altogether.

Three of the most prominent Chicago-based bandleaders during the 'twenties were Charles 'Doc' Cooke (born Louisville, Kentucky, 3rd September 1891), Charles Elgar (born New Orleans, 13th June 1885), and Erskine Tate (born Memphis, 19th December 1895). All of them were classically trained in the pre-jazz era.

Elgar, now at eighty-eight the oldest surviving bandleader, initially studied violin at various musical colleges. In 1903, he appeared in his home town with the Bloom Philharmonic Orchestra. After a variety of musical jobs in New Orleans, Elgar left for Chicago in 1913 along with trombonist George Filhe and multi-instrumentalist Manuel Manetta. The journey there proved eventful, because Filhe knew a porter on the train who agreed to allow them to travel at half the normal fare. Part of the bargain was that the three men were at first hidden in a closet of a lounge car. Filhe in particular was amply proportioned, and before their release by the porter, the three came close to suffocation. In 1915, Elgar and Filhe obtained a job at the Arsonia Cafe in Chicago, sending to New Orleans for Manuel Perez (cornet), Eddie Atkins (trombone), Lorenzo Tio Jr (clarinet) and Louis Cottrell (drums). This was one of the only two occasions on which Perez, a famous New Orleans brass band cornettist, played away from his home town for any length of time.

A section of the Erskine Tate band in 1926. The trumpet player is Louis Armstrong.

Apart from a trip to Europe with the Southern Syncopated Orchestra, Elgar worked almost exclusively in Chicago. He secured lengthy residencies at such venues as Harmon's Dreamland, the Arcadia Ballroom, Savoy Ballroom and Sunset Cafe. His out of town activities were mainly confined to trips to Milwaukee during 1925-27 and 1928. Clarinettist Barney Bigard worked with him there in the summer of 1927. In 1922, Elgar's band included Joe Suttler (trumpet), Darnell Howard (clarinet, violin), Clifford King (clarinet), and Jerome Pasquall (saxophone). Suttler proved to be his biggest attraction, with a style Pasquall described as 'loud and rough'. In 1923, Elgar handed over the musical direction of his current band to James P. Johnson. It then became an integral part of the musical show 'Plantation Days' which was resident in London from March to May 1923. Suttler (sometimes spelt Sudler) was a member of that group, as were trombonists Bert Hall and Harry Swift, and bassist Wellman Braud.

In the 'thirties, Elgar turned increasingly from bandleading to teaching, an activity he maintained during the succeeding decades. He was for many years president of Local 208 of the American Federation of Musicians in Chicago and retired from involvement in musical affairs only when advanced age made it impossible for him to continue.

The prominent Chicago bands of the 'twenties generally fared less well than their New York counterparts in securing recording opportunities. Elgar's band only entered the studios once, in September 1926. The splendid version of *Nightmare* from this date features a complex score that was to form the basis of Alphonso Trent's recording of the number a few years later. The performance also offers spirited ensemble playing, an unexpected variety of musical textures, and a good theme statement by Suttler. *Brotherly Love* is only slightly less interesting. In it, we find rhythmic

unison work by the cornets and a driving closing ensemble passage which highlights a good clarinettist. Rhythmically, these recordings are advanced for the period, and the balance between ensemble and solo parts is well handled. If these titles are typical of Elgar's performances, it is sad that he did not record more frequently.

Erskine Tate, whose early musical training was similar to Elgar's, began to play the violin professionally in Chicago during 1912. In 1919, he opened at the Vendome Theatre, leading his Vendome Symphony Orchestra, a unit which, in time, doubled in size from its original nine pieces. Tate was based at the Vendome until March 1928. Two year residencies at the Metropolitan Theatre and then the Michigan Theatre followed. During the 'thirties, he led a band at a variety of theatres and ballrooms, including the Triangle Cafe, usually with a line-up of twelve. In 1945, he opened a music studio, offering tuition in most instruments, and was still active as a teacher only two or three years ago.

At one time or another, virtually every leading jazz musician in Chicago worked with Tate. Because he led bands in theatres, many musicians doubled with him and went on to play at late night clubs after the final show. The most famous example is provided by Louis Armstrong who, from sometime in 1926 until April 1927, combined working with Tate at the Vendome Theatre with a variety of other jobs. There can be little doubt that the job with Tate helped Armstrong considerably in developing his stage presentation. He was well featured in the stage shows both as instrumentalist and as singer. One of his routines consisted of his donning a frock coat and announcing himself as the 'Reverend Satchelmouth'. This was the preamble to a mock preacher act, for many years a staple of coloured vaudeville shows.

Tate's personnel at the Vendome in 1921 consisted of James Tate (trumpet), Fayette Williams (trombone), Alvin Fernandez (clarinet, soprano saxophone), Joseph McCutchon (soprano saxophone), Raymond Whitsett (alto saxophone), Norvell Morton (alto and baritone saxophone), Harry Johnson (bass saxophone), Adrian Robinson (piano), John Hare (brass bass), Walter Dyett (banjo), Jimmy Bertrand (drums), Erskine Tate (violin, banjo). Buster Bailey worked with Tate from 1919 to 1923. He went with him on a trip to New York, and his absence from the personnel given above must have been temporary. In June 1923, Tate recorded two titles for the Okeh label with a smaller personnel of James Tate, Freddy Keppard, Williams, Fernandez, Bailey, Morton, Robinson, himself and Bertrand. A second, and final, recording date took place three years later. Then, the line-up was Louis Armstrong, James Tate (trumpet), Fayette Williams (trombone), Alvin 'Angelo' Fernandez (clarinet), Stump Evans (alto and baritone saxophone), Norvell Morton (tenor saxophone), unknown (alto saxophone), Teddy Weatherford, unknown (piano), Frank Ethridge (banjo), John Hare (brass bass), and Jimmy Bertrand (drums). Darnell Howard told me that he was sure that he had recorded with Tate, but in the light of his known movements it must have been for a session that remains unissued. Soon after the last recording, Teddy Weatherford and Alvin Fernandez left the band and were replaced by Walter Johnson and an unknown musician. Armstrong's predecessor, Reuben Reeves, returned to play with Tate for a few months from mid 1927. In an interview with Jacob S. Schneider, Reeves commented, 'Erskine Tate had the best band I ever played with. He was a master, and the people used to stand for hours applauding. After each rendition there was a five to ten minute wait for the applause to stop. People came through storms, snow and hail to hear Tate's orchestra.' Allowing for a slight exaggeration, Reeves's remarks only confirm what others have said of Tate's popularity. Apparently, it was quite commonplace for people to come for the stage show and leave without seeing the film.

Early in 1928, Freddy Keppard made a brief return to the band, and violinist Eddie South was present from the autumn of 1927 until January 1928. From 1928 until 1930, both clarinettist/saxophonist Omer Simeon and drummer Wallace Bishop were regular members of Tate's band at the Metropolitan Theatre. At some point in 1929, trumpeter Jabbo Smith was in the personnel. Stump Evans had been forced to leave the band as a result of illness early in 1928, at a time when banjoist/guitarist Bud Scott was present for the second of two brief stays. In 1929, Tate's personnel at the Metropolitan Theatre consisted of Bob Shoffner, James Tate (trumpet), Lewis Taylor (trombone), Vance Dixon, Omer Simeon (alto saxophone, clarinet), Kenneth Anderson (tenor saxophone), Jerome Carrington (piano), Quinn Wilson (brass bass) and Walter Bishop (drums). The

smaller size of the band probably reflects the onset of the depression years. The groups that Tate led at a number of ballrooms during the early 'thirties are not well documented, and by all accounts personnel changes were frequent. However, Elmer Crumbley has reported that when he was with Tate at the Savoy Ballroom, Chicago, for a short time early in 1932, the other musicians in the band included, at different times, Raymond Hobson, Guy Kelly, Doll Vine (trumpet), Jimmy 'Hooks' Hutchinson (tenor saxophone), Teddy Wilson, Zinky Cohn, Cassino Simpson, Jerome Carrington (piano), Milton Hinton (bass) and Pete Brown (drums). The fact that Charlie Beal also worked with Tate during 1932 indicates a great deal of change among piano players. The last reference I have seen to a Tate band dates from early 1940, when he led his 'Walkathon Boys'. The only musicians mentioned were George Hunt (trombone) and Hillard Brown (drums).

For a musician who led bands for over two decades, a recorded output of four titles is unusually small. *Cutie Blues* and *Chinaman Blues* from June 1923 are strongly in the mould of the Oliver Creole Jazz Band, and mainly consist of ensemble passages interspersed with breaks. Their chief interest lies in the strong lead work of Keppard and his breaks on *Chinaman*. Of considerable curiosity value is a review of these titles that appeared in the music and theatre weekly, New York Clipper, of 31st August 1923.

'Erskine Tate's Orchestra debuts with this disk as a new Okeh recording combination. They hail from Chicago where the band is a feature of the Vendome Theatre in the Windy City's Ethiopian quarter. Played by a dusky aggregation, it is only to be expected that these "blues" bear the genuine African stamp from every angle. Corking for dance purposes, both.'

The review, discovered by Len Kunstadt during his researches into early musical publications, was written by Abel Green, who was later to be the dominant figure of the magazine Variety. It must be amongst the earliest notices of its kind. The slightly condescending attitude towards black musicians was commonplace at the time.

It appears that the Tate band recorded again, this time for the Paramount label, during 1923. Walter C. Allen found a reference to a session in the Pittsburgh Courier of 29th September 1923. Unfortunately the titles, whatever they were, must have been rejected.

The date in May 1926 produced *Static Strut* and *Stomp Off, Let's Go*. These items are familiar to most collectors because of Louis Armstrong's presence in the line-up. The spirited performances are dominated by Armstrong's solos and strong ensemble playing. They must be typical of the stomp items that were familiar to the patrons of the Vendome Theatre. Purist jazz considerations aside, it is a pity that the Tate band never recorded some of its light classical repertoire when Armstrong was present, for it would have been fascinating to hear how he and other prominent jazz musicians sounded in such performances.

Charles 'Doc' Cooke (his name was always spelled Cook on

record) was active as a composer-arranger in Detroit as early as 1909 and moved to Chicago a few years later. He is now best recalled for his lengthy residency from 1922 to 1928 at Harmon's Dreamland. During the next two·years, he continued to lead bands at theatres and ballrooms. Early in 1930, Cooke found that engagements were becoming hard to obtain and moved to New York City. He had intended the shift to be temporary, but he never returned to Chicago. He worked until the early 'forties as a staff arranger at R.K.O. and Radio City Music Hall, then retired to New Jersey. He became a Doctor of Music at the Chicago College of Music in 1926, and was clearly a very highly skilled musician, though by all accounts his piano playing was solid rather than inspired. He died, probably in New Jersey, in about 1956.

During his stay of almost six years at the Dreamland Ballroom, owned by Paddy Harmon, Cooke had within his ranks a number of great jazz musicians. Most renowned were the near legendary cornettist Freddy Keppard, and clarinettist Jimmie Noone. Keppard was in the band for

two years from the autumn of 1922, except for a brief spell with Erskine Tate. He rejoined Cooke from late 1925 until early 1926 and again from the spring of 1927 until September, while Noone worked in the band from the summer of 1920 until the autumn of 1926, and again in 1927. During part of his stay with Cooke, Noone also led his own small group at the Nest Club. Jerome 'Don' Pasquall joined Cooke at the start of the Dreamland Ballroom engagement in the summer of 1922. He lists the band's personnel as Elwood Graham, Ax Turner (trumpet), Fred Garland (trombone), Jimmie Noone, Clifford King, Joe Poston, himself (reeds), Jimmy Bell (violin), Anthony Spaulding (piano), Stanley Wilson (banjo), Bill Newton (tuba), and Bert Green (drums). Keppard replaced Turner after a few weeks, and this group recorded six titles for the Gennett label in January 1924. In the latter year, Johnny St Cyr (banjo) and Andrew Hilaire (drums) replaced Wilson and Green.

Cooke's personnel remained fairly constant until 1926. From then on, however, despite the retention of such long-serving musicians as Graham, Poston, St Cyr, Newton and Hilaire, changes became more frequent. George Mitchell had been a member of Cooke's trumpet section for close on a year from the summer of 1924, and returned in Sep-

A publicity shot of Cook's Dreamland Orchestra, probably dating from about 1926.

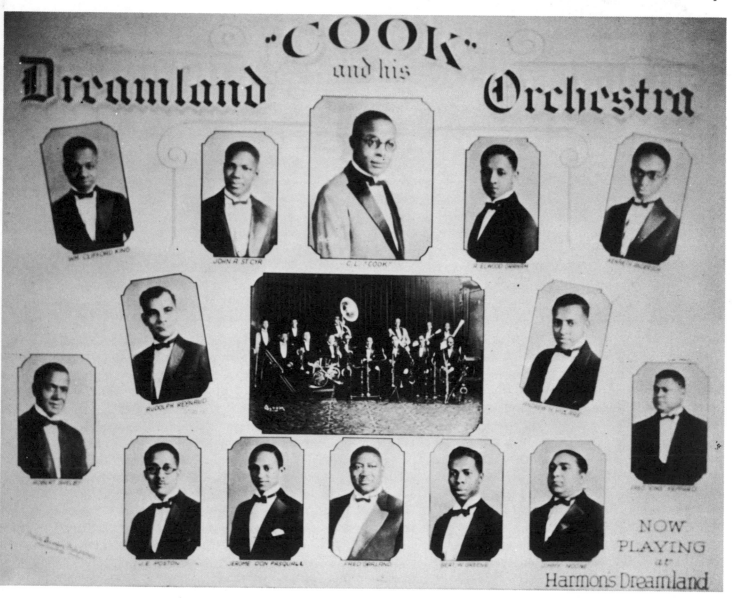

tember 1927, in time to be present at the band's final recording session. Jerome Pasquall met Cooke again late in 1929 and was persuaded to rejoin the band, then resident at the White City Amusement Park. For a while, he doubled with his own group at the Club Ambassador. He gave Cooke's line-up at this time as Charlie Allen (trumpet), William Dawson (trombone), Billy Butler, Joe Poston (alto saxophone), himself (tenor saxophone, clarinet), Wyatt Houston (violin), Sterling Todd (piano), Stanley Wilson (guitar), Bill Newton (tuba), Andrew Hilaire (drums), and Cooke (director, arranger). In 1930, the White City Amusement Park closed down and Cooke left for New York. Pasquall reports that his first job there was as staff arranger at the Palace Theatre. He adds that Cooke opened his own office in New York and scored for many prominent Broadway productions, including several that featured Eddie Cantor and Mike Todd's 'Hot Mikado'.

It is worth noting that the Dreamland Ballroom was owned by Paddy Harmon who was also the maker of Harmon mutes; Freddy Keppard and Elwood Graham of Cooke's band had been the first musicians to try them out. The band travelled to Richmond, Indiana, to make six titles for the Gennett company, and Pasquall comments, 'Since it was our first time and since recording hadn't reached the state of perfection that it has today, we had no

Left: *Doc Cook's Doctors of Syncopation at the White City Ballroom, Chicago, 1927; left to right: Billy Butler, Jerome 'Don' Pasquall, Joe Poston, Stanley Wilson, Wyatt Huston, Sterling Todd, Andrew Hilaire, Charles 'Doc' Cook, William Newton, William Dawson, Charlie Allen and Elwood Graham.*

Right: *King Oliver's Dixie Syncopators, 1926; left to right: George Filhe, Bert Cobb, Bud Scott, Paul Barbarin, Darnell Howard, King Oliver, Albert Nicholas, Bob Shoffner, Barney Bigard and Luis Russell.*

way of knowing that we weren't using the best techniques. As it was I think we tried to do too many sides. We made several tests and, I think, three masters each of six different tunes. By the end of the afternoon everybody was missing notes and making mistakes. The records didn't come out well and we were all disappointed with them. I remember Noone said, "I don't ever want to hear them anymore." '

Listening to the six titles recorded in January 1924, one can understand Noone's remark, though in fact his solo on *The One I Love Belongs to Somebody Else* provides one of the very few highspots of the session. *So This Is Venice* is dire in the extreme with a 'laughing' style wa-wa cornet solo and a quote from *O Sole Mio*. Nor can Keppard's breaks salvage an otherwise mediocre performance on

Memphis Maybe Man. Scissor-grinder Joe is rather better, mainly as a result of reasonable solos from Keppard and Noone. In general, however, this was a totally inauspicious start to the Cooke band's recording career.

In June 1926, Cookie's Gingersnaps, a six-piece unit from the full band, took part in a session that produced some much better music. Then, from July 1926 until March 1928, the full group took part in five sessions for U.S. Columbia that produced a total of eleven issued sides. The four titles from the first session are rather interesting examples of a transitional era in big band jazz. *Brown Sugar* reveals something of a New Orleans flavour in the ensemble work, and *Spanish Mama* possesses a theatrical quality typical of the production numbers that were then so much a part of the repertoire of most big bands. From the second Columbia session, *Sidewalk Blues* captures something of the flavour of Jelly Roll Morton's famous version, with pleasant solos from Joe Poston (alto saxophone) and a trumpeter. Perhaps the best performances recorded by the Cooke band are *Slue Foot,* using a fairly complex score for the period, and *I Got Worry,* which has pleasantly relaxed section passages and several creditable solos, despite featuring a very ordinary vocal trio. A notable tightening up of section work and an increase in rhythmic freedom on the later titles suggest that Cooke was keeping abreast of developments within the idiom.

King Oliver's Dixie Syncopators is not normally regarded as a big band, but it was large by the standards of the day. Between March 1926 and April 1927, it took part in eight recording sessions with a personnel that sometimes varied, particularly in the reed section, but included a firm nucleus of regulars. The transition from the great Creole Jazz Band to the Dixie Syncopators presented many problems for Oliver, not least the question of handling a conventional dance band saxophone section. The Dixie Syncopators's records are remarkably uneven. Such performances as *Lazy Mama* sound typical of conventional dance bands of the period. Curiously enough, the best use of the sax section is made in two of the earliest recordings, for on *Too Bad* and *Snag It,* Billy Paige's scores allow the saxes to be heard without letting them become obtrusive. It was in Paige's band that Don Redman made his first attempts at arranging, and Paige may have learned from his brilliant sideman. The band approaches it best in *Wa Wa Wa;* it lacks a sense of overall cohesion in *Black Snake Blues,* despite Luis Russell's highly competent score. There are, needless to say, many excellent solos to be heard on the Dixie Syncopators records. Purely in terms of big band jazz of the period, however, it is obvious that Oliver never fully solved the problems of adapting to the late idiom. On his subsequent

Victor recordings, he preferred to use a freer approach that placed little emphasis on ensemble work as such.

Carroll Dickerson, born in 1895, was another of the many violinist leaders active in Chicago during the 'twenties. He formed his first band around 1920. Two years later, his resident group at the Sunset Cafe included Eugene Hutt, Bobby Williams (trumpet), Buster Bailey (clarinet) and Andrew Hilaire (drums). He remained at the Sunset until 1924. Among the musicians who worked with him there were George Mitchell (cornet) and Mancy Carr (banjo). Late in that year, he formed a band for a long tour. The players included Natty Dominique (trumpet) and Cecil Irwin (tenor saxophone, clarinet). Early in 1926, Dickerson organised another band to go into the Sunset Cafe, with Louis Armstrong featured as both instrumentalist and vocalist. He was then resident at the Savoy Dance Hall from 1927 to 1929. In the spring of 1929, the band went to try its luck in New York and gigged there under Louis Armstrong's name before starting work at Connie's Inn which lasted until the spring of 1930. The band then broke up, and after spells with Mills Blue Rhythm Band and King Oliver, Dickerson returned to Chicago and formed a new group. During 1934 and 1935, its members included Zilner T. Randolph, Guy Kelly (trumpet), Al Wynn, Preston Jackson (trombone), Franz Jackson (tenor saxophone, clarinet), Leon Washington (tenor saxophone, clarinet), Horace Eubanks (saxophone, clarinet), Delbert Bright (alto saxophone, clarinet), Charlie Beal, Zinky Cohn (piano), Rip Bassett (banjo, guitar), Zutty Singleton (drums), and Dickerson (violin, leader). Dickerson led the band at Swingland in 1937. At this stage, his featured trumpeter was Guy Kelly. He then left music for two years, before resuming bandleading activities that continued well into the 'forties. He died in Chicago in October 1957.

Louis Armstrong recorded one title with the Dickerson band in May 1927, and a further nine titles in New York between July and November 1929. These performances, must be considered atypical, as the band functions essentially as a background for Armstrong's trumpet solos and singing. There are, however, a few creditable solos from trombonist Fred Robinson and clarinettist Jimmy Strong. *Missouri Squabble* and *Black Maria*, titles made in May 1928, display the band's abilities and weaknesses clearly enough. On the credit side, there are fine solos from trumpeter Willie Hightower, whose fine tone, relaxed phrasing, rhythmic ideas and swing suggest that he was a major artist. The ensemble playing is relaxed and the scoring is efficient if functional, though the saxophones' passages are weak. Six weeks later, there was a further session that produced *Savoyager's Stomp* and *Symphonic Raps*. Both were dominated by the brilliant solo work of Armstrong and pianist Earl Hines, with some contributions from Robinson and Strong (on tenor saxophone). The scores on this occasion are minimal, and the saxophones provide a creditable imitation of their counterparts in the Guy Lombardo band—no doubt much to Armstrong's

approval. There is proof on all these performances that the Dickerson band was highly capable. How it would have sounded with less impressive soloists is a matter for conjecture. Some musicians feel that Dickerson's best band was that of around 1934 and 1935. He did not record again after 1929.

Clarence Jones led theatre orchestras in Chicago from around 1917. Drummer Jasper Taylor worked with one of his earliest at the Owl Theatre. It appears that Jones was born in the 1880s and was in Chicago as early as 1910, when Jelly Roll Morton met him. Len Kunstadt discovered an advertisement in the Chicago Defender of December 1922 which lists Jones's personnel at the Moulin Rouge Cafe as Harry Johnson (cornet), Arthur Hill (trombone), R. Emerson Brown (saxophone), J. Wright Smith (violin), Clarence Jones (piano), William Washington (banjo), Archie Walls (tuba) and Frank Biggs (drums). The advertisement claims, 'When Clarence Jones and his aggregation of artists played *Wabash Blues* they set Chicago agog and put a tingling in its toes.' it also refers to recordings of *Downhearted Blues* and *Trot Along* made for the Paramount label, but never issued. In 1926, Jones was again resident at the Owl Theatre. A press report mentions that he was the official pianist for Southtown Station WBCN and that he was known as 'King of the Ivories'. At some point, Jones was staff pianist for the piano-roll firm Imperial, and for a short period late in 1927, and again in March 1928, Louis Armstrong worked with him at the Metropolitan Theatre, probably at the same time as Zutty Singleton (drums). Vance Dixon (reeds) was with him in 1928, but it seems that Jones left Chicago around the close of the 'twenties and moved to Detroit. It is believed that he died there sometime during the following decade.

Jones did not record a great deal, but his career was an odd one in this respect. He accompanied the vaudeville singer Ollie Powers, blues singers Monette Moore and Laura Smith, made some solo records, and recorded three titles with his Sock Four, and one with his Wonder Orchestra. He played piano while the Harmony Girls sang on *The Rosary*, a far cry from his blues accompaniments. The one title of relevance here is *The Arm Breaker*, recorded for Okeh in June 1926 with a line-up of trumpet, trombone, alto saxophone, tenor saxophone, banjo, brass bass, drums and Jones (piano). This is mainly a vehicle for Jones's piano playing, in a style that might be described as by ragtime out of Jelly Roll Morton, and has a certain charm. The band remains very much in the background throughout.

Jimmy Wade led an orchestra at Queen's Hall, Chicago in 1917, and spent most of the next five years directing the accompanying band to singer Lucille Hegamin with whom he travelled extensively. He then returned to Chicago, worked briefly with Doc Cooke, then formed his own band which was resident at the Moulin Rouge Cafe in 1923.

One of the few remaining photographs of trumpeter Jimmy Wade, who led bands well into the 1930s.

Violinist Eddie South was front man for the group until 1927, and the rest of the personnel was Wade, Ray Whetsett (trumpet), Bill Dover (trombone), Arnett Nelson, 'Stump' Evans (saxophones, clarinet), Vernon Roulette (saxophone), Teddy Weatherford (piano), Stanley Wilson (banjo, violin), Walter Wright (brass bass), and Eddie Jackson (drums). This band played at the opening of radio station WBBM in 1923, and moved to The House That Jack Built at Glenview, Illinois, a year later. In New York in 1926 and 1927, the Wade band played at the Savoy Ballroom and then the Club Alabam. In 1928, Darnell Howard worked with Wade who continued to front bands well into the 'thirties. His later career is obscure, but he died in Chicago in February 1957 when he was probably in his early sixties.

Someday Sweetheart and *Mobile Blues* were recorded in late 1923 by the personnel who played at the Moulin Rouge. They are pleasant performances with good work from Wade, Weatherford and South, though at this stage big band jazz was still in its infancy and there is little to distinguish Wade's ensemble sound from that of dozens of his contemporaries. An excellent *Gates Blues* recorded in 1928 was by a pick-up group and not Wade's regular band.

Sammy Stewart, born in Circleville, Ohio, in 1890 but raised in Columbus, formed his first band in the early 'twenties. Most of his musicians initially came from the Columbus area. Joe Glaser once claimed that he paid the Stewart band $3600 a week from the start, but one suspects the figure to be fanciful. Glaser also added, 'He would've been one of the biggest names in the business today if he didn't go wrong.' He did not offer any explanation of what he meant by this statement. Stewart worked regularly in Chicago from 1923. He played a New York engagement in 1926 and went out on fairly extensive tours.

Stewart was a classically trained musician and his band drew favourable comments from colleagues who heard it. Pianist Tommy Brookins claimed, 'For many years, it remained one of the best in Chicago. Sammy Stewart had gathered together only musicians of class and he played arrangements in a style that was sophisticated for that era. This pianist also played classical works magnificently.'

The band with which Stewart recorded in 1924 consisted of Fats Robins, Eugene Hutt (trumpet), Mancy Warley (trombone), Bill Stewart, Harley Washington, Roy Butler, Millard Robins (reeds), Paul Jordan (violin), Douglas Speaks, Sammy Stewart (piano), Lawrence Dixon (banjo), Dave Small (drums). Lawrence Dixon remained with Stewart from 1923 until 1928 and later became well known in other bands. The remaining musicians mostly drifted into obscurity. By 1926, Stewart was replacing his original Columbus personnel with Chicago musicians. Vance Dixon (reeds) worked with him in that year. When he recorded again in 1928, he led George Dixon, Walter Fuller (trumpet), Kenneth Stewart (trombone), Bill Stewart, Kenneth Anderson (alto saxophone, clarinet), Al Washington (tenor saxophone, clarinet), Alex Hill (piano), Ikey Robinson (banjo), Maurice Warley (bass), Sidney Catlett (drums). Dixon and Fuller remained with Stewart until 1930 like Sidney Catlett and Ikey Robinson, both of whom went to New York with him in 1930 and stayed there. Alex Hill, who worked with Stewart from the summer of 1929 until the spring of 1930, was presumably added for the 1928 recording. Pianist Horace Henderson was a member of the band for a short period late in 1928, at about the same time as reed man George James. Speaking of this period to Bertrand Demeusy, James recalled, 'I also played at the Metropolitan Theatre with Sammy Stewart and we had about eighteen men in the pit, but after the theatre show was over six of us played from 12 to 6 a.m. at Bill Bottom's Dreamland on State Street and we had Eugene Hutt (trumpet), myself (tenor and soprano saxophone), Kline Tindall (piano), Lawrence Dixon (plectrum banjo), Millard Robins (tuba) and Dave Smallwood (drums).'

Stewart was employed regularly at the Metropolitan Theatre. He sometimes switched to the Michigan Theatre, and was broadcasting frequently over Chicago stations in the period around 1928. In February 1930, after a summer residency in Ontario and a series of one-nighters, the band opened at the Savoy Ballroom in New York. In May, it moved to the Arcadia Ballroom. From this point, Stewart lived in New York. He led bands during most of the 'thirties, played organ at a ballroom in the early 'forties and fronted a sextet in the same decade. In the last years of his life, Stewart existed mainly by teaching. He died on 5th August 1960, at the age of seventy. I had met Stewart briefly in the autumn of 1958 when he was living in the same apartment block as trumpeter Joe Thomas. His living room was full of photographs that he had collected over the years, both of his own bands and others. However, he was not entirely coherent—I could guess what Glaser meant when he referred to his having gone 'wrong'. Despite this, some of the signed photographs from other leaders, with their congratulatory inscriptions, proved well enough that Stewart's reputation as a musician had not suffered through any personal weaknesses he might have had, and the pleasure he derived from these mementoes of his career was touching.

Sammy Stewart's Ten Knights of Syncopation, with the personnel listed above, recorded *Manda* and *My Man Rocks Me* in August 1924. A month later, they were back in the studio to record *Copenhagen*. Although the first two titles are undistinguished, from the point of view of both performance and scoring, they have trumpet solos, very much in the King Oliver manner, presumably by Hutt. *Copenhagen* is altogether more alive rhythmically; it features reasonable trumpet and bouncy ensemble playing at the close. The four titles that Stewart recorded in 1928 promise better than these earlier performances, though I have not had the opportunity to hear them.

Trumpeter Bernie Young recorded for the first time in 1923. He produced four titles under the name of Young's Creole Jazz Band and one as accompaniment to the vaudeville singer Ollie Powers. The records are pleasant but outside the scope of this book because the group operated as a sextet or septet. In 1926, Young recorded again with blues singer Hazel Meyers and with Arthur Sims and his Creole Roof Orchestra. His wa-wa work on Sims's *How Do You Like It Blues* was effective, if not particularly individual in style. The Creole Roof Orchestra was a big band by contemporary standards. Sims worked as much in Milwaukee as in Chicago, and his became the house band at the Roof Ballroom in the Wisconsin Theatre Building.

Early in 1926, Sims had a dispute with his musicians; all left him but pianist Cassino Simpson. He asked Oscar 'Bernie' Young to reorganise his band for him with Chicago musicians. In a short time, Young had taken over the band, and it is believed that Sims died around 1927. In subsequent years, Young followed the same pattern as Sims, alternating long residencies in Milwaukee with appearances in Chicago. His personnel at the Roof Ballroom, Milwaukee, in 1928 consisted of Zilner T. Randolph, himself (trumpet), Preston Jackson (trombone), Gilbert Mundy (alto saxophone), Ed Inge (alto saxophone, clarinet) Bert Bailey (tenor saxophone), Cassino Simpson (piano), 'Big Mike' McKendrick (banjo), Sylvester Rice (drums).

Possibly because Milwaukee was only two hours' journey away, Chicago musicians were not too reluctant to work there, and Randolph was a member of Young's band from 1927 to 1931, Jackson from around 1926 until the spring of 1930, and McKendrick from 1928 until 1930. Rice was with him for almost two years from late 1927, returning again for a few months during 1931-32. A year earlier, clarinettist Buster Bailey had spent a few of the summer months with Young in Milwaukee, as had bassist Quinn Wilson and drummer Wallace Bishop.

In 1930, Eddie Barefield joined Young's band for a few months, in place of Ed Inge who went on to join Billy Minor's band in Detroit. He gives the personnel at this period as Bernie Young, Zilner T. Randolph, Syd Valentine (trumpet), Preston Jackson, Doc Wheeler (trombone), himself, Gilbert Mundy (alto saxophone, clarinet), Bert Bailey (tenor saxophone), Burroughs Lovingood, Cassino Simpson (piano), 'Big Mike' McKendrick (banjo), Clinton Walker (tuba), Clifford 'Snags' Jones (drums), and states that it was an excellent band. This view is supported by the testimony of drummer Harry Dial, who told Frank Driggs: 'I joined Bernie Young's band when he came down from Wisconsin to play the Savoy Ballroom. He had one of the best bands around at the time. He was a good business man and a good manager, and knew enough to surround himself with good musicians, and not to try and do everything himself. He had Joe Suttler who was a great trumpet player. He used a Magnolia Milk can for a mute, and twisted it into the end of his horn and got all those freak sounds. I think that Paddy Harmon patented his mute from this.'

Suttler, whose playing was described by Jerome 'Don' Pasquall as 'loud and rough', was also once praised by Milt Hinton as being 'very great', and apparently he was an outstandingly well paid musician in his heyday. In later years he suffered a mental breakdown. The period of which Harry Dial speaks is either late 1930 or early 1931.

During late 1931 and early 1932, Jabbo Smith worked

Bernie Young's Wisconsin Roof Orchestra, 1928: Preston Jackson, Bernie Young, Sylvester Rice, Zilner Randolph, Mike McKendrick, Cassino Simpson, Gilbert Mundy, Edward Inge, Winston Walker and Bert Bailey.

with Young at the Roof Ballroom in Milwaukee. Then, the line-up was George Lott, Joe Thomas (trumpet), Jabbo Smith (trumpet, valve-trombone), Sam Moore, Stanford Grier (trombone), Leon Washington, George Meeks (alto saxophone, clarinet), Bert Bailey (tenor saxophone), Earl Frazier (piano), 'Red' Thomas (guitar), . . . Barbour (bass) and Sylvester Rice (drums). It is to be regretted that none of these bands were recorded, for several musicians have said that Young's musical standards were high. Certainly, he always included good soloists within his ranks. He continued to work through much of the 'thirties, and as late as 1942 was leading a small band in Milwaukee which included the saxophonist Jimmy Dudley. Sometime during the early 'forties, Young moved to Milwaukee. He may still be living there today. Nothing is known of his background, though it would be a reasonable guess that if he is still alive he must be in his early seventies.

Like most people who are nicknamed Tiny, Hartzell Strathdene Parham was of very ample proportions. He moved to Chicago from his native Kansas City, Missouri, in the mid 'twenties, and co-led a band with violinist Leroy Pickett in 1926-27. After this, he led his own bands intermittently until 1936. From that time, he normally worked as an organist. He died in Milwaukee on 4th April 1943, in the middle of an engagement, at the age of forty-three. In addition to his activities as a bandleader, Parham was in demand as an arranger. He provided scores for Earl Hines, amongst others, and for several years he had a commission to score music for the floor show at a prominent local club.

Parham's peak years as a bandleader were 1928-32. He held residencies at LaRues' Dreamland (1928), the Sunset Cafe (1930), Granada Cafe (1931) and the Merry Gardens (1931-32). In 1934-35, he was mostly at the Chicago Savoy Ballroom, and he was resident at the Club Havana in 1936. Punch Miller (trumpet) and Jasper Taylor (drums) worked with him in 1928, Jabbo Smith (trumpet) in late 1930, Eddie Mallory (trumpet) in 1931, Delbert Bright (alto saxophone, clarinet) and Harold 'Doc' West (drums) in 1932. Guy Kelly (trumpet) and Red Saunders (drums) played in his 1934 band. Saunders became a prominent leader himself in the 'forties and remained active in this role for over two decades. Eddie Mallory, for a short while director of Mills Blue Rhythm Band, took over Parham's current band in 1932, but does not appear to have kept it together for long.

Parham has always been something of a puzzle for researchers and discographers. Information on his band personnels is extraordinarily difficult to discover. The following notice appeared in the Chicago Defender of 19th December 1931 : 'Tiny Parham, pianist and arranger deluxe, is now the "fat contributor" of things musical at Al Quodback's beautiful Granada Cafe at 6800 Cottage Grove Ave. Tiny hits the air of WBBM's "Around the Town" program each night at 12 o'clock and from 1.30 to 2 o'clock. The Granada band stand has been graced by such celebrated outfits as Paul Whiteman, Guy Lombardo

and Ted Weems. Tiny does not suffer by comparison with these bands as is indicated by Mr Quodbach's mail and telegram requests.'

The paper then lists Parham's personnel as Leon Scott (trumpet), Charles Lawson (trombone), Edward Pollock (saxophone, clarinet), J. Donald Pasquall (saxophone, violin), Frank J. Woods, Wyatt Houston (violin), Tiny Parham (piano), Freddie Williams (banjo) and Freddie Bryant (drums). Jerome 'Don' Pasquall, who remained with the band when Mallory took over the leadership, adds Claude Alexander (trumpet), unknown (tenor) and unknown (bass) to the line-up, but omits mention of either Woods or Houston. This, to the best of my knowledge, is the only Parham big band personnel to be clarified.

The Pickett-Parham Apollo Syncopators recorded in late 1926, and Parham made three titles with small groups in 1927. Then, from July 1928 through to November 1930, he recorded regularly for RCA Victor. Thirty-eight titles in all were issued. Unfortunately, these records throw little light on Parham's day to day activities. The group was invariably an octet, and, even here, published personnels are open to question. Ray Hobson (trumpet), Ike Covington (trombone), Charles Johnson (alto saxophone, clarinet), Charles Lawson (trombone), Quinn Wilson (bass) and Ernie Marrero (drums) are some of the musicians who are present on many of these recordings, so that it may be presumed that they worked with Parham's big bands. The records themselves are interesting, indeed some are very good. All display Parham's talent for writing good melodies and his arranging skills. For the period in which they were recorded, however, they cannot be regarded as big band items and for this reason are not discussed here.

That Parham was an important figure on the Chicago musical scene for at least a decade from the mid 'twenties seems undeniable. However, he suffers more than most of his local contemporaries from lack of documentation, which seems remarkable in the light of his reputation. Perhaps the final irony of his career is that, while musicians who worked in Chicago during the 'twenties and 'thirties invariably speak of him in a big band context, he himself never recorded in such a setting.

Though he achieved considerable success as a leader of a touring band, to most jazz followers Walter Barnes was a relatively obscure figure during his lifetime. He is recalled, perhaps, by a handful of collectors for seven issued titles recorded between December 1928 and July 1929, or from an occasional short news paragraph in a musical periodical. Ironically, as headline news in national newspapers, his death received a degree of coverage that dwarfed anything that Barnes had known throughout his career.

Barnes was born in Vicksburg, Mississippi, on 8th July 1905. In 1922, he moved to Chicago, where he completed his education at the Wendell Phillips High School and the central Y.M.C.A. College. The Pittsburgh Courier of 4th May 1940 reported that he took a course in auto mechanics at Greer College, suggesting that initially he had not decided on a full-time career in music. Soon after his arrival in Chicago, however, he was undertaking musical studies at the Chicago Musical College and the Coleridge-Taylor School of Music. His chief tutor was Franz Schoepp. The influence of certain outstanding music teachers has been overlooked in most jazz histories, and Schoepp, referred to with great respect by Benny Goodman in his book 'The Kingdom of Swing', taught not only Barnes and Goodman but also Jimmie Noone and Buster Bailey.

In 1926, Barnes was leading a quartet; the Chicago Defender of 11th September that year listed the line-up as Wright (trumpet), Walter Barnes Jr (saxophone), Mrs Collins (piano) and Alice Calloway Thompson (drums). Trumpeter Wright is probably George Wright who played with Barnes's big bands two years later. At the time of his death, several obituary notices stated that Barnes had joined Jelly Roll Morton's touring band sometime in 1926 and had remained with it for about a year. During this time, he recorded with Morton. It is known that Morton was leading various pick-up groups at this period, and, though Barnes's association with him is shadowy, there is no reason to dispute the newspaper reports. The only issued title by Morton that could include Barnes in the personnel is the Gennett band version of *Mr Jelly Lord,* where the identity of the sax players has not been established.

During 1927, Barnes worked for a while in Detroit Shannon's band at The Merry Gardens. One report claims that he was then appointed leader and the group was renamed The Royal Creolians. Another newspaper states that he formed his first big band to play at the Arcadia Ballroom in Chicago, and the Chicago Defender of 7th April 1928 listed his personnel at the Arcadia as George Wright, James Hill (trumpet), Edward Burke, 'Hot Papa' Bradley Bullet (trombone), Lucius Williams, Earl Anderson, Erby Gage (saxophones), Paul Johnson (piano), William Hall (banjo), Charles Harkless (tuba) and William Winston (drums), with Barnes presumably leading on sax and clarinet. During that summer, the band played at The Merry Gardens, returning to the Arcadia Ballroom again on 8th September. The Chicago Defender listed the personnel in its issue of 22nd September 1928. By that time, Laurence Thomas (trumpet), Wilson Underwood (saxophone) and Quinn Wilson (bass) had replaced Hill, Anderson and Harkless. In the autumn of 1929, the band appeared at the Savoy Ballroom in New York. The Orchestra World for November listed a line-up in which George Thigpen, Leon Scott (trumpet), Richard Bates (banjo, violin) and Louis Thompson (bass) had come in for Wright, Thomas, Hall and Wilson.

Despite the fact that America was experiencing the early years of the depression, Barnes seems to have worked regularly. From late 1929 to July 1930, his band was resident at the Cotton Club in Cicero, Illinois, with an unchanged personnel. The club was run by Ralph Capone, brother of Al, and closed when Capone was prosecuted by the federal authorities. For the rest of that year and all the next, Barnes appears to have interspersed local jobs with tours of the Midwestern states. References in the Chicago Defender of 1931 give brief details of a car accident when the band was travelling between Fairmont and Huntington, West Virginia, another car accident in which Lucius Williams and Charles Barnes (Walter's brother) were injured at Pierre, South Dakota, and various engagements at venues ranging from the Rigadon Ballroom, Sioux City, to one at Brown Valley, Minnesota. The same newspaper, in its issue of 16th May 1931, gave the personnel of the touring band as Robert Turner, Claude Alexander, Leon Gray (trumpet), Augustine DeLuce (trombone), Walter Barnes, Wilson Underwood, Frank [Franz?] Jackson Lucius Wilson (saxophones), Paul Johnson (piano), Claude Roberts (banjo), John Frazier (bass) and Ralph Barrett (drums). Lucius Wilson is almost certainly the man mentioned in an earlier Chicago Defender line-up as Lucius Williams. During October 1931, the Barnes band auditioned at the Englewood Theatre, Chicago, for the R.K.O. chain. In late November, it played a date at Chicago's Savoy Ballroom in which it was pitted against the Erskine Tate band. Personnel changes now seem to be very frequent, since the line-up for the Savoy date, as given in the Chicago Defender of 21st November, was Raymond Whitsett, Doll Hutchinson, Bob White (trumpet), Charlie Lawson (trombone), Laurence Brown, Lucius Wilson, Ernest Smith (saxophone), Henry Palmer (piano), Fred Edwards (banjo), Lawson Buford (string bass, tuba), Clifford 'Snags' Jones (drums), Walter Barnes (saxophone, vocal). A month later, the band opened at the Club Congo at 35th and State, with Edward Burke (trombone), Zinky Cohn (piano) and Harry Gray (string bass, tuba) replacing Lawson, Palmer and Buford.

In 1932, Barnes developed his activities in a number of areas. Foremost was the setting up of the Walter Barnes Company Music Corporation to handle the business side of his affairs. As a southerner, he realised that the big name bands were infrequent visitors in many southern areas and conceived the idea of an annual tour covering most cities and towns of a reasonable size. From 1932 until the time of his death, he made Jacksonville, Florida, his winter headquarters, and built up a considerable reputation in the South as a result. This was an astute move financially, for, as his following increased, he was able to obtain highly paid jobs at important social functions, in addition to the more run of the mill dance hall engagements. In all probability, his earnings at this time rivalled all but those of a few top name coloured bands. The inevitable hazards of one-nighters did not escape Barnes and his musicians. The Chicago Defender of 14th May 1932 reported that as the result of lack of sleep, Barnes was involved in an accident when his car overturned, fortunately with no serious consequences to its passengers.

During 1932, the Barnes band undertook extensive touring schedules covering the Midwest and South, with returns to base at Chicago every few months. This became a kind of routine for the remaining years of Barnes's life. As a result of his absence from major entertainment centres, his activities received only occasional notice in the coloured press, but he achieved considerable popularity with his own people throughout the areas in which he toured. When he worked in Chicago, he often used several of the leading Chicago jazz musicians, but it appears that these men were unwilling to undertake gruelling tours. His line-up in 1934 consisted of the relatively little known Tom Watkins, Otis Williams, Orlando Randolph (trumpet), Richard Dunlap (trombone), Chick Gordon, Jim Coles, Joe Gauff (saxophones), Don Q. Pullen (piano), Harry Walker (banjo, guitar), Jack Johnson (bass), Bud Washington (drums), and himself (saxophone, clarinet). A year later, the trumpet and rhythm sections were unchanged, but the trombonists were now John Fryer and James Cox, and the saxophonists Les Cadwell, Wallace Mercer, Jim Coles and Chick Gordon. During 1936 and part of 1937, Barnes contributed a column to the Chicago Defender, though it was not particularly informative. The edition of 13th March 1937 mentions that his band played at the Tick Tock Tavern in New Orleans. The presence of trumpeter Punch Miller in the personnel drew crowds who were anxious to hear him after a ten years' absence from his native city. Miller joined Barnes in 1937 and remained with him until early 1940.

Barnes was mentioned for the first time in Down Beat in November 1939. It was reported that he was resident at the Savoy Ballroom in Chicago with a new band. The personnel

The Walter Barnes band in the early 1930s.

was listed as Otis Williams, Ellis Whitlock, Frank Greer (trumpet), Preston Jackson, Calvin Roberts (trombone), John Reed, Lucius Wilson (alto saxophone), James Cole, John Hartzfield (tenor saxophone), Walter Barnes (clarinet, saxophone), Clarence Porter (piano), Harry Walker (guitar) Arthur Edwards (bass) and Oscar Brown (drums). Several of these musicians accompanied Barnes on his ill-fated final tour a few months later and lost their lives.

Early in 1940, the Barnes band was once more undertaking one of its regular southern tours. On 23rd April it arrived in Natchez, Mississippi, to fulfil a dance date at the Rhythm Club. Punch Miller had left the band earlier; trumpeter Tommy Watkins, pianist Edgar Brown, and vocalist Gatemouth Moore were even luckier, according to a contemporary report, having left the day before the Natchez engagement. The band which took the stand that night consisted of Paul Stott [Scott?] (trumpet), Calvin Roberts (trombone), James Cole, John Reed, Jesse Washington, John Henderson (reeds), Clarence Porter (piano), Harry Walker (guitar), Arthur Edwards (bass), Oscar Brown (drums), Walter Barnes (saxophone, clarinet), Juanita Avery (vocalist). Though Down Beat for 15th May 1940 reported Watkins, Brown and Moore as having left the previous day, the New York Amsterdam News of 4th May had carried a different story, claiming that it was Ellis Whitlock and Frank Greer, both trumpeters, who had deserted the band on 22nd April when it reached their

home town of Louisville, Kentucky. In view of the fact that only one trumpeter played the Rhythm Club date, the News is probably correct, though the three others might well have left the band at an earlier date in the tour.

The population of Natchez in 1940 was 16,000, of whom 9,000 were coloured. By the standards of the South, the coloured population were in a reasonable economic position at this time. The admission charge to the Rhythm Club would have been far too high, at $2.50 per person, in other southern towns during this period. The following account of the Rhythm Club tragedy is considerably condensed from very full reports that appeared in the Pittsburgh Courier of 4th May 1940, and the Chicago Defender of 27th April and 4th May 1940. The Defender covered the event in great detail and, I understand, won an award for its reportage.

The Rhythm Club, originally a church, subsequently became a blacksmith's shop and then a garage. When it was finally converted into a night club, the interior was attractively redecorated; the outside, however, was not altered, and the metal sheathing on the exterior was allowed to remain in place. It was a long frame building and, to prevent anyone's entering without payment, the rear door was kept heavily bolted and the windows solidly barred. This meant that the front door was the only way in or out. It was accurately described to the Pittsburgh Courier reporter as 'the worst fire-trap that could possibly be imagined'. The band had been playing for some time when the first intimation of disaster occurred. One survivor stated that when the fire was discovered Barnes called out to the dancers to leave in an orderly manner and to avoid panic. At the same time he pressed his musicians to keep playing—the number was *Marie*—but in the event his gallant attempt to control the crowd could have been little more than a heroic gesture. It has never been ascertained with certainty what started the fire, though it was probably a lighted cigarette carelessly thrown away. In a short while, the building held an inferno. An extractor fan turning at top speed and masses of dried Spanish moss festooning walls and rafters on the interior of the galvanised-iron framework helped to spread the fire at lightning pace. Witnesses told the Courier reporter that they heard a hissing roar like a heavy gust of wind blowing through a forest, and then the entire inside of the building was filled with flame and smoke. Those inside who were not immediately by the exit had no chance of escape. Well over two hundred people died, mainly from asphyxia. Of the Barnes band, only bassist Edwards and drummer Brown survived, though three non-playing members of the Barnes organisation, including his brother Allan, also escaped. Oscar Brown described what he could remember of the events in Down Beat on 15th May 1940, and both the Pittsburgh Courier and Chicago Defender published gruesome photographs of some of the victims in addition to their full accounts. A final grim detail was the letter that Barnes had sent his wife telling her to expect him home in Chicago on 26th April. The letter arrived on that day, just a few hours before his body.

By all accounts, Barnes's great success as a touring leader owed not a little to his own personality. Many musicians described him as one in whom ever-present courtesy and amiability were paramount. When the musicians were well received, it was not uncommon for them to play considerably longer sets than their contracts stipulated, making them a welcome attraction in most of the places in which they played. Barnes was a well-schooled musician, but Punch Miller has said that in later years his playing was unexceptional and that he concentrated on showmanship. Musicians generally are unanimous in the view that the Barnes bands of the late 'thirties were the best he led, since they presented a high level of musicianship, good arrangements and a number of individual soloists. One musician who heard the band on two of its southern tours commented that, as it visited areas where the big name bands seldom played, it had in its book many cover versions of their hits. He added that it was an impressive unit when it played original material. While in Chicago, the band broadcast fairly regularly, but no transcriptions of such performances have so far come to light. The fact that it spent so much time away from Chicago probably accounts for the lack of later recordings.

The seven titles that the band did record during 1928 and 1929 are fairly typical of the secondary big bands of that period. Little can be heard that is particularly individual. *It's Tight Like That,* with reasonable solos from trumpeter Laurence 'Cicero' Thomas and trombonist Ed Burke, is one of the better titles, while the band achieves a fair rhythmic mobility on *Buffalo Rhythm.* This, too, has a competent solo from Thomas. For the rest it is not so much a question of the band's recording poorly, though this is true of *My Kinda Love* despite the saving grace of a few passable solos, as the lack of any real sense of direction or strong personality, either in solos or arrangement. In the light of views expressed by musicians who heard his band, it seems unfortunate that Barnes did not make his recordings about ten years later.

Its limited musical achievements might cause some readers to query the amount of space devoted to the Walter Barnes band. However, musical considerations aside, the Barnes story does afford more insight than most into the conditions that faced coloured bands touring in the 'thirties. It would be wrong to claim that what befell Barnes and most of his musicians is typical, but the toll of road accidents and the type of building in which these men were forced to work affected most of their colleagues at this time. It appears that only chance prevented other, similar tragedies involving touring bands. That the big band era was an exciting one, both for musicians and their public, is self-evident, but it should not be viewed in too romantic a light. Some of the less publicised aspects of what it was like to be a member of a touring band such as Barnes's will be discussed later.

Strictly speaking, Blanche Calloway is discussed in this section only because she made Chicago her headquarters for

Blanche Calloway, who fronted various bands from 1931 to 1938.

many years. The bands she used included only a proportion of Chicago musicians. Blanche, the sister of Cab Calloway, was born in Baltimore in 1905. She recorded as early as 1925, accompanied by Louis Armstrong. In the mid twenties she worked at the Ciro Club in New York, was frequently resident in Chicago, and undertook extensive tours. She was a headliner at the Pearl Theatre in Philadelphia when Andy Kirk's group was temporarily working as the house band in 1931, subsequently going out on tour with them. Kirk was aware that the manager of the Pearl Theatre had made a number of attempts to entice his musicians to become regular members of Blanche Calloway's supporting band, so that when he was told by Bennie Moten that a summer date awaited him at a resort near Kansas City he had no hesitation in accepting it. Edgar Battle, then working with Kirk, remained with Blanche Calloway and persuaded six members of the Jap Allen band to join her, filling in with other musicians. Blanche Calloway led a touring band from this point until she was forced to disband in September 1938, as a result of financial difficulties. She made one further attempt to front a big band during 1940, but worked as a solo attraction thereafter. In the early 'sixties, she became director of a Florida radio station.

The band with which Blanche Calloway toured after Kirk left for his summer residency consisted of Joe Keyes, Edgar Battle, Clarence Smith (trumpet), Alton Moore (trombone), Booker Pittman (alto saxophone, clarinet), Leroy Hardy (alto saxophone), Ben Webster (tenor saxophone), Clyde Hart (piano), Andy Jackson (banjo, guitar),

Joe Durham (brass bass) and William 'Cozy' Cole (drums). The men who came from Jap Allen's band were Keyes, Moore, Pittman, Webster, Hart and Durham. Herb Alvis (trumpet) was soon added. By the end of 1931, Henry Mason (trumpet), Ernest Purce (clarinet, alto saxophone) and Charlie Frazier (tenor saxophone) had replaced Keyes, Pittman and Webster, and Alvis had departed.

The Calloway band had undergone many changes by 1934, and the personnel for a recording date in August was Henry Mason, Archie Johnson, Clarence Smith (trumpet), Alton Moore, Vic Dickenson (trombone), Ernest Purce, Roger Boyd (alto saxophone, clarinet), Charlie Frazier (tenor saxophone), Egbert Victor (piano), Earl Baker (guitar), Abbie Baker (bass) and Walter Conyers (drums). This was the line-up with which Miss Calloway worked in Baltimore early in 1935, except that Richard Jones (trumpet) and Danny Logan (trombone) had replaced Smith and Moore. Numerous changes had occurred in the months leading up to mid 1935, when Miss Calloway was appearing in Boston, and the band now consisted of Tommy Stevenson, Archie Johnson, Richard Jones (trumpet), Vic Dickenson, Sylvester Briscoe (trombone), Chauncey Haughton, Alvin Campbell (alto saxophone, clarinet), Prince Robinson (tenor saxophone, clarinet), Ernest Purce (baritone saxophone), Clyde Hart (piano arranger), Earl Baker (guitar), Leslie 'Abie' Baker (bass) and Percy Johnson (drums). At the end of the year, when Blanche Calloway made her final records, Eli Robinson (trombone), Joe Eldridge and Billy Bowen (alto saxophone) had replaced Briscoe, Haughton and Campbell. In May 1936, with Miss Calloway headlining a show in Indianapolis, Norman Pinder (trumpet), Ben Smith (alto saxophone) and Tommy Fulford (piano) had taken over from Johnson, Bowen and Hart, Eli Robinson had left, and possibly Al Gibson (baritone saxophone) and Ted Sturgis (bass) were replacements for Purce and Baker.

After a two-year period, when personnel changes came thick and fast, the band settled down in early 1937. It appears to have remained unchanged for about eighteen months. The line-up was George Thigpen, Max Maddox, Maceo Bryant (trumpet), William Bradley, Valjean St Cyr (trombone), Scoville Brown, Tapley Lewis (alto saxophone, clarinet), Floyd Blakemore (tenor saxophone), Leslie Johnakins (baritone saxophone), Bobby Smith (piano), Earl Baker (guitar), Joe Durham (bass) and Norman Dibble (drums). Changes occurred, however, in the summer of 1938 when Charlie Hooks, unknown (trumpet), Eugene Earl (trombone), Jackie Fields, Irving Taylor (alto saxophone, clarinet), George Irish (tenor saxophone) and Amer Graves (piano) replaced Thigpen, Maddox, Bradley or St Cyr, Brown, Lewis, Blakemore and Smith and no baritone saxophone was used. Miss Calloway's final big band existed from January to September 1940. It appeared with her at the Highway Casino, Fall River, Massachusetts, the Club Harlem in Atlantic City, and the Southland Casino in Boston. Its personnel was Maceo Bryant (trumpet, trombone), Eugene Caine, Rink Johnson (trumpet), Rufus

Wagner (trombone), Ray Perry (alto saxophone, violin), unknown (alto saxophone), Frank Wess (tenor saxophone), Amer .Graves (piano), unknown (guitar), . . . Carrington (bass), and George Jenkins (drums).

The records that Miss Calloway made with the Kirk band are not impressive, less through any fault of the band than the vaudeville nature of the performances, dictated by the major role played by her. She was not a bad singer and had an agreeable rhythmic facility, but certainly lacked the stature to hold one's interest for any length of time. *Casey Jones* is almost pure hokum, *Sugar Blues* features Edgar Battle in the manner of Clyde McCoy, whose corny recording of this number was a tremendous hit, while *Just a Crazy Song* is a not very successful attempt to imitate her famous brother. *I'm Gettin' Ready For Myself* does have a good plunger trumpet solo, but the ensemble work could be matched by almost any competent dance band. Only *I Need Lovin'* shows the band at something like its best. It features driving ensemble passages reminiscent of McKinney's Cotton Pickers and an unusually forthright solo by Mary Lou Williams. The recordings with the band that includes six former Jap Allen musicians are better. *It's Right Here For You* has good solos from Pittman (clarinet), Hart and Battle, while *I Got What It Takes* displays good ensemble work. *Growlin' Dan* is a more successful vocal in the Cab Calloway manner, and the brass section plays well in the growl style. Miss Calloway's final session in November 1935 produced her best record in *Line-A-Jive*, an instrumental performance which has a fine trombone solo from Vic Dickenson and splendid section work, particularly by the saxes. Given similar opportunities, no doubt her earlier bands could have made records of equal quality, but generally they were required only to provide backgrounds to Miss Calloway's often pleasant, but equally often expendable, vocals.

APPENDIX

Chicago-based bands in general seemed to have less opportunity to record than their New York counterparts. Naturally those bands that attained national recognition while working regularly in Chicago—the Coon-Sanders Nighthawks and Earl Hines Orchestra, for example—did make frequent trips into the recording studios. On the other hand, bands with a purely local reputation, however considerable, seemed to be overlooked. One factor that militated against bands being recorded from the onset of the depression in late 1929 through to the mid 'thirties, was the financial instability of the recording industry. At this time, it was more concerned with survival than expansion. When the swing era became established, it was much easier for bands to record, even if their reputations were confined to a single city or district. Nevertheless, some of the major territorial units were never to find their way into a studio. Clearly, the sorry state of the recording industry during the depression years was partially responsible for the sparse documentation of several of the big bands then in existence, and by the law of averages, a few outstanding orchestras must have failed to find any recording opportunities. The details available on the various bands mentioned here vary considerably, ranging from reasonably full documentation to the sparsest outline. Where information is simply not available to me, I hope that the lack of data may inspire readers who have further material to forward it or even to undertake research when it is practicable to do so.

None of the twenty or so bands mentioned in this appendix ever recorded, so we can have no aural evidence of their achievements. All, however, have been mentioned by musicians at some time or other, as possessing some merit.

Boyd Atkins, believed to have been born at Paducah, Kentucky around the turn of the century, is now recalled as the writer of *Heebie Jeebies*. He alternated work for several prominent Chicago bandleaders, from 1925, with spells as a bandleader himself. He led bands at the Sunset Cafe in 1929-30, toured with his Firecrackers in 1930, had residencies in Chicago and Minneapolis during the 'thirties, and was directing the band at a club in Peoria, Illinois, for several years in the 'forties. During the next ten years, he arranged and worked with little-publicised Chicago bands, and is known to have died about ten years ago. Atkins was a violinist and saxophonist, and may have recorded on one title with Louis Armstrong in 1927, though this is not certain. Musicians have claimed that his best bands were the ones he led at the Sunset Café during 1929 and 1930 (Boyd Atkins's Chicago Vagabonds) and the touring unit of 1930. The line-up at the Sunset Café included Kid Ory (trombone), Thomas 'Tick' Gray (trumpet), Al Washington (tenor and alto saxophone, clarinet), Rip Bassett (banjo, guitar), probably Milt Hinton (bass), and Alfred 'Tubby' Hall (drums). Atkins's Firecrackers personnel for the tour in the summer of 1930 is not known, but definitely included Guy Kelly (trumpet), and George 'Scoops' Carry (alto saxophone, clarinet). Tenor saxophonist Fred Brown worked with Atkins for a couple of months in Chicago, from December 1939 to January 1940, and again during 1941 at the Greystone Ballroom, Mansfield, Ohio and in Chicago. By this time, however, Atkins was leading groups which contained almost no well-known musicians.

Fred Avendorph (or Avendorf) gained a single entry in the discographies when he replaced drummer Sonny Greer on one session with Duke Ellington in 1935. His career is obscure, but in 1932 he was leading a big band that included Thomas 'Tick' Gray (trumpet), Scoville Brown (saxophones, clarinet), and Franz Jackson (tenor saxophone, clarinet).

Violinists were particulary favoured as front men during the 'twenties. Clarence Black fronted the King Oliver band in New York, in May 1927. He returned to Chicago after a month, to lead his own group. It appears that Oliver and Black were quite closely associated for a while. The blues singer Irene Scruggs once told me that when she went to the studios to record with a section of Oliver's band in April

1926, Black was present as musical director. He recorded with Jelly Roll Morton and blues singers Henryette Davis and Nolan Welsh in 1926, with his own trio in 1928, and with Richard M. Jones in 1929. From the late summer of 1927 until at least 1929, he fronted his own band, sometimes playing at Chicago's Savoy Ballroom. Musicians who worked with Black at this time included Kid Ory (trombone), Boyd Atkins (saxophone), Lester Boone (alto and baritone saxophone, clarinet), Al Washington (tenor and alto saxophone, clarinet), Rip Bassett (banjo, guitar) and Alfred 'Tubby' Hall (drums). It is noticeable that several of these musicians joined Boyd Atkins in 1929, which suggests that Black secured no further work after the Savoy engagement terminated. Black's subsequent career is obscure, and possibly he suffered from the growing tendency of the late 'twenties, to dispense with violinists in 'hot' bands. From what I have heard of his playing on record, Black was no jazz musician himself, and if he had remained in music after the 'twenties, he would probably have been most at home in theatre orchestras.

For a short time in the early 'twenties, Mae Bradley led a popular group at the Dreamland Cafe. The exact size of the band is not known, but it is believed to have been a big band for its time. Its personnel included Freddy Keppard, Bob Shoffner (cornet), Junie Cobb (saxophones, clarinet) and Eddie South (violin).

Pianist Jerome Carrington was active on the Chicago jazz scene of the 'thirties. In 1933, he worked with the radio-studio band assembled to back vaudeville singer Frankie 'Half-Pint' Jaxon, and took part in one recording session with him. Before this, in 1931, he had led a short-lived big band that played at the Regal Theatre and possibly one or two other places, with an impressive personnel that included Reuben Reeves, Bob Shoffner (trumpet), Darnell Howard (clarinet, saxophone, violin), Lester Boone (alto and baritone saxophone, clarinet), Al Washington (tenor and alto saxophone, clarinet), Omer Simeon (alto and baritone saxophone, clarinet), Quinn Wilson (bass) and 'Big Mike' McKendrick (banjo, guitar). The band was reputedly a good one, but failed to survive long enough to achieve more than a very localised following.

Multi-instrumentalist Junie Cobb, now in his mid-seventies, worked with King Oliver and Jimmie Noone during the twenties. He made one trip to Europe in 1930, to front a band at a Paris night club for a few months. After leading his own groups in 1929 and during the early 'thirties, he decided in the depression period to disband and work as a duo with vocalist Annabelle Calhoun. For the ten years leading up to 1955, Cobb secured employment as a solo pianist. Since then he has worked only occasionally with pick-up groups. In 1929, he fronted a much larger band than was usual for him. Its line-up included Thomas 'Tick' Gray (trumpet), Cecil Irwin (tenor saxophone, clarinet), and Scoville Brown (clarinet, saxophones), and it was in

existence for only a short while before Cobb returned to leading smaller groups. He recorded a fair number of sides during the late 'twenties, with units that seldom exceeded six in number.

Ralph Cooper's Congo Knights was a popular touring band in the early 'thirties. It was booked by Joe Glaser on the RKO circuit and appeared as far afield as Denver. The band was formed in Chicago in 1931, and with Keg Johnson (trombone) and Zinky Cohn (piano) in its line-up, worked the Regal Theatre on more than one occasion. In 1932, it was well received at the Apollo Theatre and Harlem Opera House in New York, and followed with a successful tour. The personnel consisted of Bill Coleman, Bill Dillard, Henry Goodwin (trumpet), Robert Horton (trombone), Booker Pittman, Leroy Hardy (alto saxophone), Alfred Pratt (tenor saxophone), Arnold Adams (piano), unknown (bass), probably Arnold Boling (drums). However, at the end of the tour, work was hard to come by and the future of the band seemed in doubt. At this point, Irving Mills, who was then grooming Lucky Millinder to take over as leader of Mills Blue Rhythm Band, persuaded him to replace Cooper as front man, and booked the band for a long season at two prominent New York venues before it fulfilled an engagement on the French Riviera from July to October 1933. The personnel for these dates was as previously listed, except that Wilson Nyers was on bass. It was now billed as Lucky Millinder and his Orchestra. At the close of the Riviera booking, Pittman and Pratt remained in France. The other musicians went their separate ways upon returning to the United States. Cooper himself did not form another band, and was a prominent disc-jockey over a New York radio station in the 'sixties.

Around 1925, Lottie Hightower's Night Hawks was one of the best known jazz bands in Chicago. Lottie's husband, Willie, was on trumpet, as was Bob Shoffner for a while. Saxist/clarinettist Jimmy Strong and banjoist Mancy Carr were also in the group. Lottie herself was a pianist, but never recorded, though her husband did so, both under his own name in 1927, and with Carroll Dickerson a year later.

Jerome 'Don' Pasquall spoke quite kindly of Clifford 'Klarinet' King's ability on a variety of reed instruments, while mentioning that he specialised in trick routines, such as playing two instruments at once. King worked with Doc Cooke in 1924 and 1926, with Jimmy Wade at various times during 1924, 1925 and 1927, and with Eddie South for several years from 1929. He recorded with all of them. King led a big band at Harmon's Dreamland for fifteen months from early 1928. In an interview with Frank Driggs, Harry Dial described it as 'a fifteen-piece noisy band that was the worst thing I'd ever heard in my life. He [King] was very popular himself and was a good musician but didn't know anything about putting a band together. They played in an "every-man-for-himself-style". Paddy Harmon, the owner of Dreamland, eventually fired the band after we'd

Lottie Hightower's Night Hawks in 1925. Left to right: Johnny Lindsey, Rudy Richardson, Bob Shoffner, Willie Hightower, Bert Cobb, Mancy Cara, Lottie Hightower, Fred Parham, Crawford Wethington, — Buckner, Jimmy Strong.

been there fifteen months . . .' Apart from King himself, the personnel included Shirley Clay, Charlie Allen (trumpet), Jimmy Strong (tenor saxophone, clarinet), Earl Moss (piano), Cecil White (bass, tuba) and Harry Dial (drums). With such accomplished musicians in the group, it is surprising that some ensemble order could not have been achieved. In view of Dial's remarks, this may well be one example of a band where lack of recordings represents little loss to posterity.

Eurreal 'Little Brother' Montgomery is now regarded exclusively as a blues pianist and singer, but in his book 'Deep South Piano', Karl Gert zur Heide gives a great deal of new information on his career, including the fact that he led a swing style band from 1932 to 1939. The band was known as the Southland Troubadours. Originally, it consisted of Doc Parmley (trumpet), Rosser Emerson, Lucien Johnson (alto saxophone), Little Brother Montgomery (piano), H. T. Hennington (banjo), Luke Parmley (brass bass) and Henry Ross (drums). Howard Loach, a schooled musician, was soon added on trumpet, and in 1932 the band had a successful tour of Illinois, Wisconsin and Iowa, Brick Rosely (alto saxophone) replaced Johnson, and in 1933 George Guesnon (banjo) came in for Hennington. At the same time, the band reached ten in number with the addition of Louis Charles (trombone) and Doug Blackman (saxophone). J. C. Woodard was added on accordion for special occasions. In the years ahead, there were frequent personnel changes. Loach left and several saxophone players joined for stays of varying lengths. Apparently, the band became popular in the southern states. It broadcast regularly over local stations. Luke Parmley told Mr Karl Gert zur Heide that the band was offered the opportunity to record, but turned it down. Montgomery finally left in 1939,

and the band was taken over by Doc Parmley. It survived, with numerous personnel changes, into the late 'forties. In his travels, Montgomery recalls meeting such bands as those of Sidney Desvigne, Papa Celestin and George E. Lee. One surprising item of information is that Nat Towles temporarily played with the band after his own had broken up.

Clarence Moore led a band at various locations in Chicago from about 1927 to 1932, although personally he remains a shadowy figure. Banjo Ikey Robinson worked with him from late in 1928 to early 1929, to be replaced by Lawrence Dixon. In 1932, Moore was resident at the Grand Terrace Ballroom, his group at the time included Thomas 'Tick' Gray (trumpet), Keg Johnson, John Thomas (trombone), Teddy Wilson (briefly) (piano) and Everett Barksdale (guitar). Presumably the Moore band was one of the many casualties of the depression.

Jerome 'Don' Pasquall has already been mentioned on several occasions here, and his reminiscences have been helpful in identifying personnels of several Chicago bands. Mr Pasquall led his own groups, which were quintets, in Boston in 1925-27 and at the Club Ambassador, Chicago, in 1929-30. Along with many prominent Chicago-based musicians, he worked from time to time in Dave Peyton's Orchestra. Over the years, this leader must have had almost every leading Chicago jazz performer within his ranks.

Peyton was born in Louisiana around 1885. This places him in the same generation as Doc Cooke, Charles Elgar and Erskine Tate. He was working with Wilbur Sweatman in Chicago by about 1909. He led his own band at various clubs and theatres there for many years, and was resident at the Regal Theatre for a considerable length of time. In later years, he worked as a solo pianist, ran his own dry-cleaning business in the 'fifties, and died in Chicago during 1956. As well as band leader, Peyton was a musical contractor. He supplied musicians for a variety of functions, and in the mid 'twenties wrote columns for the Chicago Defender and other papers. A comment, which is often quoted, on the Fletcher Henderson band of 1926 is that their music was 'Soft, sweet, and perfect in dance rhythm . . .' and '. . . the boys get hot too—not the sloppy New Orleans hokum—but real peppy blue syncopation'. Peyton, who made these remarks, John Steiner informs us, showed a lack of sensitivity to the music of the New Orleans jazzmen on more than one occasion.

One of Peyton's first prominent theatre jobs was as leader of the pit band at the Grand Theatre around the mid 'twenties. The line-up was initially Ray Whitsett (trumpet), Eddie Atkins (trombone), Ralph Brown (clarinet, saxophones), Jimmy Bell (violin), Peyton (piano), Jasper Taylor (drums) and, occasionally, Joe Jordan (bass). In 1927-29 the following musicians all worked at various times with Peyton : Charlie Allen, George Mitchell, Bob Shoffner, Reuben Reeves (trumpet), John Thomas, Ed Atkins, Kid Ory (trombone), Bud Scott (violin), Norvell Morton (tennor saxophone, flute), Lawrence Dixon (banjo), Jasper Taylor, Jimmy Bertrand (drums). Warren 'Baby' Dodds (drums) was with Peyton in December 1927, 'Big Mike' McKendrick (banjo) in the summer of the same year, and trombonist Zue Robertson was in his band at the Grand Theatre around late 1926 or early 1927.

Jerome 'Don' Pasquall has given the personnel of the Peyton band at the Regal Theatre during part of 1930 and 1931, listing the musicians as Fats Robbins, Reuben Reeves (trumpet), Preston Jackson (trombone), Darnell Howard, Jerome 'Don' Pasquall (alto saxophone, clarinet), Norvell Morton (tenor saxophone, flute), Peyton (piano), unknown (guitar), Sudie Reynaud (bass), unknown (drums). Trumpeters Lee Collins (1931), Guy Kelly (1934) and Zilner T. Randolph (1934) were with Peyton in later years. Kelly and Randolph joined just before Peyton switched to a career as solo pianist. Curiously enough, despite his prominence in Chicago, Peyton recorded only on a single Richard M. Jones title in September 1935. However, his Regal Theatre band made two titles for the Vocalion label in April 1928. On this occasion, the band was directed by 'Professor' Stanley (Fess) Williams, who was then appearing in the Regal stage show. The titles are, incidentally, quite undistinguished and, despite his hiring of outstanding jazz musicians, one suspects that Peyton himself was essentially an organiser rather than a creative performer.

Pianist Cassino Simpson was reportedly only sixteen years of age when he started working with the Moulin Rouge Orchestra in 1925. Over the next five years, while a member of the Arthur Simm and Bernie Young bands, he established a considerable reputation as an individual stylist. In fact, Simpson's stated birth date of 22nd July 1909 must be viewed with some doubt in view of the fact that he recorded with both Bernie Young and Ollie Powers during 1923. In 1930, he was with Jabbo Smith for a short while, and also worked with Erskine Tate. In the following year, he formed a big band which he maintained until 1933, though with many personnel changes. His 1931 band included, at various times, Thomas 'Tick' Gray, Guy Kelly, Jabbo Smith (trumpet), Ed Burke, John Thomas, Keg Johnson

(trombone), Fred Brown (tenor saxophone), Franz Jackson (tenor saxophone, clarinet), Scoops Carry (alto saxophone), Jimmy Strong (tenor saxophone, clarinet) and Milt Hinton (bass). At one point, it was featured in the 'Dixie On Parade' revue. After breaking up the big band, Simpson became accompanist to the singer Frankie 'Half-Point' Jaxon. Early in 1935, he was admitted to a mental hospital in Elgin, Illinois, where he remained until his death on 27th March 1952. Simpson continued playing as an inmate of the hospital, and made solo recordings in 1944-45.

During his heyday, Simpson made a great impression on other musicians. Harry Dial told Frank Driggs, 'Cass Simpson was very good. He could imitate any piano player's style; you just give him a name and he'd sit down and play and you couldn't tell the difference. He didn't just improvise like Earl Hines, and was a real musician.'

Milt Hinton also enthused over Simpson. He is quoted in 'Hear Me Talkin' To Ya'. 'A man named Cass Simpson, he was the end on piano. He lost his mind. Last I heard he was in an insane asylum in Illinois. He was almost fanatical. He played incessantly all day. He had a terrific technique and was a fine pianist and arranger. He also had a mania for naming all his tunes after some food.' Hinton made this comment in 1955, and when I mentioned Simpson to him at a New York concert early in 1973, he spoke with the same sort of respect.

Eddie South, 'The Dark Angel Of The Violin', was a child prodigy and, from the age of sixteen, worked with several prominent Chicago bandleaders. He became the front man and musical director for Jimmy Wade's Syncopators in 1924 and stayed with Wade for three years. Subsequently,

Eddie South led a big band in 1935, and was Jimmy Wade's musical director from 1924 to 1927. South's most famous records were made in Paris in 1937.

he worked with Erskine Tate and Gilbert 'Little Mike' McKendrick before setting off on an extensive European tour with his Alabamians. Back in America in 1931, he continued to lead his own group for some years. He also accompanied a number of prominent vocalists, and in 1937 undertook further European engagements. During his stay in Europe in 1937-38, he recorded a number of records for the French Swing label that have become classics of their genre. He continued regular work in major American cities during the 'forties and 'fifties, appearing regularly on television in Chicago during the later years. His health deteriorated steadily towards the end of his life, and he died in Chicago on 25th April 1962, at the age of fifty-seven.

For most of his career, South led small groups, but formed a big band in 1935, for an engagement at Ben Marden's Riviera in New York, playing opposite the Paul Whiteman Orchestra. The personnel of South's band was George Wingfield, Lincoln Mills (trumpet), Don Pasquall, Warner Seals (alto saxophone), Harold Scott (tenor saxophone), unknown (piano), Everett Barksdale (guitar), Norwood Fennar, Eddie South (violin), Milt Hinton (bass) and Tommy Benford (drums). The instrumentation is unusual, and it is unfortunate that the group never had an opportunity to record.

In his essay on Chicago in the anthology 'Jazz', Mr John Steiner mentions the claim of trumpeter Hughie Swift to be the first South Side group leader to have nightly remote broadcasts, over Station WSBC in 1926. His band at the time included Charlie Allen (trumpet), Roy Palmer (trombone) and Warren 'Baby' Dodds (drums). Swift led a band from 1925 to 1927—some sources list him as a trombonist —and employed good musicians such as Punch Miller (cornet), Lil Armstrong (piano), Gilbert 'Little Mike' Mc-Kendrick (banjo) and Wallace Bishop (drums). I have been told that he was no great stylist personally, and that his bands tended to roughness. Failing any recorded evidence, the justice of this viewpoint must remain a matter for speculation.

Milton Vassar was another early violinist-leader, who fronted bands at the Dreamland Ballroom and Lincoln Gardens during the early 'twenties. If, today, he is remembered at all, it is because trumpeter Tommy Ladnier worked with him in 1922, along with Ed Vincent (trombone), Jerome 'Don' Pasquall (clarinet), Willie Lewis (piano) and Eddie Jackson (drums). This Willie Lewis is not, of course, the saxist who became prominent in Europe during the 'thirties.

Other Chicago-based bands are sometimes mentioned by musicians active in that city during the 'twenties and 'thirties. Bertrand Demeusy has referred to the Sunnyland Cottonpickers (1925-26), the Drake and Walker Orchestra (1927-28), with whom trombonist Zue Robertson played, and orchestras led by Ralph Brown (1927), Robert Christian (1927), Lank Keyes (early 'thirties), Jack Ellis (1931-37) and Reuben Reeves (1929). Brown was an alto saxophonist and clarinettist who was present on the record made by 'Professor' Stanley Williams in 1928 and several titles by Eubie Blake dating from 1931. It is known that Warren 'Baby' Dodds was in his band. Information on these bands is minimal, but all enjoyed a degree of popularity in their day and warrant further research.

The last photograph taken of the Walter Barnes band. Back row: Harry Walker (guitar), Arthur Edwards (bass), Oscar Brown (drums), Preston Jackson and Calvin Roberts (trombone). Front row: John Reed, James Cole, Lucius Wilson and John Hartfield (saxes), Otis Williams, Ellis Whitlock and Frank Greer (trumpet). Walker, Reed, Cole and Roberts died in the Natchez Rhythm Club fire, Edwards and Brown being the only musicians present who survived.

3 New York City — Pioneers & Pre·Swing Era Bands

New York City was a major entertainment centre long before the big band era got under way. However, the enormous popularity of dancing and dance bands in the 'twenties led to a considerable increase in ballrooms and dance halls; most of the major hotels employed bands to attract customers.

Virtually all the big jazz bands were coloured and consequently barred from playing in the leading hotels during the pre-swing era. They also found it difficult to get regular radio outlets. The biggest single factor in offsetting this situation was the growth, from the mid 'twenties, of Harlem as an entertainment centre, where many of the leading clubs catered almost exclusively for white audiences. This was the period when white socialites and intellectuals were becoming interested in African art and all things black. Before long it became fashionable to listen to jazz in the leading Harlem clubs and watch the elaborate floor shows. A few of the visitors developed more than a superficial interest in jazz and discovered the smaller, less fashionable clubs, where it was commonplace for white jazz musicians to jam with their black colleagues in after-hours sessions.

Among the most famous theatres and clubs which opened in the 'twenties were the Alhambra Ballroom, the Bamboo Inn (formerly the Palace Garden Club until closed by the police), the Bamville Club, the Capitol Palace, Connie's Inn, the Cotton Club, the Lenox Club, the Nest Club, the Rose Danceland, the Savoy Ballroom (initially billed as 'The World's Most Beautiful Ballroom') and Small's Paradise. Conditions for musicians who worked the clubs were extremely varied. Louie Metcalf commented:

'The pure jazz musicians, except for a lucky few, were really up against it in these days. It was a heck of a deal to try to get paid on a lot of jobs and most of the places were gangster dominated, the "Damon Runyon" type. A lot of the musicians had to carry sidearms, not for aggression but for protection. Often a lot of fights with the gangsters used to begin over the wages after a gig. Those were the days before the Sullivan law and gun permits so you could order your guns by mail from Sears Roebuck.'

It will not be news to most jazz fans that even the better known clubs were gangster owned; with considerable money to be made, the competition was fierce. Around 1930, a firm of gangsters opened the Plantation Club uptown and went so far as to lure Cab Calloway and his band away from their rivals at the Cotton Club. Two nights later, the bar and fittings of the Plantation were smashed up and one of the backers was murdered. That was the end of the new club. Not all the musicians suffered in the way that Metcalf mentions, however, and those in the name bands which were featured at the major clubs were at least sure of receiving their money. There were also exceptions, like Small's Paradise and Connie's Inn owned, respectively, by Ed Smalls and George and Connie Immerman, where the owners gen-

uinely liked jazz. There, musicians were treated generously and with real respect.

Much has been written of the fact that the major clubs, such as the Cotton Club, catered exclusively for white audiences, even going so far, in the heart of Harlem, as to operate a colour bar. Some musicians who were active at the time have denied this charge. Snub Mosely, for example, stated that he used to visit the Cotton Club quite frequently. I suspect the truth to be that well known black entertainers and musicians were at least acceptable to the club owners, who would probably not have welcomed a large black clientele for fear of upsetting their white socialite customers. In any case, the cost of spending an evening at anywhere like the Cotton Club would have been a sufficient bar to the average low-paid Harlemite.

It is necessary, to get the situation in perspective, to remember that the Cotton Club, Small's Paradise and Connie's Inn were not typical of most places where the bands played in Harlem. Far more prevalent were the ballrooms and smaller clubs. These were the venues which provided work for most of the big bands, which then generally numbered nine to twelve pieces. The few major bands attracted the attention of the public and recording companies alike, although many other groups, who were little known and only recorded once or twice, if at all, lasted for years and had their own following. They were important in providing work for musicians, and many acted as training schools for those who became famous in the top bands. The groups run by Billy Fowler, Eugene Kennedy, Henry Saparo and Charlie Skeets, for example, had frequent changes in personnel and appear to have been used by name musicians as stepping stones into better known bands, or as temporary havens when work was scarce. In some instances, it seems that musicians favoured by club owners remained when a band's engagement was terminated, merely joining the band which followed.

A few of the little known bands seemed to retain key personnel for lengthy periods. Vernon Andrade and Marion Hardy led bands for several years and, according to musicians who played with them, paid more than many name leaders. Quite apart from the attraction of the salary, a band like Andrade's would appeal to musicians who did not like travelling, and the fact that a player might spend many years in a little known band is not necessarily an indication of his artistic ability.

The period roughly from the early 'twenties to 1935 is one in which new bands flourished and then, in the depression following the Wall Street crash of 1929, had to cease operation. The repeal of prohibition in the early 'thirties also affected musicians, for people no longer needed to visit speakeasies to obtain a drink. Our ability to evaluate the musical worth of the bands discussed depends on their recordings. However, recording activity in the jazz sphere virtually came to a halt for some years during the depression, so that we shall never know what most of them were really like. No period in jazz remains as poorly documented as that of the early depression years. At least during the two bans on recording in the 'forties, radio transcriptions were made and are now becoming available in record form. The fact that we cannot hear many of the bands dealt with in this chapter is, however, no excuse for not detailing their history as far as possible, although surviving information is regrettably incomplete in many instances.

The Savoy Bearcats were the first large coloured jazz band to record for RCA Victor. They entered the studios seven months before Fletcher Henderson and over a year before Duke Ellington. The band was initially called the Charleston Bearcats and had been formed by Duncan Mayers in Charleston, South Carolina, some time before it opened the Savoy Ballroom on 12th March 1926, along with Fess Williams and his Royal Flush Orchestra and guests Fletcher Henderson and his Band. January 1926, the date given for its formation by Charters and Kunstadt, in their excellent book on New York jazz, I find hard to accept; it would have been remarkable for the owners of the Savoy to hear it and bring it to New York in so short a time.

One newspaper hailed it as 'The World's Greatest Coloured Orchestra' a few months after it had opened at the Savoy, and it recorded for RCA Victor twice in August 1926. The three titles from the second date were released. Three months later, it recorded a further four numbers, one of which was not issued. After that, despite its continuing existence until 1932, no other recordings were made.

Though Duncan Mayers was the organiser, the Savoy Bearcats were fronted initially at the Savoy by violinist Leon Abbey; the remaining personnel were Gilbert Paris, Demas Dean (trumpet), James Reevy (trombone), Carmello Jejo (alto and baritone saxophone, clarinet), Otto Mikell (alto saxophone, clarinet), Ramon Hernandez (tenor saxophone, clarinet), Joe Steele (piano), Freddy White (banjo, guitar), Harry Edwards (brass bass) and Willie Lynch (drums). Recorded performances of *Stampede* and *Bearcat Stomp* by the same group are impressive for the period. They display a fiery attack by the band and include a number of well played breaks. As a result of the rarity of their records (only one title, has been reissued on microgroove to date), the Bearcats have been overlooked by most jazz writers. However, on what is admittedly slight recorded evidence, they deserve recognition as one of the important pioneer groups.

The Bearcats' personnel in succeeding years is obscure. Most of the musicians present at the Savoy had moved on to other bands by 1928 or 1929. Our knowledge of the personnel in the band's final period is due to George James, who told Bertrand Demeusy, in conversation, that his first job in New York during 1932 was with the Bearcats. He gave a line-up of Buddy Murphy (trumpet), George Stevenson (trombone), himself (alto and baritone saxophone), Glyn Paque (clarinet), Ray Bumford (tenor saxophone), Duncan Mayers (piano), Ralph Escudero (bass) and Tiny Bradshaw (drums). Not long after this, the band broke up, though trumpeter Reunald Jones was a member before it did so.

Considering their popularity and the length of their stay in such places as the Savoy, the Savoy Bearcats seem unfortunate in having been virtually forgotten. No doubt research into newspapers such as the New York Amsterdam News will provide further information, but the paucity of material on the group is surprising, in view of the knowledge available about even some of the more obscure territory bands.

Apart from the few major bands, like those of Fletcher Henderson and Duke Ellington or McKinney's Cotton Pickers, Charlie Johnson's was arguably the finest big jazz orchestra playing in the Eastern States during the late 'twenties and early 'thirties. Though the band's recording career was limited, there are sufficient records available to give at least some idea of its worth.

Pianist Charlie Johnson, born in Philadelphia on 21st November 1891, first came to New York when he was in his early twenties and worked as a trombonist with a number of orchestras. He then moved to Atlantic City, switched to piano as his main instrument and, probably from early in 1919, led his own bands in that city. Trombonist Jimmy Harrison worked with him there around this time, and trumpeter Charlie Gaines about a year later. In October 1925, Johnson arrived in New York to open at Small's Paradise, where he led the resident group until he gave up full time bandleading in 1938. It was common for the Johnson band to play a summer season in Atlantic City when Small's closed for a few months. Sometimes, in New York, it worked the club and a theatre simultaneously.

Small's Paradise is one of the few clubs from the heyday of the big band era that still exists, though its musical policy has changed completely since its great period. In his book 'The Night People' trombonist Dicky Wells has given an affectionate portrait of both Ed Smalls and Charlie Johnson. Until the depression, Small's was an immensely successful venture, and Wells recalls that Smalls gave all the musicians in the band enough money to buy new cars, telling them to return it at the rate of five or ten dollars a time whenever it suited them. Johnson himself was an exceptionally amiable man who, though he was no great musician, had an ear for talent and enjoyed leading an outstanding band. It appears that he was an inveterate gambler and was sometimes away from the bandstand, following his hunches. In addition, he was fond of more than the occasional drink; one of the advantages of this weakness, as far as the musicians were concerned, was that he sometimes paid them their weekly salary twice. The relationship between owner, bandleader and musicians at Small's was an unusually happy one, and several musicians who played there recount their experiences with nostalgia. For a while during the early depression years, the band was cut down in size, although it was back to normal by 1935. In the post-Small's years, Johnson undertook a variety of gigs but his health deteriorated and he died in a Harlem hospital at the age of sixty-eight on 13th December 1959.

In an interview, reed man and arranger Benny Waters, who was for a long time a member of the Johnson Band, was asked by the British jazz writer, Peter Vacher, how the band was rated by other musicians. Waters's reply is interesting: 'In that time, it was considered by all, next to Fletcher Henderson. We were more colourful than Fletcher. We were the ones that first started the hats and the derbies and the wa-was—all those sounds. Fletcher's band was a keen, clean swing band; ours was swinging but with different little things that we did.

'Our band was very popular in playing "comps"— college prom dances—and I remember one time when there were four bands on the campus, Fletcher, Henderson, the Dorsey Brothers, the Memphis Five, and us. Each band moved around, and that day our band was the most popular. Our place was packed. As we all know, the white musicians always played with a wonderful sonority, even in those days, and Fletcher's band was in that category. A little bit more swing but no showmanship at all. Ken McComber, the white arranger, used to do some work for us. Anyone who made a good arrangement was in the book. If Charlie liked it, he would buy it there at rehearsal. He was making so much money.'

Benny Waters was with Johnson from 1925 to 1932 and again from 1936 to 1937. He is obviously speaking about his earlier days with the band, and it is interesting to note his comment on the introduction of hats, derbies and wa-was. Apparently Duke Ellington's earliest bands came to grief when pitted against Johnson's on one or two occasions, and it is not beyond the bounds of possibility that Ellington used some aspects of Johnson's presentation in the following years. Stylistically, on the evidence of its restricted recorded output, the Johnson band came midway between those of Ellington and Henderson. It employed some of the exotic effects associated with Ellington during his Cotton Club days, while adopting Henderson's freer, swinging approach. One needs to remember, however, that both Ellington and Johnson were for years permanently based in top night clubs which featured quite lavish revues; their music as a result reflected the theatrical traditions within which they worked. The similarities that exist between the two bands may depend much less on direct influences than on the purely functional aspects of their engagements.

The Johnson band recorded for the first time in the early months of 1925, producing two titles for the Emerson label. These are extremely rare and have not to date been reissued in microgroove form, so that most collectors have to base their judgment of the band on the output of four sessions made between February 1927 and May 1929, for RCA Victor. In all, twelve titles were produced, although two were never released. Some details of personnel remain uncertain; it seems unlikely that Benny Carter was present at the first session, while the plunger trumpet soloist sounds more like Sidney DeParis than Thomas Morris. Three numbers were recorded on this date. Two are available in two takes, and all have passable, if rather indifferent, vocals by Monette Moore. The arrangements and ensemble work are best described as highly proficient. The highspots are fluent, adventurous trumpet solos by Jabbo Smith on *Paradise Wobble* and *Birmingham Black Bottom,* a well conceived trombone passage by Charlie Irvis on *Paradise Wobble,* and an excellent plunger solo, presumably by DeParis, on Jelly Roll Morton's *Don't You Leave Me Here.* The second session took place almost a year later. Carter was definitely present and Edgar Sampson had been added on violin. Apart from a solo by Jabbo Smith, *You Ain't the One* is an undistinguished performance, though it has been stated that the arrangement was by Benny Carter. *Charleston Is the Best Dance After All* is much more interesting. The ensemble passages are crisply played, the cohesion of the saxes gives a foretaste of what was soon to become the hallmark of any Benny Carter arrangement, and Smith takes a very good solo. The band's high professionalism is evident on *Hot Tempered Blues,* especially in the closing ensemble chorus. There are also reasonable solos from Irvis, Sampson (on violin), and a trumpeter who is probably Leonard Davis.

From a session in September 1928, one title was rejected, although *Walk That Thing* and, particularly, *The Boy in the Boat* rank with the best big band jazz of the period. *The Boy* begins strongly, with excellent ensemble work and a theme divided between brass and clarinets, followed by an outstanding solo from trombonist Jimmy Harrison. A plunger trumpet solo by DeParis is among the best work he ever recorded. *Walk* is slightly less successful; the solos from Benny Waters (tenor saxophone) and Ben Whittet (clarinet) are reasonable, and no more. However, Harrison is again very fine and Leonard Davis good. One title from the final session of May 1929 was again rejected, but *Harlem Drag* has attractive solos from DeParis, trumpeter Gus Aiken, and Waters (clarinet). DeParis plays open, with a full, Armstrong-like tone. The final issued title, *Hot Bones and Rice,* displays the cohesiveness of the ensemble and has worthwhile solos from trombonist George Washington and DeParis, who uses a plunger. The last two sessions certainly prove that the Johnson band of this period was a very good one and it is a pity that it did not record again. Its failure to do so can probably be attributed to the onset of the depression, a few months after the session. By the time the recording companies were once more fully active, the swing era was under way and the Johnson band was nearing the end of its existence.

Trumpeters Ward Pinkett, who seemed to move around from one New York band to another with great rapidity, and Louie Metcalf played with Johnson during 1926. Bassist Henry 'Bass' Edwards was with him from

923 to 1925. Personnel changes from 1927 to 1930 were relatively few, though they appear to have become more frequent in the early 'thirties, presumably as well-known musicians sought the better paid jobs in the depression era. Several of the finest swing period trumpeters were with Johnson at this time. They include Henry 'Red' Allen (late 1932 to spring 1933), Edward Anderson (c 1930), Bill Coleman (1930), Herman Autrey (late 1933), Roy Eldridge (early 'thirties), Bernard Flood (1936-37), Reunald Jones (early 'thirties), Frank Newton (1930-31, autumn 1933 to late 1935), and Kenneth Roane (c 1932). Trombonists Robert Horton (c 1930), George Stevenson (1932-33) Dicky Wells (1933), Alton 'Slim' Moore (1938) and Joe Britton (1936) worked with Johnson, as did tenor saxophonists Leon 'Chu' Berry (late 1932-early 1933) and Teddy McRae (early 'thirties). With such musicians present, the band should have retained high musical standards during most of the 'thirties. Unfortunately no recorded material remains to make an evaluation possible.

The brothers Cecil and Lloyd Scott, born in Springfield, Ohio, on 22nd November 1905 and 21st August 1902 respectively, first played together as members of a trio, with pianist Don Frye, at their local high school in 1919. Three years later they were together leaders of Scott's Symphonic Syncopators. Their usual line-up was Gus McClung (trumpet), Earl Horne (trombone), Cecil Scott (reeds), Buddy Burton (violin), Don Frye (piano), Dave Wilborn (banjo) and Lloyd Scott (drums). Locally their only serious rivals were the Synco Septet, later to become McKinney's Cotton Pickers. Like them, they initially featured comedy routines and gimmicks at the expense of music, though the brothers soon realised that the future lay with bands which combined high standards

Scott's Symphonic Syncopators in the mid 1920s. Left to right: Lloyd Scott, Earl Horne, Gus McClung, Don Frye, Dave Wilborn, Buddy Burton and Cecil Scott. Right: *another shot taken at the same time.*

of presentation and musical proficiency.

With a few changes in personnel, the band went outside the Ohio area in the spring of 1924. It played for a while at the Royal Gardens in Pittsburgh before moving on to New York for a four-month residency at Herman's Inn at 145th Street and 7th Avenue. At the end of this engagement, the members of the band returned homesick to Ohio. They worked around Springfield for most of the next year, before setting off again to play a date in Pittsburgh en route to New York. The band had now had its membership increased to ten, and two important players were picked up during the journey to Pittsburgh. Trombonist Dicky Wells joined at Louisville, Kentucky, and trumpeter Frank Newton at Huntington, West Virginia. In New York, the band, now billed as Lloyd Scott's Symphonic Syncopators, played for a short time at the 101 Club on 139th Street, then moved into the Capitol Palace on Lennox Avenue between 139th and 140th Streets, where it remained for most of the next two years. The Capitol Palace was a well known club which became something of a haunt for musicians from other bands because of its long opening hours. Cecil Scott, in later years, stated that it never closed before dawn—not infrequently, jam sessions lasted there until six or seven o'clock in the morning. At first, to become known, the band also played matinée and evening stage shows at theatres, sometimes also working as the relief band at such noted ballrooms as the Savoy or the Roseland. Cecil Scott told the American jazz writers Thurman and Mary Grove, 'Sometimes we merely had to pick up crumbs by playing continuous dance music while bands like Ellington or Henderson took an hour off Sunday afternoon for supper. But we didn't consider ourselves humble—it was our privilege to play from their bandstand.'

The Scott band recorded three titles for RCA Victor in January 1927. Its showmanship, varied book of arrangements and musical expertise soon helped it to build up its own following. Lloyd Scott, who was the business manager of the band, retired from active playing at the end of the

Cecil Scott's Bright Boys, 1930. Left to right: Dicky Wells, Arnold Bolen, Frank Newton, Jimmy Smith, Bill Coleman, Don Frye, Cecil Scott, John Williams, Mack Walker and Harold McFarren.

Capitol Palace engagement in order to concentrate on organising the band's future. He was replaced by Arnold Bolden. The group was billed as Cecil Scott's Bright Boys and worked such locations as the Savoy and Roseland, by then as a topline band rather than a relief unit, occasionally going out on tours in the New England area. A further, final, recording session had taken place in November 1929, and while at the Savoy, the band had achieved a number of victories in the band battles which frequently took place. Lloyd Scott told of two such occasions to Thurman and Mary Grove:

'While at the Savoy, we were at the peak. On one evening there in 1928, we won an extraordinary battle of music against eight bands, including those of Fletcher Henderson and Charlie Johnson, at what they termed a "South Sea Island Ball". Another contest was called the "Arabian Nights Ball"; that was in the following year, also at the Savoy. We were placed second to Ellington. These battles were fiercely contested affairs, for much prestige was at stake. Bands would have extensive preparations ahead of time for the largest of these battles and would fire their best in the way of arrangements at one another. One particularly brutal one was a good victory over three bands—Fess Williams, Cab Calloway and Fletcher Henderson. Our winning was clear cut, but only after an all-night struggle which ended at seven o'clock Sunday morning.'

During 1931, the Scott band played the Renaissance Ballroom and then returned to the Savoy. Its final dispersal, soon afterwards, resulted from a combination of circumstances. The depression was at its worst and the public generally had little money to spend, least of all on luxury outings to clubs. This inevitably meant that most bands had to take large cuts in salary even when they were fortunate enough to find work. Apart from the economic conditions, personal factors influenced the Scott brothers in their decision to disband. At this time, Lloyd was suffering from ill health and Cecil was involved in an accident that resulted in the amputation of his leg. Lloyd never went back to working in bands, though Cecil remained a musician for the rest of his life. He had a varied career in big bands, small groups and as a music teacher until his death in New York on 5th January

1964. Outside music, his greatest pride was in his thirteen children.

The personnel of the Scott band during its heyday was unusually stable, but there were other musicians, not present on the two recording sessions, who worked with the Scotts for brief periods. Among these were trumpeter Joe Thomas (1928) and Roy Eldridge (late 1930), alto saxophonists Johnny Hodges (c 1926) and Joe Eldridge (early 'thirties), tenor saxophonist Leon 'Chu' Berry (early 'thirties), and violinist Juice Wilson (late 1928).

In 1927, the Scott band recorded *Harlem Shuffle, Symphonic Scronch* and *Happy Hour Blues. Harlem Shuffle,* by trumpeter Kenneth Roane, was in the book of several of the leading bands of the day. Apart from the period baritone solo by Cecil Scott with which the performance begins, this is an excellent recording. It includes a Roane solo with some unexpected twists of phrasing and a well played clarinet trio; a brief passage by Wells is his first on record, *Symphonic Scronch* also opens less than strikingly with a banjo solo from Hubert Mann. Then it improves, as the ensemble goes into a familiar riff, followed by pleasant solos from Roane and Wells. *Happy Hour Blues* is uneven, though the arrangement is good for the period, and Scott (on clarinet) and Wells have agreeable solos. The reed section again handles a trio clarinet passage with aplomb. One can hear from these recordings how the varied strands of development in big band arranging over the previous few years were now becoming part of a common pool of musical skill. The establishment of basic working methods by this date allowed the really talented arrangers to express themselves in an individual manner.

The 1929 recordings, while showing a clear linkage with those of two years earlier, display advances in rhythmic mobility and the expressiveness of some of the soloists. *Lawd Lawd* has a fleet solo from Bill Coleman which, though heavier tonally than his later work, shows that he had clarified his style by this date. In addition here is a pleasant alto saxophone solo, but too much time is spent on lengthy vocal passages from the band led by a solo singer, reputedly Frank Newton. *In A Corner* starts promisingly with a forceful, tightly scored ensemble passage that leads to an excellent solo by Wells. Unfortunately it deteriorates, after a reasonable passage by pianist Don Frye, into a feature for Cecil Scott on both clarinet and baritone saxophone. Apart from the bridge, this only consists of the repetition of a single dull phrase. *Bright Boy Blues* has a relaxed ensemble theme—at one point the melody is very reminiscent of *Chloe*—and Frye, Wells and Newton are heard in short solo sequences. *Springfield Stomp* highlights a fairly complex arrangement, an excellent solo from Coleman, a good one from Wells, and splendidly spacious ensemble playing. Cecil Scott solos on tenor saxophone on this title, here to better advantage. It is clear from this recording that, by 1929, the Scott band was a very good one. Its versatility obviously stood it in good stead at the varied venues in which it played.

Pianist Cliff Jackson, born in Washington, D.C., on 19th July 1902, is best remembered by record collectors as a solo pianist in the stride tradition. He went to New York in 1923. After working with a variety of local bands, he formed his own 'Krazy Kats' late in 1926. He led this group for several years at the Lenox Club, the Capitol Palace and other New York locations, then in the early 'thirties worked as a soloist or accompanist. Subsequently, he was featured mainly as a soloist, though he played intermittently with small groups, and worked up to the night before his sudden death, from a heart attack, on 24th May 1970.

Bingie Madison joined Cliff Jackson's band shortly after it was formed. He gives the personnel, at this time, as Cuban Bennett, Horace Holmes (trumpet), 'Moon' Jones, Bill Bonds (alto saxophone), himself (tenor saxophone), Cliff Jackson (piano), Goldie Lucas (banjo), . . . Stacey (bass horn) and Bobby Anderson (drums). Cuban Bennett, a cousin of Benny Carter, is something of a legendary figure in jazz. By all accounts, he featured a style that was very advanced for its time, though he never recorded.

Rudy Powell joined Jackson in 1928 and left in 1931, probably only a short time before the band broke up. Early in 1930, it had recorded for the Grey Gull/Radiex/Van Dyke group. The personnel at this time consisted of Henry Goodwin, Melvin Herbert (trumpet), 'Noisy' Richardson (trombone), Rudy Powell (alto saxophone, clarinet), Earl Evans (alto saxophone), Horace Langhorn (tenor saxophone), Cliff Jackson (piano), Andy Jackson (banjo), Chester Campbell (brass bass) and Percy Johnson (drums). Rudy Powell recalls that personnel changes were frequent during his stay with the band. He remembers trumpeters Jack Butler (1928 or 1929) and Lincoln Mills (1930), trombonists Charlie Irvis and Sandy Williams, banjoist Jimmy Cannon, and drummers Gary Lee, Dewey Beasley and Yank Porter as present at different times. Before Powell joined the band, that inveterate wanderer among New York bands, tenor saxophonist Happy

Cliff Jackson's Krazy Kats at the Lenox Club, New York, 1930. Cliff Jackson is standing; others from left to right: Rudy Powell, unidentified, Chester Campbell, Horace Langhorne, Percy Johnson, Nat Brown, Earl Evans, Andy Jackson and Henry Goodwin.

Caldwell, had been with Jackson for a month or two.

Today, musicians active during the late 'twenties and early 'thirties best remember the Cliff Jackson band from its stay at the Lenox Club at 143rd Street and Lenox Avenue. The Lenox featured three floor shows a night and stayed open from 11 o'clock at night to seven in the morning. Rudy Powell spoke of this period in his *Record Research* reminiscences :

'One of the highlights that sort of became legend in regard to the Lenox and which I heard about more than once, was this. It seems that the Cotton Club closed up at 2.00 a.m. and a lot of musicians from Duke's band would often come over to visit and jam with Cliff's outfit. Men such as Arthur "Chief" Whetsol, Freddy Jenkins and Joe "Tricky Sam" Nanton. Odd as this might sound to many people, Henry Goodwin would usually outswing the whole crew. After a while, Duke's boys became tired of Henry, who by that time was tagged as "The Menace", and so one night, the full Ellington brass section showed up and overpowered Henry with one brass chorus after another. Henry was finally subdued and because it was all in fun anyway, everyone had a good laugh. Among the trumpet fans, Henry was considered to be the very first rate.'

The Jackson band had twelve titles issued, ten under the name of Marvin Smolev, who is thought to have been the musical director for Grey Gull records. At least half are entirely commercial, with little to commend them to jazz fans; nevertheless *The Terror* and *Horse Feathers* do make it possible to understand why the band was so respected by other musicians. Both numbers feature driving ensemble work; Goodwin leads powerfully on *Horse,* and the arrangement for *The Terror* calls for a high degree of musical skill. *The Terror* contains reasonable solos from Richardson and the leader and, like *Horse Feathers,* mediocre ones by the sax men. Ultimately, the most impressive things about these performances are the sheer drive and vitality of the band in its ensemble role. It requires no great effort of imagination to guess how vigorous it must have sounded in person. Jackson was unlucky to record for a company which lacked the distributive outlets and publicity resources of the major labels. Presumably, he also suffered from a degree of interference in the choice of material to be recorded that led to the presentation of his band at a great deal less than its best.

Despite the fact that he was a prolific recording artist during the 'twenties, often with clarinettist Bob Fuller and pianist Louis Hooper, banjoist/guitarist Elmer Snowden remained a somewhat shadowy figure for most jazz followers until a few years ago. He was vaguely remembered as the man who brought Duke Ellington to New York from Washington, D.C., his home town. Snowden, who was born in Baltimore on 9th October 1900, took his first professional job in 1914. He moved to Washington, D.C. in 1919 and about two years later

formed his own band in which he doubled on saxophone. With this band, 'The Washingtonians', he opened at Baron Wilkins Inn on 134th Street and Seventh Avenue in September 1923, leaving six months later. He rejoined towards the end of 1924, when Duke Ellington had taken over the leadership. After a short time, he went to work with Ford Dabney, then resumed bandleading from 1925 until about 1934. At that point, he left for an eight year stay in Philadelphia because of a dispute with Local 802 of the American Federation of Musicians. After that time, he remained in music for all but a short period in the late 'fifties, playing as a soloist or as a member of small groups, as well as teaching saxophone and guitar. In 1968, he toured Europe for the first time. It should be mentioned that Snowden's own memory of his association with Ellington during the mid 'twenties conflicted with some of the information given above, but it is probable that after a lapse of so many years his recollection of dates was imperfect. He died in Philadelphia on 14th May 1973.

At one point Snowden had no fewer than five bands working under his name. The situation makes for confusion in establishing his personnels. He certainly led a number of successful bands at many New York clubs, including Small's Paradise, the Nest Club and the Bamville Club. Ironically, the only recording by any of these bands was issued under the name of the trombonist TeRoy Williams who had, incidentally, been replaced by Jimmy Harrison before the record was released. The record was made on 25th May 1927 with a line-up of Rex Stewart (cornet), TeRoy Williams (trombone), Prince Robinson (clarinet), Joe Garland (tenor saxophone, clarinet), unknown (alto saxophone), Freddie Johnson, unknown (piano), Elmer Snowden (banjo), Bob Ysaguirre (brass bass) and Walter Johnson (drums). This was the group that Snowden then led at the Nest Club with a couple of additions for recording purposes. Of the two titles recorded, *Lindbergh Hop* is the better, though that is not saying much. Two clarinets dominate the opening theme statement, and the pianos provide Billy Mayerl-like fill-ins; there follow a reasonable trumpet solo by Stewart, an average trombone passage by Williams, and a closing ensemble interspersed with scored breaks.

While discussing his career with Les Muscutt in Storyville magazine, Snowden mentioned that in attempting to list the musicians who had worked with him over the years he had reached 180 names. Obviously the task of presenting a chronological listing of Snowden's bands is almost impossible at this date, even so a number of the line-ups are known. His group at the Bamville Club in 1924 consisted of Horace Holmes, Gus Aiken (trumpet), Jake Frazier (trombone), Elmer Snowden (baritone saxophone, banjo), Ernie Bullock, Percy Glascoe, Alex Jackson (reeds), Leslie Hutchinson (piano), Bill Benford (brass bass) and Norman Buster (drums). With this band he moved to the Nest Club after a few weeks. In 1925,

Elmer Snowden

Snowden was back at the Bamville Club with Bubber Miley, Charlie Johnson (trumpet), Harry 'Father' White (trombone), Jimmie Lunceford (sax, trombone), Glyn Paque, Castor McCord (reeds), Count Basie, replaced by Claude Hopkins (piano), himself (banjo), Ernest 'Bass' Hill (brass bass) and Tommy Benford (drums).

The Nest Club offered Snowden regular work during 1927 and 1928. Early in 1927 he headed his 'Westerners' there. They comprised Henry Goodwin (trumpet), Joe 'Tricky Sam' Nanton (trombone), Jimmy Field, Happy Caldwell (reeds), Cliff Jackson (piano), Banjo Bernie (banjo), Cyrus St Clair (tuba) and Manzie Johnson (drums). Later in the same year, he was leading the band that recorded under the name of TeRoy Williams. From the spring of 1930 through to 1932, Snowden was frequently at Smalls's Paradise. His initial line-up was Gus Aiken, Red Harlan (trumpet), Herb Gregory (trombone), Otto Hardwick, Wayman Carver (reeds), Don Kirkpatrick (piano), himself (guitar), Sid Catlett (drums). At other times during this period he used Roy Eldridge (trumpet),

Dicky Wells (trombone), Garvin Bushell, Al Sears, Howard Johnson (reeds), and Dick Fullbright (bass).

In 1933, a short film was made of a floorshow, 'Smash Yo' Baggage', which had been put on when Snowden was at Small's. The band was enlarged to fourteen pieces for the occasion. Snowden recalls that it included Robert Cheek (trumpet), George Washington (trombone), and reedmen Gervin Bushell, Al Sears, Wayman Carver and Otto Hardwick. He adds that all the last four but Hardwick doubled on flute. An LP containing music by Snowden's band from the film soundtrack has recently been released in the United States.

Other noted jazz musicians who are known to have worked with Snowden include Harry Cooper (c 1925), Leonard Davis (1930-31), Demas Dean (c 1924), Charlie Green (1930), Hilton Jefferson (late 'twenties), Howard Johnson (1931), Bingie Madison (1930), Teddy McRae (early 'thirties), Frank Newton (summer 1927), Bobby Stark (c 1932), Billy Taylor (1925) and Greely Walton (1926).

Snowden's career illustrates the large part played by chance in selecting the bands which were recorded in this period; it is unlikely that at least some of his groups could not have equalled many of those that did find their way into the studios.

Bill Brown and his Brownies existed as a regular unit for at least a decade. They were formed in 1925 and finally disbanded around 1935. Ellsworth Reynolds told Bertrand Demeusy that he had been the band's musical director for a while in late 1925 and early 1926, when it was resident at the Club Swanee in New York and broadcast twice weekly. He gave the personnel as Luke Smith, Howard Scott (trumpet), Bill Brown (trombone), Ellsworth Reynolds (violin, director), Arville Harris (alto saxophone, clarinet), Jose Baretto (alto saxophone), John Wyatt (tenor saxophone), Ray Stokes (piano), John DeLeon (tuba) and Eddie Howe (drums). The band recorded in March 1927 with a line-up generally accepted as comprising Billy Hicks, Charlie Johnson (trumpet), Bill Brown (trombone), Ralph James (clarinet, alto saxophone), Malvin Wyatt (tenor saxophone), Bill Caine (piano), Harry Stevens (banjo), George DeLeon (tuba) and Oliver Tines (drums). John and Malvin Wyatt are obviously the same person. Gene Johnson (alto saxophone) worked with Brown at various times from the mid 'twenties, and, as Arville Harris was with the band from 1925 to 1928, he should be on the 1927 recording session. Later in 1927, Peter DuConge (reeds) also played with Brown.

In 1928 Ellsworth Reynolds rejoined the band. He claims that the personnel was as before, with the addition of Ray Carn (trumpet), Jim Reevy (trombone), Ray Hernandez (alto saxophone) and Gil Cornick (guitar). He says, too, that the band was now known as the Club Swanee Orchestra. DeLeon must have left at some point in 1928, for both Ernest 'Bass' Hill and John Kirby were briefly with Brown in this year. In addition, Hilton Jefferson (alto saxophone) played with him for a limited period, while trumpeter Wardell Jones was a member of Brown's band at the Alhambra Ballroom in the spring of 1929. A second recording session took place in December 1929 with a line-up of Ovie Alston, Billy Hicks (trumpet), Bill Brown (trombone), Rupert Cole (alto and baritone saxophone, clarinet), Gene Johnson (alto saxophone), Hubert Thompson (tenor saxophone), Norman Lester (piano), Donald Tathim (banjo), John Kirby (brass bass), Reggie Brown (drums). Around 1930, trumpeter Wendell Culley joined Brown, probably replacing Alston.

The last full personnel we have for Brown is one given to Bertrand Demeusy by guitarist Bob Lessey. It refers to 1933-34, when the band was at the Grand Central Palace, New York. The group had been reduced in size and then consisted of Russell Royster (trumpet), Bill Brown (trombone), Glyn Paque (alto saxophone), Hubert Thompson (tenor saxophone), Pat Armstead (piano), Bob Lessey (guitar), Charlie Drayton (bass), Reggie Brown (drums). Lessey recalls that Wyatt (to whom he refers as Melvin) replaced Thompson.

Brown's records are competent but little more. The date in 1927 produced *Hot Lips,* which contains a reasonable solo by the leader, and *Bill Brown Blues* with a good plunger trumpet theme (probably Hicks) and a well played tuba solo by DeLeon. The two titles from late 1929—*Zonky* and *What Kind of Rhythm Is That?*—are better, with greater swing in the ensemble passages. *Zonky* includes pleasant contributions by alto and trumpet, while *Rhythm* has good solos by Cole (baritone saxophone) and a trumpeter who is probably Alston. It is perhaps unfair to judge the Brown band on such slight recorded evidence, but musicians have confirmed to me the impression of a proficient but somewhat routine band as an accurate reflection of their own memories.

In contrast, Marion Hardy's Alabamians, originally formed in Chicago, are remembered by a number of musicians as a first rate unit. Cab Calloway fronted them for his New York debut at the Savoy Ballroom in October 1929. It was in this month that the band took part in its only recording session. The personnel that recorded *Georgia Pine* and *Song of the Bayou* was Eddie Mallory, Elisha Herbert (trumpet), Henry Clark (trombone), Artie Starks, Marion Hardy (alto saxophone, clarinet), unknown (clarinet, tenor saxophone), Ralph Anderson (piano), Leslie Corley (banjo), Charlie Turner (brass bass), Jimmy McHendricks (drums) and, alas, the Alabama Magpie Trio (vocal). Despite the efforts of the vocalists, the two numbers recorded show off the band to advantage. The two trumpeters shine in both solo and unison passages and the ensemble attains a fair degree of swing. The absence of further recordings can probably be ascribed to the Wall Street crash a few days after that session, followed by the depression years.

Early in 1931, Hardy's personnel consisted of Doc Cheatham, Eddie Mallory (trumpet), Fred Robinson (trombone), Artie Starks, Marion Hardy (alto saxophone, clarinet), Werner Seers (tenor saxophone, clarinet), Ralph Anderson (piano), Leslie Corley (guitar), unknown (bass) and 'Strippy' (drums). Later in the year, Jack Butler, Jock Bennett (trumpet) and Clyde Bernhardt (trombone) replaced Cheatham, Mallory and Robinson. Bernhardt remained with the band until it finally broke up, but clearly there were frequent changes in the group during this late stage of its existence. Bassist Olin Aderhold was present during 1932, presumably a few months before disbandment. He recalls Donald Christian and John Swan as the trumpeters, Bernhardt as the trombonist, Hardy, Craig Watson and Warner Seals—obviously the Werner Seers just mentioned—as the reed men, and a rhythm section of Anderson, Corley, himself and Tiny Bradshaw.

In an interview with Gilbert Gaster, Clyde Bernhardt

Marion Hardy's Alabamians, originally a Chicago group, whose members mostly settled in the New York area from the late 1920s. Left to right: Ralph Anderson, Marion Hardy, Warner Seals, Lawrence Harrison (front man), Artie Starks, unidentified, Jimmy McHendricks, Eddie Mallory, Elisha Herbert, Charlie Turner and Henry Clark. Charlie Turner later led his own big band at the Arcadia Ballroom, New York.

Bingie Madison's Tune Tattlers. Definitely present are pianist Joe Turner and banjoist Goldie Lucas. Madison is the first saxophonist; the others are probably Fred Skerritt and Henry 'Moon' Jones.

remembered that, while he worked with him, Hardy paid more than many big name bandleaders. He referred to the group as '. . . an entertaining band . . . you know, they used to do a lot of glee-club singing, and they played most of all white jobs. They played a lot of college jobs . . . college dances, and they were very popular.'

On his only record, Hardy is listed as Marlow Hardy, but all musicians I have spoken to call him Marion. I had a chance encounter with Hardy's son in New York some years ago. Unfortunately, it was very brief and I had no opportunity to do more than confirm the fact that Hardy had died sometime in the 'forties.

From the time when Bingie Madison played piano in cinemas at the age of seventeen, his varied and active career has extended over half a century. He was born in Des Moines and worked with Bobby Brown and Bernie Davis before forming his first big band in April 1926. He engaged Al Jenkins, Shorty Stanford (trumpet), Billy Cato (trombone), Bernie Davis, Arthur Davey (alto saxophone), Johnnie Bracken (tenor saxophone), Bingie Madison (piano), Goldie Lucas (banjo), Ed Burrows (bass horn), Johnnie Johnson (drums). The band was short-lived and disbanded after playing at a theatre in Newark, N.J. and a few clubs. Later that year, Madison fronted a

quintet. In 1929, Madison took over his second big band when Lew Henry, the original director, left New York. The line-up consisted of Louis Bacon, Cyril Hunt (trumpet), Ed Cuffee, replaced by Fernando Arbello (trombone), Freddie Skerritt, Henry 'Moon' Jones (alto saxophone), Bingie Madison (tenor saxophone, clarinet), Gene Rodgers (piano), Goldie Lucas (banjo), Richard Fullbright (bass), Gary Lee (drums). This group played at the Tango Palace in New York, then for a short time at the Savoy Ballroom. After that, it broke up through lack of engagements.

In late 1930, Madison became leader of a band that was already in residence at the Broadway Danceland at 60th Street and Broadway. He directed Wardell Jones, Edward Anderson (trumpet), Henry Hicks (trombone), Jobetus McCord, Sleepy Jamison (alto saxophone), Bingie Madison (tenor saxophone), Joe Turner (piano), Benny James (banjo), . . . Jackson (brass bass) and Bill Beason (drums). Not long afterwards, with a few changes in personnel and led by drummer Willie Lynch, this band became Mills Blue Rhythm Band. Madison then set about reorganising for the remainder of the Broadway Danceland engagement. He fronted Ward Pinkett, Bill Dillard (trumpet), Jimmy Archey (trombone), with the sax and rhythm sections of his earlier Tango Palace band. He has said that as these musicians were familiar with his style and arrangements, he felt that they best interpreted his music. Madison never again led his own big band, though in the years to come he played in many leading bands of the swing era. Since the mid 'forties, he has worked with small groups, both as leader and sideman. His autobiography, completed in the 'sixties, has not yet been published.

Although Madison's first three big bands failed to record, his final group took part in three sessions. None of the output was issued under his name. The first recording date, in October 1930, produced *Hot Lovin'*, *Papa De Da Da* and *Baby, Won't You Please Come Home?*, released as by Clarence Williams and his Orchestra. All feature a vocal trio of Clarence Williams, Eva Taylor and Clarence Todd. However, their contributions are relatively brief, and there is plenty of room left for instrumental solos. *Hot Lovin'* has fine solo work by Pinkett—who also takes a typically exuberant scat vocal—and good solos from Madison, Rodgers and Dillard. *Papa* has excellent work from Pinkett again, both instrumentally and vocally. There is a well conceived alto solo by Skerritt, who features on *Baby*, too. Clearly, this well rehearsed and skilful band, even apart from its soloists, must have been the equal of many major orchestras of the day.

The last two sessions by the Madison band were made with Joe 'King' Oliver as leader, though he only takes a solo on *Stop Crying* from the first date of January 1931. Buster Bailey (clarinet) and Dave Nelson (trumpet) joined the personnel for the occasion. The outstanding moments on a rather lack-lustre *Who's Blue* are provided by Bailey. The remaining titles, *Papa De Da Da* and *Stop Crying*, are much better and again highlight the quality of the band. Pinkett once more does good trumpet and vocal work on *Papa*, while Oliver, Nelson and Bailey (playing in the highest register of his instrument) play well on *Stop*. For a final session of April 1931, the last date on which Oliver appeared, Nelson and Bailey are not present and the identity of the trombonist is something of a mystery. The records were released as by The Chocolate Dandies. There are good ensemble passages and it is interesting to hear Oliver play behind the vocal on *One More Time*, nevertheless this performance and *Loveless Love* are undistinguished, not least when they feature the vocal trio of Lucas, Madison and Skerritt. The final number, *When I Take My Sugar To Tea*, is a great deal better. Pinkett performs a good scat vocal and a strong trumpet solo, while the ensemble plays with an impressive relaxation and swing. It seems likely that, given regular work and further opportunity to record, this Madison band could have become one of the leading groups of its day.

Dave Nelson, nephew of King Oliver, first led a band at the Dreamland Cafe in Chicago in 1927. His career had already included playing with Ma Rainey, Jelly Roll Morton, Richard M. Jones and Edgar Hayes. Although his first band had not lasted long, he led another on tour before settling in New York in 1928. There, he formed a big band towards the end of 1930. He had been on tour with Oliver, and rejoined him, before fronting his 'Hot Shots' in the Mae West show 'The Constant Sinner'. After a five week tour, the show opened on Broadway, only to be closed as a result of police intervention two weeks later. Until the mid 'thirties, Nelson continued to lead big bands, securing residencies in New York and New Jersey at such places as the Nest Club, Pelham Heath Inn and the Cedar Theatre. After this, he led smaller groups until about 1942, when he became a staff arranger for a music publishing company. He remained there until his death from a heart attack at the age of forty-one on 7th April 1946.

The Nelson Band used in the Mae West show included Leonard Fields (alto saxophone), Trent Harris (tenor saxophone), Lloyd Phillips (piano), Danny Barker (guitar) and Herbie Cowens (drums). Of these, however, only Barker is present on the recordings that Nelson made for RCA Victor in 1931, and he was only there for one of the two sessions. The first produced *I Ain't Got Nobody*, *When Day Is Done* and *Some of These Days*, all pleasant if unexceptional performances, recalled more for the quality of some individual solos than the impact of the band as such. It is unfortunate that Nelson chose to sing on every number, for he is an indifferent vocalist, although Sam Allen's piano accompaniment on *I Ain't Nobody* is good, as is the solo by clarinetist Buster Bailey that follows. *When Day* has a rather straight trumpet theme which could well be Nelson's. Bailey takes the fine release, and there are pleasant solos by a trumpeter, whom I take to be Melvin Herbert, and guitarist Arthur Taylor. *Some* is by far the best performance of the session, mainly because of the outstanding playing of Bailey who is heard solo and during the opening theme and closing ensemble chorus. There is also a reasonable tenor saxophone solo, probably by Charles Frazier, and a pleasant Armstrong-like trumpet solo, presumably by Herbert.

Nelson again has vocals on all the titles from a final session of June 1931 and features himself a great deal more on trumpet. Interestingly enough, his wa-wa playing on *Rockin' Chair* and *St. Louis Blues* and his muted work on *Somebody Stole My Gal* show a strong King Oliver influence. This forms something of a contrast with the improved ensemble work of the band which carries hints of the coming swing era. There are good solos by a trombonist and clarinettist (possibly Glyn Paque), and Wayman Carver is heard on flute on *Loveless Love*. These performances are interesting as a whole for the glimpse they give of a traditional era in big band jazz. Nelson's own playing and Danny Barker's use of banjo instead of guitar sound almost anachronistic in this context.

Alex Jackson is a rather obscure figure who led his own band from 1926 until at least 1931. He appeared on records by Mamie Smith (1924) and Ethel Waters (1925 and 1927), then made titles with his Plantation Orchestra in September and October 1927. The personnel of Clarence Wheeler, Lee Golden (trumpet), Joe King (trombone), Leonard Fields, Harold Scott (alto saxophone), Raymond Martin (tenor saxophone), Lonnie Smith (piano), Tommy Short (banjo), Bob Ysaguirre (brass bass) and Dick Wood (drums), heard on his records, has been identified from a photograph taken at the time of the session. I have heard two of the four released titles, *Jackass Blues* and *Missouri Squabble;* neither is outstanding. The band is competent as an ensemble, but the soloists are unimpressive. Pianist Smith makes the most impact with his neat underlining of the ensemble on *Jackass.*

In later years, contemporary papers carried almost no news of the Jackson band, though it is known that Ysaguirre was a regular member from 1926 to 1929. During 1929 and 1930, pianist Sam Allen worked with the band in Cincinnati, and Rex Stewart and Edgar Sampson joined briefly in 1930. It is to be presumed that Jackson, like many better known leaders, was one of the casualties of the depression years.

Although Joe Steele's band only recorded two titles, his career is rather better documented than that of Alex Jackson. He was the pianist on the 1926 Savoy Bearcats recordings and played regularly with this group. He switched to leading his own bands after a spell with Henri Saparo at the Bamboo Inn in 1927. Most of the musicians who are present on his record worked with him during 1928-29. In addition, Harry Carney was briefly in the band in 1927 and Walter 'Foots' Thomas in 1928. After giving up bandleading in 1930, he was a member of Pike Davis's orchestra in the 'Rhapsody In Black' show the next two years and joined the Chick Webb band early in 1933. He remained with Webb until 1936. His subsequent career, until he retired from music, is obscure. He died in New York City on 5th February 1964.

Jimmy Archey worked with Steele at the Bamboo Inn around 1928. He recalls the personnel as Herb Branch, Jack Wilson (trumpet), himself (trombone), Red Thomas (tenor saxophone), Joe Steele (piano), Frank Smith (bass), Manzie Johnson (drums). It seems unlikely that only one saxophone would be included and Mr Archey's memory probably failed him on this occasion. On another occasion Archey identified the musicians from a photograph taken around 1928 as James Elmer (trumpet), himself (trombone), Craig Watson (alto saxophone), Trenton Harris (tenor saxophone), Joe Steele (piano), Freddy White (banjo, guitar), Frank Smith (bass, tuba) Sam Frederick (drums), so that it appears that there were a number of personnel changes during Steele's residency at Bamboo Inn.

The personnel used by Steele on his one recording session is, in all probability, Ward Pinkett, Jack Wilson (trumpet), Jimmy Archey (trombone), Charlie Holmes (alto and soprano saxophone, clarinet), Eugene Mikell (tenor saxophone), Joe Garland (baritone saxophone), Joe Steele (piano), unknown (banjo, guitar), Frank Smith (bass) and Gerald Hobson (drums). Pinkett's presence has

been questioned, but it is known that he replaced Langston Curl sometime towards the end of 1928. *Coal Yard Shuffle*, a rather catchy theme by Steele, has good solos from Pinkett and Holmes and reasonable ones from Steele and Archey. The band as a whole sounds proficient without being markedly individual. *Top and Bottom* (Ward Pinkett's favourite drink) is very good indeed. There are excellent solos from Steele and Archey, and really striking playing by Pinkett, who was undoubtedly a trumpeter of the highest class. Here, he plays with an attractive full tone. His solos are a model of good phrasing and relaxation. Two takes have been issued of both titles. While there is little difference in the versions of *Coal Yard*, take one of *Top* is much better than take two. It lasts forty-two seconds longer and benefits from the considerably slower tempo.

Several of the well known music teachers who played such a major role in developing the talent of countless instrumentalists in the 'twenties and 'thirties were given the nickname of Fess, whether they were officially professors or not. In their cases, it was meant as a tribute, but the term was also applied ironically to some musicians whose talents did not match their reputations or self evaluations. 'Professor' Stanley Williams, the 'Black Ted Lewis', soon won the title, and it is impossible to resist suggesting that it was awarded by musicians with a considerable sense of humour.

Williams was born in Danville, Kentucky on 10th April 1894. He is, incidentally, the uncle of bassist Charlie Mingus. He had fairly extensive musical training and moved to Cincinnati in 1914. He led his own band from 1919 to 1923 before joining Ollie Powers in Chicago. In 1924, he formed another band to back a variety act, going with them to New York. A year later, he had a residency at the Rosemont Ballroom. When the Savoy Ballroom opened at 596 Lenox Avenue on 12th March 1926, Fess Williams and his Royal Flush Orchestra and the Savoy Bearcats were the resident groups, with Fletcher Henderson and his Band as the guest attraction. The Williams band was resident at the Savoy until January 1928, though its leader was absent for a while in Chicago. At this time the band was fronted either by Hank Duncan or Howard Johnson. Williams returned in the spring of 1929 and continued as a bandleader for the next ten years, varying residencies at the Savoy and other New York venues with touring schedules. He left full-time music to work in real estate during the 'forties, but led a small instrumental and vocal group at intervals. For a period in the 'sixties, he managed a popular vocal group. He worked at Local 802 of the American Federation of Musicians until 1964. Today, both his sons and one daughter are musicians.

For many years, Williams retained a nucleus of regular musicians. The player of longest standing was trombonist David 'Jelly' James. When Williams played the Rosemont Ballroom in Brooklyn during the summer of 1925,

The Fess Williams Band at the Savoy Ballroom, 1929. Williams is seated; others from left to right: David 'Jelly' James, Kenneth Roane, George Temple, Ollie Blackwell, Emanuel Casamore, Lockwood Lewis, Ralph Bedell, Andy Pendleton, Gregory Felix, Perry Smith and Henry 'Hank' Duncan.

he fronted George Temple (trumpet), David 'Jelly' James (trombone), Perry Smith (tenor saxophone), Harry 'Hank' Duncan (piano), Ollie Blackwell (banjo), and Ralph Bedell (drums). This was the group that opened at the Savoy in March 1926. Williams dressed in a diamond-studded suit and top hat. Though his playing of clarinet and alto saxophone was generally excruciating, he became an immense favourite with the Savoy audiences. Shortly after the opening, the management presented a 'Fess Williams Night' when more than two thousand copies of his latest record were given away. In describing his career to Harrison Smith, Williams spoke of the famous Savoy band battles. 'We never lost a battle even though most of these bands were larger and some were better musically. But when we got through setting perfect tempos and putting on our showmanship, the dancers thought we were best in every respect.' Lloyd Scott, for one, would dispute this. Incredible though it might seem, the Williams band won battles against Duke Ellington, Fletcher Henderson and King Oliver. They were aggrieved by the selection of Duke Ellington's band to appear in the film 'Check and Double Check' when they thought they had secured the job.

As bands became bigger in the late 'twenties, Williams added musicians to the group. His personnel at the Savoy in 1929 consisted of the six musicians who had opened with him there in 1926 plus Kenneth Roane (trumpet), Lockwood Lewis (alto saxophone, front man), Gregory Felix (reeds), Emanuel Casamore (tuba) and Andy Pendleton (banjo, vocal). From then on, his personnel became less stable. A year later, after a financially disastrous tour, his line-up at the Savoy was John Brown, Emanuel Clark, unknown (trumpet), David 'Jelly' James (trombone), Felix Gregory, Bob Holmes, Perry Smith (reeds), Walter 'Fats' Pichon (piano), Clinton Walker (bass) and Ralph Bedell (drums). From 1932 to 1934 bassist Olin Alderhold

worked with Williams. At this time, changes of personnel were frequent. Mr Aderhold gives the members of the band as Clarence Wheeler, John Brown, Oscar Clarke (trumpet), David 'Jelly' James (trombone), Fess Williams (clarinet, alto saxophone), Garvin Bushell, Craig Watson, Perry Smith (reeds), Lloyd Smith (probably an error in the name of Lloyd Phillips) (piano), Bill Johnson, replaced by Gene Fields (guitar), himself (bass) and Ralph Bedell (drums). He adds that Wheeler was replaced in turn by Jabbo Jenkins, Leroy Rutledge and Bob Shoffner. Bernard Flood and Rex Stewart (trumpet) were briefly in the band, as was clarinettist Albert Nicholas. Bushell was replaced by Jerome 'Don' Pasquall who was with Williams during part of 1934 when the band was playing at the Brooklyn Roseland and working odd gigs. He lists the personnel as John Clark, Leroy Rutledge, Jabbo Jenkins (trumpet), David 'Jelly' James (trombone), Jerome 'Don' Pasquall, Ben Smith (alto saxophone, clarinet), Perry Lee Smith (tenor saxophone), Fess Williams (clarinet, alto saxophone), Lloyd Phillips (piano), Bill Johnson (guitar), Olin Aderhold (bass) and Ralph Bedell (drums). Presumably John Clark is the same as Oscar Clarke.

By the mid 'thirties, Williams' popularity was beginning to decline: after a session in July 1930, he did not record for over a decade. He still kept a following at the Savoy, however, and when Jerome 'Don' Pasquall rejoined him there in 1936, he was leading Robert Cheeks, George Thigpen (trumpet), Jerome 'Don' Pasquall, Frank Powell (alto saxophone, clarinet), Jimmy Smith (tenor saxophone), James P. Johnson (piano), unknown (bass) and George Foster (drums). In the summer of 1937, saxophonist Lem Johnson came to New York and secured his first job there with Williams. He told the Swiss collector Johnny Simmen:

'He was a comedian, true, but he saw to it that each man would be featured in several numbers at length. He had a terrific little band with the great James P. Johnson on piano, a wonderful, unsung trumpet player, Elmer Edwards, and Larry Hinton on drums.'

Johnson's comment may explain why, quite apart from convenience or financial need, so many really good musicians worked with Williams through the years. Trumpeters June Clark, Demas Dean (both mid 'twenties) and Reunald Jones (mid 'thirties), baritone saxophonist Harry Carney (early 1927) and guitarist Danny Barker (1933) played with him. Lloyd Phillips thought that he sent for Jabbo Smith on one occasion, though he might be confusing Smith with Jabbo Jenkins. Williams recorded steadily from 1925 to 1927 and prolifically during 1929 and 1930. Though there are good individual solos to be heard, the strongly featured clarinet and alto saxophone work of the leader, not to mention his vocals on later records, make heavy listening. From Lem Johnson's account, it seems that in-person performances by the Williams band afforded musicians the opportunity to be heard to advantage and gave listeners a rest from Williams's own hokum playing. The links between vaudeville and jazz are demonstrated rather too painfully by such musicians as Wilbur Sweatman and Fess Williams. Nevertheless, they deserve an honourable mention in any comprehensive history of big band jazz for their encouragement of numerous fine musicians and, in Williams's case, for maintaining standards which, regrettably, did not extend to his own playing.

It might be as well here briefly to mention Leroy Smith and his Band, though its connection with big band jazz is only peripheral. It was very popular for many years, however, and Smith is an interesting example of a coloured musician of the older school who took a long time to come to terms with jazz, if in fact he ever did

The story of the Smith band was recounted to Bertrand Demeusy during the late 'sixties by Emerson 'Geechie' Harper, one of its two surviving members. Smith was already leading a dance orchestra when Harper first met him in Detroit in 1917. A year later, Harper joined his band. The first New York engagement was at Reisenweber's on 8th Avenue in autumn 1921. From 1924, the band worked at Connie's Inn where it was often resident in the following years. It went on tour with a road pro-

duction of the Connie's Inn revue 'Hot Chocolates' around 1933. During the next two years the band went out for a second season and had residencies in Cleveland, Philadelphia and again, Connie's Inn. Soon afterwards, the depression arrived and the band broke up. Smith returned to Detroit, where in subsequent years he led small dance orchestras and conducted concerts in public parks. After several years of ill health, he died of cancer on 23rd November 1962.

Though Smith came from a musical background which frowned on ad-libbing and led what was strictly a show band, he was forced to make some musical concessions. After coming to New York he added trumpeter Clifton 'Pike' Davis to his group. Charlie Gaines, Bill Dillard (trumpet), Wilbur DeParis (trombone), Louis Jordan, Arville Harris (saxes), Lloyd Phillips (piano), Kaiser Marshall and Walter Johnson (drums) were some of the jazz stylists who worked with him in later years. Mr Harper has said that Smith always featured improvisation sparingly, and only allowed the musicians he considered proficient in the style to take ad lib solos. The band recorded on four occasions. *Rhapsody In Blue* and *St. Louis Blues* released in 1928 best reflect its style. It also appeared in a short film titled 'Flying Fists' that featured Benny Leonard.

A lot has been heard about the white jazz musicians who spent their years in commercial dance bands dreaming of escape. A band like Smith's must have seemed little better to the coloured jazz stylists who worked with

Leroy Smith and his Victor recording group, 1927. Left to right: Emerson Harper, Frank Bell, Sammy Speed, Ed Beller, Leroy Smith (seated), Harold Henson, John Long, Stanley Peters, Harry Brookes, Charlie Gaines, Teroy Williams and Fred Peters.

it, however high its overall musical standards might be. On the other hand, the substantial number of coloured musicians who admired the Paul Whiteman band during the 'twenties might have viewed it in a very different light. That Leroy Smith's band should exist and succeed for so long is a salutary reminder that not all coloured big bands were jazz units. The view we have of several of the leading black orchestras might be significantly different, but for the prejudices of recording directors at this period who considered black musicians incapable of playing anything other than jazz. The more rigid jazz follower might feel that for once prejudice worked in his favour. Even so, it would have been interesting to have the opportunity to hear how Louis Armstrong sounded, for example, on the *Poet and Peasant Overture* when Erskine Tate's band tackled the number in Chicago.

APPENDIX

In view of its popularity and longevity, it is surprising that the Vernon Andrade band never recorded. For many years, it was based on the Renaissance Ballroom in Harlem, while it played, too, at the Savoy Ballroom—from which it also broadcast. In addition, there were limited tours. Andrade himself played banjo and guitar. He is believed to have started work at the Renaissance around 1925, though the personnels of his earliest bands are obscure.

George Washington (trombone) and Happy Caldwell (tenor, clarinet) joined the band in 1929. Caldwell remained until 1933. Trumpeter Louie Metcalf arrived in the band in the autumn of 1930. The line-up, as he remembers it, consisted during his rather short stay of himself and Clarence Wheeler (trumpet), George Washington (trombone), Happy Caldwell, Gene Mikell (reeds), Tom Thomas (saxophone, oboe), Julius Fields (piano), Vernon Andrade (guitar, banjo), and Zutty Singleton (drums). Although he does not mention a bassist, Al Morgan worked with Andrade from 1930 to 1932, and for several years during the 'thirties Pete Briggs, famous for his recordings with Armstrong's Hot Seven, was a member of the band. He probably took over from Morgan. Metcalf recalls how the Andrade orchestra defeated the bands of Zack Whyte, Blanche Calloway, Chick Webb and Bennie Moten at a 'battle of bands' in Philadelphia. It overcame the Missourians, fronted by Cab Calloway, the following night at the Savoy. If Metcalf's memory is accurate, Andrade's group must indeed have been outstanding.

Trombonist Clyde Bernhardt joined Andrade in January 1934 and remained with him for just over three years. He later recalled:

'Vernon Andrade had a very good band in the Renaissance Casino, and he had the best paying job to play in Harlem in those days. That was a wonderful band that could play almost anything. I'm telling you, as soon as a hit came along, Vernon had it in his book. We had some

Bobbie Brown's Society Orchestra, early 1920s. Left to right: Rex Stewart, Herb Gregory, Bingie Madison, Walter Johnson, Happy Caldwell, Goldie Lucas and Bobbie Brown.

wonderful arrangers too. There was Joe Thomas—he was one of the best—he played sax. Not the Joe Thomas who was with Jimmie Lunceford's band—he played sax too—this one was from Tulsa, Oklahoma. For about a year, Horace Henderson played piano with us, and he brought over all the arrangements he'd done for his brother, Fletcher.'

The only other musician that Mr Bernhardt names in his reminiscences is lead altoist 'Satch' Green, but it is worth noting that Horace Henderson was present during 1935 and part of 1936 and that the Joe Thomas mentioned is the brother of Walter 'Foots' Thomas and is active today in the agency business.

The subsequent history of the Andrade band is obscure. It certainly survived into the early 'forties. Cecil Scott (tenor, clarinet) played with Andrade in the mid 'thirties, and other musicians known to have worked with him include tenor saxophonist Al Sears (late 1938), trombonist Joe Britton (1938-1939) and tenor saxophonist Greely Walton (1938—c1941).

Bill Benford, brother of drummer Tommy, was considered one of the best tuba players of the 'twenties. He recorded with the Gulf Coast Seven and Ethel Waters in 1925, with Thomas Morris and the Plantation Orchestra in 1926, with Jelly Roll Morton in 1928 and 1930, and with Bubber Miley in 1930. During 1929 and 1930, he led his own band at the Rainbow Gardens in New York. The personnel, as given to Kurt Mohr by Earle Howard, consisted of unknown (trumpet), Jimmy Archey (trombone), Emmett Matthews (soprano), Morris O'Brien (alto) Noel Clookies (tenor), Earle Howard (piano), Bill Benford (tuba), Tommy Benford (drums). Archey and Tommy Benford were in the band for only a limited period; their replacements are not known. Trombonist Geechie Fields was with the band at one point, probably during the summer of 1930, but the suggested presence of trumpeter Ward Pinkett has not been definitely established.

Saxist Bobbie Brown was working in Canada late in 1920. He fronted a quartet that included Bingie Madison on piano from January 1921. Brown's home was actually in Newark, N.J. From there he led his own band—billed as Bobbie Brown's Society Orchestra or Bobbie Brown's Syncopators—until sometime in 1926. Bingie Madison, doubling piano and sax, joined the band in August 1922 and reported that until he left in December 1925 personnel changes were quite frequent. Musicians either found better jobs or were fired by Brown who appears to have been a somewhat capricious leader. Mr Madison gave a list of members during his stay with the band, mentioning that the line-up at various times included Rex Stewart, Bobby Stark, Shorty Stanford, A. Jenkins (trumpet), Herb Gregory (trombone), Happy Caldwell (tenor, clarinet), Ed Burrows (bass horn), Goldie Lucas (banjo, violin) Johnnie Johnson, Walter Johnson, Willie Knolls, Andrew James, Buster Tyler (drums). A surviving photograph of the band, showing Stewart, Gregory, Madison, Brown, Caldwell, Lucas and Walter Johnson, must date from late 1924, as this was when Stewart worked with Brown.

Jack Butler or, as he prefers to be known, Jacques Butler 'Chef d'Orchestre' is best remembered by European jazz fans for his work with the Willie Lewis band in the mid 'thirties and his subsequent activities throughout Europe. However, before joining Lewis in Paris during 1936, he had fronted bands in New York and on tour. One he led in 1934 had the trombonists Alton Moore and George Stevenson in the line-up. In 1935 he toured with another band as part of 'Connie's Hot Chocolates Road Show'. The personnel given by bassist Ellsworth Reynolds consisted of Reuben Reeves, Jack Butler, unknown (trumpet), Arville Harris (alto, clarinet), Scoville Brown (alto), Trenton Harris (tenor), Norman Thornton (baritone), Ellsworth Reynolds (bass, violin), Fred Pedru, Nestor Acivedo (violin), Baron Lee (director). It can be assumed that the absence of trombonists and three rhythm section men is due to a lapse in Mr Reynold's memory. Possibly, either or both of the two trombonists mentioned above were still in the band. Butler worked in Europe for eighteen years from 1950 and is still active as a musician in New York where I recently met him at the Wall Street office in which he has a day time job. He told me that his family still live in Europe and that he plans to return and settle down permanently in 1974.

Little is known about alto saxophonist Ed Campbell who led bands, mainly at the Bamboo Inn in New York City during 1927 and 1928, and was later a member of show orchestras. Although we know that trumpeter Demas Dean worked with him in 1927, the only full line-up of Campbell's group that has survived is one given to the Swiss collector Kurt Mohr by the late Jimmy Archey. It refers to the band he led at the Bamboo Inn during 1927, consisting of Herbert Branch, Jack Wilson (trumpet), Jimmy Archey (trombone), Ed Campbell (alto), Thomas Hodge (tenor), Arthur Gibbs (piano), Frank Smith (bass) and Jerome 'Romie' Bourke (drums). The Bamboo Inn was also for some years the location of Henry Saparo's band.

Musical shows and revues provided much work for jazz musicians during the 'twenties. One of the best known was Jimmie Cooper's 'Black and White Revue'. Cooper, a white man, mounted musical extravaganzas with a cast of seventy, made up of thirty-five white and thirty-five black artists. His musical director was Julian Arthur, leader of 'Julian Arthur's Ten Jazz Musicians', and from the summer of 1923 until the spring of 1924, trumpeter Louie Metcalf was a member of his band. During this period Metcalf recalls playing alongside such musicians as David 'Jelly' James, Jonas Walker (trombone), Jim McCleary (clarinet), Jazz Curry, Eugene Sedric (sax), Willard Hamby (piano), Walter Temple (banjo),

A poster for the Jimmie Cooper Revue featuring a band that included trumpeter Louie Metcalf.

D. Lamont replaced by Alex Alenxander (tuba), Red Muse replaced by Theodore 'Kid' Johnson (drums), and Julian Arthur (director). Temple later became prominent as a trumpeter with Fess Williams.

In *Record Research* (October 1962), Louie Metcalf wrote :

'Jimmie Cooper thought it would be a good idea for us to challenge bands from all over while we were travelling the road. Good publicity not only for our show but also for the cabarets of the bands we used to challenge. Cooper thought we were the best, so he had perfect faith in us. Plenty of advertising ahead of time heralding our coming to each town. We beat every band we came up across. Nobody came close to us until we hit Chicago. In Chicago we were invited to the Royal Gardens resident band which turned out to be Joe Oliver's Creole Jazzers with the King, Louis Armstrong, Johnny and Baby Dodds, Lil Armstrong, etc. We knew that Louis Armstrong was a powerful man on cornet. We had heard him playing on the boat in St Louis. So we knew what we were to expect from him. But what really surprised us

was that we thought Joe Oliver was through and were we surprised to see that he was playing more cornet than Louis. With the two of them together we got our lumps. But the audience was with us because of our well rehearsed routine. We were well dressed and attracted attention plus we had an overpowering ten pieces to their seven. The crowd accepted us as the winners but we went out of there with our pants taken off. If nobody else knew, we certainly knew that we had been well undressed. The Oliver band was the greatest jazz band we ever came across, and we had done plenty of travelling.'

Apart from his interesting comment on Oliver's playing at the time, Mr Metcalf's story highlights the fact that the 'winners' of band battles were by no means always the outstanding musical aggregates, as we shall see later.

Cooper's lavish revues are believed to have thrived until the onset of the depression. Two well known jazz musicians who worked in his band in later years were Hilton Jefferson (1925) and drummer Herbie Cowens (1927).

Trumpeter Clifton 'Pike' Davis spent many years working in and directing show bands. He first came to Europe in 1923 as part of the band for the Plantation Revue, returning to London three years later with the new edition of the show. From 1931 to 1934 he worked in the 'Rhapsody In Black' show, then joined Lew Leslie's famous 'Blackbirds' revue which came to Europe in August 1934. This show appeared in London and a number of provincial British towns. Davis was leading a number of excellent jazz musicians in his band. The full line-up was Pike Davis, George Wingfield, Jack Wilson (trumpet), David 'Jelly' James (trombone), Jerome 'Don' Pasquall (alto, clarinet, arranger), Ed Campbell (alto), Harold Scott, Castor McCord (tenor), Lloyd Phillips (piano), Bill Johnson (banjo, guitar), Olin Aderhold (bass), Aubrey Walks (drums), Billy Butler (director). It is interesting to note the presence of Campbell who was a leader in his own right during 1927-28; also that of pianist Lloyd Phillips who was in England as pianist for singer Pearl Bailey in 1972 and then recorded an excellent LP of stride piano for the 77 label. Billy Butler, for so long Lew Leslie's musical director, whom I met at a New York party in February 1973, told me that he now works as a travel agent. One can only regret, when contemplating a line-up of this quality, that the vogue for recording shows did not begin a few decades earlier.

Billy Fowler was in Fletcher Henderson's band throughout 1923, mainly playing baritone saxophone. He formed his own band in the following year. Harry Cooper (trumpet) and Benny Morton (trombone) were with Fowler during 1924. Morton returned from time to time in subsequent years, but Fowler's appears to be one of the bands that musicians joined when they were temporarily out of work, for few leading jazzmen stayed with him for any length of time.

Happy Caldwell (tenor), Jimmy Harrison (trombone), Freddie Johnson (piano) and Walter Johnson (drums), were with Fowler in 1925. However, his best band seems to have been one he led at Carlin's Park, Baltimore, and the Cameo Club in New York during the summer of 1926. The line-up was impressive: it included Tommy Ladnier (trumpet), Jimmy Harrison (trombone), Benny Carter (alto, clarinet, trumpet), Edgar Sampson (alto, violin), Prince Robinson (tenor, clarinet) and Freddie Johnson (piano). Robinson remained in the group until 1927, a year in which Ward Pinkett (trumpet) and Bobby Sands (tenor) were present with Fowler at the Strand Roof. After this, fewer well known musicians worked for Fowler, though clarinettist Edmond Hall was with him for three months from July 1929 in Atlantic City. Drummer Herbie Cowens (1929), banjoist/guitarist Eddie Gibbs (late 'twenties to early 'thirties), saxist Bingie Madison (early 'thirties) and guitarist Danny Barker (1931) all had short spells in the band. Pianist Gene Rodgers also played with Fowler in 1929. Musicians have told me that Fowler's best bands were those he led in the late 'twenties, and he is believed to have given up bandleading sometimes in the mid 'thirties.

Willie Grant, now in his seventies and in poor health, is one of the last survivors of the great days of the Harlem stride pianists and a mine of information about them. He first worked professionally in 1917, and in the next eight years appeared at a number of important New York clubs as soloist, accompanist, and leader of small bands. Musicians who played in his bands include trumpeters Bubber Miley and Gus Aiken, trombonist Jake Frazier and saxist Garvin Bushell. The highlight of Gant's bandleading days came in the period 1925-27 when he fronted a ten piece orchestra at New York's Cotton Club and Small's Paradise. In his line-up at this time were Ward Pinkett, Rex Stewart, Leroy Rutledge (trumpet), Joe Williams (trombone), Happy Caldwell, Fred Skerritt (reeds), Billy Taylor (bass) and Manzie Johnson (drums).

A report on the band was printed in 'Variety' on 26th May 1926:

'This Harlem night club [Small's Paradise] on Seventh Avenue and 135th Street, New York, continues as "the hottest place in town". If the former band aggregation was considered torrid, the new Willie Gant double quintet of sizzling jazzists are downright scorching.'

'Their music is irresistible and defies immobility when these coloured musicians under the affable Gant's direction "sock out" that low-down syncopation.'

Although Gant himself has reported that he recorded with his band around 1926, the only known records on which he is present date from several years earlier, when he was part of an accompanying group for singers Eliza Christmas Lee, Josie Miles and Lavinia Turner. In 1927, Grant left bandleading; as well as playing occasionally with a small group, he featured as a solo pianist at a

number of New York venues well into the 'sixties. A great admirer of the late James P. Johnson, Grant was reported to be a fine interpreter of ragtime and stride numbers as late as 1960. It is unfortunate that he was never recorded in this idiom during his peak years.

Pianist Arthur Gibbs is now best remembered for his association with musical shows and as the composer of such numbers as *Runnin' Wild* and *Rocky Road*. During World War I, Gibbs organised and directed a musical troupe that was popular in France. In the 'twenties, he directed the accompanying bands for such prominent theatrical artists as Florence Mills, Tallulah Bankhead and Bill 'Bojangles' Robinson. In 1923, Gibbs recorded four titles at two sessions for RCA Victor. The personnel consisted of Maceo Edwards, probably Gilbert Paris (trumpet), James Reevy (trombone), John Williams (clarinet), Ray Hernandez (tenor, clarinet), Percy Green or Lonnie Williams (alto, clarinet), Arthur Gibbs (piano), Leroy Vanderveer (banjo), unknown (tuba), Jerome 'Romie' Bourke (drums), Cordy Williams (violin). From the first date, *Beale Street Mama* and *Louisville Lou* are passable performances, with competent solos by a trumpeter and clarinettist but lack any real individuality or depth.

During 1929 and 1930, Gibbs and Bourke, who were in fact brothers, worked with a small group that played residencies in London, Paris, Vienna, Budapest and Barcelona. Before this, however, Gibbs led a highly proficient band at the Savoy and Arcadian Ballrooms in New York from June 1927 to June 1928. The personnel consisted of Leonard Davis (trumpet), George Washington (trombone), Edgar Sampson (alto, violin), Gene Mikell (alto), Happy Caldwell (tenor), Arthur Gibbs (piano), Paul Barnett (banjo), Billy Taylor (tuba), Sam Hodges (drums). It is a pity that this was not the band which recorded, rather than the 1923 group. From the early 'thirties, Gibbs turned increasingly to theatrical work. In later years, he suffered from ill health. He died at the age of sixty at a Welfare Island hospital on 17th March 1956.

It is curious that, despite lengthy and prominent careers, certain musicians seldom reach the recording studios. The pianist and entertainer Earle Howard is an example. During the 'twenties and 'thirties, he frequently led bands with excellent players. Howard was born in Petersburg, Virginia, on 3rd June 1904 and moved to New York with his parents at the age of fourteen. He played there with a boys' band that included Benny Carter and Benny Morton. He secured his first professional job with a touring revue at the age of sixteen and, from 1923 to 1926, led a seven piece group in Hartford, Connecticut, adding two men for engagements at the local Cinderella Ballroom. None of the musicians who worked with Howard at this time became well known in the following years.

During the rest of the 'twenties, Howard led a number of different personnels. He alternated tours with summer residencies in New England and location jobs in New York. In 1926 and 1927, trombonist Geechie Fields and tenor saxophonist Johnny Russell worked with Howard. Fernando Arbello (trombone) and Pete Brown (tenor) were with him at the Strand Danceland, Brooklyn, N.Y., during the winter of 1927-28. Gene Johnson (alto) and Charlie Frazier (tenor) worked with Howard during 1928 and 1929. He kept the size of his band down to seven pieces until a Boston engagement of May—December 1930, then led a line-up of Johnny Muse, Harold Whittington (trumpet), George Robinson (trombone), Carl Frye (alto), Larry Ringold (alto, tenor, trumpet, piano), Joe St. John (tenor), Earle Howard (piano), Arnold Canty (guitar), Jesse . . . . (bass), Dusty Neal (drums).

1931-33 were the peak years of Howard's bandleading career. The personnel of his 1931 band for engagements at the Palm Grove, Cincinnati, the Saratoga Club, New York and the Savoy Ballroom, New York comprised Albert Snaer, Henry Mason, Johnny Muse (trumpet), Nat Story (trombone), Ernest Purce, Seaton Harrington (alto), Noel Clookies (tenor), Earle Howard (piano), Harry Holt (guitar), Jesse . . . . (bass) and Dusty Neal (drums). From the spring of 1932 to April 1933, his band at the Rose Danceland, New York consisted of Ed Allen, Billy Douglas, John Brown (trumpet), Allen Jackson (alto), Cecil Scott (tenor, clarinet), Earle Howard (piano), Arnold Canty (guitar), Frank Smith (brass bass) and Paul Barbarin (drums). In the summer of 1933, Howard led his last big band. The line-up was Billy Douglas, Johnny Muse, Louie Metcalf (trumpet), Sandy Donaldson (trombone), Allen Jackson, Frank Powell (alto), Ernie Powell (tenor), Earle Howard (piano), Harry Holt (guitar), Jesse . . . . (bass) and Dusty Neal (drums).

Discussing these days with the Swiss collector Kurt Mohr, Howard remarked that Johnny Muse, Billy Douglas, Harold Whittington and Larry Ringold were all exceptionally talented musicians, though he said that their failure to achieve recognition was in part due to their own temperamental faults. Recording by Douglas a year or two later with Don Albert's band certainly proves him to have been a musician of stature. Howard feels that the band he led in 1931 was his best, and featured good arrangements with outstanding teamwork. He reports that it recorded four titles for the Gennett label which were never issued.

After the summer of 1933, Howard became musical director of Percy Nelson's band for six months. He worked with smaller groups until late 1937, went on a South American tour with Baron Lee from May to September 1938 and followed with engagements in the pit band of the 1938-39 'Blackbirds' show (which he thinks is the best band he ever worked with). He worked, too, with Leon Abbey's big band at the Apollo Theatre in the summer of 1939. From then on he was a solo entertainer; he came to Europe in 1951 and played lengthy residencies in several countries. He now lives in Sweden and is still very active as a musician.

James P. Johnson, who organised and fronted several big bands during the 1920s and early 1930s.

The late James P. Johnson is best known as a brilliant pianist and composer. During the early 'thirties, however, he sometimes led big bands, generally for brief residencies at ballrooms or for shows. The personnel of one such band, which played in the pit for the musical comedy 'Sugar Hill' in 1932, was given to Bertrand Demeusy by Olin Aderhold. It consists of Frank Belt, 'Brownie' Louis Hunt (trumpet), unknown (trombone), Howard Johnson, Harold Blanchard (alto), Teddy Hill (tenor), Sam Allen (piano), Olin Aderhold (bass), Tommy Benford (drums), Marion Cumbo (cello), John Long (French horn), Billy Tyler, Clarence Cummings, Felix Weir, Arthur Boyd (violin). From the line-up it is easy to assume that this was an orthodox theatre band, but musicians have told me that such pit bands could and often did play a fair amount of straight jazz during intermissions and before the shows.

Violinist Ralph 'Shrimp' Jones might seem out of place in a book on big band jazz, for despite having recorded with singers Martha Copeland and Ethel Waters, and the Plantation Orchestra, he played music which is hardly of great interest to jazz followers. His career was largely devoted to bands in support of leading shows. However, he is worth a brief mention for the band he led in 1923 at Broadway Jones's Club in New York. From time to time, it included Fletcher Henderson, Charlie Dixon and Kaiser Marshall. When Henderson formed his band for the Club Alabam engagement a few months later, its nucleus consisted of members of the Jones group, though we are unlikely to find out whether Jones was ever aware of the historical significance of that fact.

Joe Jordan was a ragtime 'professor' who had a flair for assessing public taste and business ability unusual in a musician. He was born in Cincinnati in 1882. In his teens, he played piano in the red light district of St Louis and at one point was a member of a piano-vocal quartet with Tom Turpin, Louis Chauvin and Sam Patterson. Chauvin and Patterson wrote the score for a show titled 'Dandy Coon' in 1903, while Jordan acted as the musical and stage director. After the show failed in Des Moines, Jordan went on to Chicago. He was an extraordinarily accomplished musician, and was playing drums and violin by 1900 in a St Louis band. He was reputedly able to write an orchestration in fifteen minutes. In Chicago, Jordan became musical director for a year at the famous Pekin Theatre. While there, he wrote all the music for the shows without additional payment. There followed a long and distinguished career, both in the theatre and business. During the depression, Jordan conducted the Negro Unit Orchestra of the Federal Theatre Project. He later conducted the orchestra in Orson Welles's production of 'Macbeth'. The best known of Jordan's many compositions is *That Teasin' Rag*; its leading strain was taken by the Original Dixieland Jazz Band and used for the trio of *Original Dixieland One-Step*.

Much of Jordan's career is outside the scope of this book, but for a while from the mid 'twenties, he sometimes led bands. Trumpeters Kenneth Roane and Pike Davis were members of one in the summer of 1930. Jordan recorded twice in 1926 with a personnel of Ed Allen, William Logan (trumpet), Joe Brown (trombone), Benny Motton, James Nichols (alto, clarinet), Clarence Miller (tenor), Joe Jordan (piano), Mike McKendrick (banjo), Ed Bergon (brass bass) and Jasper Taylor (drums). *Old Folks Shuffle*, now available on an LP, displays Jordan's professionalism in scoring—the instrumental breaks sound as if they, too, were scored in addition to the ensemble passages. The performance includes a good solo from Allen, a proficient one from Brown, and a solo passage by Jordan himself that is unexpectedly stiff rhythmically. It has to be remembered that Jordan's style dates from the pre-jazz era; possibly the formal qualities of ragtime prevented him from improvising convincingly in a jazz setting.

The name of trombonist William Cato appears in standard discographical reference for his presence at a recording session by Jelly Roll Morton in 1928 and another by Coleman Hawkins in 1940. He was better known in the 'twenties and 'thirties as Billy Kato and worked with a number of New York based bands. He also led his own groups intermittently from 1927 to about 1932. Allen Jackson (alto) and Russell Procope (alto, soprano, clarinet) had spells with him during 1927-28. Lee Blair (guitar, banjo) joined him for the first time in 1928, as did Johnny Russell (tenor). Howard Johnson (alto) was with Kato for a few months in late 1930 and early 1931. The full line-up of his band, when it was resident at the Broadway Danceland in the summer of 1931, was Bobby Cheeks, John 'Bugs' Hamilton (trumpet), Billy Kato (trombone), Johnny Russell (tenor), Rudy Powell (alto, clarinet violin), Clarence Johnson (piano), Lee Blair (guitar), John 'Mule' Falls (bass) and Edgar McIllvaine (drums). Rudy Powell has mentioned that he wrote his first score for the Kato band, because it was Johnson who first interested him in arranging. Kato did not secure any of the top residencies available in New York, and never recorded.

From 1929 to 1933, Eugene Kennedy led a band that employed a number of top ranking musicians, though like Kato's it never recorded. Initially, the line-up inclu-included Frank Newton, Lincoln Mills, Otis Johnson (trumpet), Robert Horton (trombone), Glyn Paque (saxes, clarinet), Joe Hayman (tenor, clarinet) and Ernest 'Bass' Hill (bass), though the three trumpeters are unlikely to have been in the band at the same time. After 1929, name musicians appeared with Kennedy less frequently, though Otis Johnson played with him in New England during 1930-31, and Chauncey Haughton (saxophone, clarinet), Edwin Swayzee (trumpet, arranger) and Fitz Weston (piano) were among his personnel in 1932. Weston remained with Kennedy into 1933, probably until the band broke up for the last time.

During the period 1925-27, one of the touring revues that provided employment for jazz musicians was the Lucky Sambo Show, run by one Vaughn. Jerome Bourke gave Kurt Mohr a complete personnel of Ray Conn (trumpet), Jimmy Archey (trombone), Carmelo Jejo (clarinet), Ed Campbell (alto), Cordy Williams (violin), Arthur Gibbs (piano), Chink Johnson (bass), Jerome 'Romie' Bourke (drums). At least four other well known musicians were present, at various times, in the Lucky Sambo Orchestra. They are Yank Porter (drums) in 1925, Peter DuConge (saxophone, clarinet) in early 1927, Wellman Braud (bass) and Rudy Jackson (clarinet, saxophone) during 1926-27. When Ed Campbell formed his own band for the job at the Bamboo Inn during 1927, he took with him Archey, Gibbs and Bourke.

Drummer Kaiser Marshall ran bands of his own from time to time after 1931, when he fronted his 'Czars of Harmony'. Leon 'Chu' Berry (tenor) and Bob Shoffner (trumpet) worked with him around this time, and in 1932 he shared leadership of a band with bassist Ellsworth Reynolds. His best known band and apparently his best musically, was the one he led in 1935 at the Ubangi Club and Harlem Uproar House. There was an impressive personnel that included Dick Vance, John Hamilton (trumpet), Joe Britton, Charlie Green (trombone), Lester Boone, Louis Jordan (saxes, clarinet), Jimmy Reynolds (piano), Wellman Braud (bass) and Marshall himself (drums). The jazz writer Johnny Simmen, who met him in Switzerland in 1937, has said that Marshall owned a fine book of arrangements by Edgar Sampson, Don Redman, Fletcher Henderson and others, though they were lost in a club fire. Marshall led a band again at the Apollo Theatre in the summer of 1936, and occasionally during the 'forties. He died after a severe case of food poisoning on 3rd January 1948. It is regrettable that his 1935 group was never recorded.

Pianist-arranger Charles Matson became prominent in New York during the early 'twenties. As an accompanist, he recorded with singers Mamie Smith (1922), Edna Hicks (1923), Clara Smith (1924), and the duo, Billie Wilson and Eddie Green (1924). In 1923, he was present on two titles recorded by Ted Claire's Snappy Bits Band. He also made two titles with his own group, then and again in January 1924. The recordings made by his band are *'Tain't Nobody's business if I Do and I Just Want a Daddy,* which are pedestrian, and *Lawdy Lawdy Blues* and *Jail House Blues,* both fairly creditable performances that include blues solos from one of the two cornettists and clarinettist Ernest Elliott.

From 1928 to 1933, Matson regularly led bands around the New York area. Banjoist Buddy Christian worked with him in 1928. These were the days of the depression and, from time to time, well known musicians took jobs with Matson. There is no record that any of them remained with him for any length of time. Jerome 'Don' Pasquall has given the personnel of the Matson band at the Remey Ballroom, New York from autumn 1932 to winter 1933, as Nat Brown, Audley Smith (trumpet), Don Pasquall, unknown (alto, clarinet), Johnny Russell, Castor McCord (tenor), Charles Matson (piano), unknown (guitar), 'Bass' Edwards (tuba) and Yank Porter (drums), though he states that there were numerous changes during this period. Matson's post-band career is obscure.

In 1934, trumpeter Louie Metcalf formed his own band for the first time. It spent most of the summer at the Renaissance in Coney Island, before taking winter engagements at the Harlem Opera House and other New York venues. The personnel, in addition to Metcalf, was Ward Pinkett (replaced by Herman Autrey), George Thigpen (trumpet), Jonas Walker (trombone), Happy Caldwell (tenor, clarinet), Jimmy Reynolds (piano), Billy Taylor (bass) and Wilmer 'Slick' Jones (drums). Early in 1935, Fletcher Henderson had a dispute with his brother Horace and lost most of his band to a date at the Apollo Theatre. Fletcher took his problem to Metcalf, who offered his band as the nucleus of a new group. With only three days to go, Henderson found the additional musicians to bring the band up to full strength and wrote a new book. He fronted the band on and off for the next six months.

Around the summer of 1935, Metcalf once more took over control of his band. He then led Ward Pinkett, George Thigpen (trumpet), Charlie Green (trombone), Happy Caldwell, Frank Powell (reeds), unknown (piano), Clarence Holiday—the father of Billie Holiday (guitar),

Billy Taylor (bass) and Alf Taylor (drums). Work was not plentiful and the group only stayed in existence for a short time. In the autumn of 1936, Metcalf assembled the most interesting band of his career, leading Oran 'Hot Lips' Page (trumpet), Jonas Walker (trombone), Lester Young, Rudy Powell, Happy Caldwell (reeds), Clarence Holiday (guitar), Billy Taylor (bass), Alf Taylor (drums), Billie Holiday and Orlando Roberson (vocal). The group played at the Renaissance Casino in New York and the Bedford Ballroom in Brooklyn, New York. It was Metcalf's last big band, though until the present day he has frequently been the leader of smaller groups.

Clarinettist Milton 'Mezz' Mezzrow led an interesting mixed band at the Harlem Uproar House, 52nd Street and Broadway, in November 1937, with a personnel of Frank Newton, Sidney DeParis, Max Kaminsky (trumpet), George Lugg, Vernon Brown (trombone), Eugene Sedric (tenor saxophone, clarinet), three unknown (reeds), John Niccollini (piano), Bernard Addison (guitar), Elmer James (bass), Zutty Singleton (drums) and himself. The group was known as 'The 14 Disciples Of Swing' and reports of its reception varied. Mezzrow himself claimed in his autobiographical 'Really The Blues' that the engagement failed as a result of hostility to the band on racial grounds, while 'Down Beat' of December 1937 stated that it failed to draw worthwhile crowds.

Both Aubrey 'Bobbie' Neal, who led his Dixieland Ramblers from 1926 to 1928, and Bobby Neal, who fronted bands from 1930 to 1936, are rather elusive figures, though they are remembered by some survivors of the swing era who now live in New York. Sylvester Lewis (trumpet) and William Alsop (alto) played with Aubrey, and Bill Dillard, Bill Coleman, Bernard Flood, John 'Bugs' Hamilton (trumpet), Alton Moore (trombone), Joe Garland (tenor) and Tommy Fulford (piano) with Bobby, at different times. Neither recorded, and the musical quality of the bands they led remains a matter of conjecture.

Bassist/violinist Ellsworth Reynolds first formed a band in 1926 when he fronted Elmer Chambers, Ray Carn (trumpet), Jim Reevy (trombone), Bobby Sands (clarinet, tenor), Gene Mikell (alto), Arthur Gibbs (piano), Del Thomas (bass) and Eddie Howe (drums) for a few months at the Strand Theatre Roof Garden Restaurant in New York. In the summer of 1932, he was joint leader of Reynolds's and Kaiser's Bostonians at New York's Renaissance Ballroom. The line-up was Gus Aiken, Benny Carter (trumpet), Ed Cuffee (trombone), George James, Dave McRae (alto), Cecil Scott, Castor McCord (tenor), Bill Caines (piano), Rafael Escudero (bass), Kaiser Marshall (drums) and Ellsworth Reynolds (violin). Just over a year later, he formed Ellsworth Reynolds's Band and his Eleven Bostonians for an engagement at the Lido Ballroom. Here, the personnel consisted of Gus Aiken, Jack

Wilson, Ray Carn (trumpet), Joe Britton (trombone), Dave McRae (saxophone), Eddie Campbell (alto, clarinet), Cecil Scott (tenor), Bill Caines (piano), 'Bass' Thompson (bass), Eddie Roberts (drums) and Ellsworth Reynolds (violin, director), Subsequently, Reynolds had a varied and interesting career. He spent twelve years from 1952 to 1963 as a member of Joe Garland's big band which played fairly frequently throughout New Jersey, although he did not himself lead a regular large orchestra again.

Henry Saparo, a New Orleans born banjoist/guitarist who led bands at the Bamboo Inn in Harlem from 1926 to early 1928, is presumably the same as the man who came to England with the Southern Syncopated Orchestra in 1919, and made two tests for Columbia with a Benny Peyton group that included Sidney Bechet. He is listed in early references as Henry Sapiro, and occasionally as Henry Shapiro or Henri Saparo. His band did not record, but several well known musicians played with him. Among them were Jimmy Harrison (trombone), Joe Garland, Gene Johnson and Russell Procope (saxes) in 1926, Harry Carney (briefly), Joe Eldridge, Greely Walton (saxes), Freddie Johnson (piano) and Manzie Johnson (drums) in 1927, Ward Pinkett, Otis Johnson (trumpet), Jimmy Archey (trombone), Charlie Holmes and Glyn Paque (saxes) in 1928. Joe Steele (piano) who was with him in 1927, took over as leader when Saparo left to join another band the next year.

The 7-11 Burlesque Company Orchestra was another theatre unit that gave employment to jazz musicians, in this case during the years 1925 to 1927. Its personnel, as recalled by Jerome 'Don' Pasquall, was in 1925 'Three Finger' Brown, . . . Prevost (trumpet), Sidney Bechet, John Howell, Ernest Poole, Pasquall (saxes, clarinet), 'Skinny' Johnson (piano), Wellman Braud (bass) and . . . Wynn (drums). A four-piece sax section was unusual in this period, and though we know little of the group's line-up during 1926 and 1927, Wellman Braud remained with it well into 1926.

Charlie Skeets led bands around New York for at least a decade from the mid 'twenties. He made only a single appearance in the recording studios when, in June 1926, his group produced *Tampeekoe* and *Deep Henderson* for the Edison label. These two performances are good examples of big band jazz for the period. The section work is competent and there are good solos from trumpeter Leonard Davis, presumably, and a fine trombonist who is almost certainly Jimmy Harrison. Harrison's presence is rather puzzling, for at the time he was working with Billy Fowler's band. He may well have been engaged by Skeets simply for the recording, however. The full personnel is unknown, but as Gene Johnson (alto, clarinet) and Lee Blair (banjo) were known to be with Skeets at the time, they are probably present on the recording.

In the rest of the 'twenties, the following musicians worked with Skeets: Otis Johnson, Ward Pinkett, Kenneth Roane, Edwin Swayzee (trumpet), Jimmy Archey, Geechie Fields (trombone), Joe Garland, Edmond Hall, Hilton Jefferson, Glyn Paque, Russell Procope, Bobby Sands (saxes, clarinet), Lee Blair (banjo, guitar), Dick Fulbright, Ernest 'Bass' Hill, Henry Turner (bass), Tommy Benford, Pete Jacobs, Arthur Trappier (drums). Late in 1929, pianist Claude Hopkins became leader of Skeets's band. Edmond Hall, Gene Johnson, Bobby Sands, Henry Turner and Pete Jacobs were some of the musicians who went with him.

Skeets kept going well into the 'thirties, though his personnel at this period is uncertain. Pete Brown (alto) was with him from 1930 to 1935, Alton Moore (trombone) in 1935, June Clark (trumpet) during 1936-37, and Cyrus St Clair (tuba) for a while in 1932. As the swing era got under way Skeets sank into obscurity.

The late Rex Stewart was one of the most individualistic of all the leading jazz soloists. He is now best remembered for his years as a key figure of the Duke Ellington band. He had one period as a leader of a big band, at the Empire Ballroom on Broadway between summer 1933 and autumn 1934. His line-up is an interesting one: himself (conductor, director), George Thigpen, Ward Pinkett (trumpet), Nelson Hurd (trombone), Edgar Sampson, Allen Jackson, Rudy Powell (alto, clarinet), Noel Klukies (tenor), Freddie Skerritt (baritone), Roger Ramirez (piano), unknown (bass), Sidney Catlett (drums), Sonny Wood (vocal). Klukies is obviously the man who played with Earle Howard, spelling his name Clookies. Rudy Powell has remarked on an unusual aspect of the

Rex Stewart in 1944, when a member of the Duke Ellington band. During 1933 and 1934 he led a swing style band with four 'hot' violinists.

Stewart band—that all the sax men with the exception of Skerritt doubled on violin. A swing band with a four-piece violin section must have been a great novelty in 1933-34, as indeed was a five-piece sax section at this time. It is regrettable that it was never recorded.

Ferman Tapp's Melody Lads were first mentioned to me by trombonist Russell Bowles, who worked with the group from 1926 to 1928. Tapp is an extremely obscure figure who was fronting bands around 1934 and 1935, when June Clark, Joe Thomas (trumpet), Herbie Cowens and Harry Dial (drums) all had brief spells with him. He is one of the many bandleaders who would repay further research by collectors based in New York.

Bassist Charlie Turner led his Arcadians at the Arcadia Ballroom, New York from either late 1933 or, more probably, early 1934 until 'Fats' Waller took the band over in 1936. The personnel during this period was reasonably stable. It consisted of James Smith, Otis Johnson (replaced in 1935 by Al Killian), Edward Andy Anderson (trumpet), Fred Robinson, George Wilson (trombones), Emmett Matthews (baritone, soprano), George James (alto, baritone), Gene Mikell (alto, baritone), Al Washington (tenor), Hank Duncan (piano), Gene Fields (guitar, vocal), Charlie 'Fat Man' Turner (bass) and Herbie Cowens (drums). When 'Fats' Waller used Turner's band for a tour in 1935, he initially added Gene Sedric (tenor, clarinet) and replaced Killian, Mikell, Fields and Cowens with Herman Autrey, Rudy Powell (alto, clarinet), Al Casey (guitar) and Wilmer 'Slick' Jones (drums), though other changes occurred in the succeeding months. Records of the band under Waller's leadership are discussed elsewhere.

Will Vodery led a sixty-seven-piece regimental band for the American army during World War I. He was General Pershing's band director. As early as 1914, at least one of his compositions had been recorded as a piano roll, and in January 1922 he led a band at the Manhattan Casino in New York.

From the early 'twenties, Vodery was a prominent figure on the New York Musical scene. He became best known through organising bands for various Lew Leslie productions. He invariably included a number of top jazz musicians. One band had Clifton 'Pike' Davis, Johnny Dunn (trumpet), Earl Granstaff (trombone), Rollen Smith, Herschel Brassfield (reeds), Floyd Hickman (violin), George Rickson (piano), Johnny Mitchell (banjo), Henry Hull (tuba, string bass), Jesse Baltimore (drums). This personnel was given to Harold Flakser by Johnny Mitchell and must relate to about 1923. Jerome 'Don' Pasquall joined the band for the 'Dixie To Broadway' revue of 1924-25, replacing Nelson Kincaid. He has given a line-up of Johnny Dunn, Jap Foster, Jabbo Jenkins (trumpet), Calvin Jones (trombone), himself (alto saxophone, clarinet), Eric Brown (alto saxophone), . . . Brown (tenor saxophone), Herb Johnson (bassoon), Allie Ross (violin, concert master), Will Tyler, Ralph 'Shrimp' Jones, Clarence Cummings (violin), William Grant Still (viola, oboe), George Rickson (piano), Harry Hull (bass, tuba), Jesse Baltimore (drums).

Ross himself became prominent as a director of show orchestras, while William Grant Still became better known as a straight composer.

Russell Wooding's Grand Central Red Caps had four titles issued on RCA Victor in 1931. The two which I have heard are decidedly undistinguished, not least for the vocals by one Willie Jackson. Little is known about Wooding's activities during the early and mid 'twenties, but trumpeter Demas Dean was working with him around 1923. Musicians have reported that the best band that Wooding led was one in 1932, a year in which he employed Leonard Davis (trumpet), Dicky Wells (trombone) and Bernard Addison (guitar) and was resident for a while at Connie's Inn. Shortly afterwards, Wooding concentrated on theatre work, his only other appearance on record was as conductor of a band that accompanied Ethel Waters on some titles made for the Liberty Music Shop.

The bands mentioned in this appendix by no means fully list those who played in and around New York during the pre-swing era. Bertrand Demeusy has mentioned such groups as those led by Clifford Andy Anderson (1925), Gilbert Anderson (1921-25), and Billy Butler (1925) which included Demas Dean, Bobby Stark (trumpet) and Rudy Jackson (clarinet, alto), Don David, Sam Domingo (1932), Norwood Fennar (1929-32), Bobby Hargreaves (1935-37), Reggie Johnson (1931-33), Jesse Owens-Danny Logan (1936-37), Sam Patterson (1925), Allie Ross (associated with Lew Leslie's 'Blackbirds' revues), Jimmy Smith (1935), John C. Smith, Alberto Soccaras (1928-36) and Napoleon Zias (1930-32). No doubt there were many others. It is already late in the day to start research into the more obscure bands of four or five decades ago, but unless a serious attempt is made in this area within the next three or four years, information about an important era in big band jazz history is likely to remain sketchy at best.

4 The First Flowering

By the mid 'twenties, the various strands of big band jazz development were beginning to come together, priinicipally through the combined efforts of a small number of talented arrangers, a select group of orchestra leaders, and a widening circle of distinctive soloists who were also skilled readers. From 1927 onwards, there were a number of nationally prominent black bands which might have made concessions to preserve their functional role as purveyors of dance music, but were recognised by the more aware members of the public as essentially jazz units. In fact, it is doubtful if either leaders or musicians were even conscious of tailoring their output to the requirements of dancing audiences, for the functional aspects of the music were considered so natural at this period that non acceptance would have been regarded as a form of almost incomprehensible eccentricity. The occasional black bandleader may have yearned to emulate Paul Whiteman's incursions into 'symphonic jazz', and certainly some theatre bands which included outstanding jazz soloists also presented versions of the light classics. In general, though, any black band that was jazz-oriented expected to find its audience largely amongst dancers. By the mid 'twenties, there were a number of outstanding large jazz units. Several of them made important contributions to the development of the music, but I doubt that many jazz followers would question the pre-eminence at this time of the bands led by Duke Ellington, Fletcher Henderson and Louis Russell, McKinney's Cotton Pickers and the Missourians. I have omitted the Bennie Moten band, which I feel reached its apex in the early 'thirties. Duke Ellington will be considered in a separate chapter; in spite of his towering importance in big band jazz, few will dispute that historical pride of place must go to Fletcher Henderson and his remarkable arranger Don Redman.

When U.S. Columbia issued a four LP set devoted to the Fletcher Henderson band of 1923-37 they entitled it 'A Study in Frustration', which could equally be the heading of any attempt to set the band's achievements in perspective. In general, the only consistent aspect of Henderson's considerable output is its lack of consistency : even individual sessions produce performances that vary from masterpieces to total banality. Within a period of months towards the end of the 'twenties, the recorded output of the Henderson band embraced the dreariest of stock arrangements played with little enthusiasm or finesse, Dixieland-styled performances that seemed to make a mockery of the band's own pioneering efforts, and a brilliant matching of scores with individual performances that could not be rivalled by any contemporary group. As the years went by, the contradictions became even more bewildering, for recordings of excellent material could be downright mediocre while the most dismal commercial numbers sometimes produced the creative solos from individual musicians. With a band like Ellington's one could reasonably assume that the more overtly commercial numbers recorded were unlikely to inspire the individual soloists to any great heights, but to approach the output of the Fletcher Henderson band with too many of the conventional jazz purist's conceptions leads only to a form of critical schizophrenia.

Henderson's background has been covered in a number of published sources, but a brief résumé of his career is needed to place his music in context. He was born in Cuthbert, Georgia on 18th December 1898; his parents were both middle class and intellectually above average. Fletcher, like his brother Horace (born 1904), went to college and graduated from Atlanta University in 1920 In the summer of that year, he went to New York to study at Columbia University for a master's degree in chemistry. He had already shown an interest in music, had heard such blues singers at Ma Rainey and Bessie Smith in Atlanta, and was an adequate pianist who sometimes played for school dances. In New York, he found that his savings would not last until the opening of the autumn term, and decided, in the interim, to accept the offer of a job as song demonstrator with the Broadway music publishing firm of Pace and Handy. Harry Pace left the firm in 1921, to form the first record company entirely owned by a black American. He named it Black Swan after a nineteenth century operatic star. Henderson joined the company as a musical director and accompanied most of its artists either as a solo pianist or as leader of small groups. In due course, he agreed, somewhat reluctantly, to go on the road as director of the group accompanying the singer Ethel Waters. Miss Waters, who became famous as a result of the tour, obviously felt little empathy with her musical director, forcing him to listen to piano rolls by James P. Johnson in the hope that his playing would become less formal. In this she succeeded, and Henderson, although never an oustanding individual piano stylist, became adept in the stride manner most often associated with Johnson and Fats Waller. Black musicians on tour at that time were forced to stay in the worst sections of the cities in which they played, and to carry knives or firearms for protection. It is understandable that a man of Henderson's background found the conditions disagreeable in the extreme, and he must have been relieved when he found himself back in New York unharmed.

Through his recording activities and local dance dates which he played in Harlem, Henderson collected a nucleus of musicians including trumpeter Joe Smith, tenor saxophonist Coleman Hawkins, drummer Kaiser Marshall and banjoist Charlie Dixon. His greatest discovery at this point was Don Redman, a talented instrumentalist and arranger who had arrived in the city as a member of Billy Paige's Broadway Syncopators. Redman was already working on musical ideas that were to make him one of the most important figures in the history of big band jazz. When the musicians were walking down Broadway after a recording session, an acquaintance informed them that the Club Alabam was auditioning bands for a floor show, and suggested that they try for the job. Using the

The Fletcher Henderson band, 1924: Howard Scott, Ralph Escudero, Elmer Chambers, Henderson, Charlie Dixon, Coleman Hawkins, Kaiser Marshall and Don Redman.

tunes that they had just recorded, the band auditioned for the engagement, by all accounts somewhat half-heartedly, and were successful. They selected Henderson as their leader because they considered his college background and cultured manners would be a considerable asset. The Fletcher Henderson orchestra opened at the Club Alabam in the summer of 1923 and remained there for a year.

In 1924, after a dispute with the Club Alabam management, the Henderson band moved to the celebrated Roseland Ballroom, where it was to be an almost permanent fixture for the next five years. This was the period of greatest public success for Henderson, and one in which his band was at its artistic peak. During the tour with Ethel Waters, he had heard Louis Armstrong, then an unknown New Orleans musician, playing at the Lyric Theatre in his home town, and had tried to persuade him to join his band. Because Henderson would not also engage drummer Zutty Singleton, Armstrong declined. However, in October 1924, he finally joined Henderson after leaving King Oliver's Creole Jazz Band in Chicago at the instigation of his wife Lil. Armstrong caused a sensation in New York; other musicians flocked to the Roseland to hear this remarkable man who was soon recognised as the undisputed trumpet king. Armstrong, however, was only one of the great names featured in the Henderson band during the 'twenties; others included trumpeters Tommy Ladnier, Joe Smith and Rex Stewart, trombonist Jimmy Harrison, clarinettist Buster Bailey, and saxophonists Coleman Hawkins and Benny Carter.

The customers at the Roseland Ballroom were white, and it has been reported that a few of the white bandleaders who alternated with Henderson there were none too happy at his success. Musically, though, the Henderson band offered a great deal more than the commercial white groups, notably in presenting fresh scores of contemporary popular material, a wide selection of original numbers written by Don Redman, 'Fats' Waller and others, and in highlighting the individual talents of its star soloists. It is an over-simplification to state, as some writers have done, that the commercial white bandleaders of the middle 'twenties used only stock publishers' orchestrations, for there is a fair amount of recorded evidence to the contrary. Certainly they leaned very heavily on them and clearly none had a staff arranger comparable with Redman in stature. It is interesting to note that as early as 1925 Henderson emulated the more successful white bandleaders in having a second orchestra touring under his banner: a group titled Fletcher Henderson's Rainbow Orchestra led by violinist Ellsworth Reynolds worked mostly in small towns in Pennsylvania and occasionally filled in for college dates. The band's arranger was guitarist LeRoy Harris, but most of the scores were exactly as used by Henderson's Roseland band.

By the latter part of 1927, the Henderson band could be challenged musically by only a handful of rivals, yet its records did not sell as well as those of the leading white orchestras and its individual stars were paid a good deal less than their white counterparts in the bands of, say, Paul Whiteman or Jean Goldkette. Redman, for example, received $25 an arrangement from Henderson, whereas Paul Whiteman commissioned him to write twenty at $100 a score. Redman left the band in the summer of 1927 to take over the musical direction of McKinney's

Cotton Pickers. Henderson then either called on outside arrangers or used head arrangements.

In 1928, Henderson was involved in a serious car accident in which his vehicle left the road. His injuries included a gash on the forehead that in later years led to the complete paralysis of his left side. Some musicians have blamed this accident for Henderson's increasingly erratic attention to business details in the ensuing years, but evidence would suggest that he was by nature an indifferent businessman and, like so many musicians of his generation, assumed that the good times that existed in the few years of relative prosperity and low taxation leading up to the depression would continue indefinitely. He was by all accounts a kindly man, concerned with strict musical standards but indifferent to discipline. There was an occasion when the whole of his trumpet section left the stand in the middle of a dance after some minor dispute with their leader, without subsequently incurring a single word of reprimand. The management of the band also appears to have been extraordinarily lax, and the musicians not infrequently found themselves minus engagements at a time when regular work should have been easy to find. The casual attitude of some of his personnel, who were often absent during the first hour or two of an engagement, finally led Henderson to undertake a drastic reorganisation in 1929 but, when the management of the Roseland showed less inclination to book the band because of his disinterest in business matters, he was forced increasingly to take to the road. A tour of the Midwestern states was unsuccessful because the Henderson band did not feature enough blues for local taste, but between times, there were worthwhile New York

The Fletcher Henderson Band, 1927: Henderson is on the extreme left. Back row: Jimmy Harrison, Benny Morton, June Cole and Kaiser Marshall. Front row, left to right: Charlie Dixon, Jerome 'Don' Pasquall, Buster Bailey, Coleman Hawkins, Tommy Ladnier, Joe Smith and Russell Smith.

engagements, though these were seldom very long-lasting.

From the early 'thirties, Henderson became increasingly in demand as an arranger and provided scores for numerous bands, including several of the leading white groups. He meanwhile continued to lead his own band, though personnel changes were now more frequent than they had been during the 'twenties, and in 1934 it seemed for a while that his fortunes were about to improve. It appeared likely that he would get a regular residency at the Cotton Club, which in the previous years had resulted in Duke Ellington's rise to eminence, but at the last moment Jimmie Lunceford got the job. Then a European tour seemed imminent, but again there was the disappointment of seeing Cab Calloway's band take over as a replacement. This was particularly unfortunate for, despite the loss of Coleman Hawkins who had left for a European trip that was to last five years, in 1934 Henderson had an excellent band that included such star soloists as Henry 'Red' Allen, Claude Jones, Buster Bailey, Ben Webster and Hilton Jefferson. In addition Henderson, with his brother Horace, was providing fine original material and a string of outstanding scores. Late in 1934, the position became so bad Henderson was forced to disband

Early in 1932, the American jazz writer and sometimes recording supervisor, John Hammond, had secured an important New York engagement for the Henderson band at a time when its fortunes were low, and he came once more to the leader's rescue. He persuaded Benny Goodman to commission arrangements for his new band, and also to take over some of the most popular scores that Henderson had used with his own group. It is ironical that this partnership, which lasted for six months, was probably the chief factor in Goodman's rise to fame, for the Henderson arrangements set the style of the Goodman band and, to a considerable degree, inspired the type of scoring customary in the swing era. Goodman himself acknowledged the fact on several occasions. In his book 'The Kingdom of Swing' (written in collaboration with Irving Kolodin), he states that Henderson, in addition to writing the type of arrangement for which he was best known, 'could also do a wonderful job on melodic tunes such as *Can't We Be Friends, Sleepy Time Down South, Blue Skies, I Can't Give You Anything But Love* and above all *Sometimes I'm Happy*. He had to be convinced of it himself, but once he started he did marvellous work. These were the things, with their wonderful easy style and great background figures, that really set the style of the band.' It can be imagined that Henderson must have had very mixed feelings about the success of Goodman's recordings of numbers which had aroused little public interest when he made them with his own band, but he was noted for maintaining inscrutability during both bad and good times.

In 1935 Henderson had regained sufficient confidence to form a new band, and by the end of the year again led an impressive line-up that, in January 1936, opened a lengthy residency at the Grand Theatre Ballroom in Chicago. This band, which included Roy Eldridge, Buster Bailey, Joe Thomas, Leon 'Chu' Berry and Israel Crosby, was the last really outstanding one that Henderson was to lead, and in *Christopher Columbus* it had what was by now a rarity for the leader, a hit record. In due course, however, the key soloists left and, though Henderson always led musicianly bands through the next three years, none made any great public impact. In June 1939, Henderson disbanded once more, returning to work as staff arranger with Benny Goodman. Initially he was featured as pianist in the Goodman Sextet. During the 'forties Henderson organised big bands on several occasions; one of the most successful was resident at Chicago's Club DeLisa during 1946 and 1947. The wheel turned full circle for Henderson when, after a further spell as Goodman's staff arranger, he again accompanied Ethel Waters on tour from the summer of 1948 to late 1949. With J. C. Johnson, he wrote material for the revue 'Jazz Train', leading his own band in the New York production, but though the show was seen in Europe it enjoyed only a moderate success and, from my own recollection of several performances in London, was not particularly outstanding. By the late 'forties, the big band era was virtually over—when Henderson secured an engagement at New York's Cafe Society in December 1950, he featured a sextet. On 21st December 1950, he suffered a stroke that left him partially paralysed; he was unable to resume an active role in music in the remaining two years of his life. A number of benefits were organised for him, several by Benny Goodman. However, Henderson's condition deteriorated and after frequent spells in hospital he died on 28th December 1952 at the age of 54.

John Hammond has described some of his experiences with Henderson in the booklet that accompanies the U.S. Columbia set 'A Study in Frustration — The Fletcher Henderson Story'. He mentions an early venture during the depression years, when he and two other friends took over a downtown New York theatre and instituted a policy of combining stage show with movies, booking the Henderson band for the first bill against the advice of the agency that handled its engagements. The agency's misgivings proved only too correct, for Hammond states that at the opening show only five of the thirteen Henderson musicians were present, while over fifty infringements of union rules occurred in the first week. Needless to say, the band was not booked for the second week. It is Hammond's opinion that Henderson's almost incredible laxity as a business man stemmed from his reaction to the colour bar, which made him cynical of the intentions of all white people. This may well be true, but it would also be reasonable to believe the musicians who assert that his accident in 1928 was responsible for part of his almost suicidal disregard of business affairs. John Hammond writes that whatever security Henderson enjoyed in his later years, or indeed even during his period of greatest success, resulted from the tenacity of his wife, who cajoled him into buying a first class house and, in the latter hard years, took in lodgers and became an excellent musical copyist in her own right. In the last resort, though, Henderson himself remains a curiously enigmatic figure, even if on a musical level his achievements and failures can be reasonably assessed.

It is one of the many paradoxes of Henderson's career that his easy-going nature enabled him to build up a band of outstanding instrumentalists who would probably not have survived long in orchestras led by strict disciplinarians. Another paradox is that however badly these men might often have behaved over such matters as time-keeping, or even putting in an appearance at all, they seemed to be devoted to their leader and the band. Many stuck with Henderson through very lean times when they could quite easily have obtained more lucrative jobs in other bands. The late Rex Stewart told me on one occasion how he had left Henderson to join McKinney's Cotton Pickers at a considerably increased salary, but said that when the Henderson band played in Detroit, where the McKinney's group was based, he desperately wanted to rejoin it and was only dissuaded from doing so at the last minute by Don Redman. John Hammond has written that the Henderson musicians in the peak years were so certain of the musical superiority of the band that they looked down on their colleagues in other, more economically successful bands.

Don Redman, Fletcher Henderson's chief arranger from 1924 to 1927, and the man who more than any other laid the foundations for big band jazz.

Henderson's bandleading career was variable, but one has to recall that he became a bandleader virtually by accident. The choice of Henderson as a leader by his fellow musicians owed rather more to his social background, in the first instance, than to his professional skills, though these were also recognised. From about 1924 Henderson, with the help of Don Redman, built up an orchestra that can reasonably be claimed as the most important in the history of big band jazz. His insistence on employing only highly skilled musicians who could read complex scores and attain a then remarkable standard of instrumental proficiency both as soloists and ensemble players, allied to his use of original arrangements which allowed freedom to his soloists, provided a basis for the swing era of the 'thirties. There is little doubt

that the Henderson band reached a peak in 1927-1929, declined in the next few years, was again outstanding in 1934, and attained its final moments of greatness in 1936. However, even if Henderson had given up bandleading in the latter part of 1928 and a number of worthwhile later recordings had been lost as a result, his important role in the development of big band jazz would remain unchangeable. It is also worth noting that even in the leaner years, there were occasional recordings that are very much above average, which suggests that the history of the band might have been quite different, given favourable economic conditions. Despite the unevenness, both in musical and financial terms, of Henderson's career as a leader, his development as an arranger was more consistent and alone would have assured him an important position in jazz history.

Although Henderson wrote a number of scores prior to the 'thirties—*Off To Buffalo*, for example, in 1927—he did not really emerge as an outstanding arranger until around 1933. His initial arrangements were not distinguished, being little better than average imitations of those by Redman, based on contrasting eight-bar passages for brass and saxes. The saxophone passages became difficult to develop as the number of brass increased and a reasonable tonal balance between the sections was lost. From the early 'thirties, he began to draw inspiration from the antiphony of Negro church music. The call-and-response pattern had already been used by Duke Ellington and formed the basis of accompaniments to blues singers, but within a few years Henderson was to make it the standard device of big band arranging. He also derived benefit from a greater mobility in the rhythm section and an increased flexibility in accenting made possible by the substitution of guitar and string bass for banjo and tuba. The change took place at the end of the 'twenties, and his maturity as an arranger is obvious from the many scores which he produced for his 1934 band. Leonard Feather, in 'The Encyclopedia of Jazz', aptly summarised his achievements as an arranger:

'The basic simplicity of his style involved such devices as the pitting of reed against brass section and the use of forthright, swinging block-voiced passages. The style he popularized, which was virtually synonymous with swing and greatly responsible for the rise of swing music, was soon incorporated into the mainstream of popular music. In the 'forties and 'fifties many commercial radio and TV bands featured arrangements with many Henderson characteristics, by now acceptable enough to the general public to be considered pop music rather than jazz.'

One slightly enigmatic aspect of the Henderson band, particularly in relationship to the arrangements used, is the exact role of Fletcher's brother Horace. He had been a leader in his own right since his college days, when he joined Fletcher's band in early 1933. He was a member until late 1934, and again from early in 1936 until he left in July 1937 to form his own big band for a residency at the Swingland Club in Chicago. Horace was quite

Top: *another shot of Henderson's 1927 band. Left to right: Tommy Ladnier, Jimmie Harrison, Joe Smith, Benny Morton, Russell Smith, Henderson, June Cole, Charlie Dixon, Jerome 'Don' Pasquall, Kaiser Marshall, Buster Bailey and Coleman Hawkins.* Above: *the band in 1933. Left to right: Henry 'Red' Allen, Keg Johnson, Joe Thomas, Claude Jones, Russell Smith, unknown vocalist, Horace Henderson, Walter Johnson, Fletcher Henderson, Bernard Addison, Hilton Jefferson, John Kirby, Russell Procope, Buster Bailey, Coleman Hawkins.*

often given the piano solos on Henderson's records, but he was also a talented arranger. Drummer Slick Jones, who was in the Henderson band during 1935 and the early part of 1936, told Frank Driggs: 'You had to be good to play in that band. Fletcher always wrote in very hard keys, writing a lot of sharps for the brass and flats for the reeds. Horace's stuff was easier to play because he didn't write in hard keys.' Against this, trumpeter Dick Vance told Mr Driggs that on the whole he felt Horace's

arrangements more challenging to play than Fletcher's, remarking that Fletcher's style had become somewhat stereotyped, while Horace would attempt new variations. Interestingly enough, Horace provided a number of scores for Benny Goodman; some, with the passage of time, have come to be accepted as Fletcher's. It has been reported that Horace Henderson later expressed bitterness on several occasions over what he considered to be unjustified neglect of his own contributions as an arranger, but it is now impossible to clarify the exact relationship between his own development in this field and that of his brother.

Before going on to consider some of Fletcher Henderson's recorded output, it is relevant here to comment briefly on his ability as a pianist. An early solo of *Chime Blues* (1923) is a reasonable example of its kind. Henderson employs a walking bass figure that is almost pure boogie for part of the time and interjects some neat variations. Generally, recorded evidence shows Henderson as a highly competent pianist without any marked individuality. He accompanied dozens of 'classic' blues singers on record during the 'twenties, usually performing ably if without great imagination. His band records contain few piano solos of length; his contributions were normally neat, musicianly and devoid of virtuoso flourishes. However, he could on occasion solo with some distinction in a style that owed something to Fats Waller. An example can be heard on his recording of *Stealin' Apples*. It is doubtful whether Henderson himself would have made any great claims for his solo piano work, but while it never reached any great heights of individuality or imagination, it was always musicianly and well constructed.

Henderson's first records were made for the Black Swan company during 1921 and 1922 and are, with the exception of a passable piano solo, uniformly mediocre and lacking in distinction. The records that the band made during 1923 and 1924, before the arrival of Louis Armstrong, are now of interest for historical rather than strictly musical reasons, not least in the occasional

The Fletcher Henderson Band at the Grand Terrace Ballroom, Chicago, 1936. Left to right: Leon 'Chu' Berry, Joe Thomas, Horace Henderson, Sid Catlett, Dick Vance, Teddy Lewis, Buster Bailey, Elmer Williams, Ed Cuffee, Roy Eldridge, Israel Crosby, Fernando Arbello, Bob Lessey and Jerome 'Don' Pasquall. Fletcher Henderson is at the piano.

glimpses of what was to follow. Titles such as *Gulf Coast Blues* and *Downhearted Blues* have precise lead work from cornettist Elmer Chambers, but most of the solos are poor and there is an absence of genuine improvisation or ensemble work of note. Even at this early date there are signs that attention was being given to the development of a less stiff rhythmic approach. *Just Hot* and, particularly, *You Got to Get Hot* show a marked improvement on what had gone before. *Hard Hearted Hannah* features an arranging device—the clarinet trio—that was to become a favourite with Henderson. It includes a tenor saxophone solo by Coleman Hawkins which hints at a personal development that was to come to full fruition some four years later. However, the performances that show progress are offset by many others, *Forsaken Blues* for example, which are mere period pieces, indistinguishable from those by other contemporary bands, both black and white.

In September 1924 Louis Armstrong joined the band and the effect was incalculable. Henderson himself, writing in the *Record Changer* of July-August 1950, commented: 'The band gained a lot from Louis, and he gained a lot from us. By that I mean that he *really* learned to read in my band, and to read in just about every key. Although it's common today, it wasn't usual at that time to write in such keys as E natural, or D natural, so that Louis had to learn, and did learn, much more about his own horn than he knew before he joined us.' Don Redman on several occasions spoke of the effect that Armstrong's arrival had on himself and the band as a whole, notably in relationship to swing. Certainly, recorded evidence suggests that Redman's development as an arranger received a tremendous impetus from Armstrong's presence in the band, and jazz writer Ronald

Atkins has written that *TNT* 'blends reeds and trombones, clarinets and brass, Armstrong and saxophones, with an exciting freshness that makes it arguably the first classic performance in orchestral jazz'. Not all the performances recorded when Armstrong was in the band boast outstanding arrangements, however, but while stock scores such as those used for *Araby* or *Me Neenyah* (neither features an Armstrong solo) were appallingly trite, others by Redman have numerous passages of note. What was at first remarkable was the contrast between Armstrong's brilliant solos with—for the period—tremendous rhythmic freedom, and those by his fellow musicians. As an illustration, the solos by Armstrong and Redman on *Go 'long Mule* are years apart in inventiveness and rhythmic awareness. In contrast, a title such as *Twelfth Street Blues* has a clarinet solo from Buster Bailey that is much closer to Armstrong's conception than could be achieved by most of his fellow Henderson musicians. Nowadays one listens to Henderson's 1924-25 recordings for Armstrong's solos, just as one listens to Paul Whiteman's records of a few years later for the contribution of Bix Beiderbecke, and it is fascinating to hear the variations in Armstrong's solos in different takes of, say, *Why Couldn't It Be Poor Little Me* and *I'll See You in My Dreams*. When Armstrong returned to Chicago in November 1925, Henderson lost his greatest musician, but Armstrong's influence was to shape not only the jazz to be performed by the Henderson band in succeeding years, but that of virtually all his important contemporaries.

Initially Armstrong's replacement was Rex Stewart, heard to good advantage on *Stampede*. This performance was excellently arranged by Redman and has good solos from Coleman Hawkins—probably his best on record to this date—and Joe Smith. From 1925 until 1928 the Henderson band recorded for, amongst other labels, Harmony, under the pseudonym of The Dixie Stompers. When Stewart left the band he was replaced by the gifted Tommy Ladnier, and for a time the personnel was relatively stable. The whole of The Dixie Stompers's output has been issued on two LP records and it is instructive to note the unevenness of the band's recordings, even at a period when it was at its peak. *Florida Stomp* is an average performance, though it includes a good solo from cornettist Joe Smith, but *Get It Fixed* from the same session, despite a dismal bass saxophone solo by Hawkins, has excellent contributions from Joe Smith and Buster Bailey and the ensemble riff at the close is well handled. Another title from the same date, *Panama,* has passages with a strong Dixieland flavour, while a slightly later *Nervous Charlie Stomp* seems to aim for a consciously 'white' sound. Later Dixie Stompers recordings have a similar erratic quality, varying as they do from the excellence of *Jackass Blues,* with its relaxed rhythmic quality and agreeable solos from Smith and Charlie Green, through the stiffness of *Have It Ready,* to the brilliance of *Snag It,* well arranged by Redman, with

superb solos from both Ladnier and Smith. The final Dixie Stompers recordings date from a period when Redman had left the band and Henderson himself was beginning to arrange for it. *Feelin' Good* has excellent solos from the under rated trumpeter Bobby Stark and trombonist Jimmy Harrison, in rather odd contrast with passages that seem to have been inspired by Frankie Trumbauer, while *I'm Feeling. Devilish* is striking, both for ensemble playing and individual solos; that by Buster Bailey shows a surprisingly strong New Orleans influence.

By no means all Henderson's recordings of the period were made for the Harmony label, though no others reveal the curious musical twists and turns of the band quite as starkly. Some of the titles made for other labels can justly be considered classic big band jazz performances, among them *Henderson Stomp, Whiteman Stomp, St Louis Shuffle, I'm Coming Virginia* and *Fidgety Feet. Henderson Stomp,* written by the leader and arranged by Redman, was recorded in November 1926, with solos from Ladnier and guest pianist Thomas 'Fats' Waller. It was a complex score, for the time, and required a high degree of technical skill from the reed section, who switched from clarinets to saxophones to provide textural and tonal variety. Redman's own *Whiteman Stomp,* recorded six months later, was an even more complex arrangement. The performance achieved a remarkably integrated balance between short solos and breaks—by Hawkins, Waller, Harrison, drummer Kaiser Marshall, and Bailey—and ensemble passages. It remains a tour-de-force of big band jazz to this day, and for the period was astonishingly advanced. Redman's arrangement of *I'm Coming Virginia* is also very fine, but here the attention is held by solo contributions from Joe Smith (first chorus, aided by sympathetic backing from Waller), Tommy Ladnier and Jimmy Harrison. *St Louis Shuffle* was recorded for more than one company, but the version made for RCA Victor is the most impressive, particularly as more than one take has become available over the years and it is possible to study the differences in the solos. The arrangement is good, the ensemble work forceful, and the solos, particularly by Ladnier and Harrison, excellent. *Fidgety Feet* highlights the major solo talent of the band—Bailey, Hawkins, Smith, Harrison and Ladnier in that order—and is a very spirited performance throughout. There are numerous other recordings of the 1926-1928 period that have admirable felicities of scoring or outstanding solos: *St Louis Blues* has a particularly fine passage shared by Harrison and Ladnier; *Hop Off* includes fine solos from Harrison, Bailey and Ladnier. Ladnier again excels in a solo on the imaginatively scored *Rocky Mountain Blues.*

Early in 1928, Tommy Ladnier joined Sam Wooding's band, leaving with it for Europe in June. His replacement with Henderson was Bobby Stark; that autumn Joe Smith also left the band to be replaced by Rex Stewart. Benny Carter was present in the personnel for a brief period during late 1928, and Harrison was joined in the trombone section by Benny Morton. From December 1928 comes *Come On, Baby!*, arranged by Benny Carter, with fiery trumpet passages from Stark set within the opening chorus, and solo sequences from Carter, Harrison and Hawkins. This is a splendidly aggressive performance, but the waywardness that attends Henderson's recording career is in evidence four months later on *Freeze and Melt*, with its ponderous rhythm and the unsteady tempo of the opening chorus. *Raisin' the Roof*, too, is only partly salvaged by a good trumpet solo from Cootie Williams who was shortly to become a star of the Duke Ellington band. In May 1929, on what was to be the band's last recording date for almost eighteen months, much of the old spirit is present in an excellent version of *Wang Wang Blues*, when Stark, Harrison, Williams and Hawkins contribute solos of a high order.

As the depression deepened, U.S. recording companies were concerned primarily with the problem of survival. Many soon became victims of the adverse economic conditions. In 1930, the Henderson band, with Claude Jones replacing Morton on trombone and Benny Carter briefly present once again, took part in only three recording sessions; in one instance, the titles made were never issued. John Nesbitt, formerly of McKinney's Cotton Pickers, was in New York at the time working as a free-lance arranger, and he provided the score of *Chinatown, My Chinatown*. The band's recording of the number displayed an impressive ensemble sound and the considerable ability of soloists Rex Stewart, Benny Carter, Claude Jones and Coleman Hawkins. From the same session came *Somebody Loves Me*, a rather light-hearted performance that closes with Jimmy Harrison doing his vocal impersonation of comedian Bert Williams, though there are also splendid solos from Stark and Hawkins and, as on *Chinatown*, the strength of John Kirby's bass playing is adequately caught. 1931 was one of the worst of the depression years, but surprisingly enough the Henderson band was well represented on record, entering the studios on no fewer than eleven occasions. Early in the year there were two changes in the line-up, when Russell Procope and Benny Morton replaced Carter and Harrison. The ill-fated Harrison, a major instrumentalist who had played an important pioneering role in developing the trombone as an effective solo voice in jazz, left to work with Chick Webb, but he was already a very sick man and died the following July.

The Henderson band's recorded output of 1931-32 (it took part in three sessions in the latter year) is particularly uneven. Its work for RCA Victor is generally its least impressive. This was largely due to the banality of much of the material for, though individual soloists play well, many numbers are ruined by the presence of excruciatingly poor vocalists. In any case, the greatest arranging genius would be hard pressed to make much of titles like *My Sweet Tooth Says 'I Wanna' (But My Wisdom Tooth Says 'No')*, or *Malinda's Wedding Day*, which has singularly tasteless Uncle Tom lyrics. At this time, the

influence of the Casa Loma Orchestra is frequently apparent, but the excellence of the band is best displayed in the use of its own material, particularly when advantage is taken of the maturity of Coleman Hawkins as a soloist. A new recording of King Oliver's famous *Sugar Foot Stomp*, arranged by Henderson, employs call-and-response patterns in the opening chorus, followed by several excellent solos, notably from Stewart, who takes the 'traditional' choruses associated with Oliver, and Hawkins. Horace Henderson arranged *Hot and Anxious* which has strongly cohesive ensemble work, with solos from Stark, Hawkins (on clarinet) and guitarist Clarence Holiday (father of Billie Holiday), and the splendid *Comin' and Goin'* with its superb solo contributions from Morton, Stark and Hawkins. Horace, who was the pianist on the date, proved less reticent in featuring himself than was generally the case with his brother. He achieved a cohesion of solo and ensemble by having the sections echo certain of his phrases. An interesting example of the then frequent interaction between white and black jazz musicians is provided by the April 1931 recording of *Singin' the Blues*, for Rex Stewart's cornet solo is consciously modelled after that by Bix Beiderbecke on Frankie Trumbauer's record. Stewart had listened to Beiderbecke when the Goldkette band had played at Roseland, and in later years frequently expressed his admiration for his unique talents. The last recording session in 1932 produced hard driving versions of *Honeysuckle Rose* and *New King Porter Stomp*, a head arrangement. On both, Hawkins asserts his complete mastery of his instrument in forceful solos, and trombonist J. C. Higginbotham plays to advantage in his robust, swashbuckling style. Despite Henderson's financial problems at this period and his uncertainty of musical direction, such recordings prove beyond doubt that the band was still a fine one, given reasonable freedom in choice of material and performance.

Sales of jazz records in the United States during 1933 were low; the Henderson band's most interesting sessions in that year only took place through a European demand for 'hot' recordings. *It's the Talk of the Town* and *I've Got to Sing a Torch Song*—the latter issued under Horace's name—are historically important because, though both contain brief solo passages by Henry Allen, they are essentially features for Coleman Hawkins and prefigure the rhapsodic ballad interpretations for which he became famous in the years ahead. *Queer Notions*, a Hawkins composition, illustrates what was, at the time, very advanced writing, with augmented chords used to achieve a whole-tone scale effect. On the recordings of the number, Hawkins and Allen take appropriately adventurous solos. Though it caused little stir at the time of issue, it does lead to speculation about Hawkins' possible achievement if he had chosen to work regularly as a composer.

Henderson's first recording date of 1934 produced one worthwhile performance in *Hocus Pocus*, with fine solos

Fletcher Henderson's band at the Roseland Ballroom New York, 1941. Left to right: Willie White, Russell Smith, Freddie Mitchell, George Irish, Bobby Williams, Freddie Robinson, George Dorsey, Fred Sturgess, Jonah Jones, Herbie Cowan, Rudy Powell and Fernando Arbello.

from Hawkins and Allen, but the other titles made at the date—incidentally Hawkins' last with the band—have only a number of worthwhile solos (particularly those by Hawkins) to recommend them, for the material used was trite and the arrangements by Russ Morgan and Will Hudson are mechanical and cluttered. In September came three sessions for U.S. Decca. The scores for such titles as *Shanghai Shuffle, Down South Camp Meeting* and *Rug Cutter's Swing* display Henderson's total assurance in the style of arranging which was shortly afterwards to help Benny Goodman's rise to fame and set the scene for the swing era. The band gave spirited performances on the twelve numbers that they recorded. *Shanghai Shuffle* (solos by Buster Bailey, trumpeter Irving Randolph and alto saxophonist Hilton Jefferson), *Wrappin' It Up* (solos by Jefferson, Allen and Bailey), and *Down South Camp Meeting* (solo by Allen) are particularly impressive, but the public appeared indifferent to the merit of the band and its records. As a result, a dispirited Henderson gave his musicians notice and retired temporarily from bandleading.

As we have already seen, Henderson's 1936 group was the last really outstanding unit that he led. Its solo

strength included trumpeters Joe Thomas and Roy Eldridge—who was at the time astounding his fellow musicians with his adventurous and forward-looking playing—tenor saxophonist Leon 'Chu' Berry, clarinettist Buster Bailey and, for a while, alto saxophonist Scoops Carry. The rhythm section was an exceptionally strong one, with Sidney Catlett, one of the greatest of all big band drummers, and the fine bassist John Kirby whose replacement, Israel Crosby, was equally brilliant. The first title the band recorded was *Christopher Columbus,* a tune based on a common riff, and it became a hit. Typically Henderson failed to capitalise on this. As Joe Thomas told Frank Driggs: 'Fletcher was hot, everyone was asking for him. Duke (Ellington) came by one night and told him. Fletcher should have gone out on the road then, while he was hot. By the time he got ready to come out, somebody else had something big, and Fletcher couldn't get started.'

Despite the commercial success of *Christopher Columbus,* two other recordings made at the same date are better, musically. *Stealin' Apples* is one of the few numbers Henderson recorded in which he allows himself a fair amount of solo space, and his Wallerish stride-style theme chorus is excellent. Other solos are taken by Eldridge, 'Chu' Berry and Bailey. A relaxed *Blue Lou,* taken at a very easy tempo, has superb solos from Eldridge and Berry. Three RCA Victor sessions were marred by the use of some indifferent commercial material, but there are good performances in a powerful *You Can Depend*

Above: *members of a 'Fletcher Henderson Reunion' band in 1958: trumpeters Taft Jordan and Joe Thomas, and trombonists J. C. Higginbotham, Benny Morton and Dicky Wells.*

on Me, with striking solos from Eldridge and Berry and a powerful riff by the ensemble at the close, and *Jangled Nerves*, one of the few recorded arrangements by the little known Roger Moore. Here Eldridge and Berry are again outstanding as soloists and the writing is notable for a fresh treatment of conventional techniques. Between March 1937 and May 1938 the Henderson band, now with quite frequent personnel changes, had seven recording sessions. Though such soloists as 'Chu' Berry, clarinettist Jerry Blake and trumpeter Emmett Berry are heard to advantage on such titles as *Rhythm of the Tambourine* and *Back in Your Own Backyard*, there is little individuality about the numbers as a whole. The last commercial session undertaken by the Henderson band took place in April 1941, but the titles recorded on that occasion are undistinguished.

Talking to musicians who played with Henderson at various times between 1927 and 1936, one is struck by their unanimous view that his records give a distorted picture of the actual band. It was, to quote the late Coleman Hawkins, 'a stomping band' and in ballrooms and theatres built up great momentum and excitement with individual numbers that lasted from five to ten minutes. According to musicians, the band's records quite failed to capture this excitement for, unlike Duke Ellington, Henderson found the three-minute time limit of 78 rpm records stultifying. In view of the numerous fine

records made throughout the band's career, such a judgment seems unduly harsh. However, in the summer of 1957, Rex Stewart assembled a band mainly of ex-Henderson musicians—who included Joe Thomas, Benny Morton, Dickie Wells, Coleman Hawkins, Buster Bailey and Hilton Jefferson—for an appearance at a Long Island jazz festival. A few days later, using the old scores, this band recorded exciting and hard swinging versions of such numbers as *Honeysuckle Rose, Wrappin' It Up, King Porter Stomp* and *Sugar Foot Stomp* that rank among the finest swing style performances of the post-war era. If the Henderson band was 'a stomping band', it is ironical that this record, made five years after Henderson's death, probably gives a clearer idea of how the band sounded at its peak than any with which he was himself involved.

In the summer of 1927, Don Redman left Fletcher Henderson's band to become musical director of McKinney's Cotton Pickers in Detroit. After remaining with the group in this capacity for almost exactly four years, he was replaced by Benny Carter. Redman joined McKinney's band as a fully matured arranger after his experiences with Fletcher Henderson, and it was not long before he moulded the group into one of the finest of its day. It is not unreasonable to suggest that McKinney's band, with its quota of excellent musicians and lacking temperamental stars, was by now a more satisfactory vehicle for Redman than the Henderson band would have been, for he was able to imprint his personality on the group and set its style. The band flourished for four or five years, then went into a decline. In the years prior to Redman's arrival, it had developed from a typical razz-ma-tazz group of the 'twenties into an excellent musical organisation.

The origin of McKinney's Cotton Pickers lies in a group that was very popular during the early 'twenties in the area of Springfield, Ohio. It was called the Synco Septet (later it worked as the Synco Jazz Band) and was organised by the alto saxophonist Milton Senior. Wesley Stewart (tenor saxophone), Todd Rhodes (piano), Buddy Burton (violin, vocals), June Coles (brass bass), Dave Wilborn (banjo) and William McKinney (drums) were among the earliest players. In 1924 Burton and Wilborn had come to the Synco Septet from its only serious local rival, Scott's Symphonic Syncopators, led by the brothers Cecil and Lloyd Scott. The Scotts left on a tour with a

reorganised band that subsequently made an impact on New York audiences, leaving the field free for Senior's group. As the group's fame spread further afield and it began to undertake a regular touring schedule, it switched its musical policy from novelty numbers, with the musicians decked out in paper hats and using whistles and rattles for effects, to the provision of well played dance music, using a proportion of original arrangements. McKinney, an ex-circus drummer, ceased to play in 1926 and took over the business side of the band which, incidentally, now bore his name. For a while, a girl singer called Mozelle Williams was featured with the band, but more important were the addition of drummer Cuba Austin in place of McKinney, and the arrival of the talented trumpeter-arranger John Nesbitt. A photo of the Synco Jazz Band, probably taken in 1926, shows that five members of the original Synco Septet were still present —Burton had left and McKinney had been replaced by Austin—and had been joined by trombonist Claude Jones, Nesbitt, and saxist/vocalist, George Thomas. Jones had, in fact, been an early member of the Septet and it is possible that the original personnel varied occasionally. In 1926, at White Sulphur Springs, West Virginia, the band played a special date for the Prince of Wales—later King Edward VIII—who sat in on drums for one set.

An engagement at the Green Mill in Toledo brought the band before a wider public, and there were also residencies in Michigan, Detroit, Baltimore and Dayton. When they were playing in Dayton, Jean Goldkette wired

Below: the Synco Jazz Band, the group from which McKinney's Cotton Pickers developed. Left to right: Claude Jones, John Nesbitt, Cuba Austin, Dave Wilborn, Todd Rhodes, Milton Senior, June Cole, George Thomas and Wesley Stewart.

McKinney, asking him to bring the band for a trial date at his popular Graystone Ballroom in Detroit. They were a tremendous success and Goldkette took control of the band, with McKinney now assigned a managerial role. Goldkette was responsible for the band's being heard nationwide on radio, which was unusual for black groups at the time. He also had the idea of throwing a lavish party in honour of Leroy Shields, a leading recording director for RCA Victor. Shields was so impressed by the performance of the band that he promised to bring pressure to bear on his fellow directors to put it under contract. Its initial recording session took place in Chicago, during 1928.

It was McKinney himself, rather than Goldkette, who decided to offer Don Redman the job of musical director which he took up in July 1927. The band, now billed as McKinney's Cotton Pickers, used the Graystone Ballroom as its home base for the next few years, regularly going on extensive tours that took in such major cities as New York, Philadelphia, Atlantic City and Chicago, though very seldom the South. During this period, the McKinney's musicians enjoyed both public acclaim and economic success. However, as the depression hit all sections of society in the U.S.A., the boom days receded. In 1930, Goldkette severed his connections with the band and the Cotton Pickers left Detroit on a tour that culminated in Kansas City, at that time a haven for entertainers and musicians in general because of the good time atmosphere engendered by Boss Prendergast. There followed a residency at Frank Sebastian's Cotton Club in Culver City, California. This club was a favourite haunt of Hollywood movie stars. It wrecked the morale of the band, according to pianist Todd Rhodes, who claimed that the easy living proved too much for several of the players. At the close of the Culver City residency, the band returned East via several Midwest cities. When it reached Detroit, it broke up. Some members joined Don Redman's newly formed band, while others remained to work under their new musical director Benny Carter. Carter only stayed a few months, and drummer Cuba Austin took over direction of the group for the next two years. The band was then billed as Cuba Austin's Original Cotton Pickers. It is unlikely that McKinney himself had more than a nominal interest in it.

These last years, with only a few of the original members remaining, were very different from the halcyon days of the band. Todd Rhodes recalls an experience in Freeport, Louisiana during 1933 when a policeman stopped two of the band's saxophonists in a car, asking whose vehicle it was. Because one neglected to call him

'Sir', the policeman knocked out three teeth and broke his jaw. In its peak years, the band never travelled into the deep South; Lexington, Kentucky was the furthest southward point it would play. Its final engagement was a residency at Carlin's Park in Baltimore during the summer of 1934. The line-up at the time included both Roy and Joe Eldridge. In later years there were a number of bands that used the Cotton Pickers's name, but none was associated with either McKinney or Austin. Although Cuba Austin continued to play quite regularly, well into the 'sixties, William McKinney worked in management and then severed all connections with music sometime in the 'forties. Now in his mid-seventies, he has suffered very poor health in recent years. An unexpected post-script to this brief historical outline is the news that the band has been reformed, thirty-eight years after its last engagement. David Hutson, a Detroit disc-jockey, has acquired most of the original Redman arrangements and assembled a band, including the veteran Dave Wilborn, to recreate the McKinney's sound. The band has performed at one or two public concerts and, in 1972, recorded an LP that, Wilborn claims, faithfully recaptures the old sound. A number of Redman's scores for the band can justly be considered classics of their kind, and it will be interesting to hear if contemporary musicians can rival the original performers.

The McKinney's band first recorded in Chicago during July 1928. Of ten titles cut over two days, all but one were issued. Not all the arrangements for these sessions were by Redman, for John Nesbitt who, in addition to being a very reasonable trumpet soloist was also an excellent arranger, obviously collaborated with Redman to some degree when they were together in the band. Recordings of such titles as *Milenberg Joys* and *Stop Kidding* show that the band was already excellent. The best solos on the date come from Nesbitt himself and Claude Jones. However, the scoring for the saxes is not as assured as that for the brass—common enough at this period—and one notices the lack of a major soloist. The most successful title from these sessions is undoubtedly *Crying and Sighing,* written and arranged by Nesbitt, which displays an impressively full ensemble sound with excellent intonation by the saxophone section. A good solo by Prince Robinson is rhythmically advanced for the period. Robinson was praised by the late Coleman Hawkins on several occasions; his work with the McKinney's band proves him to have been one of the few players of tenor saxophone whose development, in some degree, paralleled that of Hawkins himself. Three months later, the band recorded four titles for the Okeh label that were released, presumably for contractual reasons, under the name of the Chocolate Dandies. Lonnie Johnson joined the band on guitar and proved a considerable asset, taking excellent solos on *Paducah* and *Stardust,* which also has pleasant alto work from Redman and firm lead playing by Nesbitt. The brilliance of Redman is shown by his arrangement of Duke Ellington's

Left: *McKinney's Cotton Pickers, 1928.* Above left: *Back row: Cuba Austin, unidentified, George Thomas, Don Redman, Prince Robinson, Todd Rhodes and Ralph Escudero. Sitting: John Nesbitt, Claude Jones, Milton Senior and Langston Curl. Below left: J. Hoxley, Rhodes, Curl, Austin, Robinson, Escudero, Dave Wilborn, Jones, Thomas, Nesbitt and Redman.*

Birmingham Breakdown. Austin's punctuations help to keep the rhythm flowing during ensemble passages. A recording date one month later, the last in 1928, resulted in a mediocre version of *There's a Rainbow 'round My Shoulder* and a pleasant *It's Tight Like That,* in which Nesbitt and Jones play good solos and George Thomas takes one of his light-hearted, rather attractive vocals.

Two recording dates that took place in New York during 1929 resulted in recordings of uneven quality, the first producing versions of two numbers—*Beedle um bum* and *Selling That Stuff*—that are more characteristic of the material associated with such groups as the Memphis Jug Band. Several vocalists are heard on both titles, though Thomas is the most heavily featured. *Selling* begins impressively with a light, deftly scored ensemble chorus, and Nesbitt takes first rate solos, while *Beedle* has solos from Nesbitt, Jones and Robinson that are among their best on record to date. Three sessions on successive days in November certainly rate amongst the band's finest though of the regular line-up only Joe Smith (he had joined the band that summer), Claude Jones, Redman, Wilborn and bassist Billy Taylor were present. Redman had brought in such leading soloists as Sidney De Paris, Leonard Davis, Benny Carter and Coleman Hawkins to strengthen the group. One of Redman's best known compositions, *Gee Baby, Ain't I Good to You,* was brilliantly interpreted by the band; a beautiful lyrical theme chorus by Joe Smith precedes a contrasting, full-toned open solo by De Paris, a finely shaped alto solo by Carter, and one of Redman's curiously attractive half-spoken vocals. *Miss Hannah* opens with an alto solo from Redman against the remaining saxes; his vocal which follows is succeeded by an outstanding solo from De Paris, reminiscent of Armstrong, and one of Carter's best recorded clarinet solos. *The Way I Feel Today* opens with superb playing from the brass; contrasting solos by Jones, Smith and Hawkins are equally impressive. *Wherever There's a Will Baby* has a particularly good chorus from Hawkins. Redman was by now unrivalled as an arranger; his scores frequently forsook the conventional exchange of phrases between sections in favour of unusual instrumental blendings which produced a continuous textural variety. Compared with the strong brass figures, his writing for the saxes was sometimes rather sweet, often deliberately so, to provide contrast within a performance. The McKinney's ensemble sound is very distinctive. Redman aimed for lightness of texture allied to considerable swing.

Seven more titles were recorded in New York during January and February 1930. *When Someone's in Love* was one of the few waltzes to be made by a black band up to this time. It is a dreary performance and, though the other titles made were a great deal better, none approached the standard of those made on the previous date. However, *If I Could Be With You One Hour* became a big seller on the strength of George Thomas's popularity as a vocalist. In July, a further seven titles were recorded. Thomas's vocals again ensured good sales for *Baby Won't You Please Come Home* and *I Want a Little Girl.* Both include well-constructed solos from trombonist Ed Cuffee, but the muted trumpet solo on *Little Girl* presents something of a mystery. Joe Smith was well known for his interpretation of this tune, but the soloist here does not sound like him, although he is certainly present on other titles. The seven titles made in July were recorded over four days and it may be that Smith missed this particular session, but it does seem odd that *I Want a Little Girl* should have been done without him. One title recorded at the time, *Blues Sure Have Got Me,* was not issued until many years later, though it is a good performance of a Redman arrangement that employs a variety of ensemble textures. Thomas is heard again as the vocalist on the attractive *Okay Baby,* with strong ensemble work and good solos from Smith, Robinson and Nesbitt and from Redman on clarinet. This was the last session to include Thomas, who was killed in a car accident a few months later while driving with Joe Smith.

In the last two months of the year, the McKinney's band recorded eleven titles. More than half of them are marred by mediocre vocalists and the banality of the material. Exceptions include a superb *Rocky Road,* highlighted by outstanding brass writing from Redman and excellent solos from Rex Stewart and Benny Carter. A spirited *You're Driving Me Crazy* extensively features new-comer Edward Inge. Among neat touches in the Redman arrangement are a passage when Inge solos over trombones playing straight melody, and the final ensemble chorus with Inge's cutting clarinet riding over it in the manner of Barney Bigard and the Ellington band. There are good individual contributions on the commercial performances, Benny Carter's clarinet playing on *Never Swat a Fly* is one instance. However, only those with a taste for the horrific could appreciate Bill Coty's vocal on this title or such lyrics as :

Never harm a flea,
He may have a favourite she,
That he bounces on his knee,
The way I do with you.

A session undertaken in February 1931 produced only two mediocre titles. *Do You Believe in Love at First Sight,* from the band's final recording date, despite yet another dire vocal from a fortunately anonymous singer, is a satisfactory performance with a pleasant muted theme by Doc Cheatham and very good solos from Rex Stewart and Prince Robinson. The rhythm section of the band remained unchanged : pianist Todd Rhodes, banjoist/guitarist Dave Wilborn and drummer Cuba Austin were permanently in the line-up for the recording period, and bassist Billy Taylor appeared on at least two-thirds of the records. Despite the use of banjo and tuba until very late in the band's recording career, there is seldom any heaviness of rhythm, though clearly a great deal was

McKINNEY'S COTTON PICKERS
WILLIAM McKINNEY Director

Tour Direction
CHARLES E. GREEN
Consolidated Radio Artists Inc.

McKinney's Cotton Pickers.

owed to drummer Austin. Austin was noted for his press role and was something of a showman. He was also a sensitive drummer who could create intricate patterns without losing the essential element of direct swing. The stability of this highly professional rhythm section over the years undoubtedly played a part in making McKinney's Cotton Pickers one of the outstanding musical combinations of its time.

As a final illustration of the extent to which Don Redman was responsible for the McKinney style, it is worth considering a single title, Redman's *Cherry*, recorded in September 1928 by a pick-up group of white musicians, including the Dorsey brothers, Jack Teagarden, Frank Teschemacher, Frank Signorelli and Carl Kress. Although Redman and George Thomas were the only McKinney's members present on the date, using the score Redman had written for the McKinney's band, the sound of the group is almost a facsimile of the original. McKinney's Cotton Pickers can, with some justice, be described as an 'arranger's band'—its good fortune was to have one of the greatest arrangers in jazz history.

The Missourians cannot be considered musically on a par with either the Fletcher Henderson band or McKinney's Cotton Pickers, but they remain an important group, for their time. They introduced to Eastern audiences a concept of jazz that prevailed in the Midwest, based largely on the blues, with extensive use of riffs to generate a powerful swing. The few titles recorded serve to illustrate the difference between Eastern and Midwestern big bands during the late 'twenties.

The Missourians, originally known as Wilson Robinson's Syncopators, came from St Louis. After touring the Midwest, they arrived in New York late in 1924, fronted by violinist Andy Preer, with whom they recorded for Gennett. They were fortunate in securing the residency at the famous Cotton Club for about two and half years and finally left when Duke Ellington accepted an offer which had been turned down by King Oliver. In 1925, the band recorded for the U.S. Columbia label as the Cotton Club Orchestra, retaining the name for a time after they left that club, and went out on tour, for a while accompanying singer Ethel Waters. Returning to New York around the end of 1928, they decided to call themselves The Missourians, mainly to avoid confusion with Duke

Ellington whose lengthy residency at the Cotton Club was still in its early stages. They played at a number of Harlem dance halls, including the Savoy and the Alhambra, at this time fronted by vocalist Lockwood Lewis. Soon after a recording session in February, 1930, Cab Calloway's manager persuaded them to become Calloway's regular backing group. Three of the musicians —Andrew Brown, Walter 'Foots' Thomas and Lamar Wright—remained with Calloway well into the 'forties. Despite the individual solos, Calloway's many records with the band inevitably highlighted the leader's singing and, as a result, much of the personal identity of the group was lost. It is interesting to note that, as Frank Driggs has reported, Calloway was more popular in the Midwest at one time than any other Eastern bandleader, primarily because audiences identified themselves with the type of jazz played by the ex-Missourians personnel.

Hsio Wen Shi has written that the styles of such bands as The Missourians were heavily influenced by their work in clubs, when they had to back show dancers and singers, as well as play music for dancing. He commented : 'Show bands needed dramatic qualities that dance bands could ignore, and to create maximum excitement all these bands concentrated their ensemble sound on brass as the dance bands did around reeds. To satisfy the demand of white customers for "low life", they all adopted the "freak" brass playing of New Orleans musicians like Oliver and Mutt Carey, using a variety of mutes to produce strange tonal and expressive effects, and thereby developing what was called "the jungle style".'

The above is an interesting theory and may be partially correct. However, in the case of musicians from the Midwest like the Missourians, it should be recalled that they heard New Orleans musicians quite early in the 'twenties, and that in St Louis, for example, a trumpet tradition which included frequent use of various mutes had been established by the time that the band left for New York. In any case, I feel that the style of the Missourians, particularly on the recordings of 1929 and 1930, owes rather more to their Midwestern background than to their having worked at the Cotton Club.

An early recording of *I've Found a New Baby,* made

Cab Calloway with The Missourians. At the back : Calloway, Charley Stamps, Leroy Maxey and Jimmy Smith. Seated: Earres Prince, George Scott, William Blue, Andrew Brown, R. Q. Dickerson, Lammar Wright and De Priest Wheeler.

under the nominal leadership of Andy Preer, is undistinguished and features conventional section work. That by the saxes, particularly, is mediocre, with only adequate trumpet solos to provide compensation. The 1925 titles, as by the Cotton Club Orchestra, are also fairly ordinary. The most interesting passages are the solos from the brass men. It was almost four years before the band was to record again, by that time as the Missourians, and the twelve titles made between June 1929 and February 1930 show a tremendous improvement in all aspects of their music. The arrangements utilised riffs to good effect, though there were tricky bridge passages that occasionally sounded too cluttered. The band included R. Q. Dickerson and Lamar Wright, two excellent trumpeters who played in contrasting styles. Clarinettist William Blue and trombonist DePriest Wheeler were also capable soloists. *Ozark Mountain Blues,* credited to Dickerson, is actually Jesse Stone's adaption of *Tiger Rag* which he called *Boot to Boot;* the performance is a rousing one with fine solos from Dickerson (muted) and Wright (open). Although *Prohibition Blues* includes a passable baritone sax solo from Walter 'Foots' Thomas, again the two trumpeters provide the highlights, Dickerson with a plunger and Wright displaying his broad open tone. *You'll Cry for Me When I'm Gone* (Bennie Moten's *South*) is a good extrovert performance. The hectic *200 Squabble* is better, however, with effective solos from Wright and Blue, and final riff passages performed with enormous verve as Blue's clarinet rides over the ensemble. *Scotty Blues* has George Scott soloing on both clarinet and alto sax; there are also contributions from banjoist, Morris White, and Wright, who takes an excellent open solo over the saxes. This arrangement, as was then popular, makes use of a clarinet trio in the closing choruses in order to give the performance some textural variety.

As far as we can judge, admittedly from a small number of recordings, the Missourians attempted no great subtleties of scoring, and their material drew heavily on the blues and a few standard themes of the *Tiger Rag* variety. However, they outswung most of their contemporaries in the last, and in *Ozark Mountain Blues* created a near masterpiece in its idiom.

If Luis Russell had not won $3,000 in a Panama lottery some time in 1919, it seems unlikely that he would, ten years later, have led one of the best bands of its day in New York. He was born near Bocas Del Toro in Panama on 6th August 1902, and studied violin, guitar, piano and organ with his father, who was a music teacher. His first job was to accompany silent films in a Panama cinema, from which he graduated to work in clubs. When he won the lottery, he moved to New Orleans with his mother and sister, initially accepting any musical jobs that were offered him. He first became a leader around 1924, when he took the band over from Albert Nicholas at Tom Anderson's Cabaret. Late in that year he accepted an offer to join Doc Cooke's band in Chicago. He was with

The Luis Russell Band, 1930. Left to right: Henry 'Red' Allen, Greely Walton, Paul Barbarin, Charlie Holmes, Luis Russell, Albert Nicholas, Will Johnson, George 'Pops' Foster, J. C. Higginbotham and Otis Johnson.

Cooke for several months, but in 1925 joined the King Oliver band where he remained until the summer of 1927. He then left to work with drummer George Howe at the Nest Club, New York.

Howe's group consisted of Edward Anderson (trumpet), Harry White (trombone), Charlie Holmes (alto and soprano saxes, clarinet), Teddy Hill (tenor sax), Luis Russell (piano), Will Johnson (banjo, guitar), Bill Moore (tuba) and Howe himself on drums. Russell took over the leadership in October. In the course of the next year he brought in Louis Metcalf, J. C. Higginbotham and Paul Barbarin to replace Anderson, White and Howe, adding Albert Nicholas on clarinet. Barbarin and Nicholas were old friends of Russell from his New Orleans days. He had been responsible for bringing them to Chicago, along with Barney Bigard, to join Oliver earlier in the year. It was this group which made the first New York recordings under Russell's name.

The great days of the Russell band lasted from 1928 to 1930. During this period it worked at the Nest Club, Saratoga Club, Savoy Ballroom and Connie's Inn. At one point, in 1929, it acted as the accompanying group for Louis Armstrong. During the early 'thirties, the Russell band combined fairly lengthy New York residencies with an extensive touring schedule, retaining some of the earlier personnel, until it began regularly to accompany Louis Armstrong, in 1935. Russell himself worked with Armstrong until 1943, after which he left to form his own big band and returned to his former pattern of New York residencies alternating with touring schedules. He left full time music in 1948 and took charge of a stationery shop, although he still did occasional gigs with a small band and taught piano and organ. In 1959, he visited Panama after an absence of forty years, and gave a classical piano recital in Bocas del Toro. The fact that he worked as a chauffeur in New York upon his return suggests that he did not enjoy a great deal of economic security. He continued to teach piano and organ until a short time before his death, of cancer, on 11th December 1963.

Although Russell first recorded under his own name for the Vocalion and Okeh labels when he was working in Chicago during 1926, the output from these sessions is outside the scope of this book. The three titles from his first New York session, in January 1929, are not without interest. There are good solos by Metcalf, Higginbotham and Holmes, and Walter 'Fats' Pichon provides a vaudeville style vocal on *It's Tight Like That*. Metcalf was an interesting if minor trumpeter at this period, and his mobility and fondness for smears is in evidence on *Savoy Shout* and *It's Tight Like That*. The precision of his lead work provided a contrast to the more extrovert qualities of the other soloists; at times, this gives it a somewhat static quality. Virtually the same line-up recorded two more titles three months later—*African Jungle* and *Slow as Molasses*—this time under the pseudonym of Jungle Town Stompers. Once again, the attention is held by the solos, and the band as such has no particularly distinctive sound.

Shortly after the last session, two changes occurred that were to revolutionise the overall sound of the band and to give it an identity that is apparent on all the records made during the next two years. Henry 'Red' Allen replaced Metcalf, and another New Orleans musician, George 'Pops' Foster, took over from Moore. A session was recorded under Allen's name in July 1929, and two months later, the band made *New Call of the Freaks, Jersey Lightning* and *Feelin' the Spirit,* with Bill Coleman added as second trumpeter. These three titles, all composed and arranged by Russell, are entirely representative of the Russell band at its peak. *New Call* has excellent solos by Allen, Higginbotham and Holmes—with Nicholas, the band's major soloists. It is one of the few sides which allows one to hear much of guitarist Will Johnson in any role other than purely rhythm section. His playing is not unlike that of his namesake Lonnie. *Jersey* and *Feelin'* are both up-tempo performances with spirited solos by Allen, Holmes, Nicholas and Higginbotham. The first trumpet solo on *Feelin'* is taken by Bill Coleman. The most obvious change to have taken place since the last session is the new dominance in the rhythm section of 'Pops' Foster, whose slapped bass has such propulsive power that it frequently gives the impression of driving along the whole Russell band during ensemble passages. The late Jimmy Blanton revolutionised the use of the string bass within a jazz context during the late 'thirties and, since that date, the technical advances pioneered by later musicians have been awesome. However, though Foster's style might sound naive to a contemporary stylist, when basic jazz qualities are considered he rates as one of the greatest of all jazz bass players.

The band's second Okeh session took place in December 1929, when *Doctor Blues* was recorded; and a month later they were back in the studio to make *Saratoga Shout* and *Song of the Swanee. Song* includes a beautifully controlled and rhythmically free solo from Allen but is otherwise rather ordinary. In contrast, *Doctor* is sparked by powerful ensemble work and has first rate solos from Allen, Higginbotham and Holmes. *Saratoga Shout,* though, is the outstanding performance from this session, and in its combination of exuberant, superbly played ensemble passages and fine solos by the three men heard on *Doctor* plus Albert Nicholas, it must rate as one of the Russell band's greatest achievements. The arrangement by Russell, though functional, provides a framework for the soloists that would be hard to better.

Sandwiched between the band's Okeh sessions are a number for Victor that were issued under Henry Allen's name, and one released as by J. C. Higginbotham and his Six Hicks. In addition, members of the band accompanied blues singers Victoria and Addie 'Sweet Pease' Spivey on three occasions. The Allen recordings use the

Luis Russell in the mid 1930s.

full line-up in most instances but, despite the inclusion of a number of classic performances and outstanding solos from the leader, Higginbotham, Holmes and Nicholas, the accent is on Allen's own playing and the material was chosen for his benefit rather than that of the band as such. The late Mr Allen once told me that the Victor executives hoped at this time to build him up as a rival to Louis Armstrong. They finally dropped him when the sales of his records failed to match those Armstrong was making for Okeh.

In May 1930, the Russell band recorded its penultimate session for Okeh. The titles were *On Revival Day, Poor Li'l Me* (both ruined by the presence of a mediocre popular vocalist) and *Louisiana Swing.* Allen and Holmes (soprano sax) salvage *Poor,* which sounds as if it is being played from a stock orchestration, and Higginbotham performs the same service for *On Revival. Louisiana Swing* is the best performance from this date, with excellent solos by Holmes and Allen, although the overall sound is not entirely typical of the Russell band at its best and there seems to be a conscious attempt, at one point, to emulate the style of McKinney's Cotton Pickers. Of the four Okeh sessions on which Allen and Foster were present this was undoubtedly the weakest.

By contrast, the final Okeh session in September 1930, resulted in two recordings which can be placed alongside

Saratoga Shout. Panama captures the buoyancy of the ensemble and its immense swing to perfection. Good as the solos by Allen, Holmes and Higginbotham are, Albert Nicholas is the star on this occasion, with his beautifully flowing New Orleans style clarinet solo and his soaring above the ensemble in the final chorus. *High Tension,* written by the Belgian leader David Bee, is almost as good; the four major soloists of the band all perform at something like their peak. It includes that rarity, a Luis Russell solo, which is capable without being particularly noteworthy. In a discussion with the Belgian collector Felix Manskleid in 1956 Russell commented: 'I consider myself a rhythm man and take few solos. I prefer to step aside in order to provide for a better band.' The final number from the date, *Muggin' Lightly,* is not quite up to the standard of the other two, though the closing ensemble chorus is played with great spirit and there are pleasant solos from Higginbotham and Holmes.

Okeh obviously did not renew the contract with Russell, and the two remaining sessions that the band undertook in 1930 were released on the Melotone and Vocalion labels respectively. A single title—*I Got Rhythm*—for Melotone has little to commend it apart from a Higgin-

botham solo and eight bars by Allen. The arrangement is poor and an unidentified white female vocalist, worse. From the Vocalion session, *Honey That Reminds Me* is even more expendable; it features another unidentified singer, this time male, and the whole performance could be equalled by any competent dance band. *Saratoga Drag* and *Case On Down* (probably a misprint for *Ease on Down*), though not comparable to the better Okeh sides, at least exhibit some of the spirit associated with the band. Allen has good solos in both numbers. With Higginbotham replaced by Dicky Wells, and Holmes absent, a date took place in the Victor studios in August 1931. The best of the four titles recorded were *Freakish Blues* and *Goin' to Town. Freakish* is an attractive tune that, now and then, calls to mind the popular song *Red Sails in the Sunset.* Altoist Henry Jones plays pleasantly enough, without equalling the contributions of Allen and, particularly, Wells. Despite Chick Bullock's mediocre vocal, *Goin' to Town* is lifted out of the rut by solos from Wells and Nicholas and good drumming by Paul Barbarin. The remaining titles are a dismal *Say the Word,* on which only Allen's solo is worth hearing, and a jivy *You Rascal You* with an amusing vocal from Allen and an excellent solo by Wells. Although there are good moments on the post-Okeh output, a combination of less suitable material, poorer recording, and loss of ensemble inspiration makes it markedly inferior.

It is worth briefly considering the rest of Russell's big

The Luis Russell Band, 1932. Left to right: Bill Coleman, Jimmy Archey, Bill Dillard, Henry 'Red' Allen, Will Johnson, Luis Russell, Paul Barbarin, Albert Nicholas, Henry 'Moon' Jones, George 'Pops' Foster and Greely Walton.

band recordings for the sake of completeness. In 1934 he made six titles for ARC and they are a very mixed bag indeed. Virtually nothing remains of the sound the band achieved in the 1929/1930 recordings; the influences now seem to come from the Casa Loma Orchestra and Jimmie Lunceford. The sax section consisted of Russell stalwarts, though Nicholas was not in the band, and only one change in the rhythm section was the replacement of Will Johnson by Lee Blair. Rex Stewart, Leonard Davis and Jimmy Archey were included in the brass section; Stewart featured in a showy solo on *Ol' Man River* and a typical half-valved effort on *Primitive. My Blue Heaven* is unusual in lacking a solo. The theme chorus shows some imagination in the use of clarinets against staccato brass, although this number, like *Ol' Man River* and *At the Darktown Strutters' Ball,* is not helped by the presence of a male vocalist who sings in a high-pitched jivy manner. The best performances are *Ghost of the Freaks* which, despite a somewhat incongruous Casa Loma-ish ending, has an excellent alto solo from Holmes, and *Hokus Pokus,* clearly influenced by Lunceford, on which the main solo is given to a reasonable tenor player, probably Greely Walton. Though *Ol' Man River* proved to be a minor hit for Russell, these 1934 performances give the impression that the band had lost its identity and, despite being highly competent, was markedly less good than its leading contemporaries. Russell's last big band recordings were made in 1945 and 1946, after he left Armstrong, for the Manor and Apollo labels. I have heard only half of the twenty titles issued and must be cautious in judgment. Those that I did hear are conventional performances for their period, sometimes cashing in on the interest in jump blues that prevailed at the time, and offer nothing that could be considered individual. The records that the Russell band made with Louis Armstrong relegate it to a purely supporting role and, as a result, have not been considered here.

Most jazz followers must inevitably, at times, have their perspective distorted, simply because they are forced to rely on records to judge early artists. With bands that only recorded on one or two occasions, it was a matter of luck whether they were caught at their peak, or under favourable conditions. In the case of Russell, however, there seems little doubt that the Okeh recordings were made at a time when his band was it its finest; this is confirmed by several musicians who were in the line-up at that time. The band also had the advantage of Okeh's excellent recording, which was then superior to that of almost all its rivals, and it seems from the repertoire that there was little interference from recording supervisors.

Compared with the McKinney or Henderson bands, Russell's offered little in the way of innovatory scoring. Its arrangements were functional and highly effective but lacked refinements of texture or instrumental blending. The band's strength lay in its fine rhythm section and, the presence of at least four outstanding soloists—Henry Allen, J. C. Higginbotham, Charlie Holmes and Albert Nicholas. Allen already showed a rhythmic freedom that was years ahead of its time. Mention has already been made of Foster's role, but it would be unfair not to underline the contribution of drummer Paul Barbarin. In his discussion with Felix Manskleid, Russell commented : 'Barbarin was the greatest drummer around. Of course, he could only play with certain bands, as he wouldn't fit with others. Krupa took over everything Barbarin did.' On one occasion, discussing drummers, Louis Armstrong was full of praise for Barbarin, mentioning his superb time-keeping. It was this quality, with his invariable ability to swing, that made Barbarin such an asset to any band with which he played. It is doubtful if any contemporary group could equal the ensemble swing that Russell was able to produce with the personnel he led. The numbers that he and other musicians, within the band, contributed to its book were ideal for displaying both its surging ensemble power and the individuality of its soloists. Four of the key men in the band—Allen, Barbarin, Foster and Nicholas—were New Orleans musicians, and Russell himself had all his early training in that city. Russell, more than any other leader, succeeded in retaining some of the free-flowing quality and spontaneity of the New Orleans small groups within a big band framework.

It only remains to consider why the band deteriorated so rapidly after the final Okeh session, despite the retention of several of its leading soloists. In a discussion among some of the musicians who were with the band in 1929 and '30, all made the point that Russell was forced to change his sound to appeal to sophisticated theatre audiences and, particularly, when the more complex and spectacular music of, say, Duke Ellington and Jimmie Lunceford became popular amongst black audiences in the middle years of the 1930s. Had he had a stable base for a great part of the year, as was the case in later years with Chick Webb at the Savoy Ballroom, Russell might possibly have made fewer modifications to his basic style, but economics made it necessary for any band which relied upon theatres for much of its work to think in terms of visual appeal and musical showmanship.

Luis Russell was not alone among musicians in making his greatest contribution to jazz within a relatively short space of time. In later years his players of 1929 and '30 often spoke with affection of their leader and the band. They knew that for a couple of years they were members of a group that made its own important contribution to big band history. As Henry Allen once remarked, there may have been bands who could better Russell's in several respects, but none who could outswing it.

The Luis Russell Band, 1934.

LUIS RUSSELL

AND HIS "OLD MAN RIVER" ORCHESTRA

5 The Territory Bands

The Southern States

The role of the great musical teachers in jazz is one that has attracted little attention. Yet certain teachers have had a considerable influence on the development of the music; none more so than John Tuggle 'Fess' Whatley, whose students played in many leading black orchestras of the big band era.

Whatley was born in Tuscaloosa, Alabama, moving to Birmingham when at the age of twelve. Though poor he studied at Tuggle Institute in Birmingham and in 1917 was appointed an instructor at the Industrial High School where he organised the first public school band. This band won a considerable reputation for itself and even played on one occasion before President Warren Harding. Then Whatley formed the first black society dance orchestra to play in Birmingham. The latter, consisting of Fess Whatley, Herman Grimes (trumpet), Joseph Britton (trombone), Edward Whatley, Edward Brown, Murray Harper (sax), Curley Parrish (piano), William Scott (banjo), Walter Blythe (tuba) and Wilson Driver (drums), became extremely popular throughout Alabama and performed at both black and white social functions. Grimes, Britton and Brown all worked with major big bands in later years, while Parrish is the brother of the late Avery Parrish, famous for his role in Erskine Hawkins's band.

In 1925 Fess Whatley and his Jazz Demons were much in demand. Grimes had by now left to join Tommy Douglas, and Brown and Parrish had been replaced by Carl Ivory and Shed Harris. The band stayed together for some time, but by the early 'thirties Whatley had decided to enlarge it. Its personnel in 1934 was Herman Robinson, Fess Whatley, Sammy Lowe (trumpet), H. O. Thompson, George Hudson (trombone), Ed Whatley, James Lowe, Ed Brown, J. B. Sims (sax), Curley Parrish (piano), Henry Minnet (guitar), Walter Blythe (string bass) and Wilson Driver (drums). By all accounts one of the finest of the bands that Whatley led was the curiously named Vibra-Cathedral Band which operated from 1937 until about 1943, when the drafting of musicians led to its break up. The line-up was Arthur Miller, Johnny Grimes, Fess Whatley (trumpet), Paul Coman (trombone), John Reed, Wilton Robertson, J. L. Lowe, Amos Gordon (sax), Albert Jones (vibraphone, piano), Mary Alice Clarke (piano, vibraphone, accordion, vocal), James D. Swyne (bass, arranger), Alton 'Snookie' Davenport (drums). In a letter to Bertrand Demeusy,

Mr Whatley claimed that this '. . . was the greatest of all bands, with too much work to do.'

Fess Whatley retired from bandleading in 1962, but up to then he still fronted a big band with Dick Clarke, Hardy Matthews, Robert Barksdale (trumpet), Paul Coman, George Hudson (trombone), Amos Gordon, Teddy Smith, Newman Terrell, James Lowe (sax, clarinet), LaVergne E. Comer (piano), Clarence Whitfield (string bass), James Powell (drums) and Fletcher Myatt (vocal).

The list of Whatley's students who went on to make a name with major bands is long, and his reputation as a teacher was so great that service bands during World War II accepted his pupils without putting them through any tests. Not all of his best pupils moved to Chicago or New York, however, and Mr Whatley wrote M. Demeusy that his regard for trumpeter Rushton Miller was such that he felt Louis Armstrong could have taken lessons from him! Miller led bands in Nashville, Chicago and Denver but never recorded. Whatley himself also had no recording opportunities, a regrettable fact that has deprived jazz followers of hearing what was probably the finest big band in the southern states.

One of Fess Whatley's pupils in the early 'twenties was banjoist Carl Bunch who, in summer 1927, recorded in his brother's band for the Gennett company. The group

Right, top to bottom: (1) *Fess Whatley's first school band, early 1920s. Whatley is at the left of the second row, others include Paul Bascomb, Pete Clark, Teddy Hill, Robert Horton and Sheldon Hemphill.* (2) *Whatley's band in Birmingham, Alabama, early 1920s; left to right: Whatley, Herman Grimes (trumpet), Joseph Britton (trombone), Walter Blythe (tuba), Wilson Driver (drums), Curley Parrish (piano), William Scott (banjo), Edward Brown, Murray Harper (saxes). (3) Fess Whatley and his Jazz Demons, Birmingham, 1925; left to right, standing: Carl Ivory (sax), Walter Blythe, Joseph Britton, William Scott, Murray Harper, Fess Whatley; sitting: Wilson Driver, Edward Whatley (sax) and Shed Harris (piano). (4) Fess Whatley and his Vibra-Cathedral Band, Birmingham, late 1930s; left to right: Paul Coman (trombone), Arthur Miller, Johnny Grimes, Fess Whatley (trumpet), Alton 'Snookie' Davenport (drums), James D. Swyne (string bass), Albert Jones (vibraphone), John Reed (sax), Mary Alice Clark (piano), Wilton Robertson, J. L. Lowe, Amos Gordon (saxes).*

for the recording date was made up of Hunch Vines (trumpet), Joseph Britton (trombone), two unknown sax players doubling clarinet, Frank Bunch (piano), Carl Bunch (banjo), Ivory Johnson (brass bass) and an unknown drummer. It has been claimed that Teddy Hill was one of the sax men on the date, but this seems unlikely in view of Hill's known movements at the time. Three titles were made—*Fuzzy Wuzzy, Fourth Avenue Stomp* and *Congo Stomp*—and for their period they are good performances, particularly for a

group composed mostly of unknown musicians. The outstanding soloist is Vines, who reveals a strong tone, flexible phrasing and alert rhythmic sense. Frank Bunch has a good solo on *Fuzzy Wuzzy*. Britton's contributions are reasonable though rhythmically stiff, and the group as a whole plays with confidence in the ensemble passages. The Chicago Defender of 24th August 1929 carries a report on Bunch, who is described as the former leader of the Alabama Stompers. He had settled in Dayton, Ohio, where he was organising a new ten-piece orchestra. His subsequent career is unknown.

The Erwing Brothers Orchestra played in Birmingham, Alabama, during the middle 'thirties. It was a taxi dance-hall band that played approximately four hundred numbers a night—at taxi dancehalls one bought tickets for a specific number of dances, and melodies played were usually short. One of the best known popular songs of the 'twenties, *Ten Cents A Dance,* was written from the viewpoint of the girls employed by taxi dancehalls as hostesses or dancing partners. Some jazz musicians were still working well into the 'fifties in the few that survived.

In 1932 the Erwing Brothers Orchestra was a seven-piece unit, but a year later it had expanded to nine pieces with a line-up of Hernando Rotzquel, Monte Easter (trumpet), Rodger Hurd, Fats Dennis, Harris Erwing (sax), Jim Erwing (piano, leader), Chester Erwing (guitar), Joe Mendoza (string bass) and Jack White (drums). This was the personnel that during June 1933 in Hollywood recorded *The Erwing Blues* and *Rhythm*, released on the Vocalion label. It seems that some of the band stayed in California, Rodger Hurd working with Les Hite in 1940 and Monte Easter gaining some success in the rhythm-and-blues field around Los Angeles in the middle 'forties.

At the same time as Frank Bunch and his Fuzzy Wuzzies were recording for Gennett, another Alabama band, The Black Birds Of Paradise, entered the studios for the same company. This band hailed from Montgomery and had been formed in 1925 from an amalgamation of local musicians and students from Tuskogee Institute. It originally consisted of Philmore 'Shorty' Hall (trumpet), Willie 'Buddie' Howard (trombone), James Bell (clarinet, alto and soprano saxophone), Walter Boyd (tenor saxophone), Melvin Small (piano), Tom Ivery (banjo), Ivory Johnson (tuba) and Samuel Borders (drums). The Chicago Defender of 6th August 1927 listed the personnel and reported that it would make records for the Gennett company, with Howard as the leader. Hall, Bell, Small and Borders were the ex-Tuskogee students and had played there in the college band, but it was Howard who made it possible for the group to record.

The Black Birds Of Paradise, originally just The Black Birds, were very popular in the Montgomery area and worked for some years on Saturday nights at a white

country club just outside the town. Tom Ivery told Mr Gayle Dean Wardlow in 1968 that Howard was the outstanding musician of the group, remarking that 'He played as good with his feet as his hands. He played the slide with his feet to show off.' Ivery also recalled a band battle with the Fess Whatley Orchestra, which then included the Bunch brothers. They lost. In 1930 the band went on a tour of the middle west, finally disbanding in Omaha the following year. Not all the original members went on the tour. Howard was the only full time musician in the band. Those who returned to Montgomery presumably attempted to keep going for a while longer. Subsequently several band members were part of a new unit called the Black Diamonds under Bell's leadership. Howard remained in Omaha (where he still lives) and in later years fronted his own band. During the early 'thirties he worked with Smiling Billy Stewart and his Celery City Serenaders—a popular band of the day based on Florida.

The Black Birds Of Paradise recorded six titles at their first session and three at their second. Three were never issued and two others, though officially released, have never been traced. Of the issued titles *Bugahoma Blues* is the best performance, featuring a trombone with plunger theme by Howard, average solos by Bell, Small

The Black Birds of Paradise; Willie 'Buddy' Howard (trombone), Samuel Borders (drums), James Bell (clarinet, saxes), Philmore 'Shorty' Hall (trumpet), Thomas Ivery (banjo), Melvin Small (piano), Walter Boyd (sax), Ivory Johnson (tuba).

and Boyd, and a good trumpet solo by Hall against stop chords. *Sugar* and *Tishomingo Blues* are little more than competent, for the group on this showing lacked the cohesiveness of the Bunch band.

A Chicago Defender news item of 24th November 1928 refers to a (Black) Birds Of Paradise unit from Birmingham, listing a line-up of Bubber Evans, Charles Jones, Ernest Wood, Larnce Fulgham, Morgan Jones, Dave Blackman, Otto Williams, Pluto Brown (director) but with no indication of what instruments each played. It is likely that this group was attempting to cash in on the popularity of the band, but its history is obscure.

The Carolinas have not produced many well-known bands, the best known group from that area being the Carolina Cotton Pickers. The first area unit to record there was Taylor's Dixie Serenaders, who made two titles for Victor in May 1931. The Chicago Defender of 1st August 1931 carried the following story: 'Victor recording orchestra of Charlotte, N.C., is meeting with great success during their tour of the Southeastern States. Headquarters at present are at Cumberland, Maryland, under the booking management of W. H. Shepard, 180 Winlow St. The week of July 26 will find the bunch filling engagements in Washington Penna. and Eastern Ohio and will double back to furnish music for the grand ball of the K Of P State Convention at Altoona, Penna. on July 30.'

The U.S. researcher Mack McCormick has reported that Taylor's Dixie Serenaders, with three exceptions, was at the time of the recording made up of students at the Johnson C. Smith High School and University in Charlotte. The leader was a violinist who does not play on the issued titles—one of its members has claimed that four to six numbers were recorded—and the rest of the personnel was Lester Mitchell, Joe Jordan (trumpet), Leslie Johnakins (alto and baritone saxophone), Campbell 'Skeets' Tolbert (alto saxophone), Ernest Parham (tenor saxophone), Jimmy Gunn (piano), Guy Harrington (banjo), Harry Prather (brass bass) and Bill Hart (drums). Tolbert has said that one Jones was the regular trombonist with the band at the time, but there is no evidence of his presence on the recordings. Jordan, Johnakins, Tolbert and Prather moved to New York in later years and worked with name bands. (Tolbert, after some success in the recording field, moved to Houston, Texas, where for some years he has been a musicians' union official.) The band did not last beyond 1934 under Taylor's leadership. It was taken over by pianist Jimmy Gunn and enlarged.

The two known titles by the band are good. *Everybody Loves My Baby* starts with an efficient ensemble theme, heralding a rhythmic vocal by Parham, followed by a pleasant trumpet solo—presumably by Jordan—and an excellent closing ensemble with scored riffs. *Wabash Blues* unexpectedly has a vocal trio of Jordan, Tolbert and Harrington in the manner of Paul Whiteman's Rhythm Boys, but there are good solos from a trumpeter, Parham and Tolbert—the latter's contribution with its fine swing and assured phrasing is outstanding. It is hard to judge a band on so little recorded evidence but the impression one gets from these two performances is that Taylor's Dixie Serenaders was an extremely proficient band, with at least two soloists well above the ordinary.

Attempted research on the Jimmy Gunn band has resulted in almost total frustration, though a few years ago I learned that his widow still lives in Charlotte and has a scrapbook that covers his bandleading career. The Savannah Tribune during September and October 1934 states that Jimmy Gunn and his Dixie Serenaders (note the band title) were to appear at the Powell Hall in that city. A photograph shows a line-up of three trumpets, trombone, three reeds and four rhythm (the latter including banjo and tuba instead of the then more conventional guitar and string bass), but no names are given. In that

year James Berry (alto saxophone) was with Gunn, for a news report mentions his having left to join King Oliver, while a year later trumpeter Billy Douglas left to work with Don Albert. The only other printed reference found to date on the Gunn band appeared in the Pittsburgh Courier of 14th September 1935 and refers to a bus crash at Schenectady, N.Y., on the third of that month, in which Otis Hicks (sax), Alton Harrington (guitar) and Raymond Mason (drums) were injured. Presumably the guitarist is the same man previously given as Guy Harrington.

In June 1936 the band recorded six titles for the Bluebird label in Charlotte, the line-up from aural evidence being trumpet, trombone, two saxes and four rhythm. David Pugh and Sam Jennings are listed as vocalists and presumably are band members, and it is probable that some of the men injured in the bus accident nine months earlier were present—also possibly bassist Harry Prather. *Slat's Shuffle* is the outstanding title I have heard from the session. The group achieves a surprisingly full sound for eight pieces and has good soloists in the alto and tenor saxophonists, trombonist and Gunn himself. The most impressive aspect is the swing of the band and the fine work of the trombonist, possessor of an assured technique and many individual ideas. His style is something like that of Dicky Wells, and the title of the number raises an intriguing possibility. Over the years a number of musicians have spoken in glowing terms of a wandering trombonist whom they knew only as Slats, and it may be that this was the only time the elusive gentleman ever got into a recording studio.

The background of the Carolina Cotton Pickers was told to Stanley Dance during an interview that formed the basis on an article on William 'Cat' Anderson that appeared in a 1968 issue of Down Beat. It was one of a number of bands that came from the famous Jenkins Orphan Home School in Charleston, South Carolina, originally called merely Band Number Five. Anderson told Stanley Dance of the sterness of the teaching and general regime at the school, adding: 'As I look back on the teaching now, I know that it was inadequate in some places, that even the rudiments were not always taught properly. But the school was run on charity, and the pay was small, so there was a limit to what could be expected.'

Amplifying the above he added that he did not remember being taught about breathing or correct embouchure, but that the students helped one another.

Anderson first went on tour in 1929, starting a routine that involved three months on the road and three months at school. The band went far afield and Anderson recalls that they arrived in New York quite early. The members of Band Number Five formed their own group for dances, securing work in the area. The name Carolina Cotton Pickers arose because the members had to pick cotton on certain days, and the men in the older bands

who were free from such duties referred to them as the cotton pickers. It would seem that this name was used from about 1931.

The personnel from 1931 to late 1935, when Anderson left and was replaced by Leonard Graham, was William 'Cat' Anderson, Joseph Williams, John Henry Williams, Thaddeus Seabrook (trumpet), Julius 'Hawkshaw' Watson, Leroy Hardison (trombone), Albert Martin, Booker T. Starks (alto saxophone), Walter Bash (tenor saxophone), Clifton Smalls (piano), W. J. Edwards (guitar), Eugene Earl (brass bass), and Otis Walker (drums). The line-up of six brass and only three reeds was unusual for the period and must have given the band a brass heavy sound. Anderson describes a disastrous tour of Texas when the band got no engagements. After that it worked in Florida, but here the fortunes of the band members were only minimally better. Anderson talks about a diet of rolls and green oranges being quite normal. The band travelled in one car to which a small trailer was attached, and lacked any personality forceful enough to look after its interests. Anderson says that they were often the victims of crooked booking agents, adding 'We were hungry, and if he had five dollars, it meant everybody ate.' On stand the band uniform was sweaters (differently coloured for each of the three sections) and white trousers, while its repertoire consisted in the main of stocks and items copied off records.

The band recorded for the Vocalion label in 1937

Bob Pope and his band worked around the Carolinas during the mid 1930s. Fifth from left in this photograph is drummer Johnny Blowers, who shortly afterwards played with the Bunny Berigan band.

on two successive March days; out of a total of fourteen titles made only six were issued. Down Beat of September 1939 mentioned that alto saxophonist Francis Gray, then with Jimmy Raschel, had formerly played with the Carolina Cotton Pickers; and its issue of 15th February 1940 described it as 'the best band in the South, fronted by Wesley Jones around Birmingham, Jackson, Tennessee.' About this time the personnel had not altered a great deal, though Aaron Harvey (sax) had been added to the original group, Anderson had left, and Julius Watson, Albert Martin and Walter Bash had been replaced by Eugene Earle (who had merely switched instruments), Lew Williams and Addison White, with L. E. Thurman coming in on string bass. Whether the band now had any connection with the Jenkins Orphan Home School is uncertain, but it seems unlikely.

Porter Kilbert worked with the band from 1941 to March 1943, giving the personnel at that time as Thaddeus Seabrook, Leonard Graham, John Williams (trumpet), Leroy Hardison, Eugene Earls (trombone) himself, John Vaughan (alto saxophone), Harold Clark, John 'Flap' Dungee (tenor saxophone), Vincent Stewart (baritone saxophone), Clifton Smalls (piano, trombone), W. J. Edwards (guitar), William 'Basie' Fay (string bass)

Rock 'Otis' Walker (drums) and Wesley Jones (vocal, director). Jones was later replaced by Pha Terrell who had made his name with the Andy Kirk band. Kilbert remembers the band stayed in Kansas City for six months and also travelled as far afield as California. He said that the only change of personnel that occurred during his time with the band was the replacement of Dungee by Walter Leonard.

Little further was heard of the band, though Down Beat of 15th February 1944 mentions that a sax player called Bill Canada had been a former member, and Music Dial in the following month refers to its having a new vocalist in Count Collins and lists Hardison as the director. Shortly afterwards it is believed that it finally broke up.

The records made by the band present it in a better light than Anderson's remarks would lead one to expect, though it may be that it became more professional the longer it remained together. On *Off and On Blues* Otis Walker takes a reasonable vocal with good backing from pianist Smalls, and the standard of the section work on the riff theme is creditable. There is an effective trumpet solo over cohesive saxes at the beginning, and if the performance as a whole is not markedly individual it is at least highly proficient. *'Deed I Do* has a somewhat ordinary vocal by Walker, but Smalls has a good Hines-like solo and there are sixteen bars by a trumpeter with an excellent full tone and relaxed phrasing. Thaddeus Seabrook was reputedly a fine musician, with a range said to equal that of Anderson's, and he may well have been the trumpeter on *'Deed I Do*. The fact that over fifty per cent of the numbers recorded were rejected suggests that there were technical problems marring the sessions, but I have heard rougher performances from better known bands and on the evidence of an admittedly small number of titles the Carolina Cotton Pickers were anything but indifferent.

J. Neal Montgomery led bands in Atlanta, Georgia from 1921, trumpet/arranger Edgar Battle playing with him in that year, as did the then fifteen-year-old trombonist J. C. Higginbotham. He appears to have established himself as the outstanding leader in the area, and in 1927-28 fronted his Collegiate Ramblers both in his hometown and on tour. His personnel at this time consisted of Harold Whittington (trumpet), Pete Clark, Wayman Carver (reeds), Harold Finley, Harper Douglas, Eddie Grant, George Robinson, Joseph Watts, Clarence Beck and Nelson Jackson (unknown instruments), with presumably Montgomery playing piano.

The Chicago Defender of 13th April 1929 reported that J. Neal Montgomery Orchestra had recorded two sides for Okeh, adding that they were composed by the band's trombonist Henry Mason. In fact, Mason was a trumpeter who in later years worked in Europe with the Willie Lewis band. The group that recorded retained nobody from the Collegiate Ramblers, consisting of Henry Mason,

Karl Burns (trumpet), unknown (trombone), George Derrigotte, . . . Puckett (alto saxophone, clarinet), . . . Brown (tenor saxophone, clarinet), J. Neal Montgomery (piano), unknown (banjo), Jesse Wilcox (brass bass) and Ted Gillum (drums). The titles made were *Atlanta Lowdown* and *Auburn Avenue Stomp*. *Atlanta* has a good trumpet theme by Mason who later takes an excellent solo, average solos by trombone and alto, pleasant guitar, and a brass passage that is rather Ellington-ish. *Auburn* displays the tight ensemble sound of the band, with the leader contributing a reasonable solo and Mason again outstanding. Apparently the record did not sell too well, at which Montgomery later expressed his disappointment.

Mason and Montgomery also appeared on a few Atlanta recorded items backing blues singers, but apparently Montgomery was not too interested in blues and regarded these records as of slight importance. He was interviewed in later years, but the results have not been published, so his full career remains relatively obscure. For many years he has been seriously incapacitated by a stroke and as a result could not pursue a career in music. His greatest admiration is reserved for Fletcher Henderson and it is to be presumed that his bands attempted to emulate Henderson's methods during the late 'twenties and early 'thirties.

The Ross De Luxe Syncopators, based on Miami, Florida, is occasionally mentioned in jazz history books because it was the band with which Charles 'Cootie' Williams and Edmond Hall first came to New York. It received several mentions in the Chicago Defender in 1926 and the issue of 17th July listed its personnel as Melvin Herbert (trumpet), Eddie Cooper (trombone), Earl Evans (alto, soprano and baritone saxophone), Robert Cloud (tenor and alto saxophone), Julius Jones (alto saxophone), Alonzo Ross (piano), Robert Robbins (violin, tenor banjo), Richard Fullbright (tuba) and Frank Houston (drums). Herbert, Cloud and Fullbright all became prominent musicians in the East later in the 'twenties. On 11th September the same newspaper reported that the band was leaving Miami that day for a tour that would bring it to Chicago. Jones was omitted from the personnel and Fullbright's instrument was given as a sousaphone. Two news items in October editions of the paper stated that the band was now resident in Miami, with a line-up that had Edmond Hall (sax) added, with Cootie Williams and Casker Towie (banjo, sax) replacing Herbert and Robbins.

On 24th September 1927 both the Pittsburgh Courier and Dave Peyton in the Chicago Defender reported that the band had recorded in Savannah, Georgia, for Victor. The Defender incorrectly claimed that it had made fourteen titles. The personnels given differed, however. The Courier correctly listed it as previously noted but with Herbert returning and Robert 'Cookie' Mason (trumpet) temporarily replacing Williams. Throughout the winter of 1927 the band, with Williams back, was

When the Ross De Luxe Syncopators went to New York from their home base in Florida in spring 1928 the band included trumpeter Charles 'Cootie' Williams and clarinetist Edmond Hall (shown here with drummer Tommy Benford and trumpeter Buck Clayton). Both remained in New York and carved out distinguished careers in the big band field.

The records that the band made are not outstanding and seem unexpectedly commercial. The best titles are *Skad-O-Lee* and *Florida Rhythm,* though even on these the band sounds somewhat stiff, with one good moment provided by a trumpeter on *Skad-O-Lee,* whom I presume to be Herbert. This man takes a pleasant, wistful solo and employs the lagging phrasing that one associates with Lee Collins in his peak years. Apart from this solo and a competent one by the trombonist, little happens to differentiate the Ross De Luxe Syncopators from dozens of its contemporaries.

Probably the outstanding band in the Florida area during the 'twenties and early 'thirties was that led by Billy Stewart. It was in existence by 1925. A Chicago Defender column of 2nd January 1926 gives a personnel of Billy Stewart (cornet), B. Christian (trombone, banjo), Terry Crawford (sax, clarinet, violin), H. A. Hall (sax, clarinet), Charles Segar (piano), L. Brown (banjo, entertainer), James H. August (tuba) and W. A. Stevens (drums). B. Christian and H. A. Hall are not the well-known Buddy Christian and Herb Hall, but it is possible that Segar is the same man that recorded blues solos in Chicago eight years later.

resident at the Del Robia Gardens in Miami. In the following spring it set out for a tour that brought it to New York. After a fortnight at the Rosemont Ballroom the band broke up and Williams and Hall both joined Arthur 'Happy' Ford's band at another New York venue.

During 1928 the Chicago Defender twice mentioned Stewart's orchestra, once in June and once in July. Initially it gave a personnel of Shelton Reamey (trumpet), Charles Lockett, Henry Brown (trombone), Harry Reamey (sax), Henry Callin (piano), Verlon Bass (tuba), and Slick Jones (drums), but a month later it added Stewart on trumpet and Frank Sloan (sax, clarinet, assistant leader), gave Callin (or Callens) as playing baritone horn, and listed Slick Jones as a snare drummer and one Sweet Boy Short as bass drummer. This rather strange line-up is closer to that of a New Orleans marching band than a dance unit. There must have been a shake-up during 1928, for Frank Galbreath has mentioned playing with Stewart in that year in a group consisting of himself, Willard Thompson, Boyd 'Horsecollar' Rosser (trumpet), Bobby Hicks, Nat Allen, Frank Oxendine (trombone), Bill Johnson (alto saxophone), Freddie Williams (tenor saxophone), Billy Steward (sax), Lonnie Slappy (piano), A. Verlon (tuba), Clifton Best (guitar), Eddie Jones (drums). A. Verlon is obviously the 'Verlon Bass' of the Defender listing, and quite a number of this band went on to make reputations in name groups.

In September 1929 the Chicago Defender reported that that inveterate wanderer Theodore 'Wingy' Carpenter was with Stewart (in some reports he is called Steward) in Florida. The same newspaper on 11th January 1930 noted that Billy Stewart and his Celery City Serenaders were on tour in Florida—the personnel now Josiah Brown, Billy Stewart (trumpet), Willie 'Buddie' Howard (trombone), Charles Martin (sax, arranger), Eugene Slappy (sax), Saul Albright (piano), Jasper Harris (banjo), Verlon Bass (tuba) and Eddie Jones (drums). Two months later it again mentioned the tour, adding that the band was playing in Sanford, Florida. Freddie Williams (sax) was included in the personnel, Asa Harris (piano) had taken the place of Albright, and the tuba player was listed as Vernon Bass. In its 10th May 1930 edition it carried a news item to the effect that John Henry Brown, who apparently also doubled on bass saxophone, had replaced Josiah Brown, who had had to leave because of illness in the family. Billboard of 28th June gave the same line-up, though the tuba was played once more by A. Verlon. The band was touring Nebraska, Iowa, Wyoming, Minnesota, Colorado and Kansas.

In 1931 Theodore 'Wingy' Carpenter was back, replacing John Henry Brown, and a newspaper mentions that the band was engaged on a southern tour with a specific date in Cordele, Georgia. Saul Albright had taken over once more from Harris, and a Joe Preston (unspecified instrument) was named, perhaps as a temporary replacement for trombonist Howard. The Chicago Defender in June 1931 gave Stewart's current line-up, which included all the men on the southern tour, except Preston who had been replaced by Howard, and with the addition of R. C. Hicks, Robert Hall (trumpet) and Ernest 'Son' Leary (sax). No drummer is mentioned, but this must have been an oversight. Five months later the Defender reported that Carpenter was now in his sixth month with Stewart, but it is thought that a year or two later the band broke up and little is known of Stewart's subsequent activities. A number of musicians have said that Stewart's was a good band, particularly in 1928 and 1931, but it existed when recording opportunities in its working area were rare, and as a result it never had the chance to gain more than a local reputation.

Tennessee is not a state that has produced any outstanding jazz units, though a number of well-known musicians were born there. In late 1936 Bob Pope, a coloured guitarist/vocalist (not to be confused with the white trumpeter of the same name who after working with the Coon-Sanders Orchestra led his own band in a number of southern states), got Gene Crooke to organise a band for him in Memphis. Crooke, previously a banjoist with the Alphonso Trent Orchestra, put together a ten-piece unit that toured the southern states until some time in 1939. The band never recorded, but its personnel for 1937-39 is known—Johnny Hampton, Frank Robertson (trumpet), Heinie 'Miff' Walker (trombone), B. G. Hamlin, Alphonse Robinson (alto saxophone), Lee Pope (tenor saxophone), Gene Crooke (piano), Bob Pope (guitar, vocal), Emmett Sheperd (string bass) and Otis Bailey (drums).

In February 1940 Down Beat referred to Tuff Green, 'the south's biggest little band', as then playing its forty-seventh week at the Club Plantation, Nashville, Tennessee, with an instrumentation that included vibraphone and Hawaiian guitar. Richard 'Tuff' Green was a bassist who lived in Memphis. Seven months before, Down Beat had said that the band was heard by John Hammond at Kyle's in Nashville when it included pianist Harold Dugan. By December 1940 Green's band was still at the Club Plantation, but after that, during the war years, Green's activities went unreported.

By summer 1947 Green's band was again touring. A news item noted the addition of 'Jamaika Jive' (trombone) and Fats Watkins (piano) to his group. At about the same time Green took his band to California, where he is reported to have fronted a twelve- or thirteen-piece unit, including Sammie Jett (trombone), Irving Reason, Andy Goodwich (alto saxophone), 'Doughbelly' (tenor saxophone), Onze Horne (vibraphone, arranger), himself (string bass), Phineas Newborn Sr (drums), Marcellus Durham, Billy Taylor (vocal). The trombonist, incidentally, was a girl. In October 1948 Green was in Los Angeles with a band including Nathan Woodard (trumpet), Lem Campbell, Ben Branch (tenor saxophone) and himself, but in February or March of the following year the band were involved in a bus crash near Memphis and Campbell, Rufus Watson (piano) and Durham were killed. Clinton Waters (trumpet, arranger), Branch, Green and Newborn were injured. After this Green took up

studio work though he still led bands in the area from time to time. One of these provided the first professional job for guitarist Matthew Murphy in about 1950. In later years he became very active in the blues recording field and has not been active in jazz for close on two decades.

Oscar 'Papa' Celestin, born at Napoleonville on 1st January 1884, became a famous figure in New Orleans jazz late in his career, and performed regularly on TV and radio, obtaining most of the best work in the city, and making a command appearance before President Eisenhower. He died in New Orleans on 15th December 1954, and his funeral, which was filmed, was one of the most spectacular the city had ever known, four thousand people marching with the procession.

During the depression years, Celestin retired from music for a while, but by 1938 was again leading a band, a large one of fourteen pieces. This unit disbanded when he broke a leg in a car accident in 1941, after which he worked in the shipyard for the early war period. Soon after the war he re-formed a band and was active until shortly before his death, but the small Dixieland bands he led during this period are outside the scope of the present book.

Left: *Oscar 'Papa' Celestin.* Below: *Celestin lying in state. The funeral parade, with the traditional brass bands, was one of the largest in New Orleans for many years.*

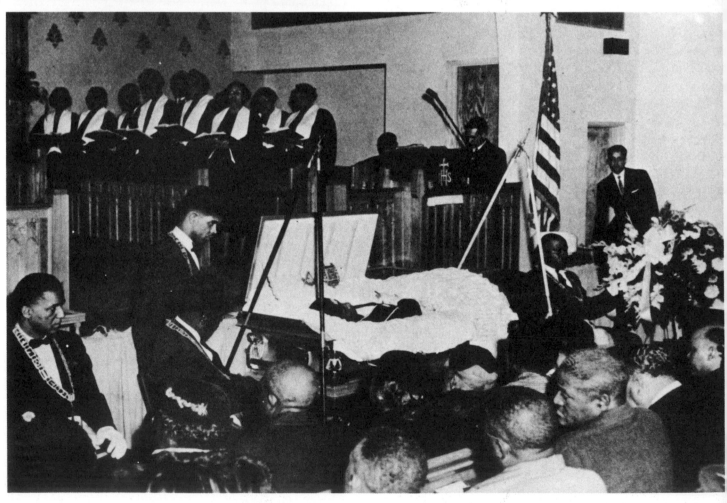

Celestin's first band was formed in 1910, and a few years later he organised a Tuxedo Brass Band in addition to his dance unit. From about 1917 Celestin and trombonist William Ridgely formed the Original Tuxedo Orchestra and remained in partnership until 1925, when Celestin went his own way, with 'Celestin's Tuxedo Jazz Band'. This was, by the standard of the 'twenties, a big band, and Amos White has provided its personnel during the early years of its existence. It generally lined up as Oscar Celestin, Hyppolite Charles, Amos White (trumpet), Buddy Johnson, Vic Gaspard (trombone), Lorenzo Tio (clarinet), ... Matthews (horn), Pete Bocage (baritone horn), Ed Jackson (brass bass), Ernest Trepagnier, Henry Martin (drums). This instrumentation suggests a brass band rather than a dance group, but from about 1926 Celestin led a dance unit that became very popular in the southern states. It continued into the early 'thirties. In his story of the Carolina Cotton Pickers Cat Anderson says that they found themselves at a disadvantage when playing an area in which a well-known band like Celestin's was working.

The Chicago Defender of 4th February 1928 carried a report on 'Celestine and his Hot Tuxedoes' appearing at the Gomez Auditorium in Mobile, Alabama, with such success that they were booked for a return engagement a month later. The personnel was listed as Mr Celestin, King Guy Kelly (trumpet), Wm Matthews (trombone), C. Hall, I. Rouzan (sax), Miss Salvoed (piano), Henry Kimble (banjo), S. Marrero (tuba), A. B. 'Chinese' Foster (drums) and Joseph Lawrence (vocal). C. Hall is Clarence Hall, I. Rouzan is Joe Rouzan, Miss Salvoed is Jeanette Salvant, S. Marrero is Simon Marrero, and 'Chinese' Foster is Abbey 'Chinee' Foster. A photograph of this band is printed in the book 'New Orleans Jazz—A Family Album, except that vocalist John Thomas has replaced Lawrence. Soon afterwards Kimble (or Kimball) left, first to be replaced by John Marrero and later by George Guesnon. Until the depression forced Celestin to break up his band the personnel remained reasonably stable.

By the late 'thirties Celestin was back in business. Down Beat in its October 1938 issue reported that he was leading a fourteen-piece band that played mostly one night stands. Just over a year later the same magazine noted that Herman Franklin, a trumpeter formerly with Alphonso Trent, was with Celestin in New Orleans, and in 1940-41 trumpeter Wallace Davenport worked with him. About the last band that Celestin led that falls within this book's scope is one of 1941, featuring himself, Jimmy 'Kid' Clayton (sometimes Albert Walters) (trumpet), Bill Matthews (trombone), John Handy (alto saxophone), Eddie Johnson (sax), Octave Crosby (piano), Ricard Alexis (string bass) and Albert Jiles (drums).

Celestin was not an outstanding trumpeter and in later years only played sporadically during an engagement. Most of his career was spent playing for white audiences and he sometimes angered his own people by his mannerisms. Nevertheless, during the years from about early 1926 to 1932 his band had a considerable reputation in the south, and was accepted as one of the best big bands in the area.

The finest records on which Celestin is present are undoubtedly those made by the Original Tuxedo Jazz Orchestra in January 1925, but these are so much in the classic mould of King Oliver's Creole Jazz Band that they hardly fall within the category of big band jazz. Celestin recorded twelve titles with his own regular band between April 1926 and December 1928, and though they are overall somewhat disappointing they include good passages. On the first four titles Foster's individual style of drumming is very interesting, while Celestin's simple but effective cornet work on *Give Me Some More* is worth hearing. On *I'm Satisfied You Love Me* Paul Barnes's alto solos is good for the period. The titles from a second session of April 1927 feature superior ensemble playing, with *Papa's Got the Jim-jams* showing a greater all-round rhythmic freedom and *As You Like It* including a well-performed duet by Celestin and Barnes and a neatly played cornet duet by the leader and Alexis. *It's Jam Up* is a relaxed performance with a strong solo from Alexis. From the final date, the otherwise routine *Ta Ta Daddy* offers an excellent cornet solo against stop time from Guy Kelly. Much of Celestin's material sounds too sentimental, but on hearing the records it is easy to understand his popularity with a wide public.

Andrew Morgan, with his sons Albert, Isaiah and Sam, formed one of the most famous of all New Orleans musical families. The latter, born at Bertrandville, Louisiana, in 1895, shared with Papa Celestin the distinction of leading the only black New Orleans big band to be recorded during the latter years of the 'twenties.

From his earliest days as a professional musician, Sam Morgan acquired a reputation as one of the finest cornet players in New Orleans, even at a time when such legendary figures as Chris Kelly, Buddy Petit, Joe Oliver and Kid Rena were in their prime. He led a small group that played regularly round the New Orleans area from 1916 to 1925, though in common with most local musicians at the time Morgan also worked in a day job. In 1925 Morgan suffered a stroke, but his band continued for a few months in his absence before finally breaking up. By late 1926 Morgan had recovered sufficiently to join his brother Isaiah's band, and within a few months took over the leadership. It soon became very popular and the 31st December 1927 issue of the Chicago Defender carried a report of an appearance at the Gomez Auditorium at Mobile, with a personnel of Sam Morgan, Isaiah Morgan (cornet), Jim Robinson (trombone), Andrew Morgan (clarinet, sax), Earl Fushay (alto saxophone), O. C. Blancher (piano), Johnnie Dave (banjo), Sidney Brown (brass bass) and Roy Edwards (drums). (The correct spelling of Fushay is Fouche.) This band, with Tink Baptiste and William Nolan in place of

Blancher and Edwards, recorded for Columbia for the first time in April 1927. Six months later it made a further four titles, with Walter Decou and Roy Evans (presumably the same man listed in the Defender report as Edwards) substituting for Baptiste and Nolan.

In 1929 the Morgan band went to Chicago, playing on the train there and back and spending a week in the city. Their presence was noted in the Chicago Defender of 22nd June, which reported that 'Morgan's famous orchestra of New Orleans gave the gang in Chicago a chance to hear their music last Tuesday night at Warwick Hall. The boys really brought us some red hot stuff from the Southland. Kid Ory, trombone in Boyd Atkins's Sunset Orchestra, was the sponsor for the affair.'

The depression years of the early 'thirties made work difficult to find in New Orleans and the band travelled more and more. George Guesnon replaced Dave on tours. In 1932 Morgan suffered a second stroke and though he tried to continue in the musical field he was forced to give up. The band folded in 1933. It appears that subsequently Morgan gave his name to bands; one that worked in New Orleans in early 1935 had a personnel of Charles Wynn, Roy Williams (trumpet), Andy Clifford (trombone), Jimmy Turner, Tony Guillelmie, Arthur Rigby (sax), Reggie McLean (replaced by Benton Overstreet in August) (piano), Henry Johnson, 'Preacher' Crawford, Willy 'Hungfish' Wright (unknown instruments, but almost certainly guitar, string bass and drums), Sam Morgan (vocalist). In February 1936 Morgan contracted pneumonia while watching the night parades the day before the regular New Orleans carnival. He died in hospital the following day, the 25th.

In Down Beat of 22nd April 1949 drummer Louis Ezell claimed that he stayed with the Morgan band from 1928 to 1934. He wrote that its personnel was Sam Morgan, Guy Kelly (trumpet), Alec Shaw, Gus Simmons (trombone), Al McCoy (sax), Andrew Morgan (tenor saxophone, clarinet), Henry McCoy (guitar), Charles Griffin (string bass) and himself (drums). He also said that he remembered making records with Morgan in 1928, though these have never been found. In as far as the band broke up in 1933, Ezell's memory is faulty, but it could be that Morgan fronted more than one band during his peak years, depending on the musicians he could secure.

The 1927 Morgan recordings are unique in big band jazz, for they used traditional New Orleans methods within a larger instrumental framework than usual. The style is essentially an ensemble one, the horn men combining to produce counterpoint in the classic manner. *Bogalusa Strut* is a superb performance, with Fouche, the band's chief soloist, providing a fine solo against stop-time. The great swing of the band is helped by the excellent rhythm section, in which Brown's string bass work is outstanding. This is clearly evident in *Sing On* and the driving *Steppin' on the Gas*. The links between this music and much later New Orleans jazz is obvious, and apart from its intrinsic merit, which is considerable, it is particularly interesting as an example of big band jazz in which regional characteristics have been totally assimilated.

Sam Morgan's Jazz Band, 1927; back: Jim Robinson, Isaiah Morgan. Front: Nolan Williams, Earl Fouche, Andrew Morgan, Johnny Dave, Sidney Brown.

A poster for the opening of the Alhambra Ballroom, New York on September 13th 1929. Among the bands playing were Roy Johnson's Happy Pals from Virginia.

Johnson's Happy Pals, from Richmond, Virginia, recorded two titles in their hometown during August 1929. They were already well known and had appeared further afield. They were one of five bands to take part in the opening of the Alhambra Ballroom, New York City, on 13th September. The Baltimore Afro-American of 12th October reported that a few days previously the band had appeared at the New Albert Casino in that city. The musicians were listed as Percy Trent, Edwin Humes (trumpet), Flemming Edwards (trombone), Harold Griffon, Nathaniel McPherson (sax), Emmett Johnson (alto saxophone, clarinet), Leroy Wyche (piano), Edward Trent (banjo), William Allen (string bass) and Roy Johnson (leader). Johnson was also the drummer in the band. This personnel differs in several respects from that normally given for the recording session, but it is probable that some musicians were brought in for the occasion.

Orchestra World of February 1931 mentioned that the band were currently playing at the Savoy Ballroom in New York, the only changes of personnel that had taken place since 1929 being the replacement of Percy Trent and Flemming Edwards by William 'Slim' Harris and 'Noisy' Richardson. According to the 11th April 1931 edition of the Pittsburgh Courier Johnson's Happy Pals had just returned to Virginia. Their line-up was the same as that in the Orchestra World, with the addition of trumpeter Chester Millingan and trombonist Flemming Edwards. In December of that year the band was back at the Savoy Ballroom.

Johnson's later career is obscure, but Down Beat on three occasions mentioned that he was working at the Roseland, Richmond, Virginia, in the early months of 1940, so he was certainly still active at that date.

Savoy Rhythm and *Happy Pal Stomp* convey an impression of a well-organised unit, with good section and ensemble work. The former title has a fine trumpet solo—as Percy Trent is named as co-composer it could well be by him—and a reasonable baritone saxophone passage, while *Happy* has good solos by trumpet and alto saxophone. In general the band sounds well rehearsed and its technical expertise suggests that it had been in existence for a year or two prior to the recording. It is unfortunate that the onset of the depression prevented further recording opportunities.

The Southwestern States

The southwestern states produced a number of outstanding bands, but in its day Alphonso Trent's was the greatest of them all. Trent was born at Forth Worth, Arkansas, on 24th August 1905, and entered music before he was eighteen, having received piano lessons as a child. After playing with various obscure local groups, he fronted a band for the first time in the summer of 1923 in Muskogee, Oklahoma. A year later he was working in Eugene Crooke's Synco Six, with Edwin Swayzee (trumpet), Lawrence 'Snub' Mosley (trombone), Joe Hayman (alto saxophone), Eugene Crooke (guitar) and Toby . . . (drums).

By 1925 Trent was working in Dallas. He was offered a job at the leading hotel there and moved in with an eight-piece group that was soon enlarged to ten. A photograph taken at the Adolphus Hotel in 1925 shows a personnel of Terrence Holder, Chester Clark (trumpet), Lawrence 'Snub' Mosley (trombone), James Jeter (alto saxophone), William Holloway (C melody saxophone), Wendell Hayman (tenor saxophone, violin), Alphonso Trent (piano, accordion), Eugene Crooke (banjo), Brent Sparks (tuba), A. G. Godley (drums) and John Fielding (vocal). The Trent band became immensely popular at the Adolphus Hotel; eventually it became the first black band to have a regular radio outlet, over station WFAA, Dallas. Late in 1926 they went on tour throughout Texas, and the following year went even further afield. Billboard for 29th January 1927 mentions their residency at the Adolphus Hotel and gives a line-up that shows only one change from that of 1925: Eunice Brigham had replaced Holder.

It was during 1927 that the late Jimmie Lunceford heard the band in Memphis, many years after paying tribute to its musicianship. Towards the end of that year Stuff Smith joined Trent in Louisville, Kentucky, though he left for a short while to work with Jelly Roll Morton in New York with Edwin Swayzee. But he returned to act as front man, vocalist and one of a vocal trio that must have been amongst the first in jazz. The solo strength of the band was augmented in 1928, and when it made its first records for the Gennett company the personnel was Chester Clark, Irving Randolph (trumpet), Lawrence

ALPHONSO TRENT'S ORCHESTRA

'Snub' Mosley (trombone), James Jeter, Charles Pillars (alto saxophone), Lee Hilliard (alto saxophone, trumpet), Hayes Pillars (tenor and baritone saxophone), Leroy 'Stuff' Smith (violin, vocal), plus the same rhythm section and chief vocalist as before—except for bassist Robert 'Eppie' Jackson who had replaced Sparks. Frank Driggs reports an occasion in St Louis in 1928 when the Trent band, playing opposite Louis Armstrong fronting Floyd Campbell's band, drew a crowd of five thousand on the steamer St Paul.

The Pittsburgh Courier of 6th September 1930 published potted information on Trent's activities over the previous years, mentioning that the band had appeared at the Greystone Ballroom, Cincinnati and the Arcadia Ballroom, Buffalo. It gave a personnel that showed few changes from 1928. (George Hudson and Alvin Burroughs had replaced Randolph and Godley, and Charles Pillars and Fielding had left.) Godley's absence was only temporary, and the former tuba player Brent Sparks was now listed as manager. Interestingly enough, it was the first time the slide saxophone had been mentioned in connection with Mosley. Between 1928 and 1930 trumpeter Herbert 'Peanuts' Holland worked on and off with Trent—as did Sy Oliver for a few months in 1931. Oliver was to be replaced by Anderson Lacey (violin, front man). Around 1930 and 1931 there were clearly other personnel changes, with Eddie Sherman (sax), Leslie Sheffield (piano) and Louis Pitts (bass) making occasional appearances.

Orchestral World for December 1931 mentions that the Trent band was then resident at the Ritz Ballroom, Oklahoma City, adding that it had recorded for Brunswick. No trace of any such recordings have ever been

Above: Alphonso Trent's band, 1932; left to right: Chester Clark, Hayes Pillars, John Fielding, A. G. Godley, George Hudson, Dan Minor, Anderson Lacy, Herbert 'Peanuts' Holland, Gene Crook, Alphonso Trent, James Jeter, Leo 'Snub' Mosely, unknown, Brent Sparks, Robert 'Eppi' Jackson. Right: Leo 'Snub' Mosely with a slide saxophone, an instrument of his own invention. Above right: Stuff Smith, the front man for the Alphonso Trent band for some while, during which he experimented with amplifying his violin to be heard above the ensemble.

found. A picture of the band taken during 1932 shows Chester Clark, Herbert 'Peanuts' Holland, George Hudson (trumpet), Snub Mosley, Dan Minor (trombone), James Jeters (alto saxophone), Hayes Pillars (tenor saxophone), Alphonso Trent (piano), Eugene Crooke (banjo), Louis Pitts (string bass), Robert 'Eppie' Jackson (tuba), A. G. Godley (drums), Anderson Lacey (violin, vocalist), John Fielding (vocal, manager), and Brent Sparks (booker). The balance of brass and saxes suggests that one or more sax men had not made the photograph session. The Pittsburgh Courier of 21st January 1933 and the Chicago Defender of 4th February 1933 both list the same personnel for the Trent band's engagement at the Casino Ballroom in Memphis, with changes where Lee Hilliard and Terry Elston had replaced Clark and Hudson in the trumpet section, trombonist Paul Butler had come in for Minor, Charles Pillars (sax) had been added along with Sheffield on piano doubling tuba (Jackson having left), and Claude Williams (banjo, violin) had replaced Crooke, now listed as an arranger only. At some time during 1933 both trumpeter Harry Edison and trombonist/arranger Gus Wilson worked with Trent, though Wilson's exact

In addition to the musicians so far mentioned, trumpeters Edwin Swayzee and Herman Franklin and saxist Charlie Fuqua played with Trent at various times—Swayzee probably when he first formed his band, and the others at unknown periods. Fuqua later became famous as one of the original members of the Ink Spots vocal group.

Considering the esteem in which the Trent band was held, it is remarkable that it never really made the big time to achieve national fame. Frank Driggs reports that Fletcher Henderson was so impressed with the band that he urged Trent to play in New York, and that the band as a result did play one week at the Savoy Ballroom. There it attracted the attention of an important booker who offered Trent a choice location job which the latter turned down for fear of losing his key men. In fact, as a glance at the personnels will confirm, Trent's musicians seemed to be extremely loyal to him, and changes of line-up were remarkably low for a territory band. It appears that Trent came from a reasonably well-to-do family and lacked the economic incentive that drove most bandleaders to seek national fame. Some of his musicians have recalled periods when they did not see him for weeks on end. By territory band standards they were paid unusually well. They travelled in an impressive array of touring cars, displaying a variety of uniforms in the course of a single night's engagement. When I first mentioned the Trent band to Budd Johnson, now a co-leader of the JPJ Quartet, his immediate reaction was to recall the envy with which other less fortunate musicians who worked the same territories viewed their Trent colleagues, not least the shining gold instruments which they always used!

It is unfortunate that the Trent band only recorded nine titles in all, one of which was never issued. Without doubt the best of these are *After You've Gone*, from a March 1930 session, and *Clementine* and *I've Found a New Baby*, recorded in March 1933. *After* displays the outstanding ensemble work and swing of the band, the best solos coming from Peanuts Holland and Snub Mosley, while *Clementine* is an outstanding performance in every way. The advanced score is by Gus Wilson, brother of Teddy, and the sound of the ensemble is Lunceford-ish. Holland has a fine fluent solo, as does Snub Mosley, and there are impressive passages from the sax section and the full ensemble at the close. *I've Found a New Baby* is almost as good, with superb playing from the brass and sax sections on the opening chorus, after which Hayes Pillars, Holland and Snub Mosley take excellent solos. The latter is an astonishing technician and plays with a facility that was years ahead of its time. It appears that the repertoire of the band was extremely varied. It ranged from special jazz numbers, through commercial ballads, to 'symphonic' orchestrations, its versatility and showmanship adding another dimension to its brilliant musicianship. If it had never made any other title but *Clementine* this alone would

tenure with the band is uncertain and may have been during 1930 or 1931.

About May 1934 Trent broke up his band, but by 1938 was back in the music business leading a septet that included Henry 'Hank' Bridges (tenor saxophone) and Charlie Christian (guitar)—it was as a result of playing with him that Christian first began to attract attention. With this group Trent worked over a wide area; locations in 1938 that have been documented include The Dome, Bismarck, North Dakota and the Gladstone Hotel, Casper, Wyoming. In the last years of his life Trent led a quintet in his hometown, though his main occupation was managing real estate. A 1958 photograph shows the quintet resident at The Branding Iron in Fort Smith, but Trent died a year later, on 14th October 1959, aged fifty-four.

Herbert 'Peanuts' Holland, soloist with Alphonso Trent's band: he has lived and worked in Europe since 1946.

qualify the Trent band's inclusion amongst a list of the greatest big bands. It is ironical that the leader of what was undeniably one of the two or three finest of all territory bands should show such a lack of interest in seeking national fame. If he had been a more assertive personality the jazz history books might read very differently when documenting the big band era.

Trumpeter Terrence Holder worked with Trent during the early years of the 'twenties, but left in 1925 to form his 'Dark Clouds Of Joy'. The personnel for the band was reasonably stable in its first year or two, with T. Holder (who was often billed in this fashion), Harry 'Big Jim' Lawson (trumpet), Allen Durham (trombone), Alvin 'Fats' Wall, John Harrington (alto saxophone, clarinet), Lawrence Freeman (tenor saxophone), Marion Jackson (piano), William Dirvin (banjo), Andy Kirk (tuba) and Edward McNeil (drums). Billboard of 29th January 1927 reported the band's presence at the Louvre Ballroom, Tulsa, Oklahoma, though its home base was Dallas. At some time during 1927 or 1928 the late Don Byas, then a teenager, worked with Holder.

By the summer of 1928, when the Chicago Defender of 16th June noted that Holder was resident at Spring Lake Park, Oklahoma City, a few changes had taken place in the line-up. Flip Benson and 'Daddy' Ross had

replaced Durham and Harrington, and Claude Williams (violin, guitar) and Billy Massey (vocal, entertainer) had been added. Late in that year John Williams (sax, clarinet) (and possibly Mary Lou Williams) had joined the band, but in January 1929 Andy Kirk took over the group after the musicians had been in dispute with Holder over financial matters.

Holder, with the assistance of Jesse Stone, built up a new band in a remarkably short time. The Chicago Defender of 9th March 1929 gave its personnel as T. Holder, Hiram Harding (trumpet), Frederic 'Keg' Johnson (trombone), Booker Pittman (alto saxophone), Albert 'Budd' Johnson (tenor saxophone), Jesse Stone (piano), Trevezant Sims (tuba) and John R. Davis (drums). Later in the year musicians of the calibre of Eddie Tompkins (trumpet), LaForest Dent (alto saxophone), Herman Walder (sax) and Herschel Evans (tenor saxophone) all played in the group.

In 1930 trombonist George Corley began an engagement with Holder that was to last almost two years. Apparently the personnel mentioned had been displaced by Jesse Stone at some point. Holder's line-up now read: himself, Jeff Carrington, Bill Dillard (trumpet), George

Corley (trombone), Wallace Mercer, Buddy Tate, Earl Bostic (reeds), Lloyd Glenn (piano), Leslie Nelson (guitar, banjo), Leslie Sheffield (tuba) and Little Joe Lewis (drums). Soon after Corley joined, his brother Reggie replaced Dillard, to be replaced in turn by Carl 'Tatti' Smith (1931) and Hugh Jones (1932), while for some months Corley played tuba after Sheffield left late in 1931 until replacement Amos Strickland arrived. For one date at least, at Des Moines in 1931, pianist Jim Youngblood was with the band.

The Chicago Defender listed the Holder personnel on three occasions during 1932, the first in its issue of 30th January when the band was playing at the Lamond Ballroom, Longview, Texas. The band for this date was Jeff Carrington, Hugh Jones (trumpet), George Corley (trombone), Thomas Lee, Buddy Tate, John Jordan (sax), Lloyd Glenn (piano, arranger), Claude Williams (banjo), Wesley Smith (violin), T. Holder (director), though one assumes that the absence of a bassist and drummer is an oversight. Williams was also a fine jazz violinist and he and Smith both played this instrument in the band. A fortnight later the band was in Little Rock, Arkansas, with Joe Brantley (bass) and Joe Lewis (drums) listed—and Bernice 'Red' Williams (trumpet), James Miller (trombone), Wallace Mercer (sax) and James Hopkins (piano) replacing Jones, Corley, Jordan and Glenn. Holder himself is now given as playing trumpet in addition to leading. The final Defender personnel, contained in its 3rd September edition, has T. Holder, Jeff Carrington (trumpet), James Miller (trombone), Earl Bostic, Jessie Washington, Buddy Tate, Thomas Lee (reeds), James Hopkins (piano), R. Knollins, Jim West Brooks, William White (rhythm instruments), and refers to a date the band was working in Longview.

Holder's bands were considered in their day to be rivalled only by the Trent group, and he himself was much esteemed as a soloist, though apparently in a sweet rather than a hot style. It is believed that his last big band of any importance broke up in late 1932 or early 1933, though he continued to front smaller groups intermittently after this date. As late as 1952 he was working with a small band fronted by Nat Towles, but his activities during the past two decades are unknown; it is not clear whether or not he is still alive.

San Antonio, Texas, was the home base for three well-known bands during the 'twenties and 'thirties, the first being Troy Floyd's. Floyd organised a sextet in 1924 that by 1926 had increased to a nine-piece unit, first playing at the Ozarks night club and then spending a great deal of time at the Shadowland club. One of his earliest soloists was Claude 'Benno' Kennedy, a trumpeter with a considerable technique and freak style, who left to form his own band in 1927 and ultimately settled in California where he played with, amongst others, Charlie Echols's orchestra. From 1927 to 1929 Floyd's personnel was reasonably stable, generally comprising

A rare photograph of Don Albert and Hershel Evans when they were members of the Troy Floyd band in San Antonio, 1929.

Don Albert, Willie Long (trumpet), Benny Long (trombone), Siki Collins (alto and soprano saxophone), Troy Flyod (alto and tenor saxophone, clarinet), Scott 'Funny' Bagby (tenor saxophone, clarinet), Allen Van (piano), John Henry Braggs (banjo), Charlie Dixon (tuba, string bass), John Humphries (drums) and Kellough Jefferson (vocal). This band broadcast regularly over station HTSA from the Plaza Hotel.

The Chicago Defender of 23rd March 1929 reported the presence of 'Troy Floyd and his 10,000 Dollars Gold Orchestra' at the Shadowland. The personnel was the same as above, except that Herschel Evans (sax) had replaced Bagby, and Wesley Smith (violin, entertainer) is listed in place of Jefferson. Changes in the personnel occurred later in 1929, and Buddy Tate gives the following line-up to cover most of that year and 1930: Willie Wagner, Al Johnson (trumpet), Burt Johnson (trombone), Herschel Evans (tenor and baritone saxophone, clarinet), Buddy Tate (alto and tenor saxophone, clarinet), Siki Collins (alto and soprano saxophone), and the rhythm section as before.

Trombonist George Corley replaced Johnson in 1932 and, during his tenure with the band, John White (trumpet) and Joe Taylor (alto saxophone) were added and Floyd himself came in again for Tate. Jefferson was the vocalist for most of the time, but he also recalls Israel Wicks and Bob Clemons singing with the band, and at some point Leonard Gay (sax, arranger) replaced one of the sax men. The band broke up during the early depression years and Floyd, not himself an outstanding musician, reverted to leading smaller groups. In later years he worked as a pool hall operator in San Diego and died in 1951.

The Floyd band recorded for the first time in March 1928, producing one thoroughly undistinguished *Wabash Blues* whose only saving grace is a good muted trumpet solo by Albert. Its other title from this date, *Shadowland Blues,* originally issued on two sides of a 78rpm record, is musically uneven, the eccentric singing of Jefferson and Long's trombone work being mediocre; but Albert has an excellent muted solo, Collins plays well, a clarinet passage is reasonable, and the ensemble work at the close is crisp. A two part *Dreamland Blues,* made more than a year later, is considerably better, with good solo work by Albert, pleasant contributions by Van and a clarinettist, and fittingly relaxed ensemble playing. Towards the close there is a tenor saxophone solo that has been credited to Herschel Evans, but certainly bears little relationship to his work with Count Basie. The impression one receives from these records is that Floyd's was a proficient band with one or two good soloists—Collins has been praised by a number of musicians who heard him with various territory bands—but that all in all it was undistinguished.

Bassist Walter Page, born in Gallatin, Missouri, on 9th February 1900, is now best remembered as a member of the famous Count Basie rhythm section from 1936 to 1942, but years before joining Basie he had led a band that was considered the finest jazz unit in the southwest after Trent's. Our knowledge of Page's early career owes much to the researches of Frank Driggs, and particularly to a long interview he undertook with Page that formed the basis of an article in the now defunct Jazz Review.

Page gained a thorough schooling in music in Kansas City, studying sax, violin, piano, voice, composition and arranging, after first mastering bass horn and string bass. In the early 'twenties he was working with Bennie Moten and Dave Lewis. On 1st January 1923 he joined Billy King's road show, as a member of a band consisting of Lawrence Williams (cornet), Ermir Coleman (trombone, leader), William Blue (clarinet), Willie Lewis (piano), himself (bass) and Edward 'Crack' McNeil (drums). Page spoke highly of this band, singling out Lewis as a particularly fine musician, and it was mentioned in the Chicago Defender of 11th October 1924, with the sax player given as William Murphy and violinist Terry Dixon added. For one tour in 1925 the band consisted of Harry Youngblood, James Simpson (trumpet), Ermir Coleman (trombone, leader), Reuben Roddy (sax), Buster Smith (alto saxophone, clarinet), and the rhythm as before. Later, Oran 'Hot Lips' Page had replaced Youngblood, Ernest Williams had taken over from McNeil, and Reuben Lynch had been included on banjo.

In 1927 the band broke up when Coleman left to go into politics. For a while Page worked the territory with a small group and then managed to get backing from influential business men in Oklahoma City to form his own big band. The initial line-up of Walter Page's Blue Devils was James Simpson, Jimmy Lugrand, Oran 'Hot Lips' Page (trumpet), Eddie Durham (soon replaced by Dan Minor) (trombone), Buster Smith, Reuben Roddy, Ted Manning (reeds), Turk Thomas (piano), Reuben Lynch (guitar), Walter Page (string bass, brass horn, baritone saxophone), and Alvin Burroughs (drums). Page told Frank Driggs : 'We started working around El Reno, Shawnee, Chickashay and all the little towns in a fifty-mile radius with just ten pieces. In Shawnee we played a little club called the Riverside for dime-dance affairs for about four months. When the summer was over, we did so well, we went out and bought a Stoddard-Dayton, a great big touring car, and drove through Texas for a couple of weeks before coming back to Oklahoma.'

Later he added that the band had cut both George Lee and Jesse Stone and that he was undisputed boss of that territory. Page was particularly anxious to battle the Bennie Moten band, but Moten avoided the encounter.

In July 1928 Count Basie replaced Thomas on piano, and about the same time Jimmy Rushing was added as vocalist. Soon afterwards Page lost several musicians to Bennie Moten, who was able to offer them much better salaries. Basie and Durham left early in 1929 and Rushing and Oran Page later in the year. For a while Page was inactive, but soon obtained good replacements. The Chicago Defender of 12th October 1929 carried a report on the Blue Devils—incorrectly referred to as a Bennie Moten unit—playing at the Cinderella Dance Palace at Little Rock, Arkansas, before going on to the Japanese Gardens in Oklahoma City. The Defender listed as personnel Oran 'Hot Lips' Page, James Simpson (trumpet), Druie 'Chap' Bess (trombone), Henry 'Buster' Smith, Reuben Roddy (sax), Charles Washington (piano), Reuben Lynch (guitar), Walter Page (string bass), Alvin Burroughs (drums), Jimmy Rushing (vocal), Thomas Owens (probably sax). A photograph taken in the same year, when the band was in Oklahoma City, has James Legrand (Lugrand?) added on trumpet, Ted 'Doc' Ross (alto saxophone, clarinet) for Owens, and Ernest Williams (vocal, director) for Rushing.

Oran Page's immediate replacement was Harry Smith, but the exact personnel of the group during 1930 and 1931 is difficult to assess. Lester Young joined in 1930 but did not stay long; drummer A. G. Godley was with it in 1930-31 and gave a personnel of Oran 'Hot Lips'

Page, James Simpson, Leonard Chadwick (trumpet), Druie Bess, Dan Minor (trombone), Buster Smith, Ted Ross, Reuben Roddy (reeds), Charles Washington (piano), Reuben Lynch (guitar), Walter Page (string bass), himself (drums), Jimmy Rushing, Ernest Williams (vocal). Godley also mentions the brief appearance in the band of a trombonist who called himself Jack Teegarden! If Mr Godley's memory was correct, and Oran Page and Rushing were still in the band, the date must be late 1929. However, the Chicago Defender of 23rd May 1931 gives a definite personnel for the period, with changes in Harry Smith, Ramon Howell and Ernest Williams for Oran Page, Godley and Rushing.

By 1931 Page felt that the band was ready for the big time and had plans to take it to New York. Unfortunately, after some quite lucrative engagements, Page fell foul of the musicians' union in Kansas City, who fined him $250.00 for failing to engage a pianist to whom he had offered a job. His reasons were that another member of the band was on bad terms with the pianist, and Page felt that their joint presence would cause too much dissension. Because of his family commitments Page was unable to continue on the salary the band could afford, and he turned it over to Simpson to finish out the current bookings. After playing with small groups Page joined Moten and remained with

him until 1934, leaving to work with the Jeter-Pillars Orchestra in the autumn of that year, and subsequently Count Basie. In his post-Basie career he undertook a variety of work until he died from pneumonia in New York City on 20th December 1957.

After Page left, Buster Smith and Ernest Williams decided to keep going. They brought in Leroy 'Snake' White as nominal leader, and billed the band as 'The 13 Original Devils'. The personnel was now Leonard Chadwick, George Young, Leroy 'Snake' White (trumpet), Druie Bess, Jap Jones (trombone), Ted Ross, Buster Smith (alto saxophone, clarinet), Lester Young (tenor saxophone), Charles Washington (piano), Reuben Lynch (guitar), Abe Bolas (string bass), Raymond Howell (drums) and Ernest Williams (vocal, director). The Chicago Defender of 9th April 1932 reports the presence of the band at the Ritz Ballroom, Oklahoma City, with a personnel as above, except that James Simpson is in place of Young.

In an interview with Don Gazzaway, Buster Smith commented: 'We built up a tough band. We were plenty tough and they [Moten] wouldn't let us catch them either. Hardly anyone would hang around to have a battle of music with us. We didn't care anything about any band till we met Andy Kirk. He had a good brass section; it was tight and it hit hard.'

The band at this time was a co-operative unit and lost a chance of wide recognition when a vote was taken on whether they should accept an offer to play on an hour and a half show with Fats Waller in Cincinnati. By a small majority the band members rejected the job on the ground that the money was insufficient. This turned out to be a disastrous decision, particularly since a tour into Kentucky and West Virginia, areas where the band

The 13 Original Blue Devils, 1932. Back row: Leroy White (trumpet), Theodore 'Doc' Ross (alto saxophone), Lester Young (tenor saxophone), Buster Smith (alto saxophone), Reuben Lynch (guitar), Abe Bolar (string bass). Front row: Jap Jones (trombone), Leonard Chadwick, George Hudson (trumpets), Ernest Williams (vocal), Charlie Washington (piano), Druie Bess (trombone), Raymond Howell (drums).

was unknown, proved something of a fiasco. Morale was low when the band played a club in Martinville, West Virginia, during 1933, only to find that they had been tricked by a booking agent into accepting a share of door receipts which were as low as thirty dollars a night. Soon their instruments were impounded by the police on the instigation of a taxi company, to whom they owed a great deal of money, and were returned only for their night's job to work the debt off. Worse followed when they were thrown out of their hotel. Shortly afterwards the band returned to Kansas City by freight train, a few lucky ones having borrowed the fare and the rest travelling in the time honoured method of the hobo. Jones, Ross, Smith and Young joined Bennie Moten and the remaining band members took what work was available. The saga of the 'Blue Devils' was over.

In view of its tremendous reputation it is unfortunate that the Blue Devils only recorded two titles, at a time when Walter Page was still leader. Even so, these give clear indication that the band was as good as musicians have claimed. *Blue Devil Blues* opens with Willie Lewis's Hines-like piano introduction to Oran Page's powerful solo, after which Buster Smith plays a fine spiky-toned clarinet solo before Rushing takes a vocal. Rushing's voice is lighter than we know it from his Basie days, but he uses some familiar phrases during his vocal. The finale has Lewis over a strong ensemble riff. *Squabblin'* has a passage by Page playing baritone saxophone, but the main interest lies in Buster Smith's clarinet and alto saxophone solos. Traditionally Smith has been named as a strong influence on Charlie Parker, and though his tone bears little relationship to Parker's his searching outlook might well have appealed to the younger man. The drive of the band, its use of blues material and riff patterns, and its general uninhibited swing must have had a considerable influence on such contemporaries as Moten, and the view that it, rather than Moten, was the real inspiration of the later Basie band is a perfectly tenable one. If Page's hopes of bringing the band to New York had been realised, the development there of big band jazz might have been radically different.

In reminiscing on his Blue Devils' days with Frank Driggs, the late Walter Page remarked: 'We used to run into some fine outfits down in Texas. Gene Coy and his Happy Black Aces were out of Amarillo with seven or eight pieces and they were really jumping. Gene played drums and his wife played piano like a *man*.'

Walter Page was not the only musician to be impressed by Ann Coy's piano playing. John Lewis, director of the Modern Jazz Quartet, told me in 1927 how as a youth he listened to the Coy band and admired Mrs Coy's work.

Coy started up his group sometime in the middle of the 'twenties, and by 1929-30 his personnel were Joe Keep, Red 'Dizzy' Thompson (trumpet), Alton 'Slim' Moore (trombone), Ted Manning, Ben Webster (alto saxophone), Odell West (tenor saxophone), Ann Coy (piano), Forrest Conley (banjo), Clyde Durham (tuba), himself (drums) and 'Bat' Johnson (vocal). By 1932 all but the rhythm section had changed, with a line-up of Carl 'Tatti' Smith, Mack McClure (trumpet), Allen Durham (trombone), Isiah Young, Aurelius Whaley, Oscar Cobb (sax), Tyree Johnson (vocal) and the same rhythm. A year later, tenor saxophonist Dick Wilson joined.

By 1938 Coy had increased his band to twelve, fronting Otto Sampson, Eddie Walker (trumpet), Allen Durham, Andre Duryea (trombone), Jack Dozer, Isiah 'Ike' Young, Herman Powell, Lester Taylor (sax), Ann Coy (piano), Junior Raglin (guitar), Clyde Durham (string bass). Raglin, who was Jimmy Blanton's replacement in Duke Ellington's band, stayed with Coy until the autumn of 1941. From 1939 until about the time that Raglin left, Coy led a full swing band of six brass, four reeds and four rhythm, made up of Prince Stewart, Claude Dunson, Otto Sampson (trumpet), Allen Durham, Andre Duryea, unknown (trombone), Isiah 'Ike' Young, Lester Taylor (alto saxophone, clarinet), Henry Powell, Charlie Lewis (tenor saxophone), Ann Coy (piano), Junior Raglin (guitar, string bass), Clyde Durham (string bass), himself (drums). After this he cut down the size of his band but continued to be popular until the later 'forties.

The Coy band made a considerable impact on musicians who heard it, and travelled extensively through Texas, Oklahoma, Michigan, Kentucky, Oregon, Washington, California and the Midwest. It made a few trips further afield, appearing in Canada and Mexico. Like most touring bands it had its rough times. Mr Leo Walker recalled in his 'Great Dance Bands' an occasion when he booked it for a dance and discovered when he paid it off at 2 a.m. that they had been unable to eat before receiving their wages. Mr Walker and the crowd who heard the band were highly appreciative. Coy at this time was based on San Francisco and leading a fourteen-piece unit playing what his business card described as 'Harlem Swing'. Coy did record in 1949, but the output bore no relationship to that of his peak years. He died in California during the 'sixties.

Eddie and Sugar Lou's Hotel Tyler Orchestra recorded six titles in 1929 and a further four in 1931, but those that I have heard are not particularly impressive. As their name implies they worked in Tyler, Texas. Buddy Tate says they owed much of their success to the fact that they had a wealthy backer who owned the local radio station and gave them plenty of airtime. Oran 'Hot Lips' Page worked with the band for a few months, but when they recorded in 1929 the line-up is thought to be Henry Thompson or Stanley Hardee (trumpet), Albert Mitchell (trombone), Adrian Kenny (alto and baritone saxophone), Charles 'Sugar Lou' Morgan (piano), Eddie Fennell (banjo, violin, arranger) and Lee Scott (drums), though aural evidence makes clear that another sax player is present. The personnel remained reasonably constant for most of the life of the band, reportedly because the leaders could pay well, though Harold 'Money' Johnson worked with the group in 1933, a year or two before it finally broke up.

KWKH Blues (KWKH was the radio station over which the band broadcast) has good trumpet, and Morgan and Kenny take competent solos, but too much time is taken up with Fennell's very average vocal, as in *Sweet Papa Will Be Gone*. *Eddie and Sugar Lou Stomp* is better, with reasonable solos from a trumpeter, Mitchell and Morgan, but on the whole the band offers little that is particularly distinctive. In view of the recording opportunities given to the band one cannot refrain from wishing that other, more important, territory units had been similarly blessed with a wealthy backer!

Don Albert, whose real name is Albert Dominique (Natty Dominique is his uncle), was born in New Orleans in 1909 and was trained as a musician by Lorenzo Tio Jr and Milford Piron. After doing some parade work he toured with Trent's Number Two band from 1925, subsequently joining Troy Floyd's band in San Antonio in 1926 and remaining with it until September 1929. In that month he went back to New Orleans to form his own band, titled Don Albert and his Ten Pals, in due course returning to San Antonio where he led it at the Chicken Plantation and the Shadowland and on one nighters.

The personnel from 1929 - 1931 was mainly unchanged

Don Albert in his early days as a bandleader.

—Don Albert, Hiram Harding (trumpet), Frank Jacquet (trombone), Herbert Hall (alto and baritone saxophone), Louis Cottrell (clarinet, tenor saxophone), Al Freeman (piano), Ferdinand Dejan (banjo), Henry Turner (tuba, valve trombone), Albert 'Fats' Martin (drums) and Sidney Hansel (vocal). In 1932 Alvin Alcorn (trumpet), Wallace Mercer (alto saxophone) and Jimmy Johnson (string bass) were added, and Philander Tillar (alto saxophone, arranger) and Sam LaBert (vocal), replaced Derbigny and Hansel.

With the break up of Troy Floyd's band in 1932, Albert found himself able to take over as the number one unit in the San Antonio area, at this time changing his billing to 'Don Albert and his Music, America's Greatest Swing Band', the first orchestra to use the word 'swing' in its title. Mr Albert told Dick Allen that before the arrival of Philander Tillar the band had used no written arrangements, but that after that they built up a large book. In 1934 James 'Geechy' Robinson (trombone) was added, and James 'Dink' Taylor, Gus Patterson (alto saxophone) and Lloyd Glenn (piano, arranger) replaced Mercer, Tillar and Freeman. A year later Albert persuaded trumpeter/arranger Billy Douglas to leave Jimmie Gunn's orchestra, and from this point Albert himself very rarely played trumpet, preferring to front the band and attend to business details. Merle Turner was brought in as vocalist in 1936, in time for the only recording session that the band made.

Although the band was based on San Antonio, playing residencies at the Shadowland and other local clubs and hotels, most of its life was spent on gruelling one night stands. Altogether it played in thirty-eight states, and in 1937 travelled outside the USA to Mexico and Canada and also made an appearance in New York. In that year, Harold Holmes (string bass) replaced Johnson, a New Orleans veteran who can be seen in the only known picture of the legendary Buddy Bolden band. Late in 1937 the band temporarily disbanded in San Antonio, reforming in the early part of 1938 with a line-up of Alvin Alcorn, Charlie Anderson, Joe Phillips (trumpet), Frank Jacquet, James 'Geechy' Robinson (trombone), Gus Patterson, Tom Johnson, Harold 'Dink' Taylor (alto saxophone), Jimmy Forrest (tenor saxophone), Lionel Reason (piano), Ferdinand Dejan (guitar), Lawrence Cato (string bass), Albert 'Fats' Martin (drums), Harry 'Buddy' Johnson or . . . Collins (vocal). Later in the year Lester Patterson, John Hardy and Herb Hall replaced Anderson, Forrest and Johnson. In 1939 Hiram Harding, Kenny Rickman (trumpet), Jay Gholson (piano) and Ernestine 'Annisteen' Allen (vocal) had taken over from Alcorn, Phillips, Reason, Johnson and/or Collins, while in the summer Hardee left to be replaced by Jimmy Bell.

Albert suffered badly from the mishandling of his business affairs by the band's booker, and late in 1939 the band broke up in Houston, though drummer Albert Martin valiantly tried to keep it going. After this Albert made a few attempts to resume bandleading on a full

time basis, but in 1941 finally gave it up. In subsequent years he worked as a booking agent, entered the civil service for a period, and opened the Keyhole Club in San Antonio, which he still owns but does not directly control. In 1948 he returned to New Orleans and, after some not too successful investments, worked for the post office for a year, going back to San Antonio in 1950. Throughout the 'forties he still organised bands for specific engagements, fronting one in New York in May 1949. Recently he has worked as a United States government inspector, but has maintained his interest in music and recorded again during the 'sixties. In June 1969 he played at the New Orleans Jazz Festival.

Unlike many bands who only had a single recording opportunity, Albert's was at its peak when it made eight titles in San Antonio during November 1936. Though three of the numbers recorded were ephemeral popular hits of the day, *Liza, Deep Blue Melody, On the Sunny Side of the Street* and *Rockin' and Swingin'* are outstanding performances. *Liza* was arranged by Douglas, and after a Glenn introduction the theme is taken by the trumpet section cushioned by the saxes, which achieve a splendid blend. Solos are by Douglas, Taylor and, briefly, Hall and Cottrell, but the impressive aspect of the performance is the swing and overall cohesion of the band. Apart from a neat solo by Glenn and an impressive

The Don Albert band on tour in the mid 1930s. Albert is in the centre of the front row. Jimmy Johnson, who played with the legendary Buddy Holden, is the middle man of the three sitting on the bonnet.

eight bars from Taylor, *On the Sunny Side of the Street* is a feature for Douglas, opening with a hoarse Louis Armstrong-inspired vocal and closing with a fine solo by Douglas. Douglas's style, particularly in its rhythmic freedom, reminds one of Henry Allen's, but apparently he was a great admirer of Cuban Bennett, and possibly developed his style as a result of listening to Bennett. *Deep Blue Melody* is a moody Ellington-ish number arranged by Lloyd Glenn, with attractive muted playing from Alcorn, contrasting effective plunger work by Harding, and an excellent flowing alto solo by Taylor in the Hodges manner. Once more the playing of the sax section is of the highest order. The complex *Rockin' and Swingin'*, with its riff theme, is something of an orchestral tour-de-force for the period, with solos confined to eight-bar passages by Cottrell, Harding and Douglas. Its chief value lies in the magnificent work of the various sections and the constantly shifting textures, especially the attractive light sound of the sax section. The other titles recorded, three with period vocals by Merle Turner, are less interesting but include such worthwhile passages as Herb Hall's baritone solo on *Tomorrow* and a beautifully scored sax passage, by Lloyd Glenn, on *You Don't Love Me.* That Albert's band was superior to a number of name units of the day can hardly be doubted on the evidence of these records.

With Albert increasingly engaged in touring schedules, the way was clear for another band to make its mark in San Antonio, and the opportunity was seized by Clifford 'Boots' Douglas. Douglas, a drummer, began playing in the late 'twenties and organised his own band in 1932, with a personnel of Percy Bush, L. D. Harris (trumpet), George Abram (trombone), Alvin Brooks (alto saxophone), David Ellis, Lonnie Hysaw (tenor saxophone), Lloyd Glenn (piano, arranger), Jeff Thomas (guitar), Walter McHenry (string bass, tuba), Clifford 'Boots' Douglas (drums) and Celeste Allen (vocal). Mr Glenn provided the above information, but he left in 1934 to join Don Albert. A photgraph exists of the band with a personnel similar to the last, but with James Wheat (alto saxophone) added, no trombonist included, and Baker Milliam (tenor saxophone) and A. J. Johnson (piano) in place of Hysaw and Glenn.

The band recorded for the first time in August 1935, the personnel generally listed being Theodore Gilders, Percy Bush, Douglas Byers, Charles Anderson (trumpet), Johnny Shields (trombone), Alva Brooks, Wee Demry (alto saxophone), Baker Millian, David Ellis (tenor saxophone), A. J. Johnson (piano), Jeff Vant (guitar), Walter McHenry (string bass), Clifford 'Boots' Douglas (drums), Celeste Allen (vocal). Whether four trumpet men are in fact present is open to doubt. During 1937-38 some changes took place, Gilders, Byers, Shields and Demry having left, replaced by C. H. Jones, L. D. Harris, George Corley and Arthur Hampton. In 1938 McHenry's place was taken by Harold Holmes. The band held together until the early 'forties. At some time Lonnie Moore (trumpet), Shelby Risher (alto saxophone) and Al Hibbler (vocal) became members. Hibbler left in 1942 to join Jay McShann.

Mr Frank Driggs once wrote that the band was frequently out of tune and sounded more like a rehearsal unit than a regular one. There is some truth in his remark, for on some records the ensemble playing gives the listener some anxious moments, but George Corley presents a different viewpoint when he nostalgically recalls the battles that Boots and his Buddies had with Don Albert, Milt Larkins, the Carolina Cotton Pickers and others, suggesting that the band could hold its own when it came to the test.

From 1935 to 1938 Douglas's band recorded quite extensively for the Bluebird label, faring much better in this respect than most territory bands. While the bulk of the output offers little in the way of felicities of scoring or technical brilliance, there is an engaging quality about it that results from the extrovert swing of the group and the presence of a number of good soloists. Foremost

Left: *Lloyd Glenn, arranger and pianist with the Don Albert band.* Right: *the only known photograph of Boots Douglas leader of 'Boots and his Buddies'.*

amongst the latter is the tenor saxophonist Baker Millians, an easily identifiable stylist with a full, dry tone and a bustling manner of phrasing, whose contributions are invariably of a high order. Another worthwhile soloist is trumpeter Charles Anderson, the possessor of a big tone and an assured technique, and both he and Millian can be heard to advantage in *The Sad Ain't Misbehavin'* is an attractive performance with a reasonable vocal by Cora Woods, solos by Anderson and a second trumpeter with a more strident tone, and an excellent passage from Millians, who swings well. Less interesting is a curious *Loveless Love* with Dixieland overtones that changes course towards the close; the final ensemble work is woefully deficient in intonation. In general, the band was at its best on blues material such as *How Long* and *Blues of Avalon,* and, if it could hardly rival the leading groups of the day in versatility and technical facility, its honest, straightforward approach provides good entertainment.

Probably the last of the great Texas big bands was the one formed by trumpeter Milton Larkins. Larkins, born in Houston, Texas, on 10th October 1910, was impressed by Bunk Johnson when he heard him with a travelling show. He subsequently taught himself to play trumpet, and while still a teenager worked with Chester Boone's band and other local groups, forming his own band in 1936 for a residency at the Aragon Ballroom. Over the next seven years, until he joined the army, he travelled with the band extensively, working at the Rhumboogie Club in Chicago for almost a year during 1941-42 and making New York for an appearance at the Apollo Theatre.

A photograph of 1936 or 1937 shows Lonnie Moore, Lester Patterson (trumpet), Milton Larkins (trumpet, vocal), Henry Sloan (trombone), Eddie Vinson (alto saxophone, vocal), Arnett Cobb (tenor saxophone), Cedric

Haywood (piano), Lawrence Cato (string bass), Charles Gardens (drums), Sammy Demerit (unknown instrument), George Layne (vocal) and two unidentified musicians. Another photograph, taken in 1938, shows Lester Patterson, Clifford Mitchell, Milt Larkins (trumpet), Willie Tompkins, Henry Sloan, Streamline Williams (trombone), Eddie Vinson (alto saxophone, vocal), L. F. Simon (alto and baritone saxophone), Frank Dominguez, Arnett Cobb (tenor saxophone) and the previous rhythm section with the addition of Bill Davis (guitar, piano, arranger).

Down Beat for July 1939 reported that the American critic John Hammond had heard Larkins's band in Beaumont, Texas, and had been impressed. (He referred to it as a fourteen-piece unit based on Houston.) In the same year Illinois Jacquet (tenor saxophone) was in the band for a short while, as were T-Bone Walker (vocal, guitar) and Joe Marshall (drums). Lester Patterson had left in December 1938 to join Don Albert. In Down Beat of 1st September 1940 a personnel of Eddie Hutchinson, Calvin Ladnier, Lester Patterson (trumpet), Henry Sloan, Richard Waters, Nelden Belding (trombone), Eddie Vinson, Frank Dominguez, Ernest Archia, Arnett Cobb (sax), Cedric Heywood (piano), Lawrence Cato (string bass), Henry Mills (drums), George Cayne (vocal) and Milt Larkins (leader) was listed. (Calvin Ladnier, incidentally, is the brother of the more famous Tommy Ladnier.)

Cedric Heywood, who worked with the band from 1936 until 1940 and again briefly in 1942, remembers Romie Lewis, Russell Jacquet, Eddie 'Googoo' Hutchinson

The Milt Larkins band at the Rhumboogie Club, Chicago, 1941. Trumpets: Calvin Ladnier (brother of Tommy), Clarence Trice, Jesse Miller. Trombones: Arnett Sparrow, 'Streamline' Williams. Saxophones: Frank Dominguez, Ernest Archey, Moses Gant, Sam Player. Cedric Haywood is the pianist, Lawrence Cato the bassist and Alvin Burroughs the drummer. Larkins is in the white jacket.

(trumpet), William Luper, Luther Williams (trombone), Gus Patterson and Kermit Scott (sax) as present at various times, in some instances very briefly, so it appears that personnel changes were relatively frequent. A photograph of the band at the Rhumboogie Club in Chicago in 1942 shows Calvin Ladnier, Clarence Trice, Jesse Miller (trumpet), Arnett Sparrow, John 'Streamline' Ewing (trombone), Frank Dominguez (alto saxophone), Sam Player (alto and baritone saxophone), Tom Archia, Moses Gant (tenor saxophone), Cedric Heywood (piano), Lawrence Cato (string bass) and Alvin Burroughs (drums).

Larkins was called up in November 1943 and played both trumpet and valve trombone in Sy Oliver's service band. The 26th August 1946 issue of Down Beat reported that he was just out of the army and rehearsing a seventeen-piece orchestra in New York City. He took this band out on tour and played at the Rhumboogie Club in Chicago, but the bottom was dropping out of the big band business and he soon cut down to a smaller group. He recorded during the late 'forties and early 'fifties, gaining one hit with his X-Rays group, then in 1956, at the Celebrity Club upstairs room, he started leading a seven-piece band, which he kept together for several years. He still does gigging around the New York area but no longer leads a regular group.

Speaking to Frank Driggs about his bandleading days, Larkins commented: 'We didn't know how good we were until we'd appear on the same stage with people like Louis [Armstrong] and we'd get just as much applause as they did. The headliners would be offstage talking to the promoters about our band and that helped us sometimes.'

Musicians with other bands have reported that Larkins's was difficult to battle with, particularly as it always included an extrovert tenor saxophone player of the Arnett Cobb, Illinois Jacquet variety, capable of rousing audiences. I would guess from what musicians have said that it was a tough, driving band, seldom given to excessive subtlety, though it built up an impressive book of arrangements which Larkins still retains. As with so many of the territory bands, Larkins's was never recorded.

The Original Yellowjackets was a band formed by pianist Chester Lane in Little Rock, Arkansas, during the early years of the 'thirties. It created a local following: Forrest Powell, Aubrey Yancey (trumpet), unknown (trombone), Monroe Fingers, Clifton Jones (alto saxophone), William Pate (tenor saxophone), Chester Lane (piano, arranger), Arthur Shelton (string bass) and Ira 'Skeets' Seville (drums), made up its personnel. Vocalist Al Hibbler obtained his first job with the band in 1935.

Lane left the band in 1936 and was replaced by Durant Allen, and in this year Earl Watkins (trumpet) and Wiley Fuller (string bass) replaced Powell and Shelton; Jesse Saville (guitar) and Fats Smith (vocal) were added, and the trombone was dropped from the line-up. A mobile unit had the band record eight titles in Hot Springs, Arkansas, during March 1937. Six titles were issued. *Swingin' at The Chat and Chew* (The Chat and Chew was a Little Rock restaurant where the band often played) opens with a growl-style trumpet solo, the release taken by a good altoist. A reasonable, but harsh toned, clarinet solo follows. Pate and a good strong toned trumpeter are heard before an ensemble close. *Cross Street Swing* is more an ensemble performance. The only solos are a few bars of muted trumpet and a good contribution by Pate; the brass men achieve surprising power in their lead work. The band generates a good swing and a full sound for nine pieces—a salutary reminder that during the 'thirties big band jazz was flourishing throughout most of the USA, not just in the major metropolitan centres. Just how long the band remained in existence is not known.

Ernie Fields, born on 26th August 1905 at Nacogdoches, Texas, formed his first band in about 1930 and maintained one longer than most of the territory leaders. His 1931 personnel was Dave Duncan, Eddie Lowery, Hubert Scott (trumpet), Ernie Fields (trombone), Luther 'Lard' West, Paul Perkinson, Leroy Bailey, Eddie Nicholson (sax), Hobart Banks (piano), O. Z. Burley (banjo), Ted Shirley (bass) and Roy Milton (drums). The Chicago Defender of 25th March 1933 carried a reference to Fields's band playing in Tulsa, Oklahoma, its home base for many years, and listed the personnel as Hubert 'Teddy' Scott, Jeff Carrington, Leon Dillard (trumpet), Ernie Fields (trombone), Leroy Bailey, John Clark, Eddie Nicholson (reeds), Salva Sanders (piano), O. Z. Burley (guitar), Theodore Shirley (string bass), Joe Walker (drums) and Pee Wee Wiley (vocal). It is believed that the line-up for the next three or four years did not differ much from the above, though Rene Hall (guitar, trombone, arranger) and Clarence Dixon (drums) replaced Burley and Walker.

Down Beat of June 1939 reported that the band had been discovered by John Hammond during a southern trip and on his recommendation had been promptly signed by Willard Alexander of the Morris Agency, who planned to give it a similar build-up to Count Basie's, three years previously. At this time Fields was appearing in Dallas, alternating at the Log Cabin Club with bands led by Don Purcell and Perry Dixon. A month later Down Beat carried a story on the band. It told its readers that the band had been scuffling for a long time and made jumps in an old worn out Dodge truck, often working on straight percentage deals—'and it's often remarkable that the boys get paid at all.' As an illustration of the gruelling touring schedule, Down Beat mentioned three consecutive one nighters—a town forty miles east of Tulsa, Wichita, Kansas, and Dallas, Texas. In August, Down Beat noted that Roy Douglas (tenor saxophone) and Rozelle Claxton (piano) had joined Fields from Bill Martin's Orchestra in Kansas City.

Fields brought his band to New York to record in August and September 1939, with a line-up of Vernon 'Geechie' Smith, Jeff Carrington, Amos Woodruff (trumpet), Edward Middleton, Russell Moore (trombone), Luther West, Hunter Gray (alto saxophone), Roy Douglas, Harry Garnett (tenor saxophone), Rozelle Claxton (piano), Rene Hall (guitar, trombone), Robert Lewis (string bass), Clarence Dixon (drums), Melvin Moore, Leora Davis (vocal), Ernie Fields (director). Fields worked around New Year for a while and then returned to Tulsa. Hunter Gray left late in the year to join another local band.

During 1940 Down Beat noted the band's whereabouts on a number of occasions, mentioning engagements in Alva, Oklahoma, Wichita, Kansas and Nampa, Idaho. At some point in the same year Claxton left, to be replaced by Hobart Banks, and it seems that Hunter Gray returned. The records did not make the impact that Fields had hoped for and numerous personnel changes occurred during 1941. Among the newcomers who worked with the band were Artis Paul (trumpet), Hal Singer, Lucky Robertson (tenor saxophone) and Lawrence Keyes (piano). Early in 1942 Aaron Izenhall (trumpet) and Gus

Chapell (trombone) were with the band in the Midwest. A full personnel is given in the June 1942 Down Beat— Eddie Walker, King Kolax, Milton Lewis (trumpet), Parker Berry, Ed Middleton (trombone), Luther West, McKinley Easton (alto saxophone), Hubert Perry, Paul Quinichette (tenor saxophone), Creon Thomas (piano), Rene Hall (guitar, trombone, arranger), Robert Lewis (string bass), Joe Marshall (drums), Melvin Moore, Estelle Edson (vocal). About a month later Helen Humes toured the Midwest with the band.

Down Beat continued to report on the band's movements throughout 1944 and 1945; locations included Baltimore, Wichita, Washington, D.C., Dallas and Los Angeles. Ed Preston has given a personnel of himself, Russell Emory, 'Fats' (trumpet), Ernie Fields, Parker Berry, 'Tang' (trombone), John White, Teddy Edwards (alto saxophone), Warren Lucky, unknown (tenor saxophone), Sy Cannon (baritone saxophone), Lee Wesley Jones (piano), unknown (string bass), Clarence Dixon (drums) for this period. He recalled that Tony Moret and Bo McMillan replaced 'Fats' and Jones just before he himself left. Music Dial of January 1945 stated that Dorothy Donegan was to use the Fields band in her own show, but it is not known if anything came of this. The turnover in the band now appears to have been rapid, suggesting that it was not doing too well, for the line-up of Julius Watkins, Rick Harper, unknown (trumpet), Phats Morris, Jimmy Wilkins, Parker Berry (trombone), Luther West, Harold 'Geezel' Minerva (alto saxophone), Bill Evans, Leon Wright (tenor saxophone), Bob McMillan (baritone saxophone), Charles Sherrill (piano), 'Bassy' McCarthy (string bass) and Clarence Dixon (drums) given by Phats Morris for 1946 includes only three men who were present a year earlier. Minerva currently plays with the Duke Ellington band.

In summer 1946 Aaron Izenhall (trumpet) and Tony Powell (trombone) joined the band in Tulsa, and in the following year Fields recorded in New York, adding a few local men to the line-up for the occasion. Though the late 'forties was a bad time for big bands, Fields doggedly kept his together. Billy Brooks toured with him in 1948 and remembered the personnel as himself, Walter Miller, Ernie Pinky (trumpet), Parker Berry, Ernie Fields, Benny Powell (trombone), Luther West, Harold Minerva (alto saxophone), Elon Watkins, Leon Wright (tenor saxophone), Leroy Cooper (baritone saxophone), Hobart Banks (piano), Freeman Lewis (string bass) and Al Bartee (replaced later by Al Duncan) (drums). The band recorded in 1949 with many of these musicians.

From February 1950 to February 1951 Fields toured with Artis Paul, Billy Brooks, unknown (trumpet), Parker Berry, himself, unknown (trombone), Luther West, Harold Minerva, Oscar Estelle (alto saxophone), Elon Watkins (tenor saxophone), Leroy Cooper (alto and baritone saxophone), Frank Haynes (tenor and baritone saxophone), unknown (replaced by Helen Stone) (piano), Ernest 'Butch' Lockett (guitar), Freeman Lewis (string bass), Jo Jo Williams (drums), Jo Jo Evans, Lawrence Stone (vocal). *Jet* for December 1953 noted that Eugene 'Upside Down' White (vocal) was touring the west coast with the Fields band, and in January 1956 the leader returned once more to Tulsa with an octet—Thomas 'Deek' Wilson (trumpet), himself (trombone), Oscar Estelle (alto saxophone), Elon Watkins (tenor saxophone), Curby Alexander (baritone saxophone), Helen Lewis (piano), Ernest 'Butch' Lockett (guitar) and William Holt (drums). Fields recorded again the following year and during 1960, but he was by then working in the rythm-and-blues field.

T-Town Blues and *Lard Stomp* are the best items I have heard from Fields's 1939 sessions, with excellent solos by trumpeter Amos Woodruff and alto saxophonist Luther West and the band swinging powerfully with strong ensemble playing. If Willard Alexander gave Fields the build-up promised, it was a signal failure, but the records suggest that the band possessed the potential for a far greater success than it ever achieved. Of the earlier territory bands, Fields's was the last to give in, and as the final survivor of a once flourishing tradition it deserves its honourable niche in big band jazz history.

The Midwestern States

Because of its geographical location St Louis was an early jazz centre, and local players were familiar with many of the New Orleans stars long before they became nationally known. Traditionally St Louis is associated with trumpet players, producing a line that starts with Charlie Creath and Dewey Jackson, continues with Harold Baker, Irving Randolph and Joe Thomas, and currently includes Miles Davis. It is interesting to discover

Below left: *SS Senator of the Streckfus Line, the boat on which Fate Marable held sway. His musicians included Louis Armstrong, Warren 'Baby' Dodds, George 'Pops' Foster and Joe Howard. Below: The Delta Queen, now the only passenger steamer operating on the Mississippi.*

that Creath, Jackson, Randolph and Leonard Davis were all trained by a Major McElroy, for this is further evidence of the influence of an important music teacher.

Charles Creath, the first of the St Louis trumpet stars, was born in Ironton, Missouri, on 30th December 1890 and initially played alto saxophone. He soon switched to trumpet and his early years were spent working with travelling shows and circuses. Later he led a band in Seattle before settling in St Louis about 1918. His first group included William Rollins on clarinet, his sister Marge on piano, and Eddie Carson, father of the famous theatrical star Josephine Baker, on drums. Around 1919 he was leading a personnel of himself (trumpet), Grant

Cooper (trombone), William Rollins, Sammy Long (reeds), Marge Creath (piano) and Alexander Lewis (drums), and this band was booked for a season in 1920 on the steamer St Paul, owned by the Streckfus Company. During the years 1921 to 1924 quite a number of musicians played with Creath on the riverboats, amongst them Ed Allen, Leonard 'Ham' Davis, Tommy Ladnier (trumpet), Dave Grant, Charles Lawson (trombone), Horace Eubanks, Hal Ester, William Thornton Blue (sax), Davey Jones (mellophone), Cran Hamilton (piano), Morris White, Pete Patterson (banjo), Lonnie Johnson (banjo, vocal), Cy McField (tuba) and Zutty Singleton (drums). Some of these musicians were with Creath for only a short time, but reed man Cecil Scott worked with him regularly during this period.

In 1921 Creath took over a band led by a girl pianist, Marcella Kyle, and fronted it at the Alamac Hall, the other musicians being Grant Cooper (trombone), Jerome Don Pasquall (clarinet, sax), Marge Creath (piano) and Robert 'Red' Muse (drums). When Pasquall left he was replaced by Eugene Sedric.

During the middle 'twenties Creath had several bands working under his name. One was a quartet of Leonard 'Ham' Davis (trumpet), George James (sax), Pauline Creath (piano) and an unknown drummer. Clarinettist Joe Darensbourg worked with Creath at the Plantation Club and Jazzland in 1924-25. (Creath enjoyed several lengthy residencies at Jazzland.)

Late in 1926 Creath joined the Fate Marable band on the SS Capitol, but illness forced him to retire from music from 1928 to 1930, and on his return usually played saxophone or accordion. He worked with Harvey Lankford's Synco High-Hatters in 1933; then he became joint leader with Fate Marable of a band from 1934 until about 1936. The personnel of this group in 1934, when it was playing on the SS St Paul, was Clifford King, Dewey Jackson (trumpet), Charlie Creath (trumpet, sax, accordion), Leon King (trombone), Leon 'Foots' Goodson, Tab Smith (alto saxophone), Kimball 'Cabbage' Dial (tenor saxophone), Fate Marable, Burroughs Lovingood (piano), John Young (guitar), Jimmy Jones (string bass) and Elijah Shaw (drums). Dewey Jackson joined the band at the Arcadia Ballrom in St Louis during 1934 and stayed for two seasons. Roosevelt Thomas (alto saxophone) was a member at one point in place of either Goodson or Smith.

In later years Creath moved to Chicago where he ran his own night club, subsequently becoming an inspector in an aircraft factory. He was in poor health for some years before he died in Chicago on 23rd October 1951.

Creath's reputation amongst other musicians was considerable, particularly during the 'twenties, and he is remembered for his power, freak half-valved effects, and mastery with mutes. He recorded ten titles between December 1924 and November 1925, and a further two in May 1927. One problem that arises in discussing them is the difficulty of positively identifying Creath's own

playing. Trumpeter Leonard Davis was added on the earliest sessions and I once read that he took most of the solos; certainly it seems to be Davis who takes the melodic blues solo on *Market Street Blues,* and he may well be the soloist on other titles. Judging from Creath's reputation the solos with mute on *Market Street Stomp* (one of his best records) and *Won't Don't Blues* are by him. As a whole the records are extraordinarily uneven, and range from Jelly Roll Morton's *King Porter Stomp* and *Grandpa's Spells* to blues, novelty numbers and a lugubrious pop song of the day entitled *Way Down in Lover's Lane.* Drummer Floyd Campbell has vocals on several titles, while Lonnie Johnson is added as a singer and violinist on *Won't Don't Blues,* a reasonable performance with good playing by Creath. *Market Street Stomp* is another good recording with a more cohesive closing ensemble passage than usual, though even here there is the anomaly of a Cranston Hamilton piano solo, pleasant in itself, that is almost pure ragtime. By the 1927 session Creath seemed much more certain of his direction. *Crazy Quilt* possesses assured ensemble playing and a good plunger solo by the leader, well backed by drummer Zutty Singleton. From the same date *Butter Finger Blues* has effective trumpet solos from Dewey Jackson and Creath (in that order), and once again it is noticeable that the ensemble passages are more relaxed than in earlier recordings.

Apart from Creath, Davis and Jackson, there are other solos on most titles. Clarinettist William Blue and trombonist Charlie Lawson do creditable jobs for the period. It is interesting to note that tenor saxophonist William Rollins, who has a very mediocre solo on the 1925 *Market Street Stomp,* had improved considerably by the 1927 *Butter Fingers Blues*—a demonstration of the changes taking place in the approach of reed men generally. As a band, judged on these records, Creath's lacked any real distinction, though the main problem was the then commonplace one of uncertain direction. On some performances there is an obvious echo of King Oliver's Creole Jazz Band; on others ragtime and the commercial dance bands of the era seem to exert a strong influence. By 1927, however, Creath's group was becoming part of the big band mainstream, and one regrets that he did not record with the band he and Fate Marable co-led. As far as his own playing is concerned one must add that there is little on his records to substantiate the great reputation he enjoyed amongst other musicians, though it may well be that his work in the recording studio was untypical of his playing on resident jobs. Those who heard Creath in his prime are unanimous in hailing him as the first of the local trumpet kings.

Dewey Jackson often worked with Creath during the early part of his career. He first joined Creath's band on a riverboat in late spring 1919. Before this Jackson, who was born in St Louis on 21st June 1900, had made his musical debut in a youth band, progressing to local

The St Louis Dixieland Six in the 1950s. Veteran trumpeter Dewey Jackson is second from left, and the bassist is Singleton Palmer.

roups. From about autumn 1919 he led a quartet which was resident at Jazzland in St Louis for two years and included drummer Floyd Casey. He then fronted his 'Gold Melody Orchestra' from 1921 to 1923. This was a sextet; the line-up included Boyd Atkins (alto saxophone, violin) and Harry Dial (drums), and for most of 1922 it worked at the Humming Bird club. In spring 1924 Jackson joined Fate Marable on a riverboat, but for the following two years led his own band on the SS Capitol. This group, consisting of Dewey Jackson, Albert Snaer (trumpet), John Lindsey (trombone), Sammy Long (alto saxophone), Willie Humphrey (tenor saxophone, clarinet), Burroughs Lovingood (piano), Pete Robinson (banjo), George 'Pops' Foster (string bass), Cecil White (tuba) and Floyd Campbell (drums) played the 1925-26 winter season out of New Orleans as the St Louis Peacock Charleston Orchestra, but on the way back to St Louis in spring 1926 it was renamed the New Orleans Cotton Pickers. At some point William Thornton Blue (clarinet, alto saxophone) came in and Andrew Luper (trombone) replaced Lindsey. After playing on a riverboat during the summer of 1926, Jackson left for New York where he worked with Andrew Preer's Orchestra at the Cotton Club for four months—this band was to become the Missourians. In his absence his band was led by Fate Marable. Before he left he had recorded with the band in St Louis with Blue present, Luper on trombone, White

absent, and Cliff Cochran (soprano and alto saxophone) replacing Long.

After returning to St Louis Jackson worked with both Marable and Creath, led his own band from 1927 to 1929, for a brief period joined Marable again, then fronted his Musical Ambassadors on the SS St Paul and at the Castle Ballroom, St Louis. Some well-known big band musicians appear at this period in his personnel, which consisted of himself, Clifford King (trumpet), Leon King (trombone), Harold Estes, Don Stovall (alto saxophone, clarinet), Earl Carruthers (tenor saxophone), Burroughs Lovingood (replaced by Cosy Harris) (piano), Pete Patterson (guitar), Cy Young (string bass) and Wilbur Kirk (drums). In 1932 and 1933 he fronted a slightly larger band—himself, Benny Starks, Clifford King, Walter 'Crack' Stanley (trumpet), Leon King (trombone), Tommy Starks, Cliff Batchman (alto saxophone, clarinet), Kimbal Dial, Elbert Claybrooks, unknown (tenor saxophone), Gus Perryman (piano), Pete Patterson (or Peterson), Floyd Smith (guitar), Singleton Palmer (string bass) and Floyd Campbell (drums), though this is a collective personnel.

Work during the depression years must have been hard to find, for in 1934 Jackson returned to playing with Creath and then in a band jointly led by Creath and Marable. In 1935 he returned to fronting groups, briefly working with trumpeter Louis Metcalf on the SS Capitol. His 1936 line-up consisted of himself, Wendell Black (trumpet), William Rollins (baritone and alto saxophone), Bradford Nichols (tenor saxophone), Cliff Batchman (alto saxophone), Robert Parker (piano),

Eugene Phillips (guitar), Singleton Palmer (string bass) and Earl Martin (drums). A year later Clark Terry (trumpet) and John Orange (trombone) had been added. The saxophone section was Fred Martin (alto saxophone), Kimbal Dial (clarinet, tenor saxophone) and Walter Martin (baritone saxophone), and in the rhythm section an unknown pianist had replaced Parker, and Phillips had left. Until 1941 Jackson led bands that played on the riverboats in the summer and at St Louis ballrooms in the winter, after which he concentrated solely on ballroom and club work. His 1941 band was himself, Wendell Black, George Hudson (trumpet), John Orange (trombone), Leon Goodson, Clifford Batchman (alto saxophone, clarinet), Ervin Williams (tenor saxophone), Eugene Porter (tenor saxophone, violin), Robert Parker (piano), John Young (guitar), Singleton Palmer (string bass) and Earl Martin (drums). Down Beat of 15th January 1942 reported that Jackson had formed a band from the nucleus of a group that played on the SS Senator, which ran between Pittsburgh and Louisville, during the previous summer. It gave a line-up similar to that listed above, except that Cy Stone (trumpet, vocal) was added and Bill Rollins (sax) had replaced Porter.

Around the middle 'forties Jackson left music, but returned to it in the following decade as a leader of his own band or as a member of Singleton Palmer's Dixie Six with whom he recorded in 1950. He continued to play occasional dates during the 'sixties, but has not worked as a musician for several years now.

Apart from the session with Singleton Palmer in 1950, all of Jackson's recordings were made in 1926-27, so that, like Creath, we are unable to hear him at the time when he was fronting orthodox big bands. *Capitol Blues* from his 1926 date has him playing capably in a style that seems to owe something to King Oliver. Most of the performance consists of solos by Luther, Blue, Lovingood and himself in that order, and a loose ensemble close. One gets the impression that Jackson was much clearer on the direction of his music than Creath appeared to be on his records, but the few titles he made can give only an inkling of how he played during the 'thirties and 'forties, and even less on the style and repertoire of his later big bands.

Considering his great reputation as a performer and trainer of musicians one has to assume that Fate Marable's only recording—*Frankie and Johnny/Pianoflage*—made in 1924, cannot possibly be representative.

Marable was of the same generation as Creath. Born in Paducah, Kentucky, on 2nd December 1890, he began playing in 1907 on the famous Streckfus Line riverboats, initially as a duo with violinist Emil Flindt and later with Tony Catalano (trumpet) and Rex Jessup (drums) added. In 1910 he replaced his three companions with Alie Ferguson (cornet), Red Robinson (violin) and Max Goempler (drums), all of whom were white. It is interesting to note that for the first ten years of his working on the riverboats Marable always led a group in which he was the only black musician, finally forming an all coloured band in 1918. This band's personnel consisted of Percy Suggs (cornet), William Moore (trombone), Eugene Derrick (clarinet), himself (piano), John Williams (drums) —John Robichaux (violin) joined shortly afterwards.

Marable's role in jazz history is a curious one, for apart from a few months in 1921-22 he spent the whole period from 1907 to 1940 working for the Streckfus brothers on their riverboats. In the book 'Hear Me Talkin' To Ya', Zutty Singleton is quoted as follows : 'There was a saying in New Orleans. When some musician would

Below left: The 14th Regiment Band, St Louis; sitting in front are Major McElroy and director P. B. Lankford. Fifth from left in the middle row is Leonard 'Ham' Davis. Andrew Webb, Wilson Robinson and R. Q. Dickerson are second, third and fourth from left in the front row, and Jerome 'Don' Pasquall third from right. Below: Fate Marable's band on the SS Capitol, early 1920s, Warren 'Baby' Dodds is on the extreme right; the cornet player is Louis Armstrong.

get a job on the riverboats with Marable, they'd say, "Well, you're going to the conservatory." That's because Fate was such a fine musician and the men who worked with him had to be really good.'

Dewey Jackson once claimed that one or more of the Streckfus brothers hired the musicians, then appointed the person they considered to be the most likely to succeed as leader; but it seems that Marable had more freedom than this. The late Henry 'Red' Allen worked with Marable before joining the Luis Russell band in New York, and while his story on this period suggests that the Streckfus family kept a close watch on what was going on—including levying of fifty dollars on each musician as a guarantee of their good behaviour—he obviously believed that Marable controlled the musical side of the business. Allen, incidentally, paid tribute to both Jackson and Creath when he told me that at one time, 'Creath, Jackson and Marable were all in the same band together, but as they were all leaders in their own right there was some tension going on. I remember once hearing them in a cabaret and when Dewey—a great blues player—ran over his horn to warm it up the people would start screaming. Then Charlie Creath would hit just one note and draw attention—his tone was so big and wide that he would pull everything together—and I thought that both were great trumpeters.'

My own belief is that Marable, by all accounts a somewhat lazy man, who turned down offers to work in Chicago and New York, was an outstanding band organiser and teacher, with an obvious flair for selecting talent. During the ten years from 1918 to 1928 the list of musicians who worked with him include many of the greatest names of the period, New Orleans stars being predominant in the early 'twenties. Amongst his most famous sidemen at this time are Henry 'Red' Allen, Louis Armstrong, Peter Bocage, Sidney Desvigne, Dewey Jackson and Manuel Perez (trumpet), Frankie Dusen, Bill Ridgeley (trombone), Johnny Dodds (clarinet), Sam Dutrey, Jerome Don Pasquall, Boyd Atkins, William Thornton Blue (reeds), Johnny St Cyr (banjo, guitar), George 'Pops' Foster (string bass), Warren 'Baby' Dodds and Zutty Singleton (drums). Armstrong first played excursion trips with Marable in the winter of 1918; then from May 1919 until September 1921 he worked regularly with him on the boats and ashore, and in the process was taught to read music by the band's mellophone player, Davey Jones.

Marable's late 1923 and early 1924 personnel of Sidney Desvigne, Amos White (trumpet), Harvey Lankford, Nat Storey (trombone), 'Paducah' Bradley (french-horn), Norman Mason, Bert Bailey, Walter Thomas (reeds), himself, Burroughs Lovingood (piano), Willie Foster (guitar), Henry Kimball (bass) and Zutty Singleton (drums) was a large one for the period, and a very similar group, with Storey and Bradley absent, and Narvin Kimball replacing Foster, recorded the only two titles Marable ever made.

From the middle 'twenties, Marable led comparatively big bands—his 1926 group was virtually Charlie Creath's regular orchestra. One can reasonably assume

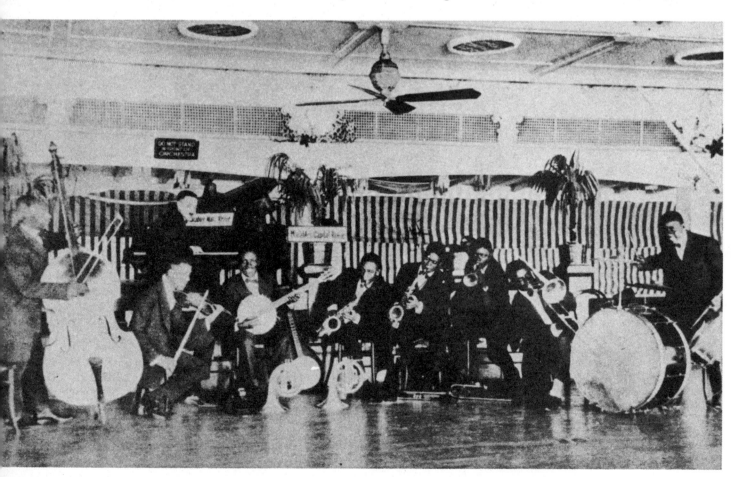

that most of his early bands were musically strongly influenced by the contingent of New Orleans and St Louis performers. Their style was what would now be considered as 'traditional'. By the closing years of the 'twenties a later generation of musicians began to work with Marable, including for a short while trumpeter Harold Baker. From the early years of the 'thirties it is likely that Marable's bands reflected current trends in the big band field, and his instrumentation became the orthodox one for the period. It is interesting to note that in the personnels that are given for four of his 'thirties bands in the following paragraph, a number of musicians are included who went on to play with name units.

A. G. Godley, a very fine if little known drummer who worked for some while with Alphonso Trent, joined Marable in 1931 and gave the line-up at this time as Walter 'Crack' Stanley, William 'Sleepy' Tomlin (trumpet), Earl Austin (trombone), Earl Carruthers, Joe Neviles, Horace Millinder (reeds), Fate Marable (piano), Bob Bell (guitar), Vernon King (string bass) and himself (drums). In passing, it is worth mentioning that Godley, whose death in Seattle, Washington, in February 1973 passed almost unnoticed, has repeatedly been referred to by Jo Jones as one of the greatest of all big band drummers. Alto saxophonist Don Stovall was a member of Marable's band from 1933 to 1935 and gave a line-up for this period of James Beard, Clifford King (trumpet), Leon King (trombone), Harold Estes (replaced by Tab Smith), himself (alto saxophone), Harold Arnold (replaced by Kimbal Dial) (tenor saxophone), Fate Marable (piano), John Young (replaced by Bob Bell) (guitar), Vernon King (replaced by . . . Barlow) (string bass), George Spotts (replaced by Wilbur Kirk) (drums), and Charles Creath (trumpet, accordion). This would have been the period when Marable and Creath were co-leaders. A photograph of the band that was taken in 1938 shows Walter 'Crack' Stanley, Benny Starks, Syke Smith (trumpet), Druie Bess (trombone), Leon 'Foots' Goodson, Tommy Stark (alto saxophone, clarinet), Elbert Claybrooks, Kimbal Dial (tenor saxophone, clarinet), Fate Marable (piano), John Young (guitar), William Moore (string bass) and Lester Nichols (drums), while another photograph a year later shows Stanley, Goodson, Tommy Starks, Claybrooks, Marable and Young still present with new men in Bob Carter (trombone), Jimmy Blanton (string bass), Robert Ross (drums) and two unidentified musicians, presumably a trumpeter and saxophonist.

Marable left the riverboats for the last time in the summer of 1940, having temporarily to retire from playing because of a poisoned finger. In the last few years of his life he performed as a soloist in several St Louis clubs. He died there on 16th January 1947 of pneumonia.

Towards the end of his life he started to write his musical autobiography on the prompting of jazz enthusiast Wilma Dobie, but was unfortunately dead before he completed more than a small fragment of it.

The musicians who have spoken highly of Marable are too many for one to be able to dismiss their opinions as mere nostalgia. By all accounts some of his bands were considered the equal of any contemporary units, and one has a special regret that he was so ill served by his only recording. Historically it would be fascinating to have recordings of the band in which Louis Armstrong played, while those of the late 'twenties and 'thirties have been spoken of with sufficient respect by musicians to make it certain that had they recorded they would have revealed Marable in a much more favourable light than his 1924 efforts. Judging musicians on recorded evidence alone, though in many instances unavoidable, has obvious drawbacks. To do so in Marable's case would lead to his dismissal as a very minor figure indeed, an evaluation which his contemporaries would consider totally unjust.

By the late 'twenties trumpeter Oliver Cobb had become one of the most popular musicians in St Louis. He recorded with his Rhythm Kings in summer 1929, leading Freddie Martin, Walter Martin (alto saxophone, clarinet), Ernest 'Chick' Franklin (tenor saxophone), Eddie Johnson (piano), Benny Jackson (banjo), Singleton Palmer (tuba) and Lester Nichols (drums). The titles made were *Hot Stuff* and *The Duck's Yas Yas Yas,* the latter a popular risqué song written by the blues pianist James 'Stump' Johnson. On both numbers Cobb takes rhythmic scat vocals, and solos with a broad tone and fluent technique that reveals the influence of Louis Armstrong. There are other pleasant solos from Jackson, Freddie Martin (on clarinet) and Franklin, the latter playing better on *The Duck's* than *Hot Stuff.* Cobb recorded a cornet solo the following year that was issued as two sides of a 78rpm record. In 1931 he was drowned.

Eddie Johnson became the leader of the band, which was now billed as Eddie Johnson's Crackerjacks, and the Chicago Defender of 6th March 1932 reported that it had 'just returned from Atlanta where they recorded 10 hits for a well-known company.' It added that the band's manager was Jesse J. Johnson of St Louis, an influential figure in the popular musical life of that city. The 'well-known company' was in fact Victor, but only two titles—*The Duck's Yas Yas Yas* and *Good Old Bosom Bread*—have ever been released. The saxes and rhythm were the same as before, but Johnson had brought in Harold Baker, James Talphy (trumpet) and Winfield Baker (trombone). Baker took an excellent solo on *The Duck's.* Late in 1932 the Chicago Defender referred to the band's performance at the Pythian Temple, Pittsburgh, on 26th December, with a return engagement set for New Year's night. The report mentioned Ed Smith (sax, arranger), who is almost certainly Tab Smith. A week later the same newspaper printed a personnel of the band, then in Columbus, Ohio, as part of a tour, naming the musicians as James Telphy, Clifford King, Leroy

McCoy (trumpet), Robert 'Buster' Scott (trombone), Don Stovall, Tab Smith (alto saxophone), Harold Arnold (tenor saxophone), Eddie Johnson (piano), Benny Jackson (banjo, vocal), Singleton Palmer (bass), Lester Nichols (drums) and James Reeve (entertainer). In its 11th February 1933 edition the Defender reported that the tour would extend to Suffolk, Virginia.

In 1933 Fats Waller broadcast with Eddie Johnson's Crackerjacks over Station WLW Cincinnati, then engaged the band for dance dates in Ohio, Kentucky and Indiana. At the time the band included Milton Fletcher, Harry Edison (trumpet), Scott, Smith, Stovall and Nicholls. Don Stovall gave Bertrand Demeusy a personnel for the 1933 period when the band was engaged on extensive one nighters throughout the USA, the only differences from the Defender listing being that he did not mention Reeves and gave Kimbal 'Cabbage' Dial (tenor saxophone, clarinet) for Arnold. In 1934 Harold Baker (trumpet), Floyd Smith (guitar) and Kermit Hayes (string bass, tuba) were members of the band, but in this year a number of musicians dropped by Eddie Johnson formed a new group which played as Winfield Baker's Crackerjacks. This band consisted of Harold Baker, Irwin Woods, Joe Anderson (trumpet), Winfield Baker (trombone, leader), Walter Martin, Freddie Martin (alto saxophone, clarinet), Ernest 'Chick' Franklin (tenor saxophone), William 'Chick' Finney (piano), William 'Bede' Baskerville (guitar, arranger), Kermit Hayes (string bass, tuba), Nick Haywood (drums), Austin Wright (vocal). A year later Finney took the band over, and until it finally broke up in 1938 it played as The Original St Louis Crackerjacks.

Frank Driggs has reported that Eddie Johnson instituted band battles with visiting groups, relying heavily on the ability of Harold Baker as a soloist and the strength of the brass section. Generally he came out on top. He also discovered from talking to musicians that the Crackerjacks used to copy the styles of other bands off records, going on first on the night of the band battle and playing in their opponents' individual manner so that when the latter took the stand they appeared to be copyists! By this ploy the Crackerjacks won many battles over musically superior bands.

The final Crackerjacks group recorded eight titles for Decca in 1936, with a brass section of Elmer King, Levi Madison, George Smith (trumpet) and Robert 'Buster' Scott (trombone). The sax and rhythm section remained unchanged from the time when Winfield Baker was leader. *Echo in the Dark* is an attractive performance, featuring two good trumpeters and Franklin in solos, and well drilled playing by the sax and trumpet sections. *Lonesome Moments*, like the more lachrymose *Blue Thinking of You*, has a period vocal by Austin Wright, but there is a good trumpet solo, rather in the Red Allen manner, and efficient contributions from Finney and Franklin. *Cracker-*

The Original St Louis Crackerjacks, 1936. Back row: Elmer Ming, Levi Madison (trumpet), Kermit Haynes (string bass), unidentified (drums), possibly George Smith (trumpet), Freddie Martin (clarinet, alto saxophone). Front row: William 'Bede' Baskerville (guitar), Walter Martin (sax, clarinet), Austin Wright (vocal), Chick Finney (piano, leader), Ernest Franklin (tenor saxophone).

jack Stomp is in much more extrovert vein and the band swings well. The impression received from these records is of a well-rehearsed, skilful band, with several good soloists and enough individuality to have merited a wider reputation.

In late 1933 James Jeter and Hayes Pillars formed the Jeter-Pillars band in St Louis, opening at the Club Plantation which was to be their location for close on a decade. The Chicago Defender for 17th November 1934 gave the personnel of the band as Lee Hilliard, Harry Edison, George Hudson (trumpet), Cardos Smith (trombone), James L. Jeter, Charles Pillars, Hayes Pillars (reeds), Warner Long (piano), Jimmy Miller (guitar), Walter Page (string bass) and Wilbur Kirk (drums). In the next year Lloyd 'Chubby' Wreath replaced Kirk, and for a short while Sid Catlett was in the band, with Kenny Clarke taking over at some point in 1936.

Floyd Smith gave Bertrand Demeusy a personnel for the 1936-38 period, listing Lee Hilliard, George Hudson, Harry Edison (trumpet), Cardos Smith, Gus Wilson (trombone), James Jeter (alto saxophone), Hayes Pillars (tenor saxophone), Charles Pillars (baritone saxophone), Warner Long (piano), himself (guitar), Vernon King (replaced by Jimmy Blanton) (string bass), Sid Catlett (drums). Blanton was certainly in the band for a short while late in 1937, but Edison left no later than the autumn of 1936 and Catlett is generally believed to have been present some time in 1935. One explanation could be that Mr Smith had more than one period with the band, then known as the Jeter-Pillars Club Plantation Orchestra.

The band's only recording session took place in August 1937. The personnel has been established as George Hudson, Ralph Porter, Walter Stanley (trumpet), Ike Covington, John Orange (trombone), the three saxes as before, Chester Lane (piano), Floyd Smith (guitar), Vernon King (string bass), Henry Ross (drums) and Ted Smith (vocal). Shortly after the session, tenor saxophonist Gene Porter was added and Blanton replaced King, to be replaced in turn by Billy Hadnott. At various times during the late 'thirties Arthur Reese (trombone), Sol Moore (alto and baritone saxophone), and vocalist Madeline Green were with the band. Madeline Green left to sing with Benny Goodman in summer 1939, according to a Down Beat report, though there is no evidence of her ever having done so.

The Club Plantation remained a permanent base for the band in the early years of the 'forties. Leon Comegys worked there with it for a few weeks in 1942 and gave the personnel as Bill Martin, Amos Woodruff, William 'Sleepy' Tomlin, Leroy Milligan (trumpet), Druie Bess, himself (trombone), Charles Pillars, Tommy Starks (alto saxophone), James Jeter, Hayes Pillars (tenor saxophone), Chester Lane (piano), Rene Hall (guitar), Bill Moore (string bass) and Henry Ross (drums). In common with most big bands of the war years the Jeter-Pillars

Orchestra had frequent personnel changes because of the call-up. The March 1944 Down Beat mentioned that former sidemen trumpeter Murriel Tarrant and trombonist Ray Torian had just joined the navy. At about this time drummer Art Blakey was in the band for a while, but left to join the Billy Eckstine band, probably in autumn 1944.

The final years of the band are slightly obscure. Down Beat of 1st February 1945 reported that it was resident at the Rhumboogie Club in Chicago on a bill which also included blues singer Gatemouth Moore. An issue of exactly five months later mentioned that bassist Carl Hogan had left the band to work with Louis Jordan, but apart from the Pillars brothers, Jeter, bassist Carl Pruitt and drummer 'Razz' Mitchell, it is uncertain who was present when it toured the Phillipines, Japan and various Pacific areas during late 1945 and 1946. It is likely that it broke up after returning from its overseas trip sometime in 1946.

The records that the Jeter-Pillars Orchestra made are very disappointing. *Make Believe* and *I'll Always Be In Love With You* have moments when the crispness of the section and ensemble work is quite impressive, but both have appalling falsetto vocals by Ted Smith, and the only worthwhile solos are from pianist Lane on *Make* and a trumpeter believed to be Walter Stanley on *I'll Always*. Hayes Pillars, who played so well on several Alphonso Trent titles, here seems content to present the melody without embellishment. The band broadcast quite frequently at one time and musicians who heard it have told me that on occasions it could play good jazz.

The last St Louis-based big band of any significance was that led by trumpeter George Hudson, who had worked with Dewey Jackson, Fate Marable and the Jeter-Pillars Orchestra before forming his own group. It made its debut early in 1942 at Tune Town in St Louis, sharing the stand with the Mills Brothers. At the time an issue of Down Beat mentioned that its personnel included Hudson, Walter Study (possibly a misprint for Stanley) (trumpet), Irvin Williams (tenor saxophone), Singleton Palmer (string bass), Earl Martin (drums), Jimmie Britton (vocal) and Glenn Bowden (arranger). All but Study, Britton and Bowden had been with Dewey Jackson's big band in the previous year. Music Dial of April 1944 reported that Jimmy Carnes was vocalist with the band, while Down Beat of 15th December 1944 mentioned that it shared a residency with the Louis Jordan combo at the Regal in Chicago.

Clark Terry was a sideman with Hudson from July 1945 until 1947. His list of the personnel during his stay was himself, Cyrus Stoner Sr, Basil Stoner, Edwin Batchman (trumpet), Fernando Hernandez, John Orange, Robert Horne (trombone), Cliff Batchman, Tommy Starks (alto saxophone), Kimbal Dial, Willie Parker (tenor saxophone), Bill Rollins (baritone saxophone), Robert Parker (piano), Singleton Palmer (string bass),

Earl Martin (drums), Jimmy Britton, Jimmy Cowans (vocal). At some point Alfred Guichard (alto saxophone, clarinet) replaced either Batchman or Starks, and around 1947-48 trumpeter John Hunt worked with the band.

During 1948 and 1949 Hudson took his band out on tour, fronting Sykes Smith, Tommy Turrentine, Paul Campbell, Edward Batchman (replaced by Cyrus Stoner Sr) (trumpet), William Seals, Bert Dabney, 'Rasputin' (trombone), Bill Atkins, Frank Dominguez (alto saxophone, clarinet), Cyrus Stoner Jr, Ernie Wilkins (tenor saxophone), Wallace Brodis (baritone saxophone), Ahmad Jamal (replaced by Robert Parker) (piano), Jimmy Royal (string bass) and Earl Martin (drums). On 7th February 1949 this group, with Parker on piano and Stoner on trumpet, recorded for the King label with vocals by Danny Knight. The third trombonist is listed as Robert Horne, and this may well be the man Tommy Turrentine could only recall by his nickname of 'Rasputin'. About three months later the band, with Hampton Reese (trombone) and Milton Whitten (sax) in place of Dabney and Cyrus Stoner Jr, was resident at the Riviera in Chicago, after which it went on to the W. C. Handy Theatre in Memphis as part of a southern tour.

Hudson kept a big band going at least during the opening years of the 'fifties. Trumpeter William Martin and trombonist Leon King were playing with him around this time. In later years Hudson continued to remain active in music, though fronting smaller groups, and it is believed that he still plays occasionally in St Louis. Unfortunately I have never been able to hear the four titles that he recorded for King, so am unable to comment on them.

Milwaukee was the home base for several leaders during the big band era, the first being Eli Rice. Rice was born in Lawrence, Kansas, on 12th April 1879 and spent his early years as a singer and dancer in road shows. In 1905 he settled in Oshkosh, Wisconsin, initially working in a variety of jobs before turning to singing with local groups throughout the state. After being with Walt Peterson's Orchestra from late 1921 until early 1925, he organised his own band for the Stecker Brothers who owned a number of ballrooms throughout Wisconsin and Michigan. At first Rice led a sextet, including at one time trombonist Preston Jackson, then during 1926 and 1927 enlarged to an octet that in the latter year had Ben Thigpen as its drummer. In 1928 his line-up was Ellis 'Stump' Whitlock, Shorty Mack, unknown (trumpet), Stanford Grier (trombone), Jimmy Dudley, Earl Keith, 'Hooks' (sax), Burroughs Lovingood (piano), Red Thomas (banjo), unknown (bass), unknown (drums).

In autumn 1928 Eddie Barefield was leading a group that played at a Stecker Brothers ballroom in Minaqua, Wisconsin, and when passing through, Rice heard it. Upon returning to Milwaukee he fired his own band and took it over. The personnel of Barefield's septet was Leroy 'Snake' White (trumpet), Finus Harris (trombone), himself (alto saxophone), Merl Williams (piano), Connie Landers (banjo), Charles Oden (bass) and Leon Lewis (drums), with the mysterious 'Hooks' being added by Rice on tenor saxophone. Eddie Barefield once told me that at this time he, like many contemporary coloured musicians, was greatly influenced by Frankie Trumbauer and that his band played various numbers that Trumbauer had recorded. By 1929 Rice had further enlarged the band, adding Johnny Wheeler and Shorty Mack on trumpet, and George Harris (replaced by Bernard Wright) on tenor saxophone, and replacing trombonist Harris and 'Hooks' with Carrol Jones and Silas McFarland.

Trumpeter Joe Thomas worked with Rice in 1930 and gives a personnel of himself, Johnny Wheeler (trumpet), Andrew Luper (trombone), Joe Moxley, Bernard Wright, Bert Bailey (reeds), Victoria Lane (piano), Connie Landers (banjo), Charles Oden (bass) and Sylvester Rice (drums). Sylvester Rice is Eli's son and is currently living in California. Eddie Barefield was in and out of the band during 1930 and 1931, first replacing Moxley and then being replaced himself by Boyd Atkins. In the latter year Eddie Tompkins (trumpet), Keg Johnson (trombone) and Sanford Beatty (banjo, guitar) replaced Wheeler, Luper and Landers.

With various changes Rice continued working with his band during 1932 and 1933, organising almost a brand new personnel early in the latter year. Paul Webster, soon to become well known as a member of the Jimmie Lunceford band, was with Rice in 1934 and gave a personnel of himself, Walter Bennett (trumpet), Jap Jones (trombone), Milus Walker, George Derricotte, Lem Johnson (reeds), Earl Fraser (piano), Leroy Dixon (string bass), Sylvester Rice (drums), Dick Rice, Edna Crump (vocal). The famous Claude 'Benno' Kennedy worked with Rice in 1936, as did trombonist Teddy Nixon and saxophonist Lem Johnson in 1937. From 1938 it appears that Rice gave up organising his own bands, instead fronting already existing groups. The last known was that of pianist Joe Broadfoot. When the USA entered World War II Rice disbanded and went into defence work. There is no record of his re-forming a band in the post-war years. He died in Minneapolis on 28th August 1951 at the age of 71.

Eddie Barefield has described Rice's as a very fine band, particularly when he returned to it in 1930 and the personnel included Eddie Tompkins, Keg Johnson and Shorty Mack. He referred to the latter as a cross between Louis Armstrong and Jabbo Smith stylistically, his nickname being derived from the fact that he was a dwarf. According to Barefield, Rice was of ample proportions— '. . . as big as Jimmy Rushing, but he was more muscular and he was tall'—and a powerful singer who could make himself heard above the band when it was playing at its loudest. Several musicians who heard the Rice band support Barefield's evaluation of it, and once again one can only regret that it never recorded.

Grant Moore formed his first band in 1926. The Chicago

Defender of 4th September reported that it was playing in Milwaukee and gave its personnel as Bill Lewis (cornet), Jack Rhodes (trombone), Grant Moore (clarinet, sax), Gerald Casey (sax), Eddie Davis (piano), Jack Jefferson (banjo), Jack Buerill (tuba) and Red Nelson (drums). The same newspaper in its 2nd July 1927 issue mentioned that the band was playing in Minneapolis with drummer Spencer 'Red' Nelson, and on 15th October reported that Lewis had left to return to New York. During 1929 and part of 1930 Eddie Barefield oscillated between Moore's and Eli Rice's bands, giving its personnel at this time as Leroy 'Snake' White, Shorty Mack, 'Story' (trumpet), Earl Keith, himself (alto saxophone), Willard Brown (tenor saxophone, clarinet), Norman Ebron (piano), Edgar Pillows (bass), unknown (drums). During 1930 this line-up was resident for a while in Sioux City, Iowa.

Trombonist Elmer Crumbley worked with Moore in 1930 and 1931 in Milwaukee, recalling the line-up as Robert Russell, Ellis 'Stumpy' Whitlock (trumpet), himself (trombone), Earl Keith, Willard Brown (alto saxophone), Lem Johnson (tenor saxophone), Norman Ebron (piano), Harold Robbins (banjo), Lawrence Williams (tuba) and Harold Floyd (drums). The band recorded two titles for the US Vocalion label in May 1931, and some confusion exists as to its exact personnel at this time. In an interview, trumpeter Bill Martin claims that he was present on the recordings with drummer Jo Jones, who certainly did work briefly with Moore during 1931. Lem Johnson says that he joined in November 1931 and that the personnel then was Robert Russell, Sylvester Friel (trumpet), Thomas 'Buddy' Howard (trombone), Earl Keith, himself (alto saxophone), Willard Brown (tenor and baritone saxophone, clarinet), and the rhythm section as previously listed. Johnson says that he replaced Moore, who from that point merely fronted the band, and adds that in 1932 he switched to tenor saxophone when Brown left but cannot remember who replaced him on alto. I suspect that Mr Crumbley has confused the period when he worked with Moore, and that it was somewhat later than the date he gives.

Moore's band, known as Grant Moore's and his Original New Orleans Black Devils, toured a circuit of ballrooms owned and operated by Tom Archer in Sioux City, Des Moines, Omaha, Oklahoma City, North and South Dakota, and also worked in Minnesota for the Stecker Brothers' circuit. In February 1933 Sylvester Rice left his father's band and joined Moore. Its personnel at that time was Robert Russell, George Lott, Gary Taylor (trumpet), Dick Heard (trombone), Earl Keith, Willard Brown (alto saxophone), Lem Johnson (tenor saxophone), Willie Lewis (replaced by Orvella Moore) (piano), Harold Robbins (guitar), Lawrence Williams (string bass), himself (drums). Rice left to rejoin his father's band in August. Soon afterwards Lem Johnson departed, though he did work briefly again with Moore during 1935. It is not certain when Moore finally gave up bandleading, but it was probably before the close of the 'thirties.

Moore's only record is not distinguished. *Mama Don' Allow* is a novelty number given over in the main to a band vocal, the only solos being by pianist Ebron and banjoist Robbins. *Original Dixieland One-step* is some what better and the reed section comes over well in ensemble passages, but the solos on tenor, trombone piano, trumpet and alto are brief and the individual musicians have little opportunity to shine. The closing ensemble passage has considerable drive, which suggest that the band was capable of better things.

Speed Webb's band was considered an outstanding unit during the 'thirties, and the fact that we know a great deal about it is due mainly to the US jazz follower and photographer Duncan Schiedt who, for a long period, conducted interviews with Webb and several of his sidemen that resulted in one of the best in-depth articles that have ever appeared on a territory band. What follows is almost solely based on Mr Schiedt's researches, with a few extra details that have come to light in the course of Walter C. Allen's researches into black newspapers.

Lawrence Arthur Webb—his nickname was derived from his prowess at baseball—was born in Peru Indiana, on 18th July 1906, and as a youth became proficient on a number of musical instruments. With a friend he played in a short-lived group during 1923, but then concentrated on his studies at the University of Illinois, though to eke out his means he led a small band which played local engagements. His family had decided that he was to become a mortician (undertaker) and he studied this subject by day, turning to music at night. He finally decided that he would spend a year or two in music prior to becoming a full-time mortician, and in summer 1925 joined a co-operative unit called the Hoosier Melody Lads. This band was resident throughout the summer at Forest Park, Toledo. Its personnel consisted of Nelson Douglas (trumpet), William Ernest McCormick (trombone), Harvey Scott, George White (alto saxophone) Herman Berry (piano), Cliff Levi (brass bass), Lester Smith (banjo) and Webb (drums). Within a short time Webb was elected its business manager and director, and during the Forest Park engagement the band built up a good book of arrangements, most of them the work of McCormick.

In the autumn the Hoosier Melody Lads were sent out by a booking agency to tour a number of Midwestern states. Though they usually met with success, they came to grief in Cleveland where they proved insufficiently skilled to play a show book at a local theatre which was featuring a revue with Ethel Waters as its star. Miss Waters left the management in no doubt about her opinion of the band and it was swiftly fired. With Parker Berry, Fitz Weston and Bob Robinson replacing McCormick, Herman Berry and Smith, and the addition of trumpeter Earl Thompson, tenor saxophonist Ernest Green and alto and baritone saxophonist Leonard Gay the band now numbered eleven in all and in April 192

The Hoosier Melody Lads, 1925; left to right: Cliff Levi, Ernest McCormick, Lester Smith, Speed Webb, Herman Berry, Nelson Douglas, Harvey Scott, George White.

it recorded four titles for the Gennett label that were never issued. Its presence at the Valley Inn, Toledo, was noted in the 21st April issue of Variety, and during their summer there the trumpet section was brought up to three with the addition of Theodore 'Wingy' Carpenter.

The owners of Forest Park, Toledo, had meanwhile purchased two Dancelands at Pico and Culver City in California, and at the close of the season sent the Hoosier Melody Lads straight to California to work these locations. Altogether the band remained in California for three years, undergoing a number of personnel changes in the process. In summer 1927 the team was Earl Thompson, Teddy Buckner (trumpet), John Thomas (trombone), Sherman Williams (alto saxophone), Leonard Davidson (tenor saxophone, clarinet), Fitz Weston (piano), Frank Watkins (banjo), Reggie Jones (bass) and Webb (drums). Billboard of 11th June 1927 reported that it was resident at one of the Dancelands, adding that the original ten-week engagement had been extended another six months and that the ten members of the band—one would guess that the personnel just quoted lacked one sax player—between them performed on twenty-one instruments.

With good location work and regular radio broadcasts over local stations the band prospered, and before long came to the attention of an MGM scout. Through this contact they appeared in at least seven films while in California, the most outstanding being a musical spectacular called On With The Show which, ironically, featured Ethel Waters in her film debut. Mr Webb told Duncan Schiedt that he had a vague recollection of recording while in California, but was unable to recall any details.

With the end of the California engagement in 1929 Webb conceived the ambitious idea of forming a new orchestra that would rival the great ones of the day, relying on his savings, business acumen and the publicity derived from appearances in films to carry him over the initial period. He discovered the nucleus of his new band at Fort Wayne, Indiana, where he took over a group led by his former sideman Leonard Gay. Curiously enough Teddy Wilson told me in 1958 that the actual leader was banjoist/guitarist William Warfield, but it seems that this was a lapse of memory. Adding to this nucleus Webb spent some time rehearsing the band in Peru, Indiana, and when it opened at Forest Park, Toledo, in the summer of 1929, it had the impressive line-up of Roy Eldridge, Reunald Jones, Steve Dunn (trumpet), Vic Dickenson, Gus Wilson (trombone), Leonard Gay (alto saxophone, clarinet, flute, oboe), Ben Richardson

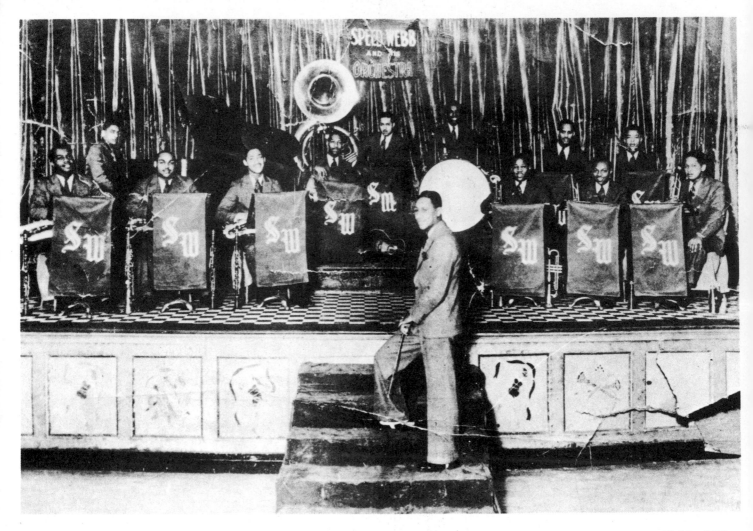

(alto saxophone, clarinet), Clarence 'Chuck' Wallace (tenor saxophone), Teddy Wilson (piano), William Warfield (banjo, guitar, occasional sax), Melvin Bowles (string bass, tuba) and Sam Scott (drums), with Webb himself fronting the band and taking the odd vocal. From October, Angelus Babe, a singer and dancer who had been featured in On With The Show, was added. Mr Schiedt quotes a handbill of the period which told of his 'flashing frenzy, mellow crooning joyousness, and tireless swift-footed ecstasy'.

This band was an immediate success, both musically and financially. Teddy Wilson told me that the group that formed the nucleus of the band was adept at playing Red Nichols's repertoire, and apparently this policy was maintained by Webb. Apart from this the musical policy of the band was shaped by the presence of several talented arrangers within its ranks, all of whom were able to display its great solo strength to advantage. The reputation of the band was enhanced when it engaged in musical battles with McKinney's Cotton Pickers, Jimmie Lunceford and Cab Calloway, reputedly emerging as winners in each instance. Mr Webb told Duncan Schiedt that the only band battle his group ever lost was, surprisingly, against Mal Hallett. When asked in later years if there was any band with which Webb's might be compared, Teddy Wilson replied that it would be the original Count Basie's band. Mr Wilson is not prone to making

Above: *Speed Webb and his band, 1929. Teddy Wilson (piano), Melvin Bowles (tuba), William Warfield (guitar), Samuel Scott (drums); Vic Dickenson, Gus Wilson (trombone); Chuck Wallace, Leonard Gay, Ben Richardson (saxes); Roy Eldridge, Reunald Jones, Steve Dunn (trumpet). Speed Webb is in front.* Right: *Speed Webb with Jack Jackson's Pullman Porters, 1934. Jack Jackson, Trim Cunningham, A. B. Townsend (saxes); Jimmy Hemphill, Earl 'Mouse' Melvin, unknown (trumpet); 'Pappy' (guitar), William Pate (string bass), unknown (drums), Henderson Chambers (trombone), Sylvester 'Wimpy' Harris (piano). Speed Webb is standing in the centre, and the bandboy is by the piano.*

statements in which judgment is clouded by nostalgia, and the fact that he could speak of the Webb band in such terms underlines just how good it was.

The trappings of the era show in a banner which had the band name lettered in mother-of-pearl buttons on black velvet, and in Webb's billing as the 'little giant of geniality'. Two recording dates were undertaken for the Okeh label, one in Cleveland and one in Chicago, but unfortunately the results were never issued. In its autumn tour the band finally reached New York, playing at the Arcadia Ballroom, and wherever it performed it drew enthusiastic audience reaction. At about this time it began to display posters reading 'We don't make records, we break 'em.' One band booker, Lee Rainey, reminiscing

with Mr Schiedt, said that the three hottest bands he ever heard were Fletcher Henderson's, Claude Hopkins's and Speed Webb's. In view of its popularity with public and bookers alike the question arises why the band never really achieved national prominence.

As far as one can gather the Webb band seldom played long in any major city, which is probably the key factor in its failure to attain the success it deserved. Virtually every band that became nationally known was fortunate enough to obtain an important location job in either Chicago or New York at some point or another, but such luck eluded Webb. Quite why this should have been so is hard to discover, but it certainly appears that the promotion of the band left something to be desired. Recordings with a major company could have partly made up for inadequate promtion, but here again Webb was unlucky in not having any of his records issued. In all probability Webb started just a little too late, for within a month or two of the formation of the band the depression struck the USA, one result being that record companies severely cut their output and were reluctant to take risks with new artists. By constantly being on the move, the Webb band would also have had little chance to broadcast, and a combination of circumstances prevented its gaining sufficient publicity to break through into the big time. It is ironic that with his considerably less impressive earlier band Webb had access to all the outlets that could

well have made him a national entertainment figure a few years later.

By summer 1930 a few changes had taken place in the personnel. Trombonist Eli Robinson came in temporarily to bring the trombone section up to three, and trumpeter Steve Dunn was replaced first by Syd Valentine and then by John Nesbitt. Billboard of 6th September 1930 reported that the band was playing at Walrose Park, Ambridge, near Pittsburgh. Here the personnel was different from that listed for its summer 1929 opening engagement in having Nesbitt—referred to as Ollie Nesbit—Buddy Johnson (tenor saxophone, clarinet, flute), and Joe Eldridge (alto saxophone, clarinet, oboe) replacing Dunn, Richardson and Wallace. Billboard, which three weeks later mentioned that the band had been booked into The Willows, Pittsburgh, refers to 'Speed Webb and his Brunswick Recording Orchestra', making one wonder if yet another recording session was made that remains unissued. In the next few months other changes of line-up took place. Chick Gordon (alto saxophone) was added and Wheeler Moran, an unknown trombonist, and bassist Joe Butler replaced Gus Wilson, Dickenson and Bowles respectively. For a brief period Sy Oliver played trumpet in the band. Early in 1931 the death knell of the band was sounded when Eldridge, Reunald Jones, Gay and Teddy Wilson all left together, and a few months later Webb disbanded.

In October 1931 Webb resumed working as a leader, with a new band called the Hollywod Blue Devils Orchestra, using Indianapolis as his base as the result of securing regular bookings there at the 'Showboat'. While the band lasted, its personnel was Eddie Washington, ... Stokes (replaced by Bill Miller) (trumpet), Fred Chandler (replaced by unknown) (trombone), Skippy White, Sam Barnett, Chick Gordon (alto saxophone, clarinet), Perry Swanson (tenor saxophone), Bobby Benson (piano), William Warfield (replaced by 'Cat' Glenn) (guitar), Bert Summers (replaced by Pete McFarland) (string bass), Sam Scott (replaced in turn by Bill Bundle and 'Fox' Eatherly) (drums) and Webb (director). Webb's name was still good enough to ensure regular bookings but the depression was now at its height and times were hard. On occasions the musicians only got a few cents for a night's work. Though outwardly prosperous, with excellent clothes and band uniforms, the musicians recall several dates on which what they earned was attached by creditors for services. Mr Webb told Duncan Schiedt of an occasion when the band was playing at the Renaissance Ballroom in Harlem when, after paying for dinner for the musicians, he had only seventeen cents left. In these circumstances the band only lasted for a few months and Webb started to hire existing groups to fulfil bookings.

Initially Webb fronted an Indianapolis band called the 'Brown Buddies', sometimes as co-leader with Jean Calloway, then took over Bernie Young's Dixie Rhythm Kings with which he opened the Cotton Club in Cincinnati. This band included Jimmy Mundy, and later, under the leadership of vocalist Clarence Carter, became popular in the Midwest. At one point Fats Waller teamed up with Webb and they fulfilled a few dates together. During 1933 and 1934 Webb fronted Jack Jackson's Pullman Porters, a group from Nashville, Tennessee, with a personnel of Jimmy Hemphill, Earl Melvin, unknown (trumpet), Henderson Chambers (trombone), Jack Jackson, Trim Cunningham, A. B. Townsend (saxes), Sylvester Harris (piano), 'Pappy' (guitar), William Pate (string bass) and an unknown drummer. This band went out on a tour of West Virginia, not an area beloved of musicians, and *en route* picked up Al Hibbler, who was later to become famous with Duke Ellington.

Subsequently Webb fronted a band led by Rupert Harris, the co-leader of the 1923 group which had marked his entry into music, and went on a disastrous southern tour. During winter 1937-38, he formed his last band, made up of musicians from the Cincinnati area, and then left music. For several decades now he has been a mortician in Indiana, part-owning a chain of funeral parlours, and has also gained prominence as a columnist, radio personality and political candidate. Musicians who worked in his 1929-30 band still insist it was the equal of any band then in existence, which makes it doubly regrettable that the records made have never become available and, presumably, the masters were long ago destroyed.

Leonard Gay has already been mentioned several times in connection with Speed Webb, and his name also occurs in the personnels of other Midwestern bands. From time to time he ceased to be a sideman and fronted his own groups, the first in 1929. Billboard, in its 7th September issue that year carried a story about Leonard Gay and his Chocolate Playboys who were then in the nineteenth week of a residency at Broadway Gardens, Madison, Wisconsin. It listed a personnel of Reunald Jones (trumpet), Vic Dickenson (trombone), Leonard Gay, Clarence 'Chuck' Wallace, J. Smith (sax), H. Selden (piano), William Warfield (banjo), P. Thompson (bass) and Sam Scott (drums). This was the group that formed the nucleus of Webb's most famous band, though neither Smith, Selden or Thompson worked with Webb.

Gay returned to bandleading in the late 'thirties. Down Beat reported that he was resident with his group at the Club Congo, Milwaukee, from July 1938 to October 1939, after which he went to the Cotton Club in Cincinnati. The final printed mention of Gay occurs in the 1st November 1945 issue of Down Beat and refers to his eight-piece group, including Lincoln Stokes (trombone, arranger), Bobby Burdette (tenor saxophone), Gene Bradshaw (alto saxophone), and himself (reeds). It is reasonable to assume that the line-up would be completed by a trumpeter, pianist, bassist and drummer. None of Gay's own bands ever recorded, but if still alive he should be a valuable source of information on the Midwestern bands of the 'twenties and 'thirties.

Omaha, Nebraska was the base for three well-known territory bands, the oldest being Red Perkins and his Dixie Ramblers. Frank Shelton 'Red' Perkins was born at Muchakinock, Iowa, on 26th December 1890, moving to Buxton, Iowa, with his family in 1900. As a youth he learned to play trumpet, piano and organ. In 1910 he joined a minstrel show that toured extensively throughout the States, and within two years became band master. By 1915 he had returned to the Midwest, where because of his marriage he worked in non-musical occupations until 1919, but then he worked as a duo with a pianist/vocalist and as a member of The Five Jazz Monarchs, with whom he went on tour. From 1920 to 1922 he was with a quartet at an Omaha cabaret spot, at the same time doubling with a brass band. He then formed his Melody Five. His Dixie Ramblers came into existence in 1923, and until 1925 he alternated between local engagements and tours of Nebraska, Iowa, etc. At the start the Dixie Ramblers was a sextet, but from 1925 to 1928 it became a septet, and after that an octet, billed from 1925 as Red Perkins and his Original Dixie Ramblers.

Perkins's personnel from 1930 to 1933 was constant, and the group which recorded four titles for the Gennett label in May 1931 consisted of Red Perkins (trumpet, alto, vocal), A. C. Oglesby (trombone), Jesse Simmons (alto saxophone, clarinet), Joe Drake (tenor saxophone, clarinet, trumpet, arranger), Howard Fields (piano),

…ed Perkins and his Original Dixie Ramblers, 1925; left to …ght: Joe Drake (saxes, trumpet, arranger), Harold Robbins …banjo, guitar, trumpet, cello), Tommy Roulett (saxes), Red …erkins (trumpet, sax), Earl Cason (piano, clarinet), Shirley …ennedy (drums).

…harles 'Goodie' Watkins (banjo, guitar), Eugene Freels …uba, trumpet), Harry Rooks (drums). During 1933-34 …erkins added trumpeters Louis Vann and Sylvester …reels, and alto saxophonist Clarence Gray to his line-up, …ernard Wright replacing Simmons, and from late that …ar spent months touring with a revue. At this time …bbo Smith was with him for a few months, and pianist …rnest 'Speck' Redd had replaced Fields.

From 1936 the Original Dixie Ramblers had an ortho-dox big band instrumentation of three trumpets, three trombones, four saxes and four rhythm. The 1936-37 line-up was Bill Osborne, Bob Hall, Sylvester Freels (trumpet), Sam Grevious, Louis Evans, Bob Cansler (trombone), Bernard Wright, Clarence Gray (alto saxophone), Leslie Cansler, Jim Alexander (tenor saxophone), Johnny Redd (piano), Frank Perkins Jr (g), Eugene Freels (string bass), Richard Hart (drums), Red Perkins (vocal, director). He continued to lead until the United States entered World War II. For his last group of 1940-41 the personnel was Joe Anderson, Albert Kerchival, Herb Wiggins (trumpet), Jay Green (trombone), Jim Alexander, Harrington Hamm (alto saxophone), Francis Whitby (tenor saxophone), Frank Perkins Jr (piano),

Willie Parr (string bass), Eugene Freels (drums), Red Perkins, Annie May Winburn (vocal).

For close on twenty years Perkins seems to have worked steadily throughout the Midwest, seldom, it seems, going further afield. Frank Driggs has reported that some of his success was due to the presentation of floor shows and various acts as part of his programme, but adds that his bands were generally good. In discussing Perkin with Jo Jones I learned that he was held in high esteem by many musicians. Jones commented on the extreme versatility of several of Perkins's sidemen. This is borne out by the extraordinary amount of doubling that they undertook, particularly in the early days. After leaving music Perkins worked in several fields, including photgraphy, and when last heard of was a TV service man in Minneapolis.

Hard Times Stomp and *Old Man Blues,* from the band's 1931 Gennett session, both impress through the fullness of sound that the eight-piece group achieves. All the solos are effective, those by trombonist Oglesby being the most forceful, and the cohesiveness and swing of the band is admirable. One gets an impression of a highly organised group, able to achieve considerable variety through the doubling ability of its members, and it is a pity that it only had the opportunity to record four titles during a lifetime of close on two decades. It is unlikely, though, that Perkins's band was the equal of the really top territory bands of his day.

Lloyd Hunter's Serenaders worked out of Omaha for more than twenty years, but only managed to get into the recording studio on one occasion, in April 1931. It is believed that the band was formed in 1923, and trombonist Elmer Crumbley has given its personnel for the 1923-26 period as Lloyd Hunter (trumpet), himself (trombone), Robert Welsh (C-melody and tenor saxophone), Burton Brewer (piano), Julius Alexander (banjo), and Amos Clayton (drums). Clayton was replaced during Crumbley's first period with the band by Holland Harold. Elmer Crumbley left Hunter for six months in the early part of 1926, returning six months later and remaining until 1929. During his absence George Crumbley (trumpet) had been added to the line-up, as had Wallace Wright (tuba), and George Madison (piano) had replaced Brewer. Later Reuben Floyd took over from George Crumbley, and when Elmer Crumbley left at the same

time as Harold they were replaced by Dan Minor and Dewitt 'Debo' Mills. In an account of his career told to Frank Driggs, Elmer Crumbley spoke enthusiastically of Brewer: 'Burton Brewer, the original pianist from Fairbury, Nebraska, was the end on piano. The first time we went to Chicago he moved Earl Hines right off the stool . . . and this was when Earl was the greatest thing in jazz. He went to Denver in 1929 and died of tuberculosis.'

Hunter's Serenaders made no great musical impact for several years. Commenting on the territory bands that he heard in early 1930 Tommy Douglas told Frank Driggs: 'Hunter's Serenaders, the Omaha Night Owls and Red Perkins were all around Lincoln, Nebraska then, but they sounded pretty much the same, because they were using stock arrangements.'

In 1931 Hunter's Serenaders got their big break when they were booked by the blues singer Victoria Spivey to back her on a nationwide tour. At the time Miss Spivey was married to Reuben Floyd, and this may have been the reason she chose the band. Having just made a successful film appearance in Hallelujah Miss Spivey was a top-line attraction, and by this time she had a string of best selling records behind her. She contracted the band to a well-known booking agency, helped buy it four sedan cars, and had every musician fitted with brand new uniforms. She was also responsible for getting it the opportunity to record. Recalling these days Miss Spivey wrote: 'We had the best Eastern and Western advance agents and they certainly paid off. We played from Canada back to the Dells in Wisconsin, most of Illinois, Iowa, and at least one quarter of Ohio. We went into upper New York State and down into Virginia. We didn't miss anything in Pennsylvania, either. We played the best dance pavilions and western and Ivy League colleges. We were sold out everywhere we went and many times we did return engagements. At times, we had as many as 3000 paid customers. Quite a haul! We lived in the best hotels, ate the best food, always had a good time on and off the job, and my musicians and I were well paid.'

This was undoubtedly the period of greatest success for Hunter's Serenaders, but around November 1931 the association with Victoria Spivey came to an end. She has said that it was due to a 'minor misunderstanding' with some of the musicians, not including Hunter himself, but Elmer Crumbley, who returned to the band in late 1931 and remained until September 1932, claims that it was due to an argument over booking agencies. Whatever the reason, it led to a period when Hunter's Serenaders fell on hard times. Crumbley left when it was stranded in Milwaukee.

The opening of the tour with Victoria Spivey was noted in the Chicago Defender of 31st January 1931, and it gave a personnel of Lloyd Hunter, George Lott, Ted Frank, Elmer Crumbley (brass), Noble Floyd, Harold Arnold, Archie Watts (sax), George Madison,

Above left: *Red Perkins's Original Dixie Ramblers, Omaha, 1938; left to right: Earl Cason, Cecil Brewton, Joe Drake, Red Perkins, Eugene Freels, Eddie Sanders and Harold Robbins.* Left: *the Harriet Calloway Revue, 1934-5 at the Orpheum Theater, Omaha. The band is Red Perkins's Dixie Ramblers; left to right: Bernard Wright (alto saxophone), Sylvester Freels (trumpet), Eddie Gray (alto saxophone), Jabbo Smith (trumpet), Joe Drake (tenor saxophone, arranger), Louis Vann (trumpet), Harry Rooks (drums), Red Perkins (leader), Charles Watkins (guitar), A. C. Oglesby (trombone), Eugene Freels (tuba), Ernest 'Speck' Red (piano).*

Walter Harrold, Robert Welch (rhythm), Henry Woode (accordion). There are a couple of surprises here, principally the fact that Crumbley was present and no banjoist/guitarist is mentioned. Ted Frank is almost certainly a trumpeter, while the correct spelling for the bass player and accordionist/arranger/pianist is Robert Welsh and Henri Woode respectively. Bertrand Demeusy tells me that Hunter's regular drummer at this time was J. Westbrook McPherson, but because of his youth he did not go on tour with the band. Some difficulty has always been experienced in discovering the exact personnel of the band on its recording date, but the Chicago Defender reported the session in an issue that went on sale eleven days later, listing Lloyd Hunter, Reuben Floyd, George Lott (trumpet), Joe Edwards (trombone), Horace 'Noble' Floyd, Archie Watts, Dick Lewis (sax), George Madison (piano), Herbert Hannah (banjo), Robert Welsh (bass) and Henri Woode (arranger). It is reasonable to accept this line-up, with the addition of an unidentified drummer, who is not likely to have been Jo Jones, though he did work with Hunter briefly—probably late in 1931. Elmer Crumbley has given a personnel for the post-Victoria Spivey period which differs from the last given in having George Crumbley himself, 'Pee Wee' (possibly a nickname for Lewis), Harold Arnold and Pete Woods in place of Floyd, Edwards, Watts, Lewis and the unknown drummer. (It may be that Woods was on the record.)

For the next five years Hunter's personnels are shrouded in obscurity, though drummer Gus Johnson told Bertrand Demeusy that he played bass with Hunter in 1935—'Debo' Mills was then the drummer and the bass chair was the only one vacant—and it is possible that some of the sax and rhythm men from earlier days remained with the band. A photograph taken in 1937 reveals almost an entirely new personnel of Lloyd Hunter, Willie Long, Richard Harrison (trumpet), Ray Byron (trombone), Leslie 'Jack' Holt, Holsey Dorsey (alto saxophone), Jimmy Bythwood (tenor saxophone), Sir Charles Thompson (piano), Dave Finney (guitar), Ed Hammonds (string bass), Dewitt 'Debo' Mills (drums) and Red Rivers (vocal). In summer 1939 tenor saxophonist Hal Singer, currently resident in France, was with Hunter, and pianist Lawrence Keyes was in the band during 1941 at the same time as drummer Johnny Otis. A photograph taken at Topeka, Kansas, in 1941 shows an incomplete personnel of Bob Merrill (trumpet), Rudy Morrison, Ray Byron (trombone), Jack Holt (alto saxophone), Jimmy Bythwood (tenor saxophone), Dave Finney (guitar), Mutt Reeves (string bass), Bobby Parker (drums) and Orvil Cox (vocal).

The last full personnel we have for Hunter's band appeared in the 15th January 1942 issue of Down Beat, and consists of Willie Long, Harold Wilkerson, Lloyd Hunter (trumpet), Ray Byron, Rudy Morrison (trombone), Preston Love, Jim Alexander, Jim Bythwood, Frank Perry (sax), Lawrence Keyes (piano), Dave Finney

(guitar), Willie Parr (string bass), Bob Parker (drums), Orvil (or Orville) Cox and Anna Mae Winburn (vocal). We know something of Hunter's activities at this time, mainly from the reminiscences of Preston Love, who had joined the band in June 1941, remained until April 1942, then returned in the following September and stayed until the summer of 1943. Love described the band as 'an excellent group with good arrangements, good soloists and good singers', but is realistic about Hunter's defects and the conditions the musicians had to cope with: 'Lloyd's bus was a 1933 Ford school bus and very inadequate for sixteen and seventeen adults and luggage, but we spent many carefree and happy moments travelling to the engagements although the conditions were most uncomfortable physically. In the winter we were very cold and we were always cramped, but the band almost always played inspired even in the middle of cornfields and in cow barns where many of the dance halls were located in the Midwest. Each man's incentive was always the hope of being discovered by a name band and escaping "small time" conditions.

'Lloyd was a beloved individual and it was felt that the only things that prevented his moving into a higher bracket were his carelessness about the appearance of the band and his own appearance, because great notice is always taken of a band's physical appearance, the appearance of their transportation and other equipment. Lloyd was never an urbane person in his dealings with agents and operators who hired the band, although they usually liked him, they never took him or his band seriously.'

Hunter continued to lead bands almost up to his death in 1961, working in Omaha and going out on regular tours. Towards the end of his career he was forced to cut the size of his bands and front small groups. He was considered an excellent lead trumpeter, but left most of the solo work to others. One can add nothing to Preston Love's analysis of the reasons for Hunter's failure to make the big time, though it is impossible not to feel sorry that nearly forty years of bandleading produced so little in the way of recognition or economic reward for such an amiable and kindly personality.

The two titles that the Hunter band recorded—*Sensational Mood* and *I'm Dreaming About You*—display the surging swing that seems a characteristic of Midwestern bands. Edwards solos well on both titles, as does one of the alto players on *Sensational*, but the finest individual contributions come from two trumpeters, one playing open and one with plunger, who must be Reuben

Left: *Alto saxophonist Preston Love and drummer Johnny Otis outside Lloyd Hunter's band bus c1941*. Right: *Nat Towles c1940*. Below: *the Nat Towles Band, Dreamland Ballroom, Omaha, 1937. Left to right: Buddy Tate (tenor saxophone), Siki Collins (alto and soprano saxophone), 'Sir' Charles Thompson (piano), Lemuel Tally (sax), Casey Smith (guitar), C. Q. Price (alto saxophone), Nat Williams (drums), Duke Groner (vocal), Tom Pratt (string bass), Nat Towles, Paul King (trumpet), Henry Coker, Archie Brown (trombone), Harold 'Money' Johnson, Walter Snead (trumpet).*

Floyd and George Lott, though I cannot specifically identify their solos. Miss Spivey takes a pleasant vocal on *I'm Dreaming*, after which the ensemble plays with considerable drive. If Hunter's later bands were as good as this, and there is fair evidence available that some at least were, big band jazz is the poorer for his not having recorded more.

After leaving Lloyd Hunter in April 1942 Preston Love joined Nat Towles. He described the move in the following terms: 'Towles had a better bus, paid a bit more money, played a few more, bigger towns, had a greater book [repertoire] and was generally a more glamorous band than Lloyd's, but all in all it was still the minor league and the "sticks".'

131

Love then went on to describe Towles's personality: 'Where Lloyd had been loved by his musicians, Nat never enjoyed much affection from his sidemen nor did he seek any from them. Where agents and operators were charitable but disrespectful in their relationship with Lloyd, they treated Nat with the utmost respect and admiration. Nat was a stickler for good appearance in his band, both for his personnel and equipment, and although Towles' sleeper bus was somewhat overcrowded and at times odorous inside, it made a very glamorous appearance externally.'

The Nat Towles band is considered by the musicians who played in it and by others who heard it one of the greatest of all territory groups, and Towles's failure to achieve national recognition seems mainly due to a curiously schizophrenic attitude on his own part when confronted with such a possibility.

Towles was born in New Orleans on 10th August 1905, the eldest of ten children, and both his mother and father were musicians who led a family band in their hometown that was quite well known during the 'thirties. Nat studied the violin from the age of nine, but shortly switched to string bass. His first professional job was with the Melody Jazz Band in 1922. In the following year he worked with Henry 'Red' Allen, but like most New Orleans musicians of his day moved from band to band depending on who had work available. Towles formed his Creole Harmony Kings in 1923 and until at least 1927 led this group in New Orleans and on tours of the southwest, on one occasion playing for three months in Yucatan, Mexico. This group was a sextet that usually included Herb Morand (trumpet), Bill Matthews (trombone) and Frank Pashley (banjo). Sometimes it was brought up to seven pieces by the addition of clarinettist Ernest 'Kid' Moliere. In a Down Beat interview that appeared in an issue dated 15th June 1944, Towles had some interesting comments on early New Orleans jazz as he recalled it: 'That story about two-beat drummers being all the rage in New Orleans is nothing but a myth. Why, Kid Faco and Zutty (Singleton) both played four-beat regularly! That Faco was some drummer, and Red Happy was even better, the greatest drummer in New Orleans! He played the show, Steppin' High, and then came back home to work with old Joe Robichaux. He was killed in an accident in 1925 or 1926. Tubas weren't so popular as some like to make out, either, though Foster could sure play one like mad. I never took it up.'

In 1929 Towles left New Orleans with a band known as the Seven Black Aces, led by banjoist Thomas Benton. After it broke up in 1930 his movements over the next four years are obscure. He appears to have gigged around New Orleans, Shreveport, Dallas and, once again, Mexico, but in 1934 he joined a band led by pianist Ethel Mays in Little Rock, Arkansas, where he remained for a year. During 1935 he organised a short-lived band in Dallas that included Joe Keyes (trumpet), Buster Smith (alto saxophone, clarinet) and Buddy Tate (tenor saxophone,

clarinet), and later that year he took over a college group in Marshall, Texas, as the nucleus of a big band. In 1936 he switched his centre of operations from Dallas to Omaha. The next few years saw him achieve considerable fame throughout the Midwest.

The personnels of Towles's bands are known. His first outstanding unit comprised Nat Bates, Harold 'Money' Johnson, Weldon Snead (trumpet), Archie Brown, Henry Coker (trombone), C. Q. Price (alto saxophone, clarinet), Leon Talley (alto and baritone saxophone), Buddy Tate (tenor saxophone, clarinet), Sir Charles Thompson (piano), himself (string bass), Little Nat Williams (drums) and Duke Groner (vocal). By 1937 Towles had given up playing to front the band, brining in Tom Pratt as his replacement; Paul King (trumpet) and Fred Beckett (trombone) had taken over from Bates and Coker. An interesting addition around this time was the alto and soprano saxophonist Siki Collins, a musician with an immense reputation amongst those who heard him, though he is poorly represented on record. There do not appear to have been any further changes until early 1939 when Tate left, to be replaced by Bob Dorsey; but in 1940 there was a shake-up of personnel when the band crystallised into Nat Bates, Harold 'Money' Johnson, Hal Wilkerson (trumpet), Monroe Reed, Leo Williams, Archie Brown (trombone), Lee Pope, Siki Collins, Francis Whitby, Leon Talley (reeds), Bill Searcy (piano), Bernie Cobb (guitar), Tom Pratt (string bass) and Nat Williams (drums), with a fourth trumpeter, Franklin Green, added in April.

During the whole of 1936 and 1937 the band was resident at Krug Park in Omaha, but after this it spent most of the time on gruelling tours of Dakota, Nebraska and the southwest, setting up a series of one-nighters that often lasted six months. This was the period in which the Towles band reached its musical peak, and Buddy Tate has no doubt that if it had had the breaks it must have become one of the top groups of the big band era. In the course of an interview on his musical career with Frank Driggs he spoke of the Towles band in the following terms: 'We had a hell of a good band, and when we came to town, we just took over, in the face of the established competition because we were so much better music-wise. They had as many as five big names going at that time, Red Perkins, Lloyd Hunter, The Night Owls and a couple of others. The Dreamland Ballroom, where all the names still play today, was the spot around there and we had it sewed up.

'Basie didn't have any organised band like ours then, and ours was definitely the better band. Andy Kirk called me when John Hammond was coming to Kansas City, because we were playing a dance in Trenton, Missouri. Nat and I drove to Kansas City and contacted John, and the only reason he couldn't come up to Omaha and hear our band was that he was just stopping over before going on to California for Benny Goodman's opening at the Palomar. Hammond wanted to hear some good jazz that night and he went to the Reno Club and signed Basie on the spot, and that was it. Nat had a lot more to offer, because he had five arrangers, and all of us were writing, and many times we had several different arrangements on tunes like *Marie*. We rehearsed every day when we weren't playing. Basie wouldn't have touched our band. We caught his broadcast when he opened the Grand Terrace, and we would have torn his band apart. We played all the best territory work and all the college proms. John Hammond picked up Ernie Fields's band out of Tulsa a couple of years later, and I'm telling you, there was no comparison. Sir Charles Thompson was in that band, Fred Beckett, Henry Coker, Archie Brown, who played like Trick Sam; C. Q. Price who was a terrific alto man and could write some wonderful things. N. R. Bates was really something on trumpet, he could play first too, and was compared to Buck [Clayton] in style. That was a band that really should have made it.'

In 1968 I had the opportunity of talking to Harold 'Money' Johnson about the Towles band, and to him I am indebted for clarifying many details which were previously obscure. I questioned him about Buddy Tate's seemingly over-enthusiastic evaluation of the band, but he expressed his agreement on most points. He stressed the fine arranging of Thompson, Snead and Price, and said Towles's band was definitely musically superior to Basie's. Upon my probing a little further it became clear that it was an exceptionally well drilled, precise band, and Mr Johnson made the significant point that all the arrangers were great admirers of the Lunceford band and attempted to capture some of its qualities. It could be that the roughness of the Basie band at this time grated on them, but against this one must balance Buddy Tate's known admiration for Basie, making it unlikely that his judgment would be biased. One very interesting fact that Mr Johnson mentioned was a recording session by the band in Omaha in either 1937 or 1938, the titles including *Please Be Kind,* on which he recalls taking an eight-bar solo, and a Sir Charles Thompson original called *Chaze* (my spelling may be incorrect). Harold Johnson was quite definite about the recording date as it was the first he ever made, and said that Towles had told him that the records were to be issued in Europe.

The constant series of one-nighters was not, Mr Johnson felt, entirely the result of Towles's failure to obtain national recognition, and he thought that Towles, obsessively fearful of losing his best musicians to name bandleaders, deliberately kept to the Midwest as much as possible to ensure this did not happen. That his fears were not entirely groundless was proved in autumn 1940, when Horace Henderson took over virtually the whole of his personnel, keeping only three musicians from his own band.

During the band's peak years the national musical press paid little attention to it. One of the only references I have seen was in the 31st August 1940 issue of Billboard where, in a listing compiled by ballroom operators throughout the USA, the manager of the King's Ballroom in Lincoln, Nebraska, lists Towles along with Vincent Lopez and Harlan Leonard as producing the 'Best Patronage Reaction'. Towles must have been discouraged at the end of 1940 by the loss of his best musicians, but he started to rebuild, and as a number of former sidemen returned once more led an outstanding unit. In early 1942 his personnel was Hal Wilkerson, Harold 'Money' Johnson, Joe Sullivan (trumpet), Heywood Walker, Rudy Morrison (trombone), Siki Collins (alto and soprano saxophone, clarinet), Bill Douglas (alto saxophone, clarinet), Lee Pope, Buddy Canway (tenor saxophone, clarinet), Leon Talley (baritone saxophone), Edgar Brown (piano), Elbert Smith (string bass) and the faithful Nat Williams (drums). Though there were numerous changes in the line-up in the next year or two, Towles retained his popularity throughout the war period, apparently sufficiently overcoming his aversion to appearing in major centres to undertake a lengthy engagement in 1943 at the Rhumboogie Club in Chicago, followed by an appearance at the Apollo Theatre in New York.

Around 1942 tenor saxophonist Hal Singer joined the band after spells with Ernie Fields and Lloyd Hunter, and it was he who told me that Neal Hefti wrote arrangements for the band while he was still at high school. Mr Hefti confirmed this but could remember no details, though Harold Johnson recalled that Hefti's first scores for the band were *Swingin' On Lennox Avenue* and *More Than You Know,* adding that his most popular arrangement was a version of *Anchors Aweigh.* Mr Singer was impressed with the playing of Harold Johnson, Rudy Morrison, Bill Douglas and Preston Love, but also mentioned the many fine arrangers in the band. Interestingly enough, Preston Love, who played with both Towles and Basie, rates the former's book as the most difficult to play.

In the Down Beat interview from which I have already quoted, Towles told John Lucas that he was then being booked by Joe Glaser after a long spell with the William Morris office, and added '. . . and I'm recording for Decca'. It was generally believed for some years that the Towles band did record for Decca, and details of some of the titles were even listed, but whether a session actually took place is uncertain. During 1944 Towles was touring with Marva (Mrs Joe) Louis, fronting Artis Paul, Milton Thomas, Alvin Sheppard (trumpet), Alfred Cobbs, Warren Scott, Abe Meeks (trombone), Preston Love, Jeff Meare, Albert Martin, James Streeter (reeds), Sir Charles Thompson (piano), Curtis Counce (string bass) and Nat Williams (drums). For a brief period in 1945 Walter Page worked with Towles, but by now the personnel was constantly changing, though the popularity of the band in the Midwest survived through the early post-war years.

Towles's line-up of 1946-47 had only Nat Williams left from the band of two years previously. It consisted of Billy Brooks, George Tyron, Russell Emory, Harold Bruce (trumpet), Danny Kelly, Felix Leach, another (trombone), Clarence Johnson, Albert McLean (alto saxophone), George Williams, Claude Miller (tenor saxophone), Richard Keith (baritone saxophone), 'Pres' (possibly Roosevelt Lovett) (piano), Albert Winston (string bass) and Nat Williams (drums). The big band he led (probably his last) during 1950 included Emory, Bruce and Williams from the above personnel, trombonist George 'Buster' Cooper and saxophonists Oliver Nelson and Noble Watts. After this Towles was forced to front smaller groups and, in the early 'fifties, added another territory band veteran, Terence Holder, to his line-up. He finally gave up leading in 1959 and it is said that Nat Williams assumed his role with those musicians who remained active. Towles moved to California where he ran his own bar. He had a heart attack in January 1963 and died in Berkeley, California.

There are a number of other musicians who played with Towles at one time or another. He himself mentioned to the Swiss collector Kurt Mohr pianists Eddie Heywood Jr, Lloyd Glenn and Mike Lacey, bassist Lowell Pointer, saxophonists Billy Taylor and Freddy Greer, trumpeters Walter Dunkin, Leo Shepherd and Hosea Sapp, and trombonists Bertrand Adams and Joe McLewis. Unfortunately it is impossible at present to know exactly when they were with his band.

Although neither the results of the recording session made in Omaha or that for U.S. Decca, if it ever took place, have come to light (Buddy Tate recently informed me that he thought that Towles did a session for John Hammond while he was with the band), we do have some evidence of how the band must have sounded. This can be heard on the session that Horace Henderson made with four-fifths of the Towles personnel, and the titles are discussed in Chapter 8. After hearing them one needs no persuasion to accept the reports of just how fine a band Towles led at this time. It is sad that his fear of having musicians stolen prevented him from making a more determined effort to be heard in major cities such as Chicago and New York in the early years of the band, for when he did finally play them it was too late. Given reasonable good luck and the support of a major agency Towles's band should have become one of the leading groups of its day, for if the 'Horace Henderson' performances are in any way representative this was a band superior to more than one that enjoyed national prominence. It may have been, economically speaking, what Preston Love has described as 'minor league', but musically it belonged with the majors.

The only regular band to make Denver, Colorado, its base was that led by violinist George Morrison. Morrison moved there when he was eighteen—he was born in Fayette, Missouri, in 1892—and after leaving university formed a string trio and then a band. Frank Driggs reports that Morrison had a very successful European tour with his band, and that in 1920 it recorded for U.S. Columbia. The session took place in New York on 2nd April 1920.

An issued title of *I Know Why* (introducing *My Cuban Dreams*) is of no jazz interest, though the unissued *Royal Garden Blues* might have been. Eleven days later the band did a test session for RCA Victor, where it again recorded the latter number, plus a popular song of the day titled *Jean*, but the results were not released.

Jimmie Lunceford is present on these recordings and worked with Morrison during the early 'twenties, as did Andy Kirk about 1925 and John Harrington in 1927. Apparently Morrison was very popular around his home area. Occasionally he organised a second band led by trumpeter Leo Davis. A 1930 photograph of the band shows Joseph Miller, Samuel Franklin (trumpet), Booker Christian (trombone), Gene Greenwald, Elliott Buie (or Boil) (alto saxophone), Quinton Pennington (tenor saxophone), Lester Grant (piano), Lloyd Scott (banjo), George Morrison (guitar, violin), Ferdinand Randall (tuba, string bass) and Eugene Montgomery (drums). Billboard in its issue of 10th May 1930 lists a very similar personnel, though Grant is left out and drummer Chandos Caldwell replaces Montgomery, while the September 1930 Orchestra World gives the last personnel plus Grant, but with Charles Waller replacing Buie and Montgomery now included as a vocalist. The Chicago Defender of 1st February carried a report that Morrison's band of eleven men had been hired to play at the funeral of Denver showman John R. Crabbe.

Apparently Morrison was active in music into the 'forties, but after 1930 his bands were not given a high rating. One would guess that he was a transitional jazz figure, occupying much the same position in his community as the more sedate uptown bandleaders who were his contemporaries in New Orleans At the time of writing Morrison is still alive in Denver.

Kansas City ranks with New Orleans, Chicago and New York as a famous jazz centre, for reasons that are briefly outlined in the introduction to the present chapter. Some of the greatest big bands in the history of jazz emanated from Kansas City, the most famous undoubtedly being Bennie Moten's. Whether in fact Moten's was musically the finest of the Kansas City bands, at least before 1931, is open to debate, but unlike all its contemporaries it recorded regularly, and as a result became accepted as *the* Kansas City band amongst collectors who until quite recently were unaware of the full history of jazz in the Midwest and southwest. Some consideration will be given to the musical development of Moten's band in a later discussion of some of its representative recordings.

Moten was born in Kansas City, Missouri, on 13th November 1894, and by 1906 was playing baritone horn in a local juvenile brass band. His mother was a pianist and in due course he started to specialise on this instrument, receiving tuition from two men who were admirers of the ragtime composer Scott Joplin. In his teens he worked with local bands and by 1918 was leading a trio at the Panama Club that became very popular locally.

The Bennie Moten Band, 1925; left to right: Willie McWashington, LaForest Dent, Vernon Page, Thamon Hayes, Lamar Wright, Bennie Moten, Harlan Leonard, Woodie Walder. Right: *the Bennie Moten Band, Kansas City, 1926; left to right: Thamon Hayes, Lamar Wright, Willie McWashington, George 'Banjo Joe' Tall, Bennie Moten, Harlan Leonard, Vernon Page, Woodie Walder, LaForest Dent.*

During the early 'twenties he led a quintet, gradually increasing the personnel as the decade wore on. Drummer Leroy Maxey worked with Moten around 1922, while trumpeter Sylvester Lewis has claimed that he was one of the original members of the Moten band, possibly around 1924. While dealing with musicians who claimed to have worked with Moten in the early years it is worth noting that in a Jazz Hot article Don Byas said that he started with him as a teenager, presumably around 1927. None of these three said that they had recorded with Moten, but in a 1945 interview with the late George Hoefer the alto saxophonist Chick Gordon asserted that he was present on a number of Victor recordings made before Count Basie joined the band, though his name has never been mentioned in this connection.

Moten recorded for the first time in September 1923 as part of a sextet consisting of Lammar Wright (trumpet), Thamon Hayes (trombone), Woodie Walder (clarinet, tenor saxophone), himself (piano), Sam 'Banjo Joe' Tall (banjo) and Willie Hall (drums), with Harry Cooper (trumpet) and Harlan Leonard (alto saxophone, clarinet) bringing the group up to eight pieces by its next recording just over a year later. LaForest Dent replaced Tall in 1925 and Vernon Page (tuba) and Willie McWashington (drums) replaced Cooper and Hall, though a year later Tall returned and Dent switched to alto and baritone saxophone.

By 1925 Moten had the leading band in Kansas City, and over the next two years built it up into a big band using the conventional instrumentation of the time. Its line-up in 1927 was Ed Lewis, Paul Webster (trumpet), Thamon Hayes (trombone, vocal), Harlan Leonard (alto and soprano saxophone, clarinet), LaForest Dent (replaced by Jack Washington) (alto and baritone saxophone, clarinet), Woodie Walder (clarinet, tenor saxophone), Bennie Moten (piano), Leroy Berry (banjo), Vernon Page (brass bass) and Willie McWashington (drums). With Booker Washington (trumpet) replacing Webster this was the band that went with Moten on its first eastern tour, on which it was resident for most of the time at a Buffalo ballroom. Upon its return to Kansas City, Ira 'Buster' Moten—Bennie's nephew—joined the band as front man, vocalist and accordionist, and 1929 saw such important additions as trombonist/guitarist Eddie Durham, trumpeter Oran 'Hot Lips' Page, pianist William 'Count' Basie, and vocalist Jimmy Rushing.

Moten had a stable personnel from 1929 to 1931. Two photographs taken at the Fairyland Park, Kansas City, and at a theatre in Philadelphia in 1931 show the same musicians as in the last list. With his first eastern tour a success and his Victor records selling well, Moten went east for a second time during the summer of 1929, remaining resident in Jamestown, N.Y., for nine months. A personnel listed in the Pittsburgh Courier of 9th May 1931, covering a period when the band was at the Hotel Bailey in Pittsburgh, does not mention 'Hot Lips' Page or McWashington but includes Lyman Wardner and John Birch. The latter is a Kansas City musician who normally played tuba and was possibly a temporary replacement for Vernon Page. Nothing is known about Wardner.

During his eastern tour in winter 1931 Moten bought a number of arrangements from Benny Carter and Horace Henderson, and around the end of the year replaced Booker Washington, Woodie Walder, Harlan Leonard and Vernon Page with Joe Keyes, Ben Webster, LaForest Dent and Walter Page. Eddie Barefield had already come in for Jack Washington, trombonist Dan Minor had replaced Hayes, and Ed Lewis was replaced in turn by Joe Smith and Dee Stewart. It is possible that trombonist George Hunt was briefly in the band prior to Minor, and Walter Page mentioned one 'Sax' Gill as being present during 1932. The changes improved the band musically, but the change in emphasis from the former two-beat

135

style to a straight four-four, coupled with its generally more 'modern' approach, displeased its public, leading to a disastrous defeat by the newly formed Thamon Hayes Kansas City Rockets at the annual Kansas City Musicians' Ball in May 1932. When the band set out on its eastern tour that year it was poorly received for the same reason, and it was in low spirits when it recorded its final session for Victor in December 1932. The personnel on this occasion was Joe Keyes, Dee Stewart, Oran 'Hot Lips' Page (trumpet), Eddie Durham (trombone, guitar, arranger), Dan Minor (trombone), Eddie Barefield (clarinet, alto saxophone), Jack Washington (alto and baritone saxophone), Ben Webster (tenor saxophone), Count Basie (piano), Leroy Berry (guitar), Walter Page (string bass), Willie McWashington (drums) and Jimmy Rushing (vocal), with Josephine Garrison and the Sterling Russell Trio added as vocalists for the recording session only. Ironically, despite the demoralisation of the band, the session produced the greatest records that Moten ever made.

After this the band just made it back to Kansas City. The Chicago Defender of 18th February 1933 reported that it was in Memphis and would open at the Champion Theatre in Birmingham, Alabama, the next day. It gave a personnel differing from that for the recording session of the previous December in that Earl Bostic and Herschal Evans had replaced Barefield and Webster, and E. Ewing had taken over from Berry. There is no doubt that 1933 and the early part of 1934 were poor years for Moten, though in the second half of 1933 Jap Jones (trombone), Lester Young, Buster Smith and Theodore Ross (sax) joined him from the now disbanded Original Blue Devils. For a short period in 1934 Moten brought in George E. Lee as co-leader, presumably relying on his popularity as an entertainer to help regain his following. Despite everything, his 1934 personnel of Joe Keyes, Oran 'Hot Lips' Page, Dee Stewart (trumpet), Dan Minor (trombone), Eddie Durham (trombone, guitar), Tommy Douglas, Jack Washington (alto and baritone saxophone, clarinet), Lester Young, Herschal Evans (tenor saxophone, clarinet), Count Basie (piano), Leroy Berry (guitar), Walter Page (string bass), Jo Jones (drums) and Jimmy Rushing (vocal) was impressive, but late in that year most of these men went with Basie to play at Little Rock, Arkansas. When the job folded the men drifted back to Kansas City and Moten re-formed, gaining from an upsurge of public favour and better bookings. When he secured a choice location job in Denver it seemed that he was on the way back, but he decided to remain behind in Kansas City temporarily for a minor tonsil operation. The surgeon who performed the operation severed his jugular vein and Moten died on 2nd April 1935.

For a while Buster Moten and Walter Page attempted to keep the band going, but in the summer of 1935 it finally disbanded.

Though by all accounts an astute business man, Moten was often generous in helping other bandleaders, sometimes providing them the opportunity to secure engagements that had initially been offered to him. With the exception of the 1932-34 period Moten's band enjoyed a popularity in Kansas City that no others could match, and for this reason it has become accepted over the years as the archetype of the Kansas City tradition.

From 1923 to 1925 Moten recorded for the Okeh label, producing a total of fourteen titles plus a few accompaniments to blues singers. It would be unrealistic to expect too much from the big band viewpoint at this early date, for this was a period when the foundations of big band jazz were only just being laid. *Vine Street Blues* and *Tulsa Blues* are good performances in their own right, the band playing with cohesion and relaxation, and the solos from Lammar Wright, Thamon Hayes and Harlan Leonard are generally well conceived. *Kater Street Rag* has a pleasant theme and features Moten's ragtime playing effectively. The records from this period are generally variable and the band shows stylistic influences ranging from ragtime to King Oliver's Creole Jazz Band. Walder in particular is a chameleon-like soloist, on one number—*Vine Street Blues,* for example—playing in a Dodds manner, on others—*Crawdad Blues, Elephant's Wobble*—indulging in a variety of hokum effects.

The band switched to recording for Victor in 1926, but that year's eight titles were as uneven as ever. Apart from a few ugly phrases from the saxes in the opening chorus, *Harmony Blues* is a charming performance, displaying adept scoring and several reasonable solos, notably from Wright. By contrast, the version of Jelly Roll Morton's *Midnight Mama* is stiff and uninteresting. The eight titles recorded in 1927 are similarly variable, but on *New Tulsa Blues* we catch a glimpse of a smoother rhythmic approach, though with *Ding Dong Blues* we are back to showbiz, with a humming duet backed by kazoo-like effects from Walder. 1928 saw the release of *South,* destined to be Moten's most popular single recording, and one is aware of a tightening up of the ensemble work and greater rhythmic mobility, though every so often florid banjo solos and hokum clarinet effects remind one that Moten was still some way behind the best of the contemporary big bands. A session of July 1929 produced a good version of *Terrific Stomp* with nice solos from trumpeter Ed Lewis and, more surprisingly, accordionist Buster Moten, yet *It Won't Be Long,* recorded the next day, reverts to a Dixieland-style ending that would have been considered old-fashioned by many big band leaders of the time.

In autumn 1929 Eddie Durham and Count Basie joined the band, and it is primarily due to the former's arrangements that the band takes a leap forward. 'Hot Lips' Page and Jimmy Rushing arrived soon afterwards, though Page was not featured much as a soloist until 1932. From the first session on which Durham is present he brings a more modern rhythmic approach. *Band Box*

The Bennie Moten Band, Kansas City, 1929: Count Basie and Bennie Moten are at the pianos with Jimmy Rushing between them.

Shuffle has an excellent guitar solo by him, but more importantly includes section patterns at the close which are new to the band. One still finds such incongruities as the stiff tenor theme with its *High Society* quote on *Rit-Dit-Ray,* contrasting oddly with the assured solos that follow from Ed Lewis and Basie, but by now the ensemble passages and solos are more at one and there is a drive engendered by the rhythm section that spurs the soloists along. By autumn 1930 the shape of things to come is clear, for the band was producing excellent overall performances such as *That Too, Do, New Moten Stomp* and *Somebody Stole My Gal.* Ed Lewis is in fine form on *That,* though one suspects that the 'preaching' trumpet near the close is by Page, and Rushing has a fine vocal with excellent backing from Durham. *Somebody Stole* has strong ensemble playing, particularly by the brass section, and Basie takes a scat vocal with answering phrases from Harlan Leonard's alto. *New Moten Stomp* underlines the new rhythmic vitality of the band, as does *Liza Lee* with its pleasant Rushing vocal and good solos from Lewis and Leonard, who can be heard at one point on soprano sax. It is worth noting that Leonard, who took virtually all the alto solos on Moten's records until 1931, has received little credit for his con-

tributions, though by comparison with most alto saxophone players of his era he was advanced.

Though from autumn 1929 Moten's records showed considerable progress in several respects, notably in the rhythmic sphere, if one judges them on the highest standards of their day they suggest that he was musically conservative at this time. This is excusable on several grounds, particularly when one considers the reaction of his audiences when he modernised his band in 1931, but it does raise the issue of whether he was in fact the spiritual heir of the Basie band as has so often been assumed. In an essay in the book 'Jazz', Hsio Wen Shih suggested that it was such bands as Walter Page's Blue Devils that really spawned the Basie band of the 'thirties. There is some truth in this. There can be little doubt that Page's band, on the evidence of a single recording, was a great deal more advanced than Moten's at the time, as were some of the other Midwestern bands that recorded prior to 1932. However, I think that the single figure who transformed the Moten band was Eddie Durham, whose arrangements and whole conception made the remarkable 1932 recordings possible. Durham, aided by Eddie Barefield, wrote nearly all the scores used on Moten's final session.

Toby, Moten's Swing, Lafayette and *Prince of Wales,* to name but four of the ten titles recorded on Moten's final December 1932 session, are now recognised classics of big band swing. It is not only that by this period

Bennie Moten's Band at the Pearl Theatre, Philadelphia, 1931; left to right: Count Basie, Jimmy Rushing, Oran 'Hot Lips' Page, Willie McWashington, Booker Washington, Ed Lewis, Leroy 'Buster' Berry, Thamon Hayes, Harland Leonard, Eddie Durham, Jack Washington, Vernon Page, Woodie Walder, Bennie Moten and Iris 'Bus' Moten.

Moten had a galaxy of major soloists—'Hot Lips' Page, Barefield, Durham, Ben Webster, Basie, etc.—but that they were provided with scores that set off their solos to the best possible advantage. The swing of the band is phenomenal, its ability to develop basic riffs astonishing, and it possessed soloists equal to the challenge of the scores. All these factors are remarkable enough, but above all there is Durham's injection of sophistication into the band's outlook. One does not wish to overstate the influence of a single figure, but to me it is inconceivable that this final set of recordings would have been so extraordinary if Durham had not been a member of the band. It may be argued that if such is the case why did he not achieve this transformation earlier, but he needed the spur of major soloists able to interpret his scores, and until Moten revamped his band they simply were not present in sufficient force. When Durham finally left Moten the latter requested him to leave him a batch of new arrangements, and Durham worked on this in his final weeks with the band. When he first heard the Basie band after it arrived in New York he recognised many of the arrangements as those he had written for Moten. Durham, of course, was drawing on traditions which had been developed by many musicians, both known and unknown, but without wishing to over-simplify the links between the Moten band and Basie's, it seems clear to me that Durham was the key figure involved.

Apart from Bennie Moten, George E. Lee was the first Kansas City based bandleader to build up a considerable reputation, though musically his bands could not compare with Moten's. He was born locally, on

28th April 1896, and at first played in a U.S. army band in 1917, concentrating on piano and baritone saxophone. Upon returning home he began to lead small groups, securing a lengthy residency at the Lyric Hall with a trio that was probably completed by his sister Julia as pianist and vocalist and Bruce Redd as drummer. A photograph of his band during 1924-25 shows Chester Clark (trumpet), Thurston 'Sox' Maupins, unknown (trombone), Clarence 'Tweedy' Taylor (clarinet, C-melody saxophone), Julia Lee (piano, vocal), himself (tuba, banjo, vocal) and Abe Price (drums). This instrumentation of one trumpet, two trombones, one sax and rhythm was unusual for the period.

Lee's peak period seems to have been from about 1927 to roughly 1932. Budd Johnson has supplied a personnel for his 1927 band, consisting of Sam Auderbach (sometimes given as Otterback) (trumpet), Thurston Maupins (trombone), Budd Johnson, George E. Lee (tenor saxophone, clarinet), Julia Lee (piano), Jim 'Daddy' Walker (guitar), Clinton Weaver (tuba) and Abe Price (drums), and in that year Lee recorded for the first time, with Clarence Taylor (alto and soprano saxophone), Jesse Stone (piano) and an unknown banjoist replacing Johnson, Julia Lee and Walker, though Julia Lee is present as a vocalist. The Kansas City Call of 27th

July 1928 gave the line-up of George E. Lee's Novelty Singing Orchestra at that time as Sam Auderbach, Robert Russell (trumpet, mellophone), Clarence Taylor, Herman Walder (reeds), George E. Lee (tenor saxophone, guitar, vocal), Julia Lee (piano, vocal), Charles Rousseau (banjo), Clint Weaver (sousaphone) and William D. Woods (drums), and when the band recorded again in 1929 Harold Knox (trumpet) and Budd Johnson (tenor saxophone) had replaced Russell and George E. Lee, and Jimmy Jones (trombone) and Jesse Stone (director) had been added. For much of this period Lee was working locally at the Reno Club.

At some point during 1929 Lee's band underwent a shake-up, with LaForest Dent, Herman Walder and Jesse Stone joining from Terrence Holder, though Dent did not stay long and was not present on the recording session just mentioned. Soon afterwards Elmer Crumbley and Baby Lovett replaced Jones and Wood, and the personnel settled down for a while to George Crumbley, Paul King (trumpet), Elmer Crumbley (trombone), Herman Walder, Tommy Douglas (alto saxophone, clarinet), Budd Johnson (tenor saxophone), George E. Lee (baritone and bass saxophone, ukelele), Julia Lee (piano, vocal), Jesse Stone (piano, accordion, director), Charles Rousseau (guitar), Clinton Weaver (tuba) and Baby Lovett (drums). This group was relatively unchanged until the winter of 1930, when Earl Thompson and Ben Smith replaced George Crumbley and Herman Walder, though a personnel of Earl Thompson, George Crumbley, Paul King (trumpet), Jimmy Jones (trombone, vocal), Tommy Douglas, Herman Walder (alto saxophone), Albert 'Budd' Johnson (tenor saxophone), Julia Lee (piano, vocal), Jesse Stone (accordion, director), Tom Tolbert (banjo), Clinton Weaver (brass bass), Baby Lovett (drums) and George E. Lee (manager, entertainer) listed in the Chicago Defender of 31st January 1931 suggests that George Crumbley and Walder stayed on a little longer than has generally been assumed. Lovett definitely left the band around February 1932 to join Thamon Hayes's Kansas City Rockets. At about the same time trombonist Ted Donnelly worked for a while with Lee.

During 1934, Lee briefly co-led with Bennie Moten, but generally his activities during the middle 'thirties are poorly documented and it may well be that he returned temporarily to leading smaller groups. In 1938 Lee's band was resident at the Brookside Club and a year later at the Reno Club. Down Beat for July 1938 reported that Professor Buster Smith had joined Lee after working at Lucille's Place in Kansas City. The same magazine mentioned that Lee was resident at Martin's in Kansas City from late 1938 to about the spring of 1939, and its July 1939 issue noted that the band had moved to Milton's Tap Room following sister Julia's departure for Chicago. Tommy Douglas has said that around 1938-39 he organised a band for Lee that played at Krug Park, Omaha, Nebraska, but I suspect that the date was a little earlier. Down Beat for 15th November 1939 carried

a news item that Lee's band was then playing gigs around town and 'having it tough'.

Lee was billed at one time as 'The Cab Calloway Of The Middle West' and was by all accounts a powerful singer, but he featured a type of novelty jazz that must have sounded dated by the end of the 'thirties. Early in the 'forties he left music altogether and moved to Detroit where he became manager of a bar during the 'fifties He died in 1959.

Down Home Syncopated Blues from Lee's 1927 recording session is mainly a vocal performance, with brief, rather mediocre solos, and *Merritt Stomp* is not much better, though Auderbach takes a reasonable solo and Jesse Stone is heard in a competent piano solo. The band on the 1929 session is a great improvement. Auderbach and Jones have efficient solos, but it clearly was no match for the better Midwestern bands of the day. Despite his musical background Lee was first and foremost an entertainer, and as such would be less likely to concentrate on building bands than Moten and other contemporaries

Jesse Stone, born at Atchison, Kansas, in 1901, went to school in St Joseph and Kansas City and formed his Blues Serenaders while in high school around 1920. He was a well-schooled musician and a fine arranger, and from 1920 to 1928, working out of Atchison, became very popular in Kansas and Missouri. His band, with a line-up of Albert Hinton, Slick Jackson (trumpet), Druie Bess (trombone), Jack Washington, Glenn Hughes (alto saxophone, clarinet), Elmer Burch (tenor saxophone), Jesse Stone (piano, arranger), Silas Cluke (banjo), Pete Hassel (tuba) and Max Wilkinson (drums), recorded four titles for the Okeh label in April 1927, two of which were never issued. During 1928 Budd Johnson (tenor saxophone, clarinet) and LaForest Dent (alto saxophone) replaced Burch and Washington.

The sequence of events from 1928 is confusing. Frank Driggs has reported that Stone lost a battle of music to Walter Page's Blue Devils in that year, after which he disbanded and moved to Texas to assist Terrence Holder in building a new group. Stone himself told Bertrand Demeusy that in the summer of 1928 his band was playing at Cristal City Park in Tulsa, Oklahoma, then moved on to a big hotel in Muskogee for three months, and finally to Dallas, where it broke up because the government closed down the place in which they were working. It is known that he was leading his Blue Moon Serenaders in and around Dallas, Texas, but its personnel at this point is uncertain. It appears that Stone did not join Holder immediately after breaking up his own band, but worked instead with George Dungee in Kansas City at the Edgewood Chicken Dinner Farm for almost a year. After this he did join Holder. It is certain that he was George E. Lee's arranger and musical director during part of 1930 and all of 1931, and he was co-director of Thamon Hayes's City Rockets from 1932 to 1934.

In 1934 Stone moved to Chicago and formed a new

band which he called Jesse Stone's Cyclones, working at the Morocco and other clubs until 1937. The Chicago Defender of 11th August 1934 reported that the Stone band was back at the Morocco Club, and that two new members of the personnel were Albert Wynn (trombone) and Antonio Maceo Cosey (alto saxophone, clarinet, violin), who had just returned from Europe. Jazz Tango for October of the same year mentioned that the band would soon leave for a trip to the east. Around 1935-36 its line-up was Jabbo Smith (trumpet), Albert Wynn (trombone), Budd Johnson (tenor saxophone, clarinet), Willie Randall (sax, arranger), Jesse Stone (piano, arranger), unknown (string bass) and Richard Barnett (drums).

In 1937 Stone made his debut with a big band at the Apollo Theatre in a show that co-starred Buck and Bubbles. A contemporary newspaper report remarked that it was 'one of the few coloured bands that is thoroughly rehearsed, possessing a large repertoire of novelty numbers for stage presentations'. The personnel was Bob Shoffner, Clarence Wheeler, George Wingfield (trumpet), David James, John Anderson, Alton 'Slim' Moore (trombone), Phil Tiller, Terry Smith, Dorlan Coleman (tenor saxophone), Bobby Holmes (alto saxophone, clarinet), Sonny White (piano), Leroy Harris (guitar), Olin Alderhold (string bass), William McIlvaine (drums) and Jesse Stone (accordion, arranger), and it recorded three titles for the Variety label—Stone claims more titles were made—of which two were issued.

From this point it appears that Stone organised various big bands for specific engagements and tours. His line-up at the West End Theatre in New York City around 1940 included Freddy Mitchell (tenor saxophone), George Duvivier (string bass) and Harold West (drums). He continued to lead bands of various sizes during the 'forties, at one point undertaking a USO overseas tour, but from the early 'fifties he worked mainly as an arranger and a-and-r man for record companies, switching his activities to the rhythm-and-blues field. One of his compositions, Idaho, has become a frequently played and recorded standard.

There are various gaps in the chronology of Stone's musical career. Ben Smith (alto saxophone, clarinet) worked with him during the 'twenties, as did Wingy Carpenter (trumpet) and Dave McRae (alto and baritone saxophone) during the mid 'thirties. In an interview, Budd Johnson gave a personnel which he thought was for 1926 of Eddie Tompkins, Terrence Holder, Hiram . . . (trumpet), Eddie Durham (trombone), Booker Pittman, Roger Boyd, LaForest Dent (alto saxophone, clarinet), himself (tenor saxophone), Jesse Stone (piano), and unknown (guitar, string bass and drums). The date is certainly too early, and this group is most likely the Holder band of 1929 which Stone helped to organise. The trumpeter Hiram is almost certainly Hiram Harding who later played with Don Albert.

The two issued titles from Stone's 1927 Okeh session are both outstanding. Starvation Blues and Boot to Boot —the latter based on Tiger Rag—have fine solos from trumpeters Hinton and Jackson and trombonist Bess, who were all much admired at the time, but equally impressive is the excellent scoring by Stone and the hard-hitting ensemble playing. It is said that Stone actually wrote the solos out, which makes the performances even more remarkable, but apart from this they are accepted as classics of their period and a tribute to the development of big band jazz in the Midwest. The 1937 Wind Storm and Snaky Feeling, though well played, tend towards novelty and are in no ways comparable.

Pianist Paul Banks, born in Kansas City before the turn of the century, started out as a drummer by playing in local brass bands, then worked as a duo with pianist Andy Miller at Emanon Hall. When he told his story to Frank Driggs in the late 'fifties he said that he switched to piano because of the clumsiness of his drum kit, but added that it was some years before he could read music. During World War I he went to Chicago with a road show and was impressed by bands like Erskine Tate's On his return to Kansas City he formed a six-piece group which he claims was only the second organised jazz unit to play there. Banks mentions Herbert Ashby (trumpet), Ira Jones (unknown instrument), his brother Clifton Banks (alto saxophone, clarinet), and James Everett (drums) as among the first musicians to play with him and a photograph taken around 1926 or 1927 shows all the above except for Jones, the line-up being completed by Robert Simpson (trombone), Alf Denny (alto and baritone saxophone), Miles Pruitt (banjo) and Jap Allen (sousaphone). During the summers of 1927-28 Tommy Douglas (alto saxophone) worked with Banks, and so did alto and baritone saxophonist Jack Washington at an unknown date.

Below: Paul Banks's Syncopating Orchestra, c1927; left to right: Robert Simpson, Jap Allen, James Everett, Herbert Ashby, Paul Banks, Miles Pruitt, Alf Denny, Clifton Banks Right: a publicity shot of Clarence Love from the 1940s

Banks played well paid location jobs at a number of Kansas City hotels. Ike Bell remembers: 'I started playing with him in 1926 and played steadily with him until 1930. We played mostly white jobs, like at the country club, so his bands have never gotten the publicity the other Kansas City bands had. The band played more on the commercial side than the other coloured bands, but we did a lot of breaks and improvised. We played tunes like *Mississippi Mud, Dinah, Sweet Sue* and *I Got Rhythm.*'

A photograph taken during Bell's stay shows a line-up similar to the last, but with alto saxophonist Richard Thompson and Ike Bell (banjo) replacing Denny and Pruitt. Bell also recalled that prior to Allen—shown in one photograph playing string bass—the bassist was one Cooper. At some time in the late 'twenties trumpeter Ed Lewis was with Banks.

Paul Banks's Rhythm Aces in Kansas City during May 1930 were Paul Webster, Alex Ashby (trumpet), J. C. Williams (trombone), Clifton Banks, Booker Pittman (alto saxophone, clarinet), Bill Saunders (tenor saxophone), himself (piano), unknown (banjo), Julius Banks (bass) and Baby Lovett (drums).

Banks continued to lead bands into the early 'forties, but they received little attention compared to those of other better known Kansas City leaders. One interesting fact that Banks told Frank Driggs was that he had the famous ragtime composer James Scott take down his numbers for him. Banks never recorded with any of his bands but can be heard accompanying the singers Lottie and Sylvester Kimbrough on sessions made during 1926 and 1929. He died in 1967.

For two decades Clarence Love fronted bands in the Midwest, several of which were highly rated by other musicians. He was born on 25th January 1908 in

141

Muskogee, Oklahoma, but moved with his parents to Kansas City four years later. He studied violin as a youth, later taking up the mellophone, and led his first band for dances at his high school from about 1925. Frank Driggs has reported that he secured his first real break through visiting a local booking agency and being given the opportunity to open at the Egyptian Club in Omaha, fronting Milton Fletcher (trumpet), Richard Thompson (alto saxophone, clarinet), himself (tenor saxophone), Charles Washington (piano), Leonard Murdoch (banjo), John Cooper (bass) and Martin McKay (drums). The bassist might well be the man mentioned by Ike Bell in connection with the Paul Banks band. After working at the club the band moved on to the Hotel Fontenelle and, with changes in personnel, a slightly larger group toured extensively until 1930, going as far afield as Canada and Oregon.

From 1930 Love worked a number of the better location jobs in Kansas City, invariably before white audiences. Lester Young and Count Basie worked with him briefly around 1932. Basie was fired because he was not a good enough reader. In the same year his personnel for much of the time was Clarence Trice, Cyrus Stoner (trumpet), Walter Monroe (trombone), William McCall, Ben Kyard (alto saxophone, clarinet), Clarence

Above: *Clarence Love's Band at Murphy's Egyptian Club, Omaha, Nebraska, 1928. Left to right: John Cooper (tuba), Leonard Murdoch (banjo), Charlie Washington (piano), Clarence Love (tenor saxophone), Richard Thompson (clarinet, alto saxophone), Martin Luther McKay (drums) and Milton Fletcher (trumpet).* Right: *the Clarence Love Band, Kansas City, 1933. Left to right: Emile Williams, Viola Anderson, Clarence Love, William McCall, Jim 'Daddy' Walker, Ben Kynard, Martin Luther McKay, Clarence Trice, Cyrus Stoner, Trevesant Sims, Walter Monroe and O. C. Wynn.*

Love (tenor saxophone), Emile Williams (piano), Jim 'Daddy' Walker (guitar), Tresevant Sims (brass bass), Martin Luther McKay (drums), Viola Anderson (vocal) and O. C. Wynne (vocal, director). The Chicago Defender of 25th February 1933 reported that the band was at the El Torreon Ballroom in Kansas City, giving the line-up as that listed above, except that Joe Smith (trumpet) and Tommy Douglas (alto saxophone) were added and no mention is made of Anderson or Wynne.

Love moved away from Kansas City late in 1933, settling down after a tour to work in Dallas. In 1934 Kenneth Rickman (trumpet), Joe McLewis (trombone) and Pete Woods (drums) replaced Smith, Monroe and McKay, and a year later pianist Eddie Heywood Jr came in for Williams. It was in 1935 that the ex-Claude Hopkins vocalist, Orlando Roberson, took over the band for an extensive tour. A 1935 photograph shows Clarence Trice, Cyrus Stoner, Kenneth Rickman (trumpet), Thomas Howard (trombone), Clarence Love (tenor saxophone, leader), Ben Kynard, Charles Bruton, William McCall (alto and baritone saxophone, clarinet), Eddie Heywood (piano), Jim 'Daddy' Walker (guitar), Trevesant Sims (bass), Pete Woods (drums), Orlando Roberson and O. C. Wynne (vocal). This band broke up at the end of the year, and Love picked up a new group in Tyler, Texas, that included trumpeter Artis Paul and saxophonist Jerry Bates. Over the next few years Love made Indianapolis his home base but toured widely in the south, at one point working a lengthy location job in Blair, North Carolina. The saxophonist Curby Alexander told Kurt Mohr that he worked with Love in Oklahoma around 1938-39 and added that most of the personnel at this time consisted of musicians from the Al Denny band. Pete Johnson (piano) and Bob Moore (piano, vocal) worked with Love at unspecified dates, but presumably earlier than this period. During the summer of 1939 Down Beat reported the band's presence at the curiously named Cafe Drug in Dallas.

The 15th February 1942 issue of Down Beat gives the personnel for Love's band at that time as Ralph Porter, Eldridge Morrison, Merrill Laswell (trumpet), Jay Jay Johnson (trombone), Clarence Love (sax, violin), Vincent Stewart, Richard Walker, William Stafford (sax), Harold Malone (piano), Jesse Starks (bass), Oliver Napier (drums) and Otis Johnson (vocal), and two months later

reported that it was touring the deep south fronted by ex-Andy Kirk vocalist Pha Terrell. Around this time tenor saxophonist Sam Dutrey worked with the band, and Waldron Joseph has given a personnel of Jack Willis (trumpet), Waldron Joseph, Clement Tervalone (trombone), Sam Dutrey (tenor saxophone, clarinet), Charles Sherrill (piano) and John Leffish (bass). He was unable to recall the remainder of the group. Frank Driggs has said that Love was deprived of the leadership of his band by an agent, so it may well be that a 1st July 1942 Down Beat story about a coming theatre tour by singer Helen Humes with his band dealt with a non-event. For the next year or two Love worked for a large booking agency in Indianapolis, controlling an all-female band called the Darlings Of Rhythm until early 1946. This band toured throughout Canada, Mexico and the USA before disbanding. Music Dial for November 1944 noted that it was then in California and during October would be resident at the Club Silver Slipper in San Diego.

Family matters led Love to return to Tulsa in the early months of 1946, and in 1947 he organised his last band, which was in existence for about a year. A photograph of this 1947 band includes Tommy Ross, Eddie Cooper (trumpet), Clarence Love, Ernest 'Sugar Man' Carter (alto saxophone), Chris Gillum (tenor saxophone), Bumps Love (piano), Arthur Bates (string bass), Duke Hyde (drums) and Joe Hammonds (vocal). For the next decade Love ran successful night clubs in Tulsa and later worked occasionally as a musician, but he was chiefly involved in non-musical occupations.

Love never recorded, though he was signed to a Decca

contract in 1934. Because the band only once reached New York, and then for a very brief period (never returning either there or to Chicago, where Decca did most of its recording), the contract was later cancelled.

John Williams was born in Memphis, Tennessee, on 13th April 1905, but was educated in Kansas City, where he worked with little known groups in his teens before joining Paul Banks in 1922. From 1923 to 1928 he led his own bands, the first a quintet which included trumpeter Shirley Clay and drummer Edward Temple. Soon after becoming a leader, Williams married pianist Mary Lou Burleigh and she worked with him for a year or two. His second band consisted of Henry McCord (trumpet), Sylvester Briscoe (trombone), himself (alto, soprano and baritone saxophone, clarinet), Mary Lou Williams (piano), Joe Williams (banjo) and Edward Temple (replaced by Abie Price) (drums). Two issues of the Chicago Defender in January 1926 mentioned that the Williams band was working in Kansas City, giving a line-up as above except that James White (trumpet) was in place of McCord and Carl Moody was added on sax.

Around 1926 the Williams band worked as part of Buzzin' Harris's 'Hits And Bits' show. At one point the personnel included trumpeter Doc Cheatham. The band later toured the Keith circuit as the accompanying unit for Seymour and Jeanette. Upon the former's death in November 1926 the band worked with Jeanette for a short while, then moved to Memphis where it worked at the Pink Rose Ballroom for the rest of 1927. Under the name of John Williams's Synco Jazzers it recorded for the Paramount label around April 1927. The Chicago Defender of 14th May reported this and listed a personnel of Henry McCord (trumpet), Bradley Bullett (trombone), John Williams (sax), Mary Lou Burley (= Mary Lou Williams) (piano), Joe Williams (banjo) and Robert Abie Price (drums). The band also recorded on four occasions for the Gennett label, but only two titles were released. A 1929 recording issued under Williams's name is in fact by the Andy Kirk band.

During 1928 Williams gave up bandleading and joined Terrence Holder in Oklahoma City. A year later he joined Andy Kirk when the latter took over the band and remained with him until 1939. After temporarily being out of music he worked with Cootie Williams's big band in 1942, but has been musically inactive for many years.

Of the four issued titles by the Williams band, *Now Cut Loose* is typical. It has reasonable alto and piano solos from John and Mary Lou Williams respectively, and, given the period, an assured trombone contribution by Bullett. The ensemble work is proficient. There is nothing particularly individual about the band, but it sounds a highly competent secondary unit.

When telling the story of his musical career to John Beaman, Jasper 'Jap' Allen began : 'I was probably very lucky, from a jazz point of view, to have been born when and where I was. The when was 1899; the where was Kansas City. Naturally, I did not know it at the time, but by playing right guard on the Lincoln High School football team I got to be good friends with the center, a big 200-pounder named Walter Page. Walter got me interested in music and although he had started out on trumpet, he was the number one sousaphone (that's what we called the tuba then) player in the school band. From his influence I also learned to play the sousaphone. Since my family had started me several years before on violin, I was able to read music and I picked it up quite fast.'

Allen did not intend to take up music professionally. After leaving high school he worked for the postal authorities in Kansas City. While in this job he played occasionally with a local group sponsored by the hod carriers' union, but noticing that several friends were making good money as musicians he decided to try his hand in this sphere, and at some time around 1927 he was offered a job as tuba player with Paul Banks. He recounts that he did not possess an instrument and was standing in a local ten cent store wondering how to raise the money when he saw $55.00 lying on the ground. Presumably, forsaking efforts to trace the original owner of the money, Allen made his way to an instrument shop and used it as a deposit on a tuba.

Ike Bell, talking about his own career to Tom Stoddard, mentioned that a number of the musicians in the Banks band became dissatisfied with its policy, feeling that it should operate more in the vein of Bennie Moten or Walter Page. Inspired by trombonist Jerome Brooks, pianist Henri Woode, and Bell, several musicians started rehearsing. They selected Jap Allen as leader because he was still working in the post office and could help the others buy needed items. (In his own story, Mr Allen does not mention this practical reason for his assuming leadership!) In due course the band began playing around Kansas City and started to attract attention. Ike Bell said its original line-up was Joe Keyes, Dee Stewart, himself (trumpet), Jerome Brooks (trombone), Booker Pittman, Alan Thomas (reeds), Henri Woode (piano) and Jap Allen (tuba, string bass), though one feels that it must also have had a drummer and possibly an extra reed man. After a while Allen approached Bennie Moten and asked him whether he could help in getting engagements for the band. Moten helped him to secure a long term contract at the Casa Loma Ballroom, Tulsa. Some confusion exists on location work at this point; Ike Bell claims that the band moved into the Crystal Springs Ballroom at Crystal City Park, just outside Tulsa, from 3rd July 1930 for the summer season. Bell himself left at the end of this engagement.

During the 1930-31 period the band varied between location work in Tulsa and touring schedules that embraced Oklahoma City, Kansas City, Sioux City and Sioux Falls, South Dakota, amongst other cities. Fronted by vocalist/entertainer O. C. Wynne it was known as

Jap Allen and his Cotton Club Orchestra. Its personnel at this time was Joe Keyes (replaced by Paul Webster), Dee Stewart, Eddie 'Orange' White (trumpet), Alton 'Slim' Moore (trombone), Booker Pittman, Alfred Denny (replaced by Tommy Douglas) (alto saxophone, clarinet), Ben Webster (tenor saxophone), Clyde Hart (piano), Jim 'Daddy' Walker (guitar, banjo), Jap Allen (bass), Raymond Howell (drums), O. C. Wynne (vocal, director). Joe Durham replaced Allen in the rhythm section when Allen decided to concentrate on the various business activities that press upon the leader of a band.

As a result of the depression good bookings became more difficult to find, and in 1931 Edgar Battle was able to lure Joe Keyes, Alton Moore, Ben Webster, Pittman and Clyde Hart away from Allen to join Blanche Calloway's band in Chicago. Allen himself has said that he encouraged them to accept the offer in view of the poor economic situation. Shortly afterwards blues singer Victoria Spivey engaged the Allen band to accompany her on a tour. Two of the replacements for those who had left were Bill Martin (trumpet) and Kimball Dial (clarinet, sax). At the end of the tour Allen disbanded, and after working with Tommy Douglas moved to St Louis where he secured a lengthy residency in a Chinese restaurant and also occasionally played with Dewey Jackson and Fate Marable. Of the latter Allen commented : 'He could put together a band better and quicker than anyone I ever knew. He was strict and wouldn't hire a man unless that man could read music and could blend in with the rest of the band. Tab Smith played with Fate then, and he was great! In fact the musicians wanted him to take more solos on his alto horn just so they could listen to him.'

From the closing years of the 'thirties Allen worked in and around the Chicago area with numerous leaders, and later bought a farm outside Chapel Hill, North Carolina, where he still lives. He was working locally as a part-time musician in Durham, North Carolina, at least until the early 'sixties. Though his 1930-31 band was, by all accounts, a very fine one, with Clyde Hart's magnificent arrangements, it never had the opportunity to record.

Thamon (Jap Allen insists it is Thaymon) Hayes is probably best remembered as the composer of *South* and for his many years of playing with Bennie Moten, but ironically he was responsible for one of Moten's worst defeats in a band battle. In winter 1931 Moten gave notice to several of his musicians, including Hayes, and they joined company with others in Kansas City to form the Kansas City Rockets. They rehearsed at Hayes's home, Jesse Stone writing many of their arrangements, and before long were working around Kansas City, including one residency at Fairyland Park. In May 1932 an annual musicians' ball took place at the local Paseo Hall, and it was at this event that the Kansas City Rockets decisively defeated Moten.

The Kansas City Rockets, under Hayes's leadership, began rehearsing in February 1932 and for a while had a stable line-up of Ed Lewis, Richard Smith, Booker Washington (trumpet), Thamon Hayes, Elmer Crumbley (trombone), Herman Walder, Harlan Leonard (alto saxophone, clarinet), Woodie Walder (tenor saxophone, clarinet), Jesse Stone (piano, arranger), Jim 'Daddy' Walker (guitar, banjo), Vernon Page (tuba, string bass), and Sam 'Baby' Lovett (drums). Crumbley was later replaced by Vic Dickenson, who left in 1933, and Walker by Charles 'Crook' Goodwin. After their triumph against Moten, the Kansas City Rockets went on tour, initially with some success, but in Chicago they ran into various union problems inspired by gangsters who were concerned at their popularity and saw it as a threat to the bands which they controlled. Despite the offer of an important club engagement this union hostility made it difficult for the band to remain in Chicago, and Hayes handed over leadership to Harlan Leonard soon afterwards. Stone remained in Chicago, his place being taken by Rozelle Claxton.

The significance of the Rockets' defeat of Moten is hard to assess, particularly as they never recorded. Frank Driggs has mentioned that at the time Moten had one of his best ever bands but that his audiences did not take too kindly to his forward-looking musical policies. The personnel of the Kansas City Rockets included many former Moten sidemen, and it may well be that its musical policy was closer to what the audience had come to accept as the norm from Moten himself. Moten's defeat might have been, given these circumstances, a triumph for conservatism rather than a reflection of musical values.

In his pioneering chapter on 'Kansas City and the Southwest' in the book *'Jazz'*, Frank Driggs refers to Tommy Douglas as 'another unsung musical giant, reedman and arranger'. He also remarked, in an introduction to Douglas's life story that appeared in Jazz Monthly, that he 'has solved musical riddles sometimes years ahead of his contemporaries, while being unable to capitalize on his ability'. The fact that Driggs, who more than any other jazz writer has made a study of the Kansas City musicians and bands, rates Douglas so highly is a reasonable indication of his stature.

Douglas was born in Eskridge, Kansas, on 9th November 1911. He first went to school in Topeka. From 1924 to 1928 he studied at the Boston Conservatory. He became friendly with Harry Carney, Otto Hardwicke and Johnny Hodges, who were then active in Boston, and took courses in composition, harmony and theory. To make ends meet he undertook a variety of menial jobs, but in summer 1926 was working with Captain Wolmack's band in Buffalo, New York, and on tour. Towards the end of the 'twenties he moved to Kansas City and worked for a while with Paul Banks, and then became a sideman with George E. Lee, Jap Allen, Jelly Roll Morton and Clarence Love. He formed his first band at Lincoln, Nebraska, during 1930 and it remained in existence for several

months. Its line-up comprised Paul King, Herman Grimes, George Crumbley (trumpet), Elmer Crumbley (trombone), Tommy Douglas (alto saxophone, clarinet), probably two other reeds, Jay Golson (piano), Tom Finney (banjo), Skeets Morgan (tuba) and Jo Jones (drums). Douglas told Mr Driggs that despite a few defects this was an above average band, principally because it was using original material.

The exact chronology of Douglas's bandleading efforts is uncertain, but around 1931 he again led a big band with a line-up of Paul Webster, Eddie Tomkins, Paul King (trumpet), Joe Edwards, Jimmy Jones (trombone), Odell West, himself (tenor saxophone, clarinet), Bill Saunders (tenor saxophone), unknown (piano), Cliff McTier (guitar), Dan Andrews (tuba, string bass), unknown (drums). In later years both Webster and Tomkins were to play together in the Jimmie Lunceford band. Douglas, like many other musicians, has praised Tomkins as one of the finest trumpeters of his era, though it appears that he passed his peak by the time he joined Lunceford. After disbanding this last group Douglas worked with Clarence Love at the El Torreon Ballroom, Kansas City, during 1932 and 1933, writing many of the arrangements that the band used. In 1934 he once again formed a big band, this time comprising Paul King, two unknown (trumpet), unknown (possibly Ted Donnelly) (trombone), Odell West, Tommy Douglas (alto saxophone, clarinet), Bill Saunders, Orlando Beck (tenor saxophone), Jesse Gibson (piano), Charles Russeau (guitar), Jap Allen (string bass) and Kenneth McVey (drums). Again the band was short lived, and Douglas moved on to spend a brief period with Bennie Moten.

Douglas's big chance came in 1935 when he took over

Above: *the Tommy Douglas Orchestra at Fergus Halls, Minnesota, 1938. Left to right: Harry Norris, Bill Martin, Fred Beckett, Curtyse Foster, Bill Douglas, Roy 'Buck' Douglas, Tommy Douglas, Bill Searcy, Clifford McTier, Paul Gunther and Lowell Pointer. Right: a 1938 poster.*

a band directed by Jimmie Keith, and rehearsed it until it became a top class ensemble, able to perform as he wanted. After being on the road it secured a location job at the Casa Loma Ballroom in Tulsa, where a sympathetic radio manager arranged for local airings, promising a national hook-up within the month. Douglas felt that this was his big opportunity, but a local business man persuaded the other members of the band, which was run on a co-operative basis, to appoint him their agent and to continue touring. The results were disastrous and the agent was jailed for selling furniture that was not his property, forcing Douglas and the band to seek work further afield as a result of the bad publicity. Ultimately Douglas handed the band back to Keith as a result of union problems in Kansas City, and later it became very successful under Harlan Leonard's leadership. While it existed Douglas had some private recordings made of the band, but unfortunately they were stolen.

For a time in 1936 Douglas fronted a septet that included Charlie Parker, then once more organised a big band. Its personnel was Robert Hibbler, Harry Ferguson, William Smith (trumpet), Fred Beckett, Lawrence 'Frog' Anderson (trombone), Bill Douglas, Tommy Douglas (alto saxophone, clarinet), Buck Douglas, Paul Jones (tenor saxophone), Bill Searcy or Henri Woode (piano), Lowell Pointer (string bass) and Cliff Love (drums). During 1938-39 he worked at Fergus Falls,

KXBY — Kansas City
RADIO FAVORITES

GETS HOT ★ STAYS HOT

Harlem's
ARISTOCRATS OF
RHYTHM ★ NOVELTIES
Singing Sizzling Swinging Syncopating

Park Region Orchestra Service, Battle Lake, Minn.

ROSCOE HALL
18th AND PROSPECT
SUNDAY, JULY 4th
ADMISSION 50 Cents -- ---- *Advance Tickets 35 cents*
—— Hours - - - 9 Until ? ? ? ——

Minnesota, with a line-up of Bill Martin, Harry Norris (trumpet), Fred Beckett (trombone), and the saxes and rhythm as listed above, except that Curtyse Foster and Paul Gunther replaced Jones and Love, Searcy is the pianist, and Cliff McTier is added on guitar.

It is possible that Douglas's memory is, not surprisingly, slightly awry on dates. The preceding details were related to Mr. Driggs for the Jazz Monthly article. Down Beat provides evidence that Douglas was leading his band at a club called Antler's in Kansas City for much of 1938. Its July 1938 issue noted that the band had just left that location for a tour into Canada. Three months later it reported that the band was back after its northern tour and was resuming work at Antler's and mention of its presence there occur in several later issues. The February 1939 Down Beat carried a story about the break-up of the band, reporting that Douglas had lost many of his best men. It was presumably after this that Douglas organised a band for George E. Lee which played at Krug Park,

Omaha. Curby Alexander gave Kurt Mohr a personnel for the 1938-39 period quite different to that Douglas told Frank Driggs, listing Bob Merrill, Onis Panky (trumpet), Floyd Hayes (trombone), Curby Alexander, Tommy Douglas (alto saxophone), Everett Gaines, Arthur Lee O'Neil (tenor saxophone), Louis Powell (piano), Thurber Jay (replaced by Commodore Lark) (string bass) and Jack 'The Bear' Parker (drums). One suspects that both personnels are correct and that Douglas was organising and disbanding with frequency at this period.

In 1940 Douglas led an eight-piece group at a restaurant in Kansas City, enlarging to ten pieces the following year for an engagement at the College Inn which lasted into 1944. Tenor saxophonist Hal Singer worked with Douglas in 1941. The 15th April issue of Down Beat reported that he had revamped his band and was being booked by the newly formed McCronkie office. Teddy Stewart has given a personnel of Douglas (alto saxophone, clarinet), John Jackson (alto saxophone), Sleepy Wilcox (piano), Effergee Ware (guitar) and himself (drums) for 1942. Other musicians known to have been in Douglas's group at about this time are Tiny Davis (trumpet), Emile Williams (piano, accordion) and Effergi Stephany (guitar)— the latter possibly an error for Effergee Ware. In the second half of 1944 Douglas directed a big band with unknown personnel, then fronted an eight-piece group at the Cuban Room, Kansas City, from 1945 until 1950. He led small groups into the 'sixties and may still be playing today. For three weeks in March 1951 he temporarily replaced Johnny Hodges in the Duke Ellington band.

Douglas recorded for Capitol in 1949 with his octet, but the performances are in a rhythm-and-blues vein and apparently quite untypical. He also took part in recording sessions with singer Julia Lee, but again does not consider his playing on these as representative of what he can do. By all accounts a brilliant instrumentalist, organiser, arranger and leader, Douglas has never been recorded as he wished, and one regretfully has to assume that at this late date is unlikely to be. His bands were modern for their day, reflecting Douglas's forward-looking views, but failing the unlikely event of the missing private recordings being found it is only the work of researcher Frank Driggs that enables one to realise the importance of Douglas's role in big band history.

Oliver Todd, born in Kansas City on 7th January 1916, represents a generation of musicians later than most of the others mentioned in this section. As a youth he worked in local bands led by Bill Nolan and others. From 1935 through 1936 he led his own Hottentots, the usual personnel being Elmer Price, Orville 'Piggy' Minor, himself (trumpet), Henry Heard, Mearl Rollins (alto saxophone, clarinet), William Scott (tenor saxophone), William Smith (piano), Gene Ramey (string bass) and Frank Sutton (drums). A year later alto saxophonist Charles Greene took over the band. Todd also worked locally with a variety of leaders. The Hottentots were reduced to a sextet in 1938, then increased to a septet with the addition of alto saxophonist Cleophus Berry the following year, and survived until the autumn of 1940. During the early war years Todd led a band on tour that went as far as Chicago and Springfield, Illinois; then for the remaining years of the 'forties he worked with his own band—a septet—at local clubs. Since the 'fifties he has concentrated on piano playing, working mainly as a single.

Gene Ramey, for one, has told me how good Todd's band of 1935-36 sounded, and his wartime groups were considered about the best then working regularly in Kansas City. Although numerically his units were hardly big bands, they apparently continued something of the Kansas City traditions which had been established by the pioneer leaders. None of Todd's groups ever recorded, but he himself took part in a 1944 Capitol session with Jay McShann, contributing a pleasant, relaxed solo to a version of *Moten Swing*.

Although he was never really successful, Buster Smith is a musician whose name is known to many jazz followers, though one suspects mainly because he has been quoted as an important influence on Charlie Parker. Smith was one of the first important arrangers in big band jazz, in addition to being an outstanding instrumentalist in his own right, and his name has occurred many times in the present chapter. He was born at Ellis County, Texas, on 26th August 1904, and first played piano and organ, later switching to clarinet and alto saxophone. After working with a variety of groups in Dallas he left for Oklahoma City to join the Blue Devils, where he remained from 1925 until late 1933 under several leaders. He then joined the short-lived Bennie Moten-George E.

Buster Smith at his home in the early 1960s.

Lee band in Kansas City, worked briefly with Ira 'Buster' Moten, and co-led The Barons of Rhythm with Count Basie. At the end of 1936 Smith went to Iowa to play with Claude Hopkins, a short-lived job, moving on to New York City for the first time to become an arranger for Count Basie and to work very briefly for Andy Kirk.

Back in Kansas City during 1937 Smith formed an eleven-piece band consisting of . . . Davis, Andy Anderson (trumpet), Fred Beckett (trombone), Charlie Parker, himself (alto saxophone), Odell West (tenor saxophone), unknown (tenor saxophone), Jay McShann (piano), Charles 'Crook' Goodwin (guitar), Billy Hadnott (string bass) and Willie McWashington (drums). This existed for about a year and a half. When it went out on tour it was reduced to a sextet, but playing locally for dancers it was at full strength and was resident at different times at Lucille Band Box, from which it broadcast, and Antler's Club. Emile Williams replaced McShann after a while, and the August 1938 issue of Down Beat gave a personnel of Orville 'Piggy' Minor (trumpet), Buster Smith, Charlie Parker (alto saxophone), Odell West (tenor saxophone), Harry Taylor (piano), Bill Smith (string bass) and Bill Nolan (drums), which suggests that the line-up and size of the group fluctuated quite considerably. After finishing a residency at the Antler's Club in September 1938 Smith once more went to New York.

Smith's major job in New York during 1939 was to provide arrangements for 'Hot Lips' Page's big band, but he also wrote scores for Gene Krupa and gigged around with various groups. He left for a while to lead a band in Virginia, and Down Beat for November 1939 reported that he was playing at the time in Fry Spring Studio, Charlottesville. But soon he returned to New York, where he worked with Eddie Durham and Don Redman amongst others. In 1942 he went back to Kansas City and formed a new band which was resident for some while at the Club Shangrila, and since the late forties he has led small bands all over Texas, Oklahoma and Arkansas.

Smith has recorded on a number of occasions, the last time in Forth Worth, Texas, in 1959, though oddly enough never in a big band context other than with Walter Page's Blue Devils. He is considered to be one of the earliest musicians to base some of his solo work on chord sequences as well as melody, using phrasing which was complex for the period. The stress on his 'modern' qualities and his influence on Parker has, possibly, been overdone, for while his recorded solos reveal him as a fine musician they are clearly in the swing tradition. His alto work has some affinity with that of Willie Smith. Though he could, with a little determination, have become much better known to the public at large, he apparently prefers the less hectic life he leads away from the major entertainment centres.

Harlan Leonard's first important job was with George E. Lee in Kansas City during 1923, but later that year he joined Bennie Moten and remained with him until 1931 when, along with three others, he was given notice. He then worked, as has been mentioned, with Thamon Hayes's Kansas City Rockets, taking over the leadership around late 1934, when Hayes had become disillusioned with the treatment they met with from Chicago union officials. When the band worked at the Cotton Club in Chicago in 1935 it retained Ed Lewis, Booker Washington, Richard Smith (trumpet), Harlan Leonard, Herman Walder (alto saxophone, clarinet), Woodie Walder (tenor saxophone, clarinet), Rozelle Claxton (piano), Charles Goodwin (guitar), Leonard 'Jack' Johnson (string bass) and Samuel 'Baby' Lovett (drums) from the original personnel, adding trombonist Carlos Smith from St Louis and tenor saxophonist William Saunders from Kansas City. The band broke up upon its return to Kansas City in 1936.

It is usually said that Leonard took over Jimmie Keith's band in 1938, but it might well have been at some point in 1937. This was the band that Tommy Douglas had so assiduously drilled into a first-class unit, only to experience the frustrations and disappointments already outlined. Initially it consisted of Edward 'Peeney' Johnson, James Ross, Sidney Miller (trumpet), Richmond Henderson (trombone), Harlan Leonard, Charlie Parker or Franz Bruce (alto saxophone, clarinet), Freddie Culliver, Jimmie Keith (tenor saxophone), Rozelle Claxton (and temporarily Countess Johnson) (piano), Effergee Ware (guitar), Ben Curtis (string bass) and Edward Phillips (drums). When the band replaced Count Basie in a Kansas City club in August 1938 only two changes had taken place: Darwin Jones (alto saxophone) and Bernie Cobb (guitar) had come in for Parker or Bruce and Ware respectively. Four months later Parker returned in place of Jones, and Richard J. Smith and Winston Williams replaced Miller and Leonard Jack Johnson, who had filled in for Curtis for a brief period.

Early in 1939 the band was resident every Sunday night at Dreamland on Vine Street. At other times it gigged around the Kansas City area, while during May and June it played at Street's Blue Room. During September further changes in personnel took place, the line-up becoming Edward Johnson, Richard J. Smith, James Ross (trumpet), Richmond Henderson (trombone), Harlan Leonard, Darwin Jones (alto saxophone, clarinet), Henry Bridges, Jimmie Keith (tenor saxophone), William Smith (piano), Effergee Ware (guitar), Winston Williams (string bass) and Jesse Price (drums). At the same time the band opened at the Century Room in Kansas City and was signed up on a long term contract by MCA who began to plan its bookings from January 1940. Just before this the band had achieved a great triumph in Louisville, where Maxine Sullivan sang with it.

MCA booked the band into Chicago's Aragon Ballroom and Savoy Ballroom during January 1940, and while in that city it took part in its first recording session for RCA Victor's Bluebird label. An important addition to the band was trombonist Fred Beckett, and Ernest Williams, a splendid big band blues shouter, was added as front man. *Hairy Joe Jump*, from the band's first session, became a minor hit, and its success seemed assured, not least because MCA had booked it into the Golden Gate Ballroom in New York City for a six-week engagement from 10th February. When in New York it recorded for the second time, with Stan Morgan replacing Ware on guitar and Myra Taylor being added as a vocalist, but for some reason the band failed to make any impact there and never again returned. In summer 1940 Billy Hadnott (string bass) and Tadd Dameron (arranger) came into the band, the former replacing Williams, but Williams was back by the time of its final recording session in Chicago in November and Walter Monroe had replaced Beckett.

In Kansas City once more, the band was resident at College Inn until April 1941. During June and July it played at the Trocadero before setting out on a tour that included a location job at the Club Lido in South Bend, Indiana. By the end of 1941 it was again in Kansas City, taking part in a battle of bands at a New Year jamboree held at the Muny Auditorium. The morale of the band must have been shaken by its lack of success in New York, for during August 1941 William H. Smith, Walter Monroe, Henry Bridges, Darwin Jones, Stan Morgan and Jesse Price had all left. Their replacements were Carlos 'Little Dog' Johnson (trumpet), Curtis Foster (sax), Freddie Hopkins (guitar) and Raymond Howell (drums), thus reducing the instrumentation to three trumpets, one trombone, three saxes and four rhythm, with Ernest Williams and Myra Taylor retained as singers. A successful Midwestern tour did something to erase memories of the New York debacle. In 1942 the band was resident in Kansas City at the Mayfair Club for March and April, the Fairyland Park from June to September, and the College Inn during October and November.

In May 1943 Leonard took a band to play at the Hollywood Club in Los Angeles, for the first time acting as front man himself. Most of his personnel was new and consisted of Miles Jones, Norman Bowden, James Ross (trumpet), Russell Moore, James Wormick (trombone), Harlan Leonard, Earl Jackson (alto saxophone, clarinet), Jimmie Keith, Merill Anderson (tenor saxophone), Arvella Moore (piano), Rodney Richardson (string bass) and Jesse Price (drums). Three months later Price left to join Louis Armstrong's band. Ernie Williams temporarily replaced him until Johnny Otis could take over. Towards the end of the year Richardson left for Count Basie, being replaced by Bob Kesterson, while in April 1944 Price returned when Otis went to work with Stan Kenton. From early in 1944 until the middle of the year, the Leonard band played at the Club Alabam in Hollywood. Merril Anderson died in Oakland, California, and his place was taken by Jack McVea, while other changes during 1944 involved Teddy Buckner

149

coming in for one of the trumpeters; P. Q. Wilson, from Oklahoma City, replacing Earl Jackson, though the latter rejoined later on for a brief period; and Kenny Bryan playing piano in place of Arvella Moore. For an engagement at Zukor's Tavern, Hermosa Beach, Horatio McFerrin, alsia 'El Baron', replaced Miles Jones for two weeks.

Early in 1945 Leonard's personnel was Ed Preston, Norman Bowden, Miles Jones (trumpet), Jab Jones (trombone), Harlan Leonard, Earl Jackson (alto saxophone, clarinet), Jack McVea, Preston Love (tenor saxophone), Arvella Moore (piano), Bob Kesterson (string bass) and Nat 'Monk' McFay (drums). This band played at Shep's Playhouse in Los Angeles, but when the engagement ended, Leonard left music, becoming· chief of the cashiers' section of the Los Angeles Department Of Internal Revenue, a position which he held until his retirement a few years ago.

Harlan Leonard and his Rockets recorded twenty-four titles in four sessions between January and November 1940. Two have never been released. Sixteen of the band's performances have been issued on a single LP, and they leave no doubt that it was a very fine group. In James Ross and later Tadd Dameron the band possessed two fine arrangers, though Richard J. Smith also contributed good scores, and it also had a full complement of top class soloists, amongst whom William H. 'Smitty' Smith, Fred Beckett, Henry 'Hank' Bridges and Jimmie Keith are outstanding. The individual sections are good, with the saxes blending particularly well, and ensemble passages are performed with power and swing. Stylistically the band sometimes shows a strong Lunceford influence, though at others there are echoes of Basie.

From its first session the band's version of *Southern Fried (Hairy Joe Jump)* and *Rockin' with the Rockets,* both arranged by James Ross, are excellent, the former displaying relaxed section and ensemble work and pleasant solos from trumpeters Smith and Ross, tenor saxophonists Keith and Bridges, and pianist Smith, the latter effective solos from the same men but without Ross. Fred Beckett can be heard playing muted on *Rockin',* and it is easy to understand why he enjoyed such a considerable reputation in his lifetime. From the second session, *Ride My Blues Away,* arranged by Buster Smith, has a really fine shouting vocal by Ernie Williams, and Bridges has an outstanding solo, while *Parade of the Stompers,* arranged by Rozelle Claxton, is Lunceford-like in conception and once more reveals Bridges to have been a great soloist. One of the best known of all Leonard's records is *A-La-Bridges,* a melodic number arranged by Tadd Dameron which is mainly a feature for the soloist of that name. Fred Beckett contributes a good short solo, but for the rest Bridges is heard in a rhapsodic solo, rather in the vein of Herschal Evans on Basie's *Blue and Sentimental.* Dameron's *400 Swing* is more extrovert, featuring excellent solos from the two tenor men—Keith's tone is a little drier than Bridges's—short passages by Beckett, and a

well played chase sequence by Ross and Smith. No doubt deliberately, the work of Bridges and Keith on this number recalls Herschal Evans and Lester Young of the Basie band, but on *Take 'um,* from the final Bluebird session, Bridges has a solo which shows that he too was influenced by Young. This number was apparently written to spotlight Bridges's tenor playing in its most jaunty vein. From the same date *Keep Rockin'* features the powerful, incisive trumpet work of William 'Smitty' Smith, on this occasion displaying a distinctly Harry Edison influence. It is worth drawing attention to *My Gal Sal* for its superb Fred Beckett solo, but there is not really a weak performance amongst Leonard's Bluebird output, and one is puzzled why New York audiences reacted so coldly to the band. Our knowledge of the individual soloists and arrangers on Leonard's records owes much to the researches of the Swiss jazz enthusiast Johnny Simmen, and I would like to express my indebtedness to him.

Leonard did not record again commercially, but two titles have been issued on an anthology LP that come from a public performance by his band in Los Angeles during 1943 or 1944. *Specs and Spots* turns out to be a version of Eddie Durham's *Harlem Shout,* very similar to the Lunceford recording, with solos from a trombonist, trumpeter (possibly James Ross), and tenor saxophonist whom I imagine was Jimmie Keith. The other number is *Play, Fiddle, Play,* taken at a fastish tempo, and this has reasonable solos from a trumpeter and tenor saxophonist. On both titles the playing of the saxophone section is excellent, but much of the individual character of the band has been lost and it sounds only an average swing group of the period.

Jay McShann's was the last of the great Kansas City bands, and probably the final territory band to achieve a degree of national recognition. McShann was born at Muskogee, Oklahoma, on 12th January 1909, and started to play the piano from the age of twelve. As a youth he went to Tulsa for four months to work with the Al Dennis band, after which he devoted a year to studying at Southwestern College, Winfield, Kansas. From about 1932 until 1934 he toured Arizona and New Mexico with Eddy Hill's band. When the band broke up he worked in Kansas City with drummer Elmer Hopkins at Monroe Inn. There is some uncertainty about the exact chronology of McShann's activities during the mid 'thirties, but in 1937 he was working with trumpeter Dee Stewart's band at the Club Continental in Kansas City and then spent nine months at Wolfe's Buffer on 18th Street. Trumpeter Ed Lewis has said that he worked with McShann as part of a trio completed by drummer Murl Johnson during 1937.

In April 1938 McShann formed a septet said to consist of Bill Smith (trumpet), Earl Jackson, Bill Scott (alto saxophone), Bob Mabane (tenor saxophone), himself (piano), Gene Ramey (string bass) and Pete McShann (Jay's cousin) (drums). This group went into Martin's-

On-The-Plaza for a two-week trial and stayed eighteen weeks before moving on to the Club Continental. Gene Ramey has said that McShann wanted bassist Billy Hadnott and drummer Gus Johnson from the start, but that as neither was available used himself and Pete McShann, though Johnson did take over from the latter after a short while. Down Beat for July 1938 gives a different personnel of Bill Smith (trumpet), Edward Hale, Bob Mabane (sax, vocal), Jay McShann (piano), Allen Anderson (string bass) and Gus Johnson (drums), stating that the band was heard regularly over local radio stations WHB, KXBY, and KCMO and that it had made many records privately for local collector Walter Bales. This particular personnel is confusing in as far as it claims that Smith had replaced Ramey, for while Ramey did play trumpet in his youth he was certainly not doing so at this time, and once he joined McShann always played string bass. However, he did leave McShann briefly in the middle of 1938 and his temporary replacement may well have been Anderson. Ramey also told me that before John Jackson joined—presumably Earl and John Jackson are one and the same—an alto player nick-named 'Dripnose De Bobo' was with the septet. He might possibly have been Edward Hale. This gentleman received his unfortunate nickname as the result of a habit which I will not describe.

One can trace most of the activities of McShann's band from the summer of 1938 through to the early 'forties from Down Beat reports. The issue of September 1938 reported that it had moved into Eddie Spitz's Club Continental, adding William Scott (tenor saxophone, arranger), and that it 'went big on a recent guest spot with WHB's Vine Street Varieties, best local ozone show of the summer.' A month later Down Beat carried a news item that McShann's group had left the Club Continental, and several issues covering December 1938 to February 1939 reported that it was resident at Martin's-On-The-Strand, had added vocalist Selma Long, and played with success at a local Christmas party. Gene Ramey told me that Martin's-On-The-Strand was an exclusive club operating a colour bar and that the local white union made several attempts to get the McShann group out of there. It was here, Ramey reports, that important contacts with business men were made that enabled McShann to form a big band in 1940.

McShann's personnel in January 1939 was Orville 'Piggy' Minor (trumpet), Earl Jackson (alto saxophone), Bob Mabane, William Scott (tenor saxophone), Jay McShann (piano), Gene Ramey (string bass) and Gus Johnson (drums). In the following month McShann took a trio of himself, Ramey and Johnson to the Off-Beat Club in Chicago and remained there for several weeks. In his absence the band continued under Scott's leadership. In May 1939 the only change was that William Smith was substituted for Minor, but two months later Minor was back and vocalist Mildred McCoy had been added. Down Beat reported that it was proving to be

the biggest draw in Kansas City. Most of the members of the band had worked together in Countess Johnson's group before joining McShann, so it should have been a cohesive unit from the start.

Martin's-On-The-Strand proved to be a lucrative job for the McShann band, though an echo of Ramey's report of union interference is contained in an item in the August 1939 Down Beat: 'Jay McShann's 7-piece orchestra was pulled from Martin's last month by Local 627 AFM when it was learned that a pianist hired to substitute for Jay when McShann played Chicago's Off-Beat Club last winter had been paid under scale. The boys in McShann's band were fined; they paid 20 dollars each and are back in the groove again.'

The band left Martin's-On-The-Strand in October 1939 and moved over to the Club Continental. Down Beat for 1st November 1939 noted that it had been signed to a Decca recording contract, 'the first K.C. outfit to go on wax since Count Basie and Andy Kirk left town'. The same magazine had a news item in its 15th January 1940 edition to the effect that the band's first Decca records were due out soon—in fact it did not record until April 1941—and that it was being featured on the Vine Street Varieties Show over station WHB. For the first four months of 1940 the band was resident at Kansas City's Century Room, and in February 1940, with the help of local backing, McShann increased to twelve pieces. Trumpeter Bernard 'Buddy' Anderson, a musician who had played with Gene Ramey's college band and was described by Ramey as 'immensely talented', was one of the new men, joining the band from Tulsa, and he gave a personnel for this period of himself, Harold Bruce, Orville Minor (trumpet), Joe Taswell Baird (trombone), John Jackson, Charlie Parker (alto saxophone), Bob Mabane, William Scott (tenor saxophone), Jay McShann (piano), Leonard 'Lucky' Ennois (guitar), Gene Ramey (bass), Gus Johnson (drums) and William Nolan (vocal), who was soon replaced by Walter Brown whom McShann had heard singing in a local bar.

The impressario at the Century Room, and now manager of the band, was John B. Tumino, and he staged band battles at his club which McShann invariably won. Down Beat for 15th May 1940 reported that 'Missouri University's century old prejudice against Negroes took a horrible beating May 3rd when Harlan Leonard and Jay McShann took bands to Columbia for a jam battle that had the Joes and Susies jumping like they never had before.' From June 1940 until the next spring the band went on frequent tours. Down Beat for 1st November 1940 mentioned that it had returned to Kansas City for a one-nighter at Lincoln Hall after playing the Trocadero Club in Wichita to which it would return that month. It also mentioned that at River View in Des Moines it outdrew Ella Fitzgerald three to one. Gene Ramey recalls these tours and says that during them there were band battles with Earl Hines, Milton Larkins and

Nat Towles, all of which they won, adding that its one reverse was at the hands of the Ellington band which, he ruefully comments, 'sliced' them. In April 1941 McShann was resident at the Casa Fiesta Club in Kansas City, and on the 30th the band travelled to Dallas to make its first Decca records. William Scott had left for the army the previous month and his place had been taken by Harry Ferguson, but transcriptions made by an octet from within the band late in 1940 do have Scott on certain titles, and also one Bud Gould, a trombonist doubling on violin, who remains a somewhat mysterious figure.

As far as one can ascertain McShann's band made its debut in New York City in March 1941, shortly before the first recording session. Down Beat for 1st April 1941 says that it 'had been jumping mightily at the Savoy, Harlem' and was due to play the Apollo and other leading coloured theatres throughout the country. The following July it was playing at Jubilee Junction (presumably a club or ballroom) in Jefferson City, Missouri, by now being booked by the Moe Gale Agency. Bob Merrill had replaced Harold Bruce in March, and soon afterwards Freddie Culliver replaced Ferguson, and Lawrence 'Frog' Anderson (trombone) was added. This was the line-up when the band played in Chicago during November 1941, though it is possible that Jimmy Coe (baritone saxophone) had also joined by this time. Eight titles were recorded for Decca while the band was in Chicago, but all but one were features for singer Walter Brown on which he was backed by the rhythm section. Orville Minor and Charlie Parker were added on *One Woman's Man*.

A note in the 15th January 1942 Down Beat to the effect that the William Morris Agency was angling to sign the McShann band is interesting in view of what Gene Ramey once told me. He said that the band was jointly owned by McShann and manager Joe Tumina, but that when it was first booked by a major agency there was an attempt on Tumina's part to gain ownership. When this failed the agency deliberately sent it out on a rough tour, and in Augusta , Georgia, and a town in North Carolina the promoters ran off with the money and the local police arrested the band and made them pay for the hire of the dance hall. Mr Ramey said that musicians in bands the agencies owned were getting as little as forty dollars a week, while the McShann musicians were receiving thirty dollars or more a night. As a result a number of well-known musicians, including the late Dick Wilson, were anxious to join McShann. The efforts of the agency to destroy the morale of the band almost succeeded and it came close to breaking up. Ramey also remarked that when the band first hit New York the musicians were raw and badly dressed by big city standards, but it was a type of family band which gave it a degree of resilience. Just before their New York debut the band received a telegram from Lucky Millinder, against whose band they would be playing at the Savoy,

reading 'We're gonna chase you hicks right back to the sticks.' As it happened it was Millinder's band that got the worst of the encounter.

In March 1942 the McShann played a week at the Paradise Theatre in Detroit, then made its way to New York where it opened at the Savoy Ballroom on 5th April and switched to the Apollo Theatre for the week of 17th April. After this it was at the Royal Theatre, Baltimore, from 24th April to 30th April and at the Howard Theatre, Washington, from 1st May to the 7th. By now alto and baritone saxophonist Jimmy Coe was definitely in the band. Bob Mabane left for the army around May 1942, and in June Harold 'Doc' West replaced Gus Johnson. After a Midwestern tour the band was in New York in the first few days of July, taking part in a recording session on which vocalist Al Hibbler made his debut. The standard discographies list Mabane as being present on this date, but it seems certain that he had been replaced by Jimmy Forrest in May. The band's arrangers at this time were Jimmy Coe, Archie 'Skip' Hall and Shay Torrent. Following the New York date the band left to open at King's Ballroom in Lincoln, Nebraska, on 14th July.

One photograph of the band taken during 1942 poses a problem, for it shows Mabane and Jimmy Forrest together, along with Coe and John Jackson on alto saxophone. There is no record of Culliver having left, and it may be that Forrest joined a week or more before Mabane departed and that Mabane taught him the book, a not uncommon practice in big bands at the time. Parker did leave for a while in 1942 but had returned by September. Joe Evans gave a personnel for 1942 of Bernard Anderson, Bob Merrill, Orville Minor (trumpet), James Taswell Baird, Lawrence 'Frog' Anderson, Clyde Bernhardt (trombone), Freddie Culliver, Jimmy Forrest (tenor saxophone), Charlie Parker, himself (alto saxophones), Alba 'Beau' McCain (baritone saxophone), Jay McShann (piano), Leonard 'Lucky' Ennois (guitar), Gene Ramey (string bass), Gus Johnson (drums), Al Hibbler, Walter Brown (vocal) and Archie 'Skip' Hall (arranger). One would guess that this was the line-up during the second part of the year.

Early in 1943 Gene Ramey left for four to six weeks. His replacement is not known, but this was the period when the call-up was causing frequent changes of personnel in all the big bands. In any case McShann was not finding things too easy and Don Redman had fronted the band to help out on several occasions during 1942. In December 1942 Charlie Parker, John Jackson and Bernard Anderson all left to join Earl Hines's band, and its line-up for an engagement at the Band Box in Chicago in May 1943 was Bob Merrill, Curtis Murphy, David Mitchell (trumpet), Clyde Bernhardt, George Bell (trombone), Joe Evans, Walter Bell (alto saxophone), Hal Singer, John 'Flap' Dungee (tenor saxophone), Jay McShann (piano), Gene Ramey (string bass), Gus Johnson (drums), Debby Robinson, Walter Brown

The Jay McShann band at the Savoy Ballroom early in 1942. Left to right: Jay McShann, Leonard 'Lucky' Ennois, Gene Ramey, Gus Johnson, Bob Mabane, Charlie Parker, Buddy Anderson, John Jackson, Orville Minor, Freddie Culliver, Lawrence 'Frog' Anderson and Taswell 'Little Joe' Baird.

(vocal) and Archie 'Skip' Hall (arranger). For a date in Oklahoma the band was down to nine pieces, but it had been increased to twelve by the time it opened at the Congo Club in Detroit in September 1943. From October, trombonist Leon Comegys was in the band for a month, giving its personnel then as Bob Merrill, Alonzo Fox, Dave Mitchell, Jesse 'Jeep' Jones (trumpet), himself, Alonzo Pettiford (trombone), Joe Evans, Rudolph 'Schoolboy' Dennis (alto saxophone), Paul Quinichette, Leon 'Stoogie' Goodson (tenor saxophone), Jay McShann, Archie 'Skip' Hall (piano), Gene Ramey (string bass) and Gus Johnson (drums). Around this time Ira Pettiford (trumpet) was briefly in the band, but Frank Driggs has given a personnel for November 1943 of Bob Merrill, Dave Mitchell, Willie Cook, Jesse 'Jeep' Jones (trumpet), Alonzo Pettiford (valve trombone, trumpet), Alphonso Fook, Leon Comegys, Clyde Bernhardt (trombone), John Jackson, Raye Bradley (alto saxophone), Paul Quinichette, Rudolph 'Schoolboy' Dennis, Leon 'Stoogie' Goodson (tenor saxophone), Jay McShann, Archie 'Skip' Hall (piano), Gene Ramey (string bass), Dan . . . (drums),

Earl Coleman (vocal). On 1st December the band took part in its final Decca recording session.

The final five months of the band are well documented in the pages of Down Beat. Issues ranging from 15th January 1944 to 15th May 1944 carry reports of it playing at the Two Spot Nite Club in Jacksonville, Florida, from 1st to 13th February; at the Club Plantation, Los Angeles, from early March until 20th April, when it took over from Andy Kirk and was itself replaced by the Fletcher Henderson band; at the Casa Madrid, Louisville, from 3rd to 9th May; and at the Band Box, Chicago, on 14th and 15th May. The personnel of the band for the March-April Club Plantation engagement was listed in the April 1944 Metronome as Bob Merrill, William Hickman, Jesse Jones (trumpet), Nathaniel Clayton, Al Morgan (trombone), John Jackson, Rudolph Dennis (alto saxophone), Paul Quinichette, John Sparrow (tenor saxophone), Bradbury Taylor (baritone saxophone), Jay McShann (piano), Gene Ramey (string bass), James Skinner (drums), Walter Brown and Kenny Williams (vocal)—a fifty percent turnover in four months. Music Dial for May 1944 mentioned that the ex-Andy Kirk vocalist Pha Terrell sung with the McShann band at the Club Plantation, and as he was working as a single on the West Coast at this time it is more likely that he used it as a backing group for a previously arranged booking. According to the 1st May 1944 Down Beat bassist Aaron Bell had just joined the army, and had formerly worked with McShann—a surprising piece of information. The same magazine fourteen days later reported that McShann, before leaving Los Angeles, had purchased a share in the new Furnace Club, a Central Avenue night spot. The band broke up in May 1944 and McShann left for army service.

Gene Ramey has commented that in its latter days the McShann band lost its distinctive sound, veering more towards the Lunceford style. He thought that this was due to the gradual replacement of the Kansas City musicians by others from Chicago and New York, citing the Basie band as another which went through a similar process. He himself recalled the early jam sessions in Kansas City with nostalgia, though claiming that they were called spook breakfasts at the time—a spook was anyone who was regularly out and around after midnight! He added that he used to jam with Jimmy Blanton, though a natural caution led him to play the rhythm background while Blanton improvised.

McShann was only in the army for six months before receiving his medical discharge. Down Beat of 1st December 1944 said that he was planning to reorganise with a twenty-piece band including former vocalist Walter Brown. Immediately upon his discharge he took part in a recording session in Kansas City with a pick-up group that included Oliver Todd, Tommy Douglas, Walter Page, Baby Lovett and Julia Lee. Another mystery is provided by a news snippet in the 15th January 1945 Down Beat claiming that one Pompey 'Guts' Dobson (drums) who had just joined the army was a former McShann musician. The same issue noted that McShann was instituting a big band policy at the Down Beat Club on 52nd Street, where he would be resident for eight weeks. A month later the magazine reported that the experiment had badly failed. A photograph in the 1st February issue shows the band in rehearsal at the Down Beat Club, with three trumpets, two trombones, five saxes (including Paul Quinichette), McShann himself, bass, and Gus Johnson (drums). It was presumably this band

Reunion in Montreal, June 1971, when Jay McShann and Jimmy Witherspoon were in the 'A Festival of American Folklife' programme at the U.S. Pavilion. Left to right: Orestes Tucker (trumpet), Little Brother Montgomery, unknown, Jimmy Witherspoon, Jay McShann, Claude Williams (violin) and 'Fats' Dennis (tenor saxophone).

that also appeared at the Paradise Club in Detroit from 9th to 15th February.

It is not quite clear when McShann finally broke up his big band, but he opened at a club in California on 18th August 1945 with a small group, and for the rest of the 'forties worked and recorded extensively in California with groups ranging from six to eight pieces as a rule, many of them featuring blues shouters of the Jimmy Witherspoon, Crown Prince Waterford type. Early in the 'fifties McShann returned to Kansas City and has worked at clubs there regularly ever since. He came to Europe in 1969 and since then has made semi-regular trips there, usually with quintets or sextets. He has recorded in the USA, Canada and Europe in recent years, proving himself still to be an excellent pianist.

A curiosity of McShann's Decca output is that of twenty-one titles recorded only ten are by the full band. From the first session of April 1941 *Dexter Blues* and *Swingmatism* are outstanding. Orville Minor, McShann and John Jackson have solos on the former, and McShann and Charlie Parker on the latter. McShann's neat blues-based solos are very effective, the band generates a powerful swing, and Gus Johnson's drumming is marvellous. Parker also takes a good solo on *Hootie's Blues* before the pleasant jazz-blues vocal by Walter Brown, behind which

Anderson plays excellent trumpet. From the second session of July 1942 the best performances are *The Jumpin' Blues,* with good solos from Parker and McShann and another agreeable Brown vocal, and *Lonely Boy Blues* with its strong ensemble work and very fine blues solo from Parker. The band does sound slightly less distinctive on its final December 1943 session, but Paul Quinichette make his recording debut with distinction and McShann has a nice understated solo on *Say Forward I'll March,* while Walter Brown and trumpeter Bob Merrill are heard to advantage on *Hometown Blues.* Merrill takes the vocal on *Wrong Neighbourhood,* Quinichette soloing well in a less Lester Young-derived manner than usual. It is worth noting that Jackson was highly regarded in his own right. Gene Ramey once told me that when he started with the band he usually played straight melody solos, but under Parker's influence emerged as a fine improviser. Apparently the success of Walter Brown led to the Decca executives insisting on a high percentage of blues material being recorded which, though generally excellent, led to many of the band's better arrangements and numbers being neglected at its few sessions. Even so the quality of the band is clear from its records, and if it was indeed the last of the real territory bands it saw an era and tradition out in fine style.

The Eastern States

The best known big band to be based on Boston was undoubtedly Sabby Lewis's, but the first to record was George Tynes's (sometimes spent Tines). Pianist Tynes began leading a group in Boston in 1926. At this time his line-up included Audley Smith (trumpet), John Cook (trombone), Bill Tinney, Jerome Don Pasquall (saxes) and Eddie Deas (drums, vocal, co-leader). The Chicago Defender of 17th August 1929 carried a news item that Tynes's current band was working at Revere Beach, Massachusetts, listing the personnel as Bob Chestnutt, J. Smity (trumpet), John Cook (trombone), Wilbur Pinkney, William Tinney (clarinet, sax), George Tynes (piano, leader), Jackie Jackson (banjo, guitar), Albert Burse (tuba) and Eddie Deas (drums, vocal).

In January 1930 the band recorded for the Harmony label—Harmony was U.S. Columbia's cheap mark—the four titles made being issued as by the 'Georgia Cotton Pickers'. Such geographically misleading pseudonyms were not uncommon at this period, as witness the many records by the California Ramblers and Arkansas Travel-

lers, neither of which contained musicians from California or Arkansas . In his 'Jazz Records 1897-1942' Brian Rust lists the personnel for these records. This differs from the Revere Beach residency only in that James Tolliver (piano, arranger) and an unknown tenor saxophone player have been added, leaving Tynes as front man. The 'J. Smity' of the Chicago Defender listing is in fact Jay Smith, and Chestnut's name is spelt with one t. I have heard a tape of *Snag It* and *Louisiana Bo Bo,* and they are creditable performances without being particularly noteworthy.

Orchestra World of September 1930 reported that the band, featuring Eddie Deas, was touring New England, but either late in that year or early in 1931 Deas left to form his own band and was replaced by Dave Chestnut. It appears that the band folded in 1933, at a time when its personnel included (according to Ray Culley) Bob Johnson (first trumpet), Bill Tinney (alto saxophone, clarinet), George Tynes (piano), Jackie Jackson (guitar), Albert Burse (string bass), and himself on drums.

After leaving Tynes, Deas went on to form his Boston Brownies Orchestra, recording four undistinguished titles for Victor in October 1931. Buster Tolliver gave Bertrand Demeusy a personnel for the band at this time—Bob Johnson, Jabbo Jenkins, Howard Callender (trumpet), Chester Burrill (trombone), George Matthews, Wilbur Pinkney (alto saxophone, clarinet), Buster Tolliver (tenor saxophone), Preston Sandiford (piano, arranger), Vic Hadley (guitar), Hubert Pierce (string bass), Eddie Deas (drums, vocal, leader). Brian Rust lists an unknown personnel for the Victor recordings, but it was probably as above, minus one of the trumpets. At some point in the next year or two drummer Dave Chestnut worked with Deas, as did Norman Lester (piano) in 1933, but the Orchestra is believed to have disbanded by the middle of the 'thirties.

William Sebastian 'Sabby' Lewis has led bands in Boston for over thirty years, though during the past two decades they have usually been small groups. He was born on 1st November 1914 in Middleburg, North Carolina, though his family moved to Philadelphia while he was still a boy and he was educated there. In 1932 his family moved on again, this time to Boston, and Lewis, having to forego hopes of a career in law or medicine because of economic difficulties, began to work as a pianist. His first professional band job came in 1934, as a member of Tasker Crosson's Ten Statesmen. Almost a quarter of a century later Lewis recalled these days in an interview

Sabby Lewis in the early 1940s.

with the U.S. jazz writer Bob Porter: 'Tasker Crossan was not a full time musician, but he did have a lot of college and high school jobs in the area. Most of the fellows in his band gradually drifted away to other jobs but there was one outstanding musician in the band, Jabbo Jenkins, who later played with McKinney's Cotton Pickers. He was one of the first high note trumpet players. In those days, the brass players were not as well equipped technically as they are today, but once they heard Louis playing all those high notes, they began to come around. Jabbo Jenkins had a terrific range and I recall one time when he had Roy Eldridge really sweating.'

Lewis formed his own band in either late 1936 or early 1937, opening with a residency at the Black Cat in Wilmington, Massachusetts, leading Clarence 'Tex' Thomas (trumpet), Clifford Turner (alto saxophone, clarinet), Jerry Heffron (tenor saxophone, clarinet), himself (piano), George Wellington (string bass), Clarence Terry—replaced after a year by Chris Cruickson—(drums), Marie Hawkins (vocal). He told Mr Porter that much of his early book was written by Heffron, a while musician, whose clever arrangements for the group provided it with as full a sound as possible.

From 1939 the Lewis band was usually heard at the Savoy Cafe in Boston, acting as house band and sometimes featured attraction for three years. Maceo Bryant (trumpet, trombone) had been added to the personnel, and Gene Caines (trumpet), Elliott 'Ricky' Pratt (tenor and baritone saxophone), Joe Booker (drums) and Julie Gardner (vocal) had replaced Thomas, Turner, Terry and Marie Hawkins respectively. The latter later became Mrs Nat Cole. The Savoy Cafe job was a good one for Lewis and he recalls many famous name musicians sitting in ·with him at this time, including Benny Goodman, whose presence caused the manager to tell the bartender that he must be got rid of because customers were listening rather than drinking. During the Savoy residency further good fortune came Lewis's way when the band won a contest sponsored by a men's hairdressing company and appeared on the nationwide Fitch Bandwagon radio programme as a result. It was this regular broadcasting that led to the band getting engagements in New York and further afield.

In February 1942, when the band was playing at Kelly's Stables in New York (incidentally being billed above the Nat Cole Trio), bassist Al Morgan replaced Wellington, remaining with the band, except for a few short trips, more than ten years. The war years were difficult ones for all bands, but Lewis was more fortunate than most, telling Bob Porter: 'A lot of fellows liked playing with us because we worked pretty steady around Boston, we paid good money and we weren't very far from New York so they could visit their families. A lot of fellows who were tired of the road would come into the band for a while.'

It is hard to document all the personnel changes that

The Sabby Lewis band at Club Harlem, Atlantic City in the summer of 1946. Back row, left to right: Rufus Jones, John 'Shorty' Haughton, Maceo Bryant, unknown, Eugene 'Sugar' Caines. Saxes: Bill Dorsey, Paul Gonsalves, George Fauntleroy, Dan Turner. Jimmy Crawford is the drummer, Al Morgan the bassist, and pianist and leader Sabby Lewis is at the microphone.

occurred during the middle years of the 'forties, but Elwyn Frazier (alto saxophone) was added in May 1943 and stayed for ten months, when his chair was taken over by Benny Williams. Caines had been drafted into the army in the summer of 1942, but his immediate replacement is uncertain, and drummer Osie Johnson worked with the band during some part of 1942-43. Down Beat of 1st April 1943 gives the line-up of the band for its residency at the Famous Door in New York as Maceo Bryant (trumpet, trombone), Cat Anderson (trumpet), Jackie Fields (alto saxophone), Jerry Heffron (tenor and alto saxophone), Rickie Pratt (tenor saxophone), Sabby Lewis (piano), Al Morgan (string bass), Joe Booker (drums). This group apparently went on to play at the Top Hat in Toronto. Music Dial for March 1944 reported that Benny Williams had gone into the army and a month later noted that Beverly Peer had replaced

Al Morgan. About this time trumpeter Buddy Anderson was briefly with the band at the Cafe Zanzibar, New York City.

The Lewis band, augmented with New York musicians to twelve pieces, stayed at the Zanzibar from the end of 1943 until April 1944 before returning to the Savoy in Boston. Its personnel was Freddie Webster, Irving Randolph, Idrees Sulieman (trumpet), Maceo Bryant, Howard Scott (trombone), George James (alto saxophone), Jerry Heffron, George Nicholas (tenor saxophone), George Fauntleroy (baritone and alto saxophone), Sabby Lewis (piano), Beverly Peer (string bass), Joe Booker (drums), Evelyn White (vocal). It then remained resident at the Savoy for ten months (where its line-up included one Sherman Freeman (sax)) before going out on a series of one nighters.

Early in 1946 the band, consisting of Eugene Caines (trumpet), Maceo Bryant (trumpet, trombone), Jimmy Tyler (alto saxophone), Paul Gonsalves (tenor saxophone), Bill Dorsey (baritone saxophone), Lewis (piano), Al Morgan (string bass), Eddie Feggans (drums) and Evelyn White (vocal), came to New York to record four titles for the Continental label, *Boston Bounce* being the most musically satisfying. Further recordings the following year saw Dan Turner (tenor saxophone) and Joe Booker (drums) in place of Gonsalves and Feggans, with Tyler and Dorsey also playing tenor. The latter personnel remained unchanged until some time in 1948, when Ray Perry (sax) replaced Tyler, who left to form his own band, and Joe Perry replaced Dorsey, who joined the Illinois Jacquet band. That Lewis often enlarged his personnel for out of town residencies is shown by his line-up of Maceo Bryant, Eugene Caines, unknown (trumpet), Rufus Jones, Shorty Haughton (trombone), Paul Gonsalves, George Fauntleroy (alto saxophone), Dan Turner (tenor saxophone), Bill Dorsey (baritone saxophone), himself (piano), Al Morgan (string bass), Jimmy Crawford (drums), with which he worked the Club Harlem in Atlantic City in the summer of 1946.

During the final years of the 'forties the Lewis band alternated residencies at such Boston clubs as the Hit Hat and Show Boat, with trips to Atlantic City and New York, where it recorded for the Mercury label in April 1949. Trombonist Al Hayes was briefly with Lewis at the end of 1949, and in January 1950 trumpeter Lenny

A later shot of the Sabby Lewis band at the Original Tic Toc Club, Boston, c1948. Left to right: Joe Booker (drums), Al Morgan (string bass), Evelyn White (vocalist), Eugene 'Sugar' Caines (trumpet), Dan Turner (tenor saxophone), Maceo Bryant (trumpet), Jimmy Tyler (alto saxophone), Bill Dorsey (baritone saxophone).

Johnson joined, subsequently telling Kurt Mohr that the personnel then consisted of himself, Hiawatha Lockhardt (trumpet), Elwyn Frazier (alto saxophone), Danny Potter (tenor saxophone), George Perry (baritone saxophone), Sabby Lewis (piano), Champ Jones (string bass), Alan Dawson (drums) and Evelyn White (vocal). Johnson was a member of the band until 1953, apart from a two-month job filling in for Cat Anderson in Duke Ellington's band in the summer of 1951, when his place was temporarily taken by Joe Gordon.

There appears to have been a great deal of coming and going in the Lewis band early in the 'fifties. Down Beat of 10th March 1950 reported that he was leading a new band at Wally's Paradise, Boston, his former personnel having left to join Jimmy Tyler's recently formed group, then playing at the Hit Hat club. Stella Dennis was his singer at Wally's Paradise, but three years later his group at the Showtime Club was mainly made up of such familiar names as Lenny Johnson, Herbie Williams (trumpet), Danny Potter (tenor saxophone), Bill Dorsey (baritone saxophone), himself (piano), Al Morgan (string bass), Alan Dawson (drums). During the 'fifties, Lewis worked for a while as a disc jockey in Boston, but continued to lead groups, as he has done down to the present day. Since the 'sixties he has mostly worked with trios and quintets and nowadays plays mainly cocktail music, though he includes jazz numbers in his book.

Lewis's records include pleasant versions of *Boston Bounce, I Can't Give You Anything But Love, Minor Mania* and *Clayton's Bounce,* all of which reveal the proficiency of the band to advantage. His biggest hit was *Bottoms Up,* a reworking of *Flying Home* with a tenor solo by Jimmy Tyler that led to his forming his own group as a result of the popularity of the record in the Boston area. It is a pity that the Lewis band did not record its most challenging material, but over the years it certainly was a highly musical unit and from time to time included many well-known soloists within its ranks, including saxophonist Sonny Stitt and drummer **Roy Haynes.**

From 1921 to at least 1927 drummer Eugene Primus led one of the most successful bands that worked around Buffalo, New York. His most famous musical alumni were Theodore 'Wingy' Carpenter, the late J. C. Higginbotham, and Juice Wilson. He was working at the Paradise Ballroom in Buffalo during 1921 with a personnel of unknown (trumpet), Ed Slocum (trombone), Mylon Sutton (alto saxophone), Bud Johnson (tenor saxophone), Juice Wilson (violin), Percy Johnson (piano), . . . Edison (banjo), and himself. Five years later he was resident at the same ballrom, his brass section now consisting of Theodore 'Wingy' Carpenter, Walter Temple (trumpet) and J. C. Higginbotham (trombone). The rest of the group was the same as in 1921 except that an unknown alto saxophonist had been added, Slocum had switched to bass, and an unknown banjoist had replaced Edison. Carpenter had persuaded Higginbotham to join the band late in 1926 and he remained with it for seven months.

The last known mention of Primus appeared in the Chicago Defender of 20th August 1927, and it gave a personnel for his Birds Of Paradise that differed little from the above, except that Slocum had returned to trombone, Temple was doubling on banjo, the unknown alto player and Slocum on bass were replaced by Vernon Johnson and Sylvester Turpin, and Horace Millinder was added on alto saxophone. There is no record of the Primus band ever having recorded.

Cincinnati was the home base for many years of one of the most famous of all territory bands, Zack Whyte's Chocolate Beau Brummels, but other bands, foremost amongst them being those led by Wesley Helvey and Clarence Paige, worked out of the town for a number of years and included musicians who were later to gain national or international fame in the jazz sphere.

Helvey, a saxophone player, operated from 1924 to 1930, and our knowledge of his earliest personnels owes much to Bill Coleman. Coleman first worked with Helvey around 1925. The line-up at this time was Bill Coleman (trumpet), 'Pluto' (trombone), John L. Henderson (alto saxophone), Wes Helvey (alto and baritone saxophone), Edgar 'Spider' Courance (tenor saxophone), Vincent Thomas (piano), Jimmy . . . (banjo), John Hargrave (drums). Courance in later years spent some time in Europe, and was still in the band a year later when George 'Buddy' Lee (trumpet) and Louis Thompson (tuba) had been added, and J. C. Higginbotham (trombone), Henry Jamerson (alto saxophone) and Slaughter Campbell (banjo) had replaced 'Pluto', Henderson and the banjoist.

The Pittsburgh Courier of 19th May 1927 reported that Helvey's Famous Troubadours were to play a lodge dance at Columbus, Ohio, on 26th May, adding that it was a ten-piece unit. Two years later Billboard carried a news item that Helvey's band had concluded an engagement at the Swiss Gardens, Cincinnati, and was going to play in Buffalo. It mentioned the presence of drummer Gerald Hobson. The Chicago Defender for 4th May 1929 also reported this fact, saying that Hobson and Joe Henderson had been injured in a car accident. Two months later the same paper mentioned that saxophonist Milton Senior had been added to the band, while the Chicago Defender of 10th August stated that trombonist Vic Dickenson had left Helvey to join Leonard Gay's band in Madison, Wisconsin. Quentin Jackson was a member of the band from August to December 1929. He has listed the personnel during his stay as George 'Buddy' Lee, Steve Dunn (trumpet), himself (trombone), Henry Jamerson, John L. Henderson (alto saxophone), Fred Jackson (tenor saxophone), Wes Helvey (clarinet, alto and baritone saxophone), Vincent Thomas (piano), Sam Helvey (banjo), Brent Sparks (tuba), Gerald Hopson (drums). Dunn was one of the earliest high note trumpeters, and a musician who appears in several band personnels during the 'thirties. At some point during the 'twenties trumpeter Theodore 'Wingy' Carpenter was with Helvey, as was Jonah Jones briefly in 1930, the year in which the band finally broke up. Helvey's subsequent career is unknown.

Saxophonist Clarence Paige formed his band in the same year as Helvey, but is known to have continued as a leader until at least the close of 1936. Theodore 'Wingy' Carpenter worked with Paige during the 'twenties, but the first full personnel we have comes from Bill Coleman, who was with Paige for a time from 1924 to 1926 when the band was playing in Cincinnati. Subsequently he went on a tour of West Virginia and Kentucky. The band then consisted of Bill Coleman, . . . Nassau (trumpet), Danny Logan (trombone), Wilbur Cocksey, Jimmy Smith (alto saxophone), Clarence Paige (C-melody saxophone), William Smith (piano), Bob Robinson (banjo), Clarence Logan (tuba) and Edgar James (drums).

Paige worked with Zack Whyte from about 1928 for several years, then resumed his former career. His band in Cincinnati in December 1933 consisted of Archie Johnson, Sleepy Grider, Steve Dunn (trumpet), Bob Kinley, Vic Dickenson (trombone), Earl Tribble, Fred Jackson, William Gill, Clarence Paige (reeds), William King (piano), Lawrence Gray (guitar, tenor saxophone),

Earl Baker (string bass), Bill Tye (drums). This was, by all accounts, a very good band, and Thomas 'Fats' Waller took it on the road as his supporting group in 1933 when he was working at radio station WLW in Cincinnati. Bill Coleman returned to the band for three months in summer 1935 and recalls himself, Thomas 'Sleepy' Grider, Melvin . . . (trumpet), Bob Kennerly (trombone), Earl Tribble (alto saxophone), Clarence Paige (tenor saxophone) and Tommy Smith (drums) as amongst those present. Paige called his band the Royal Syncopators. In 1936 he was working at the Cotton Club in Cincinnati with Ed Savage, Jimmy Hemphill, Steve Dunn (trumpet), Ike Covington, unknown (trombone), Herman 'Poncho' Pettis (alto saxophone), Jack Jackson, Clarence Paige (tenor saxophone), Nelson Goode (piano), unknown (guitar), Willie Wilkins (string bass), Jimmy Jackson (drums) and . . . Connelly (vocals, front man). As with Helvey, Paige's post-bandleading career is totally obscure.

Zack Whyte was born in Richmond, Kentucky, in 1898, and in the early 'twenties studied at Wilberforce, Ohio, where he met Horace Henderson and became a member of his collegiate band, playing banjo and providing arrangements. After this he went to Cincinnati and for a year was out of music. The Pittsburgh Courier of 19th November 1932 carries a rather curious story on Whyte: when Fletcher Henderson was touring in his area at some time in the middle 'twenties Whyte engaged him for a week, and made such a profit that he decided to form his own orchestra.

The exact year in which Whyte formed his band is uncertain, but it would seem to be 1924. Much confusion exists about Whyte's personnels over the years. I have conducted a series of interviews with musicians who played with the band, but I have unearthed such conflicting evidence that the task becomes even more difficult. The most valiant attempt to sift the details that I have read is by Mr Theo Zwicky and appeared in Storyville magazine, a source to which I shall refer frequently in the course of this section. Mr Zwicky has a note of Whyte leading a quintet in Michigan prior to 1924 (the personnel including trumpeter Bill Coleman), and mentions that J. C. Higginbotham mixed with Whyte's musicians around 1924-25. In fact, I think the date here should be 1926, though I would not care to be too dogmatic. What is certain is that at some point around 1928 the Whyte band became a real force. Melvin 'Sy' Oliver became a member early that year. He joined Whyte at Huntington, West Virginia, and has said that at this time the band used only head arrangements. He remained in the band for three years until 1930, left to join Alphonso Trent, and then returned for a few months in the same year. What little evidence we have of Oliver's stay with the Trent band suggests that it was during 1931, and I suspect that he is a year out in his statement. Speaking to Mr Zwicky of his early days with the band Oliver said: 'Zack's band was very successful and very popular. They had a

sort of arrogance and a belief in themselves that was a challenge to any youngster. It was like a close club. You walked in and you had to make it. We came to New York shortly after I joined the band. We played the Savoy twice and I couldn't wait to get out of New York. I think that was because the place frightened me then.'

The first definite personnel we have of the Whyte band comes from a photograph that must have been taken in late 1928, for it advertises an appearance at a dance hall in January 1929. The line-up is Henry Savage, Bubber White, Sy Oliver (trumpet), Floyd 'Stump' Brady (trombone), Earl Tribble, Clarence Paige (alto saxophone), Ben Richardson (clarinet, alto saxophone), Al Sears (tenor saxophone), Herman Chittison (piano), Montgomery Morrison (tuba), William Benton (drums), Zack Whyte (banjo, leader). This is the group that made the first records for the Gennett company. A few months later Richardson was probably replaced by Fred Jackson, and this was almost certainly the personnel that appeared at the opening of the Alhambra Ballroom in New York on 13th September 1929, in company with the bands of Luis Russell, Benny Carter, Roy Johnson, and The Missourians.

According to trombonist Quentin Jackson he, Fred Jackson and George 'Buddy' Lee joined Whyte on 1st January 1930, and he gives the personnel for the whole of 1930 as George 'Buddy' Lee, Henry Savage, Sy Oliver (trumpet), himself (trombone), Earl Tribble, Clarence Paige (alto saxophone), Fred Jackson (tenor saxophone), Herman Chittison (piano), Charlie Anderson (banjo), Montgomery Morrison (tuba), William Benton (drums), Zack Whyte (leader). The Baltimore Afro American for March 1930 reports the band's presence on 6th March at the New Albert Auditorium, Baltimore, listing the line-up as above, except that George Oliver is included on trumpet, and John L. Henderson, instead of Jackson, on saxophone. George Oliver is probably a misprint for George Lee, but Henderson is almost certainly correct.

In December 1930 Lee and Quentin Jackson left for McKinney's Cotton Pickers, to be replaced by John Nesbitt and Vic Dickenson respectively. Nesbitt only stayed a short while and his place was taken by Steve Dunn. In 1931 Fred Jackson had certainly come in for Henderson, and William King (piano) and Madison Lennon (string bass) had replaced Chittison and Morrison. Late in the year Melvin Hampton (guitar) and Wilbur Cartwright (string bass) took over temporarily for Alexander and Lennon.

In the latter part of 1931 the Whyte band was joined by Bennie Moten's band, Blanche Calloway's band, Roy Johnson's Happy Pals, and Chick Webb's band for a tour involving nightly band battles. Sy Oliver remembers that each band in turn had its nights of triumph. One can only regret that tape recorders were not available at the time of this tour!

Vic Dickenson has identified a photograph of the Whyte

ZACK WHYTE & HIS CHOCOLATE BEAU BRUMMELS
Jan. 22, 24 & 27, Tue., Thur., Sun. Mat.
CRYSTAL DANSANT

Zack Whyte and his Chocolate Beau Brummels, early 1929.
Back row: left to right: Al Sears (tenor and baritone saxo-
phone), Henry Savage, Sy Oliver, Bubber White (trumpets),
Earl Tribble, Ben Richardson, Clarence Paige (saxes). Front
row, left to right: Floyd Brady (trombone), Herman Chittison,
(piano), Montgomery Morrison (tuba), William Benton
(drums), Zack Whyte (leader, banjo) is sitting.

band as containing Sy Oliver, Dunn, himself, Tribble, Paige, Fred Jackson, 'Bim' (piano), 'Tarzan' (guitar), 'Rockin' Chair' (string bass), Benton and Whyte. 'Rockin' Chair' was Lennon's nickname, and 'Bim' and 'Tarzan' are presumably William King and Charlie Anderson respectively, so the picture was certainly taken during 1931. Some confusion exists as to when Dickenson left the band, but it seems likely to have been early in 1932. In that year it is known that the following musicians worked with Whyte—Henry Savage, Sy Oliver, Archie Johnson (trumpet), Gus Wilson, Elmer Crumbley (replaced by Eli Robinson) (trombone), Earl Tribble, William Gill (alto saxophone), Fred Jackson (tenor saxophone), William King (replaced by Belford 'Zinky' Hendricks) (piano), Sam Alexander (guitar), Montgomery Morrison (string bass), Truck Parham (string bass, vocal),

William Benton (drums), with 'Snake' McConnell (vocal, front man, entertainer) being added in May.

It appears that late in 1932 Vic Dickenson returned to the band for a period of a few months and, more surprisingly, Sy Oliver was present around the same time. During 1933 the following musicians are known to have played with Whyte—Sy Oliver, Henry Savage, Andy Gibson (replaced in turn by Leroy 'Snake' White and Jimmie Shaw) (trumpet), Vic Dickenson, Eli Robinson, Gus Wilson (replaced for a short while by Floyd 'Stump' Brady and then in the spring by Oliver 'Slim' Rhodes) (trombone), Eddie Barefield, Ben Richardson (replaced by Jerry Blake and George Johnson respectively during the summer), Delbert Lee (tenor saxophone), Charlie 'Rev' Williams (piano), Sam Alexander (guitar), Montgomery Morrison, Truck Parham (string bass), William Benton (replaced by Bill Baldwin at his death) (drums).

By 1934 many of the most prominent of the former Whyte sidemen had gone on to join nationally famous bands, but his personnel for that year included Dick Wilson who was soon to become famous as a member of Andy Kirk's group. It has been reported that trombonist Henderson Chambers was with Whyte for a while around this time, but for most of the year he led Henry

Savage, Ellis 'Stump' Whitlock, probably Paul King (replaced by Harry DeShazer) (trumpet), Oliver 'Slim' Rhodes, Ike Covington (trombone), Herman Pettis, Earle 'Buddy' Miller (alto saxophone), Delbert Lee, Dick Wilson (tenor saxophone), Nelson Goode (piano), Jerry Lane (guitar), Truck Parham (replaced by . . . Lucas) (string bass), Bill Baldwin (drums). Whyte's 1935 personnel showed little change—John Thomas (trombone) and Fred Jackson (tenor saxophone) replaced Rhodes and Wilson, Lee and Parham left, and J. Burroughs was added to double on trombone and string bass. After this Whyte's career seems largely undocumented, possibly because as a result of the rise of the swing bands his own group no longer attracted the attention it had in years past. At some point in the 'thirties pianist/arranger Tadd Dameron worked with Whyte, as apparently did tenor saxophonist George Kelly and drummer 'Kid Lips' Hackette. It is not even known with any certainty when Whyte finally gave up bandleading, but he had been out of the music business for many years when he died in Kentucky on 10th March 1967, aged either sixty-eight or sixty-nine.

The foregoing lists of personnels might appear finicky to some readers, but it is given in detail for two reasons. The first is to show just how many jazz musicians who subsequently became famous worked with Whyte; the second to demonstrate the difficulty of pinpointing changes in line-ups with accuracy decades later. Despite the esteem in which Whyte's band was held it only took part in five recording sessions, and only seven titles were released. It is unfortunate that the issued titles all date from 1929, for the evidence of musicians makes it clear that the band did not reach its peak for another couple of years and that recordings undertaken during the 1931-33 period would have given a much better idea of the real worth of the band. (There was, in fact, a session in November 1931, but the three titles made were rejected and in any case do not look too promising.) This does not mean that the records were totally disappointing, for they do give clues that it was an excellent unit. The first issued title, *Mandy*, has efficient ensemble work, though the saxes are rather too close in intonation to Guy Lombardo's for comfort. The highspots are the contributions of a good alto player and an excellent strong-toned trumpeter, whom I take to be Henry Savage. Savage gained a considerable reputation as one of the first specialist high note trumpeters, but never worked with a nationally famous band. *Hum All Your Troubles Away*, from a second session, is mundane, but has a fine trombone solo from Floyd Brady. *It's Tight Like That* and *West End Blues*, from a third date, are pleasant without being outstanding. The best issued title by the band is *Good Feelin' Blues*, opening with a bright lead to a trumpet theme that is notable for its relaxed phrasing and good tune, presumably played by Savage. Later there are other good solos by Chittison, an alto player, and a second trumpeter who uses a plunger. The latter could be Oliver, but it is equally possible that it is White, about whom we

know very little. *Wailin' Blues* is almost as good, again featuring the same two trumpeters and a highly proficient alto player.

Andy Gibson told Stanley Dance that when he was in the band Sy Oliver was already writing in the style that became associated with the Jimmie Lunceford band, adding that in his opinion Sy's scores were interpreted better by Whyte's band than by Lunceford's. Dance subsequently took this up with Oliver who agreed with Gibson, adding that a virtuoso element in the Lunceford band sometimes became predominant. Mr Zwicky quotes Eddie Barefield as further support : 'This was a very fine band indeed and it has not received its fair share of recognition. The style of the band was set by Sy Oliver, and the arrangements were much the same as those Jimmie Lunceford used later. In fact, when Sy got an offer from Lunceford, he took his arrangements with him.'

Just before joining Lunceford Oliver wrote a few arrangements for his band, which he described as 'just rehashes of the things I'd done for Zack's band'. A number of other musicians have confirmed this point, leading one to speculate on what might have happened if Whyte had recorded at his peak for a major company. Perhaps what we now accept as the 'Lunceford Sound' would instead have been known as the 'Whyte Sound'. The arrangements used on Whyte's issued recordings are quite simple and it is doubtful whether Oliver had much hand in them, but these titles were made at a time when he was probably still learning his trade. It seems clear that Whyte could potentially have become one of the outstanding names of the big band era. He was unfortunate never to have had the opportunity to record for the right company at the right time.

Cleveland was not a town that spawned many bands. The best known units were probably those of Jack Carter (1938), Evelyn Freeman (late 'thirties) and Marion Sears (c 1930-36). Sears is the brother of tenor saxophonist Al Sears, and in 1930 led a band unusual for the day in having numerous musicians who could double. Trumpeter Francis Williams, still active as a musician in New York City, was with Sears in 1930 and gave the personnel during his stay as himself (trumpet, piano), Heads Adams (alto saxophone, trumpet), Marion Sears (clarinet, tenor saxophone, oboe), Andy Anderson (alto and baritone sax, string bass), Buster Harding (piano), 'Smitty' (guitar), Snaggs Williams (drums). The oboe was not a common instrument for jazz groups at this period, or indeed at any time, and it would be fascinating to know what the band sounded like.

In October 1933 Earle Warren joined Sears's band, listing its personnel as Leroy 'Snake' White (trumpet), himself (alto saxophone), Andy Anderson (tenor saxophone, string bass), Marion Sears (clarinet, tenor saxophone), Charlie Ross (piano), Shavers Gardner (guitar), unknown (drums). Reminiscing on this period for the magazine Coda, Warren recalled: 'We worked for gangsters and our salary was only $10.00 a week. Our money came from the girls who danced on the floor. They split the tips with the band each night. I didn't know I was getting into this when I first went to Cleveland. You never talked about quitting if you were working for a club run by a big shot.'

Later, after speaking of the long hours and hard working conditions, he added: 'We had a tap dancer who would "Tom" and they'd throw money. He had red pants and looked like a minstrel tap dancer and talked real Southernish. He was a real "Tom" but he did get the money. I ended up with more money than I ever dreamed I would make. Some weeks it would be $80 and $90, which was fabulous in those days. It didn't last for long because the whole city regime changed.'

Warren left the band in spring 1935, about the same time that White went to join the Eddie Barefield band in California, to be replaced first by Pee Wee Jackson and then by Freddie Webster. He returned for a brief period in 1936, but the band was no longer getting good bookings and he left just before its break-up.

By contrast to Cleveland, Detroit was a town with outstanding local bands, among the best being the various Jean Goldkette aggregations and McKinney's Cotton Pickers. For much of the 'twenties a popular local favourite was the band led by violinist Earl Walton. A photograph taken of it at the Palais de Dance, Detroit, in 1923, shows Charlie Gaines, Harry Owens (trumpet), John Tobias (trombone), Bernard Calloway (alto saxophone), Fred Culley, Al Goines (sax), Earl Walton, unknown (violin), Robert Bush (piano), Earl Foley (banjo), Clyde Hayes (brass bass), George Robinson (drums). The band seems to have been permanently based at the Palais de Dance and used the name in its title. A Chicago Defender news item of 26th March 1927 mentions that cornetist Thornton Brown was a member of its personnel. In 1928 Tobias and Robinson from the 1923 group were still present—Tobias was Milt Buckner's uncle—and one of the saxophonists was Fred Kewley. After this date little was heard of the band though it was certainly in existence in 1930, for Milt Buckner wrote his first arrangement for it that year—a time when he was being brought up by drummer George Robinson. At some time in 1928 Joe Eldridge (alto saxophone) was a member of Walton's band, his replacement being Ted Buckner, who later made a name with the Lunceford band. From Milt Buckner's recollections Walton broke up his band in the early 'thirties, and afterwards opened a club.

The standard discographical reference books list a single session, recorded in November 1932, by Jimmy Raschel and his Orchestra, from which one title—*It Don't Mean A Thing (If It Ain't Got That Swing)*—was issued. Apart from the fact that the vocal was by Estelle Galloway nothing is known of the personnel.

Raschel began his bandleading activities about the middle of the 'twenties. Chick Gordon (alto saxophone) started his professional career with him at this time when Raschel was working out of Danville, Illinois. Within a few years he had made Detroit his base and there he led bands right into the early 'forties. His 1928 band included Henry Savage (trumpet), George Johnson, Hubert . . . (alto saxophone), Jimmy Raschel, Arthur Raschel (reeds), and 'Popcorn' Crawford (drums) (list supplied by George Johnson). Unfortunately, no information exists on Raschel's personnel at the time of his recording session.

Milt Buckner was with the band during 1935 and part of 1936 and it is to him that we owe a knowledge of its line-up at this period. He has identified the personnel from a 1935 photograph as Reginald Emmett, Cedric Couch, Orlando Dyer (trumpet), Johnny Orange (trombone), Hobart McLardy, Willard Brown, Arthur 'Nanny' Raschel (reeds), himself (piano, vibraphone), 'Scotty' (guitar), Tom McNary (string bass), George Bacon (drums). Another photograph from the same period has also been identified by Buckner, the line-up differing from the above in having Tig Whaley (trombone), Ted Buckner (alto saxophone), Arthur Russell (tenor saxophone), Alfonso McKibbon (guitar) and . . . McKey (drums) in place of Orange, McLardy, A. Raschel, 'Scotty' and Bacon respectively, with Toby Bowen (baritone saxophone) added. It is possible that 'Scotty' is in fact McKibbon. It is not certain which of these photographs was taken first, but I suspect that it was the former.

In 1936 the personnel had changed little. Jake Wiley (trombone) and Arthur Raschel (sax) had replaced Whaley and Russell, Bacon is now shown fronting the band, and McKey (or Mackay) is drummer. Milt Buckner remembers that the band went on tour in 1936 under the name of McKinney's Cotton Pickers, appearing at St Louis, Kansas City, Oklahoma City, Tulsa, Dallas, Houston and other Texas towns. One trip, from Corpus Christi to Amarillo, involved a journey of 700 miles in a single day. At the end of this particular tour the men had difficulty in getting paid by Raschel, which led to a fight between the leader and his brother Arthur (whose nickname 'Nanny' arose from the fact that he showed an inordinate liking for a drink not normally associated with musicians of this period—milk). Shortly afterwards Buckner left the band.

During 1937 trombonist James 'Trummy' Young was with Raschel, but the band was seldom mentioned in the press. In 1939 and 1940 Down Beat carried short news items on Raschel on several occasions. The February 1939 issue reported that the band was '. . . gaining favor through this section, and will hole up at the Knickerbocker late this month, after a series of one-niters all over Michigan, Indiana and Illinois.' The Knickerbocker was a club in Flint, Michigan. Seven months later the same magazine noted that Francis Gray (ex-Cotton

Jimmy Raschel and his Orchestra, 1935: Johnny Orange (trombone), Reginald Emmett, Cedric Couch, Orlander Dyer (trumpet), Tom McNary (string bass). George Bacon (drums), Hobart McLardy, William Brown, Arthur 'Nanny' Raschel (reeds), 'Scotty' (guitar), Milt Buckner (piano, vibraphone), Inset in bass drum: Jimmy Raschel. Left: Jimmy Raschel's Orchestra with George 'Lazy Bones' Bacon, 1936: Arthur 'Nanny' Raschel, Tubby Bowen, Ted Buckner, Willard Brown (reeds), Tom McNary (string bass), Milt Buckner (piano, vibraphone), . . . Mackay (drums), George Bacon (director), Orlander Dyer, Cedric Couch, Reginald Emmett (trumpet), Jake Wiley (trombone), Al McKibbon (guitar).

Pickers) was first alto with Raschel, and in the first six months of 1940 the band was reported as playing at various locations in Michigan. Buckner rejoined the band for a while in 1940, listing the personnel as Christie Taylor (trumpet), Michael 'Booty' Wood, James Wormick (trombone), James Robinson, Herman Barker (alto saxophone), Wardell Gray (tenor saxophone), himself (piano), Tom McWeary (string bass), Skipper Everett (drums). Within a few months Howard McGhee (trumpet) had been added, to be replaced by Reginald Emmett; Bernie Peacock (alto saxophone) and George Nicholas (tenor saxophone) replaced Robinson and Gray. This was the personnel when Wood left the band shortly after Pearl Harbour, and it is believed that Raschel gave up band-leading soon afterwards. By all accounts the bands he led during the middle and later 'thirties were highly proficient units, but without regular radio outlets they failed to come to the attention of record company scouts and never had the opprtunity to record.

All known references to the Willie Jones Orchestra, a band that worked mainly in the Indiana territory, date from 1927. The group must have been formed by 1926 for the Chicago Defender of 8th January 1927 refers to Leonard Gay (ex-Speed Webb orchestra) joining Jones's sax section and states that he was under contract until the following May. Billboard of the same date reports that the band was playing at the Arcadia Ballroom, Fort Wayne, Indiana, until 1st May, with a personnel of Ed White (trumpet), L. Gay, V. Bassett, Ray Dickerson (sax), Oscar Johnson (piano), Tom Smith (banjo), C. Peterson (bass), Willie Jones (drums). Late in May, Billboard announced that the band was at the Palais Royale, South Bend, Indiana, with Ed White, Ted Shame (trumpet), V. Dickerson, S. Scearce (trombone), Leonard Gay (sax, director), V. Bassett, S. Richardson (sax), H. Seldon (piano), W. Warfield (banjo), C. Peterson (bass), Willie Jones (drums). V. Dickerson is of course Vic Dickenson. In its issue of 27th August 1927 Billboard states that the band was at Saginaw, Michigan, for the summer and would be stopping at Richmond, Indiana, to record for the Gennett company. This session took place in November and three titles were recorded and issued. The later history of the band is unknown.

Michigan Stomp and *Bugs* are both performances which make use of tight scores. The arrangement of *Bugs* is quite complex for the period. The solos are short and there are not too many of them, though breaks are more numerous. A trombonist is heard on *Michigan Stomp*. Since he bears little stylistic resemblance to anything we know of Dickenson, he was more probably the obscure Scearce (or Seearce). Seldon has a creditable solo on *Bugs*, a slightly fussy theme, and there are several breaks by a good trumpeter. Overall the band has a rather white sound, reminding one a little of contemporary Trumbauer, but its technical expertise is never in doubt and the section playing is of a high standard. Presumably it was Leonard Gay who shaped the band's music, in which case he proves himself to have been an excellent organiser.

For two decades Frank Terry led bands that often included musicians who went on to greater fame with name units, generally working around the Ohio area. The first known reference to him concerned the Terry and Roberson Orchestra which, with a line-up of Fletcher 'High Note Henry' Devore (trumpet), Frank Terry (trombone), Leonard Davidson (clarient), Muny Smith (piano) and Roy Roberson (drums, xylophone), was working in Omaha during 1919. Davidson is probably the same man who in later years played with Sonny Clay in California.

It is not certain what Terry did during the next few years, but Billboard for 29th January 1927 reported that J. Frank Terry's Chicago Nightingales, a ten-piece band, were playing at Canton, Ohio, and were going on to New York. The Chicago Defender of 7th May 1927 gave the personnel of Terry's orchestra at the time as Roy Shelton, Harry Haskins (trumpet), J. Frank Terry (trombone, sax, director), Arthur Watkins, Bernard Wright, Millard Lacey (reeds), Wendall Strong (piano), Harrison Hall (tuba), Harry Johnson (drums). The same newspaper mentioned that Terry was resident at the Red Mill, Akron, Ohio, five months later, with Frogeye Roulette, Wendall Bulley, Cary O. Taylor, Emmett Hogan and Charles Peek replacing Shelton, Haskins, Watkins and Hall, though what instruments the five newcomers played is not stated. In its issue of 4th February 1928 the Chicago Defender noted that saxophonist Clarence Jackson had joined Terry's band. It wrote that Jackson was an ex-member of the P. G. Lowery circus band and came from Henderson, Kentucky. On 22nd September a news item in the same paper mentions that Terry's band had spent the summer at Forest Park, Toledo, Ohio, and included Frank Woods (piano, violin) and Bert Cobb (tuba). Cobb is best known for being a member of King Oliver's Dixie Syncopators before this date. Early in 1929 Terry was resident in Toledo, Ohio; the Chicago Defender gave a personnel of William J. Austin, Charles Clark,

James H. Nevils Jr, Clarence Jackson, Lester Smith, Frank Woods, Ben Thigpen, Raymond Mack, Roy Shelton, Bert Cobb and Silas White. Shelton, Jackson, Woods, Cobb and Thigpen played trumpet, sax, piano/violin, tuba and drums respectively.

For several months in 1931, Eddie Barefield played alto saxophone with Terry in Toledo, and remembers the other members of the band as Churchill Harris, . . . Taylor (trumpet), Frank Terry (trombone), Rube Wardell (alto saxophone), unknown (tenor saxophone and piano), Milton Fore (tuba), . . . Price (drums). During the summer of 1932 Terry's band left Toledo for a tour of New York state, breaking up in Amsterdam, N.Y. Emmett Berry has told Bertrand Demeusy that he was a member along with trumpeter Reunald Jones, trombonist Eli Robinson and saxophonist Ben Richardson. From 1933 to 1936 Terry, still retaining the Chicago Nightingales billing, led his best band. Trumpeter Francis Williams has given the personnel when he joined as Dick Vance, himself, Willie Lewis (trumpet), John 'Rocks' McConnell (trombone), Bill Crump, James Willis (sax), Gene Revels (tenor saxophone), Darrell Harris (piano), Connie 'Bama' Landers (guitar), Milton Fore (string bass, tuba), Phil Keeble (drums), Bill Simpson (vocal, dancer, director); but within a short time Al Gibson, Howard Watson, James Shirley and Howard 'Bunny' Fields had replaced Revels, Harris, Landers and Fore. Apparently Terry quite frequently left the band for weeks or even months at a time while he concentrated on other work, secure in the knowledge that his absence would make no difference to its performances. It finally broke up early in 1936.

From February 1936 to September 1938 Terry led an entirely different group: Joe Bail, Willard Thompson (trumpet), himself (trombone), 'Sax' Garrison, Leon Goodson (alto saxophone), Chauncey Graham (tenor saxophone), Ed Taylor (piano), Joe Lucas (string bass) and 'Chink' Lowden (drums) in Buffalo, N.Y. Four issues of Down Beat, from September 1938 to January 1939, carried a note that Terry was resident at McVans, Buffalo, presumably with the above personnel. After this no more was heard of Terry, but he is believed to have retired from bandleading in the early 'forties.

Philadelphia has been the base for a number of bands that have been well spoken of by musicians. One of the earliest was the White Brothers Orchestra. It played several seasons at the Roadside Inn. In summer 1925 it consisted of Gene Prince (trumpet), Harry 'Father' White (trombone, sax), Willie White (sax, trumpet), Warren Adams (sax, violin), Gil White (sax), Eddie White (piano), . . . Nelson (banjo), . . . Booth (tuba) and Tommy Miles (drums). Eddie, Harry and Willie White were brothers, and Eddie and Gil White were their cousins. The following summer the band, minus Willie White, Adams, Gil White, Nelson and Booth, but with Jimmy Mundy (sax) added, played at the Belmont Cabaret in Atlantic City. From 1927 to 1933 the personnel of the band remained reasonably stable, usually with Warren Jefferson (trumpet), Harry White (trumpet, trombone, alto saxophone), Willie White (alto saxophone, guitar, banjo), Jimmy Mundy (tenor saxophone), Eddie White (piano), Mason Hawkins (guitar), . . . Booth (tuba, string bass), and Tommy Miles (drums). They divided their time now between winter seasons in Newark, N.J., and residencies in Washington, D.C., where trumpeter Arthur Whetsol played with them before he joined Duke Ellington.

Orchestra World of October 1929 reported that the band, listed in the news item as Eddie White and Orchestra, was then resident at the Roseland, Newark, after dates in Washington, D.C., Atlantic City and Philadelphia. It gave a personnel of Warren Jefferson, Elton Hill (trumpet), Eugene Simon (trombone), Morris White, James Mundy, Adrian Loftis (sax), Mabel White (vocal) and the piano, guitar, string bass and drums as previously noted. Two months later it noted that Lester 'Shad' Collins (trumpet) had replaced Hill. Its issue of January 1930 reported that the orchestra was going to play at the Arcadia Ballroom in New York City and while there would record for the Brunswick company. Whether the band did record is not known, but no titles were ever issued.

Harry 'Father' White frequently worked in New York when not appearing with the band, and during 1929-30 led his own orchestra at the Nest Club. For this residency the late Glyn Paque gave a collective personnel of Harry Noisette, Willie 'Sparks' White (trumpet), Harry White (trombone), Glyn Paque, Russell Procope, Morris White (alto saxophone), Johnny Russell, Gilbert White (tenor saxophone), Don Kirkpatrick, Joe Turner, Eddie White, Fitz Weston (piano), Danny Barker (guitar), Simon Marrero (string bass), 'Cripple Spitty' (drums), Hannah Sylvester and Mattie Hite (vocal). Apparently Joe 'King' Oliver once or twice used the band for New York dates. From 1931 Harry White worked with name bands such as Cab Calloway's and Mills Blue Rhythm Band, though it is probable that the White Brothers Orchestra still continued for a while after this.

For well over a decade George 'Doc' Hyder led a band that worked around the New England states, frequently being resident in Philadelphia. Pianist Earle Howard told the Swiss collector Theo Zwicky that he had heard Hyder's band in Atlantic City in 1924 or 1925, presumably soon after it was formed, and Mr Zwicky has noted that Doc Hyder's Southernaires were playing in a revue with singer Lucille Hegamin in Philadelphia early in 1927. The New York Age of 16th June 1928 reported that the Hyder band would appear at the Lafayette Theatre for a week from 18th June. Unfortunately the personnels of Hyder's early bands remain completely unknown. Interest was aroused in Hyder's band of the 1933 period because it became known that some of the musicians took part in recording sessions by the Wash-

board Rhythm Kings. Finally, Mr Zwicky managed to obtain details of the line-up from the late Bernard Archer and Ben Smith. It was established that a number of well-known musicians were with Hyder in 1933, the full personnel consisting of Taft Jordan, Herman Autrey, Lincoln Mills (trumpet), Bernard Archer, John 'Shorty' Haughton (trombone), Dick Taylor, Stewart Scott (alto saxophone), Alexander 'Puny' Gray (tenor saxophone), Ellis Reynolds (piano), Lynnwood Barnes (guitar), Wesley Fitzgerald (string bass, tuba), Shorty Wilkins (drums). Hyder himself was a violinist but it is doubtful whether he actually played with his band in later years.

The February and April 1937 issues of Tempo reported that the Hyder band was resident at the Ubangi Club, Philadelphia, but unhappily did not name any musicians. Charlie Gaines has mentioned that trumpeters Dave Riddick and Alex 'Puny' Stevens, reedmen Ben Smith and Craig Watson, and banjoist Steve Washington were with Hyder during the 'thirties. For many years after giving up bandleading Hyder was an official in Philadelphia for the musicians' union.

Although in later years Jimmy Gorham's band made Philadelphia its home base, his original group came from North Carolina and included Campbell 'Skeets' Tolbert (clarinet, alto saxophone) and Andrew 'Mule' Maize (drums). This band worked in New York City during the 1929-31 period. By 1932 Gorham was in Philadelphia and Taft Jordan and Dave Riddick were with him before they went to work with Doc Hyder. It appears that Gorham's personnel from 1935 to 1938 was reasonably stable—his line-up, provided by Leon Comegys and Bill Doggett, being Chiefie Scott, Johnny Lynch, . . . Cooper (trumpet), Burt Clagett, Leon Comegys (trombone), Ted Barnett, John Brown (alto saxophone), Ivey Wilson, James Cawthorne (tenor saxophone), Bill Doggett (piano), Roscoe Fritz (guitar), Wallington Lawrence (string bass), Rossiere 'Shadow' Wilson (drums) and Grace Granger (vocal). When the band went to New York in 1938 it was taken over by Doggett.

Down Beat of 15th February 1940 reported that Jimmy Gorham's Kentuckians 'a Philly bunch discovered by Willie Bryant', were playing opposite the Count Basie band at New York's Golden Gate. The personnel was Johnny Lynch, Adriano Taggart, Jerome Taggart (trumpet), Raymond W. Richardson, 'Porky' Hinson (trombone), Neal Myers, Silas Johnson (alto saxophone), James Cawthorne, James Adams (tenor saxophone), Charles Harp (piano), Wellington Lawrence (string bass), Berisford Shepherd (drums), Miriam Hutchinson (vocal), Jimmy Gorham (leader and several instruments).

Eddie 'Lockjaw' Davis, for many years a key member of the Count Basie band, worked with Gorham in Philadelphia from 1940 to September 1942, recalling the three trumpeters and Hinson from the personnel listed above plus 'Ford' (alto saxophone), James Cawthorn (tenor saxophone) and James 'Coastville' Harris (drums).

In May 1944 Down Beat reported that trombonist Lionel Corbin was with Gorham; the last reference to the leader so far found occurred in the 1st December 1944 issue of the same magazine, which says: 'Another maestro shining up his baton is Jimmy Gorham. Although not in uniform, the draft cracked his old band, but the wave of service discharges may put it back on the ball.' As nothing more was heard of Gorham we may presume that the Down Beat report was over optimistic.

Pianist Lonnie Slappy formed a band in Philadelphia in April 1937. His 1937-38 group included several musicians who were destined to become well known. His personnel at the time was Frank Galbreath (trumpet, vocal), Joe Wilder (trumpet), Ernest 'Son' Leavy, Jimmy Hamilton (alto saxophone, clarinet), Freddie Williams (tenor and baritone saxophone, clarinet), Alex 'Puny' Gray (tenor saxophone), himself (piano), Skeeter Best (guitar) and Rudy Traylor (drums). On some dates Pearl Bailey worked with Slappy as a vocalist and dancer.

During the middle 'forties, Slappy cut down the size of his band to a septet, with tenor saxophonist Happy Caldwell, trumpeter Johnny Lynch and drummer Garry Lee as regular members. Music Dial for April 1944 stated that Slappy had been resident at Red Hill Inn, Pensauken, N.J., for the past three years, and it is believed that he worked with small groups throughout the 'forties. The big band of 1937-38 attracted some attention and test records were made, but regrettably they were never released.

Pittsburgh has produced many famous jazz musicians but few of the bands that were formed there gained other than a purely local reputation. Billy Page's Broadway Syncopators have rated an occasional mention in jazz history books because it was with this band that Don Redman first came to New York. It has been claimed that even at this time he was a very skilful arranger. The Pittsburgh Courier of 20th January 1923 mentions that Page's band was booked to appear at the local Temple Casino on 5th February. Two months later it arrived in New York. The New York Age of 21st March noted its presence, reporting that Page had previously worked with Lucille Hegamin and that the band was booked by Paul Specht, a prominent white bandleader and booker of the day. It was working at the Lincoln Theatre and the band members were Leroy White (trumpet, french-horn), Elmer Warner (trombone), Billy Page, Don Redman (sax, clarinet, oboe), Roy Cheeks (piano), Sam Ringold (banjo), Chester Campbell (tuba), Wm Cleveland (drums, manager). In April the New York Clipper noted that the band was to appear at the Beau Arts Cafe in Philadelphia. In February 1924 the Pittsburgh Courier reported that Page was to reorganise his Broadway Syncopators in Pittsburgh.

The 26th April edition of the Pittsburgh Courier carried a story that the band, with a new personnel of Clarence Dorsey, Rex Stewart (trumpet), Henry Robinson (trombone), Billy Page (clarinet, sax), Harrison Jackson, Fred Washington (sax), Danny Wilson (piano), Elmer Turner (banjo), Henry Jackson (tuba) and Rebert Drew (drums), was a hit in New York and that from 4th May it would be starting a six-month residency at the Capitol Palace Club on Lenox Avenue. A month later it mentioned that Floyd Fitch had joined the orchestra and that it was due to record *Chicago Gouge* and *Burning Kisses* for the Okeh label. These titles were recorded but never issued. Page closed at the Capitol Palace in October 1924 and returned to Pittsburgh, but some time in the following year he seems to have given up leading a band. Page (sometimes spelt Paige) is possibly the same man who worked with King Oliver in 1926 and went to China with Jack Carter's band.

The West Coast

The big band developments on the West Coast of the USA seemed from the start to be centred around Los Angeles, and during the whole of the big band era the city was the focal point for the jazz musicians who worked in California. Given its size and population this is hardly surprising; but there was the important additional factor of the film industry, which had taken root in Hollywood, a suburb of Los Angeles, and became an important source of employment for musicians and entertainers of all types. It might have been assumed that there would have been some degree of sympathy on the part of the burgeoning film industry towards jazz, an art form whose growth had some rough parallels with its own, but the results of Hollywood's flirtations with jazz have been almost uniformly detrimental.

Curiously enough, no big coloured band from the West Coast ever succeeded nationally. The two leaders who came closest were probably Les Hite and Floyd Ray. For most of the 'twenties the Los Angeles based bands did not travel very far afield, possibly because there were only a limited number of cities on the West Coast with large coloured populations. On the other hand, it is worth remembering that a high proportion of those musicians who pioneered jazz in the Far East and Australia were from California, or at least worked in the state.

Four musicians share most of the credit for the growth of jazz and big band music on the West Coast—Reb Spikes, Paul Howard, Sonny Clay and Curtis Mosby— and of the four Spikes was the pioneer. Benjamin J. 'Reb' Spikes, now in his eighties, was involved with his brother Johnny in show business during the first decade of this century and by 1910 was touring several western states with the Spikes Brothers Comedy Stars, one of the cast being the young Hattie McDaniels. A year later the brothers operated a theatre in Muskogee, Oklahoma, and left town with Jelly Roll Morton in a minstrel show called McCabes' Troubadours.

Both Reb and Johnny Spikes became proficient instrumentalists, and in 1915 Reb was billed as the 'World's Greatest Saxophonist' with 'The Original So-Different Orchestra'. The title was taken from the San Francisco night club in which it played. In interviews when asked about this period, Reb Spikes has praised the playing of Adam Mitchell, a clarinettist from Martinique who worked with him again in later years. He said also that when a prominent local booker heard the band he cancelled a coming appearance by the Original Dixieland Jazz Band in its favour. While fulfilling this engagement in Watts, a Los Angeles suburb, the then unknown dancer who worked in the floor show was Rudolf Valentino. In 1918-19 Johnny Spikes worked at Bill Brown's Cabaret on Central Avenue with the singer Lucille Hegamin. One of the other musicians was Paul Howard.

The 3rd July 1920 issue of the Chicago Defender mentioned that Red Spikes's So-Different Orchestra was playing at the Alhambra, Seattle. Over the next few years it built up a reputation as the outstanding local group. Leonard Davidson (clarinet, saxophone) was briefly in the band during 1924, and in the following year George Orendorff (trumpet), Les Hite (saxophone) and Jimmy Strong (clarinet, tenor saxophone) worked with Spikes. Strong was only present for a short while before returning to Chicago, but Hite remained with Spikes for a year or two.

In 1925 the orchestra received unwelcome publicity and the 16th September issue of Variety reported that three of its members had been arrested for contributing to the delinquency of three under-age white girls.

In about 1927, after being stranded with a touring band at Hastings, Nebraska, Lionel Hampton came to the coast to join Reb Spikes, but shortly afterwards he switched to play with Paul Howard.

The peak years of Spikes's bandleading activities were from the middle 'twenties until the onset of the depression. Reb Spikes's Majors And Minors Orchestra was resident at the Follies Theatre on Main Street, Los Angeles, for a number of years. A photograph taken in 1927 or 1928 shows George Bryant, Addison O'Neil (trumpet), William Woodman Sr, Eddie Morgan (trombone), Adam 'Slocum' Mitchell (clarinet), Fitz Weston, . . . Gordon (piano), William Robinson, . . . Bruce (banjo), George Morgan (tuba), Lawrence Craig (drums), and Reb Spikes (leader). With the above instrumentation plus two more reed players, one of whom may well have been Spikes himself, the band recorded two titles for Columbia in October 1927 and also appeared in a short film at about the same time.

Whatever the qualities of Spikes's bands during the 'twenties—and musicians have said that some at least were excellent—his activities in other directions were probably more significant in the long term in the development of jazz on the West Coast. In the early 'twenties he had formed, with his brother Johnny, a business embracing all aspects of music. They opened a music store on Central Avenue that became a focal point for local musicians. This almost imperceptibly developed into a booking agency with as many as seven or eight bands under their control. Talking about the early days of the store— though I think his date of 1919 is a year or two out— Reb Spikes told Floyd Levin : 'Back in those days—this was about 1919—there was no place in town where one could purchase recordings by Negro artists. As a result we did a huge record business. Wealthy Hollywood people would drive up in long limousines and send their chauffeurs in to ask for "dirty records". When the local Columbia distributors received a shipment of Bessie Smith records, we'd take the entire lot . . . a few hours later they'd be gone !'

As a result of their success in selling 'race' records the Spikes brothers decided to form their own label, and in June 1922 recorded the first titles by a genuine New Orleans band, in this instance led by trombonist 'Kid' Ory. Most of the five thousand copies pressed were sold on their Sunshine label over the counter of their record shop. Soon afterwards they went into music publishing, arranging and adding lyrics to Jelly Roll Morton's *Froggie Moore* and *Wolverine Blues,* collaborating with other musicians on various numbers and, under their own name, producing their biggest hit in *Someday Sweetheart.* The many recordings of *Someday Sweetheart* over the years have meant healthy regular royalty cheques. The brothers also branched out into the restaurant business, owning the Wayside Park Cafe, Reb's Club and The Dreamland Cafe, amongst others. In addition Johnny was extremely active teaching music and arranging for various bands. In fact there was no corner of jazz activity in Los Angeles in which one or other of the brothers was not deeply involved.

The depression years caused a severe curtailment of the Spikes brothers activities. Failing eyesight led to Johnny becoming totally blind in 1935. Since then he has lived in Pasadena, where he has spent much time writing an opera. During the 'thirties Reb worked in the promotional field, though he had severely to limit his

Reb's American Legion Club 45's. Left to right: Leon White (trombone), Bill Perkins (guitar), unidentified (drums). Russell Massengail (trumpet), Bob Spikes (sax), Max Shaw (tuba), Eugene Wright (piano) and Edgar Williams (trombone). Vocalist Herman Higgs is kneeling.

activities for some years through ill health. In the middle 'forties he revived his Sunshine label, but without success, and took up work as a talent scout until his retirement. As late as the closing years of the 'sixties he retained an interest in music and a clear memory of past events in which he had been involved. Though not himself producing any records of special value, his role in the establishment and development of California based jazz is a key one.

Reb Spikes recorded with his Legion Club 45's around late 1924, leading Russell Massengail (trumpet), Leon White, Edgar Williams (trombone), himself (clarinet, saxophone), probably Les Hite (alto saxophone, clarinet), Eugene Wright (piano), probably Bill Perkins (banjo), Max Shaw (bass saxophone) and an unidentified drummer. The two titles recorded were for a small label and are extremely rare. The 1927 session for Columbia produced *My Mammy's Blues* and *Fight That Thing. My Mammy's Blues* is superior through the powerful playing by one of the trumpeters and the drive of the whole group.

Of all the Californian bands recording during the late 'twenties and early 'thirties, Paul Howard's was the one most obviously in the mainstream of contemporary big band development. Paul Leroy Howard, who was not a native Californian, was born in Steubenville, Ohio, in 1895, and did not live in California until 1911 when he came to Los Angeles to stay with an uncle. All Howard's family were musical and in his youth he played cornet in a choir. By the time he was fourteen he was recognised as something of youthful virtuoso. In Los Angeles he switched to saxophone and clarinet, but his first contact with jazz was not until 1915, when he heard Freddie Keppard and the Original Creole Orchestra. A year later he obtained a job with Wood Wilson's Syncopators who were billed as a 'Famous Jass Band'. Later he worked with several other local groups before joining the Black and Tan Orchestra around 1918.

The Black and Tan Orchestra was originally a ragtime brass band from Texas that reached Los Angeles with a carnival. It stayed there and was reorganised in a jazz manner by trombonist Harry Southard. Howard has given the personnel for 1918 as Ernest Johnson Coycault (trumpet), Harry Southard (trombone), himself (tenor saxophone), James 'Tuba Jack' Jackson (piano) and Leon White (drums), though the date may be slightly early. There are a number of references to the band in black newspapers of the early 'twenties; the first traced

is in the Chicago Defender of 6th March 1920, which refers to the orchestra's presence at the Cadillac Cafe, Los Angeles with Johnnie Mac Venton included. Just over a month later it carried a report that Ed Rucker and the Black and Tan Orchestra were still at the Cadillac, though both Mac Venton and Rucker are somewhat mysterious figures. The same newspaper in an issue of 20th May 1922 noted that Leon Hereford (alto saxophone, clarinet) had been added to the group and, five months later it mentioned the addition of Wood Wilson (bass, clarinet).

While he was with the Black and Tan Orchestra, Howard also gigged with other groups. He finally left in 1923 to take a quartet known as the Quality Four into a local cafe. Under pianist Harvey Brooks's name this group recorded six titles early in 1924. With the addition of banjoist Thomas Valentine the group became the Quality Serenaders. Late in the year they went on tour with blues singer Hazel Myers but it ended in disaster in Amarillo, Texas, a month or two later. Upon returning to Los Angeles Howard worked for a short while with Sonny Clay before reforming the Quality Serenaders. The line-up soon became George Orendorff (trumpet), Louis Taylor (trombone), Paul Howard (tenor saxophone, clarinet), Leon Hereford (alto saxophone, clarinet), Harvey Brooks (piano), Thomas Valentine (banjo), Henry 'Tin Can' Allen (drums), but when the band moved into the Nightingale Club in 1926 Lionel Hampton had replaced Allen. Hampton was a close friend of Orendorff, who was responsible for bringing him to the West Coast, and first worked with the Spikes Brothers Orchestra.

During 1926 Howard started on what was to prove an important association with Frank Sebastian, who bought the Nightingale Club and renamed it the Little Cotton Club. A year later he bought the Green Mill Club and after much redecoration this opened as the New Cotton Club. Howard's band became resident there and stayed for two years. Sebastian, with a clientele that

included a number of Hollywood stars, booked the top attractions at the New Cotton Club and mounted lavish floor shows. In 1929 Howard's band moved into the Kentucky Club on Central Avenue, making some alterations to his line-up so that when it recorded for RCA Victor for the first time it consisted of George Orendorff (trumpet), Lawrence Brown (trombone), Paul Howard (tenor saxophone, clarinet), Charlie Lawrence (alto saxophone clarinet), Harvey Brooks (piano), Thomas Valentine (banjo), James 'Tuba Jack' Jackson (brass bass) and Lionel Hampton (drums, vocal, occasionally piano). A few months later Earl Thompson (trumpet) and Lloyd Reese (alto saxophone, clarinet) had been added, and Reginald Foresythe (piano) had replaced Brooks, while by summer 1930 guitarist Charlie Rousseau had replaced Valentine.

Charlie Lawrence has said that the peak of the Howard band's career came in 1930 when it secured a residency at the Montmartre in Hollywood, an exclusive and inordinately expensive room much favoured by the leading film stars of the time. Soon after this the depression led to the demise of the club and the Quality Serenaders was forced to disband. Howard himself worked for a while with Ed Garland's band, led his own trio during 1934, joined Lionel Hampton in 1935 and was with Eddie Barefield's big band during 1936-37. After this he worked with Charlie Echols before once again leading his own group, which stayed at a club called Virginia's from 1939 to 1953. The group that Howard fronted on tenor saxophone and clarinet was normally a quintet. Down

Above: *the Sunnyland Jazz Orchestra: Clarence Williams (string bass), Charlie Lawrence (alto saxophone), Buster Wilson (piano), Jesse Smith (tenor saxophone), Bem Borders (drums), Howard Patrick (banjo), James Porter (trumpet), Ashford Hardie (trombone), unidentified entertainer.*

Below: *Paul Howard's Quality Serenaders at the Montmartre Club, 1930; left to right: Lawrence Brown, Harvey Brooks, George Orendorff, Earl Thompson, Lionel Hampton, Charlie Lawrence, Thomas Valentine, Lloyd Reese, James 'Tuba Jack' Jackson, Paul Howard.*

Beat of 1st November 1942 listed the rest of the personnel as Earl Willis (piano), Buddy Harper (guitar), Ted Brinson (string bass) and Willis McDaniels (drums). Howard continued to play until at least the early 'sixties, but from 1937 his chief occupation has been Financial Secretary to the Los Angeles branch of the musicians' union.

In ensemble work or individuality of arrangement, Howard's recordings are unexceptional, though not notably deficient. The arrangements, mostly the work of Charlie Lawrence, are functional and efficient, while the ensemble passages are played with technical expertise. The outstanding soloist of the band is unquestionably Orendorff, and his contributions on such titles as *Moonlight Blues* (incidentally containing Lionel Hampton's first recorded vocal), *Overnight Blues, New Kinda Blues* and *Charlie's Idea*, usually in plunger style, are well conceived, swinging and nicely balanced. Lawrence Brown has typically smooth solos on *Overnight Blues, Harlem, Cuttin' Up* and other titles, performing with the assurance that he was later to display with Duke Ellington. The saxophone solos are competent but no more; the clarinet solos are somewhat better; Brooks is pleasant in a solo role. Rhythmically the band improves on the later sessions. On *Harlem*, for example, the ensemble displays more drive than before. The substitution of guitar for banjo on the final date gives more flexibility to the rhythm section. Rousseau has a solo on *Gettin' Ready Blues* that points to the influence of Eddie Lang. Earl Thompson wrote *California Swing*, and as the Bix Beiderbecke-like trumpet solo on this is untypical of Orendorff, it can reasonably be presumed that it is played by the composer. One of the best integrated performances is *Charlie's Idea*—in fact *Tiger Rag*—and there is no doubt that on this and other numbers the band shows itself to be a well-disciplined unit that, on recorded evidence, was by far the most professional band then playing on the West Coast.

William Rogers Campbell 'Sonny' Clay was born at Chapel Hill, Texas, on 15th May 1899. His interest in music arose when his family moved to Phoenix in 1908 and he became involved with a local band. At first Clay played drums, then studied piano, xylophone and C-melody saxophone, becoming accomplished on them all. After leaving high school he began working as a musician around Phoenix, one of his first stints being in a dance studio locally established by Arthur Murray. He told John Bentley that one of the early jobs he recalls with pleasure was an engagement at a Phoenix club where he was paid a dollar a tune after the first thirty, leading to many a number being presented in an unusually abbreviated form.

From 1918 to about the end of 1920 Clay led a wandering existence, often working with a clarinettist called Charlie Green, and he varied his routine of playing around Phoenix with trips to Algodones, San Diego, and several Mexican towns, including Tijuana. It was in

Above: *Sonny Clay, 1926.*
Right: *Sonny Clay in the early 1960s.*

Tijuana that he first met Jelly Roll Morton. Early in 1921 Clay joined Reb Spikes's Famous Syncopated Orchestra, travelling with it on a disastrous tour, after which he went back to gigging around Los Angeles. By now he had added trumpet and trombone to his instrumental armoury, but worked chiefly as a pianist or drummer. In 1922 he went as far as El Paso with George Morrison's band, returning to play with Kid Ory's Sunshine Orchestra in July and August in place of the temporarily sick Ben Borders. A month or two later he formed his own group and continued to lead bands around the Los Angeles area until some time in the middle 'thirties.

The Chicago Defender of 11th November 1922 carries a report that Sonny Clay's Eccentric Harmony Six had recently played at the Hiawatha Academy, Washington, and on Central Avenue, Los Angeles, giving a line-up of William Hansett (cornet), Archie Grant (trombone, piano), Cash Green (almost certainly Charles Green) (clarinet, saxophone), Theo. Bonner (saxophone), W. B. Woodman (trombone) and Sonny Clay (piano, drums, saxophone, various instruments). In the following year the band was mentioned in the 28th July Pittsburgh Courier, musicians mentioned including Charles Green,

Clarence Williams (bass), Harold Lee (drums) and Clay himself. Leonard Davidson worked with Clay frequently from 1924 and has given a personnel of Ernest Coycault (trumpet), Leon White (trombone), himself (clarinet, saxophone), James 'Jazz' Carson (tenor saxophone), Sonny Clay (piano), James 'Tuba Jack' Jackson (brass bass) and Willis McDanicls (drums) as being fairly regular over the next few years. In January 1925 Paul Howard came into the band for a short period, replacing Charlie Mosley and giving the drummer at the time as Ben Borders. A year later trombonist Luther Graven commenced working with Clay.

At some point in 1928 Clay was resident at the Vernon Country Club in Los Angeles. His band then included Les Hite (alto saxophone), who was doubling with Curtis Mosby, and later that year pianist Fitz Weston was present in Clay's line-up. At the beginning of the year Clay had taken an augmented band to Australia. The Chicago Defender of 14th January had reported that it had set sail. The vocalist with the group was Ivie Anderson, who was later to become famous with Duke Ellington, and the band must have stayed in Australia for about three months altogether. It was probably the first black jazz group ever to tour that continent.

It is clear that upon Clay's return to Los Angeles his band underwent changes of personnel. Benny Morton (saxophone, clarinet)—not to be confused with the well-

known trombonist of the same name—and Eddie Nicholson (drums) were with him in 1928 and 1929 respectively. During the 1929-30 period he formed a new band. Teddy Buckner has given the line-up as himself, Red Mack (trumpet), James Williams (trombone), Albert Baker (alto saxophone), Leonard 'Big Boy' Davidson (tenor saxophone, clarinet), Sonny Clay (piano), Bert Holloway (tuba, string bass), Willis McDaniel (drums) and Jimmy Warren (violin). This unit was resident at the Creole Palace in San Diego, and also made some film soundtracks. Variety of 14th July 1931 reported that Clay was then leading his band at Hartford's Ballroom in San Francisco, and it was around this time that he made his final recordings.

From the middle 'thirties Clay, now not in the best of health, increasingly worked as a solo pianist. During World War II he led a U.S. army band, returning to club work upon his discharge. After a lengthy period in hospital during the 'forties he took a daytime job in the post office, making a bit on the side by tuning pianos in his free time. Occasionally during the 'fifties and early 'sixties he undertook brief engagements as a solo pianist, but has been inactive musically for a decade now.

Clay's first recordings for the local Sunset label are very rare. The first appears to have been two accompaniments for singer Camille Allen. In 1923 two titles by his group were issued as by the California Poppies, after which he made four titles for the Sunset label in May 1925 which were released as by the Stompin' Six. Though strictly outside the scope of the present book, these performances are quite interesting. Clay and trombonist Woodman have reasonable solos on *Jimtown Blues* and *Creole Blues*. On three occasions in 1925-26 Clay recorded for the Vocalion label. *Chicago Breakdown* is mostly an ensemble work by a nine-piece group. In January 1928 Clay again took part in a session for Vocalion, but only two of the six titles made were issued. These were recorded on 12th January, and if the Chicago Defender report of the band having set sail by the 14th is correct the session must have been about the day before the group left for Australia. One of the unissued titles is *Australian Stomp*. Clay's final recording session took place around August 1931, and on this occasion he fronted a ten-piece group. It achieves an excellent full sound on *St Louis Blues,* with the brass and saxes trading two-bar phrases in the opening chorus, and there are good solos by a clarinettist whom I think was Davidson and a trumpeter who performs well in the plunger style. Behind Frank Watkins's rather mediocre vocal an alto saxophone and the brass build a good riff background. Both trumpeters—Doc Hart and James 'King' Porter—solo well on *Cho-King,* and the alto shines in ensemble passages. At one point the band introduces an unexpected rumba-like phrase, and the section work is again excellent. There are some pleasant felicities of scoring on these performances, almost certainly the work of Clay himself, and one regrets that he only had this one opportunity of recording in a big band setting. On this showing he had much to offer in the idiom.

Drummer Curtis Mosby came from Kansas City, Missouri, where he was born in 1895, but he established his reputation mainly in Los Angeles. Around 1918 he led his own band in Chicago after touring with the Tennessee Ten, but soon afterwards moved to California where he resumed leadership of a band and ran a music shop in Oakland during 1921. He then toured for two years with Mamie Smith's Jazz Hounds before settling in Los Angeles and forming his Dixieland Blue Blowers. A news item in the 9th September 1925 issue of Variety reported that Mosby's Dixieland Blue Blowers were then in their eleventh month at Solomon's Dance Pavilion De Luxe, Los Angeles, with Harry Barken (trumpet), Lloyd Allen (trombone), H. L. Brassfield (saxophone), Henry Starr (piano, leader), Fred W. Vaughn (banjo) and Curtis Mosby (drums). The same paper eight months later mentioned that they were still resident at the same place, 'playing opposite a Texas cowboy band, that is not as good'.

Mosby led his band for some years, occasionally switching to violin, and recorded with it at three sessions during October 1927, March 1928 and January 1929. Alto saxophonist Les Hite joined Mosby early in 1928 at a time when his band opened at the Lincoln Gardens, Los Angeles. A Chicago Defender story in its 21st April 1928 edition said that Charlie Hite was with Mosby, presumably referring to this fact. During 1929, at a period when trombonist Lawrence Brown was a sideman, Mosby's band appeared in the film 'Hallelujah' and recorded the musical soundtrack. Variety of 26th February and 24th September 1930 noted that the band was then resident at the Apex Club, Los Angeles, and a personnel of James 'King' Porter, Doc Hart (trumpet), Lawrence Brown, Parker Berry (trombone), Marshall Royal, Leo Davis (alto saxophone, clarinet), Johnny Mitchell (tenor saxophone), Walter Johnson (piano), Ceele Burke (guitar), Ike Perkins (string bass) and Baby Lewis (drums) for the 1930-31 period has been given by Marshall Royal.

During 1933-34 Mosby fronted the band for the show 'Change Your Luck' which went on quite an extensive Midwestern tour. His line-up consisted of Leroy Huston, Gene Prince, Theodore 'Wingy' Carpenter (trumpet), Baron Willie Moorehead (trombone), William Johnson, Clester Wells, John Mitchell (reeds), Wilbert Baranco (piano), William Dirvin (guitar), Julius Harris (string bass) and Red Saunders (drums). Soon after this he started to run his own clubs and entered the promotion field. Down Beat of 15th January 1941 carried the following news: 'Curtis has reopened the Club Alabam, Los Angeles, the Central Avenue spot in which Mosby and his band held forth in their heyday. Mosby is operating the spot himself. The name Mosby's Blue Blowers has been revived for the band which was organised here by Baron Moorehead.'

Mosby ran this club until about 1947 when he left music for a couple of years, after which he opened the Oasis Club. He died during the 'fifties. It appears that his initial band title was Mosby's Dixieland Blue Blowers, but that at least during 1929 it was known as Mosby's Kansas City Blue Blowers.

Mosby first recorded for US Columbia in October 1927, but the personnel for that date is uncertain. In 'Jazz Records 1897-1942' Brian Rust lists the line-up as James Porter (trumpet), Ashford Hardee (trombone), Charles Hite, Leo Davis (alto saxophone, clarinet), Bumps Myers (tenor saxophone), Attwell Rose (violin), Henry Starr (piano, vocal), Thomas Valentine (banjo), Ike Perkins (tuba) and Curtis Mosby (drums), but as Myers was only fifteen at the time his presence is unlikely, while Hite (in fact Les Hite) did not join until later. One of the alto players could have been Charles Moseley, and Davis was almost certainly present, but I would not like to guess the identity of the tenor saxophonist. Of the four titles made on the date the best by far is *Tiger Stomp* (actually *Tiger Rag*), which has a pleasant reedy low register clarinet solo, a reasonable plunger solo by Porter, and jaunty ensemble work of an uninhibited nature. *Whoop 'em Up Blues* is also quite good, despite a certain rhythmic stiffness, with the same clarinettist and trumpeter soloing most effectively. A second date of March 1928 almost certainly has Les Hite (alto saxophone, clarinet) present, possibly partnered by Charlie Lawrence. For the rest, Walter Johnson (piano), Freddy Vaughan (banjo) and an unidentified tuba player are said to replace Starr, Valentine and Perkins, but though no violin is listed one can be heard on *Hardee Stomp*. *Blue Blowers Blues* is about the most relaxed performance that Mosby recorded and features the three reed men on clarinets. There are solos by Porter, Hardee and a guitarist. *Hardee Stomp* has the violinist much to the fore and is an extrovert affair in which both banjo and guitar can be heard. On a final January 1929 session trombonist Country Allen is said to replace Hardee, and certainly the trombone work on the two released titles sounds to be by a different man, as indeed does that by the trumpeter. *Between You and Me (And the Deep Blue Sea)* is a dismal effort, not least the vocal by an unidentified male singer accompanied by a Hawaiian guitarist. Brian Rust notes that Hawaiian artists recorded on the same day, and as a banjo can also be heard it is to be presumed that Mosby asked one of them to sit in. *Louisiana Bo Bo* is better, though hardly memorable. In general Mosby's recordings have about them an engaging enthusiasm, but despite their instrumentation are outside the mainstream of big band jazz. It is possibly unfair to judge them by such standards.

Trumpeter Charlie Echols formed a band in Los Angeles in spring 1931. The Chicago Defender of 21st March gave its line-up as Charlie Echols (trumpet), James Williams (trombone), James Wynn, Babe Carter, Herman Pettis (saxophone), Lorenzo Flennoy (piano), Joe Lewis (banjo), Sid Carter (tuba), Preston Prince (drums, vocal) and Russell Jones (entertainer). A month later it repeated this personnel but added trumpeter McClure Morris, also known as Red Mack Morris or just Red Mack, reporting that all the musicians were under twenty-three years old. By the following year, if a photograph has been dated correctly, the line-up seems to have been almost totally changed and consisted of Charlie Echols, Milton Ellsworth (trumpet), Parker Berry, Edward 'Kid' Ory (trombone), Grover Diggs, Hershel Coleman, Hubert 'Bumps' Myers (reeds), Eddie Beal (piano), Joe Lewis (guitar), Joe Mendosa (bass) and Preston 'Peppy' Prince (drums).

Red Mack Morris was with Echols during 1933 and 1934 and has given a personnel for the period of himself, Bernie Brice, Claude 'Benno' Kennedy (trumpet), A. J. Williams, Bert Johnson (trombone), Emerson Scott (alto and baritone saxophone), Jack McVea (alto and baritone saxophone), Don Byas (or C. Puss Wade), Buddy Banks (tenor saxophone), Herb Williams (piano), Buddy Harper (guitar), Burt Holiday (string bass) and Alton Redd (drums). Mr Morris identified this group from a photograph, but must be in error about Don Byas, who did not join the band until a year or two later. Incidentally, when Mr Morris rejoined Echols after playing with Erskine Tate in Chicago he initially worked as a drummer. At this time the band was often resident at Papkie's Club in Los Angeles. (Papkie was an ex-prize fighter.) Jack McVea recalls this period, remembering that when Lorenzo Flennoy took over the band it included Charlie Echols, himself, Jim Wynn (alto saxophone), Oliver 'Big Six' Reeves (tenor saxophone), Lorenzo Flennoy (piano) and Otis Flennoy (drums).

Having lost his band to Flennoy, Echols organised a new one that has been identified from a photograph by Red Mack Morris as containing himself, Bernie Brice, Charlie Echols, Andrew Blakeney (trumpet), Country Allen (trombone), Paul Howard, Emerson Scott, two others unknown (reeds), Buster Wilson (piano), Ceele Burke (banjo, guitar), Johnny Miller (string bass) and Lionel Hampton (drums). Billboard of 17th November 1934 carried a news item which stated that Echols and his band were then resident at the New Cotton Club, Culver City and added that Lionel Hampton and an all-Creole floor show were featured. In the following year Echols seems to have got his own back on Flennoy, for when the latter's band broke up he took it over. As a result he led an impressive line-up of himself, Bernie 'Pee-Wee' Brice, Claude 'Benno' Kennedy, Buck Clayton (trumpet), Jack Jones, Tyree Glenn (trombone), Emerson Scott, Hugo Dandridge (alto saxophone), Don Byas, Herschal Evans (tenor saxophone), Jack McVea (baritone saxophone), Herb Williams (piano), Buddy Harper (guitar), Burt Holiday (string bass) and Alton Redd (drums). This personnel has been confirmed by both Don Byas and Jack McVea.

Echols continued to lead bands for the rest of the 'thirties, and in 1938 was fronting himself, Ernie Royal, Raymond Tate (trumpet), Lee McCoy Davis, Hubert 'Bumps' Myers (alto saxophone), Paul Howard (tenor saxophone, clarinet), Edyth Turnham (piano), Al Morgan (string bass) and Lee Young (drums) at the Cotton Club in Los Angeles. In 1939 he was in charge of virtually the same personnel at the Long Beach Dance Hall, San Francisco. His later activities are obscure, but it is believed that he gave up bandleading in the 'forties.

Several musicians have told me that the band with Buck Clayton, Tyree Glenn, Herschal Evans, etc. was outstanding and should have been recorded. Unfortunately it never was.

While on the subject of bands that worked around California but did not record, a brief mention of Sammy Franklin's Rhythm Rascals is in order. In fact it is not strictly true that Franklin never entered the recording studio, for in 1944 he did make a few titles for the Black and White label, but on this occasion he used only a small group and the performances are apparently atypical of his work in the big band era. Franklin was active from 1936 to 1953, generally leading a medium size group that was considered very proficient. At different times over the years the musicians who played with him include Leroy 'Snake' White, Teddy Buckner (trumpet), William B. Woodman, Keg Johnson (trombone), Leslie Jack Holt, Emerson Scott (alto saxophone), Leonard Davidson (tenor saxophone, clarinet), James Jackson (tenor saxophone), Bill Perkins (guitar), Ted Brinson (guitar, string bass), Douglas Fines (string bass) and Everett Walsh (drums). Franklin has not been active in music for many years now, but by all accounts was a competent trumpeter and saxophonist.

While working with Cab Calloway in California early in 1936, Eddie Barefield was taken ill, and after recovering he decided to remain there for a while. Initially he had intended to work with the Lorenzo Flennoy band but was prevented from doing so by local union regulations that required a six-month residency in the area before membership would be granted. Barefield spent the time arranging for numerous bands, including Jimmy Dorsey's and Benny Goodman's, and then decided to form his own big band. Incidentally Mr Barefield remembers meeting Buck Clayton for the first time during this period, and says that he was then 'a real high note man'. The nucleus of his own band came from seven members of the current Charlie Echols group, and when it finally began working after rehearsals it comprised Red Mack Morris, Bernie 'Pee Wee' Brice, another (trumpet), Tyree Glenn, Country Allen (trombone), Eddie Barefield (alto saxophone, clarinet), Hugo Dandridge (alto saxophone), Don Byas, Jack McVea (tenor saxophone), Paul Howard (tenor and baritone saxophone), Dudley Brooks (piano), Buddy Harper (guitar), Al Morgan (string bass) and Lee Young (drums).

175

Eddie Barefield, leader of an outstanding West Coast big band during the mid 1930s.

Eddie Barefield is a brilliant band organiser, and also a fine arranger, and within a short while his group was attracting attention. Frank Sebastian, owner of the New Cotton Club and the most important employer in the area, heard the band and asked Barefield to start working in his club. A condition of the deal was that Lionel Hampton should replace Lee Young in the band, and Barefield turned it down as a result. Within a short while Sebastian capitulated and the band moved into the New Cotton Club for a residency that lasted seven or eight months. After the job was over Barefield signed with a local booking agency and the band played up and down the coast, on one occasion going as far afield as Tucson, Arizona. After a while Barefield felt that insufficient progress was being made towards the band becoming other than a localised attraction and late in 1937 he ended the venture.

Apart from Barefield, pianist Dudley Brooks wrote arrangements for the band, and several musicians described it as outstanding. It did make some records for Al Jarvis of 'Make Believe Ballroom' fame, but nobody knows what became of them. There seems little doubt that with proper promotion and the odd lucky break Barefield's band might have become prominent during the swing era.

The best known and most successful of the Californian based bands of the 'thirties was undoubtedly Les Hite's.

Hite was from DuQuoin, Illinois, where he was born on 13th March 1903, and after school in Urbana he continued his studies at the University of Illinois. His mother, father, sisters and brothers played in a family band and in due course he was added on saxophone, later working with the Detroit Shannon band before going on the road with Helen Dewey and a five-act show. In 1925 the show made its final appearance in Los Angeles and Hite, George Orendorff and Jimmy Strong elected to remain there rather than return to Chicago, though Strong remained only a short while. Hite initially worked with Reb Spikes, then in the next three years was a sideman with several local leaders, including Mutt Carey, Paul Howard, Vernon Elkins, Curtis Mosby and Henry 'Tin Can' Allen. He joined the Allen's group either in late 1928 or early 1929 when it was working at Solomon's Penny Dance Palace in Los Angeles, and when Allen died Hite was elected leader. Late in 1929 Hite broke this group up and made new arrangements for a job at the Cotton Club (previously the Green Mill Club). His personnel at that time included Lloyd Reese (trumpet), himself, Marshall Royal, Charlie Lawrence (reeds), Harvey Brooks (piano) and Lionel Hampton (drums). Later Hubert 'Bumps' Myers (tenor saxophone) joined the band.

In the autumn of 1930 Hite got his big break when, with his Californian Syncopators, he took over from Vernon Elkins at Frank Sebastian's New Cotton Club. This was to be his base in the years ahead and his band would often back such guest stars as famous as Louis Armstrong and Fats Waller. It also found lucrative work in the Hollywood film studios, recording soundtracks and making visual appearances. In October 1930 the Hite band recorded for the first time as a backing unit to Louis Armstrong, with a line-up of George Orendorff, Harold Scott (trumpet), Luther 'Sonny' Graven (trombone), Les Hite (alto and baritone saxophone), Marvin Johnson (alto saxophone, clarinet), Charlie Jones (tenor saxophone, clarinet), Henry Prince (piano), Bill Perkins (guitar, banjo), Joe Bailey (string and brass bass) and Lionel Hampton (drums, vibraphone). At the close of 1930 Orendorff left for a month's leave in Chicago owing to a family bereavement. His replacement was Red Mack Morris who is present on one of the recording sessions made with Armstrong.

In 1931 Lawrence Brown (trombone) and Marshall Royal (alto saxophone, clarinet) joined the band. Royal later took over in the sax section from Hite, who from this point concentrated on leading. The Pittsburgh Courier of 12th December 1931 mentioned that the band was still at the New Cotton Club and had just made an appearance in the film 'Taxi Please', confirming the personnel just named, except that it adds trumpeter James 'King' Porter and pianist Harvey Brooks. This same line-up is recorded in the 16th January 1932 Chicago Defender, though in all probability Porter and Brooks were added only for the film. At some point in 1932 pianist

The Les Hite Cotton Club Band, 1931. Back row: Charlie Jones (tenor saxophone), Luther 'Sonny' Graven (trombone), George Orendorff (trumpet), Louis Armstrong, Henry Prince (piano), Les Hite (alto saxophone), Harvey Brooks (piano). Front row: Bill Perkins (guitar), Harold Scott (trumpet), Lionel Hampton (drums), Joe Bailey (string bass), Marvin Johnson (alto saxophone). Louis Armstrong was using the Hite band as his backing group during this engagement.

Harold Brown took over from Prince, while in the following year Lawrence Brown left to join Duke Ellington and was replaced by Parker Berry. During 1933 the band appeared in the film 'Sing, Sinners, Sing' and a photograph taken at the time shows James 'King' Porter, George Orendorff (trumpet), Luther 'Sonny' Graven (trombone), Marvin Johnson (alto saxophone, clarinet), Charlie Jones (tenor saxophone, clarinet), the rhythm as before minus a pianist, Daisy Mae Diggs (vocal) and Les Hite (leader). It is likely that Parker Berry, Marshall Royal and the pianist missed the photographic session.

Hite's personnel remained unusually stable for several years, for when it appeared at the Paramount Theatre, Los Angeles, in 1935 the only changes from the last line-up were that Lloyd Reese had been added on trumpet, Henry Prince had returned on piano and Preston 'Peppy' Prince (drums) had replaced Hampton. Parker Berry and Marshall Royal were still present. During 1935 the band supported Fats Waller at Sebastian's Cotton Club, and there were no personnel changes in 1936. Tempo in its April 1937 issue noted that the band was still present at the club, the personnel it gives showing

only the single change of vocalist June Richmond for Daisy Mae Diggs, though later that year Eddie Barefield came in in place of Marvin Johnson. In April 1938 Tempo again mentioned that the band was resident at the Cotton Club. By now Hubert 'Bumps' Myers had joined to bring the saxophone section up to four. In July 1938, Down Beat reported that Hite's band was on a one-night touring schedule, with apparently little success at Portland, Oregon, but a sell-out at Salem. It added that it was then heading north and east. In its 1st February 1939 edition the same magazine mentioned that the band was currently playing at Culamola, Hollywood, and reported the presence of Orendorff, Graven, Royal, Johnson (who presumably returned when Barefield left), Myers, Phil Moore (piano), Bailey and Lee Young (drums). Seven months later Down Beat noted that recently 'Les Hite used his thirteen-piece band combined with eight studio men out at MGM for the background music in the Marx Brothers' movie "A Day At The Races".

The reason for the unusually few personnel changes in the Hite band during the 'thirties probably lies in both the security of its long residencies at Frank Sebastian's Cotton Club and in the extra money earned in the film studios, particularly as these were depression years when most musicians were struggling to survive. In September 1939, however, Hite dismissed his band and took over Floyd Turnham's, adding a few men of his own choice. His new personnel consisted of Walter Williams, Forrest Powell, Paul Campbell (trumpet), Allen Durham, Britt Woodman, Luther 'Sonny' Graven (trombone),

Floyd Turnham (alto saxophone), Leo Trammel (alto saxophone, clarinet), Rodger Hurd, Qudellis Martin (tenor saxophone), Sol Moore (baritone saxophone), Nat Walker (piano), Frank Pashley (guitar), Al Morgan (string bass) and Oscar Bradley (drums), and it opened in Dallas at the end of the month. While the band was in Texas it picked up Aaron 'T-Bone' Walker, the blues singer and guitarist, and then in January went to New York City where it was resident at the Golden Gate Ballroom from the 9th to the 25th and at the Apollo Theatre from the 26th to the 31st. Down Beat of 1st February 1940 carried a report in the following terms:

'Les Hite has never been further East with his band than Denver, Colorado, until two weeks booking in New York City at the Golden Gate. The boys did not want to come East because they did not want to lose movie studio connections (35 dollars for three hours) and they had plenty of it. They are in New York City for air time and to make records for Decca. They'll play the Apollo and unless a booking for the Famous Door materialises they'll be on the way home again. Les Hite writes some of the band's best arrangements (Example : *The lick*). At one time he played alto, tenor and clarinet, but an auto smash wrecked his lower lip and he's too scared of

Frank Sebastian's New Cotton Club Revue with Thomas 'Fats' Waller (centre front), the Les Hite band (back row) and entertainers.

playing out of tune, only blowing on occasional one-niters when the mood gets him. His new star is T. Bone Walker with choruses on *I wonder why she don't write to me*. Hite's first Decca waxings will include his own original theme *It must have been a dream*, plus Harry White's grand number *Evening*.'

In fact the band did not record for Decca, but for the Varsity label, and *Evening* was not one of the numbers made. *The Lick* is actually titled *That's the Lick*.

During spring 1940 the Hite band was touring the Midwest, and over the next eighteen months changes took place in the personnel. In September 1940 Nat Jones (alto saxophone) replaced Leo Trammel, but left a few months later when probably John Brown took his place. In April 1941 Al Morgan left to be replaced first by Jimmy Butts and then Joe Booker, while six months later Ellis 'Stumpy' Whitlock (trumpet) was added and Joe Wilder (trumpet), Alfred Cobbs (trombone) and Coney Woodman (piano) took over from Campbell, Graven and Walker. Hite by this time does not seem to have been working much in California. Down Beat of 1st August 1941 reporting an appearance at the Yankee Lake, Brookfield, Ohio, while the same paper of 15th April 1942 noted that Hite was at the Strand Theatre in Brooklyn and would be in the Manhattan area for several days before touring New England.

In March 1942 Dizzy Gillespie came into the band in place of Whitlock, and trombonist Leon Comegys and

pianist Gerald Wiggins replaced Britt and Coney Woodman, though Comegys only remained two weeks. Three musicians have independently confirmed the personnel of the band when it made its final records for the Hit label in April 1942, listing Joe Wilder, Dizzy Gillespie, Walter Williams (trumpet), Leon Comegys, Allen Durham, Alfred Cobbs (trombone), John Brown, Floyd Turnham (alto saxophone), Qudellis Martin, Rodger Hurd (tenor saxophone), Sol Moore (baritone saxophone), Gerald Wiggins (piano), Frank Pashley (guitar), Benny Booker (string bass) and Oscar Bradley (drums). In fact Walter Williams arrived late and is only present on the last two titles, which meant a last-minute switch on *Jersey Bounce,* where Gillespie takes Williams's usual solo. Some reports from this period refer to Johnny Brown (baritone saxophone) replacing Sol Moore, but it is uncertain whether this is a switch by the John Brown who normally played alto or a new man of the same name entering the band.

Down Beat of 1st August 1942 and Metronome of October 1942 both have reports of Hite reorganising his band during the previous July. Metronome also noted that he had began an engagement in Los Angeles on 10th September. The band was said to have four trumpets and six saxophones. Among the men mentioned were Gerald Wilson, Fred Jack Trainor (trumpet), John Ewing, Jimmy Robinson (trombone), Buddy Collette (alto and baritone saxophone) and Gerald Wiggins (piano). All these were Los Angeles based, suggesting that Hite had recruited his new personnel there. Trumpeter James 'Snookie' Young joined in October, remaining until some time in 1943, and he remembered band members just listed plus Walter Williams (trumpet) and Luther 'Sonny' Graven (trombone). Down Beat of 1st March 1944 reported that trombonist Ralph Bledsoe had been called up in the U.S. army and referred to him as an ex-Les Hite musician.

Hite once more went back to working almost exclusively in the Los Angeles area until 1945, when he disbanded and concentrated on business activities, though still occasionally gigging with other groups. For the five years before his death in Santa Monica, California, on 6th February 1962 he was in charge of a booking agency.

Hite's band recorded twice for the American Record Company in 1935, but on each occasion the titles were rejected. Early in 1940 six titles were made for the Varsity label in New York, including *T-Bone Blues,* with vocal by T-Bone Walker, *That's the Lick, It Must Have Been a Dream* and Dudley Brooks's *Board Meeting.* Varsity, run by the ex-RCA Victor a-and-r man Eli Oberstein, was not a long-lived label and the titles are extremely rare, never having been reissued in microgroove form. I recall hearing some many years ago and being impressed by the spirit of the band and several of the soloists, notably an alto player who was almost certainly Floyd Turnham. In March 1941 the band made four titles for the Bluebird label, all repeats of numbers done at the earlier Varsity date. *Board Meeting* and

That's the Lick are excellent, according to notes I made at the time of hearing them, and are scheduled for microgroove release in the near future. The four numbers recorded for the Hit label in 1942 are also very rare, and I remember that on the only occasion I heard them I felt they were inferior to the Varsity and Bluebird performances. Admirers of Dizzy Gillespie would, of course, find *Jersey Bounce* of interest for his solo. It is to be hoped that the Varsity recordings will become available again, for they represent the best of Hite's output.

The final band to be dealt with in this section, Floyd Ray's, could as well appear in other parts of the present chapter, but as it enjoyed its greatest success while working in California I am including it here. The history of the band into the early 'forties has been detailed by Frank Driggs in an article in Coda, and he recounts that Ray, born in Grand Rapids, Michigan, started out as a dancer until an injury made it impossible for him to continue. In 1934 he started a seven-piece group called the Harlem Dictators that worked at a club in Scranton, Pennsylvania. In the next two years he augmented it for residencies at Binghampton N.Y., and the Circle Ballroom in New York City. In summer 1936, when the band went out on a tour that ended in California, its line-up was Eddie Vanderveer, Emerson Warden, James 'Chippie' Outcalt (trumpet), Gilbert Kelley, Clayton Smith (trombone), George Fauntleroy (alto saxophone, clarinet), Johnny Alston, Carroll Ridley (tenor saxophone), Sol Moore (baritone and alto saxophone), Kenny Bryant (piano), Gene Brown (guitar), Benny Booker (string bass) and George Ward (drums).

In California the band was selected to go out on tour with the black actor Clarence Muse, gaining considerable popularity throughout the state as a result. It was now known as Floyd Ray's Orchestra, and the addition of a female vocal trio—Ivy, Vern and Von—added to its commercial appeal. Down Beat of July 1938 reported that Ray's band had 'opened an engagement at the Kansas City Club, Kansas City on June 16th. Reg Marshall of Hollywood booked the band. It's the first time in twenty years that a colored band has been dated at the spot.' Two months later Down Beat mentioned Ray's appearance at the third Hollywood swing concert sponsored by American Legion Musician's Post 424, Local 47, held at the Palomar, Hollywood, Sunday afternoon 31st July, noting that it now included a girl trio. The same magazine reported Ray's presence at the Domar, Hermosa Beach, California, in its October 1938 issue, and the fact that it was touring in its editions of December 1938 to February 1939.

Several changes of personnel took place between 1936 and 1939, with Outcalt and Alston leaving, and trumpeters Cappy Oliver, Rush Miller, Joe 'Red' Kelly, Charlie Jacobs and Granville Young, alto saxophonist Shirley Green, and vocalist Joe Alexander coming in at various times. When the band recorded for Decca in New

179

York City during February 1939 its line-up was Joe 'Red' Kelly, Granville Young, Eddie Vanderveer (trumpet), Gilbert Kelley, Clayton Smith (trombone), George Fauntleroy, Shirley Green (alto saxophone, clarinet), Carroll Ridley (tenor saxophone), Sol Moore (baritone saxophone), Kenny Bryant (piano), Gene Brown (guitar), Benny Booker (string bass), George Ward (drums), Ivy Ann Glascoe, Joe Alexander, Ivy, Vern and Von (vocal). By the time of a second session two months later Eddie Byrd had replaced Ward.

Between April 1939 and the close of 1940, when Ray disbanded, numerous changes took place in the band, though the two trombonists were unchanged to the end. Sir Charles Thompson replaced Bryant, probably in 1940, and Russell Jacquet came in for Vanderveer, while Sol Moore and Benny Booker left to be replaced by unknown musicians. At some point in 1939 Bob Moore (piano, vocal) was with Ray, presumably after Bryant left and before Sir Charles Thompson joined, and drummer Chico Hamilton was present for a while in 1940. Lammar Wright Jr was also briefly with Ray around this time, and Down Beat of 1st August 1941, when mentioning one Gilbert 'Pinocchio' Johnson, referred to him as an ex-Ray musician. Though Ray broke up his band in 1940, his own popularity was so great that he fronted Milt Larkins's group on a tour. When it appeared in Seattle, Washington, on 1st January 1941, its personnel was Calvin Ladnier, Milt Larkins, Lester Patterson (trumpet), Dick Waters, Nolden Bolding, William Luper (trombone), Eddie Vinson, Frank Dominguez (alto saxophone), Ernest Archia, Arnett Cobb (tenor saxophone), Cedric Haywood (piano, arranger), Bill Davis (guitar arranger), Lawrence Cato (string bass), Henry Mills (drums), George Layre (vocal) and Floyd Ray (director).

Mr Driggs has mentioned that, after disbanding, Floyd Ray studied orchestration and string bass at the Los Angeles Conservatory, entering the armed services when America became involved in World War II. He was misinformed, however, when he was told that Ray did not form a big band again after his discharge, for various references in Down Beat issues of 1944-45 refer to the fact. Tenor saxophonist Jay Peters worked with Ray during 1944-45, when his band wts known as Floyd Ray and his Californians, and remembers touring California with a partially recalled line-up of John Smith, 'Chops', 'Red' (trumpet), Charles Greenlea, Lester Bass (trombone), Howard Martin, unknown (alto saxophone), himself, Arthur Simmons (tenor saxophone), 'Curly' (string bass) and others. Music Dial of October 1944 mentioned that Donald J. Lucas (saxophone, clarinet) had just gone into the army after working with Ray, while Down Beat of 1st December reported that the Ray band had started a ten-day residency at the Plantation Club, Los Angeles, the previous day. The same magazine of 1st August 1945 carried the following story : 'Floyd Ray is stranded without a wardrobe. He has filed a complaint against a cleaning firm which took his clothes without his permission

then sold them because he did not call for them in time.'

On another page of this edition there is a story about a booking mix-up at Shepp's Playhouse, Los Angeles, that was likely to see Tab Smith's visit cancelled, with Ray getting the job. This in fact happened, for in the 15th September Down Beat there is a note that Gerald Wilson was set to follow Floyd Ray at this venue when he closed on 10th September.

After this no further reports on Ray's activities can be traced, and it is reasonable to assume that he did in fact finally retire from bandleading. Since that time he has been a prominent disc-jockey in Los Angeles, a role he was following as late as 1969, and has also involved himself with innumerable business interests.

In all Floyd Ray's band recorded eight titles for the US Decca label, most having somewhat undistinguished vocals by Ivy Ann Glascoe, Joe Alexander and the trio of Ivy, Vern and Von. However, the soloists are heard on all titles, and the arrangements by Dudley Brooks are excellent. The style of the band at this time showed a strong Jimmie Lunceford influence, and it was clearly a powerful, hard swinging unit. The best title it made was undoubtedly *Firefly Stomp*, a Ray number taken at up tempo with a wild but driving solo by Granville Young —on this showing a Roy Eldridge admirer—and a pushing, Chu Berry-like contribution from Carroll Ridley. Sol Moore and Shirley Green are heard in eight-bar bridges, and the ensemble swings well. Ridley is less impressive on *Jammin' the Blues*, never really organising his solo, and Ivy Ann Glascoe's vocal with its string of traditional blues phrases is far too effete; but the ensemble, with wa-wa brass prominent, is in good form and Young brings the performance to a close with an unrestrained solo which is exciting. *Blues at Noon* does not benefit from the vocal by the female trio, but Ridley is back to form, there is a good growl trumpet solo, and Young— incidentally the elder brother of the better-known James 'Snookie' Young—rises over the ensemble in an extrovert manner at the close. Good as Ray's limited output was on the whole, one regrets that his band did not get more opportunity to be heard in purely instrumental performances.

There were of course other big bands which played on the West Coast, most of them based on Los Angeles, though Saunders King, Ben Watkins and Jimmy Wynn used San Francisco as their base. The Los Angeles bands which would merit research include those led by Bob Dade, Earl Dancer, Vernon Elkins, Elmer Fain, Ed Garland, Leon Herriford, Bert Johnson, Cee Pee Johnson, George 'Happy' Johnson, Claude 'Benno' Kennedy, Jelly Roll Morton, Johnny Otis, Bob Parrish, Edith Turnham, Floyd Turnham and Gerald Wilson, for though some were very short lived all contributed to the development of big band jazz in their area. Unfortunately, to deal with all the bands active in the areas covered in the present chapter would require a volume, or several volumes, of encyclopaedic proportions.

6 The White Bands

It would obviously be difficult to maintain a rigid distinction between jazz and dance music in the output of big bands in the 'twenties and early 'thirties, but at least in virtually all the prominent black bands the basic orientation is clearly towards jazz. With the white bands of the period, except probably the Casa Loma Orchestra, the position is more complex: while many were perfectly capable of producing good jazz performances and included in their ranks soloists undeniably of a jazz persuasion, none really set out to gain public recognition primarily on the strength of its jazz potential.

Almost every prominent white band was conscious that a public existed for 'hot' music—jazz. While leaders were quite happy to cater to this taste—some probably did so to keep their musicians contented—they viewed such incursions only as part of an eclectic musical policy aimed at pleasing as wide a public as possible.

Over the years, leaders and sidemen of prominent black bands have stated that recording directors expected them to play jazz and were reluctant to allow them to record out-and-out commercial performances. However, the recorded output of most of the major black bands of the pre-swing era seems to show plentiful evidence of commercial concessions, which became more noticeable in the swing era. It is interesting to discover, though, that almost no black popular singers of the type of Harlan Lattimore and Dan Grissom reached a mass white audience until well into the 'thirties. Perhaps what the jazz purist could see as commercial concessions on earlier recordings might in fact be nothing more than the use of prevailing convention. The converse of this situation is that if recording directors typed all black bands as jazz or 'hot' units, they could equally view the major white bands in a different role and discourage them from recording too high a proportion of jazz scores. This certainly seems to be the case with the Jean Goldkette band, though at this distance in time it is unlikely that the full impact of recording directors with the major companies can be assessed with total accuracy. There may have been no white bands of any prominence pursuing a totally uncompromising jazz policy in the pre-swing era, but there were certainly a number that made a point of giving prominence to jazz musicians and jazz-inclined scores.

One of the pioneers in the field was the drummer Ben Pollack. He was born in Chicago on 22nd June 1903 and, after playing with school bands and obscure local groups, joined the famous Friars Inn Orchestra (later the New Orleans Rhythm Kings) in 1922; subsequently he worked with the Harry Bastin band in California for almost a year. He returned to Chicago with the intention of working in his family's fur business, but at the last moment decided to continue his musical career and went to New York where he received an offer to take over the Bastin band. From October 1924, he fronted the band in California. He was joined in August 1925 by the sixteen-year-old Benny Goodman on the recommendation of Gil Rodin. When Pollack returned to Chicago in 1926, work

was scarce and he initially took odd jobs as a sideman. By May of that year, however, he was in residence at a local hotel and until late 1927 secured steady work as a leader in his home town. On 6th March 1928, the Pollack band opened at the Little Club in New York City, and in September of that year started what was to prove a lengthy engagement at the Park Central Hotel, doubling from December in a Broadway show. With a reasonably stable personnel, Pollack recorded for RCA Victor from 1926 to 1929, then for other labels until 1931. Late in 1928, he added the New Orleans drummer Ray Bauduc to his line-up so that he could concentrate on leading and on business matters. This band, with various changes of personnel, survived until December 1934, when it broke up in Chicago, and many of its members became the nucleus of the Bob Crosby orchestra. I am primarily concerned here with Pollack's RCA Victor recordings of 1926 to 1929, for in some respects they are among the most strongly jazz-inclined performances produced by any regular white big band of the period.

The first issued recordings by the Pollack band were made in December 1926 with a line-up that included Glenn Miller, Fud Livingston and Benny Goodman—Jimmy McPartland and Larry Binyon did not join the group until late in the following year. The second issued title, *Deed I Do*, is in many respects typical of the overall output of the band. Good solos by Goodman and others are juxtaposed with ensemble passages that are competent but uninspired. Pollack himself features in the first of many lamentable vocals. For recording purposes, two violins were added, reportedly at the insistence of arranger Glenn Miller, who was out to emulate the sound of the then enormously popular and commercially successful Roger Wolfe Kahn orchestra. The use of a small string section on many of Pollack's later recordings proved unhelpful from a jazz viewpoint. It is also unfortunate that Fud Livingston, a first rate arranger, apparently provided no scores for the band, for he would have been capable of using its jazz talent in a manner that could only have been beneficial. Throughout Pollack's RCA Victor output, one is constantly aware that much of it represents an uneasy compromise between jazz and commercial dance

Top: *Ben Pollack and his Central Park Hotel Orchestra, 1929. Back row, left to right: Eddie Bergman, Larry Binyon, Jack Teagarden, Al Beller. Front row: Al Harris, Harry Goodman, Jimmy McPartland, Benny Goodman, Dick Morgan, Vic Breidis, Gil Rodin. Pollack is sitting.*

Above: *the Ben Pollack band in the early 1930s. Front row: Al Beller, Barney Weinstein (violin), Doris Robbins (vocal), Ray Bauduc (drums), Ben Pollack, Gil Rodin, Matty Matlock, Eddie Miller (reeds). Back row: Jerry Johnson (string bass), Gil Bowers (piano), Hilton 'Nappy' Lamare (guitar), Ralph Cropsey, Jack Teagarden (trombone), Sterling Bose, Charlie Spivak (trumpet). Many of these musicians went on to become members of the first Bob Crosby band.*

music. Members of the band have said that Pollack was genuinely proud of his jazz contingent and aware of the potential of his group, but that, not surprisingly, he also hankered after commercial success and felt that this would not be achieved by highlighting jazz scores. As a result, one now listens to these records for individual solos, suffering the numerous dire vocals and indifferently scored passages. Examples are *Sentimental Baby*, which has excellent playing by McPartland, Goodman and trombonist Jack Teagarden, and *Bashful Baby*, with worthwhile solos by Goodman and McPartland, sandwiched between very poor vocals and hackneyed ensemble passages. Yet there are a few records which hint at the full capabilities of the band. In *My Kinda Love*, apart from Pollack's expendable vocal, the performance eschews overtly commercial effects; it contains outstanding solos from Goodman and Teagarden, as well as crisp ensemble passages underlined by a good rhythm section in which Ray Bauduc plays a notable part. Such unlikely looking titles as *She's One Sweet Show Girl, Song of the Blues* and *True Blue Lou* contain passages which reveal felicities of scoring and section work of a high standard, such as the brass work in the closing ensemble of *True Blue Lou*, but too often they are surrounded by much that is banal. Pollack's *From Now On*, apart from a really excellent Teagarden solo and good drumming by Ray Bauduc, is a thoroughly undistinguished performance, but listeners interested in the possible origin of popular songs will note its quite remarkable resemblance at times to the tune of *Red Sails in the Sunset*.

Listening sympathetically to Pollack's RCA Victor recordings of 1926–29 some four decades or more after they were made, one can intermittently discern the band's jazz potential, and occasionally more than just potential. However, in general the scores lack imagination, and, regrettably, the commercial trappings were sometimes retained. The band did, however, make recordings for other labels, often with a reduced personnel, under a variety of pseudonyms of which The Whoopee Makers is perhaps the best known. Some of the performances, such as *Makin' Friends* and *St James Infirmary*, are straightforward jazz of high quality, and though the arrangements used are functional rather than imaginative, the potential of the band becomes obvious even to the most casual listener. Other titles curiously combine jazz with the kind of deliberate corn demanded by recording directors, who had been very taken with burlesque playing by the musicians on one occasion. In later years, Pollack spoke with pride of his bands of 1926–34 claiming that he was a pioneer of big band jazz. This is in part true, but much as he liked jazz, Pollack also sought commercial success, and his musical direction wavered between a degree of idealism and attempts to please the less discerning members of his audiences. Pollack closed some of his RCA Victor recordings by intoning in a rather nauseatingly ingratiating voice, 'May it please you. Ben Pollack.' If Pollack had been a little less anxious to please everyone,

the records that his band made might have been more satisfactory to jazz followers, whose predilection for artists prepared to starve for their ideals is not, understandably enough, shared by the musicians themselves.

During 1933 and 1934, Pollack again recorded, this time for U.S. Columbia, but the results were unimpressive apart from a session featuring the black musicians Shirley Clay and Bennie Morton which produced good performances of *Deep Jungle* and *Swing Out*. He continued to lead bands until 1942, recording for U.S. Vocalion in 1936 and for U.S. Decca in 1937 and 1938, but despite the presence of excellent musicians in his line-ups, the performances are seldom more than competent. The last Pollack band with real potential was one of 1936 that included trumpeters Harry James and Shorty Sherock, trombonist Glenn Miller, clarinettist Irving Fazola, and tenor saxist Dave Matthews, all of whom were shortly to win recognition with other bands or as leaders in their own right. Its recorded performances of *Song of the Islands* and *Jimtown Blues* are worthy of reissue on microgroove. Pollack subsequently complained that whenever he organised a good band during the 'thirties, other leaders raided his personnel, but it may be that by this time he was no longer a convincing front man. In 1942, he finally gave up leading big bands, and for a while directed a touring unit that accompanied the comedian Chico Marx. In the following year he opened his own booking agency and formed the Jewel Record Company. The advanced Boyd Raeburn band recorded for his label in 1945 and 1946. From 1949, Pollack was again active as a musician, leading small Dixieland styled groups, and he opened his own club in Los Angeles. In his final years he ran a restaurant at Palm Springs, California. Visitors reported that he was embittered by his lack of recognition. His bitterness, combined with personal and financial problems, led him to take his own life on 7th June 1971.

It occasionally happens that just once in his career a bandleader finds himself with a trend setting group. This occurred with Jean Goldkette for a period between September 1926 and September 1927. Goldkette was born at Valenciennes on 18th March 1899, and left France for the United States in 1911. Some reports claim that as a youth he lived in both Greece and Russia. He was neither a jazz musician, nor even particularly adept at dance music. His main interest lay in the classics, which he played as a solo pianist during the 'thirties. Nevertheless, he secured work in a dance unit in Chicago and was playing in Detroit by 1921. Early in 1924, he was leading his own band, which included trombonists Bill Rank and Tommy Dorsey, reed men Jimmy Dorsey and Don Murray, and violinist Joe Venuti. The first recordings were for RCA Victor in March. During November 1924, the legendary cornettist Bix Beiderbecke joined Goldkette for a while—he can be heard taking a pleasant solo on a recording of *I Didn't Know*. The association was not a happy one, though, and Beiderbecke soon left to join

An early RCA Victor publicity shot of the Goldkette band.

the Charlie Straight band in Chicago. Goldkette never worked in his own bands and, by the late 'twenties, was basically an entrepreneur. He had control over some twenty bands, including the famous McKinney's Cotton Pickers. The records that appeared under Goldkette's name from March 1924 to September 1926 were made by two distinct groups. His number one band included numerous excellent musicians, but even their recordings are generally quite undistinguished. The most interesting looking title, *Jig Walk,* was unfortunately never issued. During this period Goldkette was hailed as the Paul Whiteman Of The West; certainly his musical interests seemed closely to parallel those of Whiteman.

In autumn 1926, Goldkette secured an engagement at the Roseland Ballroom in New York City. For much of the time his band was to play opposite the Fletcher Henderson group, and aware of the interest in hot music, he asked saxist Frank Trumbauer to organise a small jazz contingent within the full orchestra. One of Trumbauer's conditions was that Goldkette should engage Bix Beiderbecke, and this time the association was altogether more successful. The band also included Bill Rank, Don Murray, Joe Venuti, Eddie Lang, Steve Brown and Chauncey Morehouse. It opened at the Roseland in September 1926 and returned there after a tour of New England before finally breaking up exactly twelve months later. It was, by all accounts, a very expensive band to maintain, as well as including in its ranks a fair sprinkling of prima donnas, and much as he may have admired the quality of the music that it produced, Goldkette was

first and foremost a businessman. His band recorded a total of twenty-one titles for RCA Victor; eighteen have been issued over the years, some with alternative takes, but little of its recorded output gives more than a passing clue as to why the band was so highly regarded. The reason is simply that the band's recording director refused to allow it to record its best arrangements. One of its members, Stanley 'Doc' Ryker, commented upon this in an interview given to a collector in 1967:

'He [the Victor recording director] wanted it strictly Stock, commercial . . . I don't really know why he hired the band at all. The stuff he didn't want, why that was our style. We didn't get a chance to do anything we wanted until right at the end, when he let us put down *Clementine* and *My Pretty Girl.* Both of those were worked out in the manner I described. But there were so many other gems—*Spanish Shawl* was one, *Baby Face* another. . . .'

'Working out' refers to Mr Ryker's earlier account of how he rehearsed the various sections of the band, allowing them to fill in on arrangements lightly sketched out by Don Murray. The band's recorded material, which includes waltzes and mediocre novelty numbers and other casual-sounding performances, certainly bears out Ryker's remarks. Significantly, two of the most promising titles it made—*Stampede* and *Play It, Red*—were never released. In spite of everything, some of the performances contain excellent passages of ensemble playing; even some of the most dreary numbers have worthwhile solos. For example, behind an appalling vocal by one Frank Bessinger on *Idolizing* there is fine guitar work from Eddie Lang; the opening ensemble passage on *Sunday,*

Above: *Jean Goldkette and his band in the early 1930s.*
Below: *the Jean Goldkette Orchestra, 1926-7. Left to right: Bill Challis (arranger), Spegan Wilcox (trombone), Andy Riskin (piano), Bix Beiderbecke (cornet), Don Murray (clarinet,* *sax), Howdy Quicksell (banjo, guitar), Doc Ryker (sax), Chauncey Moorhouse (drums), Fred Farrar (trumpet), Ray Lodwig (trumpet), Bill Rank (trombone), Frankie Trumbauer (sax), Steve Brown (string bass).*

presumably scored by the talented Bill Challis, has an open textured quality that is impressive; Beiderbecke has excellent solos on *Proud of a Baby Like You* and the otherwise dismal *In My Merry Oldsmobile*; and bassist Steve Brown, pushing the ensemble along well on several titles, displays a rhythmic drive on string bass that was by no means common for the period. *Clementine,* certainly the most striking performance recorded by the band and presumably most typical of its in-person work, offers splendid ensemble playing and a brilliant, driving yet lyrical solo from Beiderbecke. We can only regret that the band's surviving musicians and individuals who heard the band at the Roseland are alone in being able to recall the achievements of its heyday.

An interesting point made by 'Doc' Ryker in discussing the band was that, as Beiderbecke was an indifferent reader, another trumpeter had to be engaged to play the second trumpet parts. This virtually accidental use of three trumpets instead of the then more conventional two to a section led other bands who heard them in New York to follow suit. Ryker also said, 'Same thing happened with Steve Brown on bass. At that time, all bands were using tubas, but when they heard him they all switched to string bass. None of them could equal Steve slapping the bass. He had a really distinctive style and uncanny sense of rhythm. He'd get out in front of the band for some feature number or other and everybody, all the dancers, everyone, would gather around the bandstand and watch. He was even better known to most people at that time than Bix was; in a way he was the star of the band, although the people who knew Bix knew how good HE was'. Mr Ryker summed up his reminiscences, 'So long ago; all of it . . . but what a band that was . . . like nothing you've ever heard . . .'

Though the disbandment of the group was a blow to Goldkette, he continued to lend his name to several bands for a few more years, producing recordings until late in 1929. However, he was no longer a significant force in his field, and while combining work as an agent with appearances as a concert pianist, he receded into partial obscurity. Some bands he led—at least nominally—during the mid 'forties and part of the 'fifties were unsuccessful, and in 1961 he moved to California. He died at Santa Barbara on 24th March 1962. Just three years before his death, he organised a band to record a long play item, using the original scores from his heyday in the 'twenties. The personnel included a few of the musicians who had been present on the occasion when they were first used. The current nostalgia for music of the 'twenties and 'thirties was then lacking, and the record only enjoyed a limited success.

When the Goldkette band broke up, Beiderbecke and Trumbauer joined a short-lived big band led by multi-instrumentalist Adrian Rollini. This was an idealistic venture and the leader's policy was to give jazz stars a lot of freedom. Success eluded him, however, and in late October 1927, both Beiderbecke and Trumbauer joined the Paul Whiteman band. They found themselves in the company of the Dorsey Brothers, Eddie Lang, clarinettist Izzy Friedman, and the former Goldkette arranger Bill Challis. To the public, Paul Whiteman had been the 'King Of Jazz' since about 1924. The description infuriated jazz followers then and in the years ahead, though the arrival of Beiderbecke meant that Whiteman had at last acquired the services of a major jazz artist to give some point to his title. Trumbauer remained until 1932, and in later years Whiteman always included jazz musicians within his ranks. Among them were Jack Teagarden, Bunny Berigan and Red Norvo, but the 1927-29 records featuring Beiderbecke are virtually the only ones from the enormous output of the Whiteman band that are sought after by jazz enthusiasts.

Apart from an absence of four months through ill health, Beiderbecke remained in the Whiteman band until September 1929. He was in many ways an archetypal figure of the 'Jazz Age'. His astonishing and individual talent expressed itself in cornet solos of great beauty and invention, and in a small number of highly idiosyncratic piano compositions. In his personal life, however, he was almost totally undisciplined and his death at the age of twenty-eight was precipitated by alcoholism. Apart from possibly Louis Armstrong, Duke Ellington and Charlie Parker, more has been written about Beiderbecke than any other jazz musician. His life was even romanticised by Dorothy Baker for a novel, 'Man With a Horn' that was later made into a film. Beiderbecke benefitted financially from joining Whiteman's band, receiving a weekly salary that was very high for the day. But, musically, he could never have been too happy within the massive Whiteman organisation. It has already been mentioned that Beiderbecke was at best an indifferent reader, and what he made of the ponderous, often pretentious, orchestrations used by Whiteman, frequently in what was described as a 'symphonic jazz' style, can only be imagined.

In a sense it would be true to say that Whiteman never made a real jazz record in the whole length of his band-leading career, but the 1927-29 performances which feature Beiderbecke, Lang, Trumbauer and others are interesting enough to merit a brief examination in this chapter. In fairness to Whiteman, it should be said that he did commission scores from Bill Challis, for example, with the intention of featuring Beiderbecke, and that by employing the finest musicians and arrangers, and paying them well, he undoubtedly helped to raise the standards of dance bands, even jazz styled ones, considerably. It would be unrealistic to expect most of the musicians in the Whiteman band to equal their counterparts in Fletcher Henderson's or Duke Ellington's groups on jazz terms, though their technical expertise enabled them to approach such scores as Don Redman's *Whiteman Stomp* with creditable results.

Many of the Whiteman records, which are now beloved of jazz followers for the Beiderbecke solos, probably sold

Above: *a typical posed still of the Paul Whiteman band, 1928.* Right: *Paul Whiteman with the Dorsey brothers in a scene from the film 'The Fabulous Dorseys'.*

to the general public at the time of issue because of the popularity of The Rhythm Boys, a vocal trio composed of Bing Crosby, Harry Barris and Al Rinker. It is ironical that a title such as *Mississippi Mud,* containing an excellent solo by Beiderbecke, has lyrics that would now be considered deeply offensive to all black Americans, yet even the jazz contingent within the Whiteman band, some of whom played regularly in jam sessions with black musicians, presumably did not consider them worthy of protest at the time. Bill Challis, who had already proved his talent with Goldkette, scored many of the titles on which Beiderbecke is well featured. He reduced the size of the unit on occasions to achieve a greater mobility. He was not always successful. On *Changes* and *Lonely Melody,* for example, one is always conscious of the ponderous playing of the ensemble, despite the attraction of Beiderbecke's lyrical solos. At other times—particularly when Steve Brown was brought to the fore to impart a greater rhythmic drive—though the band may not have achieved genuine swing, at least it produced a rather heavy-footed, playful momentum. Indeed, attractive scoring touches can be heard on performances such as *Lonely Melody, From Monday On* and *Dardanella.* Brown is well recorded on *Monday* and *Dardanella,* but Beiderbecke's contributions are the feature that effectively ensured their recognition as partial classics. In one form or another, these performances have remained in catalogue for decades. Whiteman's versions of such numbers as *Lonely Melody, Dardanella, 'Tain't So, Honey, 'Tain't So* and *Because My Baby Don't Mean Maybe Now* are pleasing on several levels, and individual passages from other musicians are good. However, it is hard to believe that they would have become virtually a permanent part of

the worldwide RCA Victor catalogue if Beiderbecke had not been present.

A soured critic once wrote that Whiteman's orchestra played everything, but nothing well. This is unjust, for however absurd some of the more pretentious offerings may sound today, his records are usually irreproachable from the technical viewpoint. *Whiteman Stomp,* a Fats Waller composition arranged for Whiteman by Don Redman, raises an interesting question of how the band would have sounded if Whiteman had permanently used an arranger of Redman's jazz standing. Certainly this is an impressive performance on all counts. The alto saxophone solo from Jimmy Dorsey is unusually assertive, and the band handles the tricky score well. In later years, Whiteman always included jazz soloists in his band and at one point even featured a small jazz group in personal appearances. However, though Bunny Berigan is well featured on *It's Only a Paper Moon,* the Teagarden brothers and Frankie Trumbauer on *Announcer's Blues,* and Jack Teagarden on *Ain't Misbehavin',* the scoring and ensemble backgrounds only highlight the fact that the 'King Of Jazz' was an imposter. Whiteman was a large, genial man who enjoyed life in the classic showbiz manner, complete with such success symbols as Cadillacs equipped with cocktail cabinets and large boxes of cigars to offer to cops who might query the speed at which they were travelling. In all probability, he genuinely liked jazz and enjoyed having outstanding jazz musicians in his orchestra. He was as much a figure of

tne period in which he gained his success as was Beider-becke, though in a very different manner, and when the president of the American Federation of Musicians referred to him, at his memorial service, as the 'King Of The Jazz Age' he was not being too fanciful.

The influence of the Whiteman band, even over some quite irreproachable jazz groups, is something that most jazz followers are not anxious to admit. Throughout the history of jazz and dance music in general, jazz musicians are far less purist in their tastes than their fans, who may find Louis Armstrong's admiration for Guy Lombardo's saxophone section, or the adulation that generations of alto saxophone players bestowed on Jimmy Dorsey, almost inexplicable. The answer lies simply in the readiness of musicians to pay tribute to outstanding technicians, usually with little regard to the ideological and musical standards set up by jazz followers. Jazz enthusiasts, faced with a situation similar to the above examples, either ignore it, or take refuge in the argument that even the greatest of geniuses have their aberrations. This has led, at times, to the presentation of less than the full facts on certain aspects of development of the music in standard jazz histories. Seldom has this been more strikingly illustrated than in the references made to the Casa Loma

Orchestra. It can certainly be argued that this orchestra was, overall, a bad influence on big band jazz, but to ignore it, or to pretend that its impact was only marginal, is to disavow the facts. There is abundant recorded evidence of the wide influence of Casa Loma perform-ances. Such outstanding coloured bands as those of Fletcher Henderson and Earl Hines, to name only two, attempted at one time to produce a facsimile of them. There can be little doubt that, before the arrival of the swing bands, the Casa Loma Orchestra was the white group that most impressed its black counterparts. Its admirers' claim that it pioneered much that became commonplace in the swing era is not entirely without foundation. From a jazz viewpoint, for better or worse, it is the most important white big band to have appeared in the years before Benny Goodman's success.

The Casa Loma Orchestra started life as a Jean Gold-kette unit in Detroit during the late 'twenties, changing its name when it secured an engagement (that ultimately failed to materialise), at the Casa Loma Hotel in Toronto, Canada. In 1929, it commenced a touring schedule and registered as the Casa Loma Orchestra Inc. in the form of a co-operative. Glen Gray (real name Glen Gray Knoblaugh) was elected by the members as president of the company. For some years Gray chose to play in the sax section and violinist Mel Jenssen acted as front man, but in 1937 Gray took over from Jenssen and the band was billed as Glen Gray and the Casa Loma Orchestra.

The importance of arrangers in setting the style of bands hardly needs stressing, and in Gene Gifford the Casa Loma Orchestra had a man who, more than any other, was responsible for the individual sound it achieved. Gifford, born in Memphis, Tennessee on 31st May 1908, was a banjo player and guitarist. When he joined the Orange Blossoms Band in 1929 (initially this had been led by Henry Biagnini), he already had a wide experience in a variety of touring bands, including one which he himself led. The Orange Blossoms became the nucleus of the Casa Loma Orchestra and as its chief arranger Gifford continued to play with the orchestra until December 1933, when he decided to devote all his time to arranging. He was a prolific freelance arranger during the 'thirties and 'forties. After U.S.O. tours overseas in the mid 'forties, he returned to work with the Casa Loma during 1948 and 1949. Gifford did not work full time in the musical field in the last two decades of his life, though he continued to do some arrangements on a casual basis, remaining in his home town until his death on 12th November 1970.

By all accounts, Gifford had been trained as a draughtsman and there is something of the draughtsman's meticulous care in his earliest Casa Loma scores. It is this aspect of his approach that led most jazz writers to dismiss the band as a purely mechanical unit. Soulless efficiency and an almost military precision were claimed as its most obvious characteristics. This is not altogether fair to Gifford, though his recorded scores show that his writing was not without flaws. What is undeniable is that Gifford's scores required a very high level of technical expertise on the part of the musicians who performed them, and this the Casa Lomans possessed in abundance. In the summer of 1930, Bix Beiderbecke, of all people, had a four day try-out with the band. In the course of an interview many years later Bill Challis recalled: 'Those guys—the Casa Lomans—just rehearsed and rehearsed. After full rehearsals they'd get off by themselves and rehearse. Bix couldn't take this. He got griped, so they'd take him out drinking. He thought that was just great, going out drinking with them. That went on for four days, and then it was all over.'

Once the band had settled down, with Gifford producing a stream of scores, it was an enormous success, particularly with the young college crowds who regarded it as the hottest thing around. The band's policy was cleverly geared to sustain the interest of as wide a public as possible. The instrumentals by Gifford and others were balanced by more straightforward performances of contemporary hit material sung by the immensely popular Kenny Sargent, who joined the group early in 1931. At the same time, clarinettist Clarence Hutchinrider, the most impressive individual soloist in the band, was also

Above: *Glen Gray, leader of the Casa Loma Orchestra, in the mid 1930s.* Right: *the rhythm section of the Casa Loma Orchestra, 1937: Stanley Dennis (bass), Jack Blanchette (guitar), Joe Hall (piano), Tony Briglia (drums), Glen Gray.*

added, bringing the sax section up to a quartet. The next few years were the best for the Casa Lomans, both musically and economically, and in 1933 the band became the first hot unit to be regularly featured on a commercial radio series. At this time it enjoyed the advantage of steady summer engagements at Glen Island Casino, where it reached a wide audience as a result of frequent radio transmissions. In the spring of 1935, Gifford was replaced as chief arranger by Larry Clinton. Others who contributed scores regularly in the following years include Dick Jones and Larry Wagner. Gray was fortunate in having to make few changes of personnel over a lengthy period. The two main additions to the ranks were Sonny Dunham, a brash, crowd-pleasing trumpeter who was present from 1934 until he left to form his own band in 1940, and trombonist/alto saxophonist Murray McEachern who came over from the Benny Goodman band in January 1938 and remained for three years. In February 1939, the orchestra received the accolade of being selected to act as supporting group to Louis Armstrong on a recording session, rather to the dismay of most jazz followers, as I recall.

Once the swing era got under way, the Casa Loma Orchestra began to lose some of its popularity as a hot unit, though it still held a loyal following for its performances of ballads. In comparison with such bands as Benny Goodman's and Tommy Dorsey's (it has to be remembered that its public would base evaluations on the work of other big white bands, generally knowing little of the great black jazz orchestras), its swing style performances began to sound somewhat stiff and dated, and it had few star soloists of the kind that graced the ranks of its contemporaries. During 1942 and 1943, there were several changes of personnel. Trumpeter Corky Cornelius and tenor saxophonist Lon Doty strengthened the jazz side of the band; arrangers Tutti Camarata and Harry Rodgers gave a more modern sound to its book. Unfortunately, this was the period of the first recording ban by the American Federation of Musicians so that surviving air shots provide our only idea of how the band sounded at this time. In 1944, guitarist Herb Ellis was a member and both Red Nichols and Bobby Hackett were temporarily present in the band, but its great days were over and the public acclaim of its peak years was never regained. In 1950, Glen Gray finally decided to disband and retired from bandleading, though he achieved some success six years later with a series of long play records by a studio band, recreating many of the past successes of the Casa Loma Orchestra. Gray died at Plymouth, Massachusetts on 23rd August 1963, at the age of fifty-seven.

In his book, 'The Big Bands', George T. Simon attributes much of the band's technical brilliance to the trombonist Billy Rausch, a musical perfectionist who insisted that all other members perform faultlessly. He also comments that, contrary to appearances, the band had its share of weak readers who needed a long time to perfect their parts. This was certainly not apparent either to musicians or public; early tributes to the band came from such prominent names in the jazz field as Benny Goodman and Don Redman. Goodman states unequivocally in 'The Kingdom Of Swing' that it was the Casa Loma Orchestra which inspired his booking agent Willard Alexander to consider building up a band that could play good jazz. 'It was,' said Goodman, 'the band we had started out to buck.' He achieved his ambition in 1936 when he replaced it on the Camel Caravan radio show. Jazz purists might not regard Benny Goodman's views very highly, but they would possibly find it harder to dismiss those of the New Orleans clarinettist Albert Nicholas who, many years later, recalled first hearing the Casa Lomans in 1933, when he was playing at the Roseland Ballroom. He expressed his delight in their arrangements, describing them as 'very modern at that time'; he went on to praise the precision of the band and the abilities of clarinettist Clarence Hutchinrider 'whose feeling stood out even in the theme song.' Many musicians

who were active during the swing era have told me of the impact that the band made when they first heard it. Fletcher Henderson expressed it in musical form by recording *Casa Loma Stomp* and several other numbers in the Casa Loma style, and the Blue Rhythm Band made a whole series of records which clearly illustrate its debt to Gene Gifford.

In the light of Benny Goodman's remarks, it is very interesting to hear his recording of *Cokey,* made in November 1934. This took place only six months before he made the first of his RCA Victor titles, using arrangements by Fletcher and Horace Henderson to set the style that made him famous. Even the most cursory hearing of *Cokey* makes it clear that the Casa Loma Orchestra was still influencing his music. It suggests that at this comparatively late stage in his career he was still uncertain of his musical direction. The impact of the Casa Loma was, if anything, even greater in Europe than it was in the U.S.A., however. The Lew Stone band in England, probably the finest all round dance orchestra in Europe at the time, gained a considerable reputation as a jazz inclined unit through playing many of the Casa Loma scores. In Germany the James Kok band was styled almost exclusively on the Casa Loma Orchestra, and in those European countries where dance music and jazz were played, Gene Gifford's scores became accepted as the best in hot music. It is easy, in retrospect, to blame the European leaders for ignoring the music of the major black bands, but it has to be remembered that well into the 'thirties the type of jazz best known to European musicians was that of white stylists based in New York. Only a small minority of jazz record collectors were familiar with the output of bands like those of Luis Russell, Fletcher Henderson and McKinney's Cotton Pickers.

From the start, though, the records of the Casa Loma Orchestra were poorly received by jazz enthusiasts and, in over thirty-five years of avid reading of the international jazz press, I can recall less than half a dozen favourable references to the band. One of the very few exceptions to the general attitude of disdain adopted by jazz writers is contained in the late Marshall Stearn's 'The Story Of Jazz':

'With the skill and foresight of such arrangers as Southern-born-and-bred Gene Gifford, the band learned to read harmonized solos and play riffs, the brass and reed sections calling and responding to each other in a variety of ways. What is more, they learned to roll along together, generating considerable swing as a whole. The Goldkette band and the Casa Loma band came from Detroit and played the same arrangements. "The Casa Loma band could swing more," Don Redman once told me, "perhaps because they were a great team without so many highly paid and temperamental stars." '

Stearns goes on to suggest that Gifford's success in the jazz idiom could be ascribed to his early years spent on tour in the Southwest, listening to the blues and call-response patterns used by black bands. His view is plausible, though one must take leave to doubt that the Jean Goldkette band and the Casa Loma Orchestra played the same arrangements, even though Gifford was a Goldkette staff arranger for a short time before joining the Orange Blossoms Band.

Judging from a small representative selection of Casa Loma recordings, one feels that the peak years of the band were from 1931 to around 1936. Its first records were made in the autumn of 1929 under the Okeh label; Henry Biagnini was named as the director. The output from the first two sessions was thoroughly undistinguished, but a performance of *San Sue Strut* on the third Okeh date displayed the precision of the individual sections. The closing ensemble made use of recurring riff patterns in the manner which Gifford was to exploit consistently in the years ahead. The band's final Okeh session of December 1930 introduced the first recording of a Gifford original in *Casa Loma Stomp,* though the first few bars of the theme are in fact taken direct from an old minstrel song. There were reasonable, if not particularly individual, solo contributions from trombonist Pee Wee Hunt, tenor saxophonist Pat Davis, and an unidentified trumpeter and clarinettist. An ensemble build up at the close was in the familiar riff style. From early 1931 until the summer of 1934, the band recorded for American Brunswick. In 1933, there were also several sessions for RCA Victor. This was the period in which the band built up a large, and at times fanatical, following. From September 1934 until it disbanded, it recorded regularly for U.S. Decca.

A Brunswick session of March 1931 produced the initial recording of Gifford's famous *White Jazz*. He followed up the success of this number with themes in a similar style, entitled *Black Jazz* and *Blue Jazz. Maniacs Ball* was another typical and popular Gifford instrumental number from the same period. In addition, he made his own arrangements of standards such as *Royal Garden Blues* and *Alexander's Ragtime Band. White Jazz* and *Black Jazz* display all the essential characteristics of Gifford's arranging. Both are riff themes in which the opening ensemble statements are in the call-and-response pattern, with the sections trading phrases. The solos that follow are interspersed with brief ensemble or section passages, played with great precision, and while Hunt and one or more of the trumpeters are effective in a solo role, it is immediately apparent that the strongest solo voice is Hutchinrider's and the weakest Davis's. Hutchinrider was a fluent technician and his solos are invariably interesting. His broad, powerful tone occasionally calls to mind Edmond Hall. He was adept at varying his phrasing. Sometimes he combined a staccato approach with a cutting tonal edge; at others he employed longer lines and a more mellow sound. He is best known for the driving, agitated type of solo heard on the faster instrumental showpieces. However, performances like *Always* or *I May Be Wrong* proved that he possessed a flair for neat melodic variations. By contrast, Davis who featured almost as often as Hutchinrider on record, was rather a mediocre soloist. His jerky method of phrasing was inimical to genuine swing, and he substituted an illusion of excitement for real ideas.

The main criticisms levelled at the instrumental numbers recorded by the Casa Loma are that the band sounds mechanical and that it does not really swing. There is some justification for both views for, lacking the great jazz talent of the leading coloured bands, the Casa Loma personnel achieved much of their effect with a precision that resulted from extensive rehearsal. This did give an impression of mechanical efficiency, on occasions, rather in the manner of the current Count Basie band. Nevertheless, it was not always the case and by the mid 'thirties there are quite a few instrumental recordings that are reasonably relaxed. Gifford added to the stilted nature of performances at times by rather overdoing the riff endings, extending them to the point where they became merely tedious. As to the subjective question of whether the band genuinely swung, my personal response is that it did so quite well on occasions, in spite of a rhythm section that was heavy and inflexible, at least initially. One of the last Gifford originals to be recorded was *Stompin' Around,* made for Decca in September 1934. There is a notably more relaxed quality about the whole performance that even has Davis playing with an unusual degree of coherence.

When Larry Clinton became the Casa Loma's chief arranger in the spring of 1935, the policy of the band remained much as before. Clinton was a journeyman arranger who met with some success in subsequent years through his ability to produce catchy riff tunes almost at will. Themes like *Jungle Jitters* and *Zig-Zag* veer dangerously close to novelty numbers, despite some neat scoring touches that show a greater variety of method than that used by Gifford. *A Study in Brown* is one of Clinton's best numbers for the band and, as well as creditable solos by Hutchinrider and Dunham, it offers some imaginative scoring touches, particularly in the use of low register clarinets and the balanced contrast of reeds with muted trumpets. For Decca, the Casa Loma Orchestra re-recorded such earlier successes as *Casa Loma Stomp* and *Royal Garden Blues,* although it is in versions of standard themes, like *Rose of the Rio Grande* and *Copenhagen,* that it sounds at its most relaxed. By the mid 'thirties, the Casa Loma was increasingly tailoring its output to exploit the commercial popularity of Kenny Sargent, though one of its best selling records of 1938, a version of *Memories of You,* is mainly a vehicle for trumpeter Sonny Dunham. It also includes an accomplished trombone solo from Murray McEachern. With the swing era under way, the Casa Loma made some adjustments of style and the work of the rhythm section in particular was lighter and more rhythmic than in the past. Even so, its recordings hardly compared favourably with those of the leading swing bands, let alone the great coloured orchestras that were beginning to gain a lot more publicity. The last instru-

mental recording to achieve a fair degree of success for the band was a two part version of Larry Wagner's *No Name Jive.* An orthodox swing performance, it had powerful ensemble work, and solos by trumpeter Grady Watt, Hutchinrider (on both clarinet and tenor saxophone), an unidentified alto player, and Sonny Dunham. Dunham rounded off his brash contribution with some Ziggy Elman-like flourishes. In many ways this is one of the best of all the later Casa Loma recordings. Edgar Jackson concluded his 'Melody Maker' review: '. . . this is a record in which for once the prevailing trend in large white ensembles captures the spirit and music of jazz instead of being merely a technical show-off.'

Although the stress here has been on the jazz type recordings that the Casa Loma Orchestra made, it should be remembered that many of its best selling items were the entirely commercial numbers which featured Kenny Sargent. In jazz terms, it would be easy to exaggerate the worth of the band yet, on the contrary, it has received less than its fair share of praise for what it did achieve. It was certainly the first large white ensemble to stress jazz instrumentals in its repertoire; its influence on other bands, and the groundwork it laid for the swing era, deserve consideration. Gifford, for all his failings, was an individual arranger whose methods were widely copied. It is impossible to tell what he might have achieved if he had possessed a greater melodic flair and the ability consistently to handle his riff patterns in a more cohesive fashion. The stock criticisms of the band are partially accurate; sometimes it did sound mechanical and failed to swing, but this was not always so and, for its time, it was forward looking and often adventurous. Casa Loma performances of the peak years need only be compared with those of almost any other large white band of the same era to show just how advanced the orchestra was. On balance, its merits (and there were more than most jazz writers have cared to admit) earn the Casa Loma Orchestra at least an honourable mention in the history of big band jazz.

Before the swing era, one other white band made a serious attempt to play in the jazz idiom, the Dorsey Brothers Orchestra. Jimmy and Tommy Dorsey must have been amongst the most accomplished technicians of the whole dance band and swing era. Jimmy, in particular, won the admiration of jazz alto saxophonists as diverse in style as Johnny Hodges, Charlie Parker and Ornette Coleman. From the late 'twenties, they had recorded with studio groups for releases that were issued as by the Dorsey Brothers Orchestra, and occasionally organised bands for specific engagements. In the spring of 1934, they formed a group on a full-time basis that played for a running-in period outside New York before beginning a residency at a Long Island club in the following July. After a number of engagements, the band moved into the Glen Island Casino in May 1935. The feuding of the two brothers during much of their career was staple fare for music publication writers in search of a story. It flared into a violent

The Dorsey Brothers Orchestra, 1935. Tommy and Jimmy Dorsey are to left and right of vocalist Kay Weber.

quarrel in June and later resulted in Tommy's leaving the bandstand in the middle of a performance. He did return for a few days shortly afterwards, while his replacement was being sought, but for the next eighteen years the two brothers followed separate careers.

The line-up of the Dorsey Brothers Orchestra was a little unusual in that the brass consisted of only one trumpet and three trombones; there were also orthodox sections of three reeds and four rhythm. Tommy Dorsey once said that stylistically 'We were trying to hit somewhere between Hal Kemp and the Casa Loma band.' The style of the band was actually set by Glenn Miller who not only wrote most of its arrangements but introduced about half of its personnel from the Smith Ballew group with which he had been working. Assuming that the band's Decca recordings are an accurate reflection of its in-person performances, the repertoire can be divided into three groups. There were the popular numbers of the day, performed in a straightforward dance band manner with vocal choruses by either Bob Crosby or Kay Weber. Standard instrumental features such as *St Louis Blues, Dippermouth Blues* and *Milneburg Joys* were given a Dixieland-styled treatment, and a few originals contributed by members of the band looked forward to the coming swing era. The entirely commercial recordings are outside the scope of this book, but the instrumental performances make clear that in most respects this was stylistically a transitional band. Its approach combined much that was commonplace in the dance music of the day with the occasional hint of what was to come.

The arrangements that Glenn Miller contributed to the Dorsey Brothers book, and to that of the Ray Noble band shortly afterwards, are efficient but too frequently marred by fussy detail and a generally cluttered sound. One result is that the solos are not highlighted as well as they might be. *St Louis Blues,* in particular, has a messy score. On the Dixieland style performances, there are creditable individual solos from the leaders, trumpeter George Thow, and tenor saxophonist Skeets Herfurt. However, the solos are generally pretty ordinary. In spite of featuring a period vocal trio, the version of *Honeysuckle Rose* (orginally issued as two sides of a 78 rpm record) is superior to other, similar titles. Not only does it have good solos from Thow, both Dorseys, and Herfurt, but there are neat arranging touches, such as the three trombone support to Jimmy

Dorsey's clarinet solo and good use of dynamics in ensemble passages. A few recordings have Miller using the fade-in and fade-out device which he was later to employ so successfully with his own band. The most interesting titles are *Stop, Look and Listen* and *By Heck,* both of which are swing oriented. *By Heck* has excellent solo contributions from Jimmy Dorsey, both on clarinet and alto saxophone, and Thow's open passage suggests that he was happier with this material than the Dixieland numbers. Few of the fairly plentiful recordings which the band made in a period of just over a year suggest that it was in any way outstanding. In view of the excellent musicians who were present, it must be assumed that the band's full potential was never realised. Possibly, the personal bickerings of the leaders, the rather commonplace scores, and a stylistic diversity that removed much of the band's personal identity, combined to prevent its becoming a top ranking orchestra. Whatever the reasons, the wisdom of the leaders in following their own paths is amply stressed by the records that they made in the following years.

An encyclopaedic list of white bands who could sometimes turn out a creditable jazz performance in the pre-swing era would need to include several dozen more groups. To name but two well known bands, both the Coon-Sanders Nighthawks and the Isham Jones Orchestra occasionally showed an expertise in jazz styled performances that might well surprise those new to their work. They were certainly not unique. The little known Phil Baxter Orchestra, complete with featured accordionist, made a recording of *I Ain't Got No Gal Now* that makes rigid categorisation of dance music and jazz difficult to sustain. With its recordings of *Hard Luck* and *Chicago Rhythm* for Gennett in 1929, the Floyd Mills band, based on Cumberland, Maryland, showed that it was a hard stomping group with reasonable jazz soloists and a driving ensemble sound. Many other bands could be listed like this, but here we are concerned with those bands which, however erratically, pursued a musical policy that had some bearing on the development of big band jazz in general. Until the mid 'thirties, big band jazz, with few exceptions, was the music of large coloured orchestras, and of white bands; only the Casa Loma Orchestra could claim to have made any individual contribution in the field. Historically, however, the bands of Ben Pollack, Jean Goldkette, and even occasionally Paul Whiteman, performed a pioneer role in creating a musical climate which was conducive to white big band jazz. For that, they deserve some consideration in any study of the subject that claims to be even partially comprehensive. Jazz-wise, their failures might cancel out their achievements, but in the last resort they deserve credit for trying.

7 The Swing Era—
Trendsetters & Big Names

How Charlie Barnet came to play chimes on Duke Ellington's 1930 recording of *Ring dem Bells* is not clear, but he certainly did. Barnet was in his seventeenth year and had already begun an erratic early career in the music business. From the early 'thirties, he worked quite extensively on ocean liners, crossing the Atlantic on more than one occasion. He formed his first big band in 1933 for a three month residency at the Paramount Hotel Grill in New York. After this, he led other bands, but broke off in 1935 for a brief attempt at an acting career in Hollywood. He did appear in a couple of undistinguished films. Returning to music, formed a new group for a residency at the Glen Island Casino and subsequent touring.

It appears that Barnet came from a wealthy family and suffered fewer financial pressures than many leaders, though he was clearly anxious for success on a musical level. He formed another band for a job at the Famous Door in New York during 1938. In October 1939, all the band's instruments and its library were lost in a fire at the Palomar Ballroom in Los Angeles. Duke Ellington and Benny Carter were among the musicians who sent Barnet scores to help him rebuild his library. Barnet kept this band going until 1943, though not, of course, without personnel changes. He continued to assemble big bands during the 'forties, achieving his most modern styling in 1949-50. Throughout the 'fifties and most of the 'sixties Barnet put together big bands for specific engagements. The band of 1966-67 was particularly good; it was, incidentally, the last big band to include the late Willie Smith. From time to time during these years, Barnet also worked with smaller groups. Lately, he has been musically inactive, though he may well go back to fronting a big band for limited periods in the future.

Barnet's first recording in his own name were made for the American Recording Corporation group of labels—Melotone, Perfect, Banner, Romeo and Oriole—in the autumn of 1933. Further sessions were completed for them in March 1934 and May 1936. He also recorded for Bluebird—RCA Victor's cheap label—in January 1934, and on four occasions in 1936-37. Also in 1937, he took part in two sessions for the Variety label. The performances of *Surrealism* and *Overheard in a Cocktail Lounge* owe something to the popular Raymond Scott. Two coloured musicians, Frankie Newton and John Kirby, were present on the Variety dates. In the following years, Barnet regularly cut across race barriers by employing black musicians. In 1933, he was reported to be the first leader of a white band to play at Harlem's Apollo Theatre. In subsequent years, he appeared there fairly frequently.

The band formed by Barnet in 1938 initially recorded on transcriptions only. However, the first of many sessions made under new contract to RCA Victor took place on 20th January 1939; the last date for that company occurred three years later to the day. All Barnet's output was released on the Bluebird label. After expiry of the contract, the Barnet band recorded for Decca, Apollo and Capitol respectively during the rest of the 'forties.

A few of the commercial recordings made before 193? are interesting; the rest are undistinguished and suffer from commercialism. The Bluebird releases from 1939 are much nearer to jazz and, in spite of the inevitable commercial content, represent an impressive body of recorded work. The Barnet band failed to achieve the commercial success of Benny Goodman, Tommy Dorsey or Artie Shaw. It has been claimed that, in the 'forties, radio sponsors and some hotels avoided the band in case the presence of coloured musicians might offend a few of the public. Taken as a whole, Barnet's records are the most consistently jazz slanted of all those by the white swing bands, and have worn well. Barnet commented to Leonard Feather, 'I think the reason so many of these things haven't dated is that our band was never highly stylized, like Benny Goodman's or Glen Miller's . . . We had a lot more latitude than most orchestras. We created more informal "head" arrangements than any other band except Basie's I guess. And we were happy ninety per cent of the time. There were no cliques; it was just a bunch of guys having a ball.'

The musical approach owed more to the great coloured bands, particularly Duke Ellington's, than to any other contemporary white group. Barnet's own admiration for Ellington and, only slightly less, for Basie is well known; it is interesting how often Ellington numbers were recorded. In many ways, the Barnet band's recordings of these titles demonstrate how to retain the spirit of the originals without indulging in imitation. They emerge as recognisable Ellington while remaining valid performances in their own right. Ellington themes made up only a small proportion of the band's repertoire; the remainder had its own specific character.

The band included a number of competent soloists who are heard from time to time on record. Most of the solo work on the Bluebird titles was assigned to Barnet himself, trumpeter Bob Burnet, guitarist Bus Etri, and pianist Bill Miller. While short on individuality, Barnet's solo contributions were generally effective. When he recorded with Red Norvo in 1934, Barnet seemed a competent tenor saxophonist in the style of Coleman Hawkins, but he adapted his playing in the following years. On most of his records from 1939, he employs a slightly drier tone and a staccato phrasing that imparts to his solos the agitated quality of the jump style. On alto saxophone, he normally employed a smoother approach clearly influenced by the work of Johnny Hodges. On soprano saxophone, the influence of Hodges can again be discerned, though more obliquely. Barnet seldom played clarinet, but the odd recorded example shows him to be competent performer. Bill Miller is a neat, melodic pianist whose solo work maintains a good standard. Bus Etri who was killed in a car accident in the late summer of 1941, was the first white guitarist to use an amplified instrument regularly in a big band. Etri's solos are usually excellent, for he produces individual ideas and has a flair for the blues; it is a pity that he was not featured

Above: *the Charlie Barnet band in the 1940s; the futuristic background is probably from a film set*. Right: *Charlie Barnet in the late 1940s*.

more extensively. The versatile, but neglected, Bob Burnet was apparently an admirer of 'Cootie' Williams, which no doubt explains his ability as a growl style soloist. He was also impressive when playing open, combining good phrasing, tone and swing with the knack of shaping cohesive solos. Burnet worked with Barnet from 1938 to 1940, left to lead a sextet in which he was the only white musician, then rejoined Barnet during 1941.

A good rhythm section is an essential element of any successful band. Barnet was fortunate in this respect. During 1939-41 Cliff Leeman, a fine big band drummer whose sense of time has always been highly rated, formed an excellent section with Bill Miller, Bus Etri and bassist Phil Stephens. Arrangements were provided by several well known musicians from outside the band, but Barnet, Skip Martin and, later, Billy May all made important contributions to the book. Many recordings show the band to advantage, but I have chosen to deal with numbers that combine musical quality and availability.

On the second session under the terms of its RCA Victor contract, the Barnet band recorded the first of many Ellington numbers—*The Gal from Joe's*. Recording the title a year earlier, in February 1938, the Ellington band had featured Johnny Hodges. This performance has Barnet on alto saxophone, pitted against wa-wa brass at the beginning and close. As if determined to avoid direct imitation, he adopts in his solos the jump style normally reserved for his tenor playing. The band's section work is worthy, though the arrangement is not distinguished. Evan Young's score for *Echoes of Harlem,* the next Ellington number recorded, is an improvement. Apart from a good chase sequence between trumpeters Bob Burnet and John Mendell, the performance mainly features Barnet's soprano sax against a subdued ensemble background. In July 1939, the Barnet band recorded Ray Noble's *Cherokee,* achieving unprecedented recognition. The performance is in straightforward swing style, with call-and-response patterns between the sections. Barnet's featured jump tenor is effective. Ellington's influence shows in the use of wa-wa brass at the opening and close. During ensemble passages, the strength of Leeman's drumming is readily apparent. Three months later, Barnet paid musical tribute to his two greatest influences with *The Duke's Idea* and *The Count's Idea,* both head arrangements derived from themes sketched out by the leader. The former evokes more successfully the spirit of the musician honoured. Barnet plays as much like Hodges as he can, and Burnet adopts a fine growl style. *The Count's Idea* is, appropriately enough, a riff number. Miller leads into a theme followed by the saxes. Solos come from Skip Martin (clarinet), Barnet (tenor), Burnet and Spud Murphy (trombone). Burnet introduces some Rex Stewart-like inflections during his spot. Leeman sounds more like Jo Jones than usual behind Barnet's jump tenor solo.

Mary Ann McCall was Barnet's vocalist for several months from late 1939. Miss McCall, who managed better than the average female big band vocalist, is heard to advantage on *Wanderin' Blues,* which also includes an excellent solo from Etri and a good one in plunger style from Burnet. In general, the sax section was the strongest in the Barnet band. It sounds particularly good in ensemble passages when Barnet takes over the lead on soprano. This is demonstrated on Billy Moore's arrangement of *Spanish Kick,* a number based on the habanera theme from 'Carmen'. Here, Burnet forsakes his growl style to play an attractive open solo.

Billy May joined the band in the summer of 1939 and was contributing an increasing number of scores by the early months of 1940. *Lament for May* is a bluesy theme with an attractive melodic line. The solos are by Miller, Barnet (on alto) and Burnet; contrasting backgrounds are exploited when Barnet plays against the brass and Burnet against the saxes. *Pompton Turnpike* is another pleasantly melodic number; the reeds achieve a rich sound during the opening theme, and there is a good call-and-response passage between Barnet's soprano sax and May's trumpet. *Wings Over Manhattan,* a third Billy May score originally released as a double-sided 78, is a more ambitious affair. Apparently, it was conceived for the combined Barnet and Ellington bands at the New York World's Fair of 1939-40, in a concert which did not finally take place. May uses changing moods and tempos, with more than the usual single theme, rather in the manner of Duke Ellington's

extended works. Barnet is particularly fine on soprano sax, whether solo or leading the section. He also takes a solo on tenor sax in rather less extrovert a manner than usual. However, the fine playing of the individual sections and ensemble assure the success of the performance. Very few of Barnet's swing band contemporaries would have used such material, although harmonically and melodically it was quite conventional.

Leapin' at the Lincoln is a much more straightforward jump instrumental that uses the chord changes of *Lady Be Good.* The opening ensemble leads to a swinging open solo by Burnet, followed by Barnet's tenor and Martin's clarinet. Once again drummer Cliff Leeman shows his worth with assertive but controlled playing in the ensemble passages. By contrast, Barnet's own *Reverie of a Moax* is more introspective. The opening ensemble makes good use of trombones in the lower register and leads into a nice passage by Etri and a very attractive muted solo by Burnet. Barnet leads the ensemble on soprano sax and takes a very good solo. Etri contributes a striking solo just before the close by Burnet and the ensemble. This number demonstrates the impressive musicianship of the band and illustrates its use of first rate material. Billy May's *Phylisse* is a lyrical theme that recalls Ellington in mood. The rich scoring for the saxes initially catches the ear, and includes an effective moody tenor solo by Barnet who then switches to alto sax and finally to soprano. The band still played Ellington material, and a session in August 1941 includes an arrangement of the Duke's *Harlem Speaks* by Andy Gibson. The number is taken at a surprisingly fast tempo, the band swings powerfully, and Barnet solos on both tenor and alto sax. From the same date comes *Murder at Peyton Hall,* another aggresive performance, that contains Bus Etri's last recorded solo. Immediately before switching to Decca, Barnet recorded *I Can't Get Started,* his last number for the Bluebird label, well scored by Andy Gibson. For some reason, it remained unissued for about twenty-five years, but it is an agreeable performance with soprano sax work by Barnet and another good plunger style solo by the consistent Burnet. I believe this to be Burnet's last recorded solo.

During 1939-41, although Barnet's personnel had its inevitable changes, he kept his nucleus of key musicians together successfully. From early 1942, however, his line-up became much less stable. At that date trumpeter/vocalist Herbert 'Peanuts' Holland came into the band. His entertaining singing and powerful solo work were featured on such numbers as *I Like to Riff* and *Oh! Miss Jaxson.* Andy Gibson was contributing much of the band's book at this point. A good example is *Washington Whirligig,* a relaxed performance with a strong solo by Holland. Barnet plays alto in a manner which suggests that he had been listening to Willie Smith of the Jimmie Lunceford band. *Pow-Wow* continues the tradition of 'Red Indian' titles started by the successful recording of *Cherokee,* and has a jump solo by Barnet on alto sax and forceful trumpet work by trumpeter Al Killian. Less

Above: *the Charlie Barnet band during the early 1940s.* Right: *the 1943 band included several outstanding coloured stars. Shown here with Barnet: Howard McGhee, James 'Trummy' Young, Oscar Pettiford and 'Peanuts' Holland.*

frenetic is *Things Ain't What They Used to Be,* on which pianist Bill Miller provides a good introduction to the rocking ensemble theme, with outstanding sax work preceding the excellent solos by Barnet, Holland and Miller. This tune is associated with the late Johnny Hodges and, not unexpectedly, Barnet pays due homage to Hodges during his solo. Holland plays very much in the Roy Eldridge manner. Ralph Burns wrote and arranged *The Moose,* a good theme that becomes a feature for Dodo Marmarosa's melodically sensitive piano playing. There is a return to Duke Ellington with the 1944 recording of *Drop Me Off At Harlem.* Something of the character of the number is lost through the speed at which it is taken but, as well as fleet playing from Marmarosa and a jump style tenor solo by Barnet, it offers fine solo work by trumpeter Roy Eldridge, who becomes uncontrolled only at the close. *Skyliner* is probably Barnet's biggest commercial hit after *Cherokee,* and is notable for fine section work, particularly by the reeds, and for its catchy melody.

The increasingly frenetic quality of much big band swing as the 'forties progressed was not entirely absent from Barnet's post-Bluebird output, but in general he maintained a musical balance that eschewed freneticism for its own sake. His mid 'forties Apollo recordings cannot be ranked with the best of his earlier output, but his switch to the Capitol label in 1949 produced more interesting results.

At the time of his Capitol association, Stan Kenton, then immensely popular, had temporarily disbanded, and Barnet was pressed into becoming the label's 'progressive jazz' exponent. As a role, it was neither entirely congenial to him nor successful in application. Some of his recordings at the time reveal an uneasy combination of his former swing style with a rather forced progressive manner. However, some excellent performances did materialise. Among these is a striking version of *Over the Rainbow,* very well

arranged by Tiny Kahn, *Cu-ba* on which the band and soloists Danny Bank, Claude Williamson and Doc Severinsen play with genuine fire, and Claude Williamson's excellent piano showcase *Claude Reigns.* Dave Matthews wrote *Portrait of Edward Kennedy Ellington,* an attractive if somewhat superficial musical tribute to its subject that exploits certain aspects of Ellington's style rather cleverly. Paul Villepigue contributed a moody *Lonely Street* that is not without interest. On the whole, though, particularly in view of his later recordings, it is doubtful whether Barnet was genuinely involved with the music he was recording at this period.

In retrospect, it seems apparent that Charlie Barnet's Bluebird output of 1939-42 represents the most consistently excellent jazz music produced by any white swing band of its period. Some writers consider that the Ellington influence was too important in the work of the Barnet band. The implication is that it was not sufficiently individual. I do not consider that the records substantiate this viewpoint, for Barnet had the rare ability to absorb Ellington's influence without resorting to superficial imitation. In any case, as a perspicacious jazz journalist once observed, if there has to be a major influence in big band jazz, what could be better than that of Duke Ellington?

Count Basie.

Count Basie led a great band from 1937 to 1940 and a good one during the rest of the 'forties. After reforming in 1952, he led several that were technically excellent. Unfortunately the music played by the Basie bands of the past decade and a half has been as predicatable as that of the George Shearing Quintet. It has sometimes seemed that the success of the 1958 LP 'The Atomic Mr. Basie', which is pleasant enough on its own level, has led Basie to become trapped in a formula of increasing sterility. This is a personal viewpoint, but I feel that the acclaim given to recent Basie bands mainly indicates the lack of competition. Even the current Duke Ellington band is but a pale shadow of what it once was, primarily through the paucity of great soloists who were among its great strengths in former years. However, it does still have Harry Carney, Paul Gonsalves and Ellington himself to recall the glories of past days whereas, too often now, Count Basie sounds the odd man out in his own band. It is no wonder that he once told Eddie Durham that if he could get his old band back and take it out on a single tour he would retire happily. However competent his current personnel may be, I would imagine that thoughts of retirement must cross Basie's mind from time to time as he leads them through the set routines night after night. He can well be forgiven some nostalgic reflections on what once was.

The man who deserves most of the credit for introducing Kansas City jazz to a nationwide public hailed, ironically enough, from Red Bank, New Jersey. As a youth, Bill Basie—his nickname of Count was given him in the mid 'thirties—first played drums, then switched to piano and worked with various bands around the New York area. He spent several years in the early 'twenties playing with touring shows; through leaving the Gonzelle White Show in Kansas City during 1927, he first came into wide contact with Midwestern jazz developments. After a spell of ill health he began to work in theatres around Kansas City, then deputised for the regular pianist with Walter Page's Blue Devils in the summer of 1928. Soon afterwards, he joined Page and remained with him until 1929, when he worked with obscure local groups before joining Bennie Moten late in the year. Basie stayed with Moten until early 1934, when he left to lead his own band in Little Rock, Arkansas. After the engagement was over, he returned to Moten and stayed for a short while after Bennie's death when Ira 'Buster' Moten was leader.

In his immediate post-Moten days Basie worked alone, then with a trio, and eventually as joint leader of a group with Buster Smith. With Basie as leader, the band worked in the Reno Club, Kansas City, and broadcast over a local radio station on which they were heard by the jazz enthusiast John Hammond who was staying in Chicago and had tuned in to the station by accident. He was immediately struck by the power of the nine-strong band and persuaded Benny Goodman to approach Willard Alexander of the MCA office about bookings for it. In due course, Alexander and Hammond arrived at the Reno Club and signed the band to a contract. Shortly afterwards, it left Kansas City for a short residency at the Grand Terrace, Chicago, where its inexperience in playing for shows was almost disastrous. In later years, Basie has expressed his gratitude to Fletcher Henderson for help which included the loan of some scores to use during the show. After the Grand Terrace date, the band moved to a hotel in Buffalo and then to its New York debut at the Roseland Ballroom.

The personnel of the band in New York included a number of its most famous stars, but such musicians as Freddie Green, Dicky Wells, Harry Edison, Benny Morton and Eddie Durham had not yet joined. Although a number of jazz followers were aware of its potential, the band's reception was generally less than enthusiastic. George T. Simon's review in the January 1937 Metronome commented: 'True, the band does swing. but that sax section is so invariably out of tune. And if you think that sax section is out of tune, catch the brass! And if you think the brass by itself is out of tune, catch the intonation of the band as a whole!'

Mr Simon has quoted this review in later years and has explained that the poor intonation of coloured bands at the time was often because the musicians could not afford top quality instruments and were rarely able to study for any length of time with leading teachers. Musicians have often told me that their first reactions to the Alphonso Trent band were of envy at the quality of the instruments that the musicians owned.

Throughout 1937, changes of personnel strengthened

the band, though public acclaim was still slow in coming. The real breakthrough came with engagements at the Savoy Ballroom and the Famous Door Club during 1938, which laid the foundation for Basie's lengthy career as a bandleader. He led a big band constantly from 1936 until April 1950, when he worked with a small group until he formed a big band again in 1952. Since then, he has always directed a big band, frequently touring overseas from the mid 'fifties. In addition, from the mid 'sixties, the Basie band sometimes went out on tour and recorded with such popular singers as Tony Bennett and Frank Sinatra. It is still immensely popular, and likely to remain so as long as Basie chooses to remain active.

The first Basie orchestra, particularly during 1937-40, was among the greatest of all big bands, rivalled only at the time by Duke Ellington and Jimmie Lunceford, whose styles were very different from Basie's. In his essay in the anthology 'Jazz' (1959), Hsio Wen Shih suggested that the style of the Basie band when it first reached New York probably owed more to such bands as Walter Page's Blue Devils than to the Bennie Moten band. I put this point to Eddie Durham, who disagreed, commenting that although some features of the Blue Devils may have rubbed off on Moten's band, they were not an organised group like Moten's, and the Moten band was the true founder of the Basie style. He also told a story that throws some interesting light on the source of many of Basie's best known numbers in the early years.

As chief arranger for the Bennie Moten band in its later days, he wrote a batch of new scores at Moten's request before leaving. Durham heard the Basie band when it arrived in New York and recognised many of its arrange-

Count Basie's famous sax section of the 1930s. Left to right: Herschel Evans, Earle Warren, Jack Washington and Lester Young.

ments as those he had written for Moten, though most of them had been retitled. In his own words, he 'jumped salty' on Basie; as part of the straightening out process, he joined the Basie band for a period. He says that, in common with many other musicians of his generation, he never received credit for much that he wrote, partly because he was unaware of the business formalities required to register the tunes. Basie may quite well have been unaware of the original titles of the numbers that he was using from the Moten repertoire, for there was a very casual attitude to such matters at the time. Durham mentions, for example, that *One o'Clock Jump* was originally titled *Blue Ball,* and that the tune was worked up by Buster Smith, Oran 'Hot Lips' Page and himself who sketched in the parts for saxes, trumpets and trombones respectively. At the time, there was no thought of recording the tune, and Durham says that the musicians treated it as something of a joke.

The Basie band brought to New York a concept of jazz that had been nurtured and developed in the Southwest, with a repertoire heavily based on blues and riff themes, performed with a tremendous swing. Many of its numbers were worked up into loose head arrangements that allowed the maximum of freedom to the soloists, who provided more than ample compensation for section and ensemble work that was sometimes less than perfect. Trumpeters Buck Clayton, Harry Edison and Ed Lewis, trombonists Benny Morton, Eddie Durham (who also played amplified guitar) and Dicky Wells, saxophonists Herschel Evans, Earle Warren, Jack Washington and Lester Young, and Basie himself were all fine soloists, and underlining everything was the marvellous rhythm section of Basie, guitarist Freddie Green, bassist Walter Page and drummer Jo Jones. In Jimmy Rushing and Helen Humes, the band also possessed excellent vocalists, and for a period Billie Holiday was added to the roster. At its peak, the

Basie band was unique in having virtually no weaknesses—after a while the ensemble and section defects of the initial group were almost eliminated. In any case, the strength of the music did not, at this time, depend on flawless technical execution.

A considerable factor in the success of the Basie band from 1937 to 1939 was the presence of two great tenor saxophone players. Lester Young, with his light, dry tone and searching harmonic sense, has long been recognised as one of the most brilliant and influential musicians in jazz, but Herschel Evans has perhaps not been given all the credit due to him. Oddly enough, it was Evans who made the biggest impression on critics initially, probably because his full, rich tone was closer to the tradition of Coleman Hawkins, then considered the peak of tenor playing. In a review of *Smarty* and *Listen My Children* that appeared on 7th December 1937 in the British publication Melody Maker, 'Rophone' wrote that 'for variety you have the two tenor men in solos : Hersal (sic) Evans in the first title and Lester (Motor-Horn) Young on the reverse.' In due course, Young's achievements were recognised and his influence on such tenor saxophonists as Stan Getz, Brew Moore, Al Cohn and Zoot Sims led to a new era in jazz. Evans died at the age of twenty-nine on 9th February 1939 and only in recent years has once more been recognised as a brilliant musician.

The rivalry between Evans and Young has become part of the folklore of jazz. It is not certain whether it extended to any deep personal antipathy, though occasionally it might have looked that way. Buck Clayton has said that most bands at the time had their cliques; Evans and Young mixed with different musicians and never went around together. Eddie Durham did not believe that at heart the two men really disliked each other, but added : 'They wouldn't sit beside each other. We had to place the tenors at each end of the section, because they couldn't bear to hear each other. Each complained that the other's tone was wrong. The funny thing is that after I left Basie and organised another band, the leader told me I was wrong to have the two tenors together, pointing out the way Basie had them!' Whatever they felt about each other, Evans and Young were perfect musical foils, and Basie was able to use their rivalry to good effect. After Evans's death, he carried on the tradition of two contrasting tenor soloists, but none of the many fine musicians he employed in this capacity was ever quite able to recapture the brilliance of the original duo.

One should not, however, overlook such talents of Buck Clayton, Harry Edison, Benny Morton and Dicky Wells, all of whom, along with a number of slightly lesser soloists, played their part in making the Basie band a unique aggregation. Earle Warren was not such an individual solo voice but was important because of his great ability as a section leader : his arrival certainly helped to eliminate some of the faults that George Simon enumerated.

Technically, the Basie band improved out of all recognition during the 'forties; one is certainly not conscious of any of the shortcomings reported by several writers when it first reached New York. For a while, the spontaneity of performance that distinguished the band's earliest recordings was maintained within a more disciplined orchestral framework. It is only in the second half of the decade that one becomes aware of the growing influence of the arrangers in shaping the band's music. Even more important as the earlier musicians left the band was that their replacements, though fine players in their own right, frequently came from a different jazz background, so that the music gradually lost something of its original character. However, this was inevitable, and it was not until the following decade that a band which had started by owing so much to the Southwestern tradition of loose head arrangements took the path that resulted in its ending up as little more than a swing machine.

Just before going to New York, Basie recorded in Chicago as part of a quintet with vocals by Jimmy Rushing on two numbers. The items were originally released as by Jones-Smith Inc. (the group included trumpeter Carl 'Tatti' Smith and drummer Jo Jones), presumably because they were for US Columbia and Basie was already under contract to Decca. His first recording date with the full band for Decca took place on 21st January 1937. *Swinging at the Daisy Chain,* from this date, has a very good solo by Basie, which shows his roots in the stride style; Buck Clayton (muted) and Herschel Evans are also heard to advantage. A second number, *Roseland Shuffle,* sub-titled *Count and Lester,* features these two musicians in a sort of musical dialogue. Basie's solo work on these performances is much as it was in his later Bennie Moten days, influenced at times by Earl Hines and at others by Fats Waller. Shortly afterwards, he started using a technique of playing brief assertive phrases with his right hand, with only occasional left hand interpolations, leaving the guitar and bass to provide the rhythmic foundation usually supplied by the pianist's left hand. From time to time, though, he reverted to his former approach. On these early recordings, the rhythm section is a great deal less crisp than it subsequently became—here Jo Jones occasionally sounds a little like Chick Webb; the ensemble passages, though strongly swinging, sound somewhat ragged.

Almost six months later, *One o'Clock Jump* was recorded with the band's personnel now strengthened by the arrival of trumpeter Ed Lewis, alto saxophonist Earle Warren and guitarist Freddie Green. The theme has the rhythm section at its most formidable, with Basie himself using his new, economical style. There are solos from the two tenor men, both playing superbly, from trombonist George Hunt, and from Clayton. The performance ends with the ensemble swinging powerfully on the famous riff phrase. From the same date, *John's Idea* has outstanding solo work from Evans, who for once outplays Young, a good Basie solo, and a closing ensemble that highlights the increasing technical assurance of the band. By the time of the next date in August 1937, Benny

A section of the Count Basie band in 1940. Left to right: Jo Jones, Walter Page, Buddy Tate, Basie, Freddie Green, Buck Clayton and Dicky Wells.

Morton had replaced Hunt, and another newcomer, Eddie Durham, provided the scores for *Good Morning Blues* and *Topsy*. *Good Morning* is one of the best known of all Jimmy Rushing's vocal features with the band. He sings extremely well, with Clayton providing a beautiful muted theme and Basie following him with a solo notable for its impressive timing. *Topsy*, written by Edgar Battle and Eddie Durham, is a medium tempo swinger with excellent solos by Clayton, Basie, Washington and Evans. Clayton provided particularly sensitive muted playing on many of the numbers featuring Jimmy Rushing, and *Don't You Miss Your Baby* is no exception. Rushing's vocal is backed by muted trumpets and saxes; after it, Jo Jones's break leads to a fervent ensemble close.

The quality of Basie's US Decca output is almost uniformly excellent; the titles mentioned here illustrate specific aspects of the band or its soloists. By early 1938, the Basie band had certainly reached a remarkable peak. *Sent For You Yesterday (And Here You Come Today)* has a very fine vocal by Rushing, one of the greatest of all big band singers, and Evans is in magnificent form. There are other good solos from Harry Edison and Basie, and Jo Jones takes some fine breaks during the brilliant ensemble riffing. *Swinging the Blues,* a title representative of this period, was arranged by Eddie Durham and

commenced with the saxes stating the theme over a buoyant, light rhythm that gives way to various section passages interspersed with solos from Morton, Young, Clayton, Evans and Edison. The next date produced a driving *Doggin' Around,* with solos from Evans, Clayton, Washington and Young, and the famous Herschel Evans ballad feature *Blue and Sentimental.* This has Evans displaying his broad, rich tone in a lyrical performance that finds him keeping quite close to the attractive melody, while *Doggin',* which he arranged, has one of his finest recorded solos. Young, although playing well, is eclipsed by Evans on *Doggin'*; on *Blue*, he takes a wistful clarinet solo very much in keeping with the nature of the material.

During his last year with Decca, Basie also recorded a number of really excellent piano solos. A band session of August 1938 is of interest in having Dicky Wells's first recorded solo on *London Bridge Is Falling Down.* It also produced the extrovert *Jumpin' at The Woodside* (The Woodside was a hotel) on which Young has a particularly fine solo. On this number, Evans is heard on clarinet, although he was only a moderate performer on the instrument. A date three months later produced the outstanding *Panassié Stomp,* dedicated to the French jazz critic Hugues Panassié, with excellent though generally short solos from Edison, Evans, Wells, Young and Warren, plus a superb closing ensemble chorus. Evans's eight bar solo on this was his last on commercial recordings, though he was present on one further session. The band's final Decca date resulted in the fine *Jive at Five,* with striking solos from Young, Edison, Washington and Wells, and a moody *Evil Blues,* with a splendid vocal by Jimmy Rushing and good solo passages by Ed Lewis. Leon 'Chu' Berry, Evans's replacement on the recording date, can be heard behind the vocal.

In March 1939, the Basie band began recording for US Columbia, and the second title from its initial date, *Rock-a-bye-Basie,* has an excellent solo by Evans's permanent replacement, Buddy Tate. Young left the band in December 1940. to be replaced briefly by Paul Bascomb and then by Don Byas, but during 1939-40, he recorded some of his greatest solos with the band, most notably being those heard on *Twelfth Street Rag, Miss Thing* (the first tenor solo), *Clap Hands Here Comes Charlie* and *Louisiana.* From a broadcast transcription that has been released in LP form comes the superb *Take it, Prez,* notable not only for Young's magnificent playing but the brilliant manner in which the ensemble builds towards the close. In different vein is the beautifully relaxed *I Left My Baby,* with its fine Rushing vocal, and the spirited *Gone With What Wind* and *Super Chief,* on both of which Buddy Tate solos admirably. Among many other fine performances from this period, it is worth noting *The World Is Mad,* with solos from Tate, trombonist Vic Dickenson, Young and Jo Jones, and the splendid *Rockin' the Blues* with its contributions from Edison, alto saxophonist Tab Smith and Dickenson.

From 1941, though the band was still a very fine one, its recordings become more uneven, partly because of the rather mediocre material used on some occasions. *Goin' to Chicago* is a classic Jimmy Rushing performance, with Buck Clayton also at his finest. Rushing again makes the major contribution to *Take Me Back, Baby,* on which he receives fine backing from Wells and Tab Smith. *Fiesta in Blue* is uncharacteristic of most of Basie's recordings of the period, being a Jimmy Mundy feature for Buck Clayton (who plays splendidly) rather in the style of Ellington's *Concerto for Cootie. I Struck a Match in the Dark,* which features a vocal by Earle Warren, may not be a good record, but was something of a hit for the band. It was a big production number at theatres, where the lights were turned off before Warren stepped to the microphone, sang the opening line, and then struck a match. On one occasion at the Apollo Theatre, the audience was amused at the sound of matches being desperately struck in the darkness—Jo Jones had apparently taken a dislike to the number and doused the matches in water before going on stage. The band's final recording session before the 1942-44 recording ban produced such ephemera as *For the Good of Your Country* and the curious *Ride On,* but also the excellent *Rusty Dusty Blues,* a feature for Rushing, and the driving *It's Sand, Man!* with good solos from Edison and Tate.

The Basie band returned to the studios in December 1944, and took part in a further six sessions for US Columbia before August 1946. By now, many of the old stalwarts had left, but the personnel still included Harry

Count Basie after his big band 'comeback' in the 1950s.

Edison, Dicky Wells, Earle Warren, Buddy Tate, Freddie Green and Jimmy Rushing. The newer men were generally outstanding soloists. In common with most bands of the period, Basie was now carrying eight brass and five saxes, an instrumentation which inevitably imparted a heavier sound to its performances. The December 1944 date resulted in two fine performances in *Jimmy's Blues,* entirely devoted to Rushing, and Basie's own feature *Red Bank Boogie.* Ten months later came the sparkling *High Tide* with solos from tenor saxophonist Illinois Jacquet, Wells, Edison and clarinettist Rudy Rutherford. Probably the single outstanding title from its final sessions was *The King,* with the band sounding in great form and soloists Emmett Berry (trumpet), J. J. Johnson (trombone) and Illinois Jacquet all playing well.

From 1947 to 1949, there was a switch of recording contract to RCA Victor, with disappointing results. There were some excellent recordings—*House Rent Boogie* (featuring Basie), *Seventh Avenue Express* (solos by Tate, Berry and Wells) and *Robbins' Nest* (solo by Paul Gonsalves) for example—but the band had begun to lose some of its individuality. From January 1950, Basie worked for two years with smaller units.

In the big band of 1952, Basie and Freddie Green survived from the line-up of the late 'thirties. The sound of the band was now very different, but after a rather shaky start it became very popular and has remained so through the years. For a decade the new Basie band had some good soloists, including Joe Newman, 'Snooky' Young, Henry Coker, Frank Wess and Frank Foster, though they were clearly not the equal to those from the 'thirties and 'forties. To this day, it includes a few musicians who have some individuality. However, it soon became clear that the band's style was becoming formalised, and that the dominant role had passed to the arrangers. It was, and still occasionally can be, an impressive group on the level of technical expertise and swing, but too frequently over the past years it has sounded mechanical. But financially, the Basie's bands since 1952 have probably been a great deal more successful than those of the late 'thirties and the 'forties.

I once asked a musician who had filled in with Basie for a few months in the 'sixties how he thought that the leader really viewed his present band. This musician, who developed in the era of the first Basie band, told me that when he arrived for the first night's work he was taken aside by Basie who said: 'You know, don't you, that if the lights go out on this band, the music will stop!'

Bunny Berigan was undoubtedly one of the greatest trumpeters of the swing era, and, along with Bix Beiderbecke, one of the outstanding white trumpeters in jazz's history. The parallels between the lives of the two men have been mentioned often enough to need no further comment here: both displayed a brilliance that was swiftly recognised by their fellow musicians, both declined in the latter stages of their careers, and both died at an early age as a result of alcoholism.

It is astonishing to read the comments of arranger John Scott Trotter to George Simon about Hal Kemp's initial rejection of Berigan—this would have been around 1929—on the grounds that his tone was so thin and ugly. He must have made remarkable changes in a short time, probably inspired by hearing Louis Armstrong, for by the mid 'thirties, when he concentrated mainly on studio work in New York City his tone was one of the fullest in jazz. On occasions, he left the security of the studios to work with bands. The period from June to September 1935, when he was a member of Benny Goodman's band and recorded a number of brilliant solos with it, first brought him to the notice of a wide public. Early in 1937, he recorded on a number of sessions with Tommy Dorsey. His most famous solo from this period was probably on *Marie*. From February 1936 to February 1937, he also recorded with pick-up groups under his own name; one of these dates produced the initial version of *I Can't Get Started*.

Bunny Berigan appearing at a Saturday Night Swing Club broadcast over Station WABC, New York.

Berigan made his debut with his own big band at the Pennsylvania Room in New York City during the spring of 1937, and maintained it with various personnel changes for three years until he had to file bankruptcy papers. He worked with Tommy Dorsey from March 1940, until the following August, when he left to front a small group, but soon formed another big band, with which he worked continuously until he fell ill with pneumonia in April 1942. After his discharge from hospital on 8th May, Berigan resumed a one night schedule of touring with his band. On 30th May, he suffered a severe haemorrhage and on 2nd June, he died in a New York hospital at the of thirty-three.

Berigan recorded with his later big bands in the autumn of 1941 and in early 1942, but his own playing by this time had deteriorated and his supporting group was mediocre. From April 1937 until November 1939, Berigan had taken part in many sessions for RCA Victor. It is amongst this output that one finds his best work, though as a whole it is extremely uneven. Transcription material has become available from this period, but differs little from his commercial releases.

Holding a big band together and maintaining high musical standards is an arduous job; it is noticeable that most of the really successful leaders of the swing era were men with an element of iron in their souls. Tommy Dorsey, Benny Goodman and Jimmie Lunceford, to name but three, were known as strict disciplinarians, something which Berigan palpably was not. A kind, considerate man, much beloved by his musicians, Berigan was to the fore in balling it up. His prodigious drinking struck awe into sidemen who in most circles would hardly be considered abstemious. In an era when heavy drinking was considered a normal part of the jazz life, Berigan's band gained a reputation for spectacular living, a fact which caused some promoters to hesitate in booking them. Drummer Johnny Blowers worked with Berigan for several months in 1938, replacing Dave Tough who had left to join Benny Goodman. Recalling these days, he told me:

'It was a very undisciplined band. It was a band that played hard musically and otherwise. We never missed

dates, we were late on dates, but we never missed them. If we started half an hour late, we played half an hour over. Everyone in that band liked to play and we played under some pretty difficult conditions once in a while. I guess probably people wondered sometimes how did they ever put this band together, and even more how did they keep it together.'

One example of 'pretty difficult conditions' came when the band was due to play a tea dance and evening dance at a military academy in Virginia, but en route became parted from its instruments when the truck driven by their band boy, 'Little Gate' (hence *Little Gate's Special*), slithered into a ditch. For the tea dance, a variety of instruments were exhumed from the academy band stock. Berigan fronted the band on a cornet with a fibre mouthpiece, Hank Wayland played tuba, and Johnny Blowers made do with a field drum and huge bass drum, the latter 'emitting a noise like a cannon every time I struck it'. Fortunately, the errant 'Little Gate' arrived with the regular instruments in time for the evening dance.

Given the life style of Berigan and his musicians, one would hardly expect the band's music to be technically flawless or notably disciplined. This is not to say that its recorded performances are often technically poor, or that ensemble work was unusually ragged, but there is a lack of attention at times to smoothing out the rough edges. Berigan himself stands head and shoulders above the other soloists, though tenor saxophonist George Auld, clarinettist Joe Dixon (and his replacement Gus Bivona), alto saxophonist Murray Williams, trombonist Ray Conniff, and pianists Joe Bushkin and Joe Lippman were all extremely capable. Lippman, and later Conniff, were good arrangers and provided the bulk of the scores the band used. One thing that the band always possessed was a good rhythm section: at different times in its peak

Above: *a neon sign for the Berigan band at the Paradise Restaurant.* Below: *the Bunny Berigan band of 1938, with Johnny Blowers on drums.* Right: *Bunny Berigan solos in front of his 1938 band.*

years, it included drummers George Wettling, Dave Tough, Johnny Blowers and Buddy Rich. Everything considered, though, it is Berigan's own solo work that provides the chief interest on most of the band's recordings.

Berigan's first three RCA Victor sessions contain a surfeit of rather ordinary popular tunes of the day, complete with indifferent vocals. However, his fourth date during June 1937 produced good instrumental versions of *Frankie and Johnnie* and *Mahogany Hall Stomp*, although this is better known in a classic performance by Louis Armstrong. Berigan's two solos, the first muted, the second open, are well played. There is also a pleasant relaxed trombone solo from Sonny Lee and a creditable tenor solo from George Auld, then only eighteen years old. From the next session came the most famous of all Berigan's recordings—*I Can't Get Started*. He had first recorded this number in April 1936, and I am completely at a loss to understand the few jazz writers who claim that the initial version is the better of the two. Over the years Berigan's memory has become closely linked with *I Can't Get Started*—when asked to record the number, Louis Armstrong was reluctant to do so, protesting that it was 'Bunny's tune'—and if there had been pop charts in 1937, his version would probably have made the number one spot. The RCA Victor version was initially released as one side of a twelve inch record, and the band play a purely subsidiary role to their leader. Berigan's introduction and beautiful theme display his magnificent tone to advantage. Although he is hardly an outstanding singer, his vocal remains curiously attractive to this day. The highpoint is reached in his closing solo where his use of the extreme upper and lower ranges of his instrument is quite superb. Even in the high register, Berigan's tone is broad and his execution assured. By any standards, *I Can't Get Started* is a remarkable *tour-de-force*.

Late in 1937, the Berigan band recorded a good instrumental session, including *Russian Lullaby*, with pleasant solos from Auld and Dixon and a powerhouse effort from the leader. *Can't Help Loving Dat Man*, taken at an unexpectedly fast tempo, has an opening solo from Berigan on which he plays a paraphrase of the melody, and Auld, Lee and Dixon have good passages. The first recording date on which Johnny Blowers played with Berigan produced four somewhat uninspired commercial performances and a version of *Azure*, in an arrangement by Joe Lippman, which had some finely controlled low register work by Berigan over the reeds. The next date produced an unusual version of *The Wearing of the Green*—a somewhat unlikely theme to be featured by a swing band—with the theme introduced by clarinets, including a bass clarinet, before taking a more conventional course. Berigan himself has a fine solo on this number. In more conventional vein are *High Society*, with good solos from Bushkin, Berigan and Conniff, and a sympathetic account of Jelly Roll Morton's *Jelly Roll Blues*, which has a beautiful Berigan solo performed with immense power.

Late in 1938, a nine-strong section of the band went into the recording studios and made versions of Bix Beiderbecke's four piano pieces *In a Mist, Flashes, Candlelights* and *In the Dark,* and his *Davenport Blues*. Beiderbecke's introspective and impressionist piano compositions are not all that easy to transcribe into orchestral arrangements, but Joe Lippman's scores are intelligently conceived and he makes use of a number of individual voicings. The performances are very much governed by the arrangements, with solos generally of short duration and forming an integral part of the whole. *Candlelights* and *In the Dark* are probably the most successful titles, as they capture the emotional climate of the numbers well. Berigan subordinates something of his own musical personality during these performances, while remaining tonally quite distinctive; he manages to convey an impression of the unique lyricism that suffused Beiderbecke's own playing without ever attempting to directly copy him. The wistfulness of Berigan's playing during *Candlelights,* for example, is not recreated on any other of his recordings.

After the Beiderbecke set, Berigan made two further sessions for RCA Victor, in each case with his full band. *There'll Be Some Changes Made* finds him soloing with the power and broad tone that were hallmarks of his style. The other solos were by Conniff, Don Lodice (tenor) and Gus Bivona. The riff *Little Gate's Special* has Berigan in extrovert vein; it has a driving alto solo that may be the work of Bivona, and there are other contributions by Conniff, Don Lodice and an unidentified baritone saxophonist. Berigan's final RCA Victor date was made with a band that included only one musician other than himself from the session eight months before. *Peg o' My Heart* has an excellent and forceful solo by Berigan, but the outstanding performance from the date was of Juan Tizol's number *Night Song*. This is a pleasant theme and

Berigan plays superbly, using a cup mute; his instrumental command and brilliance in the upper register at this time seems quite unimpaired.

Soon after his final RCA Victor date, Berigan left the big band field for a period. By all accounts, Berigan's final year as a big band leader was painful to his admirers, for with his health fast waning, his playing inevitably suffered and the groups he led were generally mediocre. At the end, he was forced to preface his attempts to answer requests for *I Can't Get Started* with an apology for his inability to recreate his original solo.

Berigan's RCA Victor recordings contain a proportion that still sound good almost four decades after they were made. If his band was not a great one, and despite its enthusiasm and the presence of some creditable soloists it clearly was not, it generally maintained musical standards that were by no means negligible. Even on its more mundane records, there are generally such saving factors as spirited ensemble passages or reasonable solos, and above all, there are the contributions of the leader. Without doubt Berigan, with his adventurousness as a soloist, remarkable instrumental command, and brilliance of tone and execution, was a giant of his era. The evidence can be heard in almost every solo he recorded during his peak years. For that alone, one is grateful that his band entered the studios with such frequency from 1937 to 1939.

Cab Calloway had led a band for over five years when the swing era got under way, but his outstanding line-up was that of 1939-41. As for other bands which came to prominence in the decade stretching roughly from 1936 to 1946, it seems logical to cover his earlier days in the present chapter.

Calloway's band was almost unique in the fact that it primarily played a subsidiary role to its leader's vocalising. Other bands may have heavily featured their singers—Harlan Lattimore with Don Redman, Pha Terrell with Andy Kirk and Orlando Roberson with Claude Hopkins come immediately to mind—but during the 'thirties it was rare for a band to be built around one. This obviously did not please some of Calloway's personnel, though few felt quite as strongly as one of the stars of his 1941 band who told me that 'whenever we got going, and this was a band that could really swing, there he was up to all that hollerin' and yellin'!'

Transcription material that has become available during the past year or two indicates that during broadcasts and personal appearances, Calloway gave the band its head much more than in the recording studio, where it may be that recording directors had a strong say. In any case, the band would simply not have existed without Calloway. From discussions with some of his musicians, it emerges that he was very much personally concerned with the hiring of personnel and was perspicacious in his selection. If he had wished, it would have been easy to select a line-up of capable but rather anonymous musicians to provide a backdrop for his singing. It is a tribute to him

A typically flamboyant shot of Cab Calloway in the early 1930s, with Benny Payne (piano), Doc Cheatham (trumpet) and Eddie Barefield (alto saxophone). At the back are DePriest Wheeler, Leroy Maxey and Morris White.

that he never did so. How different Louis Armstrong's bands might have been if he had been similarly motivated.

A deterrent to many who recognise the excellence of Calloway's bands is the leader's singing. While he did not originate the scat style, there can be no doubt that Calloway used it more successfully (at least commercially) than any other artist; he was also a flamboyant showman. His fame with the public was largely due to such recordings as *Minnie the Moocher, Kickin' the Gong Around* and *Eadie was a Lady*—replete with references to drugs which were missed by most of the people who purchased the records. On few such performances did the band get much opportunity to shine. I should confess at this point that I have always had a weakness for the more bizarre vocalists who have graced the jazz scene. At the risk of being considered a philistine by jazz purists, I must admit to a liking for Calloway as a singer. He clearly owes a great deal to the vaudeville tradition that shaped much early jazz, but he possesses a voice of remarkable range, has excellent diction, and phrases well. Though they might object to having limited solo opportunities, his musicians sometimes had his showmanship to thank for pulling them through hard 'band battles'. Bassist Gene Ramey has told me of one engagement when he was playing with the Jay McShann band and it became involved in a battle of music with Calloway's group. McShann's band did very well in the opening exchanges and retired for the first interval convinced the battle was well won, but when Calloway came on for the second set, he made a remarkably spectacular entry, leaping over chairs, turning somersaults, and indulging in all manner of non-musical showmanship, all the while singing ('hollering', as Ramey called it) in his most eccentric manner. This so won over the audience that 'we didn't dare go on again.'

Cab Calloway had worked as a relief drummer, master of ceremonies and singer/entertainer for a few years before appearing with The Missourians in New York in 1928. After this engagement, he returned to Chicago and appeared with Marion Hardy's Alabamians at the Merry Gardens. In October 1929, he fronted this unit for his debut at New York's Savoy Ballroom. Soon afterwards, he began to regularly work with The Missourians, and in due course the billing changed to Cab Calloway and his Orchestra. A year at the Cotton Club from February 1931 to January 1932 established Calloway as a national figure, and he led a big band regularly until April 1948.

Calloway's records with The Missourians' personnel contain a high proportion in which the band is relegated to a purely supporting role, but there are very few without at least brief solo passages that are of interest and a small number are worthy of consideration purely in big band terms. From the first session to be recorded under Calloway's name, dating from July 1930, comes an engaging version of *St Louis Blues,* with excellent plunger solos from trumpeter R. Q. Dickerson and trombonist De Priest Wheeler before Calloway's high-pitched vocal. The closing ensemble has the driving trumpet lead which was so characteristic of The Missourians on their own recordings. *Some of These Days,* made five months later, contains several good solos, notably by trumpeters Lamar Wright (just after the vocal) and Wendell Culley (the third trumpet solo), and clarinettist William Thornton Blue, while *St James Infirmary* from the same date has excellent work by Culley who plays all the trumpet solos except for the coda which is by Wright. *Basin Street Blues,* from July 1931, has a very pleasant open trumpet solo in the Armstrong manner by Reuben Reeves, who had replaced Culley, and Calloway's vocal is good, as it is on *Black Rhythm,* which has a splendidly strong opening solo by Reeves.

On all the titles mentioned in the last paragraph, the excellence of the band is clear, a point underlined by a spirited version of *Bugle Call Rag* recorded in September 1931. On this number Walter 'Foots' Thomas, a long time arranger/saxophonist with Calloway, has a reasonable tenor solo, and there are well conceived trumpet solos by Edwin Swayzee (with plunger) and Reeves, as well as good clarinet by Arville Harris over the closing ensemble. This performance highlights the drive of the band and its Midwestern heritage. From November 1932, *I've Got the World on a String* and *I've Gotta Right to Sing the Blues* are both notable for the lyrical trumpet solos of 'Doc'

Cheatham, an individual and curiously underrated musician, who had just replaced Reeves. By now, Harry White had been a member of the band as second trombonist for some while, and Benny Payne (piano) and Al Morgan (string bass) had strengthened the rhythm section. In 1933, the addition of Eddie Barefield to the saxophone section gave the band an additional soloist of stature. From September 1933 to January 1934, the band recorded for RCA Victor; most of the numbers were tailored to Calloway's vocal acrobatics. A version of *Minnie the Moocher* remained unreleased for well over a quarter of a century, in all probability because of a brief passage when Calloway goes into the Jewish cantor routine which he sometimes used on stage. The sensitivity of the recording company to this contrasts markedly with their acceptance of performances containing the most grotesque lyrics referring to black people.

Calloway's RCA Victor output is not designed to highlight the band, but *Long about Midnight* is an exception in displaying the drive and expertise of the ensemble, also offering excellent solos by Swayzee and White. On its penultimate RCA Victor session, the band recorded a straight instrumental, *Moonglow.* Eddie Barefield has told me that this tune was used as a signing off theme at the Cotton Club, but only existed in the book in the form of a single scored chorus. On the record date, the band found itself short of a number and it was decided to use *Moonglow;* Barefield was allocated a full chorus, with Andy Brown (bass clarinet) and Arville Harris (clarinet) getting shorter spots. Barefield took full advantage of this rare opportunity, playing a fine flowing chorus with overtones recalling Benny Carter—it is sad that at the time he had so few chances to be heard at this length. Soon afterwards the band left for a European tour, and after their return were working in Texas when Barefield heard a record of *Moonglow* being played in a bar. Struck by the alto chorus, he went in to inquire about the identity of the soloist—himself. The record became popular and Barefield had hastily to learn his chorus off it. Almost forty years later, I asked him to record the number again at a session which I was organising, and he arrived at the studio with a copy of the original 78!

It is easy to romanticise the big band days, forgetting the sickening racial problems which musicians in the big coloured bands endured. Eddie Barefield has told me of many situations which he faced when a member of the Calloway band. At this time, the coloured bands would play for members of their own race in the afternoon, and for whites in the evening. When the Calloway band was in Memphis, the usual pattern was followed, but at the dance for whites, the musicians were constantly heckled and abused by two drunken members of the audience. Finally one of the men picked up a music stand and Barefield hit him. The man slid by the music stool where Benny Payne struck at him with his knife, but missed. A fight followed, with the audience throwing bottles at the band, while outside a crowd gathered shouting 'Kill the niggers.' The band personnel had to call for the aid of some coloured mobsters from the Beale Street area who arrived with trucks to transport them and their instruments to the station. Cab Calloway had not been party to the fight and was not even present when it started, but next day a Memphis newspaper carried a headline stating that Calloway had been run out of town because he hugged a white woman. On another occasion, in St Louis, Barefield and guitarist Morris White arrived at the local police headquarters just in time to prevent their bandboy being thrown out of a third storey window after a false accusation of stealing a pair of cuff links.

The band took part in two recording dates during 1935, three in 1936, and then from March 1937 was contracted to Irving Mills. It recorded six sessions in 1937 and four in 1938; most of the performances heavily featured Calloway's own vocals. During these years, the band had been strengthened by the arrival of such musicians as trombonists Claude Jones and Keg Johnson, saxophonists Garvin Bushell and Ben Webster, bassist Milt Hinton and guitarist Danny Barker, but its greatest capture was Leon 'Chu' Berry, who replaced Webster in the summer of 1937. That the band was a fine one is obvious from such recordings as *Bugle Blues,* with good solos by Berry, trumpeter Irving Randolph and Bushell, and *Jive,* on which Berry plays superbly. In general, however, the band was still playing a subservient role to Calloway's vocals; only occasionally were the soloists allocated much space. Things started to change in 1939 with the arrival of William 'Cozy' Cole to complete one of the outstanding rhythm sections of the swing era; soon afterwards came trumpeter Dizzy Gillespie and alto saxophonist/clarinettist

Jerry Blake. On his first recording session with the band, Cole was featured in *Ratamacue,* a sort of 'concerto', in which he played brilliantly against a varied background from the ensemble. In July 1939, Cole was again heavily featured on the recording of *Crescendo in Drums,* which also has a fine solo from Berry, and four months later it was Milt Hinton's turn to be accorded the major solo space on *Pluckin' the Bass,* which features an excellent solo from Berry and a trumpet passage which may be by Gillespie.

By early 1940, the Calloway band could justly be considered one of the finest of its day; it remained so for the next two years. Its personnel for most of this period was Mario Bauza, Dizzy Gillespie, Lamar Wright (trumpet), Tyree Glenn (trombone, vibraphone), Keg Johnson, Quentin Jackson (trombone), Jerry Blake (alto saxophone, clarinet), Hilton Jefferson, Andy Brown (alto saxophone), Leon 'Chu' Berry, Walter 'Foots' Thomas (tenor saxophone), Benny Payne (piano), Danny Barker (guitar), Milton Hinton (string bass) and William 'Cozy' Cole (drums), with Buster Harding and Buck Ram providing most of the arrangements. Early in 1941 another fine soloist joined the band when Jonah Jones replaced Bauza.

The period 1940-41 saw more instrumentals being recorded by the Calloway band than at any other time, though the bulk of the releases still had the leader's vocals as their main commercial attraction. Cole, a very musical drummer, was given a further feature with *Paradiddle,* recorded in March 1940, and in the following June, 'Chu' Berry made his famous *Ghost of a Chance.* Excellently though Berry plays on this number, I have never felt that it is one of his finer solos: his enthusiastic, bustling style is best heard at a medium to medium-fast tempo. *Bye*

Bye Blues, from the same session, demonstrates the beautiful ensemble playing of the band—during the theme the reeds unexpectedly attain a sound like Glenn Miller—and there are first rate solos from Berry, Gillespie and Glenn (on vibraphone). *Cupid's Nightmare,* recorded in late August, is a fine performance but a better version exists on a broadcast transcription. From the same date comes a superb performance of Benny Carter's *Lonesome Nights,* arranged by Carter himself. Berry plays the theme over muted brass, and is heavily featured throughout in one of his greatest solos at slow tempo. The only other soloist is Gillespie, who takes the final release with mute. The saxes here are marvellously integrated and owe much to the fine lead work of Hilton Jefferson, who is given a solo feature on *Willow Weep for Me,* where he plays in a flowing elegiac style against a scored background by Andy Gibson that makes good use of textural variety. Jefferson was not perhaps an outstanding jazz improviser, but he was very good at this type of melodic variation, and was one of the finest saxophone section leaders.

Milt Hinton, one of the best all-round bassists in jazz, is given another feature—*Ebony Silhouette*—and acquits himself brilliantly on this attractive theme, which has extremely effective support from the ensemble. The next session, of March 1941, celebrated the arrival of Jonah Jones with *Jonah Joins the Cab,* on which Jones is heard in a fine solo which displays his big tone and relaxed swing to perfection. This is a very different Jonah Jones to the man who in later years became popular for his muted cocktail-jazz playing, which was no doubt the product of economic necessity. The ensemble swings powerfully behind him, propelled by Cole's excellent drumming.

Billy Strayhorn's *Take the 'A' Train*—this is a subway train that runs through Harlem—is associated, naturally enough, with Duke Ellington but the Calloway band's version is outstanding in its own right. Jones takes an excellent muted solo, Berry is heard in a driving chorus of phenomenal swing, and the ensemble at the close is brilliant. The arrangement is extremely good, with saxes and trombones at one point being scored together. In the autumn of 1941 Gillespie left, to be replaced by Lester 'Shad' Collins whose first recorded solo with the band occurs on *Tappin' Off,* written and arranged by Buster Harding. This is another excellent performance, with Collins playing powerfully, though he has to take second place to Berry whose surging solo, displaying an enormous tone, carries all before it. The closing ensemble passage demonstrates yet again that Calloway's band at this period was rivalled only by Basie's, Ellington's and Lunce-

Left: *the Cab Calloway band, 1941. Left to right: Milt Hinton, Cozy Cole, Chu Berry, Andy Brown, Danny Barker, Cab Calloway, Jonah Jones, Russell Smith, Keg Johnson, Jerry Blake, Dizzy Gillespie, Quentin Jackson and Walter 'Foots' Thomas.*

Below: *the Cab Calloway band in the early 1940s. The trumpeters are Dizzy Gillespie, Lamar Wright and Jonah Jones. Middle row: Danny Barker, Keg Johnson, Tyree Glen and Quentin Jackson. Front row: Jerry Blake, Milton Jefferson, Andrew Brown and Walter 'Foots' Thomas. Chu Berry is hidden behind Calloway, and the rest of the rhythm section are out of camera range.*

ford's. From the same session, *A Smooth One,* a number made famous by Benny Goodman, receives a spirited performance. Jerry Blake takes a typically hoarse clarinet solo and Jonah Jones plays with power and an impressive broad tone.

A broadcast transcription of January 1940 has become available in LP form, and it shows the balance of vocals and instrumentals to be more even than on commercial recordings. There are four vocal numbers and three considerably longer instrumentals. Both *Limehouse Blues* and *King Porter Stomp* are driving performances with solos of quality from Jerry Blake, Tyree Glenn, Dizzy Gillespie and, above all, 'Chu' Berry, but the really interesting title is *Cupid's Nightmare.* This was a Don Redman number which had been commercially recorded, but is considerably extended in the broadcast version. The theme is recognisably the work of the composer of *Chant of the Weed,* and the arrangement as might be expected eschews the now conventional call-and-response method in favour of textural variation. The number and score are quite complex, and the band performs magnificently; solos are by Gillespie, Blake, Glenn and Berry, all of whom play very well. That the Calloway band was prepared to feature such challenging material in the course of an afternoon broadcast does it considerable credit.

The Calloway band from late 1939 to 1942 had all the requisites of a really outstanding unit. It possessed in Benny Payne, Danny Baker, Milt Hinton and 'Cozy' Cole a fine rhythm section, it used good arrangements by Buster Harding, Andy Gibson and others, it included a number of excellent soloists and in 'Chu' Berry a great one, and it worked together long enough to establish an individual identity.

The recording ban of 1942-44 prevented the band being heard, and when it did record again, the material used was mundane in the extreme. Calloway started working with a small group after 1948, and in the quarter of a century since then has followed a varied career, including the role of Sportin' Life in George Gershwin's opera 'Porgy and Bess'. He has, though, continued to lead big bands for specific engagements over the years, invariably employing Eddie Barefield as his musical director. One such occasion was at the July 1973 Newport Festival in New York, when Calloway fronted a band as part of a 'Cotton Club' night. It was a superb band, along with the specially assembled Benny Carter band of the previous year's Newport Festival quite the best that I have heard in years, but it was sadly under-employed in a concert encumbered by soul singers and artists who did not really belong on the bill. Many of the old hands were present— Dizzy Gillespie, Tyree Glenn, Quentin Jackson, Eddie Barefield, Danny Barker, Milt Hinton and 'Cozy' Cole— and I was delighted to find that Cab Calloway's voice and showmanship had not suffered with the passing of the years. To the public at large, Calloway is recalled as a flamboyant entertainer and vocalist, known for many years as 'His Highness of Hi-De-Ho', but he invariably

backed himself with good bands, and that of 1939-42 lays claim to being one of the finest of all. As one of his musicians once commented to me, 'He used to annoy me with all that yelling and hollering when I was hoping to take a solo, but I give the man one thing, he knew how to swing himself and, more important, he always had a swinging band.'

Few musicians can be better equipped than Benny Carter to lead a big band. Recognised both as one of the greatest arrangers and alto saxophone stylists in jazz, Carter is also an excellent trumpeter and clarinettist, and can play the trombone, tenor saxophone and piano proficiently. He is in addition a fine composer, noted builder of bands, and occasional—though not very good—vocalist. But during the 'thirties it was said of any musician who was in one of Carter's bands that he was ready to play with anyone, and the successful big time leaders raided his groups with a regularity that Carter must have found depressing.

With his qualifications, it might seem inevitable that Carter would eventually have achieved public recognition, but though he led several outstanding big bands over the years, he never really made the big time. The most probable reason, as with Teddy Wilson, is that Carter is essentially a quiet, reserved personality, lacking the flamboyance or showmanship of many of the commercially successful leaders. In general, too, his music reflected his own make-up. It may well be that in an era when the big bands were part of the showbiz world, audiences expected a degree of theatricality in the presentation that Carter failed to provide.

Carter was initially inspired by the late Bubber Miley, and joined June Clark's band when he was only seventeen, in 1924. In the next four years, before forming his first band for an engagement at New York's Arcadia Ballroom, he worked for numerous leaders, the most famous of whom were Earl Hines, Charlie Johnson and Fletcher Henderson. In the early 'thirties, he played with Henderson again, spent a few months with Chick Webb, and became musical director of McKinney's Cotton Pickers in succession to Don Redman. From autumn 1932 until autumn 1934 he led his own bands, moving between residencies in New York and touring. After this, he was a sideman with several bands and a prolific free-lance arranger. He went to Paris to play with the Willie Lewis band in the summer of 1935. From March 1936, he became a staff arranger for Henry Hall and the BBC Dance Orchestra in London. In England he appeared in one concert sponsored by the magazine Melody Maker. After a year, he went to play on the Continent, returning to the United States in May 1938.

The musical scene had changed greatly by the time Carter arrived back in New York, and the swing era was firmly established. He organised a big band that made its debut at the Savoy Ballroom, and continued leading a big band until autumn 1941, when he switched to fronting a sextet. In 1943, Carter moved to the West Coast and once more reverted to leading a big band, which appeared at the Apollo Theatre in New York early in the following year. 1945 saw him settle permanently in Los Angeles.

Since the late 'forties, Carter has worked primarily as a composer-arranger for Hollywood film companies. He has also written the music for a number of American television series. From time to time, he did return to jazz, fronting bands of various sizes around Hollywood, recording, and doing occasional overseas tours for Norman Granz's 'Jazz At The Philharmonic' or as a solo artist. For many years, he has concentrated on the alto saxophone, so it was something of a surprise when, in the course of a solo appearance in Copenhagen during 1972, he started to take solos on trumpet once again. Despite his pre-eminence on alto saxophone, Carter himself has mentioned on a number of occasions that his favourite instrument is the trumpet. In June 1972, Carter made his first appearance in New York for twenty-six years to front a specially assembled group that played at the Newport Jazz Festival.

Carter first recorded as a leader of a big band for the Crown label in the summer of 1932, but only one title has ever been issued from this date. Just under four months later, he took part in another session, for RCA Victor, but none of the titles made on this occasion were released. In March 1933, his band recorded four numbers specially for English Columbia, and this time everything became available. This was not a particularly successful date, though individual solos are good enough. The best performance is of Patrick 'Spike' Hughes's *Six Bells Stampede,* on which the sax writing has the characteristic Carter flair and there are pleasant solos by trombonist George Washington and tenor saxophonist Leon 'Chu' Berry. A session seven months later, with numerous personnel changes, was a great deal better and produced excellent performances of two splendid Carter themes in *Lonesome Nights* and *Symphony in Riffs.* The former (which became a jazz standard and was recorded by Benny

The Benny Carter band at the Strand Theatre in 1941; Max Roach is on drums.

Goodman and Cab Calloway among others) has some beautifully rich scoring for the Carter-led sax section which acquits itself magnificently; pianist Teddy Wilson fills in well during the opening and closing theme statements. *Symphony in Riffs* is less elegiac in manner; it has good solos by trumpeter Bill Dillard, tenor saxophonist Johnny Russell, trombonist J. C. Higginbotham and Teddy Wilson, but once again the listener's attention is caught by the brilliance of the saxophone passages. Less than two months later, Carter again recorded, with, apart from himself, only trombonist Keg Johnson and pianist Teddy Wilson remaining from the previous personnel. *Dream Lullaby,* an attractive melody, is given a gentle performance, the solos being by Carter (on clarinet) and Ben Webster. The outstanding item from the date is the fine *Everybody Shuffle,* on which the band achieves a good swing and Carter (alto), Irving Randolph (trumpet), Ben Webster (tenor) and Benny Morton (trombone) shine during their solos.

Carter did not record again as leader of an American big band for four and a half years, but these performances reveal all the essentials of his musical approach. Many reflect the unruffled elegance of Carter's own playing; there is a discipline about them that eschews any hint of freneticism. There is, however, a notable difference in Carter's handling between brass and saxes. He is a total master of scoring for saxes, achieving a flowing quality and richness of sound that is immediately distinctive. By contrast, his use of the brass, particularly trumpets, was not so sure, and his writing for them frequently employs a staccato phrasing that lessens their impact both tonally and rhythmically. The contrast with his method for the saxes is so striking that one suspects that it is deliberate, probably with the intention of achieving variety, but it does not really succeed. In later years, Carter made fuller use of brass, though his trademark remained the majestic saxophone writing with which most collectors associate him.

After Carter's return to the United States, his regular big band recorded for the first time in June 1939, and three more sessions were made for the Vocalion label

with Carter fronting a relatively stable personnel. From the first date came a pleasant version of his theme song, *Melancholy Lullaby*, with Carter playing variations on the melody against a quiet ensemble background and pianist Eddie Heywood and trombonist Tyree Glenn taking neat solos. *Savoy Stampede* has the band swinging strongly. The sax section release in the opening theme chorus is typical of Carter, and there is a very fine alto solo by the leader and good ones by Ernie Powell (tenor), Joe Thomas (trumpet) and Glenn (vibes). This is the type of swing instrumental number that was then in vogue, but it is noticeable that Carter's disciplined approach ensures that it receives a performance in which musicianship is paramount and the type of showmanship favoured by many of his contemporaries is absent.

More Than You Know, from a session of November 1939, has a very ordinary vocal by Foy Felton, but otherwise features Carter throughout on trumpet. It is clear that Louis Armstrong was Carter's great influence on this instrument. Like all his recorded trumpet solos, that on *More Than You Know* is melodic, cleanly executed, and displays Carter's attractive, full tone. What is lacking is the complete individuality of his alto playing. A date of almost three months later produced two of Carter's finest big band performances. *Slow Freight* highlights Carter's trumpet work, both muted and open; it is a very relaxed effort with Ulysses Livingston's guitar used well in ensemble passages. *Sleep* is a superb arrangement making fine use of an excellent trumpet section. There are solos from Coleman Hawkins, who was added for the date, Eddie Heywood, Joe Thomas, drummer Keg Purnell, and Carter himself. On this occasion, he plays alto, shaping a solo that has an almost architectural sense of form, while Joe Thomas plays really well with none of the technical uncertainty that flaws some of his later work. After this date Carter switched to the US Decca label for a couple of sessions, the second of which was extremely disappointing. From the first date comes an impressive *Okay for Baby*, with good section playing and first rate solos from Carter (alto) and trumpeter Bill Coleman, and the excellent *Night Hop* which integrates solos from 'Shad' Collins (trumpet), Sonny White (piano), Stafford Simon (tenor) and Carter (alto) neatly within the overall score.

From the autumn of 1940, Carter was contracted for a year to RCA Victor, taking part in four sessions that produced sixteen titles in all. His old problem of constantly changing personnels plagued him during this period, but did not noticeably lower the quality of his output. What is interesting, though, is that generally Carter features himself more extensively on the RCA Victor recordings than on his Vocalion output. *Cocktails for Two* contains some delightful sax passages and Carter takes a quite stunning melodic alto solo with some fine melodic variations, as he does again on the pleasant *Midnight* which has a good vocal by Maxine Sullivan. *Takin' My Time* has good interplay between the sections and Carter once more shines on alto, while *My Favorite*

Blues has him playing excellent muted trumpet, followed by reasonable solos from trombonist Vic Dickenson, pianist Sonny White and tenor saxophonist Ernie Powell. Benny Morton has a good solo on *Sunday*, but the principal interest lies in Carter's delightful flowing alto solo and his fine arrangement. *Back Bay Boogie* is not distinguished overall, but Carter's alto solo has a drive about it which might surprise those who wrongly think of him as being invariably somewhat detached and concerned more with producing shapely, poised solos than expressing emotion.

Carter's Capitol recordings of 1945 are not among his greatest, though he achieved some commercial success with his melodic version of *Poinciana*. The best numbers feature Carter himself: on *I Can't Get Started* and *I Surrender Dear*, he takes all the solo space on alto and trumpet respectively. Carter's final records with a regular big band were made for the DeLuxe label. *Jump Call*, from the initial session, has a good solo from the leader and a spirited one from tenor saxophonist Hubert 'Bumps' Myers, but the freneticism which seemed to overtake most big bands around the mid 'forties had caught up with Carter and the sound of the band is untypical of his output as a whole. *Re-bop Boogie* is not helped by some heavy drumming and, for Carter, an unusually trite theme, but his own flowing solo is extremely fine and it is no criticism to remark that it sounds slightly detached from the rest of the performance. The same might be said of his alto solo on *Twelve o'Clock Jump*, which is a model of intelligent construction and melodic astuteness. One would guess, however, that the musical climate of the late 'forties was not one with which Carter could be entirely sympathetic.

For a man who so obviously had every essential musical requirement to be one of the major big band leaders, Carter's failure to achieve a real public breakthrough must have been disappointing. The 1939 band that produced such titles as *Sleep* and *Slow Freight* was probably the best integrated unit that he ever led and the one that had the greatest potential, but he was unable to maintain the stable personnel so necessary to success. Yet, musically, Carter's big bands were certainly not failures, for their excellence shows the strength of the tradition during the 'thirties and early 'forties.

After an absence of just over a quarter a century, Benny Carter returned to New York to lead a band at the 1972 Newport Jazz Festival. Though rehearsal time was limited, Carter drilled it into a memorable unit, and musicians such as Joe Thomas, Dickie Wells, Buddy Tate, Budd Johnson, Earle Warren, Teddy Wilson and Jo Jones played superbly. Carter's solos were as expected, marvellously poised, inventive and melodic. Many events at that Newport Festival were recorded and issued on record; significantly the performance of the Carter band was not. It was, in the stock phrase of the record companies, 'not commercial'.

After his appearance at the festival, Benny Carter was

honoured at a gathering at a long established musicians' club in Harlem. It was an interesting experience to be an onlooker on this occasion. In a sense, Carter was the local boy who had made good. Many of those who came to honour him had clearly not been favoured by fortune in the years since he had known them as band musicians. As he looked around, Carter might well have reflected that the Harlem of his youth was no more.

When Ben Pollack's band broke up in autumn 1934, a number of its musicians continued to play together. The musical director of the group was Gil Rodin, though for a while it was billed under the name of vocalist Clark Randall, but in 1935 it was decided to look for a front man with good commercial possibilities. Cork O'Keefe of the Rockwell-O'Keefe Agency made three suggestions, and the choice finally fell on Bing Crosby's brother Bob who, since 1932, had worked professionally as a singer with Anson Weeks and the Dorsey Brothers Orchestra. The decision proved to be an astute one : during the next year, the Bob Crosby band rose to national prominence.

In its early days, the Crosby band was a co-operative unit, though it is uncertain how long it remained so. Crosby, an adequate popular singer with a style that owed something to brother Bing, fronted the band with charm and flair. With various personnel changes, it remained in existence until late 1942. Several members of the band worked with Eddie Miller during 1943. Crosby himself was inducted into the U S Marines in the summer of 1944, returning to civilian life a year later with the rank of lieutenant. After a short acting career, he formed a new band which was featured on his radio series, then spent much of the 'fifties as a solo performer. Since then, he has organised bands for specific engagements, including a tour of Japan and the Far East in 1964. Such bands have been faithful to the style of the original unit and have generally included a fair contingent of the sidemen who established its musical identity. Crosby, now sixty, has also followed a successful business career, but clearly enjoys the occasional opportunity to reappear in his former role.

In its day, the Bob Crosby band was unique in its musical policy of featuring jazz standards of an earlier era so consistently. It always contained a hard core of jazz musicians, a number of them from New Orleans, notably tenor saxophonist Eddie Miller, clarinettist-arranger Matty Matlock, guitarist and sometimes vocalist Hilton 'Nappy' Lamare, and drummer Ray Bauduc. These men stayed with the band to the end, and others who became well known through their association with it include trumpeters Yank Lawson and Billy Butterfield, clarinettist Irving Fazola, bassist Bob Haggart, and pianist Bob Zurke. Today the band is best remembered for its Dixieland performances, though it always balanced such numbers with commercial tunes of the day and a proportion of more orthodox swing instrumentals. The Dixieland scores of Matty Matlock and Bob Haggart achieved a surprisingly

Bob Crosby at the start of his bandleading career in the middle 1930s.

successful blend of big band sound with the freedom of a Dixieland small group. The Dixieland style was also employed with success by the Bob Cats, a smaller unit from within the full band.

Throughout the whole period of 1935 to 1942, the Crosby band recorded for the US Decca label, with at least a third of its output being by various Bob Cats units. Its recordings of 1935 are mainly popular material of the day sung pleasantly but unmemorably by Crosby himself. In April 1936, it made its first Dixieland styled recordings when Bob Haggart arranged *Muskrat Ramble* and *Dixieland Shuffle* for a session that was otherwise devoted to backing vocalist Connie Boswell. Two months later, with Bob Zurke present for the first time, the band produced versions of *Come Back, Sweet Papa* and *Sugar Foot Strut,* both numbers that Louis Armstrong had recorded in the 'twenties. The former, arranged by Haggart, is typical of the band's approach to such material, and features loose-textured ensemble playing in which clarinets have a major role. The only soloist is clarinettist Matty Matlock, an excellent performer on that instrument, whose style is notable for its technical assurance and his ability to play with a full, rounded tone in all registers. Four days later, the band recorded another number associated with Louis Armstrong, *Savoy Blues,* and this has a powerful solo from trumpeter Yank Lawson.

One of the band's most popular musicians with the public was pianist Bob Zurke, who was frequently featured in boogie material. At times Zurke's playing has a mechanical quality about it—one British critic always referred unkindly to him as 'old jerky'—but he was a versatile pianist who, late in his career, recorded several solos of great sensitivity. Joe Sullivan's *Gin Mill Blues* and *Little Rock Getaway* provided Zurke with his first recorded showcases, and his playing showed considerable drive in the closing chorus of *Little Rock Getaway*. From the same date as *Gin Mill Blues* came a version of *The Old Spinning Wheel* with good solos from Matlock, Lawson and Zurke, and splendidly relaxed ensemble work. In November 1937, the band recorded for the first time what was to become its most popular number: the famous *South Rampart Street Parade*. This is a theme based on the music played by marching bands during New Orleans street parades, and has become a jazz standard. *Panama* was recorded at the same date, and Matlock's score has an attractive free-flowing quality which is enhanced by the apt solos from himself, Eddie Miller and trombonist Warren Smith.

A session of February 1938 produced a version of Fletcher Henderson's *Grand Terrace Rhythm* which includes a good solo by Yank Lawson; the use of clarinets in ensemble passages recalls the Fletcher Henderson band of an earlier era. From the same session, Matlock's score for Jelly Roll Morton's *Wolverine Blues* makes good use of a clarinet duo of himself and Eddie Miller. On this number there is an attractive solo by Matlock, ably backed by drummer Ray Bauduc. Bauduc, much influenced by Warren 'Baby' Dodds and Zutty Singleton, was an important member of the band, and his personal style helped establish its identity. With bassist Bob Haggart he took part in a famous duo recording of *Big Noise from Winnetka*.

During the 'thirties, blues and gospel records made for the black population of the United States were identified as 'race' items. Such releases were virtually unknown to white record buyers, but in March 1938 the Crosby band recorded Big Bill Broonzy's *Louise Louise* and Kokomo Arnold's *Milk Cow Blues*. Both are creditable performances, with vocals from Eddie Miller and Hilton Lamare respectively, and are virtually the only instances of a white swing band making use of such material until Benny Goodman recorded Lil Green's *Why Don't You Do Right* in 1942—in fact the number was initially derived from a recording by a little-known band called the Harlem Hamfats.

During October 1938, the full Crosby band, and various small units from within it, were busy recording material for a special album of six discs. One number included in the album was Bob Haggart's *I'm Prayin' Humble*, a musical evocation of a revivalist prayer meeting. Eddie Miller has a good solo on this, but the featured musician is trumpeter Sterling Bose, whose playing throughout is excellent. Bose, who shot himself after his later career had been clouded by a long illness, was a musician who had initially been influenced by Joe 'King' Oliver. His recorded work is of a quality that makes one regret he received so little attention in his lifetime. From the same session

comes a slightly mechanical version of Meade Lux Lewis's *Honky Tonk Train Blues* that features Bob Zurke, and one of Bob Haggart's most enduring tunes, *I'm Free*. Subsequently lyrics were added and it became a popular standard under its new title of *What's New*. This initial recording features the lyrical trumpet playing of Billy Butterfield, who plays with melodic sensitivity and an attractive tone. The only other solo is an eight bar release by Miller. Whenever Butterfield now makes a public appearance, he is inevitably requested to play *What's New*, though he confesses that he has become heartily sick of the number.

The New Orleans clarinettist Irving Fazola joined the Crosby band early in 1938 and he was featured on another attractive Bob Haggart theme entitled *My Inspiration*. Fazola, with his beautiful full, rounded tone and lyrical approach, was in the great tradition of such New Orleans clarinettists as Jimmie Noone. He plays an engaging melodic solo on this recording, as he does on Waldteufel's *Skater's Waltz*, recorded three months later. At this time, the band was in the unique position of being able to call upon the services of three fine clarinettists in Fazola, Matlock and Miller. In the same session as *Skater's Waltz*, the band also produced *Stomp Off, Let's Go*, a number best known in a recorded version of 1926 by the Erskine Tate band with Louis Armstrong. Here it is given a characteristic Dixieland treatment, with the theme carried by the reeds and trombones and breaks by clarinet and trombone. The ensemble achieves a pleasant loose-textured sound and there is a good solo from Eddie Miller who is ably backed by Bauduc. *Eye Opener*, again from this session and written by Bob Zurke and Matty Matlock, is rather curious, being somewhat reminiscent of the novelty ragtime themes written by Zez Confrey. Zurke is the main soloist, playing with spirit in his somewhat formalised manner, and there are good solos from Butterfield and Miller. Butterfield plays extremely well on the slightly later *When the Red, Red Robin Comes Bob, Bob Bobbin' Along*. Joe Sullivan, who became Zurke's replacement after Floyd Bean had temporarily held the job, is featured on the attractive *Boogie Woogie Maxixe*.

Sullivan did not remain very long; in October 1939, his place was taken by Jess Stacy. The Crosby's band's recorded output of 1940-41 is, taken as a whole, rather poor, and features an excessive number of pop songs. Muggsy Spanier was in the personnel for a few months during 1940, but recorded little of distinction while present. The group of sessions at the beginning of 1942 saw a reversion to a jazz policy. The first title recorded in that year, *Vultee Special*, starts with the trombones and rhythm leading into Yank Lawson's plunger solo, after which the soloists are Stacy, trombonist Floyd O'Brien, and Lawson once more. The performance is stylistically something of a mixture: Stacy employs a boogie rhythm at one point, O'Brien plays very well in his blues-based manner, and the ensemble sound is closer than usual to an orthodox swing approach. Both *Sugar Foot Stomp* and *Original*

Dixieland One-Step are performed in a style that is a compromise between Dixieland and swing. *Sugar Foot Stomp* has excellent solos from Stacy, Miller, Matlock and Lawson, the trumpeter taking the traditional solo with considerable panache. There is a relaxed quality to the ensemble work on *Original* and Matlock and O'Brien have agreeable solos. A considerably more sophisticated approach is noticeable in the session of February 1942. Both *Black Zephyr* and *Blue Surreal* are impressionistic themes, and Jess Stacy's *Ec-stacy* is very different to earlier features by his pianist predecessors. It is slightly introspective in mood, and Stacy plays with incisiveness and imagination against a generally subdued orchestral background, proving yet again that he was one of the finest pianists of the swing era. After this date, the Crosby band produced little else worth noting.

Following its own path, the Crosby band maintained its identity during the major part of its existence. It was fortunate in having Bob Haggart and Matty Matlock within its ranks; both were excellent arrangers and the former a songwriter of talent. The band's solo strength was always adequate and sometimes a great deal more. Its admirable rhythm section gained from the presence of Lamare, Haggart and Bauduc throughout the band's existence. Eddie Miller, with a style not too dissimilar from Bud Freeman's, though possibly more flexible and melodic, was a key soloist. After him, Matty Matlock, Yank Lawson, Billy Butterfield, Irving Fazola and, latterly, Jess Stacy, were the most individual voices in the band. An essential factor in the success of the band was its ability to perform the Dixieland standards in a fresh and inventive manner, far removed from what is currently offered in the Dixieland style. Today, some aspects of the band's music survive in the performances of the World's Greatest Jazz Band, co-led by Bob Haggart and Yank Lawson, though it seems unlikely that a big band would be able to follow a similar musical policy with success in the 'seventies.

During the 'fifties, Bob Crosby recorded on several occasions with a big band that included members of his original personnel. The records that resulted are often pleasant, with good solo passages and arrangements, but they cannot really be compared to the best of the 1935-42 output. The band of that period showed, above all, the value of individuality unmarred by gimmickry. It may not have been the equal of the greatest bands of the swing era, but because it maintained its musical integrity, it is remembered today with respect.

In his book 'The Big Bands', George T. Simon writes: 'In retrospect—and in big band history—Tommy Dorsey's must be recognised as the greatest all-round dance band of them all. Others may have sounded more creative. Others may have swung harder and more consistently. Others may have developed more distinctive styles. But of all the hundreds of well-known bands, Tommy Dorsey's could do more things better than any other could.'

This is, of course, a sweeping statement, and one that many might debate, but it is certainly a tenable viewpoint. A high percentage of Dorsey's output is outside the scope of a book concerned with big band *jazz*, but throughout the years Dorsey always included a contingent of jazz soloists within his personnel, and his own commitment to the music cannot be in doubt.

Tommy Dorsey, like his brother Jimmy, was a brilliant technician, taught from an early age by his father who, by all accounts, was a superb teacher. Tommy started out on trumpet, an instrument which he continued to play occasionally throughout his career, but soon switched to trombone. He was born in Shenandoah, Pennsylvania, on 19th November 1905. As a youth, he worked with local bands and then from 1925 alternated working in such big bands as Paul Whiteman's, Roger Wolfe Kahn's,

The Tommy Dorsey band during a radio broadcast, probably in the late 1930s.

Victor Young's and Fred Rich's with periods of free-lance activities in radio and recording. From the late 'twenties he and Jimmy co-led bands from time to time, forming a permanent group in 1934. The history of this band, and Tommy's abrupt departure from it, has already been mentioned. Tommy's first band was formed mainly from members of Joe Haymes's group, but before long he made various changes for an important debut at the Hotel Lincoln (now the Edison Hotel) in New York during 1935. He started recording for RCA Victor in September 1935 and remained with the company until 1950, when he switched to Decca for three years. Dorsey's finest recordings in the jazz vein were made between 1937 and 1945, although naturally the personnel during this period varied considerably.

Dorsey was deeply committed to the big band business and towards the end of his life felt little sympathy for new developments in popular entertainment. With various reorganisations, he led a big band from 1935 to the early 'fifties. Worsening financial conditions finally causing the two brothers to join up again from May 1953. Beset by personal problems, Dorsey's last few months were not happy. He died on 26th November 1956 from choking on his own vomit while sleeping. As a band-leader, Dorsey seems to have been something of a martinet, though this resulted in consistently high musical standards. Reports by musicians who worked with him, or by friends who knew him well, portray him as a rather

Tommy Dorsey in the film 'The Fabulous Dorseys'.

complex personality, alternately unforgiving and generous, extrovert and aloof, kindly yet capable of sustaining grudges. Unlike his brother Jimmy, who was apparently very easy-going, Tommy was dominated by a burning desire to succeed, and people he thought were obstructing his ambitions received scant consideration. He seemed to regard it as a form of treason if a musician wanted to leave his band against his own wishes, though if he respected a musician he was a generous employer both on and off the stand. Because of his devotion to jazz, he was particularly proud of his jazz contingent, tolerating behaviour from them that would have led others to be dismissed.

In the commercial side of the business, Tommy Dorsey showed considerable flair; he was not a man to suffer meekly what he saw as an injustice. In 1944, angered by the fact that the Hollywood Palladium management were not paying him as much as he felt he was worth, he bought his own ballroom, the Casino Gardens, and during an engagement at the Palladium invited the patrons to transfer to the new venue to hear him and his band. His opinion of his booking agency was a great deal less than flattering and when, late in 1950, his contract finally expired he placed a famous advertisement in the magazine The Billboard that read :

> PHEW !
> After 15 Years I am finally
> out of the clutches of . . .
> YOU KNOW WHO ! ! !
> I am being Booked exclusively by . . .
> TOMDOR ENTERPRISES, Inc.

Musically Dorsey was no great innovator : he chose instead to work within the conventions of his era, following the prevailing trend of larger personnels in the early 'forties and for a period adding a string section to his regular group—at its peak, his band numbered thirty-one musicians. Dorsey had an astute awareness of the importance of having good vocalists : he started out with Jack Leonard and Edythe Wright and went on to feature Frank Sinatra, Bob Eberly, Jo Stafford and Dick Haymes among others. It was with Dorsey that Frank Sinatra established his great reputation; during Sinatra's period with the band, the percentage of jazz recordings was lower than at any other time—not that at any time the jazz output of the band on record formed more than a fraction of the whole. During theatre and dance engagements the proportion of jazz was apparently higher than the recordings might lead one to believe. On occasions, the jazzman in Dorsey temporarily came to the fore, as in the 'Evolution Of Swing' concert that he featured during 1938. This included arrangements from Benny Carter, Fletcher Henderson and Dean Kincaide, with a segment devoted to musical history, which included items as they might have been played by a Memphis band in 1909, the Original Dixieland Jazz Band, Paul Whiteman, the California Ramblers, Jean Goldkette (reproducing a Bix Beiderbecke solo) and Fletcher Henderson. In general, though, Dorsey did not claim that this was a jazz unit, only that it featured jazz as part of an overall programme.

Dorsey's own evaluation of his jazz prowess was modest: when he took part in an all star group selected by readers' votes in the magazine Metronome and found that Jack Teagarden was on the session, he declined to take a solo, contenting himself instead with playing an obbligato role behind Teagarden. On the other hand, quite apart from early recording efforts such as the session on which he was featured on trumpet (and sounded as if he were inspired by Louis Armstrong by way of Jack Purvis), there are innumerable recorded solos by him which are extremely capable in a jazz vein. It would be foolish to claim that he was a jazz trombonist of the calibre of Jimmy Harrison, Jack Teagarden or Dicky Wells, but he could play jazz creditably on occasion, as his recordings show. He was, inevitably, greatly admired by other trombonists for his superb technique and tone, and it is interesting to read the views of Dicky Wells on his ability, taken from Wells's book 'The Night People': 'You have to give Tommy Dorsey credit, too, because for a trombone to sound like a trombone, there has to be a little Tommy there, somewhere. I've never heard enough praise for him. It's really been disgusting since he died. He gave out so much melody—the kind we need today from the trombone. After all, it's a voice-leading instrument. . . . He used to come to Harlem quite a bit, and he could swing, too, but his tone was so fine people always wanted to hear him play pretty. His breathing was so good.'

Later Wells summarised his feelings about Dorsey's musicianship: 'There was nothing stiff about Tommy's style. It was very flexible, and there was that beautiful, flowing tone. Everything he did was just perfect. And he really had a tougher way to go than the guy who was just swinging along, because to play the horn right, and still have people love it—that was something else.'

This is another illustration of the fact that musicians are less concerned with categorisation than most jazz followers. Many of these have been puzzled, if not dismayed, that alto saxophone players as diverse in style as Johnny Hodges, Charlie Parker and Ornette Coleman have been unstinting in their praise of Jimmy Dorsey, a musician whom the purist jazz fan views with disapproval. The truth is that musicians are swift to recognise technical perfection in others, irrespective of style, and both the Dorseys were widely admired on that score.

The Tommy Dorsey band recorded quite extensively during its first year, with the bulk of its output confined to popular tunes of the day, generally including vocals by Edythe Wright or Cliff Weston (replaced by Jack Leonard), with a few instrumental performances of jazz standards. *Weary Blues,* made at the first session, was a highly competent performance with reasonable solos from clarinettist Sid Stoneburn, pianist Paul Mitchell, tenor saxophonist Johnny Van Eps and Dorsey, but it has little about it that is really individual. For some while, Dorsey was clearly concerned with building his band and drilling it into a first class unit, leaving individuality of style to a later date. On its fourth RCA session, the band made its famous theme song *I'm Getting Sentimental Over You,* a supreme example of Dorsey's remarkable control and tone, his solo being played against a background of reeds and rhythm. The April 1936 version of *Royal Garden Blues* is an improvement on *Weary Blues,* for though the solos by clarinettist Joe Dixon and tenor saxophonist Sid Block are ordinary—Dorsey's solo is undoubtedly superior—the score allows for a greater variety of dynamics and ensemble textures, and the band achieves a lighter sound. It is not certain who wrote the arrangement, but its style suggests it might be the work of Dean Kincaide.

In January 1937, the first of a series of light classics, Rubinstein's *Melody in F,* was recorded, a thoroughly professional performance in which Dorsey plays the theme with mute and there are good solos from Berigan, Bud Freeman and Joe Dixon. Ten days later, the band made Rimsky-Korsakov's *Song of India.* Dorsey again states the theme, but this time also closes with a melodic solo. There is a powerful trumpet solo by Berigan, and the ensemble performs ably. These swing performances of the light classics caught the public's fancy, and led to a succession of similar recordings that included Mendelssohn's *Spring Song, The Blue Danube,* Dvorak's *Humoresque* and Offenbach's *Barcarolle.* These were not received with enthusiasm in all quarters: some reviewers in popular music magazines complained of the blasphemy involved in swinging the classics, just as irate Scots poured in letters of complaint to Melody Maker when they first heard Maxine Sullivan's mild swing version of *Loch Lomond.* For Dorsey, though, they were important in bringing him a great deal of publicity. When *Song of India* was issued, it was backed with *Marie,* and the band had a double hit. Max Kaminsky has said that Dorsey heard this version of *Marie,* with the band chanting responses behind a solo vocalist, performed by the Sunset Royals band when it was sharing a bill with him at a Philadelphia theatre. He had his arranger copy it, and the recorded version with vocal by Jack Leonard and the band and solos from Dorsey, Berigan and Freeman became immensely popular, leading in due course to *Who, Yearning* and other performances in the same vein.

Throughout 1937 and 1938, Dorsey's recorded output remained commercially slanted in the main, although the percentage of jazz titles did increase. *Beale Street Blues,* from May 1937, was released on a twelve inch record in a version with a slight Bob Crosby flavour. Dorsey has a solo that is definitely good jazz, Pee Wee Erwin plays with something of Berigan's fire, and Bud Freeman takes an excellent solo against a background of clarinets. It is unfortunate that instrumental versions of Willie 'The Lion' Smith's *Passionette* and *Morning Air,* made two months later, were never released. *Boogie Woogie,* arranged by Dean Kincaide, though somewhat synthetic, provided the band with another hit recording. Soon afterwards came

221

a pleasant version of Bix Beiderbecke's *Davenport Blues,* with Dorsey playing particularly well, and a theatrical version of *Hawaiian War Chant.* This, with its wa-wa brass and insistent tom-tom rhythm, is the sort of number that the swing bands liked to have in the books for stage appearances. Drummer Maurice Purtill is much to the fore, and there are good solos from tenor saxophonist Babe Russin and trumpeter Yank Lawson, who plays in his familiar plunger style.

Early in 1939 the band recorded a good version of Jelly Roll Morton's *Milenburg Joys,* released on two sides of a disc. There is a strong Dixieland feeling about much of the performance, but there are a number of good solos, notably by Russin and Dorsey, and the work of the sax section in particular is impressive. 1939 was the year in which Dorsey hired Jimmie Lunceford's brilliant arranger Sy Oliver. *Stomp It Off* and *Easy Does It,* both Oliver scores, show the band on a distinct Lunceford kick, with Dorsey even managing to sound like Lunceford's Trummy Young on *Stomp It Off.* After Sinatra's arrival in the same year, the band made fewer jazz recordings, but Buddy Rich was featured in the 1940 *Quiet Please,* and Sy Oliver provided scores for *Swing High* and *Swanee River,* both recorded at a session in October. *Swanee* is an inventive performance, mainly because of Oliver's fine arrangement; it is taken at a gentle pace with solos from Dorsey, an unidentified tenor saxophonist, probably Don Lodice, and trumpeter Ziggy Elman who had just arrived from the Goodman band. *Swing High* is very different, an exhibitionistic performance with Elman playing at his most extrovert.

The Dorsey band reached its peak in the early 'forties, both as a commercial unit and as a jazz group. By now, Dorsey was using the almost obligatory eight brass, five reeds and four rhythm, adding a string section in 1942. Dorsey's instrumental recordings were tending fashionably towards increasing freneticism, as in the wild *Well Git It,* with its screaming trumpet close by Elman and Jimmy Zito. *Blue Blazes,* recorded at Dorsey's last session before the recording ban, is spirited and includes some effective solos, but overall is inferior to an earlier version by the Jimmie Lunceford band.

On his first session after the ban was lifted, Dorsey produced two of his most popular recordings. *On the Sunny Side of the Street* depends for its success on Sy Oliver's brilliant arrangement, for there are no solos as such and the Pied Pipers vocal group are given the major role. Buddy De Franco and Milt Golden are heard on clarinet and piano respectively in *Opus No. 1,* another superb Sy Oliver score which has the band playing with immense technical assurance and verve. A string section is used on both these recordings. In autumn 1945, with Charlie Shavers now one of the band's featured trumpeters, a driving version of *Chloe* was recorded, with Shavers and clarinettist Buddy De Franco as the main soloists. The ensemble is dominated by the powerful trumpet section, though the use of De Franco's high

register clarinet against the ensemble near the end recalls an earlier tradition. After this, the band continued to make good recordings, including the attractive 1946 *At Sundown* and Dorsey's 1947 feature *Trombonology,* but it seemed to have passed its peak, and the Decca titles of 1950-53 are generally competent rather than inspired. It is as if the changes in the world of popular entertainment had left their mark on Dorsey, so that his involvement in the big band scene lacked some of its former confidence.

Tommy Dorsey was both a superb musician and a fine builder of bands. Despite his own liking for jazz, his concern was primarily to direct a band that would be capable of performing on various levels, though there is little doubt that he was proudest of its jazz achievements. The very versatility of his bands probably prevented their becoming completely individual in a jazz sense, but they produced such a body of entertaining and musically impeccable big band jazz recordings over the years and included so many fine jazz soloists within their ranks that they are ensured a secure place in big band history.

Billy Eckstine won national popularity through his appearances and recordings with the Earl Hines band. Before joining Hines in 1939, mainly at the instigation of Budd Johnson, Eckstine had worked professionally as a singer in Buffalo and Detroit and had been resident for two years at the Club De Lisa in Chicago. Eckstine occasionally played trumpet during his stay with Hines and, with Johnson, was responsible for the introduction of Charlie Parker, Sarah Vaughan and other modernists to the band. He left Hines in 1943 and began his career as a solo attraction. The following spring, with Johnson's aid, he formed a big band which he kept together until January 1947.

Eckstine's band is something of a legend in jazz history, for in its time it included most of the prominent bop or modernist musicians of the era, notably trumpeters Miles Davis, Kenny Dorham, Dizzy Gillespie and Fats Navarro, alto saxophonist Charlie Parker, tenor saxophonists Gene Ammons and Dexter Gordon, baritone saxophonist Cecil Payne, drummer Art Blakey and bassist Tommy Potter. Sarah Vaughan was the band's vocalist. Its chief arrangers were Tadd Dameron, Budd Johnson, John Malachi and Jerry Valentine. Eckstine not only sang and fronted the band, but also played trumpet and valve trombone.

In various interviews, Eckstine has described his problems in keeping the band together. It was not only that its modern style failed to appeal to conservative audiences—on recorded evidence, it sounds basically a late swing era band with a contingent of modern soloists—but that a number of the musicians were unreliable and could not get to jobs on time because of drug problems. In the end, weary of fronting a big band at a difficult time, Eckstine gave up and returned to the career as a popular ballad singer that has made him an international figure in the entertainment world. Over twenty-five years after giving up his band, he retains his deep interest in jazz.

Unfortunately little of the brilliance of Eckstine's band comes across on its commercial recordings. After an initial date for the DeLuxe label, Eckstine signed a contract with National and completed eight recording sessions between May 1945 and late 1946. Well over forty titles have been released from these dates. Not only are the recording sound and balance indifferent, but also most of the numbers feature the band purely as an accompaniment to Eckstine's vocals. There are individual solos of interest on some titles, but they are often short. Taken as a whole, Eckstine's National recordings give little idea of the quality of his band.

The regular band's only DeLuxe session did give it the chance to record two good numbers—John Malachi's *Opus X* and Jerry Valentine's *Blowing the Blues Away*. Despite the dull recording, *Opus X* gives an impression of the band's drive. There are good solos by Dizzy Gillespie and alto saxophonist John Jackson. *Blowing* has a good chase sequence by tenor saxophonists Gene Ammons and Dexter Gordon following Eckstine's vocal. Eckstine sings pleasantly enough, and the material includes a number of good standard ballads, but it is not possible to single out any individual performances in the work of the band. These recordings give little idea of the qualities attributed to the band by people who actually heard it. Fortunately an LP is now available made up of airshots from the time when the band was playing at the Club Plantation in Los Angeles during February and March 1945.

Above: *Billy Eckstine appears to find playing the trumpet hot work!* Below: *the Eckstine band in the early 1940s; the trumpet soloist on the left is Fats Navarro.*

The original announcements retained on the LP are delivered in the hip talk of the period. The master of ceremonies, Ernie 'Bubbles' Whitman, described by a station announcer as 'The stomach that walks like a man', is never at a loss for the leaden joke or hip aside. The sound is better than that achieved by the studio recordings and, though a fair proportion of numbers are devoted to vocals by Eckstine or Sarah Vaughan, the backgrounds can be heard. Despite the contingent of modernist soloists, the sound of the band comes essentially from the late swing era. The section scoring is generally conventional. Unlike the Dizzy Gillespie band, which was really far more bop oriented, Eckstine's has high quality ensemble and individual section work, at this time no doubt partly the work of musical director Budd Johnson. Whereas many of the records by Gillespie's big band are marred by sloppy intonation and ragged ensemble passages, the radio material by Eckstine's group contains numerous examples of technical expertise. The work of the saxophone section on *Love Me or Leave Me*, the trumpets on *Blue 'n' Boogie*, and the trombones on *Mr Chips* provide good instances. Ensemble interludes are performed cleanly and with fine intonation, leaving no doubt that this was a very good band indeed.

Among the highlights of the LP is a new version of *Blowing the Blues Away*, with a neat solo from pianist Malachi and a good chase by Gene Ammons and Budd Johnson. *Opus X*, also rearranged, is much better than the studio version. It has an eight bar solo from Fats Navarro and excellent playing by John Jackson, late of the Jay McShann band. Tadd Dameron wrote the arrangement of *Airmail Special*—the same one that George Auld recorded—and the band is in fine form. The performance reaches its climax with a beautifully phrased and articulated solo by Fats Navarro, certainly the finest trumpeter to emerge from the bop movement. Sarah Vaughan has two excellent vocals on *Mean To Me* and *Don't Blame Me*. The trumpets are heard to advantage on *Don't Blame Me* and *Without A Song*, sung by Eckstine. The outstanding performance is a Jerry Valentine arrangement of *Love Me or Leave Me*, which opens with a theme played well by both trumpet and sax sections. Then follow solos by Gene Ammons, Malachi, and a superb one from Navarro, which displays to perfection his attractive broad tone, fluent technique and flow of individual ideas. There is not a weak performance on the whole LP apart from Whitman's announcements—and we must be thankful that the material survived.

The claim is often made that big band jazz had begun to languish by the mid 'forties. There is plenty of recorded evidence to refute this and, judging from the Club Plantation LP, the music of the Billy Eckstine band was good enough to do so.

'Dizzy Gillespie has come to symbolise the bop revolution more than any other and no doubt a large part of its rapid diffusion is due to his efforts. Dizzy thrived in the time of revolution and anarchy, where his perverse comedy lightens and expands the more generally dark sounds of

Dizzy Gillespie and Harry James talk over the big band life at the 1958 Monterey Jazz Festival.

the new movement of the time. In front of a big band he showed that it was possible to advance while retaining the impulse of the swing era, experiment and communicate strongly without for the most part just pandering to the crowd.'

Terry Martin's opinion, expressed in a review of three Dizzzy Gillespie records written in 1965, forms the most succinct summary I know of Gillespie's role during the 'forties. The British jazz critic Alun Morgan once commented, 'Dizzy is, by nature, a compulsive big band leader.' The truth of his assertion has been stressed by the casual nature of much of Gillespie's playing since his big band days. Gillespie, the revolutionary of the 'forties, has become the conservative of the 'seventies, totally out of sympathy with post-bop developments in jazz. In any case, for Gillespie, the attraction of big bands is understandable in view of his musical background. His roots are very firmly in the swing era.

John Birks 'Dizzy' Gillespie was living in Philadelphia when he obtained his first important professional job with the Frank Fairfax band at the age of eighteen. One of his companions in the trumpet section was the late Charlie Shavers. At the time (1935), he was strongly influenced by Roy Eldridge, though 'he never could play as high as me', Eldridge told me firmly on one occasion. Early in 1937, he replaced Eldridge in the Teddy Hill band, and toured England and France that summer. Subsequently, he paid tribute to Bill Dillard, one of his associates in Hill's trumpet section, who taught him a great deal, he said. Several members of the Hill band took part in some famous recording sessions in France, but Gillespie was not considered for them. After returning to the U.S.A., Gillespie gigged around New York City, joined the Cab Calloway band late in the summer of 1939 and remained with it for over two years.

Gillespie's reputation was made with Calloway. He was heavily featured as a soloist in the band but left abruptly after firing spitballs at the leader on stage. In the summer of 1973, as a member of the Calloway reunion band at the Newport Jazz Festival, Gillespie delivered a belated but poetic apology for the spitball incident thirty-two years earlier. After leaving Calloway, he worked with such big bands as those of Benny Carter, Ella Fitzgerald, Les Hite, Charlie Barnet and Lucky Millinder. By that time, his style was evolving towards what became identified as bop, and early in 1943 he worked alongside a number of other modernists in the Earl Hines big band. After playing in small groups, he joined Billy Eckstine's big band in 1944, and soon afterwards became a guru of the bop movement.

Although bop is generally associated with small groups, and most of Gillespie's famous early bop recordings were made with a quintet or sextet, he formed his first big band briefly in 1945. He tried again in 1946 and managed to hold the band together until early 1950, taking it to Europe early in 1948. The public was not really ready for the band's music, though there was the occasional

triumph, and Gillespie had a hard struggle for survival. After six years' work with small groups, Gillespie fronted a big band organised by arranger Quincy Jones in 1956 and undertook two tours to the Middle and Far East and, later, South America under the auspices of the U S State Department. He kept the group in existence until January 1958. Since then, he has only fronted a big band for special concerts or recording dates.

Gillespie's big band recordings incorporate various bop elements but, while his personnel included many musicians involved with the new developments, Gillespie also employed players who were basically swing musicians. The first recording session with his big band produced an interesting version of Tadd Dameron's Our Delight. Gillespie's own virtuoso solos are in the bop manner, while the section and ensemble work recall the swing era. In July 1946, the band recorded the famous Things to Come, a spectacular performance with brilliant playing from Gillespie and the whole trumpet section and a coda that is startling at a first hearing. Emanon has less immediate impact, but good solos from Milt Jackson (vibraphone) and Gillespie, a reasonable effort from tenor saxophonist, James Moody, and more fine work from the trumpets. These titles were recorded for the Musicraft label. In 1947, Gillespie secured a contract with RCA Victor that lasted for two years.

Although Gillespie's big band was at its best on the RCA Victor releases, it was not always well recorded and people who heard the band claim that much of its impact was lost on record. The first RCA Victor date produced good versions of Two Bass Hit and Stay On It, along with a lighthearted Oop-Pop-A-Da, one of many scat bop vocals that Gillespie made at this period. In the late 'forties, jazz musicians were increasingly fascinated by Latin-American rhythms, and on its second RCA Victor date the band recorded the two-part Cubano Be and Cubano Bop, written by George Russell and including some of the most impressive scored passages of the band's recorded output. The performance highlights superb conga drumming by the Cuban percussion virtuoso Chano Pozo. A few days later, the exciting Manteca featured brilliant work from Pozo. The band also recorded a good version of Minor Walk. Sessions on 22nd and 30th December 1947 produced the best studio recordings by the Gillespie big band.

In February 1948, the band was recorded at a concert at the Salle Pleyel in Paris. The material is familiar and the sound is poor at times, but the excitement that the band generated does come across. A version of Things to Come has a greater impact than the earlier studio version. The performances as a whole are uneven. Highspots are Gillespie's own playing on I Can't Get Started, a fine Algo Bueno with excellent drumming by Kenny Clarke, and a likeable version of Thelonious Monk's 'Round Midnight with a pleasing alto solo in the Benny Carter tradition from Howard Johnson. Five months later, the band was recorded at another concert, this time at the Civic

Auditorium in Pasadena. There emerged a sparkling version of *Manteca*, with brilliant playing by Pozo, a good *Emanon* with reasonable tenor work from James Moody, and an interesting *Stay On It*, a feature for Cecil Payne's baritone saxophone.

After a year away from the RCA Victor studios, the band returned in December 1948 to record four titles. The best was *Lover Come Back to Me*, a solo feature for Gillespie in which he exhibits excellent control and taste. From the next date comes a roaring version of *St Louis Blues*, as arranged by Budd Johnson, which incorporates *Parker's Mood* into the theme statements. Gillespie has a fluent solo, but the solos by Yusef Lateef (tenor saxophone) and Cecil Payne are undistinguished. The band's final RCA Victor date produced an amusing *In the Land of Oo-Bla-Dee*, complete with a mercurial solo by Gillespie and a good vocal from Joe Carroll, as well as a somewhat ragged *Jumpin' With Symphony Sid*, which is salvaged by excellent solos from Gillespie and trombonist J. J. Johnson. After this, the band made a couple of mediocre sessions for Capitol and then broke up.

In general, Gillespie's band of 1956-58 was better organised than those of the earlier years, but it lacked their individuality and seems at times to follow the style of Count Basie's band. It produced some agreeable recordings. The relaxed *Groovin' for Nat* has fluent solo work by Gillespie, whose tone is fuller than usual on a new version of *I Can't Get Started*. Lush performances of *Stella by Starlight* and *My Reverie* are both arranged by Melba Liston, who sounds like a female Bennie Green in a solo on *Reverie*. It was basically an efficient group with a number of competent soloists. Too often, though, its members give the impression of a lack of musical involvement.

Gillespie suffered because his bandleading days came near the close of the big band era. His groups of 1946-50 can never rank alongside the outstanding big bands; they too often sounded ragged and technically uncertain. However, they mirrored developments that were taking place in jazz at the time, and proved capable of vital and exciting music on occasions. A big band is a perfect medium for Gillespie's personality and music, and it is a pity that recent years have provided him with so few opportunities to work in the setting which so obviously inspires him.

When Benny Goodman formed his first regular band in 1934, he already had twelve years of professional experience behind him. Goodman was a child prodigy; he took up the clarinet at twelve and joined the musicians' union a year later. In his native Chicago, he was taught by Franz Schoepp, a famous teacher whose other pupils included Buster Bailey and Jimmie Noone. Before this, Goodman had appeared in a talent contest with an imitation of Ted Lewis.

Goodman's impoverished background made him need to turn his musical accomplishments to financial advantage. From the time he was thirteen, in 1922, he began working with local bands, securing regular engagements with Charles 'Murph' Podalsky. In summer 1923, he met Bix Beiderbecke for the first time while working on a riverboat. During the next two years, he played with Arnold Johnson and Art Kassel; at some time during this period, he was heard by Gil Rodin, who recommended him to Ben Pollack. When Fud Livingston temporarily left the Pollack band, Goodman was hired in his place. Goodman left Chicago in August 1925 to join Pollack at the Venice Ballroom in Los Angeles and returned with the band four months later. During 1926, Goodman worked intermittently with Pollack, and rejoined the band as a full-time member early in 1927. After going with the band to California that summer, he left once more, late in the year, and spent two months with Isham Jones before he was induced to return to the Pollack group. He travelled with it to New York in March 1928.

In September 1929, Goodman left the Pollack band for the last time. Soon afterwards, he spent three months with Red Nichols. In the early 'thirties, Goodman was extremely active as a free-lance musician; he appeared on innumerable radio shows, played with orchestras in Broadway theatres, and took part in many recording sessions. Though this was the period of the depression, Goodman's professionalism stood him in good stead and he was never without work. In 1932, he organised a band to accompany the singer Russ Columbo and played with it frequently. Occasionally, he also fronted bands for recording sessions and outside engagements. By now, he had formed a strong desire to lead a big jazz band. Though the times were hardly propitious for such a venture, he was fortunate enough to secure a residency at Billy Rose's Music Hall from June to October in 1934. This was to prove vital for Goodman.

His personnel for the job varied, but included a few of the musicians who were to be with him when he made his great breakthrough in the following year. However, after changes in the management at Billy Rose's, he was given notice in October and found himself out of work. There was a plan for him to take an all-star jazz group to Europe, with a line-up that would include Henry 'Red' Allen, Bill Coleman, Jack Teagarden, J. C. Higginbotham, Benny Carter, Edgar Sampson, Leon 'Chu' Berry, Teddy Wilson, Gene Krupa, Red Norvo and Bessie Smith, but nothing came of it. Obtaining a couple of outside engagements in the New York area, Goodman struggled to keep the band together, bolstered by the hope of being selected as one of the bands to play on a new radio programme being planned by the National Biscuit Company. After a month of nervous waiting, the band was auditioned in November and won a place on the programme by a single vote—a story, no doubt apocryphal, has it that the sponsors originally gave the same number of votes to Goodman's and another band, settling the issue by calling in a member of their office staff to cast the deciding vote.

Left: *Benny Goodman leads his band in a 1936 broadcast.* Right: *the Benny Goodman band, late 1941. At the left are pianist Mel Powell, vocalists Art Lund and Peggy Lee, bassist Sid Weiss and Goodman. The saxes are Vido Musso, Clint Neagley, Julie Schwartz, George Berg and Chuck Gentry; the trombonists Lou McGarity and Cutty Cutshall; the trumpeters Jimmy Maxwell, Billy Butterfield and Al Davis. Ralph Collier is on drums, and guitarist Tommy Morgan is hidden behind Goodman.*

The National Biscuit Company's 'Let's Dance' programme was broadcast nationwide and lasted for three hours, with the bands of Xavier Cugat, Kel Murray and Benny Goodman playing alternating sets. The first programme went out on 1st December 1934, and the last on 25th May 1935. With the security of the series, Goodman was able to set about tightening up his personnel and commissioning as wide a variety of good arrangements as possible. Although the broadcasts were bringing the band a growing following, other engagements were still extremely modest, such as the dance date that it played on Easter Monday 1935 for the Whitehall Elks Lodge at Whitehall, New York. In late December 1934, Gene Krupa joined the band, replacing Stan King. The personnel was now almost identical with that which made the first RCA Victor records.

With the close of the 'Let's Dance' series, the Goodman band was booked to appear at the Roosevelt Hotel in New York. The booking was a disaster: the Roosevelt was best known for the lengthy residencies by Guy Lombardo and his Royal Canadians, and the music of the Goodman band shocked management and patrons alike. Although Goodman was given notice on the opening night, the engagement dragged on for three weeks. Goodman may have been dismayed but he did not waver from his swing policy. After a week at a Philadelphia hotel in July, the band set out on a long tour.

The band's reception during the first six weeks of its road trip varied from mild enthusiasm to indifference. In August, it reached California; on 21st August, it opened at the Palomar Ballroom in Los Angeles. Benny Goodman has described the opening night to Nat Shapiro and Nat Hentoff:

'We had just laid a big egg in Denver and were pretty low. And we figured that the further West we went, the worse it would get. Before we hit L.A. we played a few one-nighters, one in San Francisco that wasn't too bad. When we opened at the Palomar we had a "What've we got to lose" attitude and decided to let loose and shoot the works with our best things like *Sugar Foot Stomp, Sometimes I'm Happy,* and the others. Actually, though, we were almost scared to play.'

'From the moment I kicked them off, the boys dug in with some of the best playing I'd heard since we left New York. I don't know what it was, but the crowd went wild, and then—boom!'

'That was the real beginning.'

Goodman's triumph at the Palomar was the beginning of the swing era. Night after night, the crowds poured in to applaud the band, and the original engagement was extended another month. After leaving the Palomar, the band played at a Los Angeles theatre for a week, did a few one-nighters in Texas, then crossed the country for an opening at the Congress Hotel in Chicago on 6th November. It is said that the management of the Congress Hotel had been persuaded to book the band without hearing it, on the advice of some musicians who worked in the local union and wanted to hear it themselves. In fact, it was well received, and on 8th December, it played a concert at the Congress Hotel, bringing in some guest musicians from the Fletcher Henderson band which was playing at the Grand Terrace. This occasion may well have been the first jazz concert ever presented in the United States. In the same month, the magazine Metronome carried a readers' poll in which Goodman's was voted the best swing band.

The band stayed at the Congress Hotel until May 1936, then returned to New York. From this point, success after success followed. The band was soon booked to make its first film appearance in 'The Big Broadcast Of 1937'. In January 1938, the famous Carnegie Hall concert took place; happily, most of it was recorded. With occasional lay-offs, Goodman led regular big bands until 1949. In the 'fifties and 'sixties, he organised groups only for tours and specific engagements. He appeared overseas on a number of occasions, sometimes leading small groups and sometimes big bands (in which he once or twice used European musicians). He has been, for instance, to Japan, Thailand and Burma from late 1956 to January 1957, to Europe, including the Brussels World Fair, in May 1958, to the Soviet Union in 1962, and to Japan in 1970. In the winter of 1973 he brought a sextet to Britain and other European countries for a short tour. Outside jazz, he has been played as a soloist with a number of classical ensembles, and has recorded regularly over the years.

On many occasions Goodman has made clear the debt that he owed to Fletcher Henderson in the formative period of the band. In his autobiography 'The Kingdom Of Swing', written with Irving Kolodin, Goodman discusses the problems that he was facing on the 'Let's Dance' programmes through not having a sufficient variety of material scored in the right manner, and goes on to add : 'It was then that we made one of the most important discoveries of all—that Fletcher Henderson, in addition to writing big arrangements such as the ones I have mentioned [Goodman refers here to having purchased scores of such jazz standards as *King Porter Stomp* and *Big John's Special* from Henderson], could also do a wonderful job on melodic tunes such as *Can't We Be Friends, Sleepy Time Down South, Blue Skies, I Can't Give You Anything But Love* and above all *Sometimes I'm Happy.* He had to be convinced of it himself, but once he started he did marvellous work. These were the things, with their wonderful easy style and great background figures, that really set the style of the band.'

The factual proof of this statement lies in the early recordings of the Goodman band. It recorded on several occasions during 1934, and its output certainly shows that it was by no means certain of its musical direction at the time. A performance such as *Cokey,* for example, is very much in the style of the Casa Loma Orchestra, while *Like a Bolt from the Blues,* arranged by Jiggs Noble of the Isham Jones band, though smoothly played, has little distinctive about it. *Take My Word,* better known as *Lonesome Nights,* is a well-known Benny Carter number, and the band uses the composer's score, Goodman sitting in with the sax section on alto. The handling of Carter's arrangement is first rate, particularly the sax passages, but again the performance bears little relationship to what we now think of as a typical Goodman sound. Goodman used the period of the 'Let's Dance' series to good effect, leading the band in regular and intensive rehearsals, and spent as much money as he could on strengthening its book. By the time of its first RCA Victor sessions, the band's style had been set, thanks to Fletcher Henderson.

The first Henderson scores to be recorded were *Blue Skies, Sometimes I'm Happy* and *King Porter Stomp,* though on the previous session Goodman had used two by Horace Henderson in the same vein. They exhibit all the trademarks of Henderson's style, with the familiar call-and-response patterns and the use of one section to carry the basic theme at the start, with another filling in. It was his insistence on the highest standards of musicianship

that enabled Goodman to keep on top for so long; certainly, at this stage, the precision that the band achieves does not sound mechanical. There are very fine solos by Bunny Berigan on all these performances, with excellent backing from Krupa in two instances, and Goodman himself plays with a cutting edge to his tone and produces some good ideas. It has often been said that Goodman is a rather cold musician, that however technically skilful his clarinet work might be, it invariably conveys an impression of detachment. I cannot agree with this view. When he is playing well, there seems little doubt of Goodman's involvement with his music. I cannot help feeling that much of the criticism against Goodman comes from people who have never listened carefully to most of his best recorded work. Other arrangers than Fletcher Henderson made important contributions to the Goodman book, notably Horace Henderson, Jimmy Mundy and Edgar Sampson, whose *Stompin' at the Savoy* was recorded in January 1936. It is a relaxed performance with an attractive, well-phrased solo by trombonist Joe Harris and shorter ones by Goodman and tenor saxophonist Arthur Rollini.

Gordon Griffin joined the band in May 1936, Ziggy Elman in the following September, and Harry James in January 1937. For the two years they remained together, they made up a really formidable trumpet team with its own recognisable sound. Though they switched the lead around, it is sometimes possible to distinguish the recordings on which James is in the leader's role. He has never been given sufficient credit for his quality as section leader. The first session on which all three men were present produced fine versions of *I Want To Be Happy* and *Chloe,* which has a particularly striking Goodman solo beautifully backed by pianist Jess Stacy. Six months later, the band recorded its famous version of *Sing, Sing, Sing,* originally released as two sides of a record, with Krupa's exhibitionistic solo work being matched by the flamboyance of most of the solos and the powerful ensemble playing, particularly that of the brass. *Sugar Foot Stomp* has one of James's best solos with the band; the Fletcher Henderson score uses one of his favourite early devices of a clarinet trio against brass. By now, the band was turning out a succession of fine recordings such as Edgar Sampson's *If Dreams Come True.* The best solos are from Goodman and trombonist Vernon Brown. After Brown's solo, there is a passage which shows off the brilliance of the trumpet team.

The recordings of the famous Carnegie Hall concert of 16th January 1938 include performances by the Trio and Quartet, a 'Twenty Years of Jazz' capsule history, and a jam session with Buck Clayton, Lester Young, Count Basie among others, plus the regular full band. This recording really conveys an impression of the excitement of the band in person, and the sheer vitality of the playing on *Don't Be That Way* sets the mood for much that follows. *Loch Lomond,* with the ensemble producing an appropriate Scottish sound in its introduction, has a pleasant vocal by Martha Tilton well backed by Stacy; James takes a neatly controlled solo. *Bei mir bist do schoen* again features Miss Tilton, but aside from the fine short solo by Stacy, it is most interesting for introducing Ziggy Elman in the type of playing which he was to feature extensively in later years. Elman incorporated elements of Yiddish *fralich* into his solo style, achieving a curious wailing effect, which served its purpose of making him instantly identifiable. He could, on occasion, play with sensitivity, and was also an excellent section man. From the band's viewpoint, the highlight of the concert was its lengthy version of *Sing Sing, Sing* where, after all the flash and showcasing by Krupa and James, Stacy suddenly sets off on a brilliant piano solo that eclipses everything that had gone before. Stacy seemed to be in particularly fine form at this concert—his playing throughout is a model of taste and inventiveness.

One of the numbers played at the concert was *Big John's Special.* Four months later, a studio recording was made. James is heard in his brashest manner, but Stacy has a fine solo despite over-enthusiastic punctuations from Krupa. Stacy again shines in a slightly later recording of Benny Carter's *Blue Interlude,* both behind Goodman's attractive theme solo and Martha Tilton's vocal; the trumpets are again outstanding as a section. In December 1938, the band turned to offbeat material in Alec Templeton's *Bach Goes to Town,* a recording which became very popular. Nowadays, when one musician makes a good living out of playing jazz versions

of Bach compositions, it is difficult to realise just how much of a novelty *Bach Goes to Town* was in 1938.

Gene Krupa had left Goodman in February 1938 and in December James also departed to form his own band. They were undoubtedly the two most popular sidesmen in the Goodman band; it was some while before James was adequately replaced. Though never as brilliant a jazz soloist as Bunny Berigan, James was a key member of the band for two years. He was very heavily featured as a soloist, though in this role he is something of an enigma. There is no doubt about his ability to communicate with his public. His playing with Goodman certainly avoided the excesses that were to follow when he led his own band, but the brashness of his style, while often exciting, sometimes leads one to wish that he would pay a little more attention to the content of his music. There are recordings where he performs with taste and control, but too often with Goodman James's solos had a quality of self-indulgent theatricality about them.

If James was sometimes guilty of lapses in taste, so, on an even larger scale, was Ziggy Elman. He was heavily featured in what one critic at the time described as his 'wailing wall' style on *And the Angels Sing* and *Who'll Buy My Bublitchki,* though at the close of *Angels,* he shows his power in a more orthodox passage. Elman's more eccentric solos are really so outrageous that I, for one, cannot avoid a sneaking taste for them, just as I rather enjoy the more bizarre vocalists of the Orlando Roberson variety. The band still produced excellent swing instrumental recordings; one of its last before leaving RCA Victor and switching to Columbia was *Rose of Washington Square,* with Goodman and Stacy as soloists. By this time, the music of the Goodman band had almost certainly become formalised: it needed far greater variety in its approach. A number of first rate recordings were cut by

A scene from the film 'The Benny Goodman Story'. This is a re-enactment of the 1938 Carnegie Hall concert, with Teddy Wilson, Gene Krupa and Lionel Hampton as themselves, but actor Steve Allen playing Benny Goodman. The trumpeter on Krupa's right is Buck Clayton.

the band during 1940, notably *The Man I Love, Benny Rides Again* and *Superman,* but Goodman's most exciting and stimulating music at this time was with his sextet, which featured the brilliant guitarist Charlie Christian and latterly Cootie Williams. The three band titles just mentioned were all arranged by Eddie Sauter, who was the key figure in Goodman's finest band, that of 1941-42.

Sauter, who had established his reputation a few years earlier with the brilliant and subtle arrangements he provided for the Red Norvo band, was outside the mould of Goodman's established arrangers. Sauter's harmonic and contrapuntal innovations were highly individual, but once the band had become familiar enough with his methods to interpret his scores, it achieved a freshness of sound that made it one of the half dozen outstanding units of the swing era.

Sauter not only produced fine originals, but also possessed a rare ability to apply to his techniques to popular song material of the era, enriching many otherwise ordinary numbers. Helen Forrest had joined the band late in 1939 and the combination of her extremely pleasant singing and Sauter's arranging resulted in such attractive recordings as *More Than You Know, I Hear a Rhapsody* and *Perfidia. The Fable of the Rose* is typical of the harmonic subtlety of Sauter's scores; Elman contributes a sensitive muted solo, and Goodman himself, apparently revitalised in his solo work, plays thoughtfully.

Goodman's 1941-42 band had a strong group of soloists, notably trumpeters Billy Butterfield and Cootie Williams, trombonists Lou McGarity and Cutty Cutshall, tenor saxophonist Vido Musso, and pianist Mel Powell, who soon made his presence felt with *The Earl,* a tribute to Earl Hines, and the popular *Mission to Moscow.* Sauter wrote *Clarinet à la King* for Goodman, whose solo virtuosity remains an impressive testimony to his ability as a clarinettist. Peggy Lee had replaced Helen Forrest in the late summer of 1941, and Sauter wrote some superb scores for a number of tunes on which she was featured, foremost among them *That's The Way It Goes, I Got It Bad* and *My Old Flame.* The numerous other fine records made by the band at this time include *I'm Here,* with excellent solos by Williams, Goodman, McGarity and Cutshall, the last two in a chase sequence, and *Something New,* with contributions from Goodman, Jimmy Maxwell (trumpet), Les Robinson (alto saxophone), Butterfield, George Auld and Williams. A version of *Serenade in Blue,* with vocal by Dick Haymes, has some beautiful scoring by Sauter. The Goodman band at this time reached a peak of perfection, both technically and artistically, though there were such occasional lapses as the gruesome *Buckle down Winsocki* on which Goodman was unwise enough to sing. The entry of the United States into World War II presented Goodman with the same problem as all other leaders, and he found himself unable to maintain a stable personnel during the next few years.

With the recording ban, Goodman was away from the studios for over two years after his session of July 1942.

He recorded quite prolifically during 1945-47. His line-ups at this time underwent frequent changes; though some good records were made, they cannot be compared to those by the 1941-42 band. In 1948-49, Goodman dismayed his more conservative followers by leading a big band with strong bop overtones; he even had many of his most popular early numbers rescored in the bop manner. It is doubtful if Goodman himself really felt any involvement with the music this band was playing and he soon broke it up, reforming later in 1949 with what was to be his last regular personnel. During the past two decades, there have been some excellent recordings made by some of the specially assembled Goodman bands, but these are outside the scope of this book.

Goodman's relations with his musicians over the years were often stormy. He was by all accounts a hard bargainer over salaries—'Benny still has the first dollar he ever earned,' a musician once commented to me, though without malice—and his perfectionism led him to be intolerant of the slightest musical shortcomings. On the other hand, he had a great respect for certain musicians and could be generous in coming to the aid of those who needed help. Goodman, like most of the really successful bandleaders of the swing era, had a degree of ruthlessness in his make-up; a determination to maintain the highest possible standards is seldom a characteristic of the easygoing. The significance of Goodman's breakthrough in 1935 and its consequences is discussed elsewhere. It is surely time that he received a little more credit for his achievements from those jazz critics who tend to write them off so casually. On the strictest musical terms, Goodman's 1941-42 band must be rated as one of the finest of the big band era, and that of 1937-38 was an extremely good one. When all the exaggerated praise and 'King Of Swing' publicity is discounted, the basic fact of Goodman's enormous contribution to the development of big band jazz still remains a reality deserving of recognition.

Lionel Hampton's career in California, from his initial job with the Spikes Brothers to the lengthy spell with Les Hite, has already been covered in outline. After leaving Hite, he worked for a short while with Charlie Echols, then formed his own band which played around the Southern California area until 1936. While Hampton was resident at the Paradise Cafe in Hollywood, Benny Goodman and Gene Krupa came in to jam, a meeting that led to an initial recording by Hampton as part of the Benny Goodman Quartet in August 1936. Soon afterwards, Hampton was asked to join the Goodman organisation. From November 1936 until July 1940, he was a regular member of the quartet and an occasional drummer in the full band.

The nationwide reputation that Hampton gained as a result of working with Goodman led to an RCA Victor contract in 1937, and from that year until 1941 he recorded regularly with small to medium sized pick-up groups that featured the leading stars from the major big bands. A number of these recordings subsequently became recognised as classics of their kind. When Hampton finally left Goodman, he returned to California to organise a big band, thus following the path taken by Gene Krupa and Teddy Wilson, his former associates in the Benny Goodman Quartet. The band made its debut in Los Angeles the following November.

Hampton led a big band without break until the early 'fifties, and many musicians who later became well known obtained valuable experience under him. He continued to front big bands throughout the 'fifties and much of the 'sixties, though these were assembled for specific tours or engagements, with lay-offs between. He took his band overseas on many occasions, including visits to Africa, the Middle East, Australia, Japan and Europe. In the past few years, Hampton, who reached sixty-four on 12th April 1973, has been less active musically. However, he still emerges to play concerts and take part in radio and TV shows : in autumn 1972, the original Benny Goodman Quartet was reunited for the last time in a special TV spectacular sponsored by the Timex watch company.

Although he started out as a drummer, Hampton achieved eminence as a vibraphone player. He is one of the small band of jazz musicians to have made this instrument their major vehicle, and at his finest must be considered one of the outstanding jazz soloists of the swing era. Musicians of a later generation—notably Milt Jackson—have followed Hampton's lead in selecting the vibraphone as their main instrument, but its acceptance

Lionel Hampton at the drums during a British appearance with a big band.

within jazz certainly owes more to Hampton than to any other individual.

Hampton has always been an extrovert personality and a considerable showman, a fact which has been reflected in much of the music by his big bands. At the conclusion of his RCA Victor contract in 1941, he signed with US Decca, making his first appearance in the studio with his big band on Christmas Eve of that year. In May 1942, after a sextet date in March, Hampton led the full band at a session that produced its first recording of *Flying Home.* Over the years, this number has become associated with Hampton, who has recorded it many times (the first was under his own name with a section of the Benny Goodman band in February 1940), but this version with the obligatory tenor saxophone solo played by Illinois Jacquet and high note trumpet from Ernie Royal remains amongst the best, not least because it is exciting without degenerating into musical chaos. From the same session comes a hard driving performance of the riff theme *In the Bag,* with solos by Karl George (trumpet), Jacquet, Marshall Royal (clarinet) and Harry Sloan (trombone). The ensemble generates a tremendous swing on this number, and Hampton himself contributes some aggressive passages. These performances are archetypal Hampton, showing the musical policy that he was to maintain.

The Hampton band returned to the studios in 1944, after the recording ban. Few of the men present in the 1942 line-up now remained. *Chop-Chop* is one of the band's unsophisticated but effective up-tempo performances, with solos by Earl Bostic (alto saxophone), Al Sears (tenor saxophone) and Joe Morris (trumpet), but *Hamp's Boogie Woogie* introduces Hampton in the role of pianist. From time to time, Hampton has made records like this on which he plays the right hand piano part with a stabbing, percussive style that duplicates his vibraphone playing, while the regular pianist—in this case Milt Buckner—plays the left hand part. Although it might seem gimmickry to a listener who has never heard a performance, the actual results are entertaining and highly rhythmic. The later *Beulah's Boogie* is in similar style, though this time the second pianist is Dardanella Breckenridge and there are also solos from trumpeter Al Killian and tenor saxophonist Arnett Cobb, but *Tempo's Boogie,* a fine example of Hampton's great rhythmic ability, features him throughout on vibraphone.

Hampton has always been an outstanding ballad interpreter; and on *I Know That You Know,* he plays with considerable taste and drive. Quite different is the band's recording of Duke Ellington's *Rockin' in Rhythm,* originally issued as two sides of a record. The first part has excellent solos from Hampton, Cobb and alto saxophonist Ben Kynard; the second has short solos from the five trumpeters and four trombonists in sequence and closes with a rousing finale featuring trumpeter Joe Morris and Hampton playing drums alongside his regular percussionist. Another two part recording soon followed, this time of another number that has come to be associated

with Hampton—*Airmail Special*. The performance is a wild one, particularly in its later stages which feature Hampton and Cobb, but the band works up an exciting swing. *Adam Blew his Hat,* as its title indicates, is another extrovert affair, with solos from Cobb, Hampton, and trumpeters Jimmy Nottingham and Leo Sheppard. Among the best of the band's 1949 recordings are *New Central Avenue Breakdown,* a performance devoted to Hampton's hard hitting piano work, and *Hamp's Boogie Woogie No. 2* on which he shares the keyboard with the great boogie pianist Albert Ammons. During 1948, incidentally, the bop trumpeter Fats Navarro had worked for a while with Hampton, but no commercial recordings with him exist. Hampton stayed with Decca until 1950, a year from which one of his best recordings is the two part *Turkey Hop,* arranged by Sy Oliver, and featuring solos by Duke Garrette (trumpet), Al Grey (trombone), Jerome Richardson (alto saxophone), Benny Bailey, and Leo Sheppard (trumpet), Johnny Board (tenor saxophone) and Hampton himself.

The Hampton band's US Decca output of 1942-50 has not been too well served by reissue programmes until quite recently. Although it contains the inevitable percentage of ephemera, many fine performances deserve to be better known. The titles mentioned in the previous paragraph are by no means the only ones worthy of note.

After a spell with MGM, Hampton started recording in the early 'fifties for Norman Granz's Clef and Norgran labels. Apart from working with his regular band, he took part in many pick-up dates, quite a few of which also featured pianist Oscar Peterson. Some of these are outstanding, as is a superb date that Hampton made in Paris during 1953 with some members of his band, including his brilliant guitarist Billy Mackel, plus guests Mezz Mezzrow, Alix Combelle and Claude Bolling. From about this time, though, Hampton's big band recordings become more uneven, at their worst offering frenetic performances

The Lionel Hampton big band of the 1950s. Below: *Lionel Hampton flying home!*

of such old warhorses as *Flying Home* and *Airmail Special.*

A concert recording made in Chicago in July 1954 has a magnificent ballad version of *Stardust,* featuring Hampton throughout. He had already produced one classic performance of this number, at a 'Just Jazz' concert in the summer of 1947. Here, with changing tempos and a never ending flow of ideas, he proved beyond any shadow of doubt that he could still be a brilliantly inventive musician when the mood took him. He also made some good big band records for Norman Granz, as well as several that were mediocre. Among the good ones are *Pig Ears and Rice,* a blues on which the ensemble provides

a fine, controlled swing and Hampton plays an excellent piano solo, and *Midnight Sun,* another striking ballad feature for Hampton. A slightly different version of this number, though using the same arrangement by Sonny Burke, can be heard on a concert recording made in Amsterdam in October 1954. A 1959 session for the Audio Fidelity label resulted in new versions of such old Hampton favourites as *Airmail Special, Flying Home* and *Hey-Baba-Re-Bop,* but the band is a good one and the music stays on the right side of hysteria. None of Hampton's subsequent big band recordings is comparable to the best of his earlier output.

Numerous fine musicians have played with Hampton over the years, and certainly up to the 'fifties his recorded output includes many outstanding big band performances. Conservative jazz fans have been deterred by Hampton's flamboyance and the exhibitionist nature of much of his music at public performances, but the tradition in which he chooses to work is one that has very respectable jazz antecedents. Without being on the same level as the major bands at their peak, Hampton's have produced a great deal more worthwhile big band jazz than his detractors will allow. One hopes that current reissue programmes will make this apparent to a wider public.

The 'Bama State Collegians, a band formed of students at the State Teachers' College in Montgomery, Alabama, was working around its home territory in the early 'thirties. In 1934, directed by J. B. Sims, it went to New York, but made little impact until it came under the leadership of another ex-student, Erskine Hawkins, two years later.

Hawkins, usually billed as 'The 20th Century Gabriel', started playing trumpet in 1927 at fourteen, and had already appeared in public as both drummer and trombonist. After he was appointed leader of the 'Bama State Collegians, the band's title was retained on the records made for the US Vocalion label from July 1936 until February 1938. When it switched to RCA Victor's Bluebird label in the autumn of 1938, its releases appeared as by 'Erskine Hawkins (The Twentieth Century Gabriel) And His Orchestra'. The Hawkins band remained with RCA Victor until 1950, when it temporarily switched to Coral, then recorded for King in 1952-53. Since the mid 'fifties, Hawkins has worked mainly with small groups, though from time to time he has assembled big bands for specific engagements. In the past few years he has only occasionally made public appearances.

From the late 'thirties right through to the early 'fifties, the Erskine Hawkins band enjoyed considerable popularity in the United States, particularly with coloured audiences. Extremely popular with dancers, it was resident for long periods at New York's Savoy Ballroom. In the early 'fifties, some elements of rhythm-and-blues were introduced into its style. *Tuxedo Junction*—composed by Hawkins and band members Julian Dash and William Johnson—*After Hours* and *Bicycle Bounce* were the most popular record-ings that the band made, all achieving hit status. Oddly enough, very few of Hawkins's records were released in Europe, and his was probably the least known there of all the popular coloured bands before the era of micro-groove reissues.

The records made by the Hawkins band include a high proportion of riff and blues material, much of it written by William Johnson and Sammy Lowe who, with Avery Parrish, were its chief arrangers. Over the years the band had a number of good soloists, notably trumpeter Wilbur 'Dud' Bascomb, trombonist Robert Range, tenor saxophonists Paul Bascomb and Julian Dash, alto saxophonist William Johnson, baritone saxophonist and clarinettist Heywood Henry, and pianist Avery Parrish, with Dud Bascomb and Dash the most individual. Hawkins himself was a somewhat erratic soloist, given to flashy displays in the upper register, and his tone was sometimes poor. On occasions, though, he played well, particularly with mute, though as often as not such performances were offset by others in which he sounds like a black counterpart of Ziggy Ellman in his most eccentric mood—his closing solo on *Miss Hallelujah Brown* is an example of this. Fortunately Hawkins was generous in allocating solo space to Dud Bascomb, a trumpeter with a fine, powerful tone, a fund of individual ideas (some of them considered very modern at the time) and an unerring ability to swing.

The records that the Hawkins band made for US Columbia's Vocalion label are not outstanding, being too often marred by indifferent vocals. One of the best is *Uproar Shout,* written and arranged by William Johnson, which has jaunty ensemble playing and solos of variable quality, the best being by pianist Avery Parrish. The band was clearly influenced by the Jimmie Lunceford group,

Erskine Hawkins in the late 1930s when he was billed as 'The Twentieth Century Gabriel'.

233

largely, it seems, because of arranger Sammy Lowe's admiration for Sy Oliver. Such recordings as *Rockin' Rollers Jubilee* and *Miss Hallelujah Brown* have ensemble and sax section passages very much in the Lunceford vein. Both Bascomb and Dash have good solos on these performances, and Hawkins takes off for some convoluted high note wanderings at the close. Much better are two Johnson arrangements: *Swingin' on Lenox Avenue,* with a particularly fine solo by Dud Bascomb and a good one by Dash, and the attractive *A Study in Blue.* Dash, like Paul Bascomb, was strongly influenced by 'Chu' Berry, but, unlike the latter, utilised elements of Berry's style to fashion an individual mode of expression. Drier in tone than most of his contemporaries, Dash played in a bustling manner which gave an aura of urgency to most of his solos. Although he no longer works regularly as a musician, he is still a very good soloist.

A session of July 1939 was a particularly good one, producing three outstanding performances. *Tuxedo Junction* is far superior to the better known Glenn Miller version. It has Hawkins playing the theme at the opening and close; in between are solos by Johnson, Dud Bascomb and Henry (clarinet). *Gin Mill Special* includes very good solos from Dud Bascomb and Dash. The theme is derived from a riff used by Cootie Williams during his solo on the original version of Duke Ellington's *Stompy Jones.* *Weddin' Blues* offers relaxed ensemble and section work, with solos from Robert Range, Dud Bascomb (with plunger), Dash and Hawkins, who shows more taste and control here than he often did. The band always played well on blues. *Junction Blues* was written by Hawkins and Sammy Lowe, with the latter providing the arrangement. It opens and closes with attractive guitar work from William McLemore and contains pleasant solos from Johnson, Hawkins and Henry, the use of Henry's clarinet against the full ensemble being extremely effective. *After Hours,* certainly Hawkins's most popular recording, is a feature for the excellent blues piano playing of Avery Parrish; its success led to a number of recreations by other bands.

The Erskine Hawkins band in the early 1940s. Below: Julian Dash, for many years a leading soloist in the Hawkins band.

In 1941, Avery Parrish was again featured extensively on a recording of *Black Out,* an agreeable performance, as is the spirited *Shipyard Ramble,* with good solos from Henry (baritone saxophone), Hawkins, Dud Bascomb (with plunger) and Dash. The same musicians, with Henry switching to clarinet, are also the soloists on the excellent *Bicycle Bounce,* one of the best of Hawkins's records. A month later, in June 1942, the band had a minor hit with *Bear Mash Blues.* This title has one of William Johnson's best recorded solos—he often showed the influence of Benny Carter on his playing—and there are also effective contributions from Dud Bascomb, Hawkins and Range.

The date that produced *Bear Mash Blues* was Hawkins's last before the 1942-44 recording ban. He did not return to the studios until January 1945. From 1945 to 1947 Hawkins's brass section, including himself, was either

234

nine or ten strong, though the additions made less difference to his music than it did for several of his contemporaries. Undoubtedly the band's outstanding recording of 1945 was the splendid *Holiday for Swing* with the solos only by Hawkins himself and Julian Dash. Both Dud Bascomb and Avery Parrish had by now left the band, but the tradition of featuring another trumpeter on recordings was continued with Bobby Johnson, heard in plunger passages on *Tippin' In* and *Sneakin' Out*.

In 1950, Hawkins's contract with RCA Victor was finally terminated and he then took part in three recording sessions for the Coral label. Several of the titles made were remakes of earlier successes—*Tuxedo Junction, Bear Mash Blues* and *After Hours*—but are well done, particularly *Tuxedo* with its good solos by Dash, Hawkins and Henry (baritone saxophone). *Nona*, with Bobby Johnson and Dash playing extremely well, is superior to the original recording. With rhythm-and-blues coming to the fore, there was increasing emphasis in the records that the Hawkins band made for the King label in 1952-53 on the heavy beat associated with that style, though the fact that it had always featured a great deal of blues material now stood it in good stead. *Steel Guitar Rag* has the ensemble generating a strong powerhouse sound, in the manner of many big bands of the period, but it swings well and the solos by Dash and Bobby Johnson are good. *Double Shot*, made with a nine piece group, has an excellent solo by Dash against a driving riff background, while *Down the Alley*, an obvious attempt to duplicate *After Hours*, has good alto saxophone work by Bobby Smith—very much in the style of his namesake Willie—and reasonable piano by Freddie Jefferson.

The Hawkins band was not in the top bracket, if one assesses it in comparison with the Basie, Ellington or Lunceford bands at their best, but far more than them, it concerned itself with shaping its music to satisfy dancers. It lacked the total individuality of the leading groups of its era, perhaps too often sounding derivative of Lunceford. For its public, it was highly effective, not least in its choice of tempos and material. Over the years, it produced consistently good, if seldom great, records, and its main soloists are easily identifiable. It had talented arrangers, was always technically impeccable, and never failed to swing. In the last resort, its strengths outweighed its weaknesses.

Woodrow 'Woody' Herman must have fronted more different bands than any other leader. He still regularly appears in public with a big band, as often as not consisting of unknown musicians, then disbands for a while and reappears with an almost totally new unit. It was not always this way, for during the 'thirties and 'forties Herman led several bands which retained stable personnels for quite long periods.

After working in vaudeville as a child, Herman studied the saxophone and clarinet, initially with the intention of using them in his act. He worked with a number of obscure dance bands from the late 'twenties; his longest stay was with Tom Gerunovitch from 1929 to 1933. After brief periods with Harry Sosnick, Gus Arnheim and Joe Moss, he joined Isham Jones in 1934 and remained until Jones broke up the band in the summer of 1936. Herman, with five other ex-Isham Jones musicians, then became part of a co-operative band which made its debut at the Roseland in Brooklyn late in the year and started to record for the US Decca label almost immediately. It billed itself as 'The Band That Plays The Blues' and retained the title into the early 'forties. While it certainly recorded a fair proportion of blues material during the first few years of its existence, by 1942 its repertoire was obviously undergoing the transformation that was to produce startling results three years later. In the band's output from 1937 to 1942, it is noticeable that its blues recordings were more than balanced by performances of popular song material of the day, usually with vocals by Herman or one of several female singers, and swing-style instrumentals.

Herman himself is a pleasant and highly competent clarinettist, an agreeable Johnny Hodges-influenced alto saxophonist, and a reasonable singer. He sang on most of the band's blues numbers but there is, not surprisingly, an ersatz quality about his vocals in this vein. They are acceptable enough on their own terms, which are certainly not those of the authentic blues. The first blues item the band recorded was *Dupree Blues*—better known as *Betty and Dupree*—much of which was given over to Herman's vocal. The performance does have solos from two members of the band who could play fine instrumental blues, the more interesting coming from Joe Bishop. Bishop, for some years the band's chief arranger, played flugelhorn in the brass section; the deeper tone of his instrument proved very effective in a blues setting. The other good blues player was trombonist Neal Reid, an expert with mutes, who sometimes sounded a little like Floyd O'Brien. On occasion, guitarist Hy White could also sound very effective in a blues setting, as on *Blues Downstairs* and *Blues Upstairs*, not just in solo but in his mandolin-like backing to Herman's vocal. This two-part performance has boogie playing from pianist Tommy Lineham, a pleasant clarinet solo by Herman against wa-wa brass, excellent solos by Bishop, and a reasonable contribution from tenor saxophonist Saxie Mansfield. The arrangement, by Bishop, is somewhat in the Bob Crosby manner.

Casbah Blues is a little too theatrical, but *Dallas Blues* has excellent solos from Herman and Reid; the performance as a whole is helped by the drumming of Frank Carlson. One of the more bizarre recordings that stems from this period is *Laughing Boy Blues*, with Sonny Skylar providing a curious laughing routine that is ultimately more disturbing than humorous.

The Herman band had its struggles during the first two years of its existence, but its fortunes started to improve with its highly successful recording of *At the Woodchoppers' Ball* in 1939. Herman has said that the

Woody Herman in the late 1930s.

number has haunted him through the years. However, there is no denying its importance in providing the band's first hit recording. The moody *Blue Flame,* written and arranged by Joe Bishop, proved almost equally successful in 1941; Herman plays a good clarinet solo against a background of reeds and trombones in the lower register before Reid enters for a fine muted passage.

With the mid 'forties, it was clear that Herman's band was taking a new direction. As early as 1942, it had recorded one of Dizzy Gillespie's first scores for a big band, *Down Under,* and its 1943-44 Decca issues were very different to the sound of 'The Band That Played The Blues'. Herman, always a warm admirer of the Ellington band, introduced some Ellingtonian guests on recordings at this time: Ray Nance, Johnny Hodges and Juan Tizol appeared on a delightful version of *Perdido,* and Ben Webster on the excellent *Basie's Basement.* The band now sounded a great deal more modern, with none of the Dixieland overtones that sometimes appeared on earlier performances. Other first-rate records from this period are *Cherry,* with guest Budd Johnson taking a very good solo, and the exhilarating *Ingie Speaks,* on which White is particularly impressive.

Extensive changes of personnel were taking place in the Herman band during these years, but few could have been prepared for the music that it recorded at its first two sessions for US Columbia in 1945. From these came the famous *Apple Honey* and *Caldonia,* soon followed by *Goosey Gander, Northwest Passage* and *Wild Root.* Discussing this band, Alun Morgan has written: 'The strength of the band lay in its ensemble playing and

the fact that the soloists were used to cap arrangements at the most climactic points; typical of the band's strength in this direction is Neal Hefti's *Good Earth* where the surging power of the ensemble boosts Flip Phillips into orbit for a brief but very important tenor solo.'

Few big bands could create the excitement of this group, later known as The First Herd. Its soloists included the gifted Sonny Berman, who was to die in 1947 in his twenty-third year, the frenetic Pete Candoli, trombonist Bill Harris, tenor saxophonist Flip Phillips, and vibraphonist Marjorie Hyams. The rhythm section was sparked by bassist Chubby Jackson and drummer Dave Tough; Jackson was a key figure in assembling the personnel. Many of the musicians were deeply involved in the evolving bop style, and were determined to feature modern ideas in a big band setting. However, Herman was sensible enough to maintain some balance in his repertoire, retaining a percentage of popular song material with vocals by himself or the excellent Frances Wayne. His experience also led him to realise that it was essential to present programmes in which contrasts, both of mood and tempo, were maintained. He was thus able to appeal to a fair segment of the big band audience. Listening to the First Herd's records today, one is still impressed by the tremendous vitality and enthusiasm of the band; its style, despite the modernist inclinations of some of the soloists, owed rather more to the swing era than some of its members would probably have been prepared to admit at the time. One man who was greatly impressed upon hearing the band was Igor Stravinsky. In March 1946, it presented his specially written *Ebony Concerto* at a Carnegie Hall concert.

The First Herd broke up in December 1946; nine months later, the Second Herd made its debut. Although this band could on occasion be as extrovert as its predecessor, as such recordings as *That's Right* and *Lemon Drop* well illustrate, its character was somewhat different. Several of its soloists were under the strong influence of Charlie Parker and Lester Young, and an important recording of *Four Brothers* had long-term effects on later Herman bands. This number, written and arranged for the band by Jimmy Guiffre, was designed to feature its reed section of Stan Getz, Zoot Sims, Herbie Steward and Serge Chaloff. Since then, Herman's band have invariably had a sax line-up of three tenors and one baritone instead of the more conventional instrumentation. Perhaps the best known single recording by the Second Herd is that of Ralph Burns's *Early Autumn,* primarily for Stan Getz's ethereal solo. This beautiful theme was originally part of Burns's four part *Summer Sequence,* a delightful Ellington-influenced composition that was recorded by the First Herd.

Throughout the 'fifties, Herman fronted various 'Herds', touring Europe for the first time in 1954. His band of 1952-53, with trombonists Carl Fontana and Urbie Green and tenor saxophonist Arno Marsh as its main soloists, recorded mainly for Herman's own label Mars. Ralph

Burns and Nat Pierce were then the principal arrangers, and the band turned out a succession of straightforward instrumental performances of a high order. The old favourite *Moten Swing*, in an arrangement by Burns and Urbie Green, features good solos by Fontana and Marsh. The Latin-styled *Teressita* has a pleasant alto solo by Herman. *Celestial Blues* derives its title from the fact that Pierce introduces the theme on celeste and later plays a solo on that instrument; other contributions are by Marsh, trumpeter Don Fagerquist, and Herman. The band was a good one, and its style was that of a conventional, if updated, swing group.

Another excellent Herman band was that of 1955. A session that stretched over two days in June of that year produced some particularly good performances, notably *I Remember Duke, Sentimental Journey* and Horace Silver's *Opus de Funk*. The soloists now were bass-trumpeter Cy Touff, trumpeter Dick Collins, trombonist Keith Moon, tenor saxophonist Richie Kamuca, Pierce and Herman; at this period, Herman seemed to be featuring himself more than usual on alto saxophone.

Throughout the remaining years of the 'fifties, and the whole of the 'sixties, Herman formed bands that worked for part of each year, making several more trips to Europe. His last outstanding units were probably those of 1964 and 1965. The former recorded a good LP while working at a club in Nevada. For a while, vocalist Joe Carroll was with Herman. He can be heard on the humorous *Wa-Wa Blues* and *What Kind of Fool Am I?* The band had several effective soloists, notably trumpeter Dusko Goykevich, trombonist Phil Wilson and tenor saxophonist Gary Klein, and the lead trumpet of Bill Chase was an important asset. *Dear John C,* a musical tribute to the late John Coltrane based on Miles Davis's *So What,* is an excellent all round performance, with pleasant solos from Goykevich and Klein. Bob Hammer's arrangement of the Lennon-McCartney *The Things We Said Today* brings back memories of the 1941 *Blue Flame* with its backing of saxes and low register trombones behind Herman's alto, and it was Hammer who wrote and arranged *Dear John C.*

Herman, now sixty years of age, still organises bands for specific tours and engagements, though in the last year or two, his attempts to combine big band jazz with elements of contemporary pop have not been too successful. He also faces the major problem of all the dwindling group of big band leaders—a paucity of really individual soloists. It is understandable that Herman does not wish to lead bands that would merely present second-hand versions of former hits, but his efforts to mix jazz and rock seems to have landed him in another musical cul-de-sac.

Over the years Herman has led so many outstanding big bands that it is not possible here to do more than discuss a few of them somewhat perfunctorily. It was quite a long pull, in stylistic terms, from 'The Band That Plays The Blues' to the First and Second Herds, yet the records show that the development followed a logical course. In reminiscing about his earlier bands (and it is worth recalling that a quarter of a century has passed since the demise of the Second Herd), Herman speaks of them all with affection, for each represented a particular phase in big band history. The survivors of the swing era are now few in number, and many have reached an advanced age, but I have the feeling that the last one to throw in his hand will be Herman. He, even more than Dizzy Gillespie to whom Alun Morgan applied the phrase, is truly 'a compulsive big band leader'.

If Earl Hines had retired from music instead of forming his first band in 1928, his place in jazz history would have been assured. Already through his brilliant solo recordings for QRS and Columbia and the classic titles he made with Louis Armstrong and Jimmie Noone, he had gained recognition as a superb virtuoso pianist who was years ahead of his time. Happily, Hines has remained in music to the present day, unlike many of his contemporaries, with no apparent diminution of his creativity.

Hines was born into a musical family; he started out on the cornet but studied the piano from the age of nine. In 1923, still only in his nineteenth year, he worked with vocalist Lois B. Deppe in his hometown of Pittsburgh, subsequently touring with Deppe and making his first records with him in the autumn. In 1924, he went to Chicago for the first time, and within three years was securely established there through working with Carroll Dickerson, Erskine Tate and other leaders. During part of 1927, Hines was the musical director for Louis Armstrong's Stompers at the Sunset Cafe. He also joined Armstrong and Zutty Singleton in a short-lived venture to run their own club. Late in the year he started working with clarinettist Jimmy Noone at the Apex Club. In 1928, he made a trip to New York to record his solos for the QRS company.

On 28th December 1928, his twenty-fifth birthday, Hines opened at the Grand Terrace in Chicago with his first big band. For the next eleven years, that ballroom was his home base. From time to time, the Hines band went out on tour, though its New York appearances were infrequent. He kept it together until temporarily disbanding early in 1940. A radio announcer had given Hines the nickname of 'Fatha' while he was working at the Grand Terrace during the 'thirties; it has stuck with him down to the present time.

After a month or two in 1940 running his own club, Hines formed a new big band and with many changes of personnel, kept it together for seven years. In 1943, he had a number of the pioneer bop musicians in his band, including Dizzy Gillespie and Charlie Parker, but as this was the period of the AFoM ban, the group never recorded. For a short period in 1943, Hines also included an all-female string section. When the big band era drew to a close, Hines again ran a club in Chicago for a few months, then joined the Louis Armstrong All Stars in

January 1948 and remained with them until the autumn of 1951. For a brief period during 1948, Hines led a big band that toured with the Armstrong All Stars.

During the early 'fifties, Hines led his own small groups, securing a lengthy residency at the Hangover Club in San Francisco from September 1955. His group at the club when I heard it there during the autumn of 1958 included Muggsy Spanier, Jimmy Archey and Darnell Howard, but the Hangover appeared to cater for an audience with little real interest in the music. The Hines band went through a routine of playing Dixieland standards with professionalism but little enthusiasm. Hines became a resident of Oakland, California, in 1960, running his own club there three years later. It appeared that his career from this point would be spent in relative obscurity, but in 1964 he went to New York where he scored a sensational success at concerts at the Little Theatre and a residency at Birdland. A year later, he toured Europe and since then has been a regular visitor, including one trip to Russia as leader of a sextet in 1966. He prefers these days to work with a small group, but does appear occasionally as a solo performer. He has been a prolific recording artist during the past decade, both in the United States and in Europe, and his continuing brilliance remains a source of constant pleasure to record buyers throughout the world. Curiously enough, though accepted as one of the greatest soloists that jazz has produced, Hines himself has insisted on a number of occasions that he is really a band pianist and prefers working in that setting. An inveterate showman and on-stage an outgoing personality, Hines celebrated his seventieth birthday on 28th December 1973.

The first band that Hines led at the Grand Terrace during 1929 took part in half a dozen sessions for RCA Victor; nine titles were released. On the evidence of such recordings as Beau-Koo Jack, Chicago Rhythm and Grand Piano Blues it was, for the period, an efficient group, though one without any particular identity. The highspots of the recordings are, inevitably, Hines's own solos, but the band included within its ranks such good soloists as reedmen Cecil Irwin and Toby Turner and trumpeter Shirley Clay. After Hines, it is Clay, with his powerful, broad-toned solos, who most captures the attention of a later generation of record listeners. Hines once told me that during the late 'twenties, Clay was being built up in Chicago as a possible rival to Louis Armstrong. Though Clay was undoubtedly a fine musician, the fact that his style at the time owed much to Armstrong makes the attempt seem somewhat pointless.

After the RCA Victor recordings, almost three years elapsed before the Hines band entered the studios again, by now consisting of three trumpets, two trombones, three reeds (soon increased to four) and four rhythm, with only trombonist William Franklin and reedman Cecil Irwin remaining from the 1929 personnel. Between June 1932 and March 1934, it took part in six sessions for the US Brunswick label, on one of which Hines also recorded

two piano solos. Jimmy Mundy joined in late 1932 and remained for close on four years, becoming the band's chief arranger. The Hines band seemed to be particularly well served for arrangers at this period, for scores were also regularly provided by George Dixon, Lawrence Dixon, Cecil Irwin and Quinn Wilson.

The first recording of a tune long associated with Hines—Rosetta—took place in 1933, with solos from Omer Simeon (alto and baritone saxophone), Hines and Darnell Howard (clarinet), and an attractive vocal in what was no doubt intended to be in the Armstrong manner from trumpeter Walter Fuller. The same session also produced the first of two recordings of Jimmy Mundy's Cavernism, with solos from Fuller, Hines and Howard, the latter switching to violin. Harlem Lament, written and arranged by Quinn Wilson, is notable for a solo of great rhythmic complexity and swing from Hines; the only other musician to be given a solo is trumpeter Charlie Allen, who contributes a melodic muted passage. Darkness is an Earl Hines composition, though he does not feature himself to any extent on the recording, the solos being by Simeon (alto saxophone), Dixon (muted), Fuller (open and with plunger), Howard (clarinet) and Franklin. Howard's flowing solo is particularly good, and with the New Orleans clarinettist Omer Simeon also in the band, Hines had two exceptional performers on this instrument. Simeon is featured in an excellent clarinet solo on Swingin' Down (he can also be heard on alto saxophone), a performance on which the drive of the band is impressive, particularly in the closing ensemble chorus which has crisp work by the trumpet section.

In September 1934, Hines began recording for the US Decca label. At three sessions, the band produced a total of sixteen titles. From the first date came a new version of Rosetta, with dazzling piano by Hines, a pleasant alto solo by Simeon, and another rather breathless vocal from Fuller. Quinn Wilson's arrangement of Scott Joplin's Maple Leaf Rag is particularly interesting, with Hines playing superbly, though his approach would probably not please ragtime purists. Jelly Roll Morton's Wolverine Blues finds the band in outstanding form; the solos are by Dixon, Simeon (alto), Hines, Fuller and Howard (clarinet). The same session also produced a driving version of Copenhagen with excellent individual contributions from Mundy (tenor), Fuller, trombonist James 'Trummy' Young, Hines and Howard (clarinet). Young had been added to the band in October 1933, and was already demonstrating the unique style that was to come to its peak during his subsequent years with the Jimmie Lunceford band. The final Decca date resulted in a splendid version of Japanese Sandman, with solos by Young, Simeon (clarinet) and Hines, and an attractive version of Blue Because of You with excellent muted trumpet by George Dixon and beautiful solo and supporting piano by Hines.

For some reason, the band did not record again for two years, by which time Budd Johnson had commenced

The Earl Hines band, c1940. Billy Eckstine is on the extreme right, and Hines is the only musician not shown.

what was to be an important association with Hines. During 1937 and 1938, it went into the studio on four occasions, the titles from the second date being issued only many years later. *Pianology* is one of the best of Hines's recordings from this period: apart from his extraordinary piano work, it has good solos by Budd Johnson (tenor saxophone), Howard (clarinet) and Fuller. Almost as good is *Rhythm Sundae,* with yet another superb solo from Hines and a striking contribution from Young, and the later *Solid Mama* with strong ensemble playing and attractive solos by William Randall (clarinet), Hines and Dixon.

In many ways, I find Hines's band of 1934-37 the best integrated of all those that he led, though most collectors seem to prefer his band of the 1939-42 period. It had a number of good soloists—Fuller, Dixon, Young, Simeon and Howard—most of whom were genuinely individual in style, and achieved an individual sound that I feel later bands lacked. At its best, it produced a surging yet relaxed swing during ensemble passages, and its repertoire was

extremely wide ranging. It is a commonplace of jazz criticism to blame recording directors for the poorer output of many artists, but a transcription of a broadcast by the Hines band from the Grand Terrace in August 1938 suggests that recording directors might in fact have had a very good influence on Hines when he went into the studio. Certainly the band never recorded such dismal performances as those of *Teacher's Pet, Colorado Sunset* or *Bambino* heard on this occasion, though one should add that it was called upon to play an immense variety of material during working hours, including much of the ephemera of the day.

From July 1939 until the onset of the 1942 recording ban, the Hines band was contracted to RCA Victor, and its output appeared on the low-priced Bluebird label. There were numerous personnel changes over this period, but it was one in which Hines certainly attracted the greatest public attention, particularly when his recording of *Boogie Woogie on St Louis Blues* became a hit in 1940. The band sound was now heavier, partly because of its seven brass and five reeds, and its style at times seemed to be patterned on that of the Jimmie Lunceford band. Billy Eckstine had joined in late 1939 and his singing on many recordings proved immensely popular, particularly in the case of *Jelly, Jelly* and *Stormy Monday Blues.*

Amongst the many excellent instrumental performances recorded by the Hines band during 1939-42 are *G.T. Stomp* (drummer Alvin Burroughs, trumpeter Edward Simms, Fuller), *Grand Terrace Shuffle* (trombonist John Ewing, Budd Johnson, tenor saxophonist Bob Crowder), *Father Steps In* (Simms, Crowder, Johnson—on alto—and Fuller), *Deep Forest* (Crowder, Simms, Simeon), *Windy City Jive* (Johnson, trumpeter Harry Jackson, Ewing) and *Second Balcony Jump* (Johnson, trumpeter Shorty McConnell). In each instance, I have named soloists after titles, though of course Hines is heard in a solo role as well as the men mentioned. There are many other fine recordings from this period. Of the men new to the band, the most impressive are alto saxophonist George 'Scoops' Carry, an individual soloist heard to particular advantage on *Yellow Fire,* tenor saxophonist Bob Crowder who played in a bustling style that owed a great deal to 'Chu' Berry, and the brilliant drummer Alvin Burroughs. In his earlier career, Burroughs had worked with Walter Page's Blue Devils and the Alphonso Trent band, and he is one of the drummers most often singled out by Jo Jones for special praise. Hines produced an excellent body of big band recordings at this time. Few of the band's contemporaries could match it for swing, but it just failed to make the top grade through a failure to establish a really personal identity.

Hines recorded with a regular big band for the last time in 1946 and 1947. Many of the performances made then were never released at the time but subsequently saw the light of day in the microgroove era. Several of the recordings are marred by average vocals from Dolores Parker and excruciatingly poor ones from 'Lord Essex' (Essex Scott). However, the band as a whole is a fine one, though showing a tendency to the overblown freneticism that was prevalent during the late swing era. *Blue Keys* has excellent solos by Hines, tenor saxophonist Wardell Gray and trumpeter Willie Cook; *Let's Get Started* features Gray, Hines and Carry to good effect; while *Bamby* offers fine solos from the same trio. The splendid trombonist Bennie Green has an attractive solo on the jaunty *Throwing the Switch,* on which Hines is also outstanding, and *Trick a Track* finds Gray at his best. These instrumental recordings are certainly spirited and the band swings strongly; all that is missing is the attention to dynamics and varied orchestral textures that was a hallmark of the leading bands in the preceding years. It can be exciting to hear a big band ensemble roaring out as on these recordings, but in the end one wishes for a change of pace and a switch to a less assertive mood.

Over the years, Earl Hines's big bands always included a strong contingent of jazz soloists, always swung powerfully, and always kept within the basic big band jazz tradition. Hines's playing with his bands is of so remarkable a standard and so astonishing in its unflagging creativity that it lifts even the more casual performances. If he is, in his own words, 'just a band pianist', then one need seek no further justification for the validity of big bands.

Buck Clayton once told me that when he heard Harry James for the first time in 1936—James was then playing with the Ben Pollack band—he thought that James should join Benny Goodman. A few months later James did just that, and from January 1937 until December 1938 built up an enormous following under Goodman. James's father was a conductor for various circus bands and started teaching him to play trumpet in 1926, when he was ten years old. For most of his youth, James knew only the wandering life that went with his father's employment, but in 1931 the family settled in Beaumont, Texas, and he began to work with various local bands. With one of these groups, led by a violinist called Joe Gill, James toured as far afield as New Orleans. His first major job was with Ben Pollack in 1935. When he left Pollack and became a member of the Goodman band, he joined forces with Ziggy Elman and Chris Griffin to form one of the best known trumpet sections of the swing era.

Any musician who became as celebrated as James did with Goodman inevitably began to think about forming his own band, and he was no exception. With Goodman's blessing, and some financial backing from him, James began organising a big band early in 1939 and made his debut fronting it at a Philadelphia hotel. During the early 'forties, James was particularly successful, earning as much as $12,500 for a single night's engagement and racking up huge sales with his records. He continued to lead a band until the early 'fifties, then retired for a while from full time working. He returned later in the decade and continued right through the 'sixties and into the 'seventies leading a big band for the greater part of the year. His ability to keep the band together depended on regular and lengthy residencies in Las Vegas. He did not play in New York from 1953 to 1960; since then, he has made a number of appearances there, including a concert at the Carnegie Hall in 1964. He toured Europe in 1957, and in 1972 brought his band to Britain for the first time. He has appeared with his band in numerous films, and dubbed the trumpet solos for Kirk Douglas in 'Young Man With A Horn', a film based on Dorothy Baker's novel, which was supposed to deal with the life of the late Bix Beiderbecke.

In the context of big band jazz, James presents problems. Although he always included good jazz musicians in his bands, they had little chance to shine in his early years. More than most leaders, James dominated in-person and recorded performances, particularly during most of the 'forties, when his band often provided little more than a backdrop for James's solos. All that one can really say about most of his recordings of this period is that they show his band to be a highly proficient unit, performing what it is called upon to play in an expert manner. For much of his career as a bandleader, James

Harry James, now one of the longest serving bandleaders of them all.

has followed a very commercial path and has gained his following more for saccharine-toned solos on such numbers as *You Made Me Love You* and *Three Coins in the Fountain* than for jazz performances. Paradoxically, James's bands have followed a more committed jazz policy in the years since the big band era; his current group is much more of a jazz unit than any he led at the height of his popularity.

James was always a brash soloist, but within the Goodman band, he was forced to discipline his work. Goodman would hardly have looked with favour on the style James was later to use on such hit recordings as *Flight of the Bumble Bee* and *Carnival in Venice*. During the 'forties, the musical vulgarity that usually lurked just below the surface of James's work was given a free rein, but the following decade saw a return to a more disciplined, jazz-oriented approach. At times, he seems to be unsure of his direction: his more recent recordings have veered between nostalgic recreations of past swing hits, versions of pop numbers, and original jazz material with a strong Basie influence. Yet in live appearances with his current band, there is every impression of jazz involvement. Though there is a strong overtone of Basie in much of the music, it is performed with a freshness and enthusiasm that has been absent from Basie's own recordings for many years. In any case, it is unlikely that James needs to lead a big band for financial reasons, and the fact that he chooses

to work within this format suggests genuine enthusiasm.

James first recorded under his own name with pick-up groups: three sessions had a line-up of Jess Stacy and himself from the Goodman band plus seven Basie musicians and vocalist Helen Humes. A fourth session had him fronting fellow members of the Goodman band with Harry Carney of the Duke Ellington band as a lone guest. These are probably the best jazz records issued under James's name, particularly those with the Basie men, which are quite outstanding. With his own regular band, he first recorded in February 1939. His initial title indicated the path he was soon to follow. This was a version of *Ciribiribin,* though it was a later recording of the number that became a big hit. The band that James fronted at this time was competent, if routine; his solo work carried it. It made a number of adequate instrumental recordings, amongst which are *Two O'Clock Jump, King Porter Stomp, Flash* and *Feet Draggin' Blues* —a selection of these would make an agreeable LP.

In November 1939, the James band produced two big hit recordings: a new version of *Ciribiribin,* with a vocal by Frank Sinatra, and the sugary *Concerto for Trumpet.* Then, in 1940, James signed a contract with the Varsity label, a move that could hardly have been beneficial in terms of record sales. The Varsity recordings by James are now rare; among a few jazz instrumentals and more numerous popular titles with vocals by Dick Haymes can be found his initial waxings of *Carnival in Venice* and *Flight of the Bumble Bee.* Because of Varsity's poor distribution, they did not cause much of a stir at the time. However, within a month of returning to Columbia in 1941, he made fresh versions that became enormously popular. James's playing on these numbers has nothing to do with jazz, but a few jazz instrumentals were recorded in 1941—*Jeffries' Blues, Sharp as a Tack* and *Jughead*— as they were in the following year, but these formed only a fraction of James's output. The big successes with the public were schmaltzy performances like *By the Sleepy Lagoon* and *Estrellita.*

From the autumn of 1941, James had added a string section to his band. He continued to feature it until late in the decade. No commercial recordings could be made during 1943 and most of 1944. When they were resumed late in the latter year, James had a reasonable contingent of jazz musicians in his band. Foremost was alto saxophonist Willie Smith, one of the leading stylists on his instrument during the 'thirties and an unequalled section leader. There were also tenor saxophonist Gene 'Corky' Corcoran and pianist Arnold Ross. Between 1944 and 1955, when James finally ceased recording for Columbia and switched to Capitol, the bulk of his recordings continued to be commercial in intent and performance, but there were such exceptions as *9:20 Special, The Beaumont Ride, Moten Swing, Vine Street Blues, Tuxedo Junction, Ultra* and *Roll 'em,* and even occasional items by a small jazz-orientated group. A concert recorded at the Hollywood Palladium in January 1954 finds the band in excellent form, and good versions of *Sugar Foot Stomp, Flash* and *Bye Bye Blues* were made. In contrast, the next studio date had James back in his most saccharine style on numbers like *Three Coins in the Fountain* and *Hernando's Hideaway*. At one of three sessions undertaken in December 1954 and February 1955 to provide material for an LP, a quite remarkable solo feature of *Bali Ha'i* was recorded. This features Willie Smith in virtuoso form, but the virtuosity is controlled by a keen musical intelligence and the performance has shape and discipline about it. From the same sessions come a good version of *Perdido*, with excellent solos by James and Smith, and a Basie-ish *Marchin'* with neat muted work by James.

Since the late 'fifties, the James band has made numerous LPs of big band jazz. At times, the Basie influence has seemed overwhelming, but slowly a more personal approach has become evident. Part of the Basie influence is probably because much of the band's book is the work of arrangers like Ernie Wilkins and Neal Hefti, who also played a large part in setting Basie's post-1950 style. *Blues for Lovers Only* and *Ring for Porter* (based on *King Porter Stomp*) from a 1957 date, and *Warm Blue Stream* and *Bells* from one of a year later, show the revitalised James band at something like its best. Willie Smith has fine solos on all but *Ring*, and James plays with a welcome astringency of tone. A pleasing departure from the conventional occurs on a 1962 LP where a five strong Dixieland front line, including Eddie Miller and Matty Matlock, is heard against the full band. Matlock arranged some of the numbers, including the famous Louis Armstrong showcase of the 'twenties, *Cornet Chop Suey,* and his individual approach is refreshing. Eddie Miller has pensive, melodic solos on *Two Deuces* and *My Inspiration,* and it is interesting to hear James soloing in such famous Armstrong features as *Cornet Chop Suey, Weather Bird* and *Two Deuces.* In general he disciplines himself admirably, only occasionally permitting himself a few bravura flourishes; on *Squeeze Me* he plays particularly well. James's most recent LPs have reverted to a more florid approach, but his personal appearances invariably feature him playing big band jazz.

James's bands, however good they might be on a technical level, have never really established a personal identity, but have generally reflected the conventions of their era. This may in part be due to the very strong eclecticism of James's own playing. While he can produce effective jazz solos, he has never been as totally convincing a jazz stylist as, say, Bunny Berigan. However, during the past fifteen years or so, his determination to maintain a band that works within the broad traditions of big band jazz has been self-evident, and for that he deserves the respect of all followers of this form of music.

Andy Kirk was never an outstanding instrumentalist, though he was sufficiently competent to perform as a sideman in his own and other bands for several years. Kirk was born on 28th May 1898 at Newport,

Kentucky, and moved with his family to Denver, Colorado, in his childhood. He studied piano and alto sax at the time of World War I, but did not work as a musician until sometime in the early 'twenties, when he joined George Morrison's band, doubling tuba and bass sax. Morrison's was a society band and Kirk told Frank Driggs, in an interview published in the February 1959 *Jazz Review*, that his first contact with real jazz came when Gene Coy's Happy Black Aces played in Denver. Around the same time, he heard Jelly Roll Morton perform as a soloist and was influenced a great deal by Morton's rhythmic conception. Kirk worked for a while as a postman before accepting an offer to join Terrence 'T' Holder's band in Dallas, probably in 1925 or 1926. At this stage the personnel was Terrence Holder, Harry 'Big Jim' Lawson (trumpets); Allen Durham (Eddie Durham's cousin) (trombone); Alvin 'Fats' Wall, John Harrington (alto saxes, clarinets); Lawrence Freeman (tenor sax): Marion Jackson (piano); William Dirvin (banjo); Andy Kirk (tuba, bass saxophone); Ed McNeil (drums). Kirk told Frank Driggs that Wall was an outstanding musician whom many big name leaders attempted to get for their bands, but that he would not travel and ultimately settled in Detroit.

Kirk took over the leadership of the band in Oklahoma City in January 1929; all but three of the members remained with him. Holder had apparently had some domestic trouble and left suddenly. Though Kirk enticed him back briefly, it was a question of finding a new permanent leader or losing the band's bookings. In summer 1929, the Kirk band, retaining the Holder title of 'The Clouds of Joy', was playing at the Crystal Park in Tulsa when George E. Lee came out to hear it. He was impressed and helped get Kirk an engagement at the Pla-Mor Restaurant in Kansas City, then one of the leading ballrooms in the country. While at the Pla-Mor, Kirk was asked by Jack Kapp and Dick Voynow of Brunswick Records to hold a rehearsal so that they could judge whether the band was worth recording. At the rehearsal, the band's usual pianist, Marion Jackson, failed to turn up. With Kapp becoming impatient, Kirk asked John Williams, who had replaced Wall, to get his wife to sit in. Kapp was satisfied with the band and particularly with Mary Lou Williams. He arranged a recording session for the following week at a local radio station. Kirk felt that as Mary Lou Williams had saved them at the rehearsal, it was only fair that she should take part in the record date. She told him that she had a number of ideas that she would like him to hear, and in the days before the session worked on material and arrangements with him. If the discographies are correct, six titles, *Messa Stomp, Blue Clarinet Stomp, Cloudy, Casey Jones Special, Corky Stomp* and *Froggy Bottom* were recorded over a three or four day period. Of these, four were written wholly or in part by Mary Lou Williams; *Blue Clarinet Stomp* was by Kirk himself. Kapp was well pleased with the results and signed him to an exclusive contract, on the basis that when Kirk had suitable material ready Kapp would arrange for him to record it in Chicago. Kirk fixed dance dates in or near Chicago to fit in with the recording sessions.

During 1930, the Kirk band recorded a further fourteen titles, one of which was never issued. On the first Chicago trip, Kapp noticed that the band's regular pianist, Marion Jackson, was present in place of Mary Lou Williams and insisted that Kirk send home for her to take part in the recording sessions. Mary Lou Williams did not join the band as a full-time member until a date at the Pearl Theatre, Philadelphia, in 1931. However, in addition to the recording sessions, she travelled with the band to New York in 1930 and made occasional special appearances. Initially, she shared the piano work with Jackson, an arrangement which did not work too well and Jackson left.

The line-up for the 1929 and 1930 recording sessions was Gene Prince, Harry Lawson (trumpets), Allen Durham (trombone), Lawrence Freeman, John Harrington, John Williams (reeds), Claude Williams (violin, guitar), Mary Lou Williams (piano), with banjo, tuba and drums unchanged from the final days of the Holder period. Billy Massey takes the vocals on some numbers, while Dick Robertson was specially added—to dire effect—for *Saturday* and *Sophomore*. While Mary Lou Williams's arrangements are highly proficient, at this period the band as a whole does not have much individuality. To anyone familiar with Southwestern bands of this period, it is obvious that Kirk's is part of that tradition—ensemble passages led by the two trumpets produce a sound very similiar to that of the Missourians. The first title recorded—*Messa Stomp*—proves beyond any doubt that the band could swing; on this title, Mary Lou Williams's solo is more overtly Hines-like than most of her other recorded work. The outstanding recordings from 1929-30 are undoubtedly *Messa Stomp* and two titles with particularly tight ensemble work, *Corky Stomp* and *Dallas Blues;* all of these hint at the evolution of a personal identity.

In common with most other bands of the period, the standard of brass playing is superior to that of the saxes, most notably in the solos. Lawrence Freeman is by no means a poor soloist, but his rhythmic ideas and phrasing are stiff, though on *Loose Ankles*, he shows a surprising Frank Trumbauer influence (on the same track Claude Williams's violin playing is in the Venuti mould). John Williams is a good section man but very average soloist, and Harrington is featured in the main on clarinet, playing with a strong reedy tone. Harrington's solo on *Blue Clarinet Stomp* is so stiffly phrased as to veer at times close to the border of hokum, but those on *Once or Twice* and *Dallas Blues* are a great deal more flexible and cohesive. The main soloists are Gene Prince, a powerful-toned trumpeter who uses more variety in phrasing than any other member of the band and who, while not showing any high degree of imagination is never less than com-

petent, and Mary Lou Williams. Her solos are extremely variable, ranging from the Hines-like passage on *Messa Stomp* to one on *Froggy Bottom* that has distinct overtones of ragtime in its curiously formal quality. On *Corky Stomp* her solo is lacking in rhythmic impetus and the impact of the whole performance is lessened as a result, a problem which was to recur in later years. One musician who deserves a great deal of credit is Ed McNeil, a drummer of considerable flexibility and skill, who is particularly adept at the crush roll; his playing does much to compensate for the rather leaden quality of the tuba and banjo. McNeil was by all accounts a thoroughly schooled musician and much sought after by Fletcher Henderson and other leaders before his early death from a heart attack in 1930. Overall, these early Kirk records are creditable, sometimes a great deal more. Given the opportunity, even on the most commercially slanted titles, the band could generate a good swing, but it still had a good way to go before becoming a major band.

The records that Kirk made for Kapp sold quite well. On the strength of their success, the band played at both the Savoy Ballroom and the Roseland in New York in 1930 as part of an Eastern touring schedule that lasted for almost two years. Floyd 'Stump' Brady had come over from Al Sears's group to replace Durham, remaining with Kirk until 1934. After another appearance at the Savoy Ballroom in 1931, the band temporarily became house band at the Pearl Theatre in Philadelphia, where the manager attempted to entice the musicians away from Kirk to form a regular supporting group for Blanche Calloway. During most of 1932 and 1933, Kirk did not venture far from Kansas City, happy to have residencies at most of the city's major clubs and ballrooms. This was the period when Boss Prendergast was the undisputed political tycoon in Kansas City. Kirk told Frank Driggs that even the shortest tour could be economically disastrous, but there was plenty of well-paid work to be had in Kansas City which had somehow escaped the full force of the depression. By 1934, the outlook seemed less bleak and the Kirk band, now including Irving 'Mouse' Randolph and Ben Webster (who was soon to join Fletcher Henderson), accepted an offer to play at the leading night club in Oklahoma City. While resident there, the band was heard throughout the South over a regular CBS radio outlet. On the strength of the favourable listener response, Kirk wrote to Jack Kapp asking to make more records. After the Oklahoma City engagement, the band toured throughout Kansas before returning home and soon going out on some not very successful Eastern dates set up by Joe Glaser. By this time, Buddy Tate had replaced Webster. When he returned to Texas, probably early in 1936, Kirk persuaded Dick Wilson to join him from Zack Whyte's band. Another Eastern tour in that year was more satisfactory; Kirk finally met up again with Kapp, and was given a contract with the comparatively new US Decca company. Kirk never recorded for any other firm. From his first session of 2nd March 1936 to his last of

243

The Andy Kirk band at the Rainbow Ballroom, Denver, 1936.
Left to right: Ted Brinson, Theodore Donnelly, Earl
Thompson, Paul King, Harry 'Big Jim' Lawson, Mary Lou
Williams, Booker Collins, Ed Thigpen, Pha Terrell, Dick
Wilson, John Williams, John Harrington and Andy Kirk.

2nd December 1946 a total of 135 titles were made; all but seven were issued. The Decca recordings re-established Kirk as a national attraction, and also brought him to the notice of record collectors in other countries. Kirk's working routine became similar to that of other well-known coloured bandleaders of the swing era, with constant touring and occasional residencies of a few weeks at a time at leading clubs and ballrooms. Many of the choicest resident jobs were closed to coloured bands, so that they toured a great deal more than their white counterparts and, inevitably, were paid less. Even so, Kirk was moderately successful, and he kept his band going during the war years, finally disbanding after a long and disheartening tour in 1948. For a short time, he lived on the West Coast, but then returned to New York and worked as a manager at the Hotel Theresa, occasionally reforming a band for specific engagements well into the 'sixties. He became a Jehovah's Witness during the 'sixties and has spent much time propagating his religious beliefs.

There is a good case for considering Kirk's first batch of US Decca records, made in March and April 1936, as the best of his career. The band had achieved a really personal sound that is instantly identifiable. In the Jazz Review interview with Frank Driggs, Kirk said that, during the war, 'I had to enlarge my band because the style then called for it. I had to meet the competition then, even though it was a fad. I had seven and eight brass . . . it was loud and wrong. My style is built around twelve pieces, although you can still do a good job and get away with ten.' The early Decca recordings clearly substantiate what Kirk said on this occasion.

The outstanding titles from March and April 1936—Walkin' and Swingin', Moten Swing, Lotta Sax Appeal, and Bearcat Shuffle—are notable for the subtle balance of the sections and the light ensemble sound. The brass often plays muted and as a section is no weightier than the saxes, very seldom venturing into the upper register. The band achieves a fine swing, particularly as the rhythm section was now a great deal more flexible than on the Brunswick recordings, but this swing might be more apparent to dancers than to casual listeners who might miss the surface excitement of other more extrovert bands. From 1936 to 1939, the Kirk band often played at the Grand Terrace in Chicago. One cannot help wondering how they coped with the show routines with which they were involved. It is generally assumed that Mary Lou Williams was the guiding musical influence in establishing the style of the Kirk band, but Kirk himself told Frank Driggs that some of the scores credited to her were in fact the work of Merle Boatley, who played professionally under the name of Earl Thompson. It could be, of course, that the group's style was in part a collective development, though with Williams and Thompson defining it because of their arrangements. It now seems impossible to establish Thompson's role with any accuracy, but Mary Lou Williams was certainly a key figure, both as arranger and instrumentalist.

Possibly her greatest achievement was her ability to provide a steady stream of scores that were basically conventional but enabled it to establish a personal identity. These scores are obviously the work of a skilled professional, though craft preponderates over genuine creativity. Unlike Don Redman or Sy Oliver, for example, Mary Lou Williams seldom reshaped popular song material; her scores contain little that is really unexpected—unusual voicings, or ingenuity of tempo or melodic line. During her years with Kirk (as distinct from her post-Kirk career), she did not write any really striking melodies, perhaps because, like most Southwestern groups, the Kirk band showed a strong preference for riff material. The individuality of the Kirk band lay in its overall sound and its unusual section blend. This may occasionally have led to a sameness of performance, but it never deteriorated into a mere formula, mainly because it allowed freedom of individual expression to the soloists.

In Kirk's first Decca recordings, one is initially attracted to the band's ensemble sound and subtle swing. It was not, at least in the 'thirties, a band rich in major soloists. Its outstanding performers were Dick Wilson and Mary Lou Williams. Other members of the band, such as trumpeter Paul King, trombonist Ted Donnelly, and clarinettist John Harrington were capable if not particularly inventive soloists—Harrington's work on such numbers as *Moten Swing* and *Lotta Sax Appeal* has a lighter tone and greater rhythmic flexibility than had been evident on the earlier Brunswick recordings. Mary Lou Williams was heavily featured on record, as in public appearances—the fact of a female musician playing in an otherwise all male band may sometimes have been exploited commercially. Even as late as 1936, her style retained its eclecticism, ranging from the strongly Hines-influenced manner heard on *I'se a Muggin'* to the more delicate approach, with its rather precise rhythm, used on *Walkin' and Swingin'* and *Moten Swing*. At her best, as on *Walkin' and Swingin'* she is a fine soloist, but sometimes, possibly from carrying too heavy a solo burden, her work sounds a little bland and the tension of a performance is dissipated as a result. When supporting other soloists, or filling in during ensemble passages, she is invariably excellent. As a band pianist she had few equals.

Lotta Sax Appeal, quite apart from its pleasant short solos by Donnelly, Harrington and Lawson, is notable for having Dick Wilson featured at length. Wilson, without doubt, was the most individual soloist in the Kirk band at this period, and indeed must be one of the half dozen best tenor players of the swing era. Mary Lou Williams has told about the famous battles between Coleman Hawkins and prominent Kansas City tenor stars, among whom Wilson was a major figure. In some respects, his style bridges the gap between Hawkins and Lester Young, though it is closer to Chu Berry's than to that of any other contemporary tenor player. His tone was light, and he favoured the upper register of his instrument, playing with remarkable skill that allowed him to handle intricate passages with ease. He was fond of contrasting rapidly played short clusters of notes with longer phrases; he had a happy knack of making his solos sound totally coherent. The degree of rhythmic freedom displayed in most of them makes them sound advanced for their period, but less attention has been paid to his melodic ingenuity which led to interesting solos on such trite numbers as *I'se a Muggin'* and *All the Jive Is Gone*. Quite apart from his abilities as a soloist, his very particular sound helped to give the sax section an individual character; some scores included unison parts for Wilson's tenor and an alto sax. Wilson's death from tuberculosis on 21st November 1941, when he was only thirty, was a tragedy for jazz. For Kirk, it meant the removal of a key figure whom he was never able adequately to replace.

If *Bearcat Shuffle, Moten Swing, Lotta Sax Appeal,* and *Walkin' and Swingin'* are the outstanding performances from the March and April 1936 Decca sessions, it was *Christopher Columbus* and *Until the Real Thing Comes Along* that made the greatest public impact. *Columbus* is a good version of the popular riff number, with the theme chorus well scored for muted trumpets and low register trombones. The bridge is taken by the light sounding saxes, and there are pleasant solos from Lawson, Donnelly, Williams and Wilson, whose solo starts casually but develops very well. *Until the Real Thing*, however, was to have far more long term effects on Kirk's recording activities. He had some trouble persuading Kapp to let him record the number, but it became a hit on the strength of Pha Terrell's vocal. At the next recording session, on 9th December 1936, Terrell, whom Kirk had discovered working as a bouncer in a tough Kansas City club, was responsible for another big seller with his vocal on *Dedicated to You*. Thereafter, Kapp insisted on a high proportion of recordings spotlighting Terrell, so that of the next sixteen titles recorded twelve have vocals by him. Kirk has said that this concentration on performances featuring Terrell quite frequently caused his audiences to express surprise at the quality of the jazz instrumentals played. Obviously he was not happy with the recording policy.

Early in 1937, Claude Williams left the band, while trombonist/vocalist Henry Wells and alto saxist Earl Miller were added, increasing the strength to thirteen. Instrumental recordings were a rarity during that year but *Wednesday Night Hop* and *Bear Down* have good solos and cohesive ensemble work, though there is a slightly heavier sound to the brass. The Decca recording policy did not entirely carry over into live performances, as is shown by a very interesting LP taken from broadcasts made when the band was working at the Trianon Ballroom in Cleveland during the period from 29th January to 6th February 1937. There is, inevitably, a fair proportion of ephemera—Terrell features on *What Will I Tell My Heart, Trust in Me*, a medley of four popular numbers of the day and a not very successful version of *Organ Grinder's Swing*. On the other hand, there are outstanding versions of *Swingtime in the Rockies, Sepia Jazz, Moten Swing* and *Makebelieve Ballroom*, which ends with the ensemble sounding rather Luncefordish. The arrangement, which makes use of a neat sax counter-melody, is rather unusual for Kirk, but the other three numbers are more typical. They are impressive yet again for the fine balance of the sections and the manner in which the band swings without ever becoming frenetic. The extent to which Wilson is featured is surprising: he has solos on almost every number—those on *Swingtime, Sepia* and *Moten* are among his finest. The solo on *Moten* is particularly striking; it is played against a background of muted brass, after which there is an attractive trumpet solo slightly reminiscent of Buck Clayton. Most of the performances on this LP suggest that if Kirk was not yet leading a band to equal the major ones, the gap was not all that great.

For Decca, the Kirk band recorded twenty-seven titles during 1938; only five were instrumentals. *Little Joe from Chicago* featured a pleasant boogie-woogie solo by Mary Lou Williams and has a score that seems partly modelled on those that Bob Haggart was writing for the Bob Crosby band. It was quite a popular hit, but *Messa Stomp, Twinklin', Jump Jack Jump, Dunkin' a Doughnut* and *Mary's Idea* are musically more interesting performances. *Jump* is a riff theme. The first chorus has the usual neatly balanced section playing well underlined by Thigpen. There are solos from Wilson, probably King, and Williams, with Wilson in something like his best form after the trumpet passage. *Messa* and *Mary's* are good performances, using scores hardly altered since the Brunswick recordings of the previous decade, with Harrington, Lawson and Williams playing well. Most interesting of all is *Twinklin'*, a charming Mary Lou Williams composition reminiscent of some of the better melodies by Willy 'The Lion' Smith. An intriguing side of Mary Lou's playing has always been her occasional reversion to ragtime modes, as she does in this solo.

Early in 1939, vocalist June Richmond joined the band. More important musically was the arrival of guitarist Floyd Smith, who used an amplified instrument and was a soloist of real originality, as shown by his playing on the excellent *Floyd's Guitar Blues*. Of the twelve titles recorded in that year, only three were instrumentals. Almost as attracive as *Floyd's* was *Big Jim Blues*. Big Jim was, of course, Harry Lawson's nickname, but the only soloists on this title are Smith, who plays a fine theme against muted trumpets, and Ted Donnelly, whose gentle trombone work over quiet sections is effective. By 1940, Kirk had persuaded Harold Baker to join him, adding yet another major solo voice. Fred Robinson, Edward Inge and Rudy Powell were also in the band. During 1940 and 1941, June Richmond's vocals, heard on titles like *Fifteen Minutes' Intermission* and *47th Street Jive,* were more popular than Terrell's. When Harry Wells returned, Terrell left. *Little Miss,* made in July 1940, is still in the tradition of earlier Kirk instrumental performances; apart from good solos by Lawson and Wilson, it includes passages by the reeds that retain the light, floating sound associated with the band. *Twelfth Street Rag* had excellent solos by Baker and Wilson and capable ones by Donnelly and Harrington. The last instrumental Kirk recorded before major changes in his line-up was *Ring Dem Bells,* a really splendid version with outstanding solos from Wilson and Baker. The session of 17th July 1941 was the last on which Wilson appeared. His final recorded solo, on *47th Street Jive,* is as consistent as ever, though the material is trite.

The Kirk band can be heard on two 1942 Decca sessions made just before the first recording ban, but by this time, Wilson was dead and Mary Lou Williams had left to be replaced by Kenny Kersey. From the first date

The Andy Kirk band in the 1930s. The personnel is as in the previous photograph except that an unidentified musician has been added on baritone saxophone.

came the superb *McGhee Special,* a feature for Howard McGhee who plays with real fire and brilliance. However, the reverse of the original 78 was the real hit with the public. This was a version of *Hey Lawdy Mama* with a vocal by June Richmond, and represents a very noticeable move towards rhythm-and-blues. During 1944, Fats Navarro was in the band. Mark Gardner tells me that he is featured on one title on a Caracol LP—*Peepin' Through the Keyhole.* From December 1943 to December 1946, the Kirk band, now much changed both in personnel and style, recorded a further twenty-one titles for Decca, of which fourteen were issued. *I Know,* with a vocal by the Jubalaires, was a hit, but the line-up now included eight brass, and most of the titles were heavily slanted towards the r-and-b market. The big band era was drawing to a close. Within two years of his last Decca recording session, Kirk stopped leading a full time orchestra.

The period 1936-41 was the peak one for the Kirk band, though the picture we have of it from Decca recordings is distorted by the prominence given to Terrell's vocals. One should not assume that if it had had one major soloist and an arranger in the class of Sy Oliver or Don Redman during the mid 'thirties it could have rivalled Basie and Lunceford musically. Its style could have been moulded in a totally different manner by a strongly individual arranger, but then the regular Kirk personnel might not have been the ideal interpreters. It is also possible that if the band's recorded output had included a high proportion of instrumentals, its conventional riff material would have palled, though the Jazz Society LP suggests that its normal repertoire was more varied—for both better and worse—than its commercial recordings indicate. The important thing is that the Kirk band was able to create a distinctive personal approach by using essentially conventional methods and produced a proportion of recorded performances that retain their validity to the present day.

Gene Krupa seemed to many people to epitomise the swing era. More than any other individual, he was responsible for the emergence of the showman drummer, and the image of the gum-chewing extrovert, hair awry, launching into an exhibitionistic drum solo, remained with him for the rest of his life. Offstand, Krupa was very different. Deeply concerned about his music, swift to pay tribute to the musicians who had influenced him, he was a charming, readily approachable man.

In the mid 'twenties, Krupa studied drumming with several teachers, at the same time working around his native Chicago with a variety of bands, such as the Benson Orchestra, Mezz Mezzrow and Thelma Terry. He was slightly involved with the group of musicians which became The Chicagoans. In 1929, he moved to New York, where he worked with Red Nichols in theatre bands for about two years. He then played with various well-known dance bands, including that fronted by the famous singer Russ Colombo, before joining Benny Goodman in December 1934. With Goodman, he emerged as one of the leading personalities of the swing era. His relationship with Goodman eventually became so strained that they started to argue in public performances. Inevitably, Krupa left. On 16th April 1938 he opened with his own band at Steel Pier, Atlantic City before a crowd of around four thousand.

Krupa was a popular leader for five years until he was forced to retire temporarily in May 1943, after being charged with possessing marihuana. The charge was withdrawn, however, and Krupa rejoined Goodman after spending about six months on the study of harmony and composition. Two months or so later, he started working with Tommy Dorsey. In July 1944, he set about organising a new band which made its debut late in the year. Its initial personnel included a large string section, and it continued under Krupa, with numerous changes, until 1951.

From 1951, Krupa worked frequently with Norman Granz's 'Jazz At The Philharmonic', usually in the trio or quartet format with which he appeared on overseas tours and other jobs. He was often resident at The Metropole Cafe in New York during the 'fifties. Though forced by ill health to leave music temporarily in late 1960, he continued to work as a leader of small groups during the 'sixties. From 1954, he had been active in a drum tuition school, run in conjunction with Cozy Cole. He was the subject of a film, 'The Gene Krupa Story' (1959); he recorded the soundtrack and was portrayed by Sal Mineo.

In the last year or two of his life Krupa suffered ill health. He managed to deliver a moving tribute at Eddie Condon's funeral service in August 1973, only two months before his own death from leukaemia on 16th October at the age of sixty-four. He had made his last major appearance at a reunion of the original Benny Goodman Quartet for a TV show during October 1972—his differences with Goodman had been resolved long before. In the same month, he discussed aspects of his career with the British producer John Jeremy in sequences of the documentary film 'Born To Swing'.

Krupa's 1938-40 band was not an outstanding unit. It possessed few major soloists and little in the way of individuality. Its recorded output was mainly commercial. A high proportion of it contained vocals by Irene Day. Numbers like *Wire Brush Stomp* and *Bolero at the Savoy* were designed to feature Krupa's own playing. His most successful early recording of this type was *Drummin' Man*. Irene Day, a reasonably proficient popular singer, has a vocal and there is a good trumpet solo by Corky Cornelius with some half-valved passages in the Rex Stewart manner. *Apurksody* is one of the band's instrumental numbers. There are pleasant solos by tenor saxophonist Sam Donahue and an unidentified trumpeter (probably Tom Gonsoulin) and some excellent work by the sax section. The saxes certainly appear to form the most impressive section in the band. They achieve an almost Benny Carter-ish sound on *Quiet and Roll 'em*, arranged by Sam Donahue, with pleasant solos from Donahue and clarinettist Sam Musiker. Leo Watson was with Krupa for a few months from the summer of 1938. His zany scat singing enlivens the performances of *Tutti Frutti* and a couple of other numbers.

Early in 1940, trumpeter Shorty Sherock and the excellent blues trombonist Floyd O'Brien were with Krupa. Most of the trumpet solos were assigned to Cornelius, however. Guitarist Ray Biondi arranged the riff based *Blues Krieg;* solos were allocated to Donahue and Cornelius. The performance confirms the impression that, at this stage, Krupa led an average but well-schooled swing band. Some imagination went into the decision to record Duke Ellington's *The Sergeant Was Shy*. Apart from competent solos by Musiker and trombonist Babe Wagner, this has Cornelius doing his Rex Stewart impersonation. *Who* has a pleasant chase sequence between Donahue and alto saxophonist Clint Neagley—this was made at Donahue's last session with the band in July 1940. *Hamtrack* features a wild Cornelius solo and rather ordinary offerings from Walter Bates (tenor), Wagner, Tony d'Amore (piano), Neagley and Musiker; the brass and ensemble playing is excellent. At her last session with the band, Irene Day took the vocal on the rousing *Drum Boogie,* less of a drum showcase than the title implies.

In 1941, two members joined the band at the start of its period of greatest popularity. The first was vocalist Anita O'Day, a fine husky-voiced jazz singer, whose individual hip style began by puzzling some of the band's fans. On her first session she sings a good *Georgia on My Mind,* which also has an effective plunger solo from Shorty Sherock. Two months later, the arrival of Roy Eldridge provided the band with its first major soloist. An exciting, erratic, often brilliant trumpeter, Eldridge teamed up with Anita O'Day on his first session for the popular *Let Me Off Uptown.* After the vocal passages, he takes a powerful solo. He is even more impressive on *Green Eyes*. This seems to be a cover version of the Jimmy Dorsey recording, with Howard DuLaney and Anita O'Day substituting for Bob Eberly and Helen O'Connell, but after DuLaney's vocal Eldridge goes into a magnificent solo, initially accompanied only by Krupa.

Eldridge was soon featured on a recording of his *After You've Gone.* He plays in his most flamboyant manner with the expected flurry of high notes. Shortly afterwards came his classic *Rockin' Chair.* His solo there was a masterpiece, combining the intensity of his finest work with the discipline that sometimes deserted him. *Bolero at the Savoy,* with a mannered but fine vocal from Anita O'Day, has Eldridge in a wild solo. He shows another side of his personality with a beautifully poised muted theme on *Skylark* that is unique amongst his recorded work. *That's What You Think* features an almost wordless vocal by Anita O'Day, which demonstrates her outstanding rhythmic sense. She is also excellent on *Massachusetts,* made on the final session the band made before the AFoM recording ban.

In November 1944, when Krupa next took his band into the recording studio, his personnel was entirely different. He had been joined by a number of modernist inclined musicians, captivated by the new bop sounds. At his second session he recorded *What's This,* with scat bop vocal duet by Buddy Stewart and Dave Lambert. The big success of that date was an instrumental, *Leave Us Leap.* The performance is a good one. The band swings strongly, and there are solos from trumpeter Don Fagerquist, tenor saxophonist Charlie Ventura, trombonist Tommy Pederson and Krupa himself. Ventura became a major attraction at this time and made some records with Krupa in a trio setting. Although he could play well, his solos are too often a series of musical tricks. Anita O'Day returned in the summer of 1954. Her presence was immediately felt on versions of Sy Oliver's *Opus No. 1* and the driving *Boogie Blues.* By then, the band was a highly polished unit. These recordings, *How High the Moon, Lover,* and others, established its popularity.

Krupa's flirtation with bop was really somewhat tentative, but his band probably helped to increase the following of bop by presenting it in a commercialised form. Gerry Mulligan started arranging for the band late in 1946. Although many of his best scores were not then recorded, *Disc Jockey Jump* is an exception. On this performance Mulligan sets a small group against the ensemble during the theme at the beginning and close. There are reasonable solos by Charlie Kennedy (alto saxophone), an unidentified trombonist who sounds like a refugee from the Kenton band, Krupa, Buddy Wise (tenor saxophone) and Al Porcino (trumpet). Kennedy is extensively featured on *I Should Have Kept On Dreaming,* where his playing has a slight Lee Konitz quality. At the same date, the band made the pleasant *Calling Dr Gillespie,* a riff number with solos from trombonist Urbie Green, pianist Teddy Napoleon and tenor saxophonist Buddy Wise, who is strongly influenced by Lester Young. The boppish *Lemon Drop,* with scat vocal by Frankie Foss, has the band in

Gene Krupa just after his big band days. Below right: *the Jimmy Lunceford band in the latter part of the 1930s, shown here probably in a theatre.*

good form. It was about the last big band record made by Krupa with a regular personnel that attracted much attention. The final recordings, released on the RCA Victor label, include some pleasant performances of Fats Waller numbers but are not particularly distinguished.

Krupa's best bands were undoubtedly those of 1941-42, when Anita O'Day and Roy Eldridge were present, and 1944-45. Stylistically, none of his bands possessed any real individuality, but they maintained consistent musical standards and could be relied on to swing. In the 'fifties, Krupa fronted specially assembled big bands at a couple of recording dates for Norman Granz. The first, with Anita O'Day and Roy Eldridge, recreated some of the big hits of the early 'forties. The second recorded scores that Gerry Mulligan had written for the band in the mid 'forties. *Bird House, The Way of All Flesh, If You Were The Only Girl in the World* and *Yardbird Suite* were among those not recorded earlier. They reveal Mulligan's extraordinary gifts as an arranger. It is a pity that he did not start arranging until the big band era was approaching its close, for big band music might well have been his best medium. Krupa's own work on these tracks is not always appropriate stylistically. He was possibly out of sympathy with the aims of his younger musicians in the 'forties.

As a drummer, Krupa was sometimes unsteady in his tempos. Now and then his work could be bombastic. At his best, however, he was an excellent musician, who inspired colleagues with his enthusiasm and example. His involvement in jazz was constant, and he retained an infectious optimism about its future. Understandably, Gene Krupa and the swing era are synonymous in the minds of many people.

In his book 'The Big Bands', George T. Simon refers to a famous night in November 1940 when nearly thirty leading bands, of both sweet and swing varieties, took part in a marathon concert at New York's Manhattan Center that lasted from 8 p.m. until 4 a.m. Each band was scheduled to play a fifteen minute set. All except one left the stage as planned. The exception was the Jimmie Lunceford band, as its reception prevented any other group from coming on stage until it had been allowed to play some encores. Mr Simon concludes his report of the event with the unqualified statement that 'Jimmie Lunceford's was without doubt the most exciting big band of all time.' Supporters of Basie, Ellington and no doubt other bandleaders would dispute this view with some vehemence. Certainly, though, Jimmie Lunceford led one of the greatest of all big bands.

Lunceford was born in Fulton, Missouri, on 6th June 1902. He went to high school in Denver, Colorado, and studied music there with Wilberforce J. Whiteman, Paul's father. In 1922, he played alto saxophone with George Morrison's Orchestra, but left Denver to study at Fisk University where he took a Bachelor of Music degree. In the mid 'twenties, he also studied in New York and worked there during vacations with various leaders, including Elmer Snowden and Wilbur Sweatman. In 1926, Lunceford became a music teacher at the Manassa High School in Memphis, and formed a campus band that played around the Nashville area, venturing further afield in the summer. In due course, Willie Smith, Henry Wells and Edwin Wilcox, all of whom had met Lunceford at Fisk,

joined the band. In summer 1929, during an engagement at Lakeside, Ohio, the group decided to become full-time professionals. The band then consisted of Charles Douglas, Henry Clay (trumpet), Henry Wells (trombone), Christopher Johnson, Willie Smith (alto saxophone, clarinet), George Clark (tenor saxophone), Edwin Wilcox (piano), Alfred Kahn (banjo), Moses Allen (brass bass) and Jimmy Crawford (drums), with presumably Lunceford himself playing saxophone.

The band became well known locally and broadcast regularly over a Memphis radio station, but on a trip to Cleveland that winter, things did not work out too well and Edwin Wilcox recalls that the musicians were hungry a great deal of the time. At this period, the band was jointly controlled by Lunceford, Smith and Wilcox. When it went on to Buffalo, where trumpeter Jonah Jones joined it for a short while, the need to get financial backing led to the dissolution of the partnership, and Lunceford became sole director. The band first moved to New York in 1933 for dates at the Lafayette Theatre, afterwards touring New England, then returned to New York in January 1934 for a residency at the Cotton Club. The Cotton Club date resulted in widespread attention, and for the rest of the 'thirties the band toured extensively throughout the United States, and made one overseas trip, to Sweden, in February 1937. The peak years for the band, both commercially and musically, were 1937 to 1941. A number of key musicians left in summer 1942, and the band never really regained its former popularity. Lunceford died on 12th July 1947, shortly after collapsing

in a music store where he was signing autographs. For a while, the band continued under the joint leadership of Edwin Wilcox and Joe Thomas. Subsequently, Wilcox became the sole leader, but with the big band era at its close, he disbanded in 1950.

Lunceford himself was a highly skilled musician, playing trombone, all the saxes, flute and guitar, though rarely doing so on record. He can be heard on flute in a 1939 recording of *Liza* and probably sat in on sax on a few other recordings. By all accounts he was an astute business man, though the Lunceford band never received the financial rewards that should have come to it. Even by the standards of the coloured bands of the 'thirties and 'forties, it seldom seemed to get the residencies at leading hotels and ballrooms that it deserved, spending an inordinate amount of time on tour. The musicians' poor pay led to the departure of several of its leading members in 1942, and to the much earlier loss of Sy Oliver in 1939. When Tommy Dorsey offered the job of staff arranger to Oliver, he promised a payment of five thousand dollars a year more than Oliver was already receiving, a proposal which was naturally accepted without hesitation. For most of its existence, the band's manager was Harold Oxley, who worked very hard to promote it. Whether Oxley had a financial interest in the band is not certain, though it seems very likely. The musicians themselves seem to be divided in their opinion as to who actually had the major financial control. Edwin Wilcox told Stanley Dance that when the band had a vacation it would be an unpaid one, and blamed Lunceford for its break-up. No musicians in any other major band of the swing era seem to have received such parsimonious salaries as those who worked with Lunceford.

The origin of the Lunceford style seems rather a complex question. I have already quoted Eddie Barefield saying of Zack Whyte's band: 'This was a very fine band indeed and it has not received its fair share of recognition. The style of the band was set by Sy Oliver, and the arrangements were much the same as those Jimmie Lunceford used later. In fact, when Sy got an offer from Lunceford, he took his arrangements with him.' Oliver himself has said that he wrote some arrangements for Lunceford before joining the band, and referred to them as 'just rehashes of the things I'd done for Zack's band'. The Whyte band's recordings were made too early to have any relevance.

Edwin Wilcox, in an extremely interesting interview with Stanley Dance in the 3rd October 1968 issue of Down Beat, emphatically denies that Oliver was responsible for the Lunceford style, claiming that it originated before he joined the band. 'It started between Willie Smith and myself. We didn't really hear bands that gave us ideas. It was what we wanted to do. The melodic quality I had came from studying classical piano. That was how I wanted it to sound. If you have a good classical teacher, melodic structure is implanted in you so strongly that even when you find yourself wanting to do something else, you don't lose it. Willie was influential in the way the reed section phrased from the beginning, because he was so positive in what he wanted to do, and so dominating in tone and quality. And he had good ideas. A lot of people have good ideas, but they're not positive enough in the presentation of them. Willie was always more concerned with being able to play the horn well, and arranging was a lot of work.'

Wilcox wrote many of the arrangements for the more commercial numbers the band recorded, primarily because he was better at writing vocal backgrounds than Oliver, but he was considered particularly strong in his arranging for saxes and did the score for the remarkable *Sleepy Time Gal*. A few Willie Smith arrangements were recorded in the early years of the band, and then, as Wilcox mentions, he seemed to lose interest.

The question of who was responsible for the Lunceford style is further complicated by the leader's known admiration for the Alphonso Trent band. The last recordings that Trent made are certainly very much in the Lunceford manner, and it seems certain that the scores were written by Gus Wilson. Sy Oliver worked with the Trent band at one point, so did Oliver influence Gus Wilson or was it the other way round? Just to confuse matters further, Edgar Battle is insistent that Eddie Durham was the major influence on Oliver, though Durham himself does not entirely agree.

It is hard to reconcile all the conflicting claims, but there does seem to be some substance in what Wilcox said. In 1933, the band made two tests for US Columbia which were not released for well over thirty years. *Flaming Reeds and Screaming Brass,* written and arranged by Wilcox, does have the fine writing for the sax section that is a characteristic of many Lunceford records, and the ensemble plays with much of the precision of later years. *While Love Lasts,* another Wilcox number, again has impressive ensemble work and good writing for the saxes, though there is one passage for the latter which is more sugary than was usual in subsequent recordings. I would guess that the so-called Lunceford style was already there in embryo when Oliver joined the band, particularly in the type of sax scoring which had been conceived jointly by Wilcox and Smith. Oliver added a new dimension through his brilliance as an arranger and was unquestionably the major influence during the next six years. The question of how far the music of the Alphonso Trent band played a part is now impossible to resolve.

In its peak years, the Lunceford band was the most brilliant orchestral unit that jazz has produced. Pride of place must be given to the magnificent saxophone section, led by the incomparable Willie Smith who, in addition to being one of the greatest soloists on his instrument during the 'thirties, was also virtually unequalled as a leader. The other sections were not up to the same standard, but not too far behind. Smith spent a year in the Duke Ellington band from March 1951, reportedly paining the Ellington veterans who were with him in the sax section

Top: *the Jimmie Lunceford band in a scene from a Warner Brothers short film.* Above: *the Jimmie Lunceford band in 1939. Left to right: Jimmy Crawford, Earl Carruthers, Willie Smith, James 'Trummy' Young, Elmer Crumbley, Joe Thomas, Dan Grissom, Russell Bowles, Jimmie Lunceford, Ted Buckner, unknown, Moses Allen, Ed Wilcox, Eddie Tompkins Gerald Wilson, Al Norris and Paul Webster.*

by his insistence on regular rehearsals. He imparts a personal sound to any section that he leads. Wilcox, in his interview with Stanley Dance, indicated Smith's musical standards when he told the story of Joe Thomas joining the band in Buffalo during 1933:

'Joe had a lot of personality, and a lot of tricks on the horn. He had a way of slopping over notes, too, instead of making all the notes in a run. Willie Smith·wouldn't settle for that kind of stuff. He would turn his back on you, refuse to listen if you played that way. "Play all the notes in the run, man," Willie would say. "Don't play like that." Joe was a good tenor player when we first got him, but sitting beside a man like that he naturally got better, for Willie was a perfectionist. He believed in doing everything right.'

Smith was for some years the band's one really major soloist, though trumpeters Eddie Tompkins, Paul Webster, Sy Oliver, Snooky Young, tenor saxophonist Joe Thomas, alto saxophonist Ted Buckner, and baritone saxophonist Earl Carruthers were all very capable. James 'Trummy' Young, who came into the band after a period with Earl Hines, was a second major soloist as well as being a vocalist. The rhythm section as a whole was efficient rather than inspired—Wilcox was a good band pianist but no great soloist. However, one of the rhythm section played an important role in the realisation of the Lunceford style. He was Jimmy Crawford, a fine and highly individual big band drummer who normally played in an

Above: *a section of the Jimmie Lunceford band in 1941. The trombones are Russell Bowles, 'Trummy' Young and Elmer Crumbley. Jimmy Crawford is the drummer, with guitarist Al Norris next to him. The trumpets are Paul Webster, Eugene 'Snooky' Young and Gerald Wilson. The saxophonist on the extreme right is Dan Grissom. Below: Jimmie Lunceford listens to tenor saxophonist Charles Stewart at a dance in the mid 1940s. Right: the Jimmie Lunceford sax section, c1944. Left to right: Charles Stewart, Omer Simeon, Kurt Bradford, Joe Thomas and Earl Carruthers. The musician at the far right is trombonist Fernando Arbello.*

assertive two-beat style that was a characteristic of the band's performances. There have been few drummers in jazz more capable of inspiring a big band than Crawford, and he could swing as powerfully as any. The Lunceford band, though, seldom relied on power as such, producing instead, relaxed, easy swinging performances with an infectious beat. Its orchestral brilliance was allied to a strong sense of showmanship; live performances by the band were visual as well as musical experiences.

Lunceford first recorded with his campus band in Dallas in December 1927; only Moses Allen and Jimmy Crawford of his later personnel were present. The performances of *Chickasaw Stomp,* with 'preaching' by Allen,

and *Memphis Rag* are adequate but little more. In June 1930 he recorded again, this time in Memphis, and Allen once more does his preaching routine on *In Dat Mornin'*, a performance which starts with a rather Ellington-ish ensemble passage and has good solos by a trumpeter in plunger style—presumably either Charles Douglas or Henry Clay—and an alto saxophonist. The latter is heard again on *Sweet Rhythm,* a theme written by Edwin Wilcox, a somewhat mundane performance apart from the alto passage. Willie Smith was in the band by now, but the Hodges-influenced solos on both these numbers are not typical of any of his later work; the suggestion once made that Lunceford is the soloist on these titles is worth treating with an open mind. The next time the band was in a recording studio was for the two Columbia tests.

Once the band was established in the Cotton Club in early 1934, it recorded eight titles at two sessions for RCA Victor. It attracted a fair amount of attention with its versions of Will Hudson's *White Heat* and *Jazznocracy,* but though they show off the band's precision, the numbers, very much in the Casa Loma vein, are not

252

really suited to it. Six other numbers are mainly devoted to the high, wispy singing of Henry Wells. Only *Swingin' Uptown,* written by Sy Oliver, and the Koehler-Arlen *Breakfast Ball* are themes suited to the band. *Swingin'* has Smith playing clarinet at the start and close; he takes by far the most impressive solo, sweeping in with the huge tone and technical assurance that was so much a part of his style. *Breakfast Ball* has nice muted trumpet by Tompkins, leading into the vocal by Oliver who takes a growl style solo. After an ensemble passage with fine saxes, Oliver returns with an open solo, Smith once again takes a fleet, dominating solo, and Tompkins is heard with the ensemble.

Lunceford's recordings for US Decca from September 1934 to April 1938 set the seal on the band's excellence. Few recordings made during this period, even those with Henry Wells and Dan Grissom in lachrymose vocals, are totally without interest. At its first Decca session, the band recorded three famous Duke Ellington numbers—*Sophisticated Lady, Mood Indigo* and *Black and Tan Fantasy*—plus *Rose Room* and *Stratosphere.* Willie Smith arranged *Sophisticated Lady* and plays the theme very well on clarinet, backed by muted trumpets; there is a superb unison passage by the sax section before the close by the ensemble. The version of *Black and Tan Fantasy* is different in mood from any by Ellington, with Oliver taking the theme in growl style against a background of the baritone-led sax section and trombones; other solos are by Smith (clarinet), Tompkins, Thomas and Oliver, with Tommy Stevenson coming in for a high note close. These performances of Ellington numbers are interesting, though not among the band's most striking output.

A session of October 1934 produced the three finest Oliver scores to date. *Dream of You* has an introduction by muted trumpets and clarinets to Oliver's gentle muted theme, with trombonist Russell Bowles taking the release, and the pleasant vocal by Oliver is enhanced by the quiet backing from the trombones and guitarist Al Norris. The delicate yet swinging approach to *Dream* is continued on the instrumental *Shake Your Head,* first recorded on this date but remade seven weeks later. There is a light, buoyant quality about the ensemble and section work that is unique to the Lunceford band at this time; Willie Smith's cascading solo is outstanding. *Stomp It Off* has some dazzling section work, with the individual sections cutting in and out and across each other; the solos are by Stevenson, Thomas, Oliver and Smith. In May 1935, the band recorded Wilcox's score of *Sleepy Time Gal;* his writing here gave the sax section the opportunity to provide what Ronald Atkins once called the ultimate testimony to its prowess.

In the summer of 1936, Oliver wrote one of his best known scores when he transformed the rather trite *Organ Grinder's Swing.* The record is an engaging one; Crawford introduces a humorous touch with his use of woodblocks which he returns to at various moments during the course of the performance. The inexhaustible variety of Oliver's scoring appears in such touches as following the theme, initially carried by himself and Carruthers, with the unexpected delicacy of Wilcox's celeste passage and the contrasting power of Paul Webster's trumpet solo. Eddie Durham was in the band at the time and also provided a number of scores, *Harlem Shout* being typical. Durham wrote in a far less complex manner than Oliver, generally relying on riff themes of the type associated with the Basie band. The recording of *Harlem Shout* has a fine passage for the saxes, and the main soloist is Webster who generally provided the high register passages when required. In June 1937, the band made Oliver's *For Dancers Only,* which shows the band's ability to build to a powerful close; Smith and Webster are the soloists. A few months later, James 'Trummy' Young and Ted Buckner joined the band, and both were featured on a recording of *Margie.* Buckner, a fine alto saxophonist with a smoother and more evenly phrased style than Smith, states the theme and the rest is all Young, After his rhythmic, slightly breathless vocal, he embarks on a very fine trombone solo that includes some controlled high register work. Young was one of the most original trombonists around during the late 'thirties and early 'forties; his fine technical command and adventurous style were widely admired. He has said that his style at this period was greatly influenced by Louis Armstrong. Years later, he became a member of Armstrong's All Stars, though ironically he had to modify his approach considerably to fit in with the group.

The Lunceford band switched its recording allegiance to US Columbia early in 1939. Its first date under the new contract produced two of its greatest hits in *'Taint What You Do* and *Cheatin' On Me,* both arranged by Oliver. *'Taint What You Do* is a light-hearted performance with a vocal by Young and the band, the main soloist being Buckner; it concludes with a beautifully relaxed ensemble passage and a fine solo release by Crawford. *Cheatin'* has a good solo from Thomas after the introduction, and then the vocal quartet of Oliver, Smith, Tompkins and Young go through to the close. The band had been using a trio for some years, but the addition of Young added an extra dimension. It is interesting to note that the vocal on *Cheatin'* is phrased in a manner that parallels the approach of the sax section. From the same date comes the brilliant *Le Jazz Hot,* with solos from Oliver, Young, Webster and Thomas. A session of four weeks later produced the superb *Lonesome Road,* which is taken at a surprisingly fast tempo. The highspots of the performance are a dazzling solo by Smith, the insistent drive of Crawford's drumming, and the extraordinary virtuoso playing of the band as a whole.

Jimmie Lunceford at home to friends. Behind the bar are Joe Thomas, Lunceford, Stanley Dance and Jimmy Crawford. The identity of the two ladies is not known.

Sy Oliver left the band in summer 1939. His replacement in the trumpet section was Gerald Wilson. Lunceford was lucky to have as his new arranger Billy Moore who wrote very much in the Oliver tradition. The first of Moore's scores to be recorded was *Belgium Stomp*—also called on other occasions *Dutch Kitchen Stomp* and *State and Tioga Stomp*—with a fine solo from Thomas in his straight ahead style. From the same date, *Think of Me Little Daddy* features Young both as vocalist and instrumentalist; his closing solo has some startling high register passages. A session of December 1939 produced that rarity in the Lunceford band's output, a performance based on a head arrangement. The number is *Uptown Blues,* a vehicle for Smith and trumpeter Eugene 'Snooky' Young, who had replaced Tompkins. Young plays very well indeed, but the star is Smith whose solo, with its enormous power and control, is one of the finest he ever recorded. Six months later, the band made *Barefoot Blues,* with a nice vocal by Smith and a good solo by Thomas, but it lacks the impact of *Uptown.*

In 1941, the band once more recorded for the US Decca label; before doing so, it made a version of Don Redman's *Flight of the Jitterbug* on its final Columbia date. This is a feature for Willie Smith, who for once allows his technical brilliance to lead him into waywardness. The first of the new Decca recordings included some pleasant performances, but the band reached its zenith at a date of August 1941 when it recorded Gerald Wilson's *Hi Spook* and *Yard Dog Mazurka.* Stan Kenton has always denied being influenced by the Lunceford band, but these performances strongly contradict him—*Yard Dog Mazurka* even becomes *Intermission Riff.* Both numbers include fine solos—Young and Smith on *Hi* and Wilson on *Yard* in particular—but it is the staggering virtuosity of the band that makes the impression. In some ways, these recordings represent the ultimate in one particular approach; soon afterwards, the Lunceford band started to decline. It made popular recordings of *Blues in the Night*—it appeared in the film of the same title—and *I'm Gonna Move to the Outskirts of Town,* which has one of the rare alto solos by vocalist Dan Grissom, but when such key figures as Crawford, Smith and Young left in the early 'forties, the band could no longer be rated as a top musical force. Some of its mid-'forties performances have a surface flash and glitter about them, but the content seems shallow. It has been said that just before his death Lunceford was once again leading a fine band, but no recorded evidence of this has survived.

In its peak years, Lunceford's must rank with the Basie and Ellington bands of the same period as the greatest big bands in jazz history. In Sy Oliver, it possessed an arranger of genius, seemingly capable of endless variation within the course of a single score. Its saxophone section has never been equalled as a unit, and its soloists, though including only two major figures, were consistently fine. It was for many years the most popular band in Harlem —as late as 1958 Lunceford records could still be found on juke boxes there. To hear the band in the flesh was, according to people who were fortunate to do so, an unforgettable experience; few groups established quite such a tight rapport with their audiences. The trombonist Fernando Arbello, who played with the band in the forties, has recalled those years: 'I'm telling you that was one swinging band! There were times when we played in some places and even the walls would shake!'

The Mills Blue Rhythm Band was in existence for at least eight years, but surprisingly little was written about it then, particularly in its earlier days. Henry 'Red' Allen told me that when he worked with the band from November 1934 until February 1937 it was reasonably popular, with a schedule including regular tours and club and theatre appearances, but for some reason it attracted little publicity. There is even confusion about its foundation, though this can be clarified by sifting some known facts.

Dave Nelson claimed that his 1929 band was the basis of the Blue Rhythm Band, but this hardly seems likely. In the early months of 1929, Nelson toured with his own band out of Chicago before settling in New York, where he first worked with Luis Russell and then went out on tour with his uncle Joe 'King' Oliver. He led his own band around New York in late 1930 and again in 1931, but the dates are too late and the known personnels bear no relationship to that of the Blue Rhythm Band. It is also improbable that the group he led in 1929 would include members of the Blue Rhythm Band, as they were mainly New York based musicians.

The Mills Blue Rhythm Band in 1933. Back row: Henry Hicks, George Washington (trombone), O'Neil Spencer (drums), Hayes Alvis (string bass), and Benny James (drums). Front row: Ed Anderson, Wardell Jones, Shelton Hemphill (trumpet), Edgar Hayes (piano), Eddie Mallory (trumpet), Crawford Wethington, Gene Mikell and Joe Garland (saxophone).

Much more convincing is the story that Bingie Madison told Bertrand Demeusy. In late 1930, Madison took over the leadership of a band that was already in residence at the Broadway Danceland at 60th Street and Broadway, New York. He gave the line-up as Wardell 'Preacher' Jones, Edward Anderson (trumpet), Henry Hicks (trombone), Jobetus McCord, Sleepy Jamison (alto saxophone), himself (tenor saxophone), Joe Turner (piano), Benny James (banjo), . . . Jackson (Brass bass) and Bill Beason (drums), claiming that soon afterwards, with a few changes in personnel and drummer Willie Lynch as leader, this group became the Blue Rhythm Band. A high percentage of these men did play with the Blue Rhythm Band in its early days, and if one allows for a lapse of memory by Madison about the date—it should be late 1929—his story seems quite logical.

The Blue Rhythm Band, fronted by an obscure individual called Sonny Nichols, followed the Cab Calloway band into the Cotton Club early in 1930. In April and May of that year, it backed Louis Armstrong on two recording sessions. At this point, to confuse matters further, the band was apparently known as the Cocoanut Grove Orchestra, though when it recorded for the first time in January 1931, the records were issued as by Mills Music Masters. Further records from 1931 appeared as by Mills Blue Rhythm Band or The Blue Rhythm Boys.

Mills Blue Rhythm Band was organised at the instigation of the impresario Irving Mills as a sort of relief group for his major artists, Cab Calloway and Duke Ellington. It seems that the band filled in at the Cotton Club when the others were away on tour and was always a secondary unit within the Mills organisation. Edgar Hayes joined the band at the end of 1930; he remained until the late summer of 1936 as its arranger and probably musical director. Lynch left in autumn 1931. His replacement as drummer being O'Neil Spencer, but the front man until quite late in 1933 became Baron Lee (real name, Jimmy Ferguson). Lucky Millinder took over from Lee and remained as director until the band finally broke up in 1938,

when its personnel included trumpeter Frank Newton, trombonist Fernando Arbello, tenor saxophonist Don Byas and clarinettist Edmond Hall. Recording sheets for an RCA Victor session of 1933 list trumpeter Eddie Mallory as musical director, so it is possible that he took over temporarily for a short period after Lee left, though it seems equally likely that he was merely the contractor for this particular date. After the success of the recording *Ride, Red, Ride* in 1935, Henry 'Red' Allen was offered the leadership, but because of his liking for Millinder, he declined.

Musically, Mills Blue Rhythm Band was a highly efficient unit with a number of good soloists. It failed to rise from the ranks of the secondary units of its day mainly because it never really established an identity. From one of its earliest sessions, we have evidence of eclecticism in its recordings of *Blue Rhythm,* an obvious attempt to emulate the then highly popular Casa Loma Orchestra, and *Blue Flame*, a much more successful performance with good solos from Edward Anderson (trumpet), Crawford Wethington (baritone saxophone) and Edgar Hayes (piano). *Futuristic Jungleism* is worth hearing for George Morton's engaging scat singing and the drive of the band. The same singer is heard on the attractive *Moanin'*, which has further excellent trumpet work from the underrated Anderson. *Heebie Jeebies* is an exuberant performance with Anderson again taking an impressive solo, as is *Snake Hips,* with nice solos from Wardell Jones, Anderson, Castor McCord and a clarinettist I take to be Theodore McCord. *Savage Rhythm* has some fine writing for the ensemble which sounds as if it has been influenced by Don Redman's scores for McKinney's Cotton Pickers, but the number is the sort of spurious production item that was tailored for Cotton Club patrons seeking their quota of exotica. Much better is *Wild Waves,* an Ellington-ish theme written by trombonist Harry White, with good solos probably from Shelton Hemphill (trumpet), White, Charlie Holmes (alto saxophone) and Anderson. Soloist identification on a number of performances by the band is tentative and could well be partially inaccurate.

In March 1933, Mills Blue Rhythm Band recorded two numbers by the Irish composer Patrick 'Spike' Hughes— *Weary Traveller* and *Buddy's Wednesday Outing. Weary Traveller* is a particularly attractive performance, with an excellent alto solo by Gene Mikell. Seven months later, the band took part in an RCA Victor session that produced the pleasant Ellington-ish *Love's Serenade* and the more extrovert *Break It Down* and *Harlem after Midnight,* which shows the fine musicianship of the band at this time, with the section work of a high order. *Break It Down* includes a first rate solo by baritone saxophonist Crawford Wethington. Wethington, like Anderson, never really got the credit he deserved, for though an uneven soloist, he was capable of playing really well—few other musicians on his instrument at this time could better him.

In the autumn 1934, the band's solo strength received a fillip with the arrival from the Fletcher Henderson band

The brass section of Mills Blue Rhythm band in the latter part of the 1930s. The trombonists are George Washington and J. C. Higginbotham; the trumpeters Henry Allen, Wardell Jones and Shelton Hemphill.
Right: *Red Norvo in 1936.*

of Henry 'Red' Allen and Buster Bailey, who brought with them trombonist J. C. Higginbotham. Over the next two years, the band recorded for the US Columbia label, with its sound becoming more modern as the swing era got under way. Its greatest success on record was *Ride, Red, Ride,* a feature for Allen which he concludes with an exhibitionistic solo. Allen was clearly the outstanding soloist with the band; his rhythmically adventurous playing is heard to advantage on his own *Algiers Stomp, St Louis Wiggle Rhythm* and *Midnight Ramble.* Another interesting musician was alto saxophonist Tab Smith, whose floating, light and highly distinctive style is well featured on *St Louis Wiggle Rhythm, Red Rhythm* and *In a Sentimental Mood. Blue Mood* sees a reversion to Ellington pastiche, with Buster Bailey taking the theme in the style of Barney Bigard. Mills's staff arranger Will Hudson contributed *Mr Ghost Goes to Town,* a trite theme, despite which Smith, guitarist Lawrence Lucie, and Allen have fine solos, with Allen showing unusual rhythmic freedom.

Far too many of the band's recordings at this time featured totally expendable vocals by Chuck Richards, a mannered popular singer of slight merit. However, the titles on which Richards sings are seldom devoid of solos. Smith's airy and relaxed contribution to *Jes' Natch'ully Lazy* and Allen's beautiful closing solo on *Shoe Shine Boy* provide reasonable compensation for Richard's cloying vocals. With a much changed personnel, the band made its final records for the Variety label during 1937, among them good performances of Chappie Willet's *Blue Rhythm Fantasy* and *Prelude to a Stomp.* A year later it disbanded, an occurrence which received almost no publicity.

Perhaps the very manner of its birth, as a fill-in band for bigger names, set the pattern for much that followed.

Clearly the Irving Mills office gave it none of the publicity build-up accorded to Ellington and Calloway, for example, and at times the musicians must have felt like the proverbial poor relations. Some at least of the personnel must have suffered through not playing in a bigger name group, for several of its soloists over the years were individual stylists in their own right. I am thinking primarily of such musicians as Anderson, Mikell and Wethington. The recorded output of Mills Blue Rhythm Band was too often derivative, yet there are plentiful hints that it had the potential to become a first class unit. A proportion of its records still make for very pleasant listening, and one admires the talent of individual soloists and the musicianship of the band as a whole. If it had possessed a really major arranger who could have established its own identity, and if its booking office had given it a little more attention, the history of Mills Blue Rhythm Band might have been less obscure.

Red Norvo, who was born Kenneth Norville at Beardstown, Illinois, on 31st March 1908, is the only jazz musician to have made his reputation on the xylophone. During the 'twenties and 'thirties the xylophone was used in some dance bands, mainly for effects, and there were some flamboyant vaudeville performers who played it, but in jazz it was not considered a serious instrument until Norvo proved otherwise.

As a child, Norvo studied piano before switching to xylophone; at seventeen he toured the Mid West with a marimba band. When the band reached Chicago he remained there, and worked with Paul Ash and Ben Bernie. During 1926-27, he studied mining engineering at the University of Missouri. Returning to music, he led his own band on a Chicago radio station and worked with Victor Young before joining Paul Whiteman, with whom he remained until mid-1932. During the next few years, Norvo undertook a great variety of free-lance work, making the first recordings under his own name in April 1933. At this time, he occasionally worked with the Charlie Barnet band, and sometimes played piano, as in recordings he made early in 1936 under the name of Ken Kenny.

From October 1935, Norvo led his own sextet at the Famous Door club in New York, augmenting it to ten pieces for his debut at the Hotel Commodore in May 1936. During the autumn of that year, he led this band at the Syracuse Hotel, where vocalist Mildred Bailey—his wife from 1933 to 1945—joined it, then moved to the Blackhawk in Chicago. During the next two years, with various changes in personnel, Norvo's band remained together, though by autumn 1938 only alto saxophonist Frank Simeone and bassist Pete Peterson remained from the original group. Early in 1939, Norvo's group disbanded under somewhat curious circumstances. The official reason was that many of its members were ill and that therefore Norvo did not have sufficient fit musicians to fulfil his next engagement. It was known at the time that there was dissension within the band, partly because of Mildred Bailey's presence. While she was an outstanding singer, Miss Bailey was also an extremely temperamental personality with whom musicians sometimes found it hard to get along.

Later in 1939, Norvo reorganised once more, this time with Terry Allen as vocalist, but the band was poorly booked and soon broke up. In the spring of 1940, he was back with a new ten-piece unit, then in late 1941 fronted a big band of six brass, five saxes, four rhythm, and vocalist Linda Keene. This was hailed as an outstanding unit, but it only had the opportunity of recording two titles before the American Federation of Musicians called its ban. Through a variety of adverse circumstances, it was soon forced to break up and Norvo to resume leading a sextet.

Late in 1944, Norvo gave up the sextet and went to work with Benny Goodman. From this period, he switched to vibraphone. After leaving Goodman in December 1945, he spent a year with the Woody Herman band, then moved to California where he alternated between leading his own group and free-lancing. In the early 'fifties, he achieved some success with his trio, touring Europe during 1954. In 1956, he toured Australia, then opened his own club in Santa Monica, California. He visited Europe again in late 1959 with Benny Goodman. During most of the 'sixties, Norvo worked mainly in California and Las Vegas, taking an enforced absence from music in 1968 because of an ear operation. Later that year he toured Europe as a soloist, and returned in 1969 as a member of George Wein's Newport All Stars. In the past year or two, Norvo has been beset by hearing problems.

Norvo's 1936 band was one of the most subtle musical groups of the swing era, offering abundant proof that swing groups did not have to be loud or flashy. Part of its success was due to the brilliant arranging of Eddie Sauter, who wrote scores that were harmonically advanced. Rather than fall back upon the conventional call-and-response patterns of many swing bands, he preferred to seek unusual orchestral textures in instrumental blendings that

Above: *'Mr and Mrs Swing' – Red Norvo and Mildred Bailey.*

Below: *a publicity shot of Red Norvo in his bandleading days.*

were fresh and stimulating. Norvo himself was near his peak as a soloist at the time, using a flat, vibratoless and highly rhythmic technique to build solos that never relied upon technical ostentation. The band had one or two other good soloists, notably trumpeter Stew Pletcher, clarinettist Slats Long, and tenor saxophonist Herbie Haymer, though it clearly owed much of its commercial appeal to Mildred Bailey. Though the band went over well in an intimate setting, it suffered in large arenas and theatres as its music called for a sympathetic and informed audience.

Mildred Bailey's vocals and Eddie Sauter's arrangements formed a potent combination, for Miss Bailey was among the finest of jazz singers, despite a deceptive lightness of voice. The partnership works admirably on *A Porter's Love Song to a Chambermaid*, recorded at the band's first session in August 1936, and even more so on the slightly later *Smoke Dreams*, which has one of the most brilliant arrangements Sauter ever wrote for the Norvo band, notably in its harmonic freshness. Sauter has said that he was annoyed with Mildred Bailey when he wrote it and deliberately made it difficult. *I Would Do Anything for You* is another good score, with the saxes, led by Frank Simeone, playing very well in the theme chorus; this leads into an attractive melodic solo by Pletcher; there are duets by Long and Norvo and then Haymer and Norvo, and the close has Norvo soloing against a quiet ensemble background. *Remember* is one of the band's best recordings, with a beautiful integration of Sauter's score, ensemble work, and individual solos. *Russian Lullaby* again shows the sax section to be an outstanding unit, and Norvo, Pletcher, Long and Haymer provide good solos. Haymer's style owes something to 'Chu' Berry, and he is heard in his typical bustling style on *Clap Hands, Here Comes Charlie*, which also has a thoughtful, rhythmic contribution from Norvo.

When *Tea Time* and *Jeannine* were recorded in February 1938, only bassist Pete Peterson remained from the 1936 group. *Tea Time* is a relaxed instrumental performance with good playing by the individual sections and solos by clarinettist Hank D'Amico, Norvo, tenor saxophonist Jerry Jerome, trombonist Wes Hein and trumpeter Barney Zudecoff. *Jeannine* is in a similar vein, with Norvo and an unidentified trumpeter taking good solos. Charlie Shavers's *Undecided*—so named when a recording director phoned Shavers to ask him for the title of the number and the latter said that he was undecided what to call it—is treated in a fairly conventional manner, but Norvo's solo is particularly good and trumpeter Jack Palmer is heard playing with strong attack. Another number which was first played by the John Kirby band is *Rehearsin' for a Nervous Breakdown;* the Norvo version has fine solo work from its leader, a jump style solo from tenor saxophonist George Berg and a forceful trumpet passage I take to be the work of Palmer.

Although the music of the Norvo band was by now less subtle than it had been two years previously, it still avoided the mechanical aspects of swing, with ensemble passages showing attention to shading and to varied instrumental textures. *Toadie Toddle* demonstrates the relaxed cohesiveness of the ensemble, with Norvo, Berg, Palmer and an alto saxophonist taking effective solos. The score for *There Will Never Be Another You* has some deft touches, notably the use of clarinets behind Mildred Bailey's vocal and saxes backing Norvo's discreet solo. The slightly later *Some Like It Hot* displays the mobility of the saxes. After Norvo's own thoughtful contribution, clarinettist Hank D'Amico takes one of the best solos he recorded with the band.

Jersey Bounce, one of the only two titles recorded by

Norvo's big band of 1941-42, still shows that the leader was sticking to his policy of restrained music. His own playing is as impressive as ever—it is hard to find any solo by him from this period that one could justly dismiss as trite—and there are short contributions from an unidentified trumpeter and tenor saxophonist before the brash solo by trombonist Eddie Bert. The latter seems oddly out of place in a Norvo band recording; his barking tone is like that of later Kenton trombonists, and it is noticeable that the closing ensemble passage is more brass-dominated than usual.

Red Norvo deserves praise for adhering to a musical policy of subtlety and good taste during the greater part of his career as a leader. The 1936-37 band, when Eddie Sauter was providing the scores, was certainly one of the most individual to have been active at the time, and can be reckoned among the forerunners of the later Claude Thornhill band. Norvo's career at this time was certainly a rather chequered one: he was not always lucky with his bookings and locations. The qualities which are so admirable in the band's music reflect Norvo's own personality. One regrets that success proved elusive to this most interesting and underrated of bands.

Don Redman was the most important arranger in big band history. He established the principles of scoring for a large jazz ensemble while working with Fletcher Henderson in the mid 'twenties. He was born in Piedmont, West Virginia, on 29th July 1900. By the time he arrived in New York with Billy Paige's Broadway Syncopators, early in 1923, he had received a thorough musical training at several conservatories and was a talented instrumentalist. It has been said that Redman established his arranging methods while working with Paige, but they were not fully developed until he was staff arranger with the Fletcher Henderson band from early 1924 until June 1927. After leaving Henderson, Redman became musical director of McKinney's Cotton Pickers in Detroit. He left them during the summer of 1931.

Almost inevitably, Redman turned to bandleading. He formed his first orchestra in autumn 1931, mainly employing former members of Horace Henderson's band and McKinney's Cotton Pickers. He maintained a regular band until January 1940, spending much of the time in a residency at Connie's Inn, New York. He also gained the contracts for some important radio shows. While leading his own group, he also wrote many arrangements as a free-lance arranger, for such well-known band leaders as Paul Whiteman, Isham Jones and Nat Shilkret. He concentrated on free-lance arranging for almost a year after the break-up of his band and then, briefly, organised a new group. After a period as staff arranger with Bobby Byrne, he went free-lance again, providing scores for many of the best bands of the swing era. Among big bands which he formed occasionally for limited engagements, was a group he took to Europe in September 1946. He remained there for almost a year.

Redman had his own television series in New York in the autumn of 1949. He worked as musical director for vocalist Pearl Bailey from 1951 until the end of his life, rarely appearing as a performer. He did, however, occasionally record and play at concerts. He worked on a number of extended compositions, none of which has been publicly performed. His widow still possesses the scores, together with many from his earlier days. He died in New York on 30th November 1964.

Redman was an extremely proficient performer on most of the reed instruments, though not entirely consistent as a soloist. In general, his best recorded solos are to be heard on the items he made with Louis Armstrong (in 1928) and with McKinney's Cotton Pickers.

The Redman band recorded for the US Brunswick label between the end of 1931 and the beginning of 1934. At its first session, it produced an orchestral masterpiece in Redman's best known composition, *Chant of the Weed* (marihuana), a brooding performance with solo passages closely integrated. The score makes frequent use of contrast. The first four bars of the theme are played by the saxes in unison, and the last four in harmony; Ronald Atkins has noted that 'The scampering, whole-tone passage played by a vibratoless saxophone section here is one of the most riveting moments in big-band jazz.' Few initial recordings by any band can have attracted the critical praise that greeted *Chant of the Weed,* but the title led some reviewers astray. The late Edgar Jackson, for example, in The Gramophone described 'the sinister story of the swamps of the mysterious and impenetrable jungle'. *Shakin' the African,* from the same session, was brilliant. It had a superb solo by Henry Allen who deputised on the date for Sidney de Paris. The amusing *I Heard* had a typical semi-talking vocal by the leader.

Redman never managed to equal the impact of his first session, either as bandleader or composer, but continued to produce excellent recordings for the rest of the 'thirties. Often he featured his own vocals or those by Harlan Lattimore, an immensely popular singer who was sometimes billed at the time as 'The Coloured Bing Crosby'. A lot of good titles were recorded at a session in June 1932. *Tea for Two* is very well scored, in spite of a forgettable vocal chorus by Lattimore, and as well as displaying good solos by trumpeter Shirley Clay and trombonist Benny Morton is notable for some crisp ensemble playing. *Hot and Anxious,* arranged by Horace Henderson, is a theme that introduces the familiar riff later used in *In the Mood,* and has solos by Clay and tenor saxophonist Robert Carroll, one of the many good Coleman Hawkins-inspired tenor players active in the 'thirties. *I Got Rhythm* finds the band in excellent form. The score by Redman includes such neat touches as an arresting background figure behind Morton's solo and a striking passage by clarinet against trombones. One of the three soloists is clarinettist Edward Inge, a splendid musician with a fluent technique and full, though cutting, tone that is particularly effective against the ensemble.

In April 1933, the Redman band recorded a version of Duke Ellington's *Sophisticated Lady*. It was reported at the time that Redman had taken down the melody while listening to the Ellington band at a table in the Cotton Club. His version is much more fully scored than Ellington's. It opens with Redman's clarinet over a dense orchestral background, and he later takes a pleasant alto solo. *That Blue-Eyed Baby from Memphis* is a trite pop song of the day, with a typical vocal chorus by Lattimore, but the score is good and there is outstanding clarinet work by Inge, while Sidney De Paris takes a good open trumpet solo.

The band made one session for the American Recording Company in 1933, and two more during 1936. Neither produced anything outstanding. In 1937, seven titles were recorded for Irving Mills's Variety label. Redman had pioneered what he termed a 'swing choir'. He wrote a counter-melody to which the musicians shouted a paraphrase of the lyrics. The swing choir first appears on the 1932 recording of *Nagasaki,* but is featured on no fewer than three of the Variety titles. *Exactly Like You* and *On the Sunny Side of the Street* both contain excellent melodic solos from trumpeter Harold Baker, but the swing choir soon palls. Much better are *Sweet Sue,* with its arresting counter-melody, and the more straightforward *Swingin' with the Fat Man* on which the band swings strongly; soloists Reunald Jones (trumpet), Rupert Cole (alto saxophone), Benny Morton, Gene Porter (tenor saxophone) and Harold Baker contribute effectively.

From December 1938 Redman was contracted to RCA Victor. Most of the output of his last four sessions with a regular band appear on that company's Bluebird label.

Above: *the Don Redman band, 1932. Back row: Manzie Johnson, Talcott Reeves and Bob Ysaguire. Trombones: Benny Morton, Fred Robinson and Claude Jones. Front row: Sidney de Paris, Shirley Clay, Leonard Davis (trumpet), Horace Henderson (piano), Don Redman, Edward Inge, Robert Carroll, Rupert Cole (saxophone).* Right: *Don Redman, 'The Little Giant', at Connie's Inn.* Far right: *Don Redman in the 1950s.*

There is little of the adventurous scoring heard on some of the band's earliest recordings, and the swing choir is rather too much in evidence on such titles as *Sweet Leilani* and *Auld Lang Syne.* The first date produced an interesting version of Wilbur Sweatman's *Down Home Rag,* featuring Redman on soprano saxophone, and a spirited performance of Jelly Roll Morton's *Milenberg Joys* with good solos from Inge, Reunald Jones and Redman (alto saxophone). Most of Redman's remaining RCA Victor titles are rather commercial, but from the last session came a pleasant version of *Shim-Me-Sha-Wabble* with excellent scoring and apt solos by trombonist Claude Jones and an alto saxophonist I take to be Redman himself. It is perhaps fitting that the final number Redman ever recorded with a regular big band was a new version of *Chant of the Weed.* Although lacking the emotional impact of the initial recording, it is still impressive. Drummer Manzie Johnson sustains a rhythmic figure and Redman features in an excellent alto solo. The effect of the whole is rather more ethereal and less sinister than that of the original, and is of value in showing how Redman reworked a familiar theme.

It is possible that the very brilliance of Redman's initial recordings led critics to expect too much of his later

output. Even his more commercial titles, with a few exceptions, have good solo passages and felicities of scoring. The later performances suggest that he was becoming content to follow a conventional path. In 1958, he told interviewer Frank Driggs that he had been getting tired of travelling by the mid 'thirties, adding that he had always preferred writing. And that is what he concentrated on, with a few intervals, for the last twenty years of his life.

He was modest about his own playing and remarked to Driggs, 'I never did go too much for Don Redman's playing. I could play parts, pretty things, arrangements, but there were guys like Benny Carter around, and I never fooled myself thinking I could play jazz like they could.'

Redman's importance in the history of jazz was established before he became a bandleader. However, he fulfilled the role with distinction during the early 'thirties and with complete professionalism even when he was becoming tired of it all. His own band recordings offer much of lasting value, but the question remains of his possible achievements both as composer and as leader in his later years, if he had been more fully committed. It is perhaps not surprising that Redman, an amiable and easy-going personality, felt no need to add to his earlier accomplishments in middle age. At least he had the satisfaction of spending his last twenty years or so in doing what he liked.

In an interview that appeared in the November 1939 Metronome, Artie Shaw told George Simon: 'Frankly, I'm unhappy in the music business. Maybe I don't even belong in it. I like the music part—love and live it, in fact—but for me the business part plain stinks!' He later remarked, 'I'm a musician, not a business man. If I wanted to go into business, I'd enter Wall Street and at least keep regular hours!'

Intelligent, articulate and outspoken, Shaw was always a controversial figure during the swing era, and some of his pronouncements offended fans and backers alike. Interestingly enough, the young musicians who were to form the first wave of the modern jazz movement recognised his deep commitment to his music. Trumpeter Benny Harris was once quoted as saying, 'We listened to Artie Shaw instead of Benny Goodman. Goodman swung, but Shaw was more modern.' On another occasion, Cannonball Adderley remarked that Shaw had 'one of the original cool bands'. Right from the start, Shaw set out on his own path, and the frustrations and disappointments he suffered ultimately led him to leave music altogether.

Shaw studied the saxophone from the age of twelve. He left his home in New Haven, Connecticut, when he was fifteen, in 1927 to work in Kentucky. No job was available for him there, so he worked his way home with a travelling band. In the next few months, he was a member of various little-known groups. Then, after a spell of almost two years with violinist Austin Wylie's band, he joined Irving Aaronson's Commanders, concentrating on tenor saxophone. He moved to New York soon afterwards. In his book, 'The Trouble With Cinderella', Shaw tells how he often used to sit in with pianist Willie 'The Lion' Smith at Pod's and Jerry's, while waiting to get his Local 802 card.

During the early 'thirties, Shaw worked with a number of prominent dance bands, including Paul Specht's, Roger Wolfe Kahn's and Red Nichols's. He worked in the studio with Fred Rich, toured with Roger Wolfe Kahn in 1933, then after a further spell of studio activity, left music for a year to run a farm. Returning to New York, he free-lanced again in the studios, but was prevailed upon by a New York club owner, Joe Helbock, to form a group to fill in at a swing concert Helbock was promoting at the Imperial Theatre. On the night of 24th May 1936, Shaw led his unorthodox unit of himself, two violins, viola, cello, guitar, string bass and drums on stage, performing only his own composition *Interlude in B flat*. Much to his own surprise, he was an immense success. Soon afterwards, he was offered financial backing to form an orchestra along these lines, and toured with it for about nine months. The line-up was two trumpets, trombone, tenor saxophone, clarinet, four strings and a conventional four piece rhythm section. After an initial recording session on 11th June, Tony Pastor joined Shaw on tenor saxophone, the start of a long-lasting association.

This band recorded thirty titles at eight sessions for the US Brunswick label and a further twenty—including many duplications—for radio transcriptions. This output as a whole is not entirely successful, but performances such as *Sugar Foot Stomp* and *Thou Swell* have a freshness and vitality that have survived almost four decades. Peg La Centra, though a pleasant enough commercial singer, was rather too heavily featured on this output, except on December 1936, a date when six instrumental numbers were recorded. *Sobbin' Blues* and *Cream Puff* have excellent, fluent solos by Shaw, but the outstanding performances are *Streamline* and *Sweet Lorraine,* both without the brass. *Sreamline* has a Shaw solo of great

Artie Shaw plays for a dance at the height of his fame in the late 1930s. The guitarist behind him is Al Avola.

agility; I prefer his wistful, melodic playing on the attractive *Sweet Lorraine*. Few jazz musicians have been able to handle strings very well. They are well integrated into this group and play on the whole with a welcome astringency.

In March 1937, Shaw was forced to drop the strings and reorganise with an orthodox line-up of five brass, four saxes and four rhythm. He regretted the need for this move, but found himself at a disadvantage when pitted against the brasher swing bands. He made his debut with this new band in Boston in April. Its line-up included trumpeter John Best, trombonists Harry Rogers and George Arus, reedmen Les Robinson and Tony Pastor, pianist Les Burness, guitarist Al Avola and the fine drummer Cliff Leeman. This band made a mass of transcription material and took part in eight commercial recording sessions for Brunswick label.

In the recorded performances by this band one can note how Shaw was shaping his subsequent musical policy. There is a concentration of good show material, offset by original instrumental numbers and an occasional blues. The arrangements, many by Shaw himself, stress ensemble shading and restraint rather than rousing build-ups; for the era of swing bands, there is a rather studied avoidance of musical showiness.

Night and Day and *I Surrender Dear* both feature Shaw stating the theme; the other solos by Pastor and Best (*Night*) and Arus (*I Surrender*) are comparatively short. The opening ensemble introduction to *I Surrender* sets the mood for the whole performance, which is reflective and restrained. *The Blues March,* which originally took both sides of a 78, is quite different: at times, there is a Dixieland flavour to the performance. Best has a good solo, Pastor, Burness and Arus are adequate if not particularly individual, and the highspots are Leeman's excellent drumming and Shaw's closing solo. Shaw has always been a surprisingly effective blues soloist, giving an impression of involvement with blues material that many of his more famous contemporaries could never achieve. The next session, of 17th September 1937, was one of the best by the band, not least for the eccentric but excellent scat vocalist Leo Watson. Watson has a brilliantly

rhythmic vocal on *Shoot the Likker to Me, John Boy,* and a shorter but equally effective one on *Free Wheeling.* Also recorded on this date was Shaw's theme, *Nightmare,* a moody if theatrical performance on which Shaw is the only soloist. A month later, the band recorded two instrumentals, both composed and arranged by Shaw. *Non-stop Flight* is the superior performance, with Shaw taking a highly accomplished solo; there is again a Dixieland feeling to parts of *Free for All.*

These first recordings by Shaw's orthodox line-up include several that are pleasant and one or two that are excellent. On the whole, though, their impact is not great (at times the actual recording sound seems rather dull), and there is no major soloist to support Shaw. The instrumental numbers suggest that Shaw was still slightly uncertain of his direction, though the recordings of show tunes and good popular ballads foreshadow much that was to follow. Shaw must have realised that some reorganisation was needed, for early in 1938, he made a number of personnel changes and, most important of all, hired Jerry Gray as a permanent arranger. He also started a lengthy engagement at the Roseland State Ballroom in Boston. This gave him the opportunity to do regular late night broadcasts, which were heard over most of the New York and New England areas. The band began to attract a considerable listening audience. Shaw, Jerry Gray, Harry Rogers and Al Avola set about writing new scores, and finally the band started to sound the way that Shaw wanted. Right from the start of Shaw's new recording contract with RCA Victor, his releases on the Bluebird label gained big sales.

Between July 1938 and November 1939, Shaw recorded prolifically for RCA Victor, turning out a body of work that seems a model of consistency. This period also saw his rise to eminence in the big band world. He now obtained the choice location jobs and appeared on major radio programmes. While working at the Palomar Ballroom in Los Angeles, the band also appeared in the film 'Dancing Co-Ed'

The amount of show numbers recorded by Shaw during this period increased considerably; variety was provided by the use of the better popular songs of the day and a percentage of instrumentals, most of them originals. Compared to most swing bands, Shaw's did not record very many jazz standards of the *King Porter Stomp* variety; certainly, it used less riff themes than its contemporaries. Shaw's 1938-39 recordings still sound so impressive today because, quite apart from their musical qualities, they are devoid of gimmickry and do not include stereotyped swing hits of the Larry Clinton variety.

Much against the wishes of his recording director, Shaw made a version of a little-known Cole Porter show tune called *Begin the Beguine* on his first RCA Victor date. Although the band gives it a spirited performance and Gray's arrangement has some good touches, few could have foreseen its success with the public. It was backed with a semi-humorous version of *Indian Love Call* on which Tony Pastor takes a hoarse vocal and became an enormous hit; today, it is a standard item for any anthology of swing classics. *Any Old Time,* from the same session, is notable for a superb vocal by Billie Holiday; the section and ensemble playing has a crispness lacking on earlier recordings. Billie Holiday worked with Shaw from February to October 1938, but because of contractual difficulties made no other recordings with him. In later years she spoke bitterly of the racial prejudice she met through being the only black artist with a white band; her feelings were directed against members of the public, not against Shaw, of whom she spoke highly, or his musicians.

On his second RCA Victor session, Shaw recorded remakes of *Nightmare* and *Non-stop Flight,* both superior to the Brunswick versions; on the next date, the band made an excellent version of *Softly, as in a Morning Sunrise.* In December 1938, the solo strength of the band was improved by the arrival of trumpeter Bernie Privin and tenor saxophonist George Auld. At the same time Les Burness and Cliff Leeman left, but their replacements, Bob Kitsis and George Wettling, were of comparable stature. Auld was given a solo on his first recording session with the band, contributing pleasant passages to its version of *Jungle Drums.* Despite the title, which suggests an equivalent to Goodman's famous *Sing, Sing, Sing,* the performance is a relaxed one with Shaw taking a melodic solo. The next two sessions were devoted entirely to show tunes; Shaw was the only soloist on the attractive *Vilia* and *Zigeuner.* Shaw's recorded solos at this time were always interesting. His fluent technique allowed him to move from the low to the high register with ease, and his flair for melodic variation was particularly well displayed on the show numbers he was using. *Carioca* is performed in a light-hearted manner, as is *Donkey Serenade,* with its humorous introduction by Shaw. On this the band builds up a riff close that swings well, with Shaw providing a coda in the manner of his introduction.

Shaw was lucky to have one of the most sensitive female band singers of the era working with him. Helen Forrest can be heard on numerous Shaw records of the period; some of her best vocals are on *Deep Purple, I Poured my Heart into a Song, All the Things You Are* and *I Didn't Know What Time It Was. One Night Stand,* from March 1939, is one of the band's most stirring instrumentals, with good solos by Privin—very much in the Berigan manner—Auld, trombonist Les Jenkins, Kitsis and Shaw. This is a Shaw original, as is *One Foot in the Groove,* which contains a reasonable plunger solo from trumpeter Chuck Peterson and a driving passage of jump style tenor from Auld. Shaw, who could be a very reticent soloist, takes only two eight bar releases and the coda on *One Foot.* Another popular instrumental performance was *Serenade to a Savage,* which provided drummer Buddy Rich with an opportunity to give his tom-toms a workout. Bernie Privin takes an effective plunger solo, Auld plays in his jump style, and Shaw brings the

Artie Shaw in the recording studio in the late 1930s.

recording to a close with high register work against the ensemble.

In mid November 1939, Shaw caused a sensation by announcing his retirement. The band continued for a few weeks under Auld's direction, then disbanded early in 1940. Pressures had been growing on Shaw for some while. A few months before, he had given an interview to a journalist in which he denounced jitterbugs as morons. In a later interview with George Simon that appeared in the November 1939 Metronome, he amplified his earlier statement: 'Sure, I don't like jitterbugs! I don't like business angles connected with music. I can't see autograph-hunters. I thought the Old Gold commercial was lousy for my music. And I don't like prima donna musicians!' He did add, though, that his strictures against jitterbugs were aimed at the minority who interfered with the musicians, not the majority who danced on the floor.

In 'The Trouble with Cinderella', Shaw has written in detail about this period, describing the business and other pressures as so overwhelming that he was on the verge of a physical and mental breakdown. He went to Mexico to think out his position, and returned to the United States early in 1940 with the intention of forming a sixty-five piece orchestra. Events, however, were to push him in a different direction. His RCA Victor contract still called for further recordings, so in March 1940, he went into the studio with a thirty-two piece pick-up band. One of the numbers that he recorded was *Frenesi,* an attractive tune that he had picked up in Mexico; it became a tremendous hit. At this date, he also recorded a version of *Gloomy Sunday,* probably the most morbid song ever to become popular. Two months later, he recorded again with a large pick-up group, the output this time including pleasant versions of *April in Paris* and *King for a Day.* The success of these recordings led him to organise a new band with five or six brass, clarinet, four saxes, four rhythm and nine strings.

This particular band lasted for about seven months, until March 1941. It included such excellent jazz musicians as Billy Butterfield, Vernon Brown, Jerry Jerome and John Guarnieri, but most of its output was a far cry from conventional big band jazz, consisting mainly of beautifully played standards with Shaw soloing against a background of the strings. *Stardust,* a feature for the clear-toned lyrical trumpeter Billy Butterfield, is an exception, as are the two part *Blues* and *Concerto for Clarinet.* On the former Shaw shows once again that he is a good blues soloist, but it was *Concerto* that really caught on with the public. On this number, Shaw states the theme over the strings before the full ensemble plays a bridge to Guarnieri's boogie-style solo, after which Shaw, Jerome, Brown and Butterfield are featured. The first part closes with Shaw initially in the high register against the full ensemble, scaling down to a quieter passage by him against strings. The second part is virtually all Shaw, much of the time playing over an insistent tom-tom beat by Nick Fatool; he concludes with a coda in the high register. It is a very impressive virtuoso performance, and one that led to a number of poor imitations during war years. At the same time as Shaw was recording with this large orchestra, he was playing dates with the Gramercy Five, a unit from the band: Butterfield, himself, and the rhythm section, with Guarnieri playing harpsichord.

In autumn 1941, Shaw organised a new band, this time with the coloured trumpeter/vocalist Oran 'Hot Lips' Page as a featured artist, and trumpeter Max Kaminsky, trombonists Ray Conniff and Jack Jenney, and George Auld in the line-up. Page is heard as soloist and singer on *Blues in the Night* and a two part *St James Infirmary,* which starts with Shaw taking a solo against a background of strings and saxes. Then Page has a vocal well backed by a muted trumpeter presumably Kaminsky, and there are solos from a trombonist playing in plunger style, Auld, Guarnieri, Shaw again and finally Page, who plays with a fierce attack and tone. Other good performances on record by this group include *Solid Sam, Deuces Wild* and *Sometimes I Feel like a Motherless Child.* Early in 1942, however, Shaw once more disbanded. Soon after he enlisted as a seaman in the U.S. Navy.

Shaw had not been in the navy long before he was asked to form a services band. During most of 1943, he led this band on a service tour of the Pacific war zone. Its personnel included Max Kaminsky, John Best, Conrad Gozzo, Sam Donahue and Dave Tough. In November of that year Shaw was invalided out of the navy, and Donahue took over leadership of the band.

After a period of convalescence, Shaw organised a new band. This dispensed with strings and had eight brass, clarinet, five saxes and four rhythm, with Imogene Lynn as vocalist. The personnel had a strong contingent of jazz musicians including trumpeter Roy Eldridge, tenor saxophonist Herbie Steward, pianist Dodo Marmarosa, guitarist Barney Kessel and drummer. Lou Fromm. The arrangements were provided by Ray Conniff, Buster Harding and others. It was the most modern and thoroughly jazz-orientated group that Shaw ever fronted.

The band's first recording session produced little of interest, but from the next, in January 1945, came a splendid version of *'S Wonderful.* The sound is now that of a modern swing band, and Conniff's score is excellent: at one point after Shaw's fluent solo, it introduces the various sections playing different phrases. Three months later, the rousing *Little Jazz* was recorded as a feature for Roy Eldridge ('Little Jazz' is Eldridge's nickname), who plays with great swing, power and control. Both *Tea for Two* and *These Foolish Things* contain pleasant Shaw solos, but overall are surprisingly bland, a fault that marred many of the titles that the band recorded at its frequent sessions in June and July 1945. Eldridge is heard in a very fine short solo passage on *I Can't Get Started,* and the final title the band made for RCA Victor is a beautiful version of *The Maid with the Flaccid Air,* superbly scored by Eddie Sauter.

Late in 1945, Shaw signed a new recording contract with the Musicraft label. One of his less conventional recordings for Musicraft was his own dramatised version of the Pied Piper legend, with actors, a narrator and his own orchestra. Before this, there were a number of straightforward band dates. After the first, which included good performances of Buster Harding's *The Glider* and *The Hornet,* he returned to using strings and also added Mel Torme and The Meltones as vocalists. His biggest hit for Musicraft was a two part version of *What Is This Thing Called Love* featuring Torme and the vocal group.

During the rest of the 'forties, Shaw intermittently led bands. In February 1949 he made a guest appearance with the National Symphony Orchestra at Carnegie Hall, then a couple of months later made an appearance at the Bop City club with a large string orchestra, close to forty strong, playing a concert that on the first night lasted for $4\frac{1}{2}$ hours. The repertoire included works by Prokofiev, Debussy, Morton Gould and a number of obscure composers. Not unnaturally, the jazz club patrons became restless—they were anxious to hear Ella Fitzgerald and the Kai Winding Sextet who were also on the bill. As the week progressed, Shaw's part of the proceedings was progressively cut, and he was severely criticised by the press for his programme which does seem somewhat eccentric for a jazz night club engagement.

Late in 1949, Shaw organised another orthodox big band, including a fair number of modern jazz stylists. He bought arrangements from Tadd Dameron, Johnny Mandel, Eddie Sauter and other advanced arrangers, but the public did not accept them, or the new style he was featuring, and the band soon broke up. Thereafter, whenever he took a big band out, he featured his 'thirties book, concentrating on former hits like *Begin the Beguine*. From late 1949 until 1953, Shaw recorded with a big band for the US Decca label. The results were far from impressive and Shaw himself sounds totally uninvolved on most of the performances, many made with pick-up groups. On four titles he does not even bother to take a solo. He made his last public appearance with a Gramercy Five unit at the Embers Club in New York during October 1953, and his final recordings with it in June 1954. Then he ran a dairy farm for a while. He moved to Spain in 1955 and remained there for five years. He now lives in Lakeville, Connecticut, and works mainly as a writer and adaptor for the theatre. He has not touched his clarinet for several years and has said that he is unlikely to do so in the future.

From his records it seems that Shaw's most fruitful periods were 1938-39 and 1944-45, though the 1944-45 band may never have realised its full potential. In strict jazz terms the 1938-39 band was no match for Charlie Barnet or Benny Goodman, let alone the major coloured groups. Its recordings, though, have survived the test of time better than most. Shaw's major achievement was to prove that it was possible to organise a swing band that eschewed certain of the more obvious conventions of the period, notably in showmanship and repertoire, and to succeed with a musical policy that was comparatively sophisticated. The detractors of the swing era tend to trot out familiar phrases about 'degenerate swing' and 'robot musicians', but swing encompassed a far wider variety of music than is generally realised. Shaw might not have been able to achieve all that he wished, but he did manage to produce a body of recordings in which musical values are paramount. In so doing, he triumphed more thoroughly than perhaps he ever realised over the aspects of the music business which he so disliked.

There can be few jazz followers who have not at some time wished that tape recorders had been invented earlier. When musicians describe occasions, such as Louis Armstrong's battle with Jabbo Smith, or the time when Joe 'King' Oliver defended his title against Freddie Keppard in Chicago, it would be less than human not to regret that they could not have been taped. My own dearest wish would be a recording of the battle on 11th May 1937 in New York's Savoy Ballroom between the immensely popular Benny Goodman band and the resident Chick Webb band. Goodman was at the height of his fame, and Webb was the recognised 'King of the Savoy'. The musical duel drew a crowd of five thousand people inside the ballroom and a further five thousand who were unable to get in. By all accounts the Webb band won decisively. Gene Krupa recalled Webb's drumming on that night. 'That man was dynamic; he could reach the most amazing heights. When he really let go you had a feeling that the

entire atmosphere in the place was being charged. When he felt like it, he could cut down any of us.'

Krupa's tribute was echoed by all the drummers who heard Webb. A New Yorker profile of Buddy Rich, written by Whitney Balliet in 1972, quotes Rich as saying, 'Chick Webb was startling. He was a tiny man with this big face and big, stiff shoulders. He sat way up on a kind of throne and used a twenty-eight-inch bass drum which had special pedals for his feet and he had those old gooseneck cymbal-holders. Every beat was like a bell.'

Webb's hard fight to the top was not helped by his physical problems. Born in Baltimore around 1909, he became hunchbacked because of a tubercular spine. He is said to have bought his first set of drums out of savings he had accumulated through working as a newsboy. After playing with local bands, he moved to New York around 1925, first fronting a small group at a club in the following year. He went into the Savoy Ballroom for the first time in January 1927. His 'Harlem Stompers' included Johnny Hodges and three musicians who were to gain fame with him in later years—Bobby Stark, Don Kirkpatrick and John Trueheart. A test recording made for the Vocalion label was unsuccessful.

For the rest of the 'twenties, Webb worked mainly in clubs and dance halls around New York. Early in the 'thirties, he led bands at the Savoy Ballroom, the Roseland Ballroom and on tour with a 'Hot Chocolates' revue. The first records released under his name appeared in 1931, the year in which he began regular, long residencies at the Savoy. In the following year, Webb's band went on tour with Louis Armstrong. Then, though it continued to make theatre appearances and short tours, it became almost a fixture at the Savoy Ballroom by the mid 'thirties. From 1931 until his death, Webb employed the showman Bardu Ali to front the band and take over the role of compère. It was Bardu Ali who first heard Ella Fitzgerald sing at an amateur talent contest and persuaded Webb to hire her. She joined the band in 1935. Gradually, her popularity became as great as that of the band, leading to Webb's period of greatest success. During 1938, a tour of ballrooms and theatres produced unprecedented audience reaction. Several attendance records were broken. However, Webb's health, never good, was breaking down. After one spell in hospital, he was readmitted in two months with pleurisy. Though severely weakened, he recovered and played engagements with his band almost to the time of his death, which followed a major operation in Baltimore in June 1939. His age was given as thirty, but it is likely, in view of his early career, that he was a few years older. After his death, the band continued under the nominal leadership of Ella Fitzgerald for over two years, with Ted McRae and then Eddie Barefield as musical director. Without Webb, though, it had lost its vital spark and the final break-up was inevitable.

The records made in 1931 are good, more because of the solos than any great individuality of approach. Louis Bacon (trumpet), Jimmy Harrison (trombone) and Elmer

Williams (tenor saxophone) are the soloists on both *Heebie Jeebies* (with Don Kirkpatrick on piano) and *Soft and Sweet*. They all play adequately, but it is Harrison who really catches the ear. He produces beautifully conceived solos with a warm tone and a fluent technique that under-

lines his importance as one of the great trombonists of jazz.

Late in 1933, the Webb band took part in the first of four sessions for the US Columbia label. There was a single date for the Okeh label in July 1934, before the

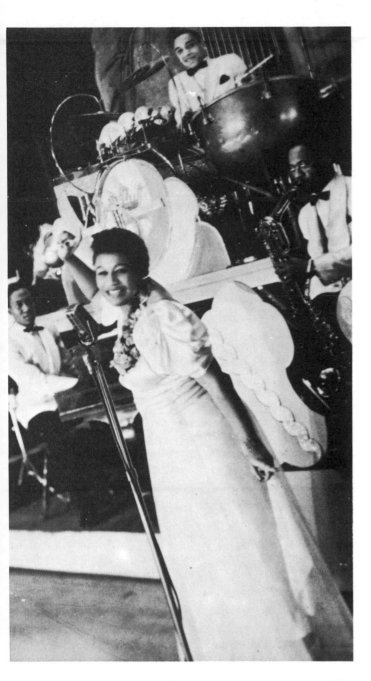

Left: *Chick Webb*, 'The King of the Savoy'. Above: *Ella Fitzgerald with the Chick Webb band.*

band signed a contract for US Decca, which lasted until its disbandment early in 1942. Until Webb's death, the personnel was relatively stable. The chief soloists were trumpeters Taft Jordan and Bobby Stark, trombonist Sandy Williams, reedmen Pete Clark, Ted McRae, Louis Jordan, Chauncey Haughton, Wayman Carver and Elmer Williams, and pianist Tommy Fulford. They were not all in the band at the same time, of course, though Jordan, Williams, Carver and Stark were all present from 1934 until after Webb's death. On a number of recordings, Carver played flute, then an unusual instrument in a big band. The reed men, though good soloists, failed to reach major stature, and the most individual solo voices were undoubtedly those of the two trumpeters and, particularly, Sandy Williams. Edgar Sampson, a very important early member of the band, was a fine arranger. He also played

alto saxophone in the section until 1936. Sampson wrote the bulk of the band's book in the early years, and composed such popular jazz standards as *Blue Lou, Don't Be That Way, If Dreams Come True* and *Stomping at the Savoy.*

If Dreams Come True (sometimes called *When Dreams Come True*) and *Stomping at the Savoy* were both recorded for Columbia during 1934. *Dreams* has a pleasant Benny Carter-like solo from Sampson and good muted work by Williams. Sampson's arrangements for both titles reveal his skill. He handles all the sections well and creates enough contrast to avoid monotony, in spite of a rather conventional approach. *Stomping* is one of the best of Webb's earlier recordings. Right from the start, the ensemble sets the pattern of the performance in an uncomplicated but swinging fashion. There are eight-bar passages by Mario Bauza (trumpet), Elmer Williams (tenor saxophone) and Pete Clark (clarinet), with main solos by trumpeter Reunald Jones and by Sandy Williams, who plays with great fluency and relaxed phrasing. Sampson also wrote the riff number *Blue Minor*, ably performed by the band. Sandy Williams is, again, the outstanding soloist. The same date produced a version of *On the Sunny Side of the Street* which featured instrumental and vocal contributions from Taft Jordan. At this time, Jordan was an Armstrong copyist; *On the Sunny Side of the Street* and the slightly later *It's Over Because We're Through* are among the best of his Armstrong-inspired efforts.

A fine version of Sampson's *Don't Be That Way* was recorded late in 1934. The band swings powerfully, and soloists Elmer Williams, Sampson, Claude Jones (trombone) and Jordan play admirably. For almost the first time on record, Webb himself comes to the fore. At the end, he pushes the ensemble along with some inspired drumming. Two other excellent Sampson scores are *Facts and Figures* with solos from Sampson himself, Clark and Jordan, and *Go Harlem*, with solos from Ted McRae (tenor saxophone), Clark, Sandy Williams and Webb. By now, the band had established its own identity. Jordan and Sandy Williams, especially, were producing consistently interesting solos. A very spirited *Clap Hands! Here Comes Charlie* was recorded in March 1937, with excellent solos by McRae and Jordan. The drive of the band at the close, with superb drumming from Webb, gives some idea of how it must have sounded at the Savoy. From the same date comes the outstanding *That Naughty Waltz* with good solos from Jordan and Chauncey Haughton (clarinet) and more superlative drumming by Webb. Charlie Dixon is the arranger in this instance and also wrote the score for *Harlem Congo*, a number performed with impressive attack by the band. Jordan has a fluent solo, making good use of flares, and passages by Haughton (clarinet) and Sandy Williams are followed by that rarity, a full chorus by Webb. He takes his opportunity brilliantly, and Hugues Pannassié's description of the solo as 'prodigious' is no exaggeration.

From the time that Ella Fitzgerald entered the band in 1935, the number of titles with her vocals gradually increased until, by the late 'thirties, instrumental numbers were recorded less frequently than before. Miss Fitzgerald was already an outstanding vocalist, and such titles as *Swinging on the Reservation, A-Tisket, A-Tasket, The Dipsy Doodle* and *Undecided* have become justly famous. However, I am concentrating on instrumental performances (though it is worth noting that many of the recordings featuring Miss Fitzgerald include solo passages).

A date that took place in May 1938 resulted in two particularly good band recordings. *Spinnin' the Webb* begins with a relaxed but swinging ensemble theme, followed by very fine solos from Bobby Stark and Sandy Williams. It has always puzzled me that Stark was given so little space on the band's recordings for, though erratic, he was capable of exciting trumpet solos, combining drive and logic. During the closing ensemble, Webb's part comes through very clearly. *Liza,* equally fine, begins with Webb's introduction and excellent solo (Jordan takes the release) before Stark once again emerges for a fierce, attacking solo. Webb is again prominent during the closing ensemble, and his drums are better recorded on this session than on most others. Three months later *Who ya Hunchin'* again has masterly drumming by Webb unusually well recorded. The last instrumental number made before his death—*In the Groove at the Groove*—is one of his few compositions. The performance is excellent, with Sandy Williams and Jordan as assured as ever in their solos and ensemble work of a very high standard. Four months after this recording session, Webb died.

Excellent as many of the records by the Webb band might be, only a percentage give any hint as to why it was such a formidable group on its own territory. It should not be overlooked that the crowd at the Savoy would be rooting for Webb, but firsthand reports indicate that it would generate a momentum in lengthy performances, sometimes lasting up to twenty minutes, that literally became overwhelming. Such performances could not be recorded before and the arrival of LPs, and the sound on a number of Webb's commercial releases is far from outstanding. Gene Krupa, already quoted, went on to say, 'For those who have never heard the Chick, I feel no small amount of compassion. Of course, records are made like *Liza,* for instance, but somehow, this genius never could get himself on wax. Chick gassed me, but good, on one occasion at the Savoy, in a battle with Benny's band, and I repeat now what' I said then, I was never cut by a better man.'

The Chick Webb band in 1938.

8 The Swing Era—
Other Bands

In the last chapter the major big bands of the swing era were discussed, but it is worth recalling that they only represented a fraction of the total number. Once swing became popular, bands claiming to play in the idiom proliferated, and by the closing years of the 'thirties there must have been literally hundreds of groups in the U.S.A. describing themselves as swing bands. A few of these were fronted by leaders who had merely jumped on the bandwagon, their only connection with swing, in some instances, being the use of the word in their billing; others were genuine enough—groups formed by musicians who had made their reputations with name bands, or longer established units who had always followed a jazz oriented policy. By the time that the swing era got properly under way there was a decline in the role of the territory bands, and recording opportunities were a rarity for units which seldom or never appeared in the major recording centres. Those territory band leaders ambitious to achieve national acclaim made a point of performing in a major city, preferably New York; no recorded evidence exists of most of the swing bands that operated on a localised basis. However, if the leader had some sort of public reputation, almost any band could reasonably expect to be recorded in New York or Chicago, and a number became prolific recorders over a period of a few years.

One or two of the bands covered in this chapter were musically superior to some of the more famous ones, but generally a combination of factors—lack of major soloists or an outstanding arranger, failure to create an individual style, too great a reliance on a well-known leader to carry the band, a tendency to fall back on stylistic gimmicks,

etc.—prevented their becoming other than secondary units. Nevertheless, most were technically highly accomplished, and almost none failed to produce records of some interest. The recorded output of the secondary bands—a term not to be confused with second-rate—underlines the high technical standards that were a commonplace of the swing era. If a high level of creativity was beyond the majority of the bands dealt with here, at least, in compensation, they generally avoided banality. They were all an essential part of the swing era and as such deserve to be remembered.

Trumpeter/vocalist Ovie Alston has already been mentioned in connection with Bill Brown and his Brownies (Chapter 2), with whom he worked from 1928 to 1930. A year later he joined Claude Hopkins and was a sideman with him until he formed his own big band late in 1936, leading it at the Plantation Club, Ubangi Club and the Roseland Ballroom over the next five years. During 1941 and 1942 his band was fronted by Noble Sissle and Eubie Blake on service tours, and he then returned to the Roseland Ballroom where he was resident until 1947. After this, Alston led smaller groups at clubs and hotels

Below: *Ovie Alston (sixth from left) with the Claude Hopkins band shortly before he left. Hopkins is at the piano, others are: Fernando Arbello (trombone), Henry Turner (string bass), Sylvester Lewis (trumpet), Bobby Sands (tenor saxophone), Walter Jones (guitar), Edmond Hall (clarinet, saxes), Eugene Johnson (alto saxophone), Albert Snaer (trumpet) and Pete Jacobs (drums).*

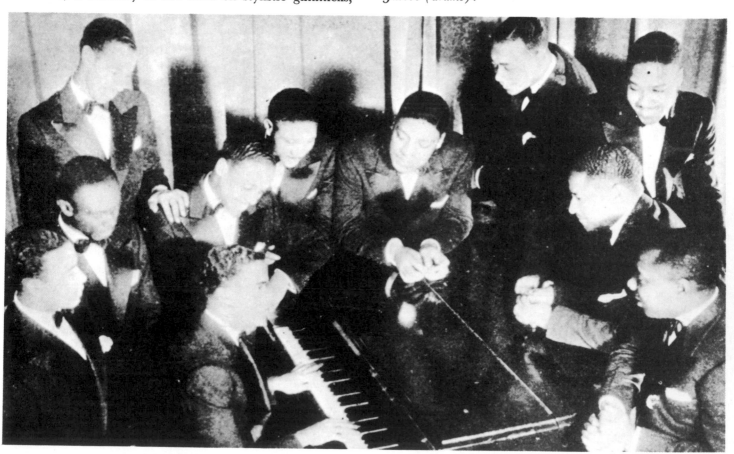

Above: *Louis Armstrong with his 1931 band at the Suburban Garden, New Orleans. Left to right: Lester Boone, Charlie Alexander, Al Washington, George James, Armstrong, Fred 'Tubby' Hall, Mike McKendrick, John Lindsay, Zilner Randolph and Preston Jackson.*

into the 1950s, retiring from full-time music at the end of the decade. There have been no reports of his having been musically active for many years now.

The musicians in Alston's big bands over the years are obscure, but in October 1938 he twice recorded for the U.S. Vocalion label, producing a total of eight titles. *Ja-da* and *Walkin' the Dog* are typical of his 1938 output, both featuring husky vocals and Armstrong-influenced solos by the leader. The band sounds well rehearsed and possessed an excellent rhythm section that provided a light, fluid beat; the work of bassist Abe Bolar and drummer George Foster were outstanding. Alston's former boss, Claude Hopkins, is present on both dates, presumably as a guest capacity. Other titles from the sessions—*Junkman's Serenade* and *Spare-ribs and Spaghetti* for example—are quite attractive and are good enough to merit reissue in a swing era anthology.

The big bands with which Louis Armstrong worked for a decade and a half frequently included excellent musicians, but not surprisingly they were mainly a back-cloth for Armstrong's own trumpet and vocal work and contributed nothing of note to big band jazz as such. His 1932-33 group, organised by trumpeter Zilner Randolph, is a case in point, for though it included musicians as good as Keg and Budd Johnson, Scoville Brown and

Teddy Wilson, it often sounded ragged in ensemble passages and the section work was frequently indifferent. There are a few occasions when it gave hints of better things—the brass introduction to *Sweet Sue, Just You* and the unison sax passage on *I Wonder Who*—but these are all too rare.

When Armstrong started recording for Decca in the autumn of 1935 his regular band was Luis Russell's, but it bore little relationship to the superb Russell band of 1929-30 and on record sounds worse than mediocre. The addition of the ex-Russell stalwarts Henry 'Red' Allen, J. C. Higginbotham and Albert Nicholas in the summer of 1937, plus the later arrival of drummer Sid Catlett, obviously brought about a much needed improvement in musical standards. The late Henry Allen once told me that at public performances the band was given a greater opportunity to shine than on record, but titles like *Our Monday Date, You're a Lucky Guy, Harlem Stomp* and *Wolverine Blues* at least display it as a well-drilled unit capable of swinging well, and one entirely agrees with the French critic, Hugues Panassie, who singled out these performances as amongst the best of Armstrong's Decca big band output for their orchestral work.

The big band that Armstrong used during 1946-47 got little opportunity to do other than fill in behind him, but at least it gave an impression of technical expertise. The sections behind Armstrong's vocal on *Endie* are well rehearsed, while the trumpets in the ensemble introduction to *The Blues are Brewin'* produce a fine sound. Although Armstrong made no commercial recordings with his regular big band of 1944-45, some LP issues

Above: *Louis Armstrong's band in the late 1930s.* Left: *George Auld in the late 1930s with Artie Shaw's band. The original caption described him as a 'Hot take-off tenor sax player'.*

exist, drawn from broadcast material. Apart from tenor saxophonists Teddy McRae and Dexter Gordon, it contained no particularly well-known musicians, but titles such as *Keep on Jumpin', Blues in the Night* and *Perdido* showlight the band effectively enough to suggest that it was possibly the best big band that he fronted. That Louis Armstrong was a unique musical genius can hardly be doubted, but his dominance was such that either by chance or design he appeared to care little about the standards of the big bands with which he played. This is sometimes painfully obvious; but it was part of his magic that as soon as he himself started to play it no longer seemed to matter.

George Auld's first big band experience was with Bunny Berigan in 1937-38, after which he worked with Artie Shaw through most of 1939, Jan Savitt during the major part of 1940, Benny Goodman for seven months from November 1940, then once more with Artie Shaw until January 1942. He then led his own band for a while, served briefly in the U.S. army, fronted a quartet, and formed a big band that was in existence from September 1943 until the summer of 1946. He has, of course, continued to work regularly down to the present day and has recorded quite prolifically, but his later activities are outside the scope of this book.

On his first sessions for the Guild label, Auld added a number of well-known musicians to his line-up for recording purposes only. A performance such as *In the Middle* is of greater interest for the solos by Erroll Garner and Dizzy Gillespie than for the work of the band. May 1945 is more instructive from the band's point of view, for here Auld uses his regular line-up, which then included baritone saxophonist Serge Chaloff, pianist Joe Albany and drummer Stan Levey. The best performance from this date is a spirited version of *Stomping at the Savoy*, featuring a hoarse-toned solo by the leader and contributions from two trombonists and trumpeter Al Porcino, the latter playing in a bop-influenced manner. The ensemble work is at times rough, the trumpets sounding superior as a section to the trombones and saxes. Five months later the band made a reasonable version of Al Killian's number *Let's Jump*, with effective solos from Auld, pianist Harry Biss, and Porcino. Biss is heard to better advantage in a performance of *Blue Moon*, recorded in January 1946, though here the band's ensemble work lacks attention to dynamics. From later dates *Just You, Just Me*, arranged by Tadd Dameron, and Neil Hefti's *Mo-Mo* are performed with spirit, but it is Dameron's arrangement of *A Hundred Years from Today*, with a really excellent vocal by Sarah Vaughan, that shows the band off at its best. Sarah Vaughan was also the vocalist on a recording of *You're Blasé*, arranged by Al Cohn—another very pleasing performance.

Auld's was hardly a top ranking band but it made a few interesting records. Though it employed a number of bop-styled musicians it was basically a late swing era group, the bop influences appearing only in occasional solos and a few passages in some arrangements, and it is probably not without significance that in later years Auld himself discarded the few elements of bop that he used at this time and reverted to his former Coleman Hawkins-influenced manner.

One is used to exaggeration in the sleeve notes of LP releases, but the following, contained in a short unsigned note to a Will Bradley Epic release, is something of a classic of its kind: 'This, in short, is a hand-picked collection of some of the greatest boogie woogie in recorded history, one that can hold its own in any musical library.'

The 'greatest boogie woogie in recorded history' includes such immortal gems as *Beat Me Daddy, Eight to the Bar, Scrub Me Mama with a Boogie Beat, Rock-a-bye the Boogie* and *Boogie Woogie Conga*, complete with hip lyrics of their era, sung by Ray McKinley.

Will Bradley, an extremely accomplished trombonist even if not a great jazz soloist, had a decade of experience behind him when he formed his band in July 1939, having worked previously with Milt Shaw, Red Nichols, Ray Noble, André Kostelanetz and several other name leaders, and also as a CBS studio musician between 1931 and 1934 and again from 1936 until he organised his new band. Bradley's group was unusual in having drummer Ray McKinley as co-leader. However, it was always billed under Bradley's name, records often having the additional line 'Featuring Ray McKinley'. The partnership lasted until early in 1942 when it was broken through disagreements on musical policy. Bradley then reorganised his band, bringing in well-known musicians —trumpeters Neal Hefti and Shorty Rogers, trombonist Bill Harris, and drummer Shelly Manne. By all accounts this was the best band he led, but unfortunately it never recorded. He broke it up in June 1942 when conscription into the armed forces led to wholesale losses. From that time Bradley has made only occasional public appearances, though he continued to record throughout the 'forties and 'fifties with pick-up groups. For many years he has worked in the New York studios, his interest in classical music leading to his writing a number of extended works in that idiom.

George Simon, reviewing the band in the April 1940 issue of Metronome, described it as the outstanding new band of the year, though he was critical of the tempos it set for ballads. There is little recorded evidence to support such an evaluation, though the band was frequently in the studios from the summer of 1939 until its break-up. Its first recording, *Celery Stalks at Midnight*, is a pleasant enough instrumental, with effective solos from trumpeter Joe Weidman and tenor saxophonist Peanuts Hucko; Bradley's score has some neat touches such as the blend of trombone in the low register with quiet trumpets at the close. *Strange Cargo*, sub-titled *Boogie-Woogie Nocturne*, was written and scored by pianist Freddie Slack and is an attractive mood number with neat section work, assured playing from Bradley, and a well-performed boogie theme by its composer. This number is not in the line of the later boogie numbers and oddly enough was later retitled *King Calypso*. Bradley's remaining output in the first nine months of the band's existence comprised popular ballads, usually with vocals by Carlotta Dale, and instrumentals which were performed adequately but with no great fire. An illustration of the latter is the band's version of *Flying Home*, arranged by Fletcher Henderson, with passable solos from Weidman and tenor saxophonist Nick Caiazza, and competent ensemble work lacking any real impact.

During 1940, boogie woogie, mainly as a result of the popularity of Albert Ammons, Pete Johnson and Meade Lux Lewis, was enjoying a vogue, and arranger Leonard Whitney, with Slack and McKinley, became interested in presenting the form in an orchestral idiom. A recording from May 1940 of a boogie-styled novelty number titled *Beat Me Daddy, Eight to the Bar*, issued initially as a two-sided 78rpm record, became a great popular success, and from then on the band concentrated on this type of material, sometimes using a smaller personnel. Though it continued to record popular songs of the day, generally played straight, it was the numbers in the boogie idiom such as *Rock-a-bye the Boogie, Scrub Me Mama with a Boogie Beat, I Boogied when I should* have *Woogied* and *Booglie Wooglie Piggly* that became favourites. Such performances combined elements of boogie with a big band setting, and invariably had vocals by Ray McKinley and solos by Freddie Slack or his replacement Billy Maxted. Today these pieces sound what they actually were—novelty ephemera—and are interesting only as a reflection of the boogie woogie craze of the period. Bradley became increasingly disenchanted by the direction the band was taking and nursed ambitions to attain higher musical standards. The differences between him and McKinley over repertoire and musical policy finally led to the break-up of the partnership. It seems certain that Bradley's technical expertise and concern for musical standards would have been better realised in a different setting, for his own solos, on most of the records the band made, are excellent of their kind. There is irony in the fact that the idiom which brought the Bradley band its commercial success was one which the leader himself did not find altogether to his liking, but his realisation that the benefits of hit recordings were not solely pleasurable was one he shared with quite a few of his colleagues. On record at least, the Will Bradley band must be considered one of the minor ones of the swing era.

Myron 'Tiny' Bradshaw, born in Youngstown, Ohio, in 1905, began his professional career as vocalist with Horace Henderson's Collegians, moving to New York in the late 'twenties and working with Marion Hardy's Alabamians, the Savoy Bearcats, Mills Blue Rhythm

Tiny Bradshaw.

Band and Luis Russell. He left Russell to form his own big band, which made its debut at the Renaissance Ballroom in New York around the summer of 1934. This band was an interesting one, comprising Lincoln Mills, Lester 'Shad' Collins, Max Maddox (trumpet), George Matthews, Eugene Green (trombone), Bobby Holmes, Russell Procope (alto saxophone, clarinet), Edgar Courance, Happy Caldwell (tenor saxophone), Clarence Johnson (piano), Bob Lessey (guitar), Ernest Williamson (string bass), Arnold Bolden (drums), and Tiny Bradshaw (vocal, leader). It recorded eight titles for the U.S. Decca label.

Bradshaw continued to lead big bands for over a decade and achieved some national popularity, but he did not record again until 1944. His personnels during this period are sometimes obscure, and much of what we know of them is due to the researches of the Swiss collector Kurt Mohr. Charlie Shavers, Carl 'Bama' Warwick (trumpet), Ed Morant (trombone), E. 'Son' Leavy, Ronald Hayes (alto saxophone), Fred Williams (tenor saxophone), John Williams (string bass), and Norman Dibble (drums) worked with Bradshaw in Baltimore during 1935, a year when Bill Johnson (alto saxophone, clarinet) and Billy Kyle (piano) were temporarily with him. Drummer Arthur Trappier, bassist William Oscar Smith and guitarist John McLean also played with him during the middle 'thirties. In 1939 he was fronting Nelson Williams, Benny Harris, Roger Jones (trumpet), Henderson Chambers, Ed Morant (trombone), Joe Allston, George Dorsey (alto saxophone, clarinet), Chink Williams (tenor saxophone), Charlie Fowlkes (baritone saxophone), Albert Allston (drums) and others, but for an engagement at the Apollo Theatre in New York he used a completely new brass section. In June of the following year his band consisted of Joe James, Paul Randle, Willis Nelson (trumpet), Edward Johnson, Henderson Chambers (trombone), Robert Plater, Jimmy Johnson (alto saxophone, clarinet), Winston Jeffrey, Lowell 'Count' Hastings (tenor saxophone), Bill Grey (piano), Tack Teaberg (guitar), Joe Brown (string bass) and Rossiere 'Shadow' Wilson (drums); and in the next couple of years John Anderson (trumpet), James Warwick (trombone), Fred Radcliffe (drums), and Walter 'Gil' Fuller (arranger) worked with him.

Musicians moved in and out of the band with frequency during 1942-44, but the line-up for a recording session for Regis in 1944 was Billy Ford, Talib Daawud, Sammy Yates (trumpet), Leon Comegys, Andrew Penn, Alfonso King (trombone), Sonny Stitt, Donald Hill (alto saxophone, clarinet), Lowell 'Count' Hastings, George 'Big Nick' Nicholas (tenor saxophone), Charlie Fowlkes (baritone saxophone), Howard 'Duke' Anderson (piano), Leonard Swain (string bass), Earl Walker (drums), and Tiny Bradshaw (vocal, leader). In 1945 Leroy Lovett was the band's chief arranger, and in 1946 alto saxophonist Gigi Gryce worked with Bradshaw.

The constant changes of personnel suggest that Bradshaw was not reaping any great success during these years, but with the entry of the U.S.A. into World War II, he was granted a commission as a major and visited many countries with a large band, performing before U.S. troops. Between overseas trips he continued to tour the U.S.A. He recorded for the last time with a big band in February 1945, and thereafter led small groups. Towards the close of the 'forties he moved into the rhythm-and-blues field and started to record for the King label. During the next year or two   had a number of hit records, working mostly in Chicago, until he suffered two strokes that forced his retirement in the late 'fifties. He died in Cincinnati, Ohio, in January 1959.

Bradshaw's Decca recordings are entertaining rather than outstanding, and too much time is taken up with the leader's Cab Calloway-type vocals. The best titles are *Darktown Strutter's Ball* and *The Sheik of Araby;* but *I Ain't Got Nobody* has good passages from a trumpeter I take to be Collins and a tenor saxophonist who is almost certainly Caldwell. The 1944 session produced a reasonable *Bradshaw Bounce,* with solos by a tenor saxophonist (probably Count Hastings), drummer Earl Walker and an unidentified trumpeter, while *Straighten Up and Fly Right* includes a forceful solo from 'Big Nick' Nicholas. Bradshaw recorded too little in a big band setting to make any overall evaluation possible, but musicians who played with him in 1939 and others who were in his 1942 personnel claim that his bands of these years were highly accomplished and as good as several name units. Failing the discovery of transcription material or private recordings one can only reserve judgment on such assertions.

Randy Brooks built up a reputation as an outstanding lead trumpeter with Claude Thornhill in 1942 and Les Brown in 1943-45. In the latter year, in the closing phase of the swing era, he formed his own band and secured a recording contract with U.S. Decca. Brooks was not a jazz soloist of any stature, his major recording hits coming quite late in his bandleading career with ballad versions of *Tenderly, More than You Know* and *The Man with the Horn,* all with his pleasant but rather syrupy solos. The rest of his recordings are mostly commercial items with vocals by Marion Hutton, Billy Usher, Lillian Lane or Harry Prime, but there are a few performances that suggest that his band had reasonable potential. Brooks did have the advantage of employing a genuinely talented arranger in John Benson Brooks, and he wrote the scores for *Thunder Rock, How High the Moon* and *A Night at The Deuces,* composing the first and third numbers. These were certainly the most interesting commercial recordings that the band made. *Thunder Rock* had section and ensemble playing of a high order, the solos being by Brooks, alto saxophonist Eddie Caine and an unidentified tenor saxophonist. The band provides a slightly modern sound, partly through some of the boppish figures used in the score, and this is evident once more in its version of *How High the Moon.* On this title Stan Getz, who had joined early in

1946, is heard in a distinctly boppish solo, and once more the ensemble playing is crisp and technically impeccable. *A Night at The Deuces,* described as being one part of John Benson Brooks's *Tales of 52nd Street* suite, is an excellent performance and begins with a boppish theme statement from the leader, Getz, and Shorty Allen on vibes, after which Brooks and Getz take effective solos. Brooks's muted solo here is quite different to his usual ballad style, showing a distinct bop influence, and Getz plays with considerable verve.

Brooks was forced to break up his band in the latter part of the 'forties. Later he married the female bandleader Ina Ray Hutton and moved to California. In later years he suffered a stroke which brought his musical career to a close. He lost his life in 1967 as the result of a fire at the house in which he was living. The recordings that he made with his band are uneven, though they invariably display high technical level skills. The band possessed a nucleus of fine musicians, notably the leader, Eddie Caine, Stan Getz and Shorty Allen, and John Benson Brooks—no relation to Randy—was that rarity a really individual arranger. If Brooks had formed his band a year or two earlier he might well have achieved greater success, but on the recorded evidence its full potential appears never to have been realised.

Willie Bryant led a good band during 1934 and 1935, though its contingent of worthwhile soloists was not matched by a really individual style. Bryant, born in New Orleans on 30th August 1908, was essentially an entertainer, and prior to forming his band in late 1934 had had eight years' experience in vaudeville, both as dancer and vocalist. Just before organising his band he had partnered Bessie Smith in a revue and had worked with the Buck and Bubbles unit. He led his own band for four years, then turned to acting and compering, also becoming a prominent disc-jockey. He undertook overseas tours as an entertainer to the U.S. armed forces

The Willie Bryant Orchestra, 1935. John 'Shorty' Houghton (trombone) and Bryant are in front; others, left to right: Edgar Battle (trumpet), Robert Horton (trombone), Benny Carter, Dick Clark (trumpet), William 'Cozy' Cole (drums), Arnold Adams (guitar), Louis Thompson (string bass), Glyn Pacque, Stanley Payne (alto saxophone, clarinet), Teddy Wilson (piano), Ben Webster Johnny Russell (tenor sax).

during World War II, organising a big band once more between 1946 and 1948. For the last decade and a half of his life he was best known as a disc-jockey in California. He died of a heart attack in Los Angeles on 9th February 1964.

Bryant's showbiz personality dominated more of the records his band made than was desirable. His vocals varied from being inoffensively pleasant to abysmal, and even when he did not take a vocal, he would often make spoken interjections that added nothing to the music. Teddy Wilson once told me that though Bryant had a quick ear and was by no means musically insensitive, he tried too hard to make characters out of his musicians, some of whom responded with a form of passive resistance. Mr Wilson considers that the band reached its peak when Benny Carter was its arranger, but concluded that it was 'never a good musical band'. Possibly he is a little harsh in his judgment, for many other musicians consider that in its earliest days, at least, it was an excellent band, even if not comparable to the best of the era. One went so far as to claim that it was potentially the finest band of its day, but he happened to be a featured soloist with it, and one must allow for a certain degree of bias!

Three sessions made between January and August 1935 present the most interesting recorded performances

Below: *Edgar Battle, trumpet soloist and arranger with Willie Bryant in the 1930s.* Right: *Benny Carter in the mid 1930s; for a short time he was arranger and sideman in the Willie Bryant band.*

of the Bryant band. Its personnel at this time harboured several good soloists who included trumpeter Edgar 'Puddin' Head' Battle (built up by Bryant as 'The Pied Piper Of Harlem'), trombonists John 'Shorty' Haughtone and Robert Horton, clarinettist Glyn Paque, tenor saxophonist Johnny Russell and pianist Teddy Wilson, and on its second session the addition of Benny Carter and Ben Webster further strengthened the line-up. The rhythm section was first rate, due in part to the presence of drummer William 'Cozy' Cole. From the first session, *A Viper's Moan* is the outstanding performance, the section work being tighter than in other numbers of this date. Solos are by Robert Horton, Russell, Battle and alto saxophonist Stanley Payne, Battle's making most impression. *It's Over because We're Through*, a pleasant pop number of the day, has one of Bryant's more restrained vocals but its main interest lies in the excellent solo work of Wilson against a background of muted trumpets.

From the second session, *Jerry the Junker* is an obvious attempt to cash in on Cab Calloway's success with numbers such as *Minnie the Moocher* and *Kickin' the Gong Around*, but although rather uninspired, it does include a good clarinet solo from Paque. Of greater value are *Rigmarole* and *The Sheik of Araby*, the first with some sharp ensemble passages and a good solo by Ben Webster, the second one of the best of all Bryant's records. Starting with an introduction by Wilson to Horton's growl trombone theme, there follows a series of excellent solos by Wilson, Webster, Battle and Paque, Paque's spiky clarinet ride-out creating a good climax. Paque's clarinet is also well featured in the final chorus of *The Voice of Old Man River* from the third session, but the highspot of this performance is an extended tenor solo by Ben Webster, amongst his best recorded work at this time. Both *The Voice* and *Long Gone from Bowling Green* have expendable vocals by Bryant, but the compensations on the latter are Paque's clarinet work and a good solo by Battle. Teddy Wilson arranged *Steak and Potatoes,* with Carter's influence clear in his writing for the saxes; and there are good solos from a trumpeter (possibly Otis Johnson), Webster, and trombonist George Matthews. The best title from this session is undoubtedly *Liza.* Wilson again wrote the score, and the solos by Matthews, Otis Johnson and Stanley Payne are all of high quality, Matthews producing some of his best recorded work on this date.

The Bryant band, with a number of personnel changes, recorded two further sessions for RCA Victor in 1936 but the titles are much more commercial and the performances generally uninteresting. There are good individual solos—Taft Jordan's on *Ride, Red, Ride* and *Mary Had a Little Lamb,* Johnny Russell's on *Cross Patch,* and Paque's on *Is It True What They Say about Dixie?,* for example—but the scores are ordinary and the band has little opportunity to shine. A final 1938 recording date with a completely new line-up (apart from guitarist Arnold Adams) produced a pleasant version of

Al Cooper's Savoy Sultans: Rudy Williams, Pat McNeil and Al Cooper (saxophones), Sam Massenberg and Pat Jenkins (trumpets), Grachan Moncur (string bass), Alex 'Razz' Mitchell (drums) and Oliver Richardson (piano).

On the Alamo, after which Bryant did not record again in a big band setting until 1946, when he made a couple of undistinguished sides for the Apollo label. Bryant's 1934-35 band came close to attaining top rank status, but musically it never quite made it and must be considered only as one of the more interesting secondary groups.

Al Cooper's Savoy Sultans were formed in 1937 under somewhat obscure circumstances, though I was told by the well-known trumpeter/arranger Edgar Battle that he was partly responsible for the band becoming organised, and had originally intended to bring it to Europe. But the European tour never materialised, and the band played lengthy engagements at the Savoy Ballroom in New York, until it broke up in 1945.

By the standards of the day the Savoy Sultans hardly qualifies as a big band at all. It started out as an eight-piece unit with two trumpets, three reeds and three rhythm, and became nine-strong when a guitar was added. Despite its limited instrumentation it achieved a full sound and musicians in many of the bands that played at the Savoy have told of the difficulty they experienced when they came up against the Sultans in band battles. The records made by the Savoy Sultans between July 1938 and December 1941 show why they were such formidable opponents for the name bands, though their prowess in this field may have caused some musicians to rate them more highly than was justified.

Essentially the Savoy Sultans were a functional group,

and one can well imagine that their hard-driving swing and basic riff material would be ideal for the Savoy dancers. Subtlety of performance or complexity of arrangement had almost no part in their music; instead they relied on a straightforward approach which almost literally outblew their opponents. One has only to hear the ferocious riffing on such numbers as *Frenzy* and *Stitches* to understand what problems other bands faced. Nevertheless, it would be unfair to imply that the Sultans won their musical battles by means of express tempo flagwavers, for part of their success lay in their ability to swing fiercely at medium tempo and to build exciting climaxes by clever use of dynamic variation. This aspect of their work is well illustrated by their recording of *Second Balcony Jump*. Occasionally they performed well at medium-slow tempo, the attractive *Jeep's Blues* and *See What I Mean?* being good examples.

Cooper himself was a versatile musician who played alto and baritone saxophone and clarinet, usually soloing on the clarinet. He also wrote and arranged many of the numbers in the band's repertoire. As a soloist he did not feature himself a great deal, but his clarinet passages on *Looney* and *Norfolk Ferry* are pleasant, *Looney* having a mellowness that one associates with New Orleans clarinettists. The major soloists in the band were alto saxophonist Rudy Williams and trumpeter Sam Massenberg, with trumpeter Pat Jenkins, pianist Cyril

Haynes and tenor saxophonists Lonnie Simmons or George Kelly performing ably on occasion.

Both Massenberg and Williams have attracted a certain amount of critical attention because of phrases they used which anticipated the post-swing era, but their work with the Sultans was essentially swing-oriented. Williams played in a jump style that made use of short phrases and occasional clusters of notes, employing a less rounded tone than was usual at this period. In more restrained vein he can be heard in good solos on *Jeep's Blues* and *See What I Mean?*, the last under a decided Willie Smith influence. At his most individual he can be heard on the faster riff type numbers such as *Jumpin' the Blues, Frenzy, Jumpin' at the Savoy* and *Stitches,* where he fashions solos that highlight his attack, swing and tonal strength. Massenberg was a musician who, like Williams, could easily have held down a job in one of the major big bands, his solo work being notable for its power and freshness. He achieved variety by use of tonal inflections and modifications of phrasing, and has fine solos on *See What I Mean?, Frenzy* (showing that he had listened to Roy Eldridge), *The Thing* and *Norfolk Ferry*, the fieriness of his work amply demonstrating why he was so respected by trumpeters who so frequently sparred with him in the Savoy band battles. The band's other trumpeter, Pat Jenkins, also possessed an attractive full tone and was extremely agile with the mute—as, for instance, in his

Left: *Rudy Williams taking a solo with Al Cooper's Savoy Sultans. The others are Razz Mitchell (drums), Pat McNeil (tenor saxophone) and Sam Massenberg (trumpet).* Above: *the Savoy Sultans with Al Cooper, far right, Pat Jenkins, far left and Rudy Williams, third from left.*

well-conceived theme on *Second Balcony Jump* and his plunger solo on *Jeep's Blues.* Lonnie Simmons's jump style was ideal for the band, although it lacked individuality; but he could, as on *Jumpin' the Blues,* produce apt solos, while George Kelly, at the time working mainly as a pianist, recorded a number of solos that are effective within the music's context. Pianist Cyril Haynes was not allocated much solo space on record, but is an effective member of the rhythm section and has neat solos on *Jumpin' the Blues* and *Second Balcony Jump,* which was performed against a riff figure by the saxes.

There was no shortage of bands during the swing era with a greater degree of musical sophistication than the Savoy Sultans, nor were bands with a stronger solo contingent hard to find. But when it came to enthusiasm and straightforward swing, the Sultans more than held their own with most of their contemporaries, and rival leaders could not contemplate playing against them at the Savoy without a degree of apprehension. Cooper, if one assumes that it was he that set the style of the band, made very intelligent use of the musical forces at his command, and by eschewing the complex and concentrating on essentials made the Sultans into a powerful force. Like Chick Webb and Erskine Hawkins, Cooper soon found that to achieve success at the Savoy it was important to win over the dancers. Once this was done his opponents

had another obstacle to overcome.

That the music of the Savoy Sultans was in the mainstream of the swing era and the big band jazz of preceding years cannot be doubted, but its jump style included elements that in due course were to lead to rhythm-and-blues and then to rock-and-roll. There is irony in the fact that this jump style, which became increasingly popular with the coloured population of the U.S.A. as the 'forties progressed, should have been part of the groundswell of a coming revolution in popular entertainment that was to bring the big band era to a close.

There were two leaders with the surname of Donahue who led swing bands in the closing years of the 'thirties and the opening years of the 'forties. The first, Al Donahue, was initially a violin-playing society bandleader who, in 1940, suddenly decided to lead a swing band, revamping his personnel as a result. The band's only well-known musicians were trumpeter Ray Anthony and guitarist Allan Ruess, and of the swing-styled records made, *Burning the Midnight Oil* and *The Blue Jump* are of mild interest. On the evidence of the few records I have heard, Al Donahue's was a competent group but one lacking any real individuality, its best soloist being a tenor saxophonist I assume to be Roy Hammerslag.

Sam Donahue has had a closer connection with big band jazz than his namesake Al. He was born in Detroit on 8th March 1918 and led his own band in that city from about 1934 to 1938. In the latter year he was offered a job in Gene Krupa's band and remained with Krupa until July 1940, the leadership of his Detroit band passing to arranger Sonny Burke. Burke brought the group to New York and it made four recording sessions under his name, on the first two of which Donahue sat in, while still a member of Krupa's band. At this time Burke was a great admirer of the Count Basie and Jimmie Lunceford bands, a fact given musical expression with a recording of *Jimmie Meets the Count.* The final date under Burke's name produced two highly competent performances in *Jumpin' Salty* and *Minor de Luxe,* both having reasonable tenor saxophone solos by Donahue.

At this point, in the autumn of 1940, the question of leadership of the band arose and the musicians decided that Donahue should resume his former role. Burke went on to arrange for Jimmy Dorsey and Charlie Spivak. In later years he had a lengthy association with Frank Sinatra at Reprise Records and became musical director for Warner Brothers. Meanwhile, Donahue continued to record, though his output became increasingly commercial. *It Counts a Lot* is interesting because Count Basie is the guest pianist on the title, while *Skooter* reveals the band as an enthusiastic if rather unpolished outfit. In 1942 Donahue took over the direction of Artie Shaw's navy band, after Shaw's discharge; no commercial records were made, but the group did record on V Discs and sounded a well-organised unit with some good soloists. From a jazz viewpoint it was unquestionably superior to Glenn Miller's AAF Orchestra.

After the war, Donahue formed a civilian band that included some members of the navy group, but the records it made during 1946 and 1947 are of slight interest. In the 'fifties, Donahue worked with Tommy Dorsey, led Billy May's band on a tour, and in the closing years of the decade again fronted his own band. During the 'sixties, Donahue became musical director of the Tommy Dorsey Band, visiting Britain with it on one occasion, but his later activities are obscure. Donahue was a big-toned tenor saxophonist whose initial inspiration was Coleman Hawkins. Many of his recorded solos swing well, although they sometimes lack discipline. None of the records made by the two Donahues or Sonny Burke has been reissued in microgroove form at the time of writing and, while not justifying, whole LPs would be worthwhile on anthologies that present a broad spectrum of the swing era.

Roy Eldridge, one of the greatest and most influential trumpeters in the history of jazz, first led his own band at the age of sixteen in 1927. After this he played with innumerable big bands over the years, amongst the most famous being Fletcher Henderson's, McKinney's Cotton Pickers, Zack Whyte's, Teddy Hill's, Gene Krupa's and Artie Shaw's. From time to time he led his own groups, which varied in size from a sextet to a big band, and in 1944 and 1946 he recorded for the U.S. Decca label with his big bands of those years. His 1946 unit played residencies in Chicago, New York, Los Angeles and other major cities, but the big band era was drawing to

Roy Eldridge; though best remembered for his work with Gene Krupa and Artie Shaw, he played with many bands including McKinney's Cotton Pickers, Fletcher Henderson's and Teddy Hill's and fronted bands of his own in the 1940s.

a close and in due course he cut down his personnel and worked with small groups.

Curiously enough, Eldridge's big band recordings of 1944 and 1946 have not been collected together on a single LP to date, only five titles having appeared in microgroove form. Inevitably, with a band fronted by a major soloist such as Eldridge, the records highlight the leader's playing, but other soloists do get the opportunity to be heard, albeit usually briefly. On the first of his 1944 sessions Eldridge recorded a big band version of *After You've Gone,* a number which he had previously made with a small group some years previously. *After You've Gone* is associated with Eldridge—he recorded it also with the Gene Krupa band in 1941—and this version is about the wildest that he made. Most of the performance has Eldridge soloing against a powerful ensemble in his most extrovert vein, with a closing chorus which showcases his upper register playing; but there is also a fluent alto saxophone solo by his brother Joe, an excellent musician in his own right. The other titles from this date— *I Can't Get Started* and *Body and Soul*—are vehicles for Eldridge's fine ballad playing, as is the moody *Twilight Time,* from a second 1944 session. From the latter comes a blues titled *Fish Market* (its meaning being mercifully unknown to the recording company!), and aside from excellent solos by Eldridge, trombonist Sandy Williams and guitarist Snags Allen, the performance gives an opportunity for the ensemble to build powerful and swinging riffs, propelled by a fine rhythm section in which drummer Cozy Cole is outstanding.

Of the twelve titles recorded in 1946, three remain unissued. Several performances again feature Eldridge almost exclusively, but the quality of the band is well displayed on a rocking *Les Bounce* and the amusing *All the Cats Join In*. It seems probable that Eldridge's regular personnel was strengthened on some of these recordings, though many of the musicians present were known to be sidemen in his bands at the time. Yet they are fine examples of their kind, and show the high degree of professionalism that was commonplace in the big band sphere as the swing era drew to its close.

Seger Ellis commenced recording early in 1925, initially as a pianist and then as a vocalist. A few of his piano solos are of mild interest, but his sentimental crooning style is about as devoid of jazz interest as can be imagined. Seger's accompaniments from 1926 to 1931 ranged from his own piano through salon orchestras to small jazz groups, the latter often including Tommy and Jimmy Dorsey, Joe Venuti and Eddie Lang. Presumably he was sympathetic

Seger Ellis and his Choirs of Brass band. The musicians are probably, in unknown order, Nate Kazebier, Don Anderson, Benny Strickler, Hank McCarthy (trumpet), King Jackson, Al Thompson, Bob Logan, John Stanley (trombone), George Siegler (drums) and Jim Lynch (string bass).

to jazz, for on two sessions he even managed to get Louis Armstrong to play in his supporting groups, but with the onset of the depression his recording activities ceased. Rather surprisingly he surfaced once more early in 1937, as leader of a swing type band known as Seger Ellis and his Choirs Of Brass Orchestra, the title being derived from its unusual instrumentation of four trumpets, four trombones, clarinet and three rhythm. With this group he recorded six titles for U.S. Decca, on two of which he made clear that his singing had not improved with the passing of the years, and then switched to the Brunswick label with a more orthodox line-up of three brass, three saxes and four rhythm, though still retaining the 'Choirs Of Brass' tag. The Brunswick recordings are of little interest, but such Decca titles as *I Know that You Know*, *Bees Knees* and *Shivery Stomp* are within the scope of the present book. *Shivery Stomp* starts with the brass playing the theme, after which there is a pleasant clarinet solo by Irving Fazola—masquerading for some unknown reason under the pseudonym of Pancho Villa—who had just left the Ben Pollack orchestra; a very indifferent piano solo by, presumably, Stan Wrightsman; and a closing ensemble chorus by the brass. The brass gives a rather top-heavy sound to the performance as a whole, and it is also somewhat deficient in swing. In January 1940, Ellis recorded for the Okeh label with a more orthodox instrumentation. The resulting *Mellow Stuff* and *Jitterbug's Jump* are competent swing-

Coleman Hawkins photographed in England many years after the period when he led a big band.

style instrumentals with a number of capable solos by unidentified musicians. Ellis achieved little commercial success with his bands and left music during the 'forties.

When the late Coleman Hawkins returned to the U.S.A. in July 1939, after his five-year European stay, he organised a medium size group to play with him at Kelly's Stable in New York. The enormous success of his recording of *Body and Soul* brought him more public recognition than ever before, and he formed a big band which made its debut at the Arcadia Ballroom in November 1939. He continued to front this band at various New York ballrooms until February 1941, when he switched to working with small groups, and until his death in New York on 19th May 1969, at the age of sixty-four, never again appeared in a big band context.

Inevitably with a soloist of Hawkins's stature his band frequently found itself in the role of a purely accompanying unit, but though it only took part in one commercial recording session there are LPs available which include items taken from broadcasts. From its Okeh session *Serenade to a Sleeping Beauty* is a melodic number written by Hawkins and Edgar Sampson which is a feature for the former's lyrical tenor saxophone playing,

with pianist Gene Rodgers contributing a pleasant solo and the band providing an efficient background. *Rocky Comfort* gives the band a little more to do, the ensemble sounding a little ragged at the close. Solos on this number are by trumpeter Joe Guy, trombonist Sandy Williams, and Hawkins, the latter employing unusually staccato phrasing on this occasion. From a broadcast of 25th August 1940 comes an interesting performance of *Chant of the Groove,* a number written by Hawkins himself. The saxes take the lead on the riff theme, with drummer J. C. Heard punctuating crisply. There are solos from trumpeter Joe Guy, Hawkins—using a very hoarse tone —pianist Gene Rodgers, and another, unidentified, trumpeter. The ensemble builds a series of Basie-like riffs between the closing solos and rides out with considerable swing. On *Can't Get Indiana Off My Mind,* Heard once more proves himself an excellent big band drummer, the closing ensemble passages using dynamics effectively and showing the band to better advantage than the faster tempoed performances; while *Passing It Around* —also recorded for Okeh—has some good reed scoring, at one point Hawkins himself leading the saxes. Although the band only has a subsidiary role on *Body and Soul,* this broadcast version of a number indelibly linked with Hawkins's name is worth mentioning, for it contains a truly magnificent solo by the leader which differs in many respects to his RCA Victor recording. The Hawkins band was not in the top bracket, but while it sometimes sounds undisciplined in ensemble passages—the sax section was better integrated than the brass—it could generate a considerable swing and gives the impression that its musicians approached their job with genuine enthusiasm. One would wish that some of its spirit could be found in the somewhat machine-like big bands that currently seem the norm.

When Edgar Hayes formed his own orchestra in 1937 he already had a decade and a half of big band experience behind him. Born in Lexington, Kentucky, on 23rd May 1904, he had won a Bachelor of Music degree at Wilberforce University at an early age, and until 1931 gained experience with a variety of bands. From time to time he led his own groups (the first in Ohio during 1924), including one that was part of a touring show. He was working with his own band in New York in 1931 when he was offered a job as arranger and musical director of Mills Blue Rhythm Band. He stayed with it until 1936, and during this period the front men were Baron Lee (Jimmy Ferguson) and Lucky Millinder. The personnel of his own band included several former Mills Blue Rhythm Band sidemen.

Hayes kept his band together until 1941, and took it on a successful tour of Belgium and Scandinavia in 1938. In 1942 he moved to California and led small groups in several clubs, but for the past two decades has worked exclusively as a solo pianist at various locations in that state. He was always a solid, dependable band pianist but one presumes that he must have modified his style since his big band days, no doubt currently playing in a jazz-influenced cocktail manner out of economic necessity.

As might be expected with someone of Hayes's musical background his band was a well-rehearsed and disciplined unit. What prevented it reaching the top rank was the usual combination of a lack of distinctive style and no major soloists. Yet its solo strength was by no means negligible, for trumpeters Leonard Davis and Henry Goodwin, trombonists Robert Horton and Clyde Bernhardt, clarinettist Rudy Powell and baritone saxophonist Crawford Wethington, if no match for the stars of the Basie or Ellington bands, were all capable of making individual contributions.

Sharing the musical direction of the band with Hayes was tenor saxophonist Joe Garland, and one of the numbers he wrote was the famous *In the Mood,* based on a familiar riff. Hayes's recording of this number is by far the best and avoided the monotony of most later interpretations, though the tune did not become popular until Glenn Miller recorded his version. The Hayes recording has the saxes leading on the theme, a neat touch being the trading of phrases between Wethington's baritone saxophone and the brass. Then follow solos from Davis and Powell, before the ensemble, with Wethington's lead work, returns to the theme and the performance closes

Below: *a 1955 photograph of Edger Hayes in California, where he has been living and working as a solo pianist.* Right: *Horace Henderson, Fletcher's younger brother, who led several big bands without attaining much public recognition.*

with Hayes soloing between section passages. The drummer with the band was Kenny Clarke, later a prominent figure in the bop era, and his swing style drumming on Hayes's recordings is of a high order. The scores that the Hayes band played often had the saxes led by Wethington's baritone, a feature of their recording of *Swingin' in the Promised Land,* which is a good performance with fine playing by the ensemble and solos from Horton, Garland and Hayes. One of the better aspects of Hayes's recordings is the attention paid to dynamic variations in ensemble passages, a point well illustrated on the excellent *Edgar Steps Out* and *Stompin' at The Renny. Stardust* is presented in an individual fashion as a straightforward swinging instrumental performance, and there are distinctive touches to the band's version of *Caravan,* which is given a far more down-to-earth treatment than usual.

Listening to the records that the Hayes band made, one is impressed by its musical expertise and ability to swing. The fact that secondary bands of the swing era could reach such admirable standards merely underlines the fact that this period was the high peak for big band jazz.

If Fletcher Henderson remains the most enigmatic personality of all the big band leaders, his elder brother Horace—born in Cuthbert, Georgia, in 1904—is also something of a mystery. The two have been linked through Horace's association with his brother's band, but it is worth recalling that he only worked with it from early 1933 to late 1934, for just over a year from 1936, and for just over nine months during 1943-44, a total of little more than three years. As a leader in his own right he began by leading a college band in the summer of 1924, continuing to front bands (except for a short break late in 1928) for the next seven years. Several of these bands included musicians who were later to become prominent during the swing era, but in 1931 Henderson's current group became the nucleus of Don Redman's band and he himself worked with Redman until early 1933. After leaving Fletcher's band at the close of 1934, Horace temporarily became a sideman with Vernon Andrade after another attempt at fronting his own band. Then, after his second tenure with Fletcher, he went to Chicago where his newly formed big band played a number of residencies at some of the more prominent clubs. In 1940 he scrapped his band and formed a new one by taking over most of the Nat Towles personnel, leading this group until the end of the year. In the post-war years he led further big bands from 1945 to 1949, and toured with one as late as the early 'sixties, though during most of the 'fifties he had fronted small groups. A year or two ago he was working in Denver, Colorado.

Although overshadowed by his brother, Horace is a fine arranger in his own right, and has written scores for, among others, Benny Goodman, Charlie Barnet, Earl Hines, Don Redman and Fletcher Henderson—some of them quite outstanding. There is disagreement amongst ex-Fletcher Henderson musicians about the relative merits of the two brothers in the arranging field, but it is significant that a number considered Horace the more advanced, though others do not accept this evaluation. It appears that Horace is bitter about the lack of recognition his own work has received, a situation exacerbated by the crediting of some of his arrangements to Fletcher. Whether there is substance in Horace's view that Fletcher received credit that should rightly have been his can only be a matter for speculation, and one which by now is unlikely to be resolved.

Some records were issued in the middle 'thirties under Horace Henderson's name, but they were by the regular Fletcher Henderson band and do not come within the scope of this chapter. With bands solely under his control he recorded twenty titles during 1940, a number of which are excellent. From his first session, *Shufflin' Joe* illustrates the precision of his band, the ensemble riffing helped by careful attention to dynamics, and there are good solos by a trumpeter and tenor saxophonist, whom I take to be Emmett Berry and Dave Young. The same date produced the attractive *Kitty on Toast,* a number on which Ray Nance has a lengthy violin solo and a short

Above and right: *Emmett Berry and Ray Nance, who worked with Horace Henderson's band in Chicago.*

trumpet passage. Henderson's own solo work on this and other titles is neat, melodic and somewhat more modern than one might expect. The outstanding titles from a second session are *Chloe* and *Swingin' and Jumpin',* the former a relaxed performance on which the highspot is a fine broad-toned trumpet solo by the underrated Emmett Berry, the latter a jaunty riff instrumental with effective solos by Berry and another trumpeter, probably Harry Jackson, and the leader himself. From the third date it is interesting to compare the scores for *Sultan Serenade* and *Ginger Belle,* by Fletcher and Horace Henderson respectively. The former is in Fletcher's typical style, with the familiar call-and-response patterns, whereas the latter makes greater use of textural variation. *Do Re Mi* illustrates even better Horace's use of textural and tonal variation whenever possible, and proves that he by no means slavishly copied his brother. Both styles of arrangement are, of course, equally valid. From the fourth session *Turkey Special* is the outstanding performance, though *Flinging a Whing Ding* and *Coquette* are

also good. The former has a particularly fiery trumpet solo by Berry, with good contributions by other musicians I cannot identify with any certainty, and the ensemble passages are played skilfully and powerfully.

The titles from these four sessions indicate that Henderson led a very good band with several excellent soloists, of whom Berry is the most outstanding. A number of titles contain felicities of scoring, but some are marred by the banality of the material. With the final session we move, on at least two titles, from the good to the brilliant. *You Don't Mean Me No Good,* arranged by Bob Dorsey, has Henderson leading into an outstanding trumpet solo by the little known Nat Bates, after which C. Q. Price launches into a striking alto saxophone solo against a beautifully scored quiet ensemble background. There follows a good trombone solo in plunger style, a reasonable blues type vocal by drummer Debo Mills, and then a superb closing ensemble in which the band generates the most tremendous swing without ever relying on sheer volume to carry it through. Equally good is Sir Charles Thompson's arrangement of *Smooth Sailing,* again featuring remarkably fine solos by Bates and Price, with complex ensemble work in the Lunceford manner

Top: *the Teddy Hill band, 1935. Sam Allen (piano), John Smith (guitar), Richard Fullbright (string bass) and Bill Beason (drums); brass section, left to right: Lester 'Shad' Collins, Bill Dillard, Frank Newton (trumpet), unknown (trombone); saxophones: Howard Johnson, Russell Procope and Leon 'Chu' Berry. Hill is holding the baton; the man leaning against the piano is unidentified.* Above: *the Teddy Hill band, 1937. Left to right: Hill, Cecil Scott, Russell Procope, Lester 'Shad' Collins, Bill Beason, John Smith, Richard Fullbright, Sam Allen, Wilbur de Paris, Dicky Wells, Howard Johnson, Bill Dillard, Frank Newton.*

that is quite remarkable in its impact. These two performances are of a quality to be compared with the finest of big band jazz, and the casual listener might well wonder what had happened to the Henderson band in the space of a few months. The answer lies in the fact that he was now fronting what was virtually the complete Nat Towles band and that the two numbers recorded were from the Towles book. The history of Towles and his bands is given in Chapter 5, and these titles provide the proof that the tremendous reputation he enjoyed was well deserved.

285

Dizzy Gillespie joined Teddy Hill's band in 1937; his first recorded solo is on Hill's King Porter Stomp.

Teddy Hill's band enjoyed a reputation amongst musicians, particularly during the 1937-38 period when it included a number of major soloists and toured England and France. Hill himself hailed from Birmingham, Alabama, where he was born on 7th December 1909, receiving his musical training from the redoubtable Fess Whatley. After touring with a vaudeville show he joined George Howe's band at the Nest Club in New York, remaining with it when Luis Russell took over the leadership in 1928. From 1932 he regularly led his own big bands in New York, though it was not until 1935 that he attracted much attention. After the 1937 European trip Hill continued as a leader for another three years, then became manager of a famous early bop club in Harlem called Minton's, a post he held for a lengthy period. Subsequently he worked in non-musical occupations.

The Teddy Hill band first recorded in February 1935, but the four titles made were disappointing, despite the presence in the group of outstanding soloists like trumpeters Roy Eldridge and Bill Coleman, trombonist Dicky Wells, and saxophonists Howard Johnson and Leon 'Chu' Berry. The numbers selected were mediocre current pop songs, some with indifferent vocals by Bill Dillard. Two sessions for the U.S. Vocalion label in April and May of 1936, with Frank Newton, Lester

'Shad' Collins and Cecil Scott replacing Eldridge, Coleman and Berry, were considerably better, not least in the material used. Hill's best known number was *Blue Rhythm Fantasy,* composed and arranged by Chappie Willett, a rather theatrical piece on which alto saxophonist Howard Johnson, clarinettist Russell Procope, Newton and tenor saxophonist Scott have good solos. *Uptown Rhapsody* and *At the Rug Cutters' Ball* show the band in a good light, both in its ensemble playing and in the contributions of the individual soloists.

In the early part of 1937 the Hill band took part in three recording sessions for RCA Victor's cheap Bluebird label. The first resulted in several disappointing commercial titles but included *Harlem Twister,* one of the best of all Hill's recordings. This performance does give one some idea of why the band was so highly regarded, for the swing and power of the ensemble is impressive and there are excellent solos from Procope, Wells, tenor saxophonist Kenneth Hollon and Collins. Wells's solo on this title is certainly the most striking he recorded with Hill. The second session produced mainly average performances, though Frank Newton's powerful solo on *China Boy* is first rate and Sam Allen's piano playing on the same number is agreeable enough. On the final date the band made four rather commercial titles with vocals by Bill Dillard and two instrumental numbers—*King Porter Stomp* and *Blue Rhythm Fantasy. King Porter Stomp* has been reissued on a number of occasions as it contains Dizzy Gillespie's first recorded solo—so very much in the Eldridge tradition—but it is a spirited performance that highlights the worth of the band, with other worthwhile solos from Howard Johnson, Wells and tenor saxophonist Robert Carroll. The new version of *Blue Rhythm Fantasy* is excellent, Willet's score being advanced for the period. Johnson, Procope, Gillespie and Carroll take good solos.

It would be interesting to know who selected most of the material that the Hill band recorded, for the preponderance of average pop numbers was hardly beneficial. The instrumental performances certainly give every indication that it was a hard swinging group with a quota of individual soloists, though whether it was quite as outstanding as some musicians have claimed must remain, on record evidence, an open question.

Claude Hopkins recently completed a half century as a professional musician and today, at the age of seventy, is a more impressive pianist than he was during the years of his greatest public success. Although born in Alexandria, Virginia, he was raised in Washington, D.C., and in his youth studied medicine and music at Howard University. He told me in the course of a 1958 interview that he, along with Duke Ellington and the late Cliff Jackson, was considerably influenced in his formative years by the playing of an obscure pianist called Clarence Bowser.

After working briefly with Wilbur Sweatman and leading his own groups, he secured an engagement at

Above: *the Claude Hopkins band, 1934. The line-up appears to be, left to right: Ovie Alston (trumpet), Fred Norman (trombone), Sylvester Lewis (trumpet), Fernando Arbello (trombone), Claude Hopkins (piano), Walter Jones (guitar), Pete Jacobs (drums), Eugene Johnson (alto saxophone), Bobby Sands (tenor saxophone), Henry Turner (string bass) and Edmond Hall (clarinet, saxophones). Right: three photographs of sections of the Hopkins band at the Earl Theatre, Philadelphia, 1937; top: Jabbo Smith, Shirley Clay and Lincoln Mills (trumpets); centre: Fred Norman, Floyd 'Stump' Brady and Vic Dickenson (trombones); bottom: Bobby Sands, Chauncey Haughton, Ben Smith and Eugene Johnson (saxophones).*

Asbury Park fronting a band consisting of Henry Goodwin (trumpet), Daniel Day (trombone), Joe Hayman (alto saxophone), himself, Ernest Hill (tuba) and Percy Johnson (drums). While there, a booker who was looking for a band to go to Europe with the 'Revue Negre', featuring Josephine Baker, heard him and signed the group mainly on the strength of their performance of *St Louis Blues*. The band sailed for Europe in September 1925, Sidney Bechet joining them in Paris, and it worked with the revue in Paris, Brussels and Berlin. At some point in 1926 the show broke up when Josephine Baker left for the Folies-Bergère, Hopkins having committed himself to take the band to the Savoy Hotel in Dresden as soon as he was free. Unfortunately for him, all the musicians other than Hayman went their own ways and he had to make the journey alone to Dresden to explain to an irate hotel manager why he could not fulfil the engagement. After this he led a band composed of Hayman, himself, and a number of European musicians in Italy and Spain.

Upon his return to New York he organised another band early in 1930, taking over the leadership of the group that was then working with Charlie Skeets. With this band, initially consisting of Ovie Alston, Sylvester Lewis (trumpet), ... Heard (trombone), Edmond Hall (alto and baritone saxophone, clarinet), Gene Johnson (alto saxophone, clarinet), Bobby Sands (tenor saxophone), himself (piano), Walter Jones (guitar, banjo), Henry Turner (bass) and Pete Jacobs (drums), he moved into the Savoy Ballroom and began to attract the attention of public and musicians alike. Within a short while

Fernando Arbello replaced Heard on trombone, and Fred Norman (trombone, arranger) and Orlando Roberson (vocal) were added to the line-up.

The Hopkins band recorded for the first time in 1932 and 1932-35 were the years of its greatest popular suc-

287

The Hopkins rhythm section, 1937: Claude Hopkins, Walter Jones, Abe Bolar and Pete Jacobs.

cess. In discussing this band Hopkins referred to its good team spirit, and mentioned that with jumps of 400 miles not uncommon during tours he hired three Lincolns complete with chauffeurs to transport the musicians from one place to another. Until 1936 the band enjoyed lengthy residencies at New York venues such as the Cotton Club and Roseland Ballroom, and only undertook tours during the summer months, but from 1937 to 1940 it toured extensively and only occasionally had the respite of an extended location job. In 1941 Hopkins reorganised the band, and worked from New York to California until it broke up late in 1942. After this he was employed for a year in an aircraft factory. He returned to lead big bands intermittently, the last being at the Club Zanzibar in 1946. In common with most musicians of his generation Hopkins then switched to working with small groups, during the 'fifties spending a great deal of time with the late Henry 'Red' Allen's band at the Metropole Café, New York. From 1960 to 1966 he led his own small group, and from 1967 to 1969 worked with Wild Bill Davison in 'The Jazz Giants', making regular appearances in Canada. Since then he has worked in various small groups, the present writer having heard him at the Rainbow Grill in New York during July 1973, still playing as well as ever and looking incredibly youthful for his age.

Claude Hopkins is quite frank about his 'thirties band, and says that it had no outstanding soloist other than Edmond Hall. Part of its commercial success was due to the popularity of its vocalist Orlando Roberson, whose falsetto style, displayed on such titles as *In the Shade of the Old Apple Tree, June in January* and *Trees,* should appeal to all lovers of vocal eccentricity. The band did, however, record a proportion of instrumental numbers, its version of Jimmy Mundy's *Mush Mouth,* from its initial session in May 1932 being typical. Trombonist Fernando Arbello takes the theme straight, and is followed by pleasant solos from alto

saxophonist Gene Johnson, tenor saxophonist Bobby Sands and trumpeter Ovie Alston. The ensemble playing on this number is highly efficient and the band achieves a light, relaxed swing that gives it a certain distinction, aided greatly by the excellent drumming of Pete Jacobs. Fred Norman's arrangement of *Washington Squabble* is very good, as are the solos on this recording by Claude Hopkins—in the Harlem stride style—trumpeter Sylvester Lewis and clarinettist Gene Johnson, while *Mystic Moan* is a pleasant mood piece well performed.

Hopkins himself is well featured on *Three Little Words,* a number which has become a stock item in his repertoire over the years; but one of the best recordings from the band's viewpoint is the version of Jelly Roll Morton's *King Porter Stomp.* The ensemble here uses the familiar call-and-response patterns of the big band era, Norman's score highlighting the fine unison work of the trumpet section. The solos by Alston and Edmond Hall (clarinet) are well conceived, and Sands is heard to advantage in his Coleman Hawkins-influenced manner. Alston, who shared the trumpet solo work at this time with Lewis, was also a quite engaging vocalist; his hoarse Louis Armstrong-inspired singing is on several recordings, typical of which are *Chasing All the Blues Away* and *Walkin' the Dog.*

An LP of transcription material (in which the bulk of the performances feature instrumental numbers) recorded by the Hopkins band in late 1935 shows it in

Claude Hopkins in the late 1950s.

an excellent light. Throughout one cannot fail to be impressed by the rhythm section of Hopkins, Jones, Turner and Jacobs; and the performances of *Swingin' and Jivin'*, *Hodge Podge* and *Farewell Blues* are particularly good, with Sylvester Lewis taking attractive solos on all these titles. Hopkins and Hall also make important contributions to *Farewell*.

There was a two-year gap between 1935 and 1937 during which the Hopkins band made no commercial recordings. Then early in 1937 it made two sessions for U.S. Decca. Numerous changes of personnel had taken place in the interim, the line-up now including trumpeters Shirley Clay and Jabbo Smith and trombonist Vic Dickenson. Smith is something of a legendary jazz figure and Mr Hopkins once told me that he was still playing brilliantly at this time, invariably stirring the public with a feature entitled *Trumpet Mania* that, unfortunately, the band never recorded. Six of the seven titles recorded in 1937 have indifferent vocals by Beverley White, the exception being an excellent version of *Church Street Sobbin' Blues* with solos by Sands, Clay and clarinettist Arville Harris. On this number the band manages a relaxed ensemble sound; the drumming of Pete Jacobs's replacement George Foster is quite admirable. Hopkins recorded for an obscure label in 1940 in a big band setting, but the results were not outstanding.

Though one has to agree with Mr Hopkins's own view that his band lacked all but a few soloists of major stature, its achievements were by no means trivial. While not in the class of the really outstanding big bands of its day it did at least possess a degree of individuality that makes it easily recognisable, and its better recordings have withstood the passing of four decades remarkably well. Possibly its success was due to the fact that its leader recognised its limitations and was wise enough to work within them.

Will Hudson came to the fore around 1934 when he was working as a staff arranger for impresario Irving Mills and producing slick, Casa Loma-ish type numbers like *White Heat* and *Jazznocracy*. He had studied arranging in Detroit and some of his first scores were taken, surprisingly enough, by McKinney's Cotton Pickers. Cab Calloway was responsible for his moving to New York in 1932, and when he became Mills's staff arranger he provided scores for most of the bands under Mills's direction, including Jimmie Lunceford's, Don Redman's and Louis Armstrong's. Late in 1935 a lyric writer called Eddie DeLange organised a band, and shortly afterwards offered Hudson partnership in the group in return for his providing regular arrangements. Although Hudson very seldom actually appeared with the band, it was billed as the Hudson-DeLange Orchestra until a disagreement between the two men led to their dissolving the partnership in 1938.

Hudson and DeLange wrote many numbers together, the most famous of which is *Moonglow*. Their swing-style instrumentals like *Organ Grinder's Swing, Sophisticated Swing* and *Mr Ghost Goes to Town* were featured by numerous bands during the 'thirties and they also wrote novelty numbers such as *Hobo on Park Avenue*—the band's signature tune—*Love Song of Half-wit* and *Definition of Swing*.

The Hudson-DeLange Orchestra recorded quite extensively between January 1936 and April 1938 and numbered trumpeter Jimmy Blake, clarinettist Gus Bivona and guitarist Bus Etri among its best musicians. They were all to make their names with better known bands shortly afterwards. Such recordings as *Mint Julep, Mr Ghost Goes to Town* and *Midnight at The Onyx* are competent swing style performances, but there is little to distinguish the band from dozens of others and most of the solos lack individuality. One of the best recordings by the band is their version of *If We Never Meet Again* which, while entirely commercial in intent, was attractively scored and performed. It has a vocal by the band's singer, Fredda Gibson, better known in later years as Georgia Gibbs.

After their disagreement Hudson became the sole leader, DeLange formed a new band of his own. Hudson took part in three recording sessions during 1938, one with a seven-piece group, but musically the results were indifferent. In 1940, with a personnel showing numerous changes, Hudson twice recorded for U.S. Decca, producing his best work in the studio. *Start Jumpin'* is a conventional swing performance, but the ensemble does swing reasonably and the solos by an unidentified trumpeter, tenor saxophonist George Berg, and alto saxophonist George Siravo are agreeable. Billy Exner's drumming is a distinct asset to the band, and he performs ably on the riff number *On the Verge*, where the solos are by pianist Mark Hyams, Berg, and the same trumpeter as on *Start Jumpin'*.

Neither Hudson or DeLange were successful with their individual bands. They joined each other again in 1941 in a bandleading venture but it did not last long. After this, Hudson returned to working as a freelance arranger (some of his scores being used by Glenn Miller's AAF Band during the war years), and has remained active in music, though not in the big band jazz field, ever since. DeLange moved to Hollywood during the 'forties and devoted himself to film music until he died in 1949.

Hudson, on the evidence of his records, was essentially a journeyman arranger-composer though his professionalism cannot be doubted. This applies equally to the musicians who formed the personnel of the bands with which he was involved either as leader or co-leader; unfortunately professionalism by itself is not enough to build a major band, and Hudson's, like so many others, is recalled for its competence rather than its creativity.

Lucius Millinder was given the nickname of Lucky, one that in the light of much of his professional experience seems singularly inappropriate. He was born at

Anniston, Alabama, on 8th August 1900, but educated in Chicago where, in the closing years of the 'twenties, he became well known as a master of ceremonies in local ballrooms and clubs. His bandleading career seems to have started in 1931 when he fronted a band that toured the RKO circuit, and early in 1932 he assumed the leadership of Doc Crawford's band, playing a location job in New York. On 29th June 1933, he sailed from New York as director of a band that worked in Monte Carlo and Paris until the following October, its impressive line-up being Bill Coleman, Bill Dillard, Henry Goodwin (trumpet), Robert Horton (trombone), Leroy Hardy, Booker Pittman (alto saxophone, clarinet), Alfred Pratt (tenor saxophone, clarinet), Arnold Adams (piano), Wilson Myers (string bass), Arnold Bolling (drums) and Freddie Taylor (dancer, entertainer).

In 1934 Millinder began his well-known association with Mills Blue Rhythm Band, initially as a front man and later as full leader, remaining with it until it broke up in 1938. In late May 1938, Millinder took over Bill Doggett's big band and toured extensively with it until the following January, fronting a personnel of William 'Chiefie' Scott, John Swan, Frank Galbraith, John Lynch (trumpet), Leon Comegys, Rocks McConnell, Burt Clagett (trombone), Ted Barnett, John Brown (alto saxophone, clarinet), Ivy Wilson, James Cawthorne (tenor saxophone,

Above: *Lucky Millinder.* Below: *the Lucky Millinder band in the 1940s.*

290

clarinet), Bill Doggett (piano), Roscoe Fritz (guitar), Jay Lawrence (string bass), and Rossiere 'Shadow' Wilson (drums). At some point Leroy Hill (trumpet) and Jack Johnson (trombone) replaced one of the trumpeters and Comegys respectively. The venture was a financial disaster. Early in 1939 Millinder was declared bankrupt.

From September 1940, when he organised a new band, until 1952, Millinder fronted a big band almost continuously, often with outstanding soloists in his line-up. For a while after 1952 he worked in non-musical jobs but a year or two later began once more to front big bands for specific club or theatre engagements, even undertaking limited tours. In the latter years of his life he combined occasional bandleading with work as a disc jockey, publicist and, less conventionally, fortune teller. He died in New York on 28th September 1966.

From 1941 to 1947 Millinder recorded for the U.S. Decca label, his best records stemming from 1941-42. For nearly a year one of his vocalists was the gospel singer Sister Rosetta Tharpe. In fact, the very first record he made featured her in a splendid version of *Trouble in Mind.* She is also heard in powerful vocals on *Rock Daniel, Rock Me* and *I Want a Tall Skinny Papa,* after which she became conscience-stricken through singing such secular material and left the band to concentrate on religious numbers. The band plays a role subsidiary to Sister Tharpe's vocals, but leaves its proficiency in no doubt. From the first two sessions come an amusing *Big Fat Mama*—presumably leading to Sister Tharpe's rejoinder *I Want a Tall Skinny Papa*—with vocal by guitarist Trevor Bacon and a good tenor saxophone solo by Stafford 'Pazuzza' Simon; and a version of *Ride, Red, Ride,* on which Millinder himself sings and Buster Bailey contributes an excellent clarinet solo. This was a number that had been something of a hit for Millinder in his Mills Blue Rhythm Band days (at that time with the trumpet and vocal of Henry 'Red' Allen). Many years later Mr Allen told me that because of its success Irving Mills had offered him the leadership of the band, but that he had declined because of his liking for Millinder.

From a February 1942 session came such eminently forgettable performances as *Fightin' Doug MacArthur* and *We're Gonna Have to Slap the Dirty Little Jap.* But a date made five months later produced two of the best titles that Millinder ever recorded: *Mason Flyer* and *Little John Special.* Both have good solos from trumpeter Dizzy Gillespie, alto saxophonist Tab Smith and tenor saxophonist Stafford Simon—some sources suggest that the tenor sax on the latter number is by Dave Young—and the band generates an impressive swing. A high register clarinet, possibly played by Ernest Purce, rides over the ensemble on *Little John Special*—a device effectively used by several bands in the swing era but rarely heard today. *Shipyard Social Function,* from an autumn 1943 session, also displays the drive of the band, and contains a fine flowing solo by Tab Smith and good

ones from an unidentified trumpeter and tenor saxophonist Mike Hedley, a Chu Berry disciple.

From 1944 the Millinder band moved increasingly into the rhythm-and-blues field, its recordings heavily featuring a number of vocalists on the titles made for Decca and RCA Victor. From 1950 it recorded for the King label, gaining some commercial success with several of its rhythm-and-blues influenced recordings. Late performances, such as *Backslider's Ball, Old Spice* and *Heavy Sugar,* usually based on blues riffs, reveal the band's power and the authority of the section work, but few opportunities to hear the many excellent jazz soloists working at the time.

The early Decca recordings are undoubtedly the best that Millinder made, though all his bands are notable for their high technical level. He was deeply respected by other musicians for his adroitness in selecting his men and in his abilities as an organiser and front man, but somehow the breaks never really came his way and one must assume that his full potential as a leader was not realised.

Several of the prominent arrangers of the swing era were tempted to try their hand at bandleading and for a brief period in 1939 Jimmy Mundy fronted a big band. Mundy is best known from his period with Earl Hines from 1932 to 1936 and for his arrangements for Benny Goodman in the following years—he was staff arranger with Goodman from 1936 to 1939—but prior to this he had a remarkably varied musical experience, beginning in 1919 when, at the age of twelve, he toured with an evangelist orchestra. A year or two later found him in Chicago where he worked with Carroll Dickerson and Erskine Tate. He then moved to Washington, D.C., where he played tenor saxophone and wrote arrangements for numerous little-known bands before joining Hines. His own band was short-lived, and afterwards he returned to arranging on a freelance basis, contributing scores to the libraries of many of the leading groups of the swing era. He has continued in this role to the present day, working for a while in the late 'fifties as a musical director for Barclay Records in Paris. However, his involvement in jazz has for many years been minimal.

When he formed his band, Mundy recruited part of his personnel from the Bill Dogger group which Lucky Millinder had led. He took part in only one recording session, for the Varsity label. Four numbers are recorded, but two are somewhat commercial, with vocals by Madeleine Greene; *Sunday Special* and *All Aboard,* on the other hand, are instrumental performances that show how proficient his band was, even if it lacked in real distinction. Both titles feature several of the musicians in solos, but they cannot be identified with any certainty. It is, of course, impossible to evaluate any band on a single recording session, but Mundy's short career as a bandleader would suggest that he himself was aware that he was perhaps ill fitted for this role.

Lyle 'Spud' Murphy is another arranger who tried his hand at bandleading in the late 'thirties and early 'forties, with little more success than Mundy. Murphy was born in Salt Lake City, Utah, on 19th August 1908, and learnt to play several brass instruments and the clarinet as a youth. His early career was adventurous, and included jobs as a sideman with a band in Mexico City and on a China-bound liner. From 1927 he worked with several well-known dance bands including those led by Russ Gorman, Austin Wylie and Jan Garber. In 1934 Murphy worked with Joe Haymes. From 1935 to 1937 he became one of Goodman's staff arrangers, after which he moved to California and led his own band from early in 1938. The band remained in existence for a few years without making any great impact, though at some point in the mid-'forties Murphy briefly organised an avant-garde band that was highly regarded by musicians but failed to please the public. Throughout the 'forties and the following decade Murphy worked mainly as a free-lance arranger, recording with small groups in 1955 and 1957. At this time Murphy was deeply involved in studies of the 12-tone system, reflected in his last records.

As leader of a conventional big band Murphy took part in three recording sessions, the first in April 1938. His line-up included few stars, the best known musicians apart from the leader being trumpeter Nate Kazebier, trombonist Joe Harris and alto saxophonist Bill De Pew, all of whom had worked with Benny Goodman. *Trans-Continental* and *Dancing With a Debutante* are novelty items in the swing idiom. The best titles from the session are the more straightforward *Quaker City Jazz* and *Cherokee* which are well performed and have capable solos. Murphy's records of 1939 are hardly memorable—*Pinetop Breakaway* is an acceptable pastiche boogie performance and *Sand Due* a well played but average instrumental number. As with many of the secondary swing bands of the period, Murphy's failed to establish an individual identity; as a result its music lacked the impact essential to the band's survival in a highly competitive field.

In an oft-quoted remark, Dizzy Gillespie once said that he regarded the late Oran 'Hot Lips' Page as an unrivalled blues player. That Page should be a fine blues trumpeter is not altogether surprising, for as a youth he was a member of Ma Rainey's accompanying band—he once said that Ma Rainey took an interest in him and helped him as far as she was able—and then went on to work the TOBA circuit with a group that backed several leading blues singers, including Ida Cox and Bessie Smith. Page, born in Dallas, Texas, on 27th January 1908, worked in several of the leading South-western territory bands during the decade before his arrival in New York, including a spell as featured artist with Count Basie's band in Kansas City.

Page was signed in 1936 by the prominent booking agent Joe Glaser, who apparently at the time had hopes of building him up to become as well known as Louis Armstrong. In August 1937 Page opened with a big band at Small's Paradise, moving on nine months later to a residency at the Plantation Club. For a variety of reasons Page never became a big name to the public. Over the next few years he led groups of various sizes and sometimes worked as a featured artist with other leaders. He spent four months with Artie Shaw from August 1941; then for the last time he returned to fronting a big band regularly for most of 1942 and the early part of 1943, though occasionally in later years he would put a band together for specific engagements. For the rest of his life Page alternated between fronting small groups, working as a single, and appearing as a featured artist with other leaders, travelling to Europe in 1949, 1951 and 1952. In his last years he suffered from poor health, partly due to alcoholism, and he died from a heart attack on 5th November 1954.

Commercially Page's most successful record was a single made with Pearl Bailey in 1949 of *The Huckle-buck* and *Baby It's Cold Outside*. Though he recorded over the years with bands ranging from Bennie Moten's to Artie Shaw's, his work is uneven, only a few of his records being worthy of his considerable reputation. He twice went into the studio for RCA Victor with his big band of 1938, each session producing six issued titles. Regrettably the results were generally mediocre, largely owing to the choice of unsuitable numbers like *Small Fry, I'm Gonna Lock My Heart, The Pied Piper* and *And So Forth,* on which Page himself usually sings engagingly, plays well, but is defeated by the banality of the material. The band normally takes a very subsidiary role, *Skull Duggery,* composed and arranged by trom-

Oran 'Hot Lips' Page.

Oran 'Hot Lips' Page at a jam session in the late 1930s. Bud Freeman is looking on.

bonist Harry White, providing it with its best chance to be heard. The reed section achieves a pleasant light sound in the theme chorus of this number and the ensemble work is effective throughout, with Page taking a powerful solo, and tenor saxophonist Ernie Powell emerging for a bustling eight bars near the close. It would be unjust to judge the band on these recordings, for it is unlikely that it would be faced with so much daunting material on its resident jobs. As with the band, which included some good if not brilliant soloists, one must look elsewhere for the best of Page's work, though it should be said in fairness that his solos on such titles as *The Pied Piper, At Your Beck and Call* and *Small Fry* are considerably better than the tunes warranted. Page was not, by all accounts, temperamentally suited to cope with the problems of leading a big band, and it is unlikely that he would have ever made any strong impact in this capacity.

Teddy Powell appears to have had a desperate desire to build a big band that would rival the major ones of the day. In the process he overcame setbacks that would have daunted a less optimistic man. He never succeeded in his ambition, though during the early years of the 'forties he led some musically excellent units.

Born at Oakland, California, on 1st March 1905, Powell

initially played violin, forming his first band at the age of fifteen. After working with various bands in Los Angeles he began an association with Abe Lyman in 1927 that lasted for eleven years, the first seven as a musician, arranger and vocalist in the band, the last four as organiser of Lyman's radio programmes. During the latter period he wrote a number of songs, some of which became very popular.

Powell formed his own band in 1939, appearing with it for the first time at a restaurant in New Jersey. It seems that it was well received in New York but failed on its out-of-town tours. Powell is said to have lost $35,000 in the first year. In 1940 Powell acquired the lease of The Famous Door, then a key night club in New York, and for a while used it as a base for his band. By now his line-up had almost totally changed, Powell wryly observing that the past twelve months had taught him much about highly paid temperamental star musicians. He seemed uncertain about his musical direction and his new group was less jazz orientated than its predecessor. In October 1941, after a nine-month residency at the Rustic Cabin in New Jersey the band lost all its instruments as the result of a fire, though fortunately Powell had kept the original manuscripts of all his arrangements elsewhere and was able to resume working after a very brief interval.

Powell's 1942 band was generally agreed to be the finest that he ever led, though the recording ban meant that it never made commercial records and the call-up

293

soon led to the loss of key musicians. By this time Powell seems to have learned a great deal from his early set-backs, and surprised critics and public alike by his ability to organise excellent musical bands at short notice. From 1945 Powell devoted much of his time to songwriting and working for Broadway shows, though a disagreement with the draft board led to an enforced fifteen-month absence from the music scene in late 1945 and for the whole of 1946. He continued to lead bands intermittently over the next decade, but from the late 'fifties has concentrated on a music publishing business that he owns.

The first Powell band took part in four sessions for the U.S. Decca label during 1939 and 1940. Several of the performances featured novelty swing-styled numbers that now sound very dated. *Teddy's Boogie Woogie,* from the band's initial session, is a better than usual big band boogie performance, with good piano by Milt Raskin and assertive tenor saxophone by Don Lodice. *Jamaica Jam* is a riff theme somewhat in the Count Basie mould and Powell's rhythm section comes across as a well-integrated one on this number. Ray Conniff scored *Feather Merchant's Ball,* a take-off of Woody Herman's well-known *Woodchopper's Ball.* This performance showed the band in a good light, with solos

Above: *a section of the Jan Savitt band at the Lincoln Hotel in the early 1940s. The vocalist is Bob Bon Tunnell.* Below: *Jan Savitt with his brass section in the early 1940s.*

by trombonist Peter Skinner, Raskin, trumpeter Jerry Neary and an unidentified tenor saxophonist.

After the Decca contract expired, Powell switched to recording for RCA Victor's cheap label Bluebird, entering the studios frequently between December 1940 and July 1942 when he made his final session. Many, indeed most, of the records made by the band are conventional swing-styled performances of no great interest, though the level of technical expertise is invariably high. A number of boogie features were recorded (the most popular of which was *In Pinetop's Footsteps*), and some instrumental numbers like *Sans Culottes* and *Ode to Spring* are reasonably distinctive. *Serenade to a Maid* found the Powell band following a tradition established by Charlie Barnet and Tommy Dorsey in mercilessly satirising the sweet bands of the day. In general, however, few of Powell's Blue-bird recordings rise above the level of competence.

Powell's 1942 line-up, the best that he ever fronted, included the New Orleans clarinettist Irving Fazola, a trumpeter called Dick Mains, who drew rave notices from the critics, a good tenor saxophonist in Roy Hammerslag, and a fine rhythm section that included pianist Tony Aless, guitarist Carmen Mastren and drummer Lou Fromm. The band's few Bluebird recordings are disappointing, but an LP has appeared that uses transcription material, and this proves the band to have been a really fine one. The same LP has performances by Powell's 1943 band, the personnel then including trumpeters Pete Candoli and Ray Wetzel and tenor saxophonist Charlie Ventura, but they are inferior to those by the 1942 group.

Whatever his failures might have been, there is no denying Powell's overwhelming enthusiasm, nor his astuteness in his later career in selecting worthwhile musicians to play in his bands. Through his own good nature and naïvety he was sometimes the victim of his musicians, a number of whom apparently despatched telegrams to themselves offering large salaries which purportedly came from such established leaders as Tommy Dorsey and Glenn Miller. When Powell was shown these telegrams his immediate reaction was to offer a rise in salary which would outbid the 'offer' contained in the telegram! In later years Powell told these stories with rueful humour, adding that it was not only his musicians who took him for money. Even allowing for his lack of business acumen, however, there can be little doubt that Powell was not the luckiest of leaders. The final irony of his career is that when, in 1942, he finally led a band that could conceivably have attained major status both commercially and musically, a combination of a recording ban and conscription denied him the advantage of the situation. There have been many leaders more musically skilled than Powell, and few with less business acumen than he possessed, but for sheer enthusiasm and optimism he was in a class of his own. If he failed to make the big time it was certainly not for lack of effort, and the 1942 transcription material proves how close he

came to achieving his ambition to lead a band that would be one of the trendsetters of the day. Alas, big band history is one in which the nice guys too seldom triumphed!

The desire to establish a personal sound led some band-leaders into the field of gimmickry, though few went so far as Shep Fields who created his 'Rippling Rhythm' effect by blowing through a straw into a fish bowl filled with water. Jan Savitt was instantly recognisable for his 'shuffle rhythm', the creation of his chief arranger, Johnny Watson, but though it became irritating on record it was never allowed to overpower musical values as did some of the gimmicks used by the sweet band-leaders.

Savitt was born in St Petersburg in 1913, his family moving to Philadelphia shortly after the outbreak of World War I. He soon revealed a precocious musical talent, played violin in a local symphony orchestra at the age of fourteen, and a year or two later went to Europe to study conducting under Fritz Reiner and Artur Rodzinski. In 1934 he was appointed musical director of a Philadelphia radio station. Three years later he moved to another local station and formed his 'Top Hatters'. The band, an immediate success, toured extensively in the following years, at one point being greatly influenced by the Jimmie Lunceford style. In the early 'forties, Savitt added strings to his line-up, though no recordings from this period exist, and for the next year or two he worked mainly in California. In 1944 he went out on tour as the supporting band for Frank Sinatra. The big band era was coming to a close, but reportedly to clear a large tax deficit incurred through an embezzling associate, Savitt went out on a series of one night tours. On his way to an engagement in Sacramento, Savitt collapsed with a cerebral hæmorrhage and died without regaining consciousness on 4th October 1948.

Although his own roots were in classical music, Savitt was respected by his sidemen as a knowledgeable and highly skilled leader who soon became proficient in a new field. His main soloists were trumpeter Johnny Austin, tenor saxophonist Eddie Clausen, and trombonist Al Leopold, all of whom are featured on many of the band's better recordings. Austin was a brash, at times wild, soloist with a style that seems to be a mixture of Harry James and Ziggy Elman, and he can be heard on *When Buddha Smiles, Alla en el Rancho Grande, Blues in the Groove, Green Goon Jive* and *Meadowbrook Shuffle* amongst other titles. On *Meadowbrook* he performs quite capably with plunger, while his muted solo on *Green Goon* benefits from a disciplined approach that was not always present in his work. Clausen played with a rather dry tone and staccato phrasing, occasionally sounding like a less extrovert Charlie Barnet, his best solos occurring on *It's Time to Jump and Shout, That's a Plenty,* and in a chase sequence with Austin on *Rose of the Rio Grande.* Leopold is a little-known musician but his solos on *Rose of the Rio Grande*, *Blues in the Groove* and *My Heart at Thy Sweet Voice* show him to have been extremely versatile and the possessor of a considerable technique. George Auld played with Savitt for a while, perhaps his best solo with the band being that on *Big Beaver*. Other musicians who are occasionally heard in a solo role are alto saxophonist Gabe Galinas, clarinettist George Bohn, trumpeter Jack Hansen, and pianists Jack Pleis and Nat Jaffe, all of whom are capable.

Savitt was fortunate in having two above average vocalists in Carlotta Dale and George 'Bon Bon' Tunnell, especially the latter. His rhythmic singing on *Vol Vistu Gaily Star* is outstanding, one scat passage pointing the way to the scat bop vocals of a year or two later, and whether featured on a ballad or catchy riff theme like *720 in the Books* he always sung with taste and rhythmic acumen.

Though the constant use of the shuffle rhythm led to a certain monotony, Savitt's rhythm section was proficient. The ensemble playing was invariably of a high order, with clean, precise work from the individual sections, and careful attention to dynamics. At its best the band swung quite powerfully, generally maintaining a balance between tension and relaxation that placed it a cut above most of the secondary swing groups. Where it failed was in its inability to achieve complete stylistic distinction—the shuffle rhythm was a trademark and not a device that could influence the brass or reed sections—its records showing influences of Basie, Lunceford and other bands. It was, though, on its own terms an entertaining and musical unit, and one that once more underlined the depth of talent that existed in the big band era.

Noble Sissle's musical association with Eubie Blake was mentioned in Chapter 1; but apart from this the veteran songwriter, entertainer and bandleader has been an active force in the popular music business for well over half a century. He was born in Indianapolis on 10th August 1889. After leading a band in his hometown, he moved to Baltimore in 1915. There he worked with a local group, before once more organising his own band to play a residency in Palm Beach, Florida, then joined Jim Europe's Society Orchestra as a guitarist and singer. He became a member of a U.S. army band

during World War I, and on returning to the U.S.A. he toured with Jim Europe until the latter's death. Subsequently Sissle formed his highly successful partnership with Blake, both as a working duo and as a songwriting combination, their most famous collaboration as songwriters being for the show *Shuffle Along*.

In 1926 Sissle and Blake went to London for an engagement at the Kit Kat Club. Sissle returned two years later with pianist Harry Revel as his accompanist. He then formed his own band, largely composed of British musicians, for a residency in Paris, returning there in 1929 with an American band that included clarinettist Buster Bailey and violinist Juice Wilson. This group played in France, Belgium and England before arriving back in New York in December 1930. For the next eight years Sissle toured with his band throughout the U.S.A. In 1938 he secured a residency at Billy Rose's Diamond Horseshoe in New York that lasted until the early 'fifties. Sissle has remained active in music to the present day, mainly as manager of his own music publishing company but also as owner of a night club and occasional

bandleader/entertainer.

Sissle's recording career started in 1920 and for the remainder of that decade he was frequently in the studios, often in the company of Eubie Blake. His first records with his own band were made in London in 1928, but the titles are of no jazz interest. With his 1929 American band he again recorded in London, and though most of the titles made have rather dire vocals by him, *Kansas City Kitty* and *Miranda* are interesting for the solos by trumpeter Demas Dean, Buster Bailey and, especially, Juice Wilson. The latter is a semi-legendary figure who spent thirty-five years in Europe and North Africa from 1929. His work on the Sissle recordings would suggest that his considerable reputation was not without justification. In 1930 Sissle once again recorded in London, but despite the presence in his band of such musicians as trumpeter Tommy Ladnier, tenor saxophonist Frank 'Big Boy' Goudie and clarinettist Rudy Jackson the results are very disappointing.

Further recording sessions by the Sissle band took place in New York and Chicago in 1931, 1934, 1936 and 1937. These are mainly of interest to jazz followers because a number feature the great New Orleans clarinettist and soprano saxophonist Sidney Bechet. Bechet was never a musician who could accept a role as a modest sideman, and his solo performances dominate most of Sissle's later recordings. The 1934 *Polka Dot Rag* has Bechet at his most assertive in a sweeping soprano solo, though James Tolliver on tenor saxophone and Ramon Usera on violin also have reasonable solos. The ensemble generates a good drive, with bassist Edward Coles playing in the hard-hitting manner of 'Pops' Foster. From the same

Left: *Noble Sissle in the late 1930s.* Below left: *Noble Sissle and his Orchestra O Belgium, 1929. Left to right: Clifton 'Pike' Davis, Demas Dean, James Reevy, Henry Edwards, Jesse Baltimore, Lloyd Pinckney, Warren Harris, Rudy Jackson, Raymond Usera, Buster Bailey. The violinists are Juice Wilson and William Roseman. Sissle is standing in front.* Below: *the Noble Sissle Orchestra in Denver, Colorado, summer 1937. Sidney Bechet is tenth from left in the back row. Sissle is in a white suit in the centre of the front row and veteran Denver bandleader George Morrison is far right at the front.*

The Noble Sissle band at Billy Rose's Diamond Horseshoe Club, 1950. Clarence Brereton, Wendell Culley and Russell Smith (trumpets); Wilbur Kirk (drums); unknown, Gene Mikell and Jerome 'Don' Pasquall (saxophones).

session comes a pleasant version of *Loveless Love*—Lavaida Carter's vocal an improvement on Sissle's own efforts. Bechet again is heard to excellent effect on soprano and there are other good solos from trumpeter Clarence Brereton, Tolliver and also saxophonist Harvey Boone. The band at this time could swing quite powerfully, though it had little personal identity (apart from Bechet's contributions). Sissle's final band recordings—*Bandanna Days, I'm Just Wild About Harry* and *Dear Old Southland*—are almost totally features for Bechet, who plays with characteristic power and intensity. The only other solos are by Brereton, a good trumpeter who might well have gained a bigger reputation if he had worked with a major band.

Over the years Sissle had many fine soloists in his various bands, and no doubt they were allowed greater opportunity to be heard during in-person performances than on record, though by all accounts his most musically impressive groups never recorded. However, Sissle is essentially an entertainer, and it must be remembered that the primary function of his bands was to provide support for him in this capacity. One regrets, though, that no recorded evidence exists of Charlie Parker's brief association with this remarkable showbiz personality!

Francis 'Muggsy' Spanier is a musician whose best known recordings have been made with small groups, but at least half of his professional life was spent playing in big bands. He was only sixteen when, in 1922, he joined Sig Meyers's band in Chicago. He remained with him for two years, and then he worked with half a dozen bands in the Chicago area before joining Ray Miller in the autumn of 1928. From 1929 until 1936 he was a member of Ted Lewis's Orchestra, then played with Ben Pollack until ill health led to his temporary retirement early in 1938. In April 1939 he made his debut with his 'Ragtimers', creating a series of famous records during their brief seven months' existence. He returned once more to Ted Lewis for a couple of months. From 1940, Spanier spent a year in the more musically congenial surroundings of the Bob Crosby band, leaving to form his own big band early in 1941. This band was quite often resident at the Arcadia Ballroom in New York, remaining in existence for two years. Apart from a final brief period with Ted Lewis from May to August 1944 Spanier never again played in a big band setting. In subsequent years he worked with Earl Hines in San Francisco (1951-59) and led his own small units until ill health forced him to leave the music field in 1964. He died in Sausalito, California, on 12th February 1967 at the age of sixty.

Spanier's formative years were spent in Chicago, one of his major influences being Joe 'King' Oliver. Stylistically he was of the pre-swing era, though his years of

working in big bands stood him in good stead when he became a leader. There are obvious similarities between his own band and Bob Crosby's. Both indulged in a form of scored big band Dixieland, and he was fortunate in securing the services of a particularly sympathetic arranger in Dean Kincaide. Only seven titles by his big band were recorded, and they are good of their kind. Initially the fine New Orleans clarinettist Irving Fazola was in the band, though his only recorded solo with it is a pleasant version of *Can't We Be Friends,* which also has contributions from tenor saxophonist Nick Caiazza —a former member of the 'Ragtimers'—and Spanier himself, the latter's open solo being slightly untypical. *More Than You Know* offers an uninspired vocal by Dotty Reid after the excellent muted theme by the leader, who is heard in his more familiar plunger style on *Little David, Play On Your Harp* and *Two o'Clock Jump.* On the last number Spanier plays with great drive and swing, the score being in a more conventional swing-band style. Generally, Spanier's big band sounds very effective in its chosen idiom. Apart from the leader the soloists were usually Caiazza, who plays in a vaguely Eddie Miller-ish style, trombonist Vernon Brown and pianists Dave Bowman or Charlie Queener. Though not attaining great heights, the Spanier band sounds a fresh enthusiastic unit on the evidence of its few records.

There are some musicians who seem born leaders and one cannot imagine them in any other role; equally there

Jack Teagarden's original 1939 band. Vocalist Meredith Blake and Teagarden are in front; at the back: Allan Ruess (guitar), Carl Garvin, Charlie Spivak and Alex Fila; in the centre: Art Miller (string bass), Cub Teagarden (drums), Mark Bennett, Jose Gutierrez, Red Bone (trombone); first row: John Anderson (piano), Art St John, John Van Eps, Ernie Caceres, Clint Garvin and Hub Lytle (saxophones).

are those who were tempted to try their hand at fronting bands during the swing era who seemed almost destined to fail, usually because they lacked organising ability. In the latter category Jack Teagarden is an obvious example, for though one of the greatest trombonists in jazz's history and a charming, amiable man, he clearly was not the person to cope with all the business problems that face any big band leader.

When Teagarden settled in New York early in 1928 he already had something of a reputation through reports from musicians who had heard him with Peck Kelley, Doc Ross and other bands. From the latter part of that year until the summer of 1933 he worked with the Ben Pollack band, also taking part in innumerable recording sessions that established him as a unique stylist, admired by musicians of different generations and inclinations. After leaving Pollack he undertook a few short-lived engagements with several groups and then joined Paul Whiteman, with whom he remained until December 1938. Teagarden had a long-term contract with Whiteman and reportedly was far from happy in the band once the swing era got under way and he saw his former colleagues riding to public success. Shortly after leaving Whiteman he organised his own big band which made its New York debut early in 1939. He continued to front large units until late 1946.

Teagarden's career as a big band leader was not a happy one. His first group included a number of well-known musicians who were unwilling to go out on lengthy tours; this necessitated various changes of personnel. Once conscription was introduced, all bands faced the loss of key musicians at short notice, and line-ups literally varied almost from week to week, a process that was given further impetus when the U.S.A. entered World War II. Teagarden also faced the problem of having to cope with transport difficulties brought about by petrol rationing, in addition to which he ran into severe financial difficulties. During 1943 there was dissension within the band, some of the sidemen wanting to switch to the more modern Kenton-Raeburn approach, and in the autumn of that year, as a result, the band underwent major reorganisation. In Howard J. Waters Jr's book, 'Jack Teagarden's Music,' a personnel listing of the years from January 1939 to November 1946 shows a staggering turnover, and there can be little doubt that by the time he disbanded Teagarden must have been a weary and disillusioned man.

After the break-up of the big band, Teagarden led a sextet for several months before working with Louis Armstrong and the All-Stars from July 1947 until August 1951, a job which restored his fortunes both musically and otherwise. For the remaining years (until his death from pneumonia in New Orleans on 15th January 1964 at the age of fifty-eight), Teagarden worked with small groups, normally as a leader. With his own All-Stars he went on a four-month tour of Asia from September 1958. He had already visited Europe in the previous autumn with a sextet which he co-led with Earl Hines.

Teagarden's best line-up was that of 1939 and this is quite well represented on record. Its very first recording was *Persian Rug*, a number arranged by the band's trombonist Red Bone. The soloists are tenor saxophonist Hub Lytle, clarinettist Ernie Caceres, Teagarden, and trumpeter Carl Garvin. As might be expected Teagarden and Caceres make the most impression, as they do on *Muddy River Blues,* though here Lytle's Eddie Miller-ish tenor solo is superior to that on *Persian Rug.* The band sounds well rehearsed and organised, though without much individual identity. Such titles as *I Gotta Right to Sing the Blues* and *Peg o' My Heart* are essentially features for Teagarden himself, his closing solo on the latter number being particularly fine. Some of Bone's scores are Dixieland styled, notably those for *Beale Street Blues,* which uses a Dixieland front line against the full ensemble at one point, and *Wolverine Blues.* Caceres plays admirably on *Wolverine,* while Garvin takes one of his most effective recorded solos on *Beale,* the latter hav-

ing fine instrumental and vocal passages by Teagarden. *Swingin' on the Teagarden Gate* is a more orthodox swing score by Fred Norman—Teagarden and Garvin taking good solos and the ensemble swinging strongly on the riff close. Curiously enough, one of the band's most successful performances with the public—*Somewhere a Voice is Calling*—has so far not been reissued in microgroove form.

With an almost entirely new personnel, Teagarden began recording for the now long defunct Varsity label early in 1940, making four titles for the even obscurer Viking company in January 1941 before switching to Decca late that month. From the first Decca session, *Chicks Is Wonderful* is a routine performance, though it includes a fine, relaxed solo by Teagarden and a pleasant one from clarinettist Danny Polo. A version of Rachmaninov's *Prelude in C Sharp Minor* in swing style attracted some attention, and Teagarden recorded big band versions of *Blue River* and *A Hundred Years from Today,* numbers with which he was associated from earlier studio group dates. Transcriptions exist of his 1944-45 bands, but such performances as *Octoroon, East of the Sun, Out of Nowhere* and *Aunt Hagar's Blues* are chiefly valuable for Teagarden's own solos and vocals, few of his sidemen making much impact. For a short while in the mid-'forties Teagarden even had his own record label, but it appears that this venture was none too successful.

When he first organised his band, Teagarden said that he wanted it to have a personal identity so that

Thomas 'Fats' Waller in the mid 1930s.

it would be as recognisable to the public as Glenn Miller's or Benny Goodman's, but a variety of adverse circumstances prevented his realising such a goal. Although his personnel usually included worthwhile soloists, and it would be wrong to overlook his ability to draw the best from the younger musicians in his later bands, at this distance in time the main appeal of the records is the brilliance of his own playing.

Thomas 'Fats' Waller, on the bulk of his considerable body of recorded work, used a small group known as 'Fats Waller and his Rhythm'. Because the record buying public are familiar with these performances it tends to be forgotten that he frequently fronted big bands on tours, sometimes taking over existing groups for specific engagements. Amongst the bands which he used in this manner are Clarence Paige's, Eddie Johnson's Crackerjacks and Charlie Turner and his Arcadians, though there were also periods when he organised big bands with his regular accompanying musicians as the nucleus. On only four occasions did RCA Victor record him with a big band, a total of twenty titles resulting.

A session producing eight titles took place in April 1938. As might be expected, several were essentially features for Waller's own vocals and piano playing, though most of these have short solos from others. The outstanding titles were *Skrontch* and *The Sheik of Araby*. In the former Waller plays the theme in stride style

Above: *Cootie Williams' band in the 1940s, with the unusually large line-up of nine brass, including himself.* Below: *a publicity shot of Cootie Williams in the early 1940s.*

accompanied only by the rhythm. After his vocal there are solos by a trumpeter I take to be John Hamilton, trombonist John Haughton, and tenor saxophonist Lonnie Simmons. An instrumental version of *In the Gloaming* has an excellent flowing alto saxophone solo by James Powell, but some of the ensemble playing is uncertain. Quite the best performance that Waller made with a big band is *Chant of the Groove*—with solos by himself, Hamilton, Powell and tenor saxophonist Gene Sedric—for here the band sounds much more cohesive than on some of the other titles. Although Waller worked and recorded with big bands on occasions, his major contributions to jazz lie in other areas, and it is unlikely that he himself would have claimed any outstanding merits for the big bands that he organised for touring purposes. At their best they included a number of excellent soloists and generated a good swing; other than that they were just competent routine groups of their era.

After over eleven years as a member of the Duke Ellington band and a year with Benny Goodman, trumpeter Charles 'Cootie' Williams, late in 1941, formed his own big band, which he managed to maintain until economic circumstances and the demise of the big band era forced him to switch, in 1948, to fronting a small group. For much of its life the band was resident at New York's Savoy Ballroom and was popular with the dancers who formed the major part of its clientele.

The repertoire of Williams's band was unusually varied and ranged from old-established standards such as *Royal Garden Blues* to Thelonious Monk's *'Round Midnight*. A recording of the latter features Williams in an attractive solo throughout, his approach to the number underlining its melodic beauty. The presence in his band of the alto saxophonist and blues singer Eddie 'Cleanhead' Vinson resulted in a number of blues-styled recordings, amongst which is a mainly vocal version of Louis Jordan's novelty jump number *Is You Is or Is You Ain't My Baby*, and an excellent *Things Ain't What They Used to Be*. *Royal Garden Blues* displays the band more fully, particularly in the riff close, and has fine solos by Williams, tenor saxophonist Sam Taylor, trombonist Bob Horton

and pianist Bud Powell. Quite a few of the band's Capitol recordings feature vocals by Bob Merrill, and there was a stylistic shift towards rhythm-and-blues. Exceptions were an interesting remake of one of Williams's famous feature numbers with Duke Ellington, *Echoes of Harlem*, and the splendid *House of Joy*.

Williams formed his band quite late in the swing era and in certain respects its records reflect the changes that were taking place in the popular music world at the time. The fact that Williams himself was its major soloist and that initially at least Vinson was featured on record gives the band a degree of individuality, though as a collective unit it never achieved an easily identifiable sound.

When Teddy Wilson left Benny Goodman in April 1939, he organised a big band which made its first public appearance at the Famous Door during the following month. It survived for a year, mostly resident at the Golden Gate Ballroom on 142nd Street, though it did work briefly in both Detroit and Washington, D.C., and toured throughout New England. In 1958 Teddy Wilson, in a discussion with me, said that the band was an excellent musical aggregation, but added that he was not an entertainer and found that reliance on good quality music was not sufficient to ensure survival. Some years later he expanded his views when talking to the Swiss jazz writer Johnny Simmen, telling him that the band was popular with dancers because of its tempos and balance of ballads and up-tempo numbers, but failed to appeal to theatre audiences who were used to showmanship and spectacular production effects.

The Wilson band has been neglected by collectors and record companies, and the first thorough article on the band that I have read was written by Mr Simmen and *Below: the Teddy Wilson Orchestra, 1939. Right: after leading big bands, Teddy Wilson worked with smaller groups in the 1940s: this photograph taken in the Pump Room of the Ambassador Hotel, Chicago, shows George James (baritone saxophone), Jimmy Hamilton (clarinet), Wilson, Bill Coleman (trumpet), J. C. Heard (drums), Benny Morton (trombone) and Al Hall (string bass).*

appeared in the December 1970 issue of the Canadian magazine Coda. It is interesting to read of the late Billy Strayhorn referring to the Wilson band as 'the most musical and cleanest big band—outside of Ellington's,' and of the enthusiasm for it still displayed by several of the musicians who were sidemen. Even more important is the fact that, as a result of discussion with various ex-band members and Teddy Wilson himself, Mr Simmen has identified soloists and arrangers for all the band's recorded titles.

From a session of June 1939—two titles were recorded during the previous month but never released—comes an excellent performance of *Exactly Like You,* with solos by Wilson, tenor saxophonist Ben Webster, trombonist Jake Wiley and trumpeter Karl George—all of a high order. From the same date *Booly-Ja-Ja* is one of the more ephemeral performances recorded by the band, sounding a little like a number that would go down well in one of the Cotton Club revues. A second date produced a moody *Lady of Mystery,* with finely controlled playing from the band and a neat Wilson solo, and the more extrovert *Early Session Hop,* which has solos from Webster, Wilson, George and Wiley and further impressive ensemble work. Wiley is a little-known trombonist whom Mr Simmen reports as having died some years ago, but judged by his solo on *Early Session Hop* alone he was a fine musician with a considerable command of his instrument. *Sweet Lorraine* is a beautiful ballad performance with a fine lyrical solo from trumpeter Harold Baker, delightful contributions by Wilson and Webster, and outstanding relaxed ensemble work. From its final session, *Cocoanut Groove* and *71* display the powerful swing that the band could achieve on up-tempo numbers, though one of the best performances of this type is heard on the earlier *Jumpin' on the Blacks and Whites.*

Musically the Teddy Wilson band was superior to most that are covered in the present chapter, and given the chance might well have become one of the major groups of its day. As we go to press, a full LP by it has become available, making it possible that its excellence will become more widely recognized.

Bob Zurke, born in Detroit on 17th January 1912, worked with a number of local bands in his hometown and Philadelphia during the latter part of the 'twenties and the early years of the following decade, but came to prominence with Bob Crosby with whom he played for over two years from January 1937. He organised his own big band in the summer of 1939 and in a brief life of just under a year it recorded thirty titles for RCA Victor. After its break-up, Zurke worked as a solo pianist in Detroit, Chicago, St Paul and Los Angeles, but he was too often beset by problems that stemmed from his somewhat wayward mode of life. He died at the early age of thirty-two in Los Angeles on 16th February 1944.

With Crosby, Zurke had become famous for his boogie woogie playing, one of his biggest successes being a version of Meade Lux Lewis's *Honky Tonk Train Blues.* Many of the records that he made with his own band were in the boogie woogie idiom, though some little known recordings that came to light after his death show that he was a far more versatile and introvert stylist than his commercial recordings might lead one to assume. On occasions Zurke's boogie solos seem rather mechanical—a British critic dubbed him, somewhat unkindly, as 'old jerky' after hearing one of his records, being unable to resist the punning opportunity his surname afforded—but this was not always the case.

None of Zurke's records are outstanding from an overall big band viewpoint, though several of those that

I have heard—I must confess that at least fifty per cent of his output is unknown to me—do contain interesting individual contributions. His chief arranger was Fud Livingston, an exceptionally talented musician who wrote some advanced scores during the early part of his career but later became a victim of alcoholism, and the most striking soloist in the line-up was trumpeter Sterling Bose. *Nickel Nabber Blues* has a good solo from Bose, a competent one by an unidentified trombonist, and one from Zurke that shows him to have been a more advanced stylist than he has been given credit for. *Hobson Street Blues* has technically adept playing from Zurke and a pleasant solo by Bose, both of whom also play capably on *I've Found a New Baby*. In the style with which he made his name with Crosby, Zurke can be heard on a new version of *Honky Tonk Train Blues* and such numbers as *Tom Cat on the Keys* and *Cuban Boogie Woogie,* on none of which is the band called upon to do much more than provide a background.

In the light of his final solo items, it becomes clear that the records that Zurke made with his big band hardly reflect his real abilities at all, their character probably being dictated by the success of his boogie features with the Crosby band. The band itself, like so many of the secondary swing groups of the period, was technically competent and well rehearsed, but lacked distinctiveness of style and any genuine spark of creativity.

9 The Expatriates

The relative speed with which the various forms of American syncopated music were accepted in Europe is well known. Nevertheless, only in recent years has any attempt been made to provide authoritative documentation of the development of ragtime, dance music and jazz within individual countries. One of the few writers to have dealt with the subject in some depth is the Finnish musicologist Pekka Gronow, whose provisional observations raise a number of interesting points. He argues that there was a crisis in European popular music at the turn of the century, chiefly as a result of rapid urbanisation which led many forms of rural folk music to become obsolete. The strong influence of American syncopated music began with ragtime at the end of the nineteenth century; records, sheet music and visiting American brass bands and minstrel shows acted as conveyers of the new music. From roughly 1905 to World War I, ragtime numbers were commonplace items in the lists of tunes written by European composers, though they were often of mediocre quality.

When jazz and dance music began to dominate American popular music, it was inevitable that the countries which maintained strong contacts with the United States (principally Britain, France, Belgium and Germany) should be first influenced. Gronow points out, however, that frequency of contact was only a secondary factor; it was of even greater importance that jazz and dance music were first accepted in urbanised industrial areas. He cites as illustration a history of Czechoslovakian jazz, broadly outlined in a set of two LPs which exclusively features musicians from the industrialised area of the country. Mr Gronow also mentions that his own country lagged far behind Sweden in industrial development, and that jazz became popular much later in Finland than in the rest of Scandinavia. He concludes that there seems to be definite evidence that the popularity of jazz in Europe has been positively correlated with urbanisation.

As was only to be expected, by virtue of its close contacts with the United States, its industrialisation and above all the lack of a language barrier, Britain was the first country to be influenced by all forms of American popular music. By the turn of the century, innumerable records had been made by British artists in the ragtime manner, and American performers were regular visitors. It has even been suggested that the great ragtime composer Scott Joplin played in British music halls at some time between 1895 and 1902, though no supporting evidence has ever been discovered. The visit of the Original Dixieland Jazz Band in 1919 is well documented, on the other hand, and its historical significance needs no underlining. From the early 'twenties, American musicians came to Europe in increasing numbers, generally as members of touring bands, but occasionally to settle and work with resident groups. The more adventurous set their horizons beyond Europe, and for the next ten years bands of American musicians could be found as far afield as China.

The full story of the expatriate musicians is fascinating, not least because it occasionally reflects political and social events in an unexpected manner. For instance, numerous White Russians found their way to such Far Eastern centres as Singapore and worked in dance bands after escaping from their own country in 1917. However, I am not concerned here either with touring bands or with individuals who settled for varying periods outside the United States but with the small number of bands who worked regularly outside their own country; some indeed existed only in Europe or the Far East.

The factors that led musicians to seek work outside their own country ranged from an enjoyment of travel to greater financial reward. Black American performers also realised that racial prejudice was generally less oppressive in Europe or Asia, at least for entertainers. In most European countries, social conditions for the 'average wage earner were abysmal during the 'twenties and 'thirties. Nevertheless, some of the wealthy were sufficiently powerful economically to support the existence of luxury hotels and night clubs in all major cities, and it was there that many of the American expatriate musicians found lucrative work. A few bands, notably that of Sam Wooding, discovered that theatres could be a remunerative field, though their music had to be geared to a form of visual presentation that would not have been necessary if they had worked in clubs. The society that made possible the existence of hotels and clubs where musicians, and entertainers in general, could command high fees was partially destroyed by the social impact of World War II and post-war developments. Although there are still a number of expatriate American musicians who make Europe their home, their working conditions are quite different from those of their pre-war colleagues. It is not entirely surprising that a few survivors among the expatriates of the 'thirties regret the passing of the old order, rather in the manner of an out-of-work Jeeves yearning for the splendours of a long departed era.

Although most of the bands to be discussed here made their reputation in Europe, for about ten years from 1925, American musicians worked regularly in China. Today, the idea of jazz groups resident in China would strike most people as bizarre. However, from the mid 'twenties, a cosmopolitan city like Shanghai contained its quota of luxury hotels and clubs catering mainly for European and American residents, but also for Europeanised sections of the Chinese community. Naturally enough, such patrons wanted entertainment with which they were familiar, and the hotel managements did not take long to realise the commercial value of providing it.

Close on half a century later, the facts surrounding some of the early jazz bands that played in China are sometimes obscure, but it appears that the first group to include coloured American musicians was led by Bill Hegamin, husband of the blues singer Lucille Hegamin. Known as the New York Singing Syncopators, it included clarinettist/saxophonist Darnell Howard, and the saxophonists Clinton Mormon and Bailey Jackson. The band left the United

States in August 1925 and returned ten months later. The full personnel is unknown, but the late Darnell Howard told me in 1958 that it was completed by trumpeter, pianist, drummer and violinist from the Philippines, with Hegamin—himself a pianist—acting as front man. It was based at the Plaza Hotel in Shanghai and also toured Japan and the Philippines.

In August 1926, another coloured band took up residency at the Plaza Hotel, this time led by drummer Jack Carter. Again, the full personnel is obscure, but the band included banjoist Frank Ethridge, the New Orleans clarinettist Albert Nicholas who has been resident in Europe for the past twenty years, and pianist Teddy Weatherford. Just how long Carter worked in Shanghai is not clear. Nicholas and Ethridge left the band after a year, playing with bands in Cairo and Alexandria and briefly in a revue in Paris, before arriving home in November 1928.

The visiting American bands who played in Shanghai during the 'twenties were of medium size. A larger swing style group arrived there in 1934, led by trumpeter Buck

Albert Nicholas, an early expatriate who went to Shanghai with Jack Carter in 1926. In 1953 he went to live in Europe, and died in Basle, Switzerland twenty years later.

Clayton. Clayton had taken over the leadership from Earl Dancer early in that year. The band was heard by Teddy Weatherford in California and booked for a residency at the Canidrome Ballroom. The unit was twelve strong and, apart from Clayton, included trumpeters Teddy Buckner and Jack Bratton, trombonist 'Happy' Johnson, reedmen Hubert 'Bumps' Myers, Arcima Taylor and Caughey Roberts, pianist Eddie Beal, guitarist Frank Pashley, bassist Reggie Jones, drummer (doubling vibraphone and trumpet) Babe Lewis, and violinist Joe McCutcheon. Although Weatherford made occasional guest appearances with the band, he was never a regular member. While in Shanghai, Clayton also led a smaller group at the Casanova Club. After a short spell of further bandleading when he returned to Los Angeles in 1936, he joined Count Basie in Kansas City. Unfortunately, his band had never recorded.

Teddy Weatherford was undoubtedly the doyen of the Far Eastern travellers. When he first went to China with Jack Carter's band in 1926, he was already recognised as a brilliant pianist. Chicago considered him the only rival to Earl Hines. Weatherford obviously found the Far East much to his liking, for he led his own bands in Shanghai, Manila and Singapore throughout the rest of the 'twenties and the early 'thirties, returning only once to America to recruit Buck Clayton for the Canidrome Ballroom residency. During the summer of 1937, he visited Paris for the International Exposition and recorded for the Swing label. Of the titles he made, *Tea for Two* and *Maple Leaf Rag* are the most interesting. *Maple Leaf Rag* is a flamboyant version of the Scott Joplin classic, which displays Weatherford's considerable technique and excellent rhythmic attack. On the evidence of the Paris recordings, Weatherford appears to have been a talented transitional piano stylist who bridged the gap between the earlier stride school and the virtuoso approach of Hines.

After his Paris visit, Weatherford returned to Asia, where he remained for the rest of his life. He had lengthy residencies at the Grand Hotel, Calcutta, and in Bombay and Colombo. In India, he recorded both under his own name and as an accompanist to popular singers. During World War II, reports of his activities appeared fairly regularly in the British musical press as a result of visits made to hear him by servicemen who were also jazz fans. He contracted cholera in 1945 and died in a Calcutta hospital on 25th April. His Indian recordings, though occasionally showing flashes of talent, are generally rather commercial in character. It appears likely that playing for so many years to uniformed audiences had discouraged Weatherford from exerting himself. On the other hand, pianist Lennie Felix, who heard him in India during the early 'forties, once told me that he could still play brilliantly if the occasion demanded it. Felix wryly recalled a night when he had sat in with Weatherford's band and the leader reappeared after a few numbers to assert his musical authority. When Felix heard the band, it included clarinettist Rudy Jackson, a musician who was at one time a member of the Ellington band and worked regularly in India and Ceylon until the end of World War II.

There were, of course, numerous other groups and individual musicians who worked for much of their career in Asia. One of the most interesting was Whitey Smith, whose career has been outlined by Edward S. Walker. Born Sven Erik Schmit in Denmark in 1897, Smith emigrated to America in 1906. After a variety of musical jobs, he arrived in Shanghai to form a band for the Carlton Club in September 1922. Smith stayed in Shanghai until 1937. It has been reported that his band played at first in a Dixieland jazz style. Later groups were more orthodox dance bands. During the mid 'twenties, Smith had started to feature westernised versions of Chinese folk songs to attract non-Western audiences. He was very successful: within a year or two, his public included many Chinese residents who, he claims, proved to be excellent dancers. Smith's story is as intriguing as that of many an early musician who worked chiefly in Asia. However, these pioneers were concerned with small groups or with straight dance bands, here outside our scope.

A contender for the position of most widely travelled bandleader was Leon Abbey, who was born in Minnesota early this century. He had worked in vaudeville and in 1926 was director of the Savoy Bearcats, then resident at New York's Savoy Ballroom and recording for Victor. A year later he took a band on a South American tour. It played in the Argentine, Brazil and Uruguay, with a personnel of John Brown, Demas Dean (trumpet), Bob Horton (trombone), Carmello Jejo (alto saxophone, clarinet), Joe Garland (tenor saxophone), Prince Robinson (alto saxophone), Earl Frazier (piano), P. Franklin Blackburn (banjo), Henry 'Bass' Edwards (tuba), Billy Lynch (drums), Greenlea and Drayton (dance team), and himself on violin.

Leon Abbey's band at the Apollo Theatre, May 1940. Earle Howard (piano), Muriel Gaines (vocal), Leslie Carley (guitar), Ellsworth Reynolds (bass), 'Puss' Johnson (drums), Gene Prince (trumpet), Horace Bush or Lester Boone (sax), Shirley Clay (trumpet), Abbey, Leslie Johnakins (alto, clarinet), probably George Hancock (trumpet), Jobetus McCord (alto, clarinet). Ed Cuffee (trombone), Fred Robinson or Jonas Walker (trombone) and Cass McCord (tenor).

The New York Age gave this line-up on 2nd July 1927 and reported six months later that Abbey had left for London with a six piece group comprising Charlie Johnson (cornet), Fletcher Allen, Ralph James (sax), Billy Gaines (piano), Harry Stevens (banjo), Oliver Tynes (drums), and himself (violin).

The New York Age refers to a three-month engagement in London. In fact, Abbey did not return to the States for twelve years. During that time, he toured extensively throughout Europe and twice visited India. The band, supplemented by Harry Cooper (trumpet), Jake Green (trombone), Peter Ducionge (sax) and John Warren (tuba), played in London, Berlin and Paris in 1928. The following year, it appeared in a number of French and Spanish cities, and in 1930, Abbey led a group at the Silver Slipper Club in London. The New York Amsterdam News of 3rd September mentions his having won a suit over false accusations concerning the deportation of some of his men. That autumn he was back in Paris. It is clear that the size of his group varied, as did its personnel, for violinist Juice Wilson told Bertrand Demeusy that he was a member of Abbey's quintet during an engagement in Italy in 1930; the line-up had the unusual instrumentation of two violins, piano, banjo and drums. An issue of Music dated December 1930 reports the arrival from Paris of Abbey's band, augmented with two unnamed musicians, to replace Sam Wooding's orchestra at the Théâtre de 10 Heures in Brussels. Little is known of Abbey's activities during 1931, but Music reported in July 1932 that Leon Abbey's Rhythm Band had begun an engagement two months earlier at the Europa Hall, a new dance hall in Prague. What Abbey was doing in 1933 remains undocumented, though there are reports of his working in both Paris and Zurich towards the end of 1934.

Early in 1935, Abbey opened at Le Boeuf Sur Le Toit in Paris. His personnel, as given in a contemporary issue of Jazz Hot, included Noel Chiboust (trumpet), Castor McCord (tenor saxophone), Peter Ducionge and Oliver Tynes. In June 1936, the same magazine reported that his orchestra had just returned from an engagement in India. Among those who had made the trip were Charlie Johnson and Fletcher Allen from his initial sextet, and Castor McCord. Shortly afterwards, Abbey was heading a new group in a Paris club. Johnson, Tynes and Emile Christian (bass) were the only Americans in the personnel. At some time in the late summer or early autumn of 1936, a band led by Abbey took part in a short film, according to a report in Music of October 1936.

Abbey's Indian trip must have been successful, for in October 1936 he set out there from Paris. A residency at the Hotel Taj Mahal in Bombay lasted until the end of April in the following year. This time, his line-up consisted of Bill Coleman, Crickett Smith (trumpet), Emile Christian (trombone), Arthur Lanier, Rudy Jackson, Anthony Cosey (reeds), Charlie Lewis (piano) and Oliver Tynes (drums). On his return, he led a septet at the Brick Top Club in Paris. His trumpeters at different times included both Jack

Hamilton and Henry Mason. Late in 1937, he led what Music (December 1937) described as a swing band in Holland, returning to Paris late in the year. In the autumn of 1938, he was fronting a rumba band in Stockholm, recording four titles for the Swedish Sonora label. Sometime in 1939, Abbey returned to the United States. Down Beat (15th February 1940) reported that he was auditioning a fifteen piece group in New York. Abbey's subsequent career will be discussed with those of other New York bands.

From the reports of jazz followers who heard some of Abbey's bands in the 'thirties, it appears that at least a few were highly accomplished in the swing style. It is unfortunate that his recordings were not in the jazz idiom, for his larger bands always included good soloists. As they were comprised of musicians who played together a great deal, they must also have offered cohesive ensemble playing.

Among bands which were based in Europe during the 'twenties and 'thirties, the Southern Syncopated Orchestra is worthy of brief consideration. Although little of its music would be recognised as jazz today, it is important historically for having within its ranks a few of the musicians who were to be instrumental in spreading jazz throughout Europe. The Southern Syncopated Orchestra was a large unit consisting of around thirty-six musicians, and its music was regarded as showing a strong ragtime flavour. Its leader, Will Marion Cook, had been prominent in New York; in common with many of his contemporaries, he led large orchestras with a repertoire varying from syncopated numbers influenced by ragtime to concert versions of Negro spirituals and light classics. These groups were as much concerned with proving to the public that black musicians could attain high musical standards as with making converts to the music of their own community. They frequently included string sections and large numbers of banjos.

The Southern Syncopated Orchestra arrived in England in June 1919. Concerts at a number of the leading London halls were followed by a Command performance for George V at Buckingham Palace. It was reported that the King most enjoyed Sidney Bechet's feature of *Characteristic Blues*. For jazz followers, the presence of Bechet is the most important single factor in the band's history. The late Ernst Ansermet made one of the most famous and prophetic comments on an early jazz musician when he described Bechet in the Swiss Revue Romande as 'this artist of genius'. Other musicians within the band who were to make their mark on the development of jazz in Europe included trumpeter Arthur Briggs. However, Bechet is the performer who must be credited with the introduction of authentic blues to European audiences.

The full history of the orchestra's European tour, which lasted into 1922, is lacking in some details, not least because numerous personnel changes obviously occurred. Some members of the band were drowned when their boat sank in the Irish Channel; they had been on their way to a concert at the Scala Theatre, Dublin in October 1921. It is not clear how many were lost in this tragedy. About eight is probable, although figures up to eighteen have been quoted. A six piece unit of members from the full band, including Sidney Bechet and led by Benny Peyton, made two test recordings in 1920 for the British Columbia label, but these were rejected. At some point in 1921, possibly after the drowning, a reorganisation of the orchestra brought in the West Indian brothers, Cyril and George 'Happy' Blake. A number of British musicians played with the band. They included Tom Smith, Ted Heath and Billy Mason, all prominent in jazz in the years ahead. Heath wrote many years later of the assistance given by members of the group to the British contingent on aspects of jazz playing. When the band finally broke up in 1922, a few of its musicians remained in Europe. Trombonist/dancer Ellis Jackson, a long time stalwart of the Billy Cotton band, became one of the best known to British audiences in later years.

Edward S. Walker recently suggested that the influence of the Southern Syncopated Orchestra on English and European jazz was in all probability as great as that of the Original Dixieland Jazz Band. He argues that English musicians played with the band for several years and that those members who remained to work throughout Europe in the subsequent years made important contributions to the spread of the music. His views can hardly be challenged, and it is worth considering the later activities of a couple of the musicians who remained in Europe.

Drummer Benny Peyton, after heading his Jazz Kings in London and Birmingham in 1921-22, led a variety of bands throughout Europe during the rest of the 'twenties and 'thirties. In early 1926, he was in Russia with a band led by trombonist Frank Withers, formerly with the Southern Syncopated Orchestra, who was billed as the 'King of the trombone'. This band, including Sidney Bechet, was by all accounts the first jazz group to play in the Soviet Union. In the following years, Peyton organised bands that were resident in France, Belgium, Switzerland and Hungary, among other countries. The details of most of these bands are obscure, but a photograph reproduced in Robert Pernet's 'Jazz In Little Belgium' shows Peyton fronting a ten piece group of Tommy Ladnier (trumpet), John Forrester (trombone), 'Pancho', Alonzo 'Lonnie'

Benny Peyton's band in London, 1919. Sidney Bechet is on the extreme left.

Williams, Fred Coxito (reeds), Lou Henley (piano), Henry Saphiro (banjo), June Cole (tuba), Will Tyler (violin) and himself (drums). This photograph is part of a handbill, which refers to Benton E. Peyton by his full name and advertises an engagement at the Hotel Atlanta in Brussels during 1929. It also mentions that the band was previously resident in Nice. Interestingly enough, the line-up includes three former members of the Southern Syncopated Orchestra, Forrester, Coxito and Saphiro in addition to Peyton himself.

Peyton returned to the United States in 1939. He was employed by Local 802 of the American Federation Of Musicians for some years and retained an interest in music up to the time of his death in January 1965, when he was in his mid seventies. Only a few of the expatriate bands ever got into the recording studios, and Peyton's was not one of them.

Trumpeter Arthur Briggs returned briefly to America at the end of the Southern Syncopated Orchestra tour in 1922. Within a few months, he was back in Europe leading his own Savoy Syncopated Orchestra in Brussels. The band left Belgium to play in Vienna two years later and was then based in Germany from 1926 to 1928. There, it recorded prolifically. However, Briggs's use of European musicians in his group places it outside the scope of this chapter. Having disbanded in the summer of 1928, Briggs worked with the Noble Sissle band both in Europe and America until 1931. In that year, he returned to Europe, co-led a band with Freddy Johnson, worked as a sideman with various groups, and again formed his own band. Briggs played mainly in France with this band, though he took it to Egypt in 1937. He was interned in a concentration camp during World War II, but continued to be a successful bandleader from 1946 until 1964. For the past eight years, he has been a professor of music at several French colleges. Apart from two brief trips to America, Briggs has been living in Europe for over fifty years, which makes him the veteran American musical expatriate.

Best known among black American bands resident for long spells in Europe were those led by Sam Wooding during the 'twenties and Willie Lewis in the 'thirties. Strictly speaking, Wooding's was not an expatriate group, though some of its individual members remained in Europe for varying periods, but it never recorded in the United States, and its leader enjoyed a greater reputation abroad than in his own country. Wooding was born in Philadelphia on 17th June 1895. He first led his own band in Atlantic City when he was demobilised in 1919. In the next six years, he led bands in Detroit and New York, and as part of a touring show. He sailed to Europe in May 1925 as director of the band accompanying the 'Chocolate Kiddies' revue, which opened at the Admirals Palast in Berlin. His line-up was a strong one and consisted of Bobby Martin, Maceo Edwards, Tommy Ladnier (trumpet), Herb Flemming (trombone), Willie Lewis, Garvin Bushell,

Above: *the Sam Wooding Orchestra in Copenhagen, 1925. Left to right: Willie Lewis, Gene Sedric, Garvin Bushell, John Warren, Sam Wooding, Johnny Mitchell, George Howe, Bobby Martin, Herb Flemming, Tommy Ladnier and Maceo Edwards.* Right: *San Wooding with Rae Harrison in Tokyo, 1967.*

Gene Sedric (reeds), himself (piano), Johnny Mitchell (banjo), John Warren (tuba) and George Howe (drums). The revue as a whole was an immediate success.

From this point until the spring of 1972, the Wooding band toured extensively throughout Europe, appearing in Hamburg, Frankfurt, Munich, Vienna, Prague, Budapest, London, Birmingham, Zagreb, Moscow, Leningrad, Rome and Copenhagen, among other places. In 1926, Wooding left the revue and the band worked on its own. A highpoint of the tour had already been reached when the revue and band arrived in Moscow, probably in late February 1926. In an interview with jazz writer Art Napoleon in 1967, Wooding recalled incidents from his past career. He often spoke of the three months he spent in Moscow and Leningrad, warmly remembering the welcome the band received, the symphony concerts and the singing Russian Orthodox Church choirs. Of the less pleasant aspects of the visit, he said, 'Some of the things we saw bothered us, sure. But today we have poor people sleeping in the streets in downtown New York—so why be amazed at hearing of people doing the same forty years ago in Russia? . . . As far as the chain gangs and oppression go, we really don't have too far to go in our own country to find that, now, do we?'

After sailing from France, the band worked in South America for a few months and returned to the United States in the summer of 1927. Wooding led bands in his own country for about a year, then set out again for Europe in June 1928 with a personnel of 'Doc' Cheatham, Bobby Martin (trumpet), Billy Burns (trombone), Jerry Blake, Willie Lewis, Gene Sedric (reeds), Freddy Johnson (piano), John Mitchell (guitar) and Ted Fields (drums). Again the tour was extensive. The band played in Germany, France, Scandinavia, Italy, Spain, Rumania and Turkey before breaking up in Belgium during November 1931. There were personnel changes during the tour: 'Doc' Cheatham and Jerry Blake left the band in Spain towards the end of 1929, being replaced by Harry Cooper and Ralph James. Albert Wynn was added on trombone in Spain and replaced in Berlin by Herb Flemming some

time in 1930. Freddy Johnson left in late 1929 (presumably Justo Baretto took over on piano), though he worked again with Wooding in Berlin during the following year. In late 1929, bassist June Cole joined the band from Benny Peyton's group. The bassist for the first part of the tour is not known. On the first tour, the band recorded a total of fourteen titles in Berlin. It doubled this output during its second tour, completing several sessions in Spain and France.

Upon his return to the States late in 1931, Wooding assembled another band, which he led until 1935; he then spent two years studying at Pennsylvania University before forming his Southland Spiritual Choir. In the interview with Art Napoleon, he explained that part of his inspiration to organise the choir had come from the Orthodox Church choirs he had heard in Russia. From 1937 to 1941, he achieved some success in his new role. He led his own vocal group during the mid 'forties, did a great deal of teaching and ran a small record label. He then formed a duo with singer Rae Harrison that took them to residencies in several European countries, Israel and Turkey in the 'sixties. They returned to America in 1966, worked in Japan during 1967, and went home again after a spell in Germany in 1968 and part of 1969.

In view of his line-up, Wooding's 1925 records are generally disappointing. He seems to have had a liking for 'symphonic jazz' of the Paul Whiteman variety, and a number like *By the Waters of Minnetonka* is played very straight. Here, Garvin Bushell's oboe is featured. *O Katharina* almost has a brass band sound, and the rhythm on *Alabamy Bound* has overtones of ragtime. *Shanghai Shuffle* is by far the best performance, mainly because it has an excellent solo by Ladnier. However, big band jazz

was still in its infancy in 1925, whereas it had made enormous progress by 1929. Wooding's records of 1929 and 1930 are only intermittently satisfactory and include a great deal of period ephemera. *Bull Foot Stomp* moves along well enough and has a few reasonable solos. The score for *Tiger Rag*, on the other hand, is over-elaborate and detracts from the contributions of the soloists. There is a nice trumpet solo, probably by Cheatham, on *Ready For the River,* and the ensemble work at the opening of *Krazy Kat* is spirited enough, but the performances are too often marred by obvious attempts to emulate Paul Whiteman, by poor material and a series of dreadful vocals. It is difficult to resist the surmise that, while benefiting socially and financially from the overseas tours, Wooding lost contact with the mainstream of big band jazz development in several of its most important years. This shows in his recordings, particularly those of 1929-30, and how he might have developed, had he remained in America at this time, must be left to conjecture. It is interesting that several of the musicians who were with him on his second tour remained in Europe, forming the nucleus of what was probably the best of all the expatriate bands, that led by Willie Lewis.

It is not certain if the Wooding band played in Spain during 1925 or 1926, but a little known American coloured band was resident there for a while in 1927. Led by violinist Wilson Robinson, a musician believed to be from St Louis, it was billed as Robinson's Syncopators. Robinson was leading a band under this title in St Louis as early as 1923, when he was joined by trombonist De Priest Wheeler. The band took part in one recording session for the Paramount label. It toured extensively throughout the United States during 1923 and 1924, coming to New York early in 1925. Under the leadership of Andrew Preer, it became known as the Cotton Club Orchestra, and later as the Missourians. It can be assumed that Robinson was not involved in that part of the story and must have returned to St Louis to form a new band. Although we know that clarinettist Angelo Fernandez was present, Robinson had few well-known musicians with him in Spain in 1927; his personnel is as obscure as his own subsequent career.

Pianist Freddy Johnson, who set out for Europe with Wooding in 1928, stayed on after the band returned to the United States, initially working as a soloist in Paris. Late in 1932, he became co-leader of a band with trumpeter Arthur Briggs. The full personnel consisted of Briggs and Bobby Jones (trumpet), Billy Burns (trombone), Peter Duconge (alto saxophone, clarinet), Alcide Castellanos (alto saxophone), Frank 'Big Boy' Goudie (tenor saxophone, clarinet), Johnson (piano, arranger), Sterling Conaway (guitar), Juan Fernandez (bass), Billy Taylor (drums). In 1933, this band recorded four titles for the French Brunswick label, and Briggs and Johnson made four more without the band. At least three of the four

Left: *Freddie Johnson in the late 1930s.* Above: *Booker Pittman worked in France during the 1930s after arriving with the Lucky Millinder band in 1933. He died in Brazil in 1969, having spent more than three decades of his life in South America.*

band numbers are creditable performances, despite mediocre vocals by Spencer Williams and Louis Cole. Briggs plays particularly well on the session, taking fluent, rhythmically bright choruses on *Sweet Georgia Brown* and *Foxy and Grapesy,* while Duconge's clarinet solos possess something of a New Orleans character. Johnson, who could sometimes be rather square rhythmically, is in good form and reveals a clear Hines influence on *My Baby's Gone.*

Johnson recorded again with a band for French Brunswick late in 1933. On that occasion, the titles were issued as being by Freddy Johnson and his Harlemites. The brass and rhythm were as before, except that trombonist Herb Flemming had been added. The reeds comprised Booker Pittman (clarinet, alto saxophone), Cle Saddler (alto saxophone), Roy Butler (alto and baritone saxophone) and Alfred Pratt (tenor saxophone). The ensemble playing is crisper than that of the previous session, especially on *Harlem Bound* and one of the two versions of *I Got Rhythm.* Pittman, on both alto and clarinet, proves a worthwhile addition to the solo strength of the band; Briggs, Flemming and Pratt contribute good passages. Without being particularly individual, Johnson's scores are highly professional, employing call-and-response patterns ably, and the band as a whole generates a good swing.

In February 1934, after a spell with Freddy Taylor's band, Johnson left to play in Belgium and Holland. He became co-leader of an international band in Holland with the Surinamese saxist Lex van Spall. This band, which included four Americans, two Russians, one German, one Dutchman and one Surinamese, recorded for Dutch Decca. After a while, Johnson took up a residency at the Negro Palace in Amsterdam, working frequently in a trio with Coleman Hawkins. During 1937 and 1938, Johnson recorded with both Benny Carter and Coleman Hawkins in Holland; he joined the Willie Lewis band in Belgium in the spring of 1939. Two years later, when Lewis took his band to Switzerland, Johnson opened his own club in Amsterdam and remained in Holland until arrested by the Nazis in December 1941. He was interned in Bavaria until February 1944 and repatriated to the United States a month later. Johnson's post-war career was varied. Until the close of the 'fifties, his time was occupied with work as a piano and vocal coach and with engagements as a soloist. He returned to Europe with a show at the close of 1959 and performed as a soloist in Holland during 1960. He was by this time very ill—at the age of fifty-seven he died of cancer in a New York hospital on 24th March 1961, some months after his return to the States.

Jazz collectors who began to buy records around the mid 'thirties will recall Freddy Taylor's vocals with the famous Quintet of the Hot Club of France, as well as a single record, made under his own name, that coupled *Blue Drag* and *Viper's Dream.* Taylor was a dancer and entertainer

312

who had worked at the Cotton Club during the 'thirties. He came to Europe with Lucky Millinder's touring band of 1933; during this visit, he received trumpet tuition from Bill Coleman. In 1935, he returned to Europe to lead his own band. It appears that he had already been a band leader for a brief period after the conclusion of the Millinder tour in October 1933, when Freddy Johnson worked with him. Taylor's band was resident for a period at the Villa d'Este in Paris, and was by all accounts a good one. Then, until his return to America in the late 'thirties, he led a band in Rotterdam, ran his own night club in Paris, and worked in various European cities as a solo entertainer. He did make a return visit to Paris in 1967, but since 1939 his career has been outside jazz.

Trumpeter Bobby Martin's early career was spent working with the Sam Wooding orchestra. He was present during both of Wooding's European tours and the band's American residencies in 1927 and 1928. Martin remained in Europe when the band broke up in Brussels in November 1931 and was almost a permanent member of the Willie Lewis orchestra from 1932 to 1936. He then returned to New York and set about forming a band to play in Europe, arriving back in June 1937. He persuaded reed men Glyn Paque and Johnny Russell, pianist Ram Ramirez, and bassist Ernest Hill to leave the Willie Bryant band, and completed his line-up with saxist Ernest Purce, drummer Kaiser Marshall, and guitarist Bobby McRae. By doubling on trumpet, McRae added ensemble flexibility to the group. Kaiser Marshall gave Martin an impressive book of arrangements by Don Redman, Benny Carter, Fletcher Henderson and Edgar Sampson among others—he had built this up while fronting his own groups from time to time during the previous six years. Their loss through fire while the band was playing an engagement at The Mephisto in Rotterdam during the spring of 1938 was a disaster which the band did well to surmount.

In 1937, the Martin band appeared in a French film, 'L'Alibi', which featured Erich von Stroheim, Louis Jouvet, Jany Holt and Florence Marlay. It also toured in France, Denmark, Switzerland and Holland until the spring of 1939, taking part in one recording session in Holland. *Crazy Rhythm* and *Make Believe Ballroom* show the band off to advantage; the punch of the ensemble and the swing generated give the effect of a larger band. There are several good solos, but the spirit and cohesion of the band are even more impressive, and the group must be rated as one of the most polished to have toured Europe during the late 'thirties. On his return to the States, Martin continued to lead bands for some years, ultimately retiring from the music scene to take charge of a family business.

One of the last expatriate bands before World War II was the Harlem Rhythm Makers, formed late in 1938 by ex-members of the Willie Lewis band. Its personnel consisted of Bill Coleman (trumpet), Billy Burns (trombone), Joe Hayman, Fletcher Allen, Edgar 'Spider' Currance (reeds),

Herman Chittison (piano), and an unknown drummer. The group left France for Egypt, appearing at the Shepherd Hotel in Cairo and the Monseigneur in Alexandria throughout 1939. Because of the outbreak of war, the musicians were unable to go back to Europe and returned to the United States in the spring of 1940; the band did not record. Since its existence almost a quarter of a century ago, both Burns and Chittison have died, Hayman, Currance and Allen have been inactive musically, and only Coleman is still a prominent jazz artist. He returned to Paris in 1948 and has made his home there ever since.

The best known, and probably the best musically, of all the expatriate bands that could be heard in Europe in the 'thirties was the one led by Willie Lewis. A member of Sam Wooding's band from 1925 until it broke up in 1931, Lewis stayed on in Brussels to lead his own band, which included several other former Wooding musicians, at the Merry Grill. Later, he appeared with it in Berlin and one or two other European cities. He went back to New York in January 1934, but was in Europe again three months later. During the next five years, he established a reputation unequalled by other expatriate groups. Lewis was frequently in residence during these years at a club in Paris, Chez Florence, described by pianist Herman Chittison as ' . . . the prestige club for Americans in Paris. It was a late hour club, formal dress required, and the only thing they served was champagne—no food or whisky. I can remember that this precedent was broken only once, when actor Edward G. Robinson threw a huge private party'. Lewis often broadcast from the club over Poste Parisienne, and I remember hearing his band regularly when programmes were relayed by the BBC.

From the summer of 1935 until March 1936, Benny Carter worked both as instrumentalist and arranger with the Lewis band; it included another major soloist, trumpeter Bill Coleman, from June 1937 to December 1938. In addition to its lengthy residencies at the club Chez Florence, the band played in a number of cities in France, Holland and Belgium, and at one point worked in Egypt for a short period. Although several musicians walked out on the band late in 1938, after disagreements, Lewis found adequate replacements, and a season in Belgium during the following year enabled him to build the group up to its former high standard. When the Nazis invaded Holland in May 1940, the band was prevented from playing for the Dutch people or German soldiers, but leading Nazi officials and high ranking German officers sometimes engaged it for private parties. Early in 1941, permission was granted for the band to leave for Switzerland; with the addition of three Swiss musicians, it played over twenty concerts there while awaiting visas for transit through France, Spain and Portugal on the way home. Swiss jazz writer Johnny Simmen has described the treatment the band received in his country. He relates that a few of the musicians, somewhat undisciplined characters, found themselves in trouble with the police. In the end,

313

Benny Carter, 1937, with : Sam Duisberg (trumpet), Roberto Monmartre (drums), George Chisholm (trombone), Louis Stevenson (alto saxophone), Carter, Jimmy Williams (alto saxophone, clarinet), Len Harrison (string bass) and Ray Webb (guitar). Sitting: unidentified Cuban percussionist, Bertie King (tenor saxophone), Cliff Wooldridge (trumpet).

the American consul in Zurich allowed the local police to imprison the whole band, innocent members included, until the visas arrived. Mr Simmen comments, 'It is out of the question that such a thing could have happened to any group of white American citizens.' Not surprisingly, when he visited the band in a Zurich jail several of its members at first refused to shake hands or speak with him. After staying in jail for two weeks, the band was taken to the station by a police escort on its day of departure.

The band played a few concerts in Portugal. It finally arrived back in the United States in October 1941. Lewis himself made a few club appearances after his return; he worked as a clarinet player in a 1951 Broadway show, 'Angel in the Pawnshop'. For most of the remaining years of his life, he was employed as a bartender. He died at the age of sixty-five in New York City in March 1971.

The Willie Lewis band, having recorded fairly regularly during the period from 1936 to 1938, made a number of recordings in Switzerland during July and August 1941. A high proportion of its output is now available on microgroove reissues. It first entered the studio on 23rd April 1935, producing two competent but ephemeral performances. Nine months later, the band recorded its only session with Benny Carter as a member. The titles include the band's signature tune, a gentle Benny Carter number called *Just a Mood,* on which both Carter and Chittison solo very well. *Stardust,* which is primarily a feature for Carter's Armstrong-inspired trumpet playing, and *All of Me* were also recorded. Carter used the same arrangement of *All of Me* nearly five years later, when he recorded the number with his own American band; the scoring for saxes during the theme statement is typical of him. Carter (on trumpet) and Chittison have good solos.

By the time the band recorded again later in 1936,

Carter was in England. Bill Coleman is present on trumpet, at this stage presumably for recording purposes only. *I'm Shooting High* has excellent solos from Coleman and altoist George Johnson; the ensemble sound of the band is crisp. Coleman's fleet, adventurous work on *Stompin' at the Savoy* is impressive, and Frank Goudie takes quite individual sounding solos on *Sweet Sue* and *Organ Grinder's Swing.* On *Sweet Sue,* there is particularly good work, again by Coleman, and the band's ensemble work has an impressive cohesiveness. From a session in 1937, *Doin' the New Low Down* is a feature for pianist Chittison, whose solo reveals a strong stride influence, while *Swinging for a Swiss Miss* displays excellent drive from the band and individual solos by Goudie, Chittison, Coleman and Jack Butler. Coleman and Butler engage in an effective trumpet chase.

Of the personnel in the 1936-38 band, only Billy Burns and Lewis himself took part in the Swiss recordings, with several Swiss musicians filling in. The ensemble sound is slightly less relaxed than before, while some of the performances sound a little casual; nevertheless, on the better numbers, the band still acquits itself well. The ensemble on *Bacon's Blues* achieves a very full sound, and trumpeter Louis Bacon has a pleasant solo. *Swingin' at Chez Florence* is more impressive, as a result of spirited playing by the band and good solos from Johnny Russell (tenor saxophone) and Henry Mason (trumpet). Russell was an excellent tenor soloist with a bustling style derived from that of Coleman Hawkins. He can be heard to advantage on *After You've Gone* and *Body and Soul,* numbers with trumpet solos taken by Mason and Bacon respectively. The presence of drummer Tommy Benford is beneficial, and the clarinet solos of German-born Ernst Hollerhagen are pleasant. The Lewis band recorded a fair proportion of ephemera, but overall it was an excellent group that did much for big band jazz in Europe.

Throughout the 'twenties and 'thirties, there were, of course, other bands of American jazz musicians working throughout Europe. Some were there for a few months on tour, like the Lucky Millinder band, while others took part in shows. As early as 1923, such musicians as Darnell Howard (violin), James P. Johnson (piano) and Wellman Braud (bass) were playing in London, Paris and Brussels with a revue; this tradition was maintained with the 'Blackbird' revue bands and many others. Other musicians like the pianist Tommy Chase, led either international bands or small groups, while some individuals preferred to work with existing bands in the various countries they visited. If a full list of American jazz musicians working abroad during the 'twenties and 'thirties were compiled it would make a formidable total indeed. The Clarke-Boland Band of recent years, which has drawn much of its strength from a later generation of musical expatriates, and the many individual American jazz musicians still living in Europe help to demonstrate that the trend set by the pioneers has become an essential part of the jazz tradition.

10 Big Band Jazz in Europe

The most important single characteristic of big band jazz in America was the way in which it developed almost entirely through the support of black audiences. If there had been no black population of the United States, clearly the very existence of jazz would be in doubt. Nevertheless, in due course the music was received with such enthusiasm throughout the world that it was no longer the exclusive property of its originators.

As soon as it was heard outside America, jazz was welcomed by the public, and by a number of dance band musicians, who swiftly attempted emulation. It first attracted serious critical attention in Europe. All the same, the number of people displaying a deep interest in jazz during the 'twenties and 'thirties was very small in comparison to the regular listening and dancing audiences that heard the popular dance bands of the day. At the time, it would have been considered either absurd or utopian to suggest that a group of musicians in any European country might successfully form a big band with an unadulterated jazz policy. In this respect, the European musicians who wished to concentrate on jazz were in the same position as their white counterparts in America, who, with very few exceptions, also had to make a living in commercial dance bands.

The jazz of the white New Yorkers, who were typified by such individuals as Red Nichols, Miff Mole and Adrian Rollini, was considered for some years the apex of jazz achievement and was initially the kind which most influenced European musicians, particularly those in Britain. Many musicians in Europe scarcely knew of the leading coloured bands such as those of Bennie Moten and Luis Russell or McKinney's Cotton Pickers, let alone the territory groups, until long after their best years were over. And even if they had been familiar with these bands, given a critical climate in which Louis Armstrong's playing was regarded as 'crude', it is unlikely that they would have been impressed. At least in this respect, the white American musicians were in a better position, for they could hardly remain unaware of the merits of, say, Fletcher Henderson's or Duke Ellington's band. In any case, from the mid 'twenties, it was not uncommon for white jazz performers to take a break from the restrictions of their regular jobs by sitting in on sessions with coloured musicians after hours.

To satisfy a yen for the jazz life, European musicians could at best hope for a job with a dance band leader who favoured a 'hot' policy. There has been a tendency among jazz fans to be supercilious about 'commercial' dance bands, but a number of the leaders of such bands were sympathetic to jazz from the beginning and liked to employ musicians who could take the occasional hot chorus. At times, leaders not noted for an adventurous musical policy even in their own sphere engaged some unlikely sidemen. For example, the late Leo Reisman featured ex-Ellington trumpeter Bubber Miley during 1930, though it could have been of little commercial advantage to him. Six years earlier, he had hired the coloured trumpeter Johnny Dunn

for a concert in Boston and seen a section of his audience walk out in protest. Similarly, Henry Hall speaks proudly, to this day, of engaging Benny Carter as an arranger for his BBC Dance Orchestra in 1936, although it could have meant nothing to his public. There are many stories of philistine bandleaders who fired jazz musicians for stepping out of line, but the opposite angle has not always been publicised.

Before the swing era, it is not always simple to categorise a band as a jazz unit or a straight dance group, and I am well aware that my own criteria are at times rather arbitrary. It has frequently been pointed out that bands such as Fletcher Henderson's and Bennie Moten's worked essentially as dance units, and certainly for much of the 'twenties and 'thirties jazz was still a functional music. Significantly, far from lamenting the fact, many musicians active during these years have claimed that they drew their greatest inspiration from their interaction with the dancing public. However, definition is complicated by a long line of bands extending from Henderson and Moten to Basie, Lunceford and Ellington, whose music is undeniably in a jazz mould and whose personnels have always consisted primarily of jazz musicians. Although these bands might feature commercial vocalists, play stock scores of the hits of the day, and observe some of the conventions of their time in the manner of the dance bands, on the whole their music is recognised as jazz. On the other hand, there are bands such as those led by Guy Lombardo, Paul Whiteman or Jack Payne which sometimes performed in a hot manner (the house record at the famous Savoy Ballroom is held by Guy Lombardo, to the intense chagrin of jazz purists), but could hardly be considered as jazz units, even in the loosest of terms.

The terminology of jazz has always been imprecise, and thus of more use in providing guidelines than strict definitions; the real problems arise in the borderline areas. There are jazz followers who dismiss the large orchestras of a Benny Goodman or an Artie Shaw as 'degenerate swing bands' and claim that they are basically commercial units. I accept that some of the successful swing bands pursued commercial policies—remember that even the most experimental leaders hope to attract enough public support to make their music commercially viable. But for me, the swing bands have sufficiently strong musical links with the big band jazz pioneers to make them acceptable on the jazz side of the fence. Curiously enough, there are jazz purists who reject the swing bands out of hand but enthuse about a hot performance from the orchestra of, say, Ben Pollack or Bert Lown. Often, a jazz follower's use of the word 'commercial' tells us about his prejudices rather than the music.

I raise this question of a distinction between jazz bands and straight dance bands at this point in the hope of making clear why I have included certain bands and not others. It is particularly relevant in a discussion of European bands, for, as I have already indicated, big jazz bands in the strict sense of the term were virtually unknown in

Europe until after World War II. Even so, a number of bands in several European countries had the capacity to perform more than ably in a hot (jazz) manner. Although detailed consideration would be out of place here, it would be helpful to look generally at some of the better bands. I believe that jazz brings an emotional depth to a performance that is normally outside the framework of straightforward dance music, but I am by no means unmindful of the achievements of the better dance bands, and have written about them elsewhere.

Between the late 'twenties and the outbreak of World War II, Britain's leading dance bands enjoyed a unique reputation; some even attracted a considerable audience in the United States. One result of the swing era in America was a dichotomy between the sweet and hot bands that was almost total. Europe, for reasons which I will discuss later, never really had a swing band craze, and the leading dance bands achieved a versatility that their American counterparts lacked. By the early 'thirties, dance bands in

the United States seemed, with few exceptions, to be in a total rut, and the swing era certainly introduced a much needed vitality into American popular music. In Europe, dance bands in various degrees pursued their own paths, after an initial period of copying American models, and by about 1932 there were a number of British bands that could justly be considered superior to their American rivals. Among these can be found several that employed excellent jazz musicians and featured material of a jazz nature.

Of all the prominent dance bands that became famous during the 'thirties, Lew Stone's is the one remembered with the greatest affection by jazz fans. Stone took over as leader of the band at the Monseigneur Restaurant in London when Roy Fox, who had formed the band, became ill. Almost a year later, he was invited by the Monseigneur management to form his own band. He used a personnel with only one change from that of the Fox band, and was an immediate success. Although he was active in the dance band field for several decades, Stone's greatest contribution was undoubtedly made in the 'thirties through broadcasts, records and theatre appearances. His band featured a hot policy more than any other at the time, employing excellent musicians like Nat Gonella, Lew Davis, Joe Crossman,

The Lew Stone band, 1933. Left to right: Ernest Ritte, Albert Harris, Jim Easton, Lew Stone, Monia Liter, Harry Berly, Tiny Winters, Joe Ferrie, Joe Crossman, Lew Davis; seated Nat Gonella and Alfie Noakes.

Albert Harris and Tiny Winters. In common with many Eurpean bands at the time, Stone's was greatly influenced by the Casa Loma Orchestra and featured such well known Casa Loma numbers as *White Jazz* and *Blue Jazz*. He also recorded outstanding versions of *Serenade for a Wealthy Widow* and *Garden of Weed,* both written by the remarkable Reginald Foresythe. A piano solo by Monia Liter on *Serenade* is harmonically advanced for the period. Other good recordings by Stone with leanings towards jazz include an excellent version of Jelly Roll Morton's *Milenberg Joys,* with precise section work and apt solos from Crossman and Davis; a well scored *Call of the Freaks* contains a particularly good clarinet solo by Crossman. Stone's jazz recordings constitute only a fraction of his work, but they have withstood the test of time well.

Roy Fox, the original band leader at the Monseigneur Restaurant, came to England from the United States in 1930, initially fronting an eight piece group. He had made some hot recordings between leaving the Monseigneur and forming a new band. The most famous is probably *Georgia on My Mind,* which features trumpeter and vocalist Nat Gonella. The best of Fox's later recordings were in a smooth, commercial vein, but a number of programmes that he made for commercial radio present his band in rather a different light, featuring a high proportion of instrumentals in the swing manner. They include a version of *Song of India,* which is in outline a copy of Dean Kincaide's score for Tommy Dorsey, and performances of *San, Basin Street Blues, Mean To Me* and *Singin' in the Rain* that are probably the nearest thing to the American swing band sound achieved by any British band. The numbers were recorded for programmes relayed from Radio Luxembourg in 1938; a selection recently appeared on LP.

Bert Ambrose led one of the finest and most versatile of all British bands for over a decade, but his jazz-inclined performances are never totally convincing, despite the presence of capable jazz musicians in his personnel. For many years, Ambrose's arranger was Sid Phillips, a talented musician, whose original work was highly acclaimed. Some of his numbers—*Tarantula, Hick Stomp* and *B'Wanga* for example—are basically novelty items. Others at the level of *Cotton Pickers' Congregation, Early Morning Blues* and *Plain Jane* are more obviously in the jazz tradition, and are enhanced by individual touches in the scoring, like the wordless vocal passages on *Cotton,* as well as by solos from such musicians as George Chisholm and Tommy McQuater. The real problem with Ambrose's band was that it never really managed to swing as a group, despite the presence of a jazz contingent.

Jack Hylton was one of the most popular among British bandleaders between the wars. He achieved financial suc-

Left: *the Roy Fox band in the late 1930s, with singer Mary Lee*. Above: *Jack Hylton's first band in the late 1920s.* Right: *the Hylton band on stage in the 1930s*

cess, and his reputation extended to a number of other European countries. Hylton first recorded in 1921 and after leading orthodox dance bands formed a show band roughly in the Paul Whiteman mould. It was this kind of orchestra that brought him fame. From time to time, he did record hot numbers; among early examples were *Tiger Rag* and *Limehouse Blues,* which had good Billy Ternent scores and a surprisingly high level of ensemble playing and individual solos. Later in the 'thirties, the Hylton band (or at least arranger Billy Ternent) was inspired by the visit of Duke Ellington's orchestra to Britain during 1933, producing *Black and Blue Rhythm,* an attractive exercise in Ellingtonia, and a medley of *Black and Tan Fantasy, It Don't Mean a Thing, Mood Indigo* and *Bugle Call Rag,* which is pastiche, skilfully performed. Hylton brought Coleman Hawkins to Europe in 1934, and his band backed the great tenor star on two titles five years later. People who knew him have said that his interest in jazz was a great deal keener than his recorded output might lead one to suppose.

For jazz fans in Britain during the late 'twenties, the great event was the presence of the Fred Elizalde band at the Savoy Hotel from December 1927 to July 1929. Elizalde, born in Manila in 1907, came to Britain with his brother Manuel in the autumn of 1926. He soon gained a reputation as an unusually progressive musician and endeared himself to the jazz followers of his day by engaging such

319

Fred Elizalde with his Savoy Hotel Band. Elizalde is at the piano. Adrian Rollini is third from the left.

American jazz performers as Adrian Rollini, Chelsea Quealey, Bobby Davis and Fud Livingston to play in his band at the Savoy. Elizalde's relationship with the Savoy management and clientele and, from time to time, the BBC was not a happy one. His musical policy offended both his regular dancing public and many radio listeners who complained to the BBC of a lack of melody in his band's performances. Elizalde's recordings are curiously uneven; several feature small hot groups from within the full band, and one can gauge the full potential of the group only on a very few titles such as *Sugar Step* and *Singapore Sorrows*. Its style was heavily influenced by the American contingent, most of whom had previously worked in the United States with the California Ramblers, and although it undoubtedly had a strong influence on some aspects of jazz development in Britain, its long term effect on big band jazz was, at best, peripheral.

For the rest, the listener in search of big band jazz during the 'twenties and much of the 'thirties had to be content with occasional hot performances from the popular bands of the day. The leaders of such groups were generally willing to provide an occasional instrumental, and now and then listeners or record buyers would be rewarded with a creditable jazz-influenced performance from the bands of, say, Henry Hall, Jack Payne or Billy Cotton. Surprisingly enough, for many years Billy Cotton employed Louis Armstrong-inspired trumpet soloists like Nat Gonella, Teddy Foster and Jack Doyle, and his early recordings of for instance, *New Tiger Rag, St Louis Blues* and *Shine* are not without merit. Occasionally a little known band would attract the attention of jazz followers. Stanley Barnett led a band at Madame Tussaud's Restaurant around 1933, producing versions of Duke Ellington's *Rockin' in Rhythm, Stevedore Stomp, Lightning* and *Echoes of the Jungle* which are, though largely derivative, brave attempts in a challenging idiom. But on the whole, British admirers of authentic big band jazz had to content themselves with recordings by the leading American exponents. The situation was made worse when a disagreement between the local musicians' union and the American Federation Of Musicians led to a total absence of touring bands in Britain after 1934. In this respect, European jazz fans were more fortunate; not only could they see and hear visiting American bands, but they also had the advantage of jazz expatriates in their midst. On the other hand, if European swing fans hoped that the swing era would be duplicated in their own countries, they were to be sadly disappointed.

Generally, trends in American popular music had been rapidly reflected in Europe after the close of the nineteenth century. When swing music became the rage in the United States late in 1935 and dominated the popular music scene there in subsequent years, people in a number of European countries must have anticipated similar happenings at home. Undeniably, swing did have a considerable influence in Europe, but the music never became dominant there and it is interesting to consider the reasons.

In attempting to explain the significance of the swing era in American society, I have argued that it was very much a reflection of the particular social and mental climate that then existed. The first fact that emerges when one compares social and economic conditions as they existed in the United States with those in most European countries during the mid 'thirties is that they differ completely. Economically, Western Europe was lagging behind the United States, and a rigid class structure still survived in most countries. The totalitarian regimes that existed in Germany, Italy and Spain were, in any case, hostile to jazz. Elsewhere, bands depended on residencies in hotels and night clubs that were effectively patronised only by a wealthy segment of society who lacked interest in musical qualities. Their attitude was reflected in a cynical observation from the late Bert Ambrose as he recalled an engagement in a Monte Carlo night club, 'If I couldn't hear the surf, I knew we were playing too loud.'

The situation in America was very different. While hotel managements might initially have been shocked by Benny Goodman or Tommy Dorsey, they soon came to realise that a large, youthful audience was ready to patronise their ballrooms and spend quite freely if it could hear the music it wanted. In a very short time, the triumphant swing bands were playing in the major American hotels to audiences who would have had trouble in getting past the doorman at similar hotels in Britain and the rest of Europe. The social climate in Britain at the time would have prevented Goodman and Shaw from taking up residencies at the Dorchester or the Savoy in London, even if the opportunity had existed. In addition, the audience for swing music in European countries simply did not exist in sufficient numbers to sustain bands playing in the idiom. Equally important was the dearth of musicians capable of convincing swing performances, for even the most chauvinistic of Europeans could hardly deny the superiority of American musicians in the jazz idiom, particularly in the pre-war years. Certainly, there was a nucleus of musicians able to play in the swing style in all European countries, but whatever the ambitions of this limited number might have been, they were prudent enough to realise that the lack of both a secure economic base and an assured audience precluded any attempt to form an out-and-out swing band. This reality is underlined by the fate of the few groups in Britain which tried to pursue a swing policy.

Pianist Eddie Carroll had given few indications of seeking adventurous musical goals before forming a fourteen piece swing band in 1938. With this group, he played in the intervals of a show called 'Choose Your Time', making an initial broadcast on 19th April; his line-up included George Chisholm, Benny Winestone and Jimmy Macaffer. He went on tour with his Swing Orchestra in September, leading a nine piece unit at a London night club the following January. He persisted with his attempts to lead a swing group until war broke out, achieving a minor success with his composition *Harlem,* based on a familiar jazz riff. Unfortunately, the rather mediocre records he made signally failed to capture the sound and spirit of the genuine article.

The West Indian leader, Ken Johnson, was another who tried to follow a swing policy, initially with some success. He led a mainly West Indian band at a London club in 1937 and made history in July 1938 by presenting his band in an uncompromising swing manner over the BBC. For the broadcast, he used arrangements specially commissioned from Adrian de Haas, who was writing for Gene Krupa, Fats Waller and Lucky Millinder at the time. In 1939, Johnson was resident with his band at the Cafe de Paris and broadcast fairly regularly, but the musical compromises that were increasingly forced on him led him to tell a Melody Maker reporter, 'I determined I'd make them like swing at the Cafe, or die in the attempt, and, boy, I nearly died.' Johnson recorded for both Decca and HMV; the versions of *My Buddy* and *The Sheik of Araby* that his band made for Decca are excellent. In March 1941, he was killed by a bomb at the Cafe de Paris.

Early in 1939, British jazz followers were excited at news of the formation of a co-operative unit, brainchild of a group of ex-Ambrose musicians, to be called the Heralds Of Swing. The band was lucky enough to secure a residency at London's Paradise Club from late February, opening there with a line-up of Tommy McQuater, Archie Craig (trumpet), George Chisholm (trombone), Dave Shand, Norman Maloney, Benny Winestone (reeds), Bert Barnes (piano), Sid Colin (guitar, vocal), Tiny Winters (string bass) and George Fierstone (drums). It met with a reasonably enthusiastic reception, and was featured in due course at one or two jazz concerts. Nevertheless, within a month the Paradise management was asking for a reduction in personnel and, unwilling to accept this, the group disbanded, since there was no alternative work in sight. After this, the band reformed for one concert engagement and a number of broadcasts during the last five days before the outbreak of war. The broadcasts were rather disappointing and only Chisholm seemed to be playing at his best. Although this idealistic venture failed, many of the Herald members found themselves together again soon afterwards in the Squadronaires.

Throughout the 'forties, big band jazz in Britain was dominated by the Squadronaires (initially and more correctly titled the RAF No. 1 Dance Band) and Geraldo.

Neither was a big band compared with those of Goodman or Lunceford, and jazz instrumentals formed only a part of the repertoire. However, these bands at their best were nearer to the real thing than any that had gone before. The Squadronaires included such musicians as Tommy McQuater, George Chisholm, Andy McDevitt and Jock Cummings, who had all figured in the British jazz scene before the war; it continued to exist as a civilian unit for some years after the end of the war. Among the many good

Top: *The Heralds of Swing; left to right: Bert Barnes, Tommy McQuater, George Firestone, Dave Shand, George Chisholm, Norman Maloney, in front: Tiny Winters, Benny Winestone, Sid Colin and Archie Craig. Above: The Squadronaires, left to right: unknown, George Chisholm, Eric Breeze, Tommy McQuater, Archie Craig, Kenny Baker, Monty Levy, Tommy Bradbury, Andy McDevitt, Jimmy Durant, Jock Cummings. The band is shown playing at a wartime dance. Right: Ray Ventura and his band in 1938.*

322

records were an individual arrangement of Spike Hughes's charming *Donegal Cradle Song,* written by Ronnie Aldrich, and spirited versions of *No Name Jive, C Jam Blues, Jeepers Creepers, Pompton Turnpike* and *Mission to Moscow.* Though it also recorded ephemera, and in its instrumentals veered from the stylistic extremes of big band Dixieland on the one hand to Stan Kenton on the other, the Squadronaires at its best was a very musicianly and versatile combination.

Geraldo, whose real name is Gerald Bright, became active in the jazz scene in 1939. He launched a series of 'Sunday Night Swing Club' sessions at a London theatre, adding jazz-inclined instrumentalists to his personnel. He had been a leader since 1930 with no apparent interest in jazz. From the early 'forties, many of Geraldo's recordings combined a high standard of ensemble playing and solo work. Alto saxophonist Harry Hayes is heard to advantage on such numbers as *Soft Shoe Shuffle* and *Idaho.* A few years later, the Geraldo band recorded swing numbers from the books of American leaders like Charlie Barnet and Stan Kenton, and by now original themes in the jazz vein were being provided by members of the band. The influence of bop became apparent in recordings of the early 'fifties. Until his retirement, Geraldo maintained a policy of featuring jazz musicians within his band.

The really successful British band in the late 'forties was that of the late Ted Heath, who commanded as high a reputation in the United States as at home. His band was strongly influenced by jazz; like that led by Vic Lewis, it was modelled on the Stan Kenton band. However, by the time these bands were in existence, the big band era as such was past.

I feel justified in devoting so much space in this chapter to British bands partly because I have more information on them than on most of their European counterparts, and more importantly, because British bands tended to dominate the European scene until the war years. This is not to say that there were not excellent bands in a number of European countries; some of them produced recordings that qualify as big band jazz.

Ray Ventura's Collegians was the leading band in France for many years. As a group, it was roughly equivalent to Jack Hylton's in Britain and, similarly, included jazz musicians from time to time. Best known were trumpeters Philippe Brun and Gus Deloff, bassist Louis Vola, and tenor saxophonist Alix Combelle. Both on stage and in recordings, it featured a few hot numbers. The best I have heard include *I Got Rhythm, Can't We Be Friends* and *Blue Prelude;* as far as I know, the band has not yet had any microgroove reissues. Of greater interest is the lesser known Gregor and his Gregorians, a band whose recording career was confined to the years 1929-33. At times towards the end of this period, the Gregorians included Philippe Brun, trombonists Leo Vauchant and Guy Paquinet, alto saxophonists Roger Fisbach and Charles Lisee, and Stephane Grappelly. Such recordings as *Harlem Madness, Put on Your Old Grey Bonnet* and *Puttin' on the Ritz* are well scored and combine spirited ensemble work with solos of high quality. Even more remarkable is *Tiger Rag;* the performance was rhythmically advanced for its day and compares favourably with the work of all but a few of Gregor's American contemporaries.

Over the years, Belgium boasted several highly skilled bands. Those led by Stan Brenders, Fud Candrix, Jean Omer and Eddie Tower produced the best recordings. Brenders led the official Belgian radio band, which acted as the supporting group for recordings by Django Reinhardt in May 1942. Candrix led a big band for over twenty years from 1936. Many of his recordings reflect the influence of popular American swing bands; several of them were ably scored by his pianist Raymond Colignon. A broadcast by the Candrix band in February 1939, relayed by the BBC, moved 'Detector' of the Melody Maker to report with alarm that 'Fud Candrix and his Orchestra showed once again that the Continental bands are getting uncom-

fortably ahead of us in this little matter of swing.' Jean Omer's full band did not record until late in 1940, but such titles as *Porte de Namur* and *Rhythm indien* offer further proof of the Belgian musicians' stylistic skill in swing. Tower's recordings are very uneven, but his band reached a peak in 1940 with versions of several titles associated with the Count Basie band.

One of the best known European bands was The Ramblers, formed by pianist Theo Uden Masman in 1926 for an engagement at an Amsterdam cabaret. By the end of the 'twenties, it was broadcasting and recording frequently. It had secured the most lucrative residencies in Holland, and toured in Denmark, Germany and Switzerland. In 1936, it became the resident dance band at the VARA radio station in Hilversum. An extensive broadcasting schedule here included relays through the BBC; one took place at the moment when the Germans invaded Holland. Initially, the band was heavily committed to a jazz policy and generally recorded jazz numbers, but the demands of broadcasting and regular stage appearances resulted in an extension of its repertoire and the jazz performances gradually became fewer and fewer. The Ramblers survived until 1964, when it was disbanded after a farewell broadcast.

Another Dutch leader, Ernst Van t'Hoff, led a popular band during the 'forties, which combined influences from some of the popular American swing units and Glenn Miller. He worked in Germany in the early war years, recording there in 1941 and 1942, and then moved to Brussels. Although his swing recordings are derivative, they show considerable technical skill in the idiom.

Switzerland produced one well known band—Teddy Stauffer and his Original Teddies. Stauffer formed his first band in 1927 at the age of twenty; two years later, he took a group to Berlin. For the next ten years he and his band led a roving existence, with summer engagements in Switzerland and tours as far afield as the United States and Cuba. The deteriorating political situation led Stauffer to decide that he would be well advised to remain within his own country from early 1939, but two years later he handed over his band to tenor saxophonist Eddie Brunner and left for America to start the career he still follows in the night club business. Frequent broadcasts during the rest of the war made the Original Teddies very popular throughout Europe. Their musical policy highlighted the hits of the well known American swing bands. The band recorded fairly regularly during the 'forties. Its output proved it to be a very accomplished unit, with a number of special scores that showed a marked individuality of approach. Brunner was a good soloist, active until his death in 1956; the other prominent soloist was clarinettist Ernst Hollerhagen, who had chosen to exile himself rather than serve in the German armed forces. The band gained from the unusual flexibility of the rhythm section.

Jazz and dance music did not develop at the same rate in all the Scandinavian countries; Finland and, to a lesser extent, Norway lagged behind Sweden and Denmark. Sweden's finest bands are generally considered to have been those led by Hakan von Eichwald, Arne Hulphers and Thore Ehrling. All have been well served with reissues.

At the start of his career and in the war years, Hakan von Eichwald led theatre orchestras, but he is best remembered for the dance bands he organised and fronted between 1930 and 1939. He was a prolific recorder and, among more than three hundred titles, he issued several in a swing vein. However, numbers such as *Nagasaki, Limehouse Blues* and *Alabamy Bound*, though expertly performed, are not convincing as big band jazz, and lack the necessary rhythmic urgency.

In January 1934, pianist Arne Hulphers took over von Eichwald's personnel, continuing as a big band leader into the 'forties. Versions of *Swingin' in the Promised Land, Don't Be That Way, Baltimore* and *I'm Coming Virginia,* recorded at a session in 1939, proved his band to be a good one. The first title is skilfully scored by trombonist Julius Jacobsen; high quality section work is underlined by a good rhythm contingent. *Baltimore,* arranged by Miff Gorling, is also notable for the assurance of the section work and agreeable solos from tenor saxophonist Erik Eriksson and trumpeter Gosta Torner. Only in some of the call-and-response passages on *I'm Coming Virginia* is a certain stiffness of execution apparent.

As a director of bands from 1938 until the mid 'sixties, Thore Ehrling was certainly the best known of all Swedish leaders. A versatile musician, he worked as trumpet player, arranger and composer. Over the years he recorded fairly extensively. Inevitably, these recordings included trivia, but the band's better titles, such as *Kansas Jump, My Buddy, Meditation, Mississippi Mood* and *Blues on Strings,* display accomplished ensemble work and a variety of effective solos. They still make good listening. Ehrling worked for a well known music publisher after he gave up bandleading. He returned occasionally to front a band in the early 'seventies and recorded again in 1972.

Thore Ehrling's Danish counterpart was the clarinettist and alto saxophonist Kai Ewans. From 1924 to 1926, he worked with Valdemar Eiberg, an important pioneer dance band leader in Denmark. He appears then to have travelled around Europe and the United States until 1931, when he joined Kai Julian's band. He switched to the Erik Tuxen band in 1933, taking over as leader in 1936. For most of the next decade, Ewans was extremely active; his band backed Benny Carter in one set of recordings and produced excellent records in its own right. The jazz-influenced items owe a great deal to the scores provided by Kai Moller and Leo Mathiesen. In his review of a broadcast relayed by the BBC in October 1938, 'Detector' of the Melody Maker warned his readers that Ewans 'has achieved for Denmark the one thing no one

Top: *Hakan von Eichwald and his Orchestra, 1930.* Above:
Arne Hulphens's band in Berlin, 1938.

here has yet suceeded in achieving for us—a swing band
whose music is a true reflection of what, rightly or
wrongly, is today considered to be the millennium of
jazz'. In fact, 'Detector' was not strictly correct, for
although the Ewans band featured a fair amount of swing
material, arranged and interpreted with finesse, its wide
repertoire made an excellent dance band rather than an
uncompromising swing group.

For close on a decade, pianist Leo Mathiesen led a highly
proficient dance band that featured a strongly jazz-
oriented repertoire Mathiesen, who usually worked with
small groups until late in the 'thirties, was greatly influenced by the late 'Fats' Waller both as a pianist and, sometimes without unqualified success, as a vocalist. Among
the better recordings by his band, *It's the Talk of the
Town, Hot Spot Blues, Harlem* and *Leo's Idea* all display
ensemble playing of a high order and first-rate solos from
several musicians who were prominent in the Danish jazz
scene.

The story of big band jazz in such countries as Finland, Norway, Poland and Czechoslovakia is still too little known. It has been reported that the Finnish bands led by Erkki Aho and Jaako Vuormaa during the 'forties were very much in the swing tradition, while visitors to Poland in 1939 were impressed by a band led by a Goodman-inspired clarinet player called Lofka Ilgowski. Unfortunately, no recordings exist of these bands. In the post-war years, the Czech bands of Karla Vlacha and Gustav Brom gained a deservedly high reputation. Earlier, a good tradition had been formed in their country, by such bands as Jan Sima's Orchestrem Gramoklubu (1936) and Ladislava Hobart's Orchestra (1945).

The European country which, with Britain and France, was most prominent in the jazz/dance band field was Germany. During the 'twenties it was a haven for musicians from Britain, Denmark, Holland, Sweden, Russia, Turkey, Canada and America. By the end of the decade, a number of good German bands existed; however, the Nazis' rise to power brought the halcyon years to a close. The outlawing of Jewish and negro music seems not to have been completely effective, for big band jazz performances continued to appear throughout the 'thirties. At this time, the most interesting band was led by the Rumanian James Kok; its style was based on that of the Casa Loma Orchestra. Recordings of *Tiger Rag*, *White Jazz* and Eddie Carroll's *Harlem* suggest that the band was the equal of almost any other European group; the standard of ensemble playing and its drive were very impressive. Kok left Germany in 1935, presumably for political reasons, and the band continued under the leadership of clarinettist Erhard Bauschke with less effective results.

During the early war years, a number of Belgian and Dutch bands worked in Germany; several recorded in the swing idiom. Even more surprising, in view of the Nazi distaste for jazz, is the fact that numerous German bands seemed to be doing the same. Records of this period by such bands as Willy Berking's, Benny de Weile's, Freddie Brocksieper's, Horst Winter's and Kurt Hohenberger's and these are by no means all, are unmistakably swing-oriented. Some passages even show that the musicians were listening to current recordings by, say, Benny Goodman or Bunny Berigan. It might be that the Nazis were well aware of the propaganda value of such bands in broadcasts to other countries, particularly to allied troops, and in any case plentiful evidence suggests that by no means all Nazi officers were hostile to jazz. Whatever the reasons, it is ironical that, for a short period during 1940-42, the swing centre of Europe should be a country in which it was officially banned.

Although the years of the big band's supremacy produced very few European orchestras that could be judged as uncompromising jazz units, within the ranks of many well known orchestras there existed a core of jazz musicians who in varying degrees made their own contributions to the development of the idiom. Today, every European country has a number of big bands that are unquestionably jazz units; identification presents no difficulty because popular music and jazz have become separate entities. Whatever their limitations—in a jazz sense—the bands mentioned here were important in creating the musical environment in which big band jazz became acceptable.

Above: *Jaako Vuormaa and his band at a VE Day celebration, 1945.*

Below: *James Kok and his band in the mid 1930s*

11 Duke Ellington—Apex of the Big Band Tradition

Duke Ellington once remarked that his main reason for keeping the orchestra together was that he wanted to hear his music performed as he had intended. Although his remark was regarded as whimsical at the time, whatever it might be that drives Ellington continually to undertake gruelling international tours at an age when most men have long retired, it is most certainly not financial pressure. The royalties alone from his extensive output of popular numbers would have enabled him to retire in comfort years ago, if he had so wished. Instead, Ellington shares with Guy Lombardo—although the association will make jazz purists wince—the record of being the longest serving bandleader.

Ellington, who was seventy-four on 29th April 1973, has been leading his own groups for half a century. Apparently, his first was billed as 'The Duke's Serenaders', though most jazz followers think of his bandleading career as beginning early in 1924, when he became director of The Washingtonians in New York. Until then, the group had been led by banjoist/guitarist Elmer Snowden—titles were recorded under Snowden's name for RCA Victor in 1923 but never issued—and interestingly enough, Mr Snowden told Les Muscutt that Ellington was a reluctant leader at first; his greatest ambition was to further his career as a songwriter. However, Snowden was at that period concerned with several bands. According to him, Ellington took over The Washingtonians in the absence of another suitable leader. Since then, Ellington has maintained an unbroken sequence as a bandleader; even in the dismal years of the late 'forties and early 'fifties, he declined to reduce his personnel significantly as Count Basie, for example, was forced to do.

During his formative musical years, Ellington worked both as a solo pianist and with small groups in his home-town of Washington, D.C.; he first went to New York with Wilbur Sweatman for a week in March 1923. He was playing as a substitute for the regular pianist Lester Dishman at the Poodle Dog Café in Washington when he wrote his first number, *Soda Fountain Rag,* and soon afterwards he followed this with his first tune with lyrics. At the Poodle Dog Café, Ellington worked with drummer Sonny Greer, as did Claude Hopkins, another musician who also substituted occasionally for Dishman at this time. Hopkins, four years Ellington's junior, told me in 1958 that Ellington, along with him and the late Cliff Jackson, was greatly influenced by an obscure Washington pianist called Clarence Bowser, though I cannot recall Ellington's ever having mentioned this musician. Once he was permanently established in New York, from the autumn of 1923, Ellington was very much taken with the playing of the leading stride stylists. Even now, he sometimes introduces such stride classics as the late James P. Johnson's *Carolina Shout* and *Snowy Mornin' Blues* into his public performances.

The great problem in writing about Ellington is that the man's talents are so enormous and diverse. His career as a bandleader has embraced so many highlights that it is possible to treat his musical achievements and history only in the most superficial manner within the space of a chapter; some commentators, indeed, have failed to do better at book length. Inevitably, too, consideration of Ellington as a composer, orchestrator, popular songwriter, bandleader and pianist, raises the question of Ellington the man; it would be a reckless writer who presumed to know anything of the real individual behind the 'We love you madly' public mask. I do not intend to provide detailed musical analysis of Ellington's compositions, to date best examined by Gunther Schuller, nor can I add to the store of biographical or anecdotal knowledge that has formed the basis of innumerable articles and even books on Ellington. I simply propose to summarise some of Ellington's manifold achievements as leader of one of the greatest of all big bands, citing representative examples of his massive recorded output in the big band era, and sketching in biographical details where relevant. Specifically, I wish to consider Ellington's band in relationship to its contemporaries and, in addition, to discuss Ellington's attitude to his public, though much of this will necessarily be speculative.

After working with Elmer Snowden in Atlantic City, Ellington accompanied him to New York late in the summer of 1923. The band secured a residency at the Hollywood Club in September. Snowden has said that the 'jungle style' associated with Ellington during the 'twenties was already in existence before he took over leadership of the group early in 1924. He gives as evidence the presence of trumpeter Bubber Miley and trombonist Charlie Irvis in the personnel. While Miley's playing was then rhythmically stiff in comparison with his recorded work of a year or two later, it is certainly his plunger solos that stand out on Ellington's initial recordings, *Choo Choo* and *Rainy Nights*. Both performances are otherwise mediocre, and it is very doubtful whether Ellington contributed much at that stage in shaping the group's musical style. Snowden might therefore be right. From then until the end of 1927, The Washingtonians, generally billed under Ellington's name, worked in a variety of New York clubs and theatres, appeared in a revue at the Plantation Cafe, and undertook regular tours throughout New England, also filling a residency at a ballroom in Salem, Massachusetts. After a New England tour in the summer of 1927, the band returned to New York to work at the Kentucky Club (formerly the Hollywood Club) and the Lafayette Theatre, then went to Philadelphia for a theatre date before opening at New York's Cotton Club on 4th December.

Most jazz followers know the story that King Oliver had turned down the Cotton Club engagement on the grounds that too little money was being offered. Familiarity does not detract from the poignancy in the contrast between the subsequent careers of Oliver, who refused the job, and Ellington, who accepted it. Ellington used the engagement as an initial impetus to a career that led in due course to his becoming an international celebrity, while Oliver went into a musical decline that culminated in the final years of misfortune and poverty before he died in Savannah, Georgia, on 8th April 1938. Just how different Oliver's later career might have been if he had accepted the Cotton Club booking is a matter for conjecture, but it should at least have extended his career and given him sufficient financial resources to cope with some of the problems of his failing health. In Ellington's case, it seems unlikely that the breakthrough could have been long delayed in any case. What is undeniable is the fact that the Cotton Club engagement was not only important to Ellington in terms of publicity and economic stability, but provided him with a unique spur as a composer.

The Cotton Club acted as a working base until February 1931, though the Ellington band continued to play theatres and go out on tour. In the summer of 1930, it went to California for residencies and film work. The late 'twenties were the heyday of Harlem as an entertainment centre, and the Cotton Club was for many years a favourite haunt of white socialites and intellectuals who had made Carl Van Vechten's 'Nigger heaven' their bible, and of entertainment celebrities who came as much to be seen as to listen. The Ellington band played not only for dancers, but also to support the many acts that appeared in lavish floorshows; as a result, Ellington gained considerable experience in many facets of show business. A surprising insight into the attitudes then prevalent is given by trumpeter Freddie Jenkins in his reminiscences, told to an unknown writer for the magazine Storyville. Jenkins sustained a serious hand injury during his youth, which necessitated the removal of his fingertips, but until he worked with Ellington, he continued to play trumpet with his right hand. He commented:

'It wasn't until years later, after joining Duke, that I started playing trumpet with my left hand. With Duke, you were in show business, and show business meant just that. You're there to perform, and nothing must interfere with the enjoyment of your patrons. You must try to hide any deformity you have which might divert their attention from what you are doing. You don't want them feeling sorry for you. You want them to enjoy your music.'

Most contemporary black musicians and many jazz writers have deplored the connection between show

The Duke Ellington band, c1926. Left to right: Sonny Greer, Charlie Irvis, Otto Hardwick, Fred Guy, Bubber Miley and Duke Ellington.

business and jazz; today it is almost non-existent, but aside from financial considerations, the question is one that has been simplified. It is very easy to assume that the calls of show business led Ellington away from other, more creative paths towards the end of the 'twenties and in the early 'thirties, but a strong case could be made to the contrary. Ellington seems at least initially to have thrived in the theatrical environment of the Cotton Club and to have been stimulated by the manifest musical tasks that he was faced with. Not to put too fine a point on it, there has always appeared to me to be a strong show business element in Ellington's personality, and I say this with no censorious intent. Given this attitude, there is no reason to suppose that Ellington was unduly restrained in any creative sense by the need to conform in part with the show business requirements of his employers. The years at the Cotton Club were, I believe, extremely beneficial to Ellington's development as a composer and orchestrator, both in providing him with the stimulus to write a great variety of material and, equally important, because he was saved the constant round of travelling that would inevitably have resulted in a more restricted output. It might be claimed, on the other hand, that Ellington has toured constantly during the last twenty or thirty years without any apparent effect on his output; however, there have been periods of inactivity between the tours that have allowed him time to work on his compositions. The position has, in any case, changed completely since the close of the 'twenties, for then Ellington was at an important formative stage of his career and could only have been helped by a long-term residency such as that provided by the Cotton Club. Ellington's talent as a composer is sufficiently immense for one to assume that its flowering could not have been prevented. Nevertheless, if he had had to face the endless grind of one nighters that befell some of his less fortunate contemporaries during the Cotton Club years, it is hard to believe that his output would not have been affected.

Freddie Jenkins's reminiscences include several fascinating insights into Ellington's working methods during the Cotton Club years. Jenkins mentions that many of the recordings were achieved by cooperative endeavour in the studio, and that if the results were good, Ellington would later write down the score from the record, sometimes adding or revising passages for use at dances or concerts. Jenkins commented:

'Did you know that Duke developed his own technique and styles mainly by utilizing the band? He used to set us on the stand and pay us union scale, maybe for five hours, just to help him formulate chords. He'd assign different notes to every instrument in the band and say —"Play that, B-a-a-m!"—and it might produce a big C-13th, what we call a Christmas Chord. Then he'd take those same notes and switch them to different instruments and while you'd still have a big C-13th, it would sure sound a lot different. Sometimes he'd do that three

or four times before he found what he wanted.'

Jenkins later added: 'One thing among many he discovered, was that if you get sounds pitched very close together they would produce a mike-tone. Like a trumpet, upper register trombone and lower register clarinet would produce a mike-tone that would sound almost like a fourth instrument. And, that's the way *Mood Indigo* came into being. Another time we worked five hours on a passage using seven different relative keys. We didn't know what that was all about at the time, but later it was the intro to *St Louis Blues,* and it worked.'

Ellington and Fred Waring—two disparate musical characters—were probably the bandleaders who most concerned themselves with recording techniques as such during the late 'twenties. This concern must have been an important factor in Ellington's production of so many recorded masterpieces early in his career. Several musicians who worked in the important large coloured orchestras of the period have commented upon Ellington's remarkable ability to recreate his in-person sound on record, but it appears from Jenkins's account that Ellington was reversing the usual process by recreating his recorded sound in person. In this ability to make full use of recording he placed himself in a position of advantage over such leaders as Fletcher Henderson who, on the testimony of his sidemen over many years, was never heard to the greatest advantage on record.

The first ten recorded titles by Ellington, made between November 1924 and June 1926, are generally undistinguished. On balance, they offer less than the contemporary output of the Fletcher Henderson band which, despite its shortcomings, usually included some good and occasionally brilliant solos. Ellington's personnel on these early recordings was variable, but generally included his friends and associates Otto 'Toby' Hardwicke (saxophone), Fred Guy (banjo) and Sonny Greer (drums), all of whom were to remain with him for many years. The first authentic masterpiece came from a session of November 1926. In the line-up were Bubber Miley (trumpet) and Joe Nanton (trombone)—both important influences on Ellington's early development. The recording was a version of *East St Louis Toodle-Oo,* a number still played regularly by the Ellington band. For over a decade this was Ellington's signature tune. In later years, he told Stanley Dance, 'The title meant, for me, the broken walk of a man who had worked all day in the sun and was leaving the field at sunset. I had never been in East St Louis then, but I thought the locale sounded right.'

Significantly, Bubber Miley is credited as co-composer of *East St Louis Toodle-Oo,* as he is on the next two important compositions to be recorded by the band, *Black and Tan Fantasy* and *Creole Love Call.* The full extent of Miley's influence on Ellington during the late 'twenties is now difficult to assess, but it was considerable. From 1926 to the time he left in January 1929, Miley's solos, along with those of Joe Nanton, dominated the bulk of the recordings; the arrival of clarinettist Barney Bigard and saxophonist Johnny Hodges in 1928 added two major voices to the band. The 'jungle style' which delighted the patrons of the Cotton Club reflected, albeit obliquely, the current interest of intellectuals in most things African. To a large extent, it was the creation of Miley, though if he had ever thought about it he would doubtless have been amused to think that his listeners considered it in such a light. *Creole Love Call,* though in the general mould of Ellington-Miley collaborations, was remarkable for the inclusion of a wordless vocal by Adelaide Hall, a device which Ellington was to use again in the years ahead. The first listeners to *Black and Tan Fantasy* (the Black and Tan was apparently a speakeasy) must have been astonished by the introduction of Chopin's *Funeral March* as a tag. Miley's solos on most of the Ellington records are models of rhythmic and melodic balance; the use of the plunger is integrated completely with the melodic line, sometimes to the extent of giving the impression of perfect musical structure.

From late 1926, Ellington's records, despite the occasional weak solo and fairly frequent rhythmic stodginess, immediately proclaimed that an important new voice had arisen in big band jazz. In the late 'twenties, only McKinney's Cotton Pickers and the bands of Fletcher Henderson and Luis Russell could, on recorded evidence, be considered his musical equals, and although Henderson and Russell might outswing the Ellington band on occasion or the McKinney's group produce a more impressive ensemble sound, their overall objectives were generally more limited. Ellington's speed in appreciating Miley's qualities, making full use of his unique tonal characteristics—and those of Nanton—is an early instance of the genius he was to develop in responding

Above: *Bubber Miley, master of the growl style and a formative influence on Ellington in his early days.* Below: *a scene from the 1929 film* Black and Tan Fantasy *with the Ellington band in the background.*

to the individual strengths of the musicians in his band and providing them with a perfect orchestral framework. Ellington was already approaching in a unique manner the basic modes such as blues and stomps. Gunter Schuller points out that, with all its faults, *East St Louis Toodle-Oo* is a genuine *composition*. From the outset the Ellington recordings frequently eschewed the more conventional approach of his contemporaries, who generally worked within a setting of opening and closing ensemble passages with solos in between. Of course, this was often a very effective medium for first class performances, depending on the imagination of the arranger, the solo strength of the band, and the quality of ensemble work. Ellington, however, swiftly revealed his concern with the way in which individual voices might be integrated into an overall band concept, employing textural variety as one of the main elements.

The first soloist to sound truly dominant in a big band context was Louis Armstrong with Fletcher Henderson during 1924 and 1925. Here, though, it was simply that he was too far advanced in comparison with most of his colleagues at this time for any real integration of his solo work to be achieved within an orchestral framework, even by as brilliant an arranger as Don Redman. Armstrong ultimately had as great an effect on the Henderson band as Miley did with Ellington, mainly in making the other musicians aware of their own rhythmic limitations. By contrast, though not yet fully ready for the task, Ellington attempted from the beginning to provide frameworks that would display Miley to the best possible advantage, and in the process achieved a fair degree of success.

By late 1928, Ellington had achieved a stability of personnel that was to last for many years. He used three trumpets, Bubber Miley (soon to be replaced by Cootie Williams), Arthur Whetsol and Freddie Jenkins, Joe Nanton and, from 1929, Juan Tizol on trombones, a three piece reed section of Johnny Hodges, Barney Bigard and Harry Carney, and a rhythm section of himself, Fred Guy (banjo, guitar), Wellman Braud (bass) and Sonny Greer (drums). Trumpeter Louie Metcalf had worked with the band for about a year during 1927-28 but made no markedly individual contribution. For some years, the Ellington band recorded for a variety of labels; one advantage was that on several occasions this resulted in more than one recording of the same number. By the close of 1928, Ellington had made enormous strides both as composer and arranger. Although Miley did not leave until January 1929, there was already plenty of recorded evidence of Ellington's lessening dependence on him. At this point, it might be as well to discuss a small selection of Ellington's recordings made while the band was mainly based at the Cotton Club.

The Mooche is in the same *genre* as *Creole Love Call*, with Baby Cox providing the wordless vocal instead of Adelaide Hall. Four versions were made in one month for four different companies, a year after the excellent recordings of *Creole Love Call*. In comparing the num-

bers, one is at once aware of the strides that Ellington had made in the handling of his orchestra, for the ensemble passages are adroitly handled in the later recordings and there are numerous characteristically personal touches. Miley is heavily featured as a soloist, playing with his customary brilliance, but now there are other solos of quality, such as Bigard's fine low register contribution, and a familiar Ellington device of a dialogue between two instrumentalists—in this case Miley and Hodges—makes its appearance. Of the four recordings in October 1928, Brunswick has perhaps Miley's finest solo, while Okeh has the added advantage of guitarist Lonnie Johnson who contributes an incisiveness to the rhythm. *Awful Sad* is historically important in being the first recording of an Ellington ballad and features the plaintive trumpet of Arthur Whetsol and fine clarinet by Bigard. In the years ahead, this type of number performed at slow tempo became increasingly prevalent in the Ellington repertoire. The moody, impressionistic quality led some writers to make fanciful comparisons between Ellington and classical composers such as Debussy and Delius. It must have disappointed those writers who made such play in the 'thirties of the similarities between Ellington and Delius to discover that he had never heard a single work by Delius up to that time.

Whetsol's gentle, lyrical style clearly drew a sympathetic response from Ellington and, a month after the recording of *Awful Sad*, he was given the major solo role on *Misty Mornin'*, a number in comparable vein. The theme is shared by the saxes and brass; the saxes are more together than on most previous recordings, and after Whetsol's solo on the Okeh version, Lonnie Johnson is heard to advantage. Johnson worked for most of his career in the blues field, but his solos, his duets with Eddie Lang, and particularly his work on a number of Louis Armstrong and Duke Ellington records make it regrettable that he was not heard more frequently in a jazz setting. His contributions to both the Armstrong and Ellington recordings add a great deal rhythmically to the performances; he was in every respect an extraordinarily fine guitarist. *Blues With a Feeling*, recorded two days before *Misty Mornin'*, proves conclusively that Ellington had by then solved most of his earlier problems in arrangement. It has beautiful playing from Nanton, Hodges and Miley. Miley's final session with the band resulted in a superb solo from him on *Flaming Youth*, and introduced the first version of Ellington's splendid *Saturday Night Function*, on which Bigard's clarinet is outstanding.

In the period between December 1927 and February 1931, when the Cotton Club was the Ellington's home base, the band took part in sixty-four commercial recording sessions, or an average of a session every two and a half weeks. Well over one hundred and fifty titles were released, each was frequently recorded for different companies, and today the collector has the opportunity of hearing different takes of many performances. Inevitably,

Left: *Duke Ellington at the Cotton Club in the early 1930s.*
Top right: *the Duke Ellington band in 1930; at the back: Joe Nanton, Juan Tizol, Sonny Greer, Fred Guy, Wellman Braud; in front: Freddy Jenkins, Cootie Williams, Arthur Whetsol, Duke Ellington, Harry Carney, Johnny Hodges and Barney Bigard.* Right: *a section of the Ellington band in the early 1930s.*

in such a considerable output, there is a percentage of ephemera, although remarkably few Ellington recordings of this period are totally without interest. The 'jungle' numbers—*Jungle Jamboree, Jungle Blues, Jungle Nights in Harlem*—were obviously titled to titillate the Cotton Club clientele in search of African exotica while seated at a comfortable ringside table—the floorshows frequently used what were considered African motifs. It is ironical that so sophisticated a musician as Ellington should produce material which appealed to a spurious primitivism on the part of his audiences, though the musical performance of such material was very far from primitive. The band also recorded other consciously produced exotica as used in the floorshows, like *Japanese Dream, Harlemania* and *Arabian Lover,* all written by Jimmy McHugh and Dorothy Fields. Apparently, many of the songs used in the shows exploited *double entendre* lyrics, in the manner of the then popular 'race' recordings, but these were

often written, under a variety of pseudonyms, by well-known songwriters, who usually forbade their publication.

Even judged by the most stringent standards, the percentage of fine recordings that the band produced at this time is remarkable, and only lack of space prevents me from discussing more than a small sample. On occasions Ellington used only a section of the band, normally a three piece front line of trumpet, trombone and clarinet backed by four rhythm musicians. From a session in October 1930 came the haunting *Big House Blues* and *Rocky Mountain Blues;* both had outstanding contributions from Whetsol, Nanton and Bigard. Whetsol was obviously a great favourite with Ellington who still frequently refers to him with respect and affection, though he died in 1940. The third title made at the same time was to provide Ellington with his first major songwriting hit, for it was the initial recording of *Mood Indigo.* It was rejected on that occasion, and though remade for the same company in just over a fortnight, was first recorded for a rival three days later. Collectors in general tend to view such Ellington recordings as *Mood Indigo, Solitude* and *In a Sentimental Mood* as of minor importance. Nevertheless, though musically slight in comparison with the finest of his output during the 'thirties, they were important to his career as a whole in leading to his acceptance by a wider public. There is also the interesting question, frequently overlooked, of whether Ellington would have been in a position to keep his band in existence throughout several difficult periods if he had not had the royalties from his popular songs to sustain him financially.

Long before the close of the Cotton Club residency, Ellington had passed beyond any dependency on the concepts of Bubber Miley, who had left the band two years earlier. As Eddie Lambert has written, '... for the rest of its career the group has reflected in a unique manner the interplay of musical ideas between the leader and the various sidemen. Often in the most complex of Ellington's scores his musicians can be heard playing with the same relaxation as if at a jam session.' Ellington's achievement is considerable, since his star sidemen over the years—Cootie Williams, Rex Stewart, Joe Nanton, Lawrence Brown, Johnny Hodges, Harry Carney, Barney Bigard, Ben Webster and so on—are extremely diverse stylists and, in some cases, highly temperamental personalities.

The final session before Ellington left the Cotton Club was curious. It produced an atypical version of *Is That Religion?* which sounds as if it could equally have been recorded by Mills Blue Rhythm Band, a rather ordinary *Peanut Vendor,* and Ellington's first recorded extended composition, *Creole Rhapsody.* In January 1929, the Ellington band had broken with convention by recording a version of *Tiger Rag* that was issued on two sides of a 78 rpm release, but *Creole Rhapsody* was a very different proposition. Just under five months later, the Ellington band again recorded the composition, this time further

extended, on two sides of a twelve inch record. In the Melody Maker of July 1931, Patrick 'Spike' Hughes said of *Creole Rhapsody,* 'It is, in fact, the first classic of modern dance music. The individual player is, for the first time, completely subservient to the personality of the composer.' For many years the first, ten inch recording of *Creole Rhapsody* was generally accepted as the better of the two, but some jazz critics later came to accept the view that the longer version was superior. This is of no great importance; the significance is in the success of *Creole Rhapsody* as an extended composition, as jazz, and as the completion of a process by which, as Charles Fox once wrote, Ellington's compositions began to impose a pattern upon his soloists.

Whatever the benefits of the long term Cotton Club residency had been to Ellington, and I believe that they were far from negligible, there can be little question that by early 1931 he was ready for change. In his profiles of Ellington and his musicians, Richard O. Boyer stated that Ellington had become weary of the tinsel glamour of the Cotton Club and was disillusioned with the music business in general. The band devoted its first year after leaving the Cotton Club to extensive touring, with residencies in Boston and California, before returning to New York for an appearance at the Paramount Theatre. Then, after more work in California, the band left for its first overseas tour, playing throughout Britain and at a number of concerts in Paris.

Ellington undertook the 1933 tour at the suggestion of several friends who were alarmed at his mood of despondency. He did not enjoy the journey across the Atlantic ocean according to Mr Boyer, particularly after a fellow

Left: *the Ellington band arriving in England, 1933. Back:*
Bessie Dudley, Bill Bailey, Sonny Greer, Fred Guy, Harry
Carney, Otto Hardwick, Barney Bigard, 'Spike' Hughes, Cootie
Williams, Wellman Braud, Johnny Hodges, Joe Nanton,
Lawrence Brown, Ivie Anderson. Front: Derby Wilson, Freddy
Jenkins, Jack Hylton, Duke Ellington, Irving Mills, Juan
Tizol, Arthur Whetsol. Above: the London Palladium, 1933:
Sonny Greer (behind), Joe Nanton, Juan Tizol, Lawrence
Brown, Fred Guy, Wellman Braud, Freddy Jenkins, Cootie
Williams, Arthur Whetsol (trumpets): Otto Hardwick, Harry
Carney, Johnny Hodges, Barney Bigard (saxophones).

passenger had told him that the ship was steered at night
by an automatic pilot. To offset this unwelcome situation,
Ellington slept by day and paced the ship at night, ready
to make a speedy departure if they hit an iceberg. In later
years, Ellington appears to have overcome his distaste
for ocean travel, though he still refuses to fly; his preference for rail travel is well known and has produced
several of his finest compositions.

The Ellington band and its music were received with
great enthusiasm in both Britain and France. The welcome
had the desired effect of restoring Ellington's confidence.
During his British tour, however, Ellington revealed a
characteristic caution in selecting his repertoire. He
featured his most popular numbers heavily and made his
more fervent followers angry as a result. Exactly a quarter
of a century later, on his second British tour with the full
band, he showed a similar lack of audacity in his choice
of material, once more upsetting a section of his audience.
Legend has it that on at least one occasion during the
1933 tour a few members of the audience were so enraged
by the 'gutter' sounds of Nanton and Williams that they
threw pennies on to the stage. I have always assumed
this story to be apocryphal, but as Fred Elizalde, a
pioneer of advanced dance music and jazz in Britain, had
fallen foul of Scottish audiences a year or two earlier,
because of his unwillingness, and probably inability, to
play reels, the story might not be without foundation.

After returning to America heartened by the willing-
ness of European critics and audiences to accept his music
on adult terms, Ellington led his band on continual tours,
appearing in Canada for the first time in 1935. In this
year, Ellington suffered the death of his mother, to whom
he was deeply attached. Once more, he sank into a state
of depression, temporarily suffering a period of self-doubt
over his deeply held Christian beliefs. After a while, he
came to terms with his loss, and continued his touring

Above: *a trick shot of Ellington in the early 1930s.* Left: *Rex Stewart, whose half-valving effects gave the band another individual sound.* Right: *the Ellington band in the mid 1930s: Rex Stewart (cornet) and Hayes Alvis (string bass) replaced Freddy Jenkins and Wellman Braud.*

schedules, observing with interest the onset of the swing era. The prophetic sentiments of his 1932 composition *It Don't Mean a Thing (If It Ain't Got That Swing)* appeared to find general acceptance amongst bandleaders and public alike.

There are few musicians from the big band era who do not have their own fund of harrowing stories about travelling conditions during the frequent round of one night stands. In his reminiscences, Freddie Jenkins suggests that the Ellington musicians were more fortunate than most in this respect:

'...we always had the best accommodation. We had either two or three sleeping cars, depending on how big a show the Duke was carrying at the time, and a baggage car, and they would switch us from line to line for our itinerary. We never had to get out of our cars unless we wanted to. If there was no diner on the train, we had our

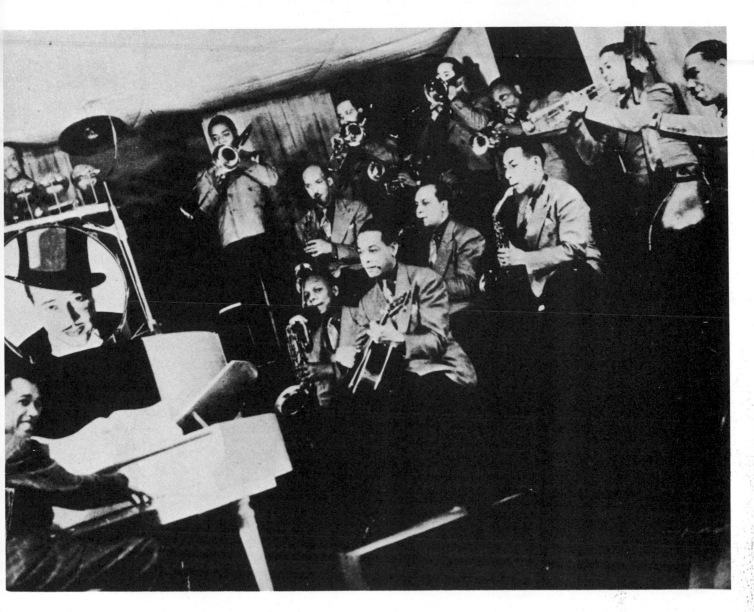

own kitchen set up in the baggage car, and our porters would serve us. So, even in the towns where we were booked, if our cars had to be set on a siding pretty far out of town, we could either get taxis to a restaurant, or eat in style in our cars.'

Other Ellington musicians have spoken of touring in rather different terms; Rex Stewart, for example, once told me of innumerable instances when the band, after a long and tiring journey, found itself unable to obtain food before a show because local restaurant owners refused to serve black musicians. Some of the worst problems of travelling may have been avoided because the Ellington musicians did not very often venture far south, but it is doubtful if life on tour was quite as light-hearted as Mr Jenkins now remembers.

Whatever the personal problems that may have beset Ellington in the immediate post-Cotton Club period, his continuing development as a composer and arranger appears to have been unaffected. The acceptance of his band as one of the greatest of all time by other musicians and by a growing section of the public grew without interruption. In a five year period from June 1931, when the extended version of *Creole Rhapsody* was

recorded, to July 1936, just before a recording contract with his manager Irving Mills, the band took part in forty-five recording sessions, which produced a good proportion of outstanding performances.

Each of the three years, 1933-35, produced one number that became immensely popular with the public at large and has continued to earn regular royalties for the composer ever since—*Sophisticated Lady, Solitude* and *In a Sentimental Mood.* Ellington's personnel had remained remarkably stable; Lawrence Brown and Rex Stewart were added in the spring of 1932 and December 1934 respectively, and Otto 'Toby' Hardwick returned, after an absence of four years, early in 1932. It is amusing to read the reviews that appeared in such papers as the Melody Maker at the time, for the arrival of Brown and Stewart was greeted by some writers with considerable lack of enthusiasm. There were laments that the styles of these musicians were unsuitable for Ellington and presaged the decline of his band.

One of the most beautiful of all Ellington's compositions, *The Mystery Song,* was recorded in June 1931. Unfortunately, he seems never to have revived it in subsequent years. The magnificent, almost ethereal

opening of the recording is perhaps not fully maintained, though the rich scoring throughout is extremely impressive. Early 1932 saw the recording of *It Don't Mean a Thing (If It Ain't Got That Swing)*, a jaunty stomp number that contains the first vocal on record by Ivie Anderson, the finest regular singer Ellington has ever employed. (Ellington's choice of vocalists is at times, to put it mildly, decidedly eccentric.) In the 'thirties, Ellington became associated with lyrical 'mood' numbers like *Lazy Rhapsody, Blue Tune, Blue Harlem, Blue Ramble, Eerie Moan, Saddest Tale* and *Blue Feeling*. All these performances feature many felicities of scoring and contain brilliant solos. My personal favourites are *Blue Feeling, Blue Tune* and *Saddest Tale,* which has an introduction and close half spoken, half chanted by Ellington himself. Though these numbers were invariably performed at slow tempo and are in a lyrical mould, they are totally free from vapidity. Williams and Nanton contribute powerful solos on *Blue Harlem,* and Whetsol's wistful muted theme is contrasted with strong passages from Williams and Hodges on *Blue Tune.* In all, such performances represent an important aspect of Ellington's output, not least for their melodic resourcefulness and impressionistic quality.

The more extrovert side of Ellington's personality was reflected in such gems as *Merry-Go-Round, Harlem Speaks, Daybreak Express, Stompy Jones* and the delightful *Showboat Shuffle. Daybreak Express* is one of his first 'train' numbers. Quite apart from the expected fine solos and brilliant scoring, such recordings as *Stompy Jones* and *Showboat Shuffle* prove conclusively that the Ellington band was by that time capable of swinging as hard as any other in existence when it chose to do so. During 1934, the Ellington band was featured in the film 'Belle Of The Nineties'; two numbers from the film, *Troubled Waters* and *My Old Flame,* were recorded in May. They feature very attractive vocals from Ivie Anderson, a sensitive singer even when her material was occasionally below standard (certainly not the case in this instance), with fine backing from Cootie Williams on *Troubled Waters.* In September 1935, the band recorded *Reminiscing in Tempo,* an extended composition by Ellington, that was issued on four sides of ten inch 78 rpm records.

Speaking of *Reminiscing in Tempo* to Richard O. Boyer, Ellington said, 'It was one of my first ambitious things. It was written in a soliloquizing mood. My mother's death was the greatest shock. I didn't do anything but brood. The music is representative of that. It begins with pleasant thoughts. Then something awful gets you down. Then you snap out of it, and it ends affirmatively.' On record, the work lasts for twelve and a half minutes and is a strongly integrated orchestral performance, beautifully scored with constantly varying

Above left: *Johnny Hodges in the 1930s.* Left: *Duke Ellington at an informal session in the mid 1930s with Arthur Whetsol.*

A little-known photograph of the Ellington band in 1934. At the back; Joe Nanton, Juan Tizol, Lawrence Brown, Arthur Whetsol and Fred Guy. Centre: Barney Bigard, Marshall Royal, Johnny Hodges, Harry Carney and Wellman Braud. In front: Sonny Greer and Freddy Jenkins flanking Duke Ellington. Royal temporarily replaced Otto Hardwick.

musical texture. Although individual musicians—Hodges, Whetsol, Carney, Brown, Stewart and Ellington himself —sometimes emerge at the forefront for brief passages, their contributions are less solos in the conventional sense than a means of switching emphasis within a tightly scored orchestral framework. When first released, *Reminiscing in Tempo* received a rather cool reception from the critics, some went as far as to claim that it was pretentious. Such a reaction seems unjustified today, as it was to a few listeners at the time. It seems that Ellington was upset by the attitude of the critics to what was, after all, an intensely personal work, and it is likely that this contributed to the conservatism with which he selected his repertoire when presenting concerts in the following years.

Although by that time Ellington had been writing with the sounds and capabilities of his major soloists in mind for about a decade, the process went a stage further in 1936 with the composing and recording of *Barney's Concerto (Clarinet lament), Cootie's Concerto (Echoes of Harlem), Rex's Concerto (Trumpet in Spades)* and *Lawrence's Concerto (Yearning for Love)*. Of these, *Cootie's Con-*

certo is the most successful, closely followed by *Barney's Concerto. Rex's Concerto* is devoted rather too much to technical virtuosity on Stewart's part and *Lawrence's Concerto* suffers from its somewhat cloying sentimentality. Two years later, Stewart was to be highlighted much more effectively in the brilliant *Boy Meets Horn,* a theme in which he employed his highly individual half-valve technique to fine effect. Two other 1936 recordings of interest are *Kissin' My Baby Goodnight,* with its highly attractive and lyrical cornet solo by Stewart, and the more aggressive *In a Jam,* on which first Nanton and Bigard and then Hodges and Williams are featured in superb musical dialogues.

Early in 1935, Ellington had broken with tradition when Wellman Braud left the band and was replaced by two bassists in Hayes Alvis and Billy Taylor, a situation that lasted for three years. In August of that year Benny Goodman scored his great triumph at the Palomar Ballroom in Los Angeles, an important event in the advent of the swing era. Ellington, and other prominent black bandleaders, could well have felt a degree of cynicism as they viewed spectacular rise to fame of a number of white bands which played a style of big band jazz that they had been presenting for years. On balance, though, the black leaders probably approved of the situation, for in the new atmosphere that welcomed big band jazz they must have foreseen the possibility that they might themselves gain the acceptance that had previously been denied them. Unfortunately, social conditions and racial attitudes continued

339

to deny them the financial rewards to which they were entitled.

During 1936, Irving Mills, Ellington's manager for many years, started his own recording company, issuing titles on the Master and Variety labels. From December 1936 until February 1940, Ellington recorded for Mills, not only with the full band but also with some of the small groups led by Stewart, Williams and others that were drawn from within the band. On 20th March 1937, the Ellington band went back to the Cotton Club for its first residency there for several years. Around this time, Ellington himself suffered another loss with the death of his father. Once more he was in a state of depression and, for a while, gave up composing altogether. As before, it was a European tour, this time covering Belgium, Denmark, France, Holland and Sweden during March and April 1939, that restored his confidence and will to continue. 'Europe is a different world' the late Rex Stewart once claimed. 'You can go anywhere, do anything, talk to anybody. You can't believe it. You are like a guy who has eaten hot dogs all his life and is suddenly offered caviar. You can't believe it.' Such a view of Europe was hardly accurate in 1939, and it is even less so in the 'seventies, but the acclaim that greeted the Ellington musicians during their European tours, in contrast to the treatment they received too often at home, easily led to an over-optimistic assessment of social attitudes there. On returning to the United States, the band started out again on tour. The personnel was substantially as before, with the exception of trumpeter Wardell Jones, who had replaced the ailing Freddie Jenkins. Billy Taylor was the sole bassist until replaced by the phenomenal Jimmy Blanton in the autumn of 1939. Late in 1939, Billy Strayhorn joined the organisation as an arranger and occasional pianist, beginning a unique working relationship with Ellington that was to last until his death in 1967.

The Ellington band occupied a rather curious position early in the swing era. Regarded with awe by almost all the successful white swing band leaders—Charlie Barnet in particular made his debt obvious in innumerable recorded performances—and by the more aware musical public, it somehow missed the wide acceptance granted to Goodman, Tommy Dorsey and Artie Shaw, for example. One reason, of course, is that as a black band, it was denied the extensive radio outlets and sponsorship that helped its white counterparts. Beyond this, the main factor lay in the social conditioning of white youngsters, who made up the bulk of the swing audience and could not yet identify totally with a black band. In addition, however brilliant its music and however many the concessions to show business, the band's output contained much that called for a degree of musical appreciation not possessed by the average follower of the swing craze.

In jazz, great composers have been rare; come to that, so have arrangers capable of stamping their personality on the music of a band. Whatever medium he chooses to work in, the jazz composer naturally stands slightly aloof from his contemporaries. No matter what he contributed to the common pool of big band devices or what he had taken from it, from the beginning of his band-leading days, Ellington pursued a course that left him slightly outside the mainstream. He was certainly not the only arranger to think in terms of orchestral texture and blending of instrumental combinations, rather than conventional trading of phrases between sections. Don Redman, Sy Oliver, and later Gil Evans are others that come to mind. It was his combination of these preoccupations with the qualities of a composer of genius that made him unique. Freddie Jenkins, among others, has spoken of his difficulty in coming to terms with Ellington's music when he first joined the band. If a musician as highly trained as Jenkins experienced this difficulty, it is easy to guess the bewilderment of a public accustomed to more conventional dance bands. I am reminded of the story told by Richard Boyer, of the Irish gentleman who found himself at the Cotton Club and, after listening for a while to the Ellington band featuring its individual repertoire, begged it to help him retain his musical sanity by playing *Mother Machree*. While musical philistinism as extreme as this was, one hopes, rare, there is little doubt that the less subtle and more straightforward approach of other big jazz bands would normally have a more immediate public appeal.

Talking to musicians who were active in the big band era makes it clear that they felt the Ellington band both to be unique and to stand slightly apart from its contemporaries. Indisputably, this stemmed from the fact that Ellington was first and foremost a composer, using his band as an instrument to perform his own music. Ellington's choice of musicians over the years has, in itself, been based on slightly different considerations from those of most leaders, for he has generally been less concerned with technical skill and sight-reading abilities, important though these might be, than with tonal characteristics and elements of musical idiosyncrasy that he felt he could utilise in his overall orchestral concepts. From the beginning, Ellington has achieved a unique interplay of musical ideas with his individual musicians, though over the years he himself has become increasingly dominant in shaping the nature of the music. In recent years, too, the death or retirement of key musicians has left him with fewer great soloists. While major soloists of the big band era could normally move from band to band without having to make too many adjustments, several Ellington stars have spoken of their initial difficulty in managing to feel at home in the band. Faced with a repertoire that included only a small proportion of jazz standards and current popular tunes, musicians needed time to adjust to a working situation that was strange to them. Ultimately, most became proud of the fact that they were part of a unique musical body where, paradoxically, their own individuality blossomed as never before within an orchestral framework ruled by the concept of a jazz composer of genius. As time went by, the Ellington musicians perceived themselves as separate from their contemporaries in other big bands, and in a musical sense the other bands accepted the fact. The situation was best summed up by a veteran of many of the finest big bands of the 'thirties and 'forties, who told me that while one could incorporate elements of arranging or general musical style from most of the big bands of his day and in the process adjust them to a personal medium, whatever one took from Ellington ended up sounding like a second-rate copy of the original. This is probably an exaggeration, for a few arrangers and leaders successfully used elements of Ellington's style without loss of personal identity. Nevertheless, such a view, reasonably common among musicians, merely underlines the fact that the Ellington band possessed characteristics that made it both part of and slightly outside the mainstream of a well defined big band tradition.

The arrival of swing, an extrovert music that reflected the *mores* and hopes of a new generation, would present no difficulties to Ellington, whose arranging skills were generally superior to those of the principal arrangers then defining the styles of the swing bands. The recordings that Ellington made for the Irving Mills labels between late 1936 and early 1940 are particularly interesting. The temptation to regard this period as 'A Time Of Transition', in the words of Demetre Ioakimidis, is hard to resist. The reason for this is that it led up to the great Victor period of 1940-42 when the Ellington band reached one of its greatest peaks and turned out masterpieces at almost every recording session. Yet it is doubtful whether Ellington himself would accept such a description, for he could well claim that everything he did had a validity on its own terms and was at base an extension of all that had gone before.

For Mills's labels, Ellington began the now well established practice of reworking older material, in this instance *East St Louis Toodle-Oo, Black and Tan Fantasy, Birmingham Breakdown* and *Doin' the Voom Voom;* the first three were prefixed with the word new. Writing of these, M. Ioakimidis, who has dealt with the Mills recordings more thoroughly and with more perspicacity than any other critic I have read on the subject, comments that '... the results, so far as *Black and Tan Fantasy* is concerned, led to a slackening of the item's links with traditional jazz and also to its enrichment from the viewpoints of general mood and tonal colouring.' While agreeing with this, I would add that these new versions of numbers strongly associated with Bubber Miley also indicate clearly the extent to which the powerful emotional impact of the originals had been due to Miley's personal contributions. Ioakimidis also mentions that on the Mills recordings Ellington made considerable use of standard precedures of the swing bands, while stamping his own personality on everything he did. He cites Ellington's distinctiveness of composition; *Hip Chic* has a thirty-two bar theme which consists of an opening and closing twelve bar blues chorus and an eight bar bridge, *Buffet Flat* has a twenty-four bar chorus, and in

Battle of Swing, the first number on which Ellington uses the *concerto grosso* style, a four piece group is pitted against the rest of the band.

Three of Ellington's compositions which were first recorded during this period—*Azure, Caravan* and *I Let a Song Go Out of My Heart*—achieved wide popularity. *Azure* is in the familiar tradition of Ellington mood numbers; highlights are the beautiful blending of Bigard's clarinet with the saxes and an attractive baritone saxophone solo by Carney. *Caravan,* with fine solos from Bigard and Williams, uses a Latin-American rhythm and has Juan Tizol's valve trombone stating the theme. Tizol, not a jazz soloist at all, collaborated with Ellington on a number of exotic themes while he was a member of the band. The Ellington Mills recordings contain a number that are quite outstanding. Among them are *Boy Meets Horn,* which features superb playing by Rex Stewart, the beautiful and wistful *Subtle Lament,* the driving *Tootin' Through the Roof,* on which Stewart and Williams are heard both in a chase sequence and in duet, and *Diminuendo in Blue* and *Crescendo in Blue,* another score for the orchestra like *Reminiscing in Tempo,* where individual musicians provide embellishments rather than solos. This is a superb performance, and almost two decades later *Diminuendo and Crescendo in Blue* was to play an important role in Ellington's later career.

Considering the brilliance of many of the recordings that the Ellington band made in about three and a half years—recordings, in fact, that would be beyond the musical capacity of almost any other band—it seems almost ludicrous to refer to them as 'transitional' in any way. Were it not for the fact that they were immediately followed by the masterpieces of the Victor period, such a term would never have been applied to them. During the autumn of 1939, the band, and Ellington himself, were stimulated by the addition of bassist Jimmy Blanton. Blanton's tragically short career lasted only just over two years, and he died in 1942. During that time, he revolutionised jazz bass playing. He was a considerable virtuoso, using the *pizzicato* bass as a melody instrument, and possessed a unique harmonic sense. Later generations of bass players have used Blanton's approach as their guideline, but unlike many of them, Blanton could subordinate his talents to the need of a conventional rhythm section, helping the ensemble and individual soloists with a powerful swinging background. Billy Strayhorn had by that time taken up his appointment as arranger and was shortly to contribute a number of important compositions to the band's book. Early in 1940, tenor saxophonist Ben Webster added his very individual voice to the sax section which then, for the first time, numbered five. There are certain big band records which are generally accepted as jazz masterpieces—the last items made in 1932 by the Benny Moten band, many of Basie's recordings of the late 'thirties, some by Lunceford in the late 'thirties and early 'forties, Henderson's of the late 'twenties, for instance—and to this body of accepted classics can be added a high proportion of those made by the Ellington band during 1940-42.

The French musician and critic Andre Hodeir devotes over twenty-one pages of 'Jazz: Its Evolution and Essence' to Ellington's 1940 recording of *Concerto for Cootie (Do Nothin' Till You Hear From Me)*, and other titles from 1940-42 have been analysed at length by a number of critics. I will therefore restrict myself to discussing some of the significant titles from this remarkable output.

The first Victor session of February 1940 produced five titles; two were ephemeral popular numbers of slight interest. The remainder—*Jack the Bear, Ko-Ko* and *Morning Glory*—are outstanding compositions, and the performances highlight the brilliance of solo and ensemble playing which the band by then produced with apparent ease. *Jack the Bear* was named after an obscure Harlem stride pianist and fittingly it is Ellington himself, well supported by Blanton, who states the theme; the later soloists are Bigard, Williams, Carney and Nanton, whose contribution is outstanding. *Ko-Ko* has been described as 'one of the monumental events in jazz music' and this is not too fanciful. Basically the theme is a twelve bar blues; the imaginativeness of the orchestration, the magnificent playing of the ensemble, with swiftly changing instrumental voices, and the striking plunger solo by Nanton combine to make it a masterpiece. *Morning Glory* has a more pastoral atmosphere and mainly features some beautifully controlled playing by Stewart, a musician whose solos over the years varied between the superb and the banal. Performances of similar quality, emerging from the next three sessions, include the famous *Concerto for Cootie, Cotton Tail* with its bustling assertive tenor saxophone solo by Webster, *Never No Lament* (later retitled *Don't Get Around Much Any More*) which has excellent solos from Hodges, Williams and Brown, the poignant *Dusk*, again capturing Stewart at his sensitive best, and the two delightful musical portraits *Bojangles (Portrait of Bill Robinson)* and *Portrait of Bert Williams*. Incidentally, Robinson was a prominent black dancer, and Williams a comedian.

There were six further recording sessions by the band during 1940 and another which featured Ellington and Blanton in duets. *Harlem Air Shaft* is a particularly fine performance, with contrasting ensemble passages and instrumental voicings; soloists Williams and Bigard are also used effectively in the fiery closing passages. *All Too Soon* and *Warm Valley* are lyrical themes which spotlight Webster and Hodges respectively, while Hodges and Williams are the soloists on a relaxed performance of what is now a well established Ellington favourite, *In a Mellotone*. The last session in 1940 produced the evocative *Sidewalks of New York*, with solos from Bigard, Nanton, Webster, Hodges and Carney.

Cootie Williams's departure from the Ellington band in November 1940 was lamented in Raymond Scott's composition *When Cootie left The Duke*. Williams was replaced by trumpeter/violinist Ray Nance, who made an impressive solo debut on the first title recorded in 1941, *Take the 'A' Train*. This is another theme that has remained a favourite with audiences ever since. From the same date came *Jumpin' Punkins, John Hardy's Wife, Blue Serge* and *After All*, which has Billy Strayhorn on piano and features a typical rhapsodic solo by Hodges. The second of the Ellington's seven recording sessions in 1941 did not produce performances of quite the same standard, with the possible exception of the engaging *Just a-Settin' and a-Rockin'* on which a relaxed Webster makes an important contribution. A session in June saw a recording of the attractive *I Got It Bad and That Ain't Good*, which was notable for the sensitive vocal of Ivie Anderson and beautiful playing by Hodges. The following session was partially devoted to tunes from a revue in which the band was to appear, entitled 'Jump for joy.' On the final 1941 date Blanton, by then seriously ill, was replaced by Junior Raglin. Highlight of the session was a fine version of Strayhorn's delightful *Chelsea Bridge*, said to have been inspired by a Whistler sketch.

The first of four 1942 Victor sessions resulted in initial recordings of two long term Ellington favourites, *Perdido* and *'C' Jam Blues*, while the last had Ivie Anderson's farewell vocal on an Ellington commercial release, a somewhat mundane *Hayfoot, Strawfoot*. That date was also the last one with Bigard in the personnel; his place was initially taken by Chauncey Haughton. August 1942 saw the termination of commercial recordings for an extended period, as a result of a dispute between the American Federation of Musicians and the recording companies. Victor, along with U.S. Columbia, held out against the AFoM demands until November 1944. One result of this unfortunate dispute is that an important era in big band jazz remains uncharted on commercial recordings. In recent years, however, a few of the gaps in our knowledge have been filled by the appearance of LPs made up from radio transcriptions of the period. By the time the Ellington band once more entered a recording studio, changes of personnel had occurred; Haughton and Webster had been replaced by Jimmy Hamilton and Al Sears respectively, and William 'Cat' Anderson had joined the trumpet section. Anderson, an iron-lipped trumpeter with a tremendous facility in the upper register, left the band in January 1947, but later rejoined for two lengthy spells from 1950 to late 1959 and from 1961 to 1971. The 'forties saw the departure of other long-serving Ellington stalwarts. Stewart and Hardwick left in December 1945 and May 1946. Hardwick was replaced by Russell Procope, who is still a member of the band. In July 1946, Joe 'Tricky Sam' Nanton, whose health had been poor for some time, died while the band was on tour, while guitarist Fred Guy left in January 1949. Since Guy's departure Ellington has never used a guitarist in his band. Perhaps the biggest blow of all came in March 1951, when Johnny Hodges, Lawrence Brown and Sonny Greer left together, to become part of a small group led

Left: *a section of the Ellington band in the early 1940s. Ray Nance is at the back behind trombonist Joe Nanton, Juan Tizol and Sandy Williams. Front row: Ben Webster, Johnny Hodges and Al Sears, with Ellington conducting.* Right: *Tyree Glenn, who worked with Ellington in the mid 1940s.*

by Hodges. The replacements for Hodges and Greer were Willie Smith and Louie Bellson. Hodges rejoined the band in August 1955 and remained until his death in May 1970, while Brown went back in May 1960 and stayed for almost a decade. Juan Tizol left late in 1953, returning only temporarily in the spring of 1960. After an absence of twenty-two years Cootie Williams rejoined as a featured soloist in the autumn of 1962 and is still with the band. Another current band member, tenor saxophonist Paul Gonsalves, joined in 1950, while trumpeters Ray Nance (1940-63) and Clark Terry (1951-59) were long-serving musicians. Of course, there have been numerous other personnel changes in the three decades since the final 1942 Victor recording session, but it is interesting to note that three members of the current Ellington saxophone section, Harry Carney, Paul Gonsalves and Russell Procope, have together contributed ninety-six years' service to the band.

Although the band made no recordings during the AFoM dispute with the recording companies, it kept very active with tours and residencies. On 23rd January 1943, Ellington introduced his new major work *Black, Brown and Beige* at the band's first Carnegie Hall concert. On the following night, the concert was repeated at the Symphony Hall, Boston. In December of that year a second concert was given at Carnegie Hall; the repertoire included extracts from *Black, Brown and Beige* and the first performance of *New World A-Comin'*. *Black, Brown and Beige* had received a lukewarm reception when first performed and, characteristically, Ellington had reacted

by featuring only sections of it at later appearances, even going so far as to reassure the audience at one concert that he was only going to play extracts. The closing years of the 'forties saw the end of the big band era. During 1946 and 1947, such long established leaders as Benny Goodman, Tommy Dorsey, Benny Carter and Woody Herman all disbanded, although they re-formed big bands for varying periods from time to time in the ensuing few years, a process that Goodman and Herman have maintained down to the present day. Ellington refused to reduce his personnel significantly, but musicians who played with him at this time have said that the morale of the band was sometimes low. It may well be that Ellington was forced to underwrite the band with money received as royalties. The fact that he, Ray Nance and vocalist Kay Davis came to Britain in the summer of 1948 and appeared at various halls is, in itself, an indication that bookings for the band had become scarce.

When the Ellington band returned to the Victor studios on 1st December 1944, after an absence of over two years, the line-up included several new musicians, notably in the trumpet section, which now consisted of Shelton, Hemphill, Taft Jordan, Cat Anderson and Ray Nance. Musically, the results were hardly spectacular; the best performance was a pleasant version of *I'm Beginning to See the Light* with a vocal by Joya Sherrill. Just over a week later, *Work Song, Come Sunday, The Blues* and *Three Dances* from *Black, Brown and Beige* were recorded. Hodges's beautiful alto saxophone playing on *Come Sunday* proved to be the highlight. During 1945, the Ellington band took part in eleven Victor recording sessions; in comparison with those of the 1940-42 period, the results were disappointing. New versions of such Ellington classics as *Black and Tan Fantasy, Mood Indigo* and *Black Beauty* were made, but generally they lacked distinction. Of greater interest is *Perfume Suite,* though even this work is only partially successful. In fact, the numerous broadcast transcriptions gradually becoming available are of far greater interest than almost all the Ellington band's commercial recordings of this period. Some of them reveal the orchestra in fine form. Two duets by Ellington and Strayhorn, *Tonk* and *Drawing Room Blues,* were recorded in January 1946 and are interesting. Of the remaining 1946 titles, only *Rockabye River,* featuring Hodges and Anderson, *Just Squeeze Me,* with solos by Jordan and Hodges, *A Gathering in the Clearing,* with solos by Anderson and Sears, and *Esquire Swank,* arranged by Strayhorn and with solos by Hodges and Anderson, are in any way outstanding.

Late in 1946, Ellington's Victor contract expired and the band made five sessions for the Musicraft label. The resulting output is worthy of attention. The first session produced a lyrical *Magenta Haze* which features a ravishing solo by Hodges, who was again given the major role on a similar *Sultry Sunset* from the second session. It is noticeable on several of these Musicraft performances that the orchestral backgrounds, though often excellent, are conventional by Ellington's highest standards. The finest of the Musicraft titles are undoubtedly the flamboyant *Trumpet No End,* a Mary Lou Williams arrangement of *Blue Skies* which features solos by trumpeters Taft Jordan, Harold Baker, Francis Williams and Cat Anderson in that order, with Ray Nance taking the release on two occasions, and, above all, *Happy-Go-Lucky Local.* This number, issued at first as two sides of a 78 rpm record, is a musical portrait based on Ellington's favourite train motif and, apart from excellent solos, features superb playing by Ellington, the ensemble and bassist Oscar Pettiford.

From August to December 1947, the Ellington band recorded numerous sessions of extremely variable quality for the U.S. Columbia label. *Hy'a Sue* has excellent solo work from trombonist Tyree Glenn, Hamilton (on tenor saxophone) and Hodges, while *Lady of the Lavender Mist* is pleasantly evocative. The best performances are probably *Three Cent Stomp,* with pleasing solos by Baker, Glenn, Nance and Pettiford, and Strayhorn's attractive *Progressive Gavotte* with outstanding work from Carney, Baker and Hodges. As a result of a further dispute between the American Federation of Musicians and the recording companies, no titles were made during 1948, and it was September 1949 before the band was once more in the studio. An interesting version of *Creole Love Call* was recorded, with a vocal by Kay Davis. However, the relatively few Ellington recordings of 1949-50 include nothing to match his greatest achievements. Not until late 1951, when it recorded the superb *A Tone Parallel to Harlem,* arguably Ellington's most successful extended work, did the band once more strike a vein of consistent brilliance. In the twenty-odd years since then, it has had its ups and downs, but masterpieces such as *Such Sweet Thunder* (1957) and the *Far East Suite* (1966) testify to the continuing vitality of the band and to the genius of its leader.

A brief note on some of Ellington's activities since the big band era ended in the late 'forties would perhaps be useful here. An apparently routine appearance at the Newport Jazz Festival during July 1956 turned into something very different when the band, stimulated by the vocal encouragement of ex-Basie drummer Jo Jones and the response of an enthusiastic audience, went into a rousing version of *Diminuendo and Crescendo in Blue,* on which Paul Gonsalves took a marathon solo of over twenty choruses. The wild acclaim of the crowd made headline news and the Ellington band received more publicity in the national press than it had for many years. Ellington himself was delighted. In 1958, the band began its second tour of Britain after a gap of a quarter of a century; it returned at regular intervals throughout the 'sixties and early 'seventies. In addition, it undertook tours to other European countries, Japan, India, the Middle East, the Far East, Senegal, Australia and New Zealand, still of course continuing the usual touring and residencies in the United States. In 1967, Togo featured Ellington on a commemorative postal stamp, and a number of honours have been accorded him both at home and abroad in recent years. Yet, at the age of seventy-four, he shows no sign of wanting seriously to curtail his touring schedules, and his creativity as a composer seems unaffected. The output of some survivors from the big band era today owes a considerable part of its popularity to nostalgia. The continuing excellence of Ellington's work requires no boost from extra-musical factors. There have, however, been subtle shifts in his career and music during the past decade or so, and it is worth considering these.

Mention has been made here of Ellington's unadventurous repertoire, in relation to his British tours and the initial critical reaction to *Black, Brown and Beige.* Sometimes he has been criticised for his conservatism—not unjustly by some members of audiences weary of the rather too familiar Ellington hit medleys. He himself justifies these medleys on the grounds that they are well received by many long-standing followers. It is essential to remember that Ellington comes from that generation of musicians who conceive it as a primary function to entertain their audiences, without running too far ahead of them in musical experimentation. With *Black, Brown and Beige,* he probably reasoned that, if critical and audience reaction was unfavourable at first, it would be better to introduce it piecemeal for a while, in the hope that it would ultimately gain reasonably wide acceptance. Time has proved him right in this instance. Since the early 'sixties, however, the position has altered, and it may well be that the demand of his European audiences for material more challenging than his popular successes helped Ellington to gain confidence. Nowadays his programmes at concerts are generally geared to the many segments of his audience, with the medleys retained only

Top left: *Clark Terry, Willie Cook, 'Cat' Anderson and Ray Nance with trombonists Quentin Jackson and John Sanders in 1954.*
Top right: *Duke Ellington in the 1960s.*
Above: *the Ellington band at the 1958 Newport Jazz Festival.*

as part of a repertoire that will almost certainly include at least one of his recent extended works. It is probably true to say that late in his career Ellington has reached a position in which he has total freedom of choice in repertoire. He has achieved the status of an international celebrity whose offerings are accepted more or less uncritically by a large part of his audience. In the popular music and entertainment world, there are a handful of artists who have lived long enough to reach a position where their physical presence on stage is almost in itself sufficient to satisfy their audiences and the content of their programme is almost of secondary consideration. Most of us have seen singers, now advanced in years, who have received rapturous receptions for croaking their way through a succession of past hits. On a human level this is engaging enough, and one feels that Louis Armstrong, for example, had gained the right to coast through the final years of his career. What is truly remarkable

345

Ellington veterans Lawrence Brown, Harry Carney and Jimmy Hamilton.

about Ellington, in contrast, is that he continues to be a totally creative and searching composer and leads a big band that currently has no rivals.

The band that Ellington leads today has fewer great soloists than those of the past, though Cootie Williams, Harry Carney and Paul Gonsalves remain and there is a strong contingent of other musicians who are more than capable soloists. Although he has recorded with such artists as the late John Coltrane, Charlie Mingus and Max Roach, Ellington has seldom included modernists in his band until quite recently, probably because the tonal characteristics he seeks are more likely to be found amongst stylists of the pre-bop era. Over the past decade or so, Ellington himself has emerged as a major pianist—indeed it would not be an exaggeration to say that he is now a great piano soloist in his own right. In fact, there have been isolated examples on record of his prowess as a soloist since the 'twenties, and he has always been recognised as an outstanding orchestral pianist. However, in the past decade he has thrown off his reticence to feature himself, possibly as the solo strength of his band dwindled. Today, he ranks with Williams, Carney and others as a major soloist within the band.

Over the years, many writers have commented upon the fact that Ellington's major soloists have seldom been able to maintain their creative musical capacity once they have left the band; with the probable exception of the late Johnny Hodges, this seems indisputable. Barney Bigard and Rex Stewart are two musicians who signally failed in their post-Ellington career to match the creativity of their work as members of the band. The reason for this probably lies in Ellington's skill in providing a setting for his musicians which displays their strengths to the full, and also in his remarkable ability to discipline, in a musical sense, even the most idiosyncratic of stylists. After Stewart left Ellington, his highly personal style degenerated in due course into eccentricity, lacking the framework that gave it its cohesion and validity. Stewart may be an extreme example, but the decline in Bigard's playing once he left Ellington was hardly less spectacular. It seems that long-term Ellington musicians become so accustomed to working within the concepts of their leader that they fail to adjust to different conditions.

Ellington the man remains the perpetual enigma; the show business trappings prove impenetrable to outsiders. Richard O. Boyer mentions Ellington's hope that winning World War II would achieve great changes in the social conditions of his people; he says that, at the time, Ellington was working on *New World A-Coming* and liked to repeat the title, adding 'And I mean it.' At the 1972 Newport Jazz Festival, he was more explicit in his announcements than I have ever heard him, referring to the fact that his was the music of the black man in the United States. Yet, paradoxically, he sees no contradiction in publicly embracing Richard Nixon at a reception that the President held in his honour. In fairness to President Nixon, it appears that he has been a long-term admirer of Ellington's music—though it can hardly be claimed that Nixon has ever been a great fighter for civil rights. Perhaps we all make the mistake of assuming that public figures conform in private life to patterns of thought and behaviour which we wish upon them, an outlook that a moment's reflection will reveal as absurd. If Ellington wishes to preserve his private life and attitudes by the donning of a public mask that is his right; what matters ultimately is that he has given to the world a body of music that is unique. If one had to defend the big band era, the fact that it produced Duke Ellington would alone make further justification unnecessary.

12 End of an Era — The Decline of the Big Bands

By the end of World War II, bands of both sweet and swing varieties had been at the centre of the entertainment scene in the United States for close on a quarter of a century. The swing bands had been dominant for a full decade. If all seemed well in the months immediately following the war, the decline, when it came, was quite spectacular; by the end of 1946, even the most optimistic observer was aware that the bands had fallen on hard times. At the beginning of 1947, a number of leaders broke up their groups within a period of four weeks. Among them were Les Brown, Benny Carter, Benny Goodman, Woody Herman, Tommy Dorsey, Harry James and Jack Teagarden. Although some reformed in the following years, several were never again to lead a regular band. As the full reality of the situation became apparent, bandleaders and ballroom operators desperately sought the reasons why the bands failed to retain their hold on the public. The answers they found were both varied and occasionally fanciful. My own view is that popular entertainment is, however obliquely, a mirror of the society in which it operates, and that changes in its form are caused in the last resort by economic and social events. I do not believe that any one of the factors that were perhaps unfortunate for the big bands could, taken in isolation, have caused them to disintegrate with such rapidity. Although some may have contributed to the decline of the bands, the real cause lies further below the surface.

During the history of popular entertainment, in all its manifestations, a very small minority of performers have survived at the top for lengthy periods. If anyone doubts this, I would suggest that he studies the hit record charts of five years ago. The majority of artists are essentially at the mercy of shifts in public taste. Jazz fans in particular, cannot help but be aware of this situation. Even such important figures as Johnny Dodds, Jelly Roll Morton and King Oliver, three pioneers, ended their days in dismal circumstances. A constant fear of most figures in the entertainment field is that their acts will suddenly seem dated to audiences. Very few are able to survive the establishment of a new direction in popular entertainment. Jazz fans may well object that music by the leading figures in any era is ill served by the application of standards of pure entertainment in evaluating it, and feel that it should also be judged by artistic criteria. This is certainly true, but it has to be accepted that the era discussed here was one in which jazz was very much a part of the general entertainment industry. This, while giving it certain strengths, also involved it in the problem of surviving what seems an insatiable public quest for the new and the novel. By the standards of popular entertainment, the bands had held sway for a lengthy period, everything considered, partly because they had been able to adapt to changing times and varying conditions. By the mid 'forties, however, there were signs that all was far from well within the bands themselves.

One of the conventional arguments advanced by bop musicians and, with even greater fervour, by their admirers was that swing was played out and held no further challenge for the rising generation of jazz performers. No one who is familiar with the evolution of jazz will be surprised to know that similar arguments were later to be advanced against the boppers themselves by the avant-garde musicians—though whether the boppers appreciated the irony is open to doubt. The followers of big bands and of middle period jazz in particular counter this with vociferous denials that the music was showing signs of degeneration. They point to the many records made in the late swing years that display numerous swing stylists at something approaching an artistic peak. The problem here is that exponents of each viewpoint are overstating their case, although each offers an element of the truth. Throughout the whole history of jazz, whole areas of music, in different eras and of varying stylistic inclinations, have failed to be explored because changing fashion has rendered them obsolete in the public eye. It would surely be naive to suggest that, by the mid 'forties, big band music had literally explored every avenue of development open to it. Yet, conversely, there is no point in denying that creativity seemed to be at a low ebb in the run-of-the-mill swing bands. This is hardly surprising, for the swing bandwagon was boarded by many leaders and musicians who were far from creative; in the most extreme instances, directors of society type dance bands announced the change to a swing policy almost overnight. The increasing size of the average band and frequently the wasteful use of all those instruments purposefully caused at least some bands to seem trapped by their very size. The complaints of ballroom operators were usually derided by the bandleaders as a form of philistinism, but it is worth at least considering what they had to say about the situation.

To begin with, it is obvious that ballroom operators more than any other element of the entertainment industry concerned with the employment of bands stood to lose by the decline of the bands. Other bookers, whether they were theatre, cinema, or hotel owners, could if absolutely necessary afford to do without bands, but owners of the lavish ballrooms that had been so much a part of the band scene faced financial ruin in the light of what was happening. In the years ahead, some of the ballrooms managed to survive, but in due course many were sold, at a considerable loss, for conversion into supermarkets or cinemas. Except for a very small minority, ballroom operators are not men who have been noted for tolerating musical experimentation; their success is measured in terms of box office receipts. In the mid 'forties more and more ballroom operators were heard to complain that the big bands were playing music that was over the heads of their dancing public. It is easy to view such comments as a further example of commercial self-seeking and lack of interest in musical standards, yet a few of the musicians who were active in the big bands were in later years prepared to admit

Duke Ellington, shown here with a section of his current band, still tours the world at the age of 74.

that their employers were not entirely unfair in their criticisms. One or two said that they themselves became bored by what they were playing and, as a result, neglected the needs of dancers in the search for material which they found more stimulating to perform. This is a problem that has faced creative musicians within the bands almost since their inception. When it alienates the audiences upon whom they rely for a living, the effects can be extremely damaging. Another sore point with the ballroom operators was the increasing cost of hiring a name band; some claimed that they could no longer afford to book them.

In a society as proud of its free enterprise system as the United States, financial rewards for the really successful entertainer have always been astronomical by European standards. It was reported that Rudy Vallee was earning as much as $7500 weekly in the worst of the depression years. The demand for music and entertainment in general reached new heights during World War II, and name bandleaders could command huge fees. Mr Leo S. Walker has reported that, towards the end of the war, leaders such as Tommy Dorsey, Benny

Goodman, Harry James and Artie Shaw were asking, and receiving, a guaranteed $4000 a night for appearances, with an option of sixty per cent of the takings, less entertainment tax, if that should prove greater. He also states that two of the leading Los Angeles ballrooms found that unless their bids for name bands were in the region of $7500 a week they had little chance of hiring one. The ballroom operators' position was not helped by the fact that they had to pay a wartime entertainment tax. True, this tax was subsequently lifted, but it happened too late to be of much help, and the only means of meeting increased costs was to raise admission prices. In fairness to the bandleaders, it should be said that they, too, were facing an economic situation of spiralling costs, both in the salaries they had to pay musicians and in travelling expenses. The really good musicians who were not called up for war service could make a lucrative living in any of the major cities, and to persuade them to travel on what could be exhausting one night stands became increasingly hard without large financial inducements. By the close of 1946, few leaders had realised that the spiral had to be broken. Harry James was one who reduced his fees, even inserting a clause in contracts to limit admission charges to ballrooms at which he appeared. Unfortunately, his example was followed only

349

by a few leaders, although it is doubtful whether a long term effect could have been achieved if all the major bands had followed suit.

What faced bandleaders, and the entertainment industry in general, was a post-war cutback in individual spending on entertainment. This is understandable enough, in view of the uncertainty of the immediate post-war period, but it is surprising that neither the musicians nor their official representatives had foreseen the possibility and. made

Top: *another survivor of the big band era, Count Basie, with his early 1960s group: Eddie Jones (bass), Eddie 'Lockjaw' Davis, Frank Wess, Marshall Royal, Frank Foster and Charlie Fowlkes (saxophones). Freddie Green (guitar), the only member who was in the 1930s band, is behind Foster. Above left: Woodie Herman still gets big bands together, with a repertoire usually slanted to contemporary trends. Above right: Harry James, a swing era bandleader who keeps a big band in existence.*

Harry James with his early 1970s line up. He and his band work at least six months of the year at Las Vegas.

some plans to meet it. It is easy, with the benefit of hindsight, to be censorious about the activities of the American Federation of Musicians during a very vital period for the big bands, but the most generous assessment of its role would need to criticise the search for short term gains, which ultimately damaged the interests of its members. For some time, the AFoM had been unhappy about recording fees, and, at the outbreak of war, its president, James C. Petrillo, gave a pledge that there would be no musicians' strikes for the duration. However, in 1942, he said that the situation had reached a point where his members were facing serious unemployment problems (because of the increase in juke boxes to nearly half a million and the use of records by the radio stations), and that he considered the record companies should set up a fund for those who found themselves without work as a result of these developments. The record companies presented a united front in the initial stages of the bargaining, refusing to meet Petrillo's demands, and on 1st August 1942 the AFoM declared a strike, and recording by major firms almost ceased. In the week before the ultimatum, most companies worked feverishly to build up a backlog of material, but inevitably this was soon exhausted. U.S. Decca was the first major company to break the common front, signing a new contract with the AFoM in September 1943; Columbia and RCA Victor held out until November 1944 before they were forced to concede defeat. The real beneficiaries of the situation were the smaller, independent companies who accepted the musicians' union terms almost immediately. In fact, the relative newcomer, Capitol Records, achieved major status as a result.

To be fair one must accept that the AFoM felt threatened by events in the booming record business, and in view of the industry's prosperity it probably assumed that its demands would be met quite swiftly. The long term effects of its action proved in many respects to be very different from those anticipated, with serious results for the interests it represented. The major companies, unable to use musicians on any sessions, attempted to keep some sort of recording activity going by featuring popular vocalists with choral backings, though in general the results were not particularly satisfactory for them in commercial terms. The smaller independents, unable to draw upon the services of the major bands, contracted to the giants of the industry, either used whatever competent bands they could find who were free of contractual obligations, or turned to areas of music such as rhythm-and-blues and country where there was a plentiful supply of artists who could be built up into national figures. The full implications of this trend will be discussed in more detail shortly, though at the time few could have possibly foreseen that it was to sound the knell of the band era.

If the first AFoM strike seems in retrospect to have been an error, the second one that lasted during the greater part of 1948 appears almost suicidal. By now the bands were in a parlous state, many having already broken up, and there were clear signs that vocalists were taking over in terms of poularity. Throughout the whole dance band era vocalists with the leading orchestras had enjoyed considerable success, but during the early years of the 'forties it was becoming obvious that singers such as Bob Eberle and Helen O'Connell with Jimmy Dorsey, and particularly Frank Sinatra with Tommy Dorsey, were becoming as important to the fans as the bands themselves. Soon leading singers began increasingly to turn to a solo career, sometimes to the displeasure of their former bandleading bosses. The recording companies had been given greater warning of this second impending strike and were able to build up a much greater backlog of material, so that almost inevitably when the strike came it seriously damaged those bands that were still trying to survive in an increasingly difficult entertainment world. If this were not enough, television was becoming immensely popular, and while it is partly true that radio made the bands, the same could certainly not be said of TV. A few leaders did come to terms with the new medium, usually the more commercially minded ones who `operated within a format in which novelty and comedy were as important to their success as music, but generally TV found little use for the bands apart from featuring a few in short spots on general programmes.

In this situation, faced with adverse trends in the general economic situation and changing social patterns, spiralling travelling costs, the closedown of many ballrooms, recording strikes, the emergence of the vocalists in their own right, and the challenge of TV, not to mention developments within jazz which led to its becoming an increasingly esoteric music, bandleaders must well have thought that the fates were conspiring against them, though there were still some who survived despite everything. Any of the above factors, singly or in combination, would have made it hard for bands to continue without facing almost insurmountable problems, but they were not the basic reasons for the decline of the bands. To discover what these were one needs to take a backward glance at developments within the entertainment business that became all important as the war years evolved.

Little research has been undertaken on the nature of the audience for the bands from the days of the foxtrot's popularity in the World War I period—a craze which launched a dancing boom lasting with only minor modifications for a quarter of a century. One presumes that the dancing public was at first concerned only with the effectiveness of the bands in their functional role, but by the mid 'twenties an audience arose who were looking for a musicianship and an individuality that lifted bandleaders, and even some sidemen, into national figures. In general, popular entertainment is the province of a relatively youthful audience, but it does appear that for the first decade of the bands' ascendancy they enjoyed the support of a wide cross-section of the public. The turning point may well have been the swing era, for the audiences became predominantly youthful, and were partisan to the extent that they, and the magazine writers who reflected their views, were scornful of the 'Micky Mouse' and sweet bands that still attracted a following amongst older age groups. It is possible, in fact, to hold the theory that the swing band induced the first awakening of the youth sub-culture so widespread today, particularly through an awareness of the leading coloured bands and what they represented

in musical and social terms. However, the long-lasting predominance of the bands should not blind one to the fact that there were many other strands in popular entertainment in the USA, some viewed with contempt by the establishment figures of the industry, but enjoyed and successful on a regional basis. One such strand—country music—incurred the special scorn of the Tin Pan Alley professionals, but from 1941 they became increasingly prominent on a national scale as a result of a dispute between the American Society of Composers, Authors and Publishers (ASCAP) and the radio networks.

ASCAP controlled most of the music written and published in the USA after 1884, but despite its great strength it was basically a conservative body which viewed most songwriters in the country and blues fields with disdain. A contract between itself and the radio networks expired on 31st December 1940, and ASCAP demanded future guarantees of around $9,000,000 annually—almost twice what it had previously called for. The radio networks refused to meet the demand and, forewarned, had set up a rival concern called Broadcasting Music Inc. (BMI), and called a ban on all ASCAP material from 1st January 1941. At first BMI was at the serious disadvantage of controlling only a minute fragment of available song material, but gradually several quite important publishers threw in their lot with it and by October 1941 it could offer 36,000 copyrights from fifty-two publishers. The deadlock between ASCAP and the radio networks was broken after ten months, but by this time BMI had destroyed the Tin Pan Alley monopoly, and writers and publishers of country and blues material found an outlet for their work that had previously been denied to them. Needless to say, the bands were affected by the ASCAP dispute, with a great part of their repertoire unavailable for broadcasts, and in face of the competition of musical forms not previously awarded much in the way of national outlets.

Country music, or hillbilly as it was often called during the 'twenties and 'thirties, had always enjoyed considerable popularity with white rural audiences, and soon after the establishment of radio there were stations in the southern USA who featured it almost exclusively. Amongst the black population of the rural south, and in the cities to which they emigrated, blues enjoyed a similar following, and though blues are an essential part of the jazz tradition there was an audience who preferred the earthier approach of relatively unsophisticated singers and instrumentalists. Most of the major recording companies built up catalogues for these audiences, usually labelled 'hillbilly' or 'race material', though such items were little known amongst general record buyers in large cities. Even during the depression years the companies continued to record this material, partly because the artists normally commanded only moderate fees and partly because they were assured of reasonable sales figures. In his excellent study, Country Music, USA, Bill C. Malone reports that during the war years young southerners in the armed

Above: *although a swing era veteran, drummer Buddy Rich took up full-time bandleading late in his career. He now leads one of the most commercially successful big bands.* Right: *Radio City Music Hall, New York: the scene of many big band concerts in the past, still occasionally used for jazz events.*

forces carried their musical tastes with them, and that by 1943 twenty-five hillbilly bands were playing to U.S. forces in Europe alone. The same is obviously true of black servicemen, many of whom listened closely to artists such as Louis Jordan, whose style of jump music was an important influence in the rhythm-and-blues that started to dominate the scene from the middle 'forties. As the 'forties evolved, rhythm-and-blues and country music became familiar nationwide to audiences who had previously been unaware of its existence. Rhythm-and-blues provided the basis for the rock-and-roll boom that ushered in a new era of popular music still apparent today.

Major changes in popular music seldom occur overnight. Their origins are so often found in developments, initially hidden from public view, which need some impetus from social and economic shifts to emerge. The

dispute between ASCAP and the radio networks, the creation of BMI, and above all the impact of World War II, when servicemen from all parts of the USA introduced their musical tastes to wide audiences, were undoubtedly the major factors in making Americans aware of the diversity of music available to them, but an attempt to create an interest in what might be termed grass-roots music had its origin in movements that had taken shape as early as the late 'twenties and received a boost from President Roosevelt's New Deal administration cultural programme.

In the USA traditional forms of song were used a great deal by militant unions, particularly by the mine-workers in their bitter struggles with reactionary mine-owners; though even before this the IWW (Industrial Workers of the World) had kept alive the use of political and satirical songs as an aid to recruitment. In the late 'twenties two southern-based schools for radicals showed a deep interest in the folk songs of their areas, tracing both traditional singers and material. Zilphilia Horton of the Highlander Folk School collected around 1300 songs from 1935 onwards (including the now famous *We Shall Overcome* from striking tobacco workers in the early 'forties). An interesting essay by T. L. Fisher on the subject appears in the August 1972 issue of Folk Review, detailing the activities of folklorists working as part of the Works Progress Administration cultural programme in the dissemination and collection of folk song. Singers such as Leadbelly (Huddie Ledbetter), Sonny Terry and Woody Guthrie became known to urban audiences, as did a considerable quantity of folk material, and much of it had a contemporary relevance. Mr Fisher summarises the situation in the following words:

'In the teeth of the Depression and the slide into war this commercial pop culture seemed trivial and inadequate to many people, and they searched for a popular culture with more excitement and relevance. If we want to find a starting point for the "counter-cultural" movement which has been so important in recent years, then this is probably the best place to put it. The search for an alternative to admass pop music found a natural solution in the folk songs that were emerging from obscurity.'

With the advent of war, folk songs were utilised in the war effort, and radio programmes made especially for British audiences introduced such singers as Josh White, Burl Ives, Leadbelly and Sonny Terry and Brownie McGhee, all of whom were becoming popular figures in their own country. By the close of the war the folk song revival was well under way in the USA and it has been an essential element in the music scene there ever since.

The emergence of country music, blues and folk into the mainstream of American popular music has profoundly altered its nature during the past two decades. There are a few diehards who view it as an unmitigated disaster, reacting to an extent that borders on hysteria. On the whole, and despite a rejection of the more messianic claims made by some partisans of contemporary pop, I feel that such trends have injected a healthy degree of realism into the music. In any case, I have always felt that the percentage of what was genuinely creative in any area of popular entertainment does not vary significantly from one decade to the next, however different its form might be. Ultimately it is as foolish for diehard band followers to deny what is valid in contemporary pop culture as it is for the spokesman of the latter to dismiss what preceded it; both are products of different eras and must be viewed accordingly.

Some readers might feel that much of this has strayed from the subject matter of the opening paragraphs of this chapter, where I outlined the practical difficulties that accrued for bandleaders by the middle years of the 'forties. In fact, it has a very direct bearing on the decline of the big band era, for while the problems that faced the bands were not easy to solve, they alone could not have led to such a fast and spectacular eclipse. In the long run, far more significant were the changing social and economic patterns, the growing financial strength of a youthful population able to create and sustain demands for forms of music different to what had gone before, and the breakthrough on a national level of types of popular music that had in the main previously been confined to regional areas and specific groups of listeners. Some writers have claimed that record companies, booking agencies and the business side of the entertainment industry are capable of creating large scale shifts in popular music forms; but the truth seems to be that they are often caught out by such movements and ultimately reflect, rather than create, current trends, particularly when, as in recent years, such trends have arisen spontaneously from a youthful sub-culture. Once any new popular musical development is seen to have a commercial potential—even including 'protest' songs against the establishment, of which the music business is a part!—the agents, record companies and bookers will move in to exploit it; but certainly in the USA the basic conservatism of the major record companies prevented them from realising the full potential in commercial terms of rhythm-and-blues. The 'conspiracy' theory of older people, dismayed that what they regard as acceptable commercial entertainment had declined, and ready to lay the blame at the feet of the grasping commercial interests manipulating public taste, has the virtue of simplicity but bears little relationship to reality.

Large scale shifts in the nature of popular music are essentially due to its sensitivity to changing social, economic and technological circumstances. Ragtime in its original form was greatly helped by the fact that the piano was the most popular instrument in middle-class American homes, thus aiding the sales of sheet music; dance music and jazz could hardly have achieved an international following without the growth of the radio and recording industries; contemporary pop would be very different if it were not able to utilise methods of amplification and recording far removed from those of the 'twenties and 'thirties. The best of popular music has always reflected, however obliquely, the society of which it is part. That small percentage which outlasts the era in which it was created does so by having qualities of creativity or a specific appeal that evokes a sympathetic response from listeners of a later generation. Anyone may feel, rightly or wrongly, that one era in popular entertainment was the highpoint and that since then there has been a decline; but, if they then ask for a return to earlier days, they are not only asking that popular entertainment be static, but that society itself should follow suit.

If by the middle years of the 'fifties the big band era was already beginning to seem remote, big bands were by no means obsolete. If most of the leaders were in retirement, or occupied with other affairs, Woody Herman continued to organise bands from time to time, Stan Kenton was dominating the big band scene, and Count Basie and Duke Ellington were gaining new plaudits. If for the past quarter of a century big bands have been outside the mainstream of popular entertainment, they have survived on their own terms, and now in the 'seventies there are signs that the interest in the bands is greater than it has been for many years. One indication is the massive reissue of records by the leading bands of the 'twenties to the 'forties; another, the increasing publicity given to newly formed big bands such as that led by Buddy Rich, and the Thad Jones-Mel Lewis group. Nostalgia, which seems to run in roughly quarter-century cycles, is undoubtedly one reason for the renewed interest in bands, but it might also be that the limited instrumentation of the average pop group is beginning to pall and that youthful listeners are seeking a less restricted medium. Jazz musicians, both young and old, appear to enjoy playing in big bands—there are reportedly some two hundred rehearsal bands in Britain alone, while college bands proliferate in the USA—and rock players are showing more than a passing interest in taking part in the band revival. At the time of writing, signs of a revival of jazz interest are increasing, both in Europe and the USA, and this will inevitably help big bands to achieve some degree of popularity.

Inevitably, the survivors of the big band era can only have a few more years of active life—Count Basie is now 68, Woody Herman 59, and Duke Ellington 73—and with the latter many of his sidemen are in late middle age. There are many musicians in their forties and fifties who can still contribute much in the field, but if the tradition is to survive it must depend on the newer and younger jazzmen agreeing on its validity. There is ample evidence that many do, and though the form that big band jazz takes in the next few years will be varied—revivalist type big bands through rock-influenced units to the avant-garde — its continuance seems assured. There can, of course, never be another big band era in the old sense for that is to assume that the social conditions of which it was a part will reappear. I would guess that permanent bands of the type of Basie's and Ellington's will be a rarity in the future, though undoubtedly there will be a few in existence, and that a more likely pattern is bands, with a regular nucleus, forming and re-forming for specific periods or engagements. The increasing number of jazz festivals held throughout the world will help provide employment for big bands, the Newport/New York Jazz Festival of 1972 setting an example by its sponsorship of several large bands organised for the occasion. It is even possible, particularly in the USA, that large public corporations might be found to sponsor a band. This has recently happened with at least one small jazz group. Whatever the future, there will be big bands playing jazz, and there is no reason to assume that some at least will not match the creativity shown by the best of their forerunners. Big band jazz has existed now for nearly half a century. While there are musicians who find the idiom stimulating or enjoyable, and audiences to whom it gives pleasure, it will continue. Its survival is the best tribute to the pioneers, both famous and obscure, who made it all possible.

The specially assembled Benny Carter band at the 1972 Newport Jazz Festival: Teddy Wilson (piano), Milt Hinton (string bass), Jo Jones (drums), Bernard Addison (guitar). Benny Carter is taking a solo, behind him are the saxaphone section, Buddy Tate, Howard Johnson, Earle Warren, Budd Johnson and Heywood Henry. The trombonists are Benny Morton, Tyree Glenn, Dicky Wells and Quentin Jackson, and the trumpeters Carl Warwick, Taft Jordan, Joe Thomas and Harry Edison.

Record Lists & References

Records marked with an asterisk are anthologies. After the name of the label is given the country of origin is indicated by the following letters:

A USA   Arg Argentina   D Denmark   E England
F France   G Germany   H Holland   Sd Sweden

Chapter 1

Records

Too Much Mustard*   Saydisc(E) SDL 221
   (Includes tracks by Jim Europe)

Unfortunately no other microgroove recordings exist that feature band performances by the artists mentioned in this chapter.

References

Jazz – A History of the New York Scene by Samuel B. Charters and Leonard Kunstadt (Doubleday & Co. Inc. New York. 1962)
Ford Dabney Discography by Leonard Kunstadt (*Record Research*, April 1955)
Wilbur Sweatman – Daddy of the Clarinet by Leonard Kunstadt and Bob Colton (*Record Research*, September/October 1959)
Wilbur C. Sweatman – 'Original Jazz King' by Harrison Smith (*Record Research*, July 1961)

Chapter 2

Records

Jazz Bands 1926–30*   Historical(A) ASC5829–16
   (Includes two tracks by Charles Elgar)
Freddy Keppard*   Herwin(A) 101
   (Includes two 1923 tracks by Erskine Tate)
Louis Armstrong – Young Louis: The Side Man (1924–1927)   Decca(A) DL–9233
   (Includes two 1926 tracks by Erskine Tate)
Doc Cook/Johnny Dunn   Vintage Jazz Mart(E) VLP–27
   (Includes all Cooke's U.S. Columbia titles)
Freddy Keppard*   Byg(F) 529.075
   (Includes four of Cooke's Gennett titles)
King Oliver's Dixie Syncopators   Ace of Hearts(E) AH–34
King Oliver's Dixie Syncopators, Volume 2   Ace of Hearts(E) AH–91
Collection of Historical Recordings*   Coral(G) epc 94259 (EP)
   (Includes two tracks by Carroll Dickerson)
The Sound of Chicago*   Columbia(A) C3L–32 (3 LP set)
   (Includes two tracks by Carroll Dickerson, one by Arthur Sims)
Jones, Jones and . . . Jones*   Audubon(E) AAQ
   (Includes four tracks by Clarence Jones)
New York and Chicago Jazz 1923–1924*   Byg(F) 529.079
   (Includes tracks by Sammy Stewart, Jimmy Wade and Bernie Young)
Big Band Jazz*   Ristic(E) 28
   (Includes three tracks by Sammy Stewart)
Walter Barnes Royal Creolians   Only for Collectors(Arg) OFC–47
Blanche Calloway and her Orchestra 1931/Dave
Nelson and his Orchestra 1931   RCA(G) LPM 10124
The Territory Bands*   Tax(Sd) m–8009
   (Includes two tracks by Blanche Calloway)

References

Jerome Don Pasquall by Frank Driggs and Thornton Hagert (*Jazz Journal*, April and May 1964)
Darnell Howard by Albert McCarthy (*Jazz Monthly*, July 1960)
The (incomplete) Story of Erskine Tate's Orchestra by Kurt Mohr and Otto Fluckiger (*Jazz Statistics*, March 1959)
Filling in Discographically by Walter C. Allen (*Record Research*, November 1968)
Reuben Reeves by Jacob S. Schneider (*78 Quarterly No. 2*, 1968)
The Jazz Record Review – Its Commencement by Len Kunstadt (*Record Research*, October 1961)
Beyond the Impressions by John Steiner (*Record Research*, June/July 1957, March/April 1958, August 1961)
The Story of Harry Dial, Part 2 – Chicago Period – As told to Frank Driggs (*Jazz Journal*, January 1959)
From The Archives – Compiled by Len Kunstadt (*Record Research*, May/June 1956)
Booker Pittman by Frank Driggs (*Coda*, October 1963)
Filling in Discographically by Len Kunstadt (*Record Research*, July 1964)
George James talks to Bertrand Demeusy (*Jazz Monthly*, February 1966)
The Life and Death of Walter Barnes by Albert McCarthy and Walter C. Allen (*Jazz Monthly*, January 1970)
Chicago by John Steiner in *Jazz* – Edited by Nat Hentoff and Albert McCarthy (Rinehart and Company, Inc. New York. 1959)
Deep South Piano – The Story of Little Brother Montgomery by Karl Gurt zur Heide (Studio Vista. London. 1970)
Jazz New Orleans 1885–1957 by Samuel B. Charters (Walter C. Allen, Belleville, N.J. 1958)
Hear Me Talkin' To Ya – Edited by Nat Shapiro and Nat Hentoff (Rinehart and Company, Inc. New York. 1955)

Chapter 3

Records

Charlie Johnson/Lloyd Scott-Cecil Scott   RCA(F) 741 065/6 (2 LP set)
The Sound of Harlem*   Columbia(A) C3L–33 (3LP set)
   (Includes tracks by Cliff Jackson, Clarence Williams (Bingie Madison Band), Fess Williams, Teroy Williams (Elmer Snowden Band).
The Sound of Chicago*   Columbia(A) C3L–32s
   (Includes one track by Joe Jordan Band)
Harlem Jazz 1921–1931*   Classic Jazz Masters(Sd) CJM–1
   (Includes one track by Cliff Jackson)
Rare Jazz of the Twenties*   Old Masters(A) TOM–5
   (Includes tracks by Marion (Marlow) Hardy, Cliff Jackson)
Elmer Snowden   Collector's Classics(Dan) CC 42
   (Includes soundtrack of film *Smash Your Baggage*. This was not available for hearing when text of present chapter was written)
Elmer Snowden   IAJRC(A) 12
   (Includes soundtrack of film *Smash Your Baggage*. This was issued subsequent to the writing of the present chapter)
King Oliver   Collector's Classics (Dan) CC 42
   (Includes all tracks recorded with Bingie Madison Band)
Clarence Williams Story 1925–1935   Vintage Jazz Mart(E) VLP–5
   (Includes three tracks with Bingie Madison Band)
Blanche Calloway and her Orchestra 1931/Dave
Nelson and his Orchestra 1931   RCA(G) LPM 10124
Byways of Jazz*   Origin(A) OJL–9
   (Includes one track by Alex Jackson)
Bubber Miley and his Friends 1929–1931*   RCA(F) 741 057
   (Includes both takes of two titles by Joe Steele)
Charles Matson   Rarities(E) RA 14 (EP)
Big Band Jazz*   Ristic(E) 28
   (Includes two tracks by Charlie Skeets)
Big Bands*   Only for Collectors(Arg) OFC–35
   (Includes four tracks by Bill Brown and his Brownies)
Fess Williams 1926–1928   Gaps(H) 100
(No LP Title)*   Jazum(A) 8
   (Includes two tracks by Savoy Bearcats)
Alex Jackson's Plantation Orchestra   Rarities(E) RA 21 (EP)
(No LP Title)*   Jazum(A) 12
   (Includes one track by Leroy Smith)

References

Jazz – A History of the New York Scene by Samuel B. Charters and Len Kunstadt (Doubleday and Co. Inc. New York. 1962)
The Night People by Dicky Wells (Robert Hale and Co. London. 1971)
They All Played Ragtime by Rudi Blesh and Harriet Janis (Alfred A. Knopf. New York. 1950)
Jerome Don Pasquall by Frank Driggs and Thornton Hagert (*Jazz Journal*, May 1964)
The Story of Louie Metcalf by Leonard Kunstadt (*Record Research*, October 1962)
The Clyde Bernhardt Story, Part 2 by Derrick Stewart-Baxter (*Jazz Journal*, October 1967)
Bingie Madison – Biography of a Career (*Jazz Monthly*, September 1964)
Ellsworth Reynolds – A Musical Career as told to Bertrand Demeusy (*Jazz Monthly*, February 1967)
Clyde Bernhardt by Gilbert Gaster (*Storyville*, December 1972/January 1972)
Notes on Arthur Gibbs by Otto Fluckiger (*Jazz Statistics*, June 1956)
This Is William D. Gant by Mike Lipskin and Leonard Kunstadt (*Record Research*, October 1960)
The Career of Earle Howard by Kurt Mohr (*Jazz-Bulletin*, March 1953)
The Musical Career of Olin Aderhold by Bertrand Demeusy (*Record Research*, November 1966)
Saga of a Sideman – as told to Ernie Smith by Rudy Powell (*Record Research*, November/December 1958)
Beyond the Impressions by John Steiner (*Record Research*, July 1961)
George James Talks To Bertrand Demeusy (*Jazz Monthly*, February 1966)
Benny Waters by Peter Vacher (*Jazz Monthly*, March 1969)
Henry James 'Hank' Duncan by Johnny Simmen (*Jazz Journal*, June 1969)
Cecil Scott and his Bright Boys by Thurman and Mary Grove (*Jazz Journal*, December 1953 and January 1954)
Discovering Elmer by Les Muscutt (*Storyville*, April/May, June/July, August/September 1968)
The Musical Career of Bob Lessey by Bertrand Demeusy (*Record Research*, October 1965)
Jimmy Archey at Bamboo Inn reported by John Steiner (*Record Research*, July 1961)
The Lem Johnson Story – as told to Johnny Simmen (*Jazz Journal*, December 1967)
The Fess Williams Story – as told to Harrison Smith (*Record Research*, October 1957)
LeRoy Smith and his Band – Emerson 'Geechie' Harper's Story as told to Bertrand Demeusy (*Jazz Monthly*, April 1969)
Notes by George Hoefer to accompanying booklet for 'The Sound Of Harlem' 3 LP set – Columbia(A) C3L–33.

Chapter 4

Records

Fletcher Henderson and his Orchestra: 'A Study in Frustration'	Columbia(A) C4L–19 (4 LP set)
Fletcher Henderson and his Orchestra: featuring Louis Armstrong 1924–25	Jazz Panorama(Sd) JPLP–21
Fletcher Henderson and his Orchestra, Vol. 1	Collectors Classics(Dan) CC–27
Fletcher Henderson and his Orchestra, Vol. 2	Collectors Classics(Dan) CC–28
Fletcher Henderson and The Dixie Stompers, 1925–26	Parlophone(E) PMC–7109
Fletcher Henderson and The Dixie Stompers, 1927–28	Parlophone(E) PMC–7056
Fletcher Henderson and his Orchestra: 'The Immortal Fletcher Henderson'	Milestone(A) MLP–2005
Fletcher Henderson 1927–1936	RCA(F) 730.584
Fletcher Henderson and his Orchestra 1934	Ace of Hearts(E) AH–61
McKinney's Cotton Pickers	RCA(E) RD–7561
McKinney's Cotton Pickers	RCA(F) 430.637
McKinney's Cotton Pickers 1929–1930	RCA(G) LPM 10.020
Chocolate Dandies	Parlophone(E) PMC–7038
The Missourians	RCA(F) 430.385
Big Band Jazz* (Includes Andy Preer item)	Ristic(E) 28 (10 in. LP)
Luis Russell and his Orchestra and Burning 8: 'The Luis Russell Story'	Parlophone(E) PMC–7025
Luis Russell and his Orchestra	Collectors Classics(Dan) CC–34

References

A Study in Frustration – The Fletcher Henderson Story. Foreword by John Hammond and Documentary Notes by Frank Driggs in booklet to 4 LP set.
Ellsworth Reynolds – A Musical Career – as told to Bertrand Demeusy (*Jazz Monthly*, February 1967)
Discographie Critique des Meilleurs Disques de Jazz by Hugues Panassie (Robert Laffont. Paris. 1958)
The Springfield Story by George W. Kay (*Jazz Journal*, July 1952)
Todd Rhodes – Then and Now by Thurman and Mary Grove (*Jazz Journal*, February 1953)
Cecil Scott and his Bright Boys by Thurman and Mary Grove (*Jazz Journal*, December 1953)
Kansas City and The Southwest by Frank Driggs in *Jazz* – edited by Nat Hentoff and Albert McCarthy (Rinehart and Co. Inc. New York. 1959)
The Spread of Jazz and The Big Bands by Hsio Wen Shi in *Jazz* – edited by Nat Hentoff and Albert McCarthy (Rinehart and Co. Inc. New York. 1959)
The Missourians by Eric P. Townley (*Jazz Monthly*, July 1958)
The Big Bands – 2 : Luis Russell by Albert McCarthy (*Jazz Monthly*, August 1960)
Luis Russell Revisited by Felix Manskleid (*Jazz Monthly*, April 1957)

Chapter 5/Southern States

Records

Celestin's Original Tuxedo Jazz Orchestra	Vintage Jazz Mart(E) VLP–33
Sam Morgan's Jazz Band/ Get-Happy Band/Blue Ribbon Syncopators*	Vintage Jazz Mart(E) VLP–32
Byways Of Jazz* (Includes tracks by Carl Bunch and his Fuzzy Wuzzies and the Black Birds of Paradise)	Origin(A) OJL–9
The Territory Bands* (Includes tracks by the Carolina Cotton Pickers)	Tax(Sd) m–8009
The Territory Bands 1926–29* (Includes tracks by J. Neale Montgomery Orchestra and Roy Johnson and his Happy Pals)	Parlophone(E) PMC–7082
Untitled LP* (Includes track by Jimmie Gunn and his Band)	IAJRC(A) 2
Untitled LP* (Includes tracks by Taylor's Dixie Serenaders and Ross De-Luxe Syncopators)	Tax(Sd) LP–4 (10 in. LP)

References

John Tuggle 'Fess' Whatley – A Maker of Musicians by Bertrand Demeusy (*Jazz Monthly*, August 1966)
The Black Birds of Paradise by Gayle Dean Wardlow (*78 Quarterly*, Vol.1 No.2 1968)
Taylor's Dixie Serenaders – Notes in 'Filling in Discographically' column (*Record Research*, March 1966)
Cat Anderson : Trumpet Astronaut by Stanley Dance (*Down Beat*, January 25th, 1968)

Chapter 5/South West

Records

Don Albert and his Orchestra/Boots and his Buddies – 'San Antonio Jazz'	IAJRC(A) 3
Byways of Jazz* (Includes tracks by Eddie and Sugar Lou's Hotel Tyler Orchestra)	Origin(A) OJL–9
Territory Bands 1929–1933* (Includes tracks by Alphonso Trent and his Orchestra)	Historical(A) HLP 5829–24
Territory Bands, Vol.2* (Includes tracks by Walter Page and his Blue Devils)	Historical(A) HLP–26
The Territory Bands* (Includes tracks by Alphonso Trent and his Orchestra)	Classic Jazz Masters(Sd) CJM–10
The Territory Bands 1926–29* (Includes tracks by Troy Floyd and his Orchestra)	Parlophone(E) PMC–7082
The Territory Bands* (Includes tracks by the Original Yellow Jackets)	Tax(Sd) m–8009

References

George Corley's Career – as told to Bertrand Demeusy (*Jazz Monthly*, February 1967)
About My Life in Music by Walter Page – as told to Frank Driggs (*Jazz Review*, November 1958)
Before Bird – Buster by Don Gazzaway (*Jazz Monthly*, January 1962)
The Story of Milton Larkins – as told to Frank Driggs (*Jazz Monthly*, December 1958)
Kansas City and The Southwest by Franklin S. Driggs contained in *Jazz* – edited by Nat Hentoff and Albert McCarthy (Rinehart and Company Inc. New York. 1959)
The Wonderful Era of the Great Dance Bands by Leo Walker (Howell-North Books, Berkeley. California. 1964)

Chapter 5/Midwestern States

Records

Jazz in St Louis 1924–1926* (Includes tracks by Charlie Creath and Fate Marable)	Parlophone(E) PMC–7157
The Territory Bands 1926–29* (Includes tracks by Jesse Stone and Charlie Creath)	Parlophone(E) PMC–7082
Riverboat Jazz* (Includes tracks by Dewey Jackson)	Coral(E) LRA 10023 (10 in. LP)
'Big Band Jazz'* (Includes tracks by Oliver Cobb and his Rhythm Kings)	Only for Collectors(Arg) OFC–35
'Big Bands'* (Includes tracks by Eddie Johnson's Crackerjacks)	Only for Collectors(Arg) OFC–7
'Big Bands'* (Includes tracks by The Original St Louis Crackerjacks)	Swingfan(G) 1005
The Territory Bands* (Includes tracks by Jeter-Pillars Club Plantation Orchestra and The Original St Louis Crackerjacks)	Tax(Sd) m–8009
Territory Bands* (Includes tracks by Hunter's Serenaders, Red Perkins and his Dixie Ramblers and Grant Moore and his New Orleans Black Devils)	IAJRC(A) 6
The Territory Bands* (Includes tracks by Red Perkins and his Dixie Ramblers. Better recorded than on IAJRC(A) 6)	Classic Jazz Masters(Sd) CJM–10
Bennie Moten's Kansas City Orchestra, Vol.1 1926–27	RCA(F) 741.056
Bennie Moten's Kansas City Orchestra, Vol.2 1927–28	RCA(F) 741.078
Bennie Moten's Kansas City Orchestra 1923–25	Parlophone(E) PMC–7119
Bennie Moten and his Band – 'Count Basie In Kansas City'	RCA(A) LPM–514
Territory Bands, Vol.2* (Includes tracks by George E. Lee)	Historical(A) HLP–26
Walter Barnes and his Orchestra (Includes one track by George E. Lee)	Only for Collectors(Arg) OFC–47
Byways Of Jazz* (Includes tracks by John Williams's Synco Jazzers and Dewey Jackson's Peacock Orchestra)	Origin(A) OJL–9
Collectors Items, Vol.2* (Includes track by John Williams's Synco Jazzers)	London(E) A1–3533
Harlan Leonard and his Rockets	RCA(A) LPM–531
Jay McShann and his Orchestra: 'The Jumpin' Blues'	Decca(A) DL–9236, Coral(E) CP–4

Note: RCA(F) are issuing all Bennie Moten's RCA Victor recordings on five LPs, the remaining three issues – not as yet allocated numbers though they will be released by the time this book is in print – will make RCA(A) LPM–514 redundant.

References

Trumpets by the River by Bob Koester (*Jazz Report*, February 1960)
The Early Years by Henry 'Red' Allen (*Jazz Monthly*, February 1970)
Eddie Barefield's Many Worlds by Frank Driggs (*Jazz Review*, July 1960)
The Eddie Barefield Story – as told to Albert McCarthy (*Jazz Monthly*, May 1959)
Speed Webb by Duncan Schiedt (*Jazz Monthly*, November 1968)
Chords and Discords by Preston Love (*Sounds and Fury*, July/August 1965)
The Hal Singer Story – as told to Albert McCarthy (*Jazz Monthly*, January 1959)
Elmer Crumbley – His Story as told to Frank Driggs (*Coda*, February 1959)
Tommy Douglas by Frank Driggs (*Jazz Monthly*, April 1960)
Blues Way Back by Victoria Spivey (*Sounds and Fury*, October 1965)
Nat Towles – Interview with John Lucas (*Down Beat*, June 15, 1944)
Discography of Nat Towles by Otto Fluckiger and Kurt Mohr (*Jazz Statistics*, May 1959)
The Buddy Tate Story – as told to Frank Driggs (*Jazz Monthly*, April 1959)
Paul Banks Tells His Story to Frank Driggs (*Jazz Journal*, August 1958)
Ike Bell in Kansas City by Tom Stoddard (*Coda*, February 1971)
Clarence Love by Frank Driggs (*Jazz Monthly*, December 1959)
Memories of Kansas City Early Jazz by Jap Allen – as told to John Beaman (*Jazz Report*, December 1958)
Tommy Douglas by Frank Driggs (*Jazz Monthly*, April 1960)
Harlan Leonard and his Rockets by Johnny Simmen (*Bulletin of the New Jazz Club Zurich*, March 1963)
The Nat Towles Story by Albert McCarthy (*Jazz Monthly*, February 1969)
Kansas City and The Southwest by Franklin S. Driggs contained in *Jazz* – edited by Nat Hentoff and Albert McCarthy (Rinehart and Company Inc. New York. 1959)
Hear Me Talkin' To Ya – Edited by Nat Hentoff and Nat Shapiro (Rinehart and Company Inc. New York. 1955)
Jazz: New Orleans 1885–1957 by Samuel B. Charters IV (Walter C. Allen, Belleville, N.J. 1958)
New Orleans Jazz – A Family Album by Al Rose and Edmond Souchon (Louisiana State University Press, Baton Rouge. 1967)
Preservation Hall Portraits by Noel Rockmore, Larry Borenstein and Bill Russell (Louisiana State University Press, Baton Rouge. 1968)

Chapter 5/East Coast

Records

Sabby Lewis and his Orchestra	Solitaire(A) LP–514
The Territory Bands* (Includes tracks by Zack Whyte and his Chocolate Beau Brummels)	Classic Jazz Masters(Sd) CJM–10
Territory Bands 1929–1933* (Includes tracks by Zack Whyte and his Chocolate Beau Brummels)	Historical(A) HLP 5829–24
Territory Bands, Vol.2* (Includes tracks by Willie Jones and his Orchestra)	Historical(A) HLP–26

References

The Sabby Lewis Band by Bob Porter (*Jazz Journal*, February 1967)
Zack Is The Name, Whyte That Is! by Theo Zwicky (*Storyville*, August/September 1969)
Earle Warren Before Basie – Reminiscences (*Coda*, May 1967)
The Milt Buckner Story – In Conversation with Peter Vacher (*Jazz and Blues*, December 1972)

Chapter 5/West Coast

Records

Paul Howard's Quality Serenaders 1929–1930	RCA(G) LPM 10 117
Territory Bands*	Classic Jazz Masters(Sd) CJM–10
(Includes tracks by The Dixie Serenaders, a Sonny Clay group)	
Territory Bands*	IAJRC(A) 6
(Includes all issued tracks by Curtis Mosby and his Dixieland Blue Blowers)	
Territory Bands, Volume 2*	Historical(A) HLP–26
(Includes tracks by Sonny Clay)	
The Kansas City Five and The Stompin' Six	Vintage Jazz Mart(E) VLP–20
(The latter is a Sonny Clay group)	
Golden Book Of Classic Swing, Volume 1*	Brunswick(G) 87 097/8/9 (3 LP set)
(Includes one track by Floyd Ray and his Orchestra)	
Golden Book Of Classic Swing, Volume 2*	Brunswick(G) 87 094/5/6 (3 LP set)
(Includes one track by Floyd Ray and his Orchestra)	

References

Reb Spikes – Music Maker by Ray MacNic (*Storyville*, February/March 1969)
The Spikes Brothers – A Los Angeles Saga by Floyd Levin (*Jazz Journal*, December 1951)
George Orendorff – Quality Serenader by Berta Wood (*Jazz Journal*, February 1957)
Charlie Lawrence by Berta Wood (*Jazz Journal*, October 1956)
Paul Leroy Howard by Berta Wood (*Jazz Journal*, November 1957)
Sonny Clay – A Veritable Giant by John Bentley (*Jazz Research*, November/December 1962 and January/February 1963)
Floyd Ray's Orchestra by Frank Driggs (*Coda*, July 1968)

Chapter 6

Records

Ben Pollack Orchestra	Only for Collectors(Arg) OFC–40
Ben Pollack and his Orchestra 1928–1929	Old Masters(A) TOM–22
The Bix Beiderbecke Legend, Vol.1*	RCA(F) 731.036
The Bix Beiderbecke Legend, Vol.3*	RCA(F) 731.131
Paul Whiteman and his Orchestra	Columbia(A) CL–2830
Paul Whiteman and his Orchestra, Vol.2	RCA(E) RD–8090, RCA(A) LPV–570
Casa Loma Orchestra	Brunswick(G) 87.534
Casa Loma Orchestra	Brunswick(G) 10304 (EP)
Casa Loma Orchestra	Decca(A) DL–8750
Benny Goodman 'Collectors Gems 1929–1945'*	Nostalgia(A) CSM 890/891 (2 LP set)
Dorsey Brothers Orchestra	
'Dixieland Jazz 1934–1935'	Coral(E) CP–27, Decca(A) DL–8631
'Collectors Items'*	IAJRC(A) 1
(Includes Phil Baxter item)	
Golden Book of Classic Swing*	Brunswick(G) 87097/98/99 (3 LP set)
Golden Book of Classic Swing, Vol.2*	Brunswick(G) 87094/95/96 (3 LP set)
(Both of above sets include track by Casa Loma Orchestra)	
Territory Bands, Vol.2*	Historical(A) HLP–26
(Includes tracks by Floyd Mills Orchestra)	

References

Benny Goodman on Record – A Bio-Discography by D. Russell Connor and Warren Hicks (Arlington House, New Rochelle, N.Y. 1969)
The Big Bands by George T. Simon (Collier-Macmillan. London. 1967)
The Kingdom of Swing by Benny Goodman (Frederick Ungar Publishing Co. New York. 1961)
The Story of Jazz by Marshall Stearns (Sidgwick and Jackson. London. 1957)
A Band Like Nothing You Ever Heard – Reminiscences of Stanley 'Doc' Ryker. (*Storyville* Magazine Issues 12 and 13. August/September and October/November 1967)
Bill Challis Speaks Out – An Interview. (*Storyville* Issue 12. August/September 1967)
Sleeve Notes to Casa Loma Orchestra LP (Brunswick(G) 87 534) by Hans Herder
The Casa Loma Orchestra by Frank Littler (*Jazz Monthly*, May 1961)

Chapter 7

Records

Charlie Barnet and his Orchestra	
'Charlie Barnet, Volume 1'	RCA Victor(A) LPV–551, RCA Victor(E) RD–7965
'Charlie Barnet, Volume 2'	RCA Victor(A) LPV–567, RCA Victor(E) RD–8088
'Skyliner'	Ace of Hearts(E) AH–157
'Hop on the Skyliner'	Decca(A) DL–8098
'Jazz Oasis'	Capitol(A) T–1403
Count Basie and his Orchestra	
'Jumpin' at The Woodside'	Coral(E) CP–106
'Jimmy Rushing With Count Basie's Orchestra'	Ace of Hearts(E) AH–119
'Swinging at The Daisy Chain'	Coral(E) CP–75
'You Can Depend On Me'	Coral(E) CP–76
'Swingmusic from The Southland Cafe, Boston'	Collector's Classics(D) CC–11
(Also featuring performances by Chick Webb and his Orchestra)	
'Early Count'	Jazz Panorama(Sd) LP–23
'Lester Young Memorial'	Epic(A) LN–6031/2, Epic(F) 66212 (2 LP set)
'Count Basie, Volume 1'	RCA(F) 731.111
'Count Basie, Volume 2'	RCA(F) 730.608
'Super Chief'	CBS(E) 67205
Bunny Berigan and his Orchestra	
'Bunny Berigan'	RCA(E) LSA–3108
'Bunny Berigan'	RCA(A) LPV–581
'Bunny'	Camden(A) CAL–550, Camden(E) CDN–159
Cab Calloway and his Orchestra	
'The King of Hi-De-Ho'	Ace of Hearts(E) AH–106
'The Man from Harlem 1930–1932'	Jazz Panorama(Sd) JPLP–22
'Cab Calloway and his Orchestra 1932'	Collector's Classics(D) CC–20
'Cab Calloway and his Orchestra 1933–1934'	RCA(G) LPM 10120
'16 Cab Calloway Classics'	CBS(F) 62950
'Erskine Hawkins/Cab Calloway 1940'	Jazz Panorama(Sd) LP–16

Benny Carter and his Orchestra	
'Benny Carter and his Orchestra 1939/40'	Tax(Sd) m–8004
'Benny Carter 1940–1941'	RCA(F) 741.073
'Benny Carter Orchestra/Cootie Williams Orchestra'	Capitol(H) 5CO52.80 850
'Dynamic Hit Sounds of the Great Benny Carter Orchestra'	Ember(E) CJS 802
'The Fabulous Benny Carter'	Audio Lab(A) 1505
Bob Crosby and his Orchestra	
'Stomp Off, Let's Go!'	Ace of Hearts(E) AH 29
'Come On And Hear, Volume 1'	Coral(E) CP 109
'Come On And Hear, Volume 2'	Coral(E) CP 110
Tommy Dorsey and his Orchestra	
'Tommy Dorsey, Volume 1'	RCA(E) DPM–2026 (2 LP set)
'Tommy Dorsey, Volume 2'	RCA(E) DPM–2042 (2 LP set)
'That Sentimental Gentleman' (Airshots)	RCA(A) LPM–6003 (2 LP set)
Billy Eckstine and his Orchestra	
'Billy Eckstine and his Orchestra'	Spotlite(E) 100
Dizzy Gillespie and his Orchestra	
'The Greatest of Dizzy Gillespie'	RCA Victor(A) LPM–2398, RCA Victor(E) RD–27248
'Dizzy Gillespie'	RCA Victor(A) LPV–530, RCA Victor(E) RD–7827
'Dizzy Gillespie Big Band in Concert'	Gene Norman(A) GNP–23, Vocalion(E) LAE–540
'In Concert'	Pye-Vogue(E) VRL–3011
'World Statesman'	Verve(A) 8174, Columbia(E) 33CX10077
Benny Goodman and his Orchestra	
'Volume 5 – The Fletcher Henderson Arrangements'	RCA(F) 741.044
'Volume 6 – The Fletcher Henderson Arrangements 2'	RCA(F) 741.059
'Volume 7'	RCA(F) 741.072
'Volume 8 – The Compositions and Arrangements of Jimmy Munday and Edgar Sampson'	RCA(F) 741.084
'Carnegie Hall Concert'	Columbia(A) OSL–160, CBS(E) 66202 (2 LP set)
'Treasure Chest'	MGM(A) 3E9 (3 LP set)
'The Famous Benny Goodman Orchestra 1937–1938'	Metro(G) 2626 003 (2 LP set)
'Clarinet a la King'	Epic(A) EE–22025

Notes: Volumes 1–4 of the French RCA series mostly feature Goodman small groups. By the time this book appears in print no doubt further volumes of big band recordings will appear. MGM(A) 3E9 and Metro(G) 2626 003 consist of the same material, but in the latter case the small group items are not included. There is a very considerable quantity of LPs available of broadcast material by the Benny Goodman Orchestra, much of it on the Sunbeam label.

Lionel Hampton and his Orchestra	
'Lionel Hampton 1 – Steppin' Out (1942–1944)'	MCA(F) 510041
'Lionel Hampton 2 – Slide Hamp Slide (1945–1946)'	MCA(F) 510.063
'Hamp!'	Verve(A) MGV–8019, Music For Pleasure(E) MFP–1040
Erskine Hawkins and his Orchestra	
'Volume 1 (1938–1940)'	RCA(F) 730.708

Note: Further volumes in the set started by the LP listed above will follow and may well be available by the time this book is published.

Woody Herman and his Orchestra	
'The Band That Plays The Blues'	Ace of Hearts(E) AH–156
'Golden Favourites'	Decca(A) DL–8133, Ace of Hearts(E) AH–78
'The Turning Point (1943–1944)'	Decca(A) DL–9229, Coral(E) CP–2
'The Thundering Herds'	Columbia(A) C3L–25 (3 LP set)
'The Great Big Bands, Volume 2'	Capitol(E) T20809
'They Heard The Herd'	Verve(A) MGV–8216, Verve(E) VLP–9062
'The Swinging Herd Recorded Live'	Philips(A) PHM–200, Philips(E) BL–7649
Earl Hines and his Orchestra	
'Swinging in Chicago'	Decca(A) DL–9221, Ace of Hearts(E) AH–159
'Hines Rhythm'	Epic(A) EE–22021
'The Indispensable Earl Hines, Volume 1 (1929–1939)'	RCA(F) 731.065
'The Indispensable Earl Hines, Volume 2 (1939–1940)'	RCA(F) 741.041
'Earl Hines et son Grand Orchestre'	Mode(F) CMDINT–9733
'Earl Hines 1932–1937 Alternate Recordings'	Jazz Archives(A) JA–2
Harry James and his Orchestra	
'Sharp as a Tack 1939–1959'	Swing Era(A) 1004
'Rhythm Session'	Columbia(A) CL–6088, Columbia(E) 33S–1031 (10 in. LP)
'Harry James at The Hollywood Palladium'	Columbia(A) CL–562, Philips(E) B.07691R
'Harry James and his Orchestra'	Columbia(A) CL–669, Philips(E) BBL–7176
'Wild about Harry'	Capitol(A) T–784, Capitol(E) LCT–6146
'An Evening of Jazz with Harry James and his Orchestra'	
Andy Kirk and his Orchestra	Polydor(E) 2682 029 (2 LP set)
'Twelve Clouds of Joy'	Ace of Hearts(E) AH–160
'Clouds of Joy'	Ace of Hearts(E) AH–105
'Andy Kirk and his 12 Clouds Of Joy – March 1936'	Parlophone(E) PMC–7156
'Live from The Trianon Ballroom, Cleveland January/February 1937'	Jazz Society(Sd) AA–503
Gene Krupa and his Orchestra	
'That Drummer's Band 1939–1947'	Sounds of Swing(A) 114
'Gene Krupa and his Orchestra 1938–1946'	Sounds of Swing 119
'Drummin' Man'	Columbia(A) C2L–29, CBS(E) BPG–62289/90 (2 LP set)
'That Drummer's Band'	Epic(A) EE–22027
'Gene Krupa – Drummer Man'	Verve(E) VSP–21/22 (2 LP set)
Jimmie Lunceford and his Orchestra	
'Jimmie Lunceford/Mills Blue Rhythm Band – Memphis to Harlem'	RCA(F) 741.045
'Jimmie Lunceford 1 – Rhythm Is Our Business (1934–1935)'	MCA(F) 510.012
'Jimmie Lunceford 2 – Harlem Shout (1935–1936)'	MCA(F) 510.018
'Jimmie Lunceford 3 – For Dancers Only (1936–1937)'	MCA(F) 510.032
'Jimmie Lunceford 4 – Blues in the Night (1938–1942)'	MCA(F) 510.040
'Jimmie Lunceford 5 – Jimmie's Legacy (1934–1937)'	MCA(F) 510.066
'Jimmie Lunceford 6 – The Last Sparks (1941–1944)'	MCA(F) 510.067
'Lunceford Special'	Columbia(A) CL–2715, Realm(E) RM–52567
'Jimmie Lunceford Orchestra'	Tax(Sd) m–8003
Mills Blue Rhythm Band	
'Jimmie Lunceford/Mills Blue Rhythm Band – Memphis to Harlem'	RCA(F) 741.045
'Mills Blue Rhythm Band'	Jazz Panorama(Sd) LP–3
'Mills Blue Rhythm Band 1934–1936'	Jazz Archives(A) JA–10
'Everybody Swing'*	Regal(E) REG–1108
(Also includes tracks by Benny Carter, Fletcher Henderson and Andy Kirk)	
Red Norvo and his Orchestra	
'Red Norvo and his Big Band featuring Mildred Bailey'	Sounds of Swing(A) LP–112
'Mildred Bailey – Her Greatest Performances'*	Columbia(A) C3L–22 (3 LP set)
Don Redman and his Orchestra	
'Don Redman and his Orchestra'	Realm(E) RM–52539
'Don Redman (1938–40) – The Little Giant of Jazz'	RCA(F) 741.061

Artie Shaw and his Orchestra
'Concerto for Clarinet' RCA(E) DPM 2028 (2 LP set)
'Artie Shaw and his Orchestra, Volume 2' RCA(E) DPM-2041 (2 LP set)
Note: It is probable that by the time this book appears in print a third double LP set will be available on RCA(E).

Chick Webb and his Orchestra
'Stompin'' at The Savoy' Columbia(A) CL-2639, Realm(E) RM-52537
'Midnite in Harlem' Ace of Hearts(E) AH-32
'Spinning the Webb' Coral(E) CP-3
'Chick Webb, Volumes 1 and 2' Decca(A) DL-9222/3
'The Golden Swing Years' Polydor(E) 423 248
'Swingmusic from The Southland Cafe, Boston' Collector's Classics(D) CC-11
(Also featuring performances by Count Basie and his Orchestra)
Note: Ace of Hearts(E) AH-32 and Coral(E) CP-3 extensively duplicate Decca(A) DL-9222/3.

References

The Big Band Era – 1: Cab Calloway by Albert McCarthy (*Jazz Monthly*, February 1960)
Cab Calloway Discography and Soligraphy by Otto Fluckiger (*Jazz Statistics*, 19/20, 1960)
Don Redman by Charles Fox (*Jazz Monthly*, April 1962)
Don Redman – An Interview with Frank Driggs (*Jazz Review*, November 1959)
Andy Kirk by Frank Driggs (*Jazz Review*, February 1959)
Andy Kirk and his Clouds of Joy by Albert McCarthy (*Jazz and Blues*,
Ed Wilcox: Lunceford Ace by Stanley Dance (*Down Beat*, October 3, 1968)
Woody Herman entry by Alun Morgan and Don Redman entry by Ronald Atkins included in *Jazz on Record* (Hanover Books, London. 1968)
The Big Bands by George T. Simon (Macmillan Co. N.Y. 1967)
Tommy and Jimmy: The Dorsey Years by Herb Sanford (Ian Allan, London. 1972)
B G on the Record – A Bio-Discography of Benny Goodman by D. Russell Connor and Warren W. Hicks (Arlington House, New Rochelle, N.Y. 1969)
The Kingdom of Swing by Benny Goodman and Irving Kolodin (Frederick Ungar Publishing Co. N.Y. 1961)
Hear Me Talkin' To Ya – Edited by Nat Shapiro and Nat Hentoff (Rinehart and Co. Inc. New York. 1955)
The Night People by Dicky Wells (Robert Hale and Company, London. 1971)
The Trouble with Cinderella: An outline of Identity by Artie Shaw (Farrar, Straus and Young, New York. 1952)

Chapter 8

Records

Louis Armstrong
'Satchmo's Greatest, Volume 3' RCA(F) 731.050
'Louis Armstrong and his Orchestra, Volume 6' Swaggie(Aust) 706
'Louis Armstrong and his Orchestra' Blue Ace(F) BA-3603
George Auld
'George Auld and his Orchestra' World Record Club(E) WRC 15
Will Bradley
'Boogie Woogie' Epic(A) LN-3115
Tiny Bradshaw*
'Tiny Bradshaw Orchestra' Swingfan(G) 1005
(Also including tracks by the Original St Louis Crackerjacks and the Washboard Rhythm Kings)
Randy Brooks
'Trumpet Moods' Decca(A) DL-8201
'Randy Brooks and his Orchestra (1944)' First Time(A) FTR-1511
Willie Bryant
'Willie Bryant and his Orchestra' RCA(F) 430.584
'Willie Bryant and his Orchestra 1936/
Teddy Hill and his Orchestra 1937' RCA(G) LPM-10116
Al Cooper
'Jumpin'' at the Savoy' Ace of Hearts(E) AH-80
Roy Eldridge
'Roy Eldridge 1943–1946' Sounds of Swing(A) 108
(The above LP has been issued subsequent to the writing of the present chapter)
Coleman Hawkins
'Stompin'' at The Savoy (The Home of Happy Feet) Collectors Classics(Dan) CC-8
(Also contains tracks by Count Basie and his Orchestra)
Edgar Hayes
'Edgar Hayes 1937–1938' Swingfan(G) 1003
Horace Henderson
'Horace Henderson 1940' Tax(Sd) m-8013
Claude Hopkins
'Harlem 1935' Jazz Panorama(Sd) LP 13
Lucky Millinder
'Lucky Days 1941–1945' MCA(F) 510.065
Hot Lips Page
'Feelin' High and Happy' RCA(A) LPV-576
Teddy Powell
'Teddy Powell 1939–1942' Sounds of Swing(A) 110
'Teddy Powell and his Orchestra 1942–43' First Time(A) FTR-1509
Jan Savitt
'The Top Hatters (1939–41)' Decca(A) DL-79243
'Jan Savitt 1938–1941' Sounds of Swing(A) 104
'Jan Savitt and his Orchestra (1938–39)' First Time(A) FTR-1505
Muggsy Spanier
'Muggsy Spanier' Ace of Hearts(E) AH-154
Jack Teagarden
'The Unforgettable Jack Teagarden' Halcyon(E) HAL-4
Fats Waller
'Fats Waller and his Big Band 1938–1942' RCA(G) LPM-10118
Teddy Wilson
'Teddy Wilson 1939–1940' Swing Era(A) 1010
Sidney Bechet*
'Unique Sidney' CBS(F) 63 093
(Includes tracks by Noble Sissle)
Big Bands 1934–1942* Swingfan(G) 1010
(Includes tracks by Claude Hopkins)
Dizzy Gillespie*
'Dizzy Gillespie, Volume 1' RCA(F) 730.676
(Includes tracks by Teddy Hill)

Golden Book of Classic Swing, Volume 1* Brunswick(G) 87 097/8/9 (3 LP set)
(Includes tracks by Al Cooper, Roy Eldridge, Edgar Hayes, Claude Hopkins, Will Hudson, Lucky Millinder and Noble Sissle)
Golden Book of Classic Swing, Volume 2* Brunswick(G) 87 094/5/6 (3 LP set)
(Includes tracks by Al Cooper, Seger Ellis, Edgar Hayes, Claude Hopkins, Will Hudson, Lucky Millinder, Teddy Powell, Muggsy Spanier and Jack Teagarden)
Night at The Savoy* Tax(Sd) m-8006
(Includes tracks by Teddy Wilson)
Sounds of Chicago* Columbia(A) C3L-32 (3 LP set)
(Includes tracks by Horace Henderson)
Sounds of Harlem* Columbia(A) C3L-33 (3 LP set)
(Includes tracks by Teddy Hill, Claude Hopkins, Cootie Williams and Teddy Wilson)
Jack Teagarden*
'King of the Blues Trombone, Volume 3' Columbia(E) 33SX1573
(Includes tracks by Teagarden's big band)
Treasury of Golden Swing* Polydor(E) 236.523/4/5 (3 LP set)
(Includes tracks by Cootie Williams)
Cootie Williams Orchestra/Benny Carter Orchestra* Capitol(H) 5C.052.80 850

References

Discography of Tiny Bradshaw by Kurt Mohr (Jazz-Publications, Reinach, Switzerland. 1961)
Discography of Lucky Millinder by Bertrand Demeusy, Otto Fluckiger and others (Jazz-Publications, Basel, Switzerland. 1963)
Jack Teagarden's Music – His Career and Recordings by Howard J. Waters, Jnr. (Walter C. Allen, Stanhope, New Jersey. 1960)
Teddy Powell by Ian Crosbie (*Coda*, October 1972)
Lesser Known Bands of the Forties – George Auld by Jim Burns (*Jazz Monthly*, June 1968)
Teddy Wilson Orchestra 1939–40 by Johnny Simmen (*Coda*, December 1970)

Chapter 9

Records

Sam Wooding Orchestra Biograph(A) BLP 12027
Willie Lewis and The Entertainers Pathe(F) C 054-11416
Willie Lewis and his Negro Band 1941 Brunswick(G) 87.530
Bill Coleman a Paris, Volumes 1 and 2* Parlophone(E) PMC 7104/5
(Includes titles by Willie Lewis and his Band)
Teddy Weatherford Jazum(A) 9
Jazz Piano a Paris* Parlophone(E) PMC 7121
(Includes solo titles by Teddy Weatherford and Herman Chittison)
Americans in Paris 1933/1938* Tax(Sd) m-8008
(Includes titles by Freddy Johnson and Bobby Martin bands)

References

Shanghai Shuffle by Edward S. Walker (*Jazz and Blues*, May 1972)
The Southern Syncopated Orchestra by Edward S. Walker (*Storyville*, August/September 1972)
A Pioneer Looks Back – Sam Wooding 1967 by Art Napoleon (*Storyville*, February/March and April/May 1967)
Herman Chittison by George W. Kay (*Coda*, January 1968)
A Portrait of Louis Bacon by Johnny Simmen (*Coda*, December 1968)
Mrs Emily Kraft Banga and Mr Kaiser Marshall by Johnny Simmen (*Storyville*, June/July 1972)
International Jazzdiscology column by Harold Flakser (*Record Research*, December/January 1973)
Jazz in Little Belgium by Robert Pernet (Editions Sigma, Brussels. 1967)

Chapter 10

Records

The following is a selection to illustrate the work of many of the bands mentioned in this chapter. It should be stressed that only a percentage of the titles on these LPs can strictly be considered as big band jazz.

Ambrose and his Orchestra/Lew Stone and his Band
'London Jazz Scene The 30's' Ace of Clubs(E) ACL 1103
Ambrose and his Orchestra 'Champagne Cocktail' Ace of Clubs(E) ACL 1246
Billy Cotton and his Band World Record Club(E) SH 141
Thore Ehrling and his Orchestra 'Thore Ehrling 1943–45' Odeon(Sd) 054-34396
Roy Fox and his Band
'At The Monseigneur Restaurant, Piccadilly' Ace of Clubs(E) ACL 1172
Roy Fox and his Band 'This Is Roy Fox' Halcyon(E) HAL 7
Geraldo and his Orchestra 'Hello Again!' Parlophone(E) PMC 7139
Jack Hylton and his Orchestra Ace of Clubs(E) ACL 1205
Leo Mathisen and his Band 'Take It Easy' Odeon(Dan) MOCK-1003
The Squadronaires 'There's Something in the Air' Eclipse ECM 2112
Lew Stone and his Orchestra 'My Kind of Music' Ace of Clubs(E) ACL 1231
Czech Jazz 1920–1960* Supraphon(Cz) DV 10177/8
(Includes titles by Ladislava Habarta, Jam Sima, Karla Vlacha)
Dansk Guldalder Jazz, Volume 2* Odeon(Dan) MOCk-1007
(Includes titles by Kai Ewans and Leo Mathisen)
Jazz in Deutschland, Volumes 3–4 and 5–6* Historia(G) H 632/3, H 634/5
(These are 2 LP sets. Vols. 3–4 include tracks by James Kok, Teddy Stauffer and Kurt Hohenberger. Vols. 5–6 include tracks by Willy Berking, Horst Winter, Benny de Weille, Kurt Widmann)
La Prehistoire du Jazz en France* Pathe(F) C 054-10656
(Includes one track by Gregor and his Gregorians)
Swing from Belgium, Volume 1, 1940–1942* Swingfan(G) 1002
(Includes titles by Fud Candrix, Jean Omer, Eddie Tower)
Swing! Volume 3 – Svenska Swingepoken 1935–1939* Sonora(Sd) SOLP 108
(Includes titles by Hakan von Eichwald and Arne Hulphers)

References

Jazz in Deutschland by Horst Lange (Colloquium Verlag Uhle und Kleimann, Lubbecke, 1960)
Jazz in Little Belgium by Robert Pernet (Editions Sigma, Brussels. 1967)

Swing Discographie by A. Schwaninger and A. Gurwitsch (Ch.Grasset, Geneva. 1946)
The Dance Band Era by Albert McCarthy (Studio Vista, London. 1971)
Fox on Lux by Alasdair Fenton (*Jazz Monthly*, August 1970)
The Finnish Jazz Scene by Pekka Gronow (*Jazz Monthly*, November 1965)
Discography as a Science by Pekka Gronow (*Jazz Monthly*, August 1968)

Chapter 11

Records

All records are by Duke Ellington and his Orchestra.

Early Duke	Jazz Panorama(Sd) LP–12
In Harlem	Jazz Panorama(Sd) LP–17
Cotton Club Days, Volume 1	Ace of Hearts(E) AH–23
Cotton Club Days, Volume 2	Ace of Hearts(E) AH–89
Cotton Club Days, Volume 3	Ace of Hearts(E) AH–166
The Duke In Harlem	Ace of Hearts(E) AH–47
Duke Ellington	Swaggie(Au) S–1231
The Works of Duke Integrale, Volume 1	RCA(F) 731 043
The Works of Duke Integrale, Volume 2	RCA(F) 741 028
The Works of Duke Integrale, Volume 3	RCA(F) 741 029
The Ellington Era, Volume 1	Columbia(A) C3L–27 (3 LP set)
The Ellington Era, Volume 2	Columbia(A) C3L–39 (3 LP set)
Duke Ellington and his Orchestra 1928–31	Jazz Panorama(Sd) LP–6
Braggin' in Brass	Tax(Sd) m–8011
Duke Ellington at the Cotton Club	Tax(Sd) m–8001
At His Very Best	Victor(A) LPM–1715, RCA(E) LSA–3071
In a Mellotone	Victor(A) LPM–1364, RCA(E) LSA–3069
Jumpin' Punkins	RCA(A) LPV–517
Daybreak Express	RCA(A) LPM–506
The Indispensable Duke Ellington	
	Victor(A) LPM–6009 (2 LP set), RCA(E) RD–27258/9
Duke Ellington and his Orchestra	
Primping for the Prom	Ember(E) EMB–3327
	CBS(F) 62 993

Note: The above refer to the period covered in the present chapter. French RCA are issuing nineteen LPs of Ellington's Victor recordings in chronological sequence, including several takes of some titles. They are being issued under the title of 'The Works of Duke Integrale' and six volumes have been released at the present writing.

References

Early Jazz by Gunther Schuller (Oxford University Press, London and New York. 1968)
Duke Ellington on Record – The Nineteen-Thirties by Charles Fox (Article in *Duke Ellington – His Life and Music*. Phoenix House, London. 1958)
Duke Ellington entry by G. E. Lambert (Included in *Jazz on Record*. Hanover Books, London. 1968)
Ellington – A Time of Transition by Demetre Ioakimidis (*Jazz and Blues*, February 1973)
Discovering Elmer by Les Muscutt (*Storyville*. April/May 1968)
Reminiscing in Tempo with Freddie Jenkins (*Storyville*. April/May 1973)
The Hot Bach (3 profiles of Ellington and his musicians that first appeared in the New Yorker during July 1944) by Richard O. Boyer.
Jazz: Its Evolution and Essence by Andre Hodeir (Grove Press, N.Y. 1956)

Chapter 12

References

American Revival – How it All Started by T. L. Fisher (*Folk Review*. London. August 1972)
Country Music, U.S.A. by Bill C. Malone (University of Texas Press, Austin and London. 1968)
The Wonderful Era of the Great Dance Bands by Leo S. Walker (Howell-North Books. Berkeley, California. 1964)